THE NEW TESTAMENT
AND ITS MODERN INTERPRETERS

THE SOCIETY OF BIBLICAL LITERATURE

The Bible and Its Modern Interpreters
Douglas A. Knight, General Editor

THE NEW TESTAMENT AND
ITS MODERN INTERPRETERS

edited by

Eldon Jay Epp

and

† George W. MacRae

SCHOLARS PRESS

Atlanta, Georgia

SOCIETY OF BIBLICAL LITERATURE

CENTENNIAL PUBLICATIONS

Editorial Board

The Society of Biblical Literature gratefully acknowledges a grant from the National Endowment for the Humanities to underwrite certain editorial and research expenses of the Centennial Publications Series. Published results and interpretations do not necessarily represent the view of the Endowment.

Library of Congress Cataloging in Publication Data
Main entry under title:

The New Testament and its modern interpreters.

(The Bible and its modern interpreters ; 3)
1. Bible. N.T.—Criticism, interpretation, etc.—
History—20th century.   I. Epp, Eldon Jay.   II. MacRae,
George W.   III. Series.
BM2350.N47   1988   225.6'09'04   ·   86-3880
ISBN: 0-89130-881-4
ISBN: 0-89130-882-2 (pbk.)

To the Memory of

GEORGE W. MACRAE, S.J.

27 July 1928 — 6 September 1985

CONTENTS

EDITORS AND CONTRIBUTORS

William A. Beardslee, Emory University (*Emeritus*), Atlanta, Georgia

Schuyler Brown, University of St. Michael's College, Toronto, Ontario, Canada

Eldon Jay Epp, Case Western Reserve University, Cleveland, Ohio

Reginald H. Fuller, Virginia Theological Seminary (*Emeritus*), Alexandria, Virginia

Victor Paul Furnish, Perkins School of Theology, Southern Methodist University, Dallas, Texas

Harry Y. Gamble, University of Virginia, Charlottesville, Virginia

Philip Edgcumbe Hughes, Trinity Episcopal School for Ministry (*Emeritus*), Philadelphia, Pennsylvania

Howard Clark Kee, Boston University, Boston, Massachusetts

Edgar V. McKnight, Furman University, Greenville, South Carolina

† George W. MacRae, S.J., The Divinity School, Harvard University, Cambridge, Massachusetts

Abraham J. Malherbe, The Divinity School, Yale University, New Haven, Connecticut

Jerome Murphy-O'Conner, O.P., Ecole Biblique de Jerusalem, Jerusalem, Israel

Birger A. Pearson, University of California at Santa Barbara, Santa Barbara, California

John H. P. Reumann, Lutheran Theological Seminary, Philadelphia, Pennsylvania

Anthony J. Saldarini, Boston College, Chestnut Hill, Massachusetts

William R. Schoedel, University of Illinois, Urbana, Illinois

Elisabeth Schüssler Fiorenza, The Divinity School, Harvard University, Cambridge, Massachusetts

D. Moody Smith, The Divinity School, Duke University, Durham, North Carolina

Charles H. Talbert, Wake Forest University, Winston-Salem, North Carolina

R. McL. Wilson, St. Mary's College, St. Andrews, Fife, Scotland.

PREFACE TO THE SERIES

The present volume is one part of a trilogy, The Bible and Its Modern Interpreters. Together with three other series—Biblical Scholarship in North America, Biblical Scholarship in Confessional Perspective, and The Bible in American Culture—it has been initiated by the Society of Biblical Literature to mark the 1980 centennial of its founding. As a whole, the Centennial Publications program aims to scrutinize the history of biblical scholarship as well as the very diverse roles that the Bible has played in North American culture. Approximately 150 scholars are contributing to about forty volumes planned for these four series—graphic witness to the current vitality of biblical studies.

Whereas the other three series are devoted primarily to North American phenomena, such as distinctive schools of thought, influential scholars, fields of special activity, various confessional contexts, and arenas of cultural impact, the three volumes that make up The Bible and Its Modern Interpreters focus on the full range of research on, respectively, the Hebrew Bible, Early Judaism, and the New Testament. Structured according to the usual subdisciplines and subject matter, each sets for itself the task of describing the course of international scholarship since ca. 1945. The essays are intended as critical reviews, appraising the current state of affairs in each area of study and calling attention to issues that scholars should face in the years ahead.

Deep appreciation goes to each person who has been involved in the planning and producing of this trilogy, most especially to the authors themselves, who have joined in this common effort to reflect on the developments in their fields. We also acknowledge gratefully the cooperation of the two publishers, Scholars Press and Fortress Press, as well as the generous support of the National Endowment for the Humanities.

DOUGLAS A. KNIGHT
Vanderbilt University

EDITORS' PREFACE

This volume has been designed both to survey and to evaluate New Testament scholarship since World War II. In several respects this period of about forty years comprises one of several eras in NT studies that were extraordinarily productive both in quantity and quality of work and also in significance of results. Similarly productive periods surely are to be identified around 1835–1840, when David Friedrich Strauss stirred up a worldwide debate on the historical Jesus and when the priority of Mark seemed secure; or around 1865, when the basic Two-Source theory of Synoptic origins seemed assured and C. Tischendorf was discovering or publishing some of the most important NT manuscripts; or around 1900, when the impressive scholarship of Adolf Harnack and the other learned "Old Liberals" set the modern standard for excellence in critical scholarship and at the same time misled two generations on the kingdom of God and the historical Jesus, and when Johannes Weiss and Albert Schweitzer effected a revolution in NT scholarship on the latter issues; or around 1920, when Karl Barth's *Epistle to the Romans* (1918) had appeared and when the stage was set by Martin Dibelius and Rudolf Bultmann for the form-critical analyses of the NT, but especially by Barth and Bultmann for new theological/hermeneutical approaches that were to have far-reaching influence in the post–World War II period and down to our own times; or, finally, around the mid-1930s—just before the war—when Rudolf Otto and C. H. Dodd emphasized (and Dodd overemphasized) the reality of the present kingdom in the ministry of Jesus, and when the Chester Beatty papyri were published and brought new life to textual criticism.

Our forty-year period began in 1945 and the immediately following years with the reestablishment of those international scholarly ties that had been broken and had lain dormant during the war years when North America and virtually all of Europe were involved in conflict. Obviously, British-American ties were quickly and almost automatically restored, but perhaps most striking in this reconnection was the early and close cooperation of German and American NT scholars. This was symbolized, for instance, in the broad use of English-language publications in the work of European scholars like W. G. Kümmel and others, but was demonstrated very concretely, for example, in the interconnection between the German "Neutestamentlicher Arbeitskreis" and the American "New Testament Colloquium." Prominent in the former group were scholars like Hans Conzelmann; the latter group emphasized "the study of issues raised by or resulting from the scholarly work of . . . Rudolf Bultmann" (as described in the

Encyclopedia of Associations, 10th ed.) and included among its senior members Hans Jonas, Kendrick Grobel, and Amos Wilder, as well as (then) younger members such as Robert W. Funk, Helmut Koester, George MacRae, Norman Perrin, James M. Robinson, and about a dozen others. Fully half of these members of the American group were either European by birth or had studied on the Continent. Renewed recognition and cooperation between those on both sides of the Atlantic were not limited, of course, to the German-American scene, but were worldwide, and no longer would any national group form an isolated "cell" of NT scholarship.

At the same time, due primarily to the encyclical of Pope Pius XII in 1943, *Divino afflante spiritu,* Roman Catholic NT scholars no longer traveled a separate path, but began to walk in the mainstream of critical scholarship (see Brown: 18–19, 117). This dramatic change can be seen, symbolically and in actuality, by observing in North America the extraordinary degree to which the memberships of the Society of Biblical Literature and of the Catholic Biblical Association now overlap—and also in recent years by the numerous Roman Catholic presidents of the former and the recent Protestant president of the latter. As a further instance, Joseph Fitzmyer, a Jesuit, has served as editor of both societies' journals, first of the *Journal of Biblical Literature* for six years (1971–1976) and then of the *Catholic Biblical Quarterly* (1980–1984). Examples could be multiplied, such as the appointment of Roman Catholic (and Jewish) NT scholars to permanent positions and endowed chairs in Protestant theological seminaries (and conversely), or the "denominationally blind" appointments now made in most of our college and university programs in the study of religion. These developments, which appear matter-of-fact to us now, could not have been foreseen or even imagined prior to World War II. Anyone who doubts this statement will find striking confirmation of its accuracy in a 1947 article in *The Study of the Bible Today and Tomorrow*—a collaborative volume similar to the present one—by J. H. Cobb on "Current Trends in Catholic Biblical Research," where the "Catholic" and the "liberal" scholars are seen as radically different in their approaches and results:

> The Catholic scholar, on the other hand, begins with Scripture and tradition, the total deposit of the faith as, and only as, this is officially interpreted by the living *magisterium* of the church. . . . He cannot doubt the reliability of the channels by which the biblical literature has been transmitted, nor can he consider portions of it as mere myth, legend, fiction, symbol, etiological explanation, or apologetic. He cannot employ one portion of it to disprove the factual character of another portion. To illustrate, when accounts of a given event, such as the resurrection narratives, differ widely in detail, he must harmonize the records in such a way as to affirm both the truth of the detail and the truthfulness of the total story of which it is a part. (117–18)

Raymond E. Brown, S.S., speaks for the current view on the relationship between the *magisterium* and the theologians or biblical scholars:

> I do not think that the members of the magisterium can speak authoritatively about matters of theology or Scripture unless they have elementary competence in the field, either by their own learning or by consultation. . . . I am saying that bishops must listen to theologians and acquire information, and pray over it, and think over it, and then teach pastorally what they judge the Church must hear. (48–49)

To be more specific, he speaks, for instance, of the Catholic Church's "acceptance of a developmental approach to the Gospels, recognizing that the final Gospels go considerably beyond the ministry of Jesus and that later Christology had been retrojected into the accounts of the ministry" (67), and he cites as one example Matt 16:18: "Today, the majority of scholars would recognize that Mark is older than Matthew and that the sentence about building the Church upon Peter is a Matthean addition (from post-resurrectional material) to an account which originally lacked it, as we see in Mark and Luke" (75). These somewhat random statements from Brown are symbolic of a fresh and refreshing ecumenical unity among NT scholars that is a distinctive feature of the postwar period.

Another refreshing change has been the steady decline of anti-Semitic expressions and anti-Jewish sentiments in NT scholarship, though the task has not been finally completed. As one example, the pejorative (and inaccurate) description of the Judaism of the general NT period as *Spätjudentum* ("late Judaism") has in our time largely disappeared from our parlance. In addition, a new openness to face the issues of anti-Semitism *within* the NT—and to face them honestly—has been evident throughout the post–World War II period, involving both Protestant and Catholic—and, of course, Jewish—participants in the continuing discussion and the growing literature.

In North America following World War II, graduate schools welcomed returning veterans—along with numerous fresh seminary and college graduates—who wished to pursue advanced degrees in religious studies. The rapid expansion within institutions of higher education provided opportunities for nearly all who were qualified and wished to teach and pursue research in the NT field. Accompanying all of this was a dramatic increase in the number of programs for the study of religion in the public universities of the United States, especially during the 1960s, including many Ph.D. programs where additional scholars were trained.

By the early 1950s NT scholarship, here and abroad, had both recovered its wartime losses and had taken giant steps forward. New journals appeared, including the prestigious *New Testament Studies* in 1954 and its monograph series, and *Novum Testamentum* in 1956, also with its monograph supplements. An old and distinguished journal, the *Zeitschrift für Theologie und Kirche,* was thoroughly reorganized in 1950 under the editorship of Gerhard Ebeling, with NT scholars like Ernst Käsemann and Erich

Dinkler on its editorial board. New bibliographical journals were initiated
to keep track of the burgeoning literature, including both the *Internationale
Zeitschriftenschau für Bibelwissenschaft und Grenzgebiete* in 1951 and *New
Testament Abstracts* in 1956.

Work resumed on interrupted projects, like Kittel's *Theologisches
Wörterbuch zum Neuen Testament,* whose first three volumes had appeared
between 1933 and 1942, but whose fifth and subsequent volumes were
published beginning in 1954, and like Walter Bauer's *Griechisch-Deutsches
Wörterbuch zu den Schriften des Neuen Testament und der übrigen urchristlichen Literatur,* whose third revised edition had appeared in 1937, but
whose monumental fourth edition was published after the War in 1949–
1952. English translations of substantial reference works such as these—
though slower in coming—offered their treasures to the non-German reader.
Bauer was available in English dress in 1957, and Kittel followed during
1964–1974, almost catching up in publication date to the last German
volume in 1973. Other projects entered new, energetic phases, such as the
edition of the Old Latin NT at the Beuron monastery under the vigorous
leadership of Bonifatius Fischer: *Vetus Latina: Der Reste der altlateinischen
Bibel* (1949ff.); the edition of the Old Latin Gospels revised and completed
after World War II by Kurt Aland: *Itala: Das Neue Testament in altlateinischer Überlieferung;* and the Corpus Hellenisticum Novi Testamentum,
which stems from the extensive collection of classical parallels in J. J. Wettstein's Greek NT of 1751–1752 and which was reestablished at Utrecht in
1956 by W. C. van Unnik (see his description of the project in *JBL* 83 [1964]
17–33). New projects were undertaken, such as the so-called International
Greek New Testament Project in 1948, which received the endorsement of
the Society of Biblical Literature in that same year; the extensive tasks
initiated by the Institut für Neutestamentliche Textforschung at Münster,
founded in 1959 under the aggressive and productive leadership of Kurt
Aland; and the numerous research projects carried on in the Institute for
Antiquity and Christianity in the Claremont Graduate School, founded by
Ernest C. Colwell and continued under the leadership of James M. Robinson. Finally, the restructuring of the Society of Biblical Literature in the late
1960s fashioned its goals more directly toward research and publication;
these far-reaching changes were effected by a forward-looking minority in
the Society, but the creative leadership of Robert W. Funk was foremost in
their actual accomplishment (see Saunders: 58–68).

These examples, however, represent merely some of the supporting
pillars of NT studies—reference works, tools, opportunities for cooperative
efforts, vehicles for publication of results, centers and learned societies
where new ideas could be tested, and so forth. The heart of the discipline
is to be found, naturally, in the substance of the articles and monographs
produced by a vast array of scholars worldwide, including—of course—those

contributing to large-scale projects and works of reference. Their achievements, across an ever-broadening range of subdisciplines, have opened the
way for new insights into the NT and its surrounding worlds of history,
society, and literature and have afforded a deeper understanding of its essential meaning. Those achievements constitute the subject of this collaborative
volume.

I once heard of a systematic theologian who, early in his graduate
student days, had toyed with the idea of becoming a biblical scholar until he
discovered that "the field was an inch wide but a mile deep." Others—once
inside—have left biblical studies out of a similar "claustrophobic" reaction.
To most on the inside, however, this complexity and almost limitless depth
present a welcome challenge and hold a genuine fascination. To them, of
course, the field appears also to be a mile wide, and both the long history
of scholarship and the meticulous attention to every aspect of the NT and
its related areas—its breadth and depth—set the discipline apart from many
others, so that what appears to outsiders to be a small, circumscribed field
is in reality a highly sophisticated discipline supported by scholars whose
competence in philology, historical criticism, literary criticism, and in the
philosophy, sociology, and history of religion is extraordinary. Such a
laudatory assessment may appear self-serving, but it comes from one who
has been responsible over a long period for nearly two dozen university
departments and programs across the humanities and social sciences, and
biblical studies by almost any measure stand the comparative test of quality
exceedingly well. And so it has been from the very beginning.

Anomalous though it is, critical NT scholarship actually reaches back to
the period before there was a "New Testament" in any proper sense of that
term. Already Marcion in the middle of the second century not only was
drawing distinctions between writings authoritative for him and similar
writings then in circulation but also was altering existing documents according to his bias. Tatian, shortly thereafter, was attempting a critical exercise
in his *Diatessaron*, though ultimately an unsuccessful one. The so-called
Marcionite prologues to the Pauline Epistles and the Anti-Marcionite prologues to the Gospels provided answers to historical questions about their
date and destination. In the mid-third century, Origen could use style criticism to argue that Paul did not write Hebrews, and Dionysius of Alexandria
could assess the differing language and style in the Johannine Apocalypse
and Gospel to argue that they had different authors. And in the next century
and a half, Eusebius and Jerome report disputes over the authorship of NT
writings (Kümmel: 14–19).

Were these rudimentary efforts the beginning of NT scholarship?
Surely not in any modern "scientific" sense. Yet W. G. Kümmel is too
restrictive when he argues that NT scholarship began only during the course
of the eighteenth century and that everything earlier "can only be referred
to as the prehistory of New Testament scholarship" (13). Jerry Bentley, in

his recent *Humanists and Holy Writ: New Testament Scholarship in the Renaissance* has argued persuasively that these humanist scholars developed "methods, principles, and insights" that were employed from their time to the present and thereby became "the founders of modern philological scholarship on the New Testament" (3). In particular, Lorenzo Valla (1407–1457) concentrated not on the NT's doctrine or moral teaching but on its *words* as they appeared in the *Greek* NT (33), and he savagely castigated medieval exegetes who based their work on the Vulgate and ignored the Greek text of the NT (60). By utilizing for the first time in modern scholarship a full analysis of Erasmus's *Annotationes*, Bentley clearly documents the fact that Erasmus (ca. 1466–1536) not only followed Valla's lead more closely than had been assumed, but that Erasmus far surpassed Valla in sophistication of critical method and results, both in NT philology and textual criticism, and in exegesis (142, 149, 161). Indeed, Bentley's conclusion is fully justified: with Erasmus "modern New Testament scholarship and scholarly methods took their first great leap forward, and this was perhaps the most enduring of all the legacies Erasmus bequeathed to his cultural heirs" (193). It was these humanist scholars, then, who treated the NT not merely as a source of doctrine but as "an object of detached literary, historical, and philological analysis," and this new historical attitude opened the world of biblical antiquity to a more accurate understanding than had previously been possible (216–17).

The period of the Reformation brought further advances. The cautious toleration of allegorical interpretation by Erasmus soon gave way to the total rejection of the multiple sense of scripture by Flacius in his 1567 *Key to the Scriptures*, which gave first place to the grammatical sense of scripture and its interpretation wholly out of its special context (Kümmel: 27–28). This emphasis found continuation in a NT commentary by Joachim Camerarius in 1572, with the added insight that the NT writings must be explained *in the light of their own times*, and Camerarius attempted to do so by reference to the Greek and Latin classical authors (Kümmel: 31). Then Hugo Grotius, in his *Notes on the New Testament* (1641–1650), utilized both Hellenistic-Jewish literature and the church fathers, in addition to the classics, to interpret the NT ideas in terms of their own historical setting, and John Lightfoot, in his writings between 1658 and 1678, added the postbiblical Jewish literature to this essential base for understanding the NT, for he concluded that "the language of the New Testament, written by and for Jews, could only be understood if one were familiar with the language of the Jews of that time" (Kümmel: 38). Finally, at about this same time, Richard Simon approached the NT history and text through dispassionate observation and critical methods, for which some have called him the "founder" of NT introduction (Kümmel: 41).

Many essential ingredients seemed in place for the full development of modern "scientific" NT scholarship in the mid-eighteenth century. That, at least, is the traditional date, though it would appear that modern NT scholarship actually evolved gradually over many, many generations rather than having burst on the scene at one point in history. For example, right at mid-century but clearly accelerating the trends already observed, J. J. Wettstein's monumental edition of the Greek NT in 1751–1752 provided a long-unsurpassed collection of classical and Jewish passages parallel to the NT (as already noted above) and at the same time required that the NT be read like any other book—in its own setting and as its first readers heard it:

> Since we read with the same eyes the sacred books and the laws given
> by decrees of the princes, as well as all ancient and modern books,
> so also the same rules are to be applied in the interpretation of the
> former as we use for an understanding of the latter. . . . If you wish
> to get a thorough and complete understanding of the books of the
> New Testament, put yourself in the place of those to whom they were
> first delivered by the apostles as a legacy. Transfer yourself in thought
> to that time and that area where they first were read. Endeavor, so
> far as possible, to acquaint yourself with the customs, practices,
> habits, opinions, accepted ways of thought, proverbs, symbolic
> language and everyday expressions of these men, and with the ways
> and means by which they attempt to persuade others or to furnish a
> foundation for faith. (Kümmel: 50)

Wettstein's characterization of the proper methodological approach to the NT is genuinely sophisticated in its conception, and what do J. S. Semler and J. D. Michaelis really add to this? They write a quarter century later and are credited with showing "the first evidences of a consciously historical approach to the New Testament as a historical entity distinct from the Old Testament," which is Kümmel's definition of the modern historical method (62), and he names Semler the founder of NT historical study and Michaelis the founder of NT introduction. They, however, follow directly in the traditions of Simon and Wettstein, though they treat more issues more comprehensively and take more daring positions in their "free" investigation of the NT.

From this point on we move to more familiar territory: Lessing's work on the Synoptic relationships (and his publication of Reimarus's radical assessment of the historical Jesus); J. P. Gabler's isolation, in 1787, of "biblical" theology as a historical discipline; Herder's insights—ahead of their time—on the oral tradition behind the Gospels and on the priority of Mark; Herbert Marsh's precursory Two-Document hypothesis; F. C. Baur's tendentious history of early Christianity; Strauss's largely misunderstood mythological interpretation of the Gospels; Lachmann's decisive break with the *textus receptus,* and Lachmann's, Wilke's, and Weiss's demonstrations of the priority of Mark; Tischendorf's manuscript discoveries and monumental critical edition of the NT; Holtzmann's classic formulation of the Two-Document hypothesis; Ritschl's attractive but wrong-headed definition of the kingdom of God; Westcott and Hort's NT text and theory and its long dominance in the field; Kähler's distinction between the "so-called historical Jesus and the historic, biblical Christ"; Dalman's attention to Jesus' native Aramaic, and Deissmann's to the everyday Greek of the time; Jülicher's massive and incisive volumes on the parables; Harnack's prodigious scholarship on the NT and early Christianity and his succinct description of the "Old Liberal" Jesus; Wrede's insights into the church's imposition of its faith on the Gospel narratives, which facilitated form criticism; J. Weiss's rehabiliation of the relevance of apocalyptic for understanding the historical Jesus, and Schweitzer's captivating — but also disappointing — reconstruction of the aims of Jesus; Cumont's, Reitzenstein's, and Bousset's placing of the NT in its Hellenistic setting, with special attention to the mystery religions; K. L. Schmidt's demonstration that the early tradition about Jesus circulated in brief, independent units; Dibelius's and Bultmann's presentations of form criticism; Billerbeck's massive commentary on the NT from the Mishna and Talmuds; Streeter's Four-Document hypothesis and his theory of "local texts"; Otto's reclamation of the presence of the kingdom in Jesus' ministry, and Dodd's persuasive but overstated "Realized Eschatology"; and, finally, Bultmann's influential essay "The New Testament and Mythology," written in 1941 and circulated in mimeographed form, though not published until after the war.

This last item, Bultmann's brief but provocative essay, serves appropriately as the pivot between the prewar and postwar phases of NT scholarship, for not only does it bridge chronologically the gap created by the war, but it is symptomatic of widespread changes that were to take place when studies resumed on a broad scale. This is evident, as examples, in renewed investigations of the Christian *kerygma* and its meaning to moderns, in hermeneutics generally and in the application of existentialist categories to the NT in particular, in the study of NT language and "language-event" and the new literary-critical approaches to the NT, in the application of Greco-Roman religion and philosophy to the study of the NT, and in the so-called new quest of the historical Jesus. Indeed, when one takes into account the other aspects of Bultmann's work — form criticism and the sayings of Jesus, NT theology, and Pauline and Johannine studies — it is obvious how pivotal he and his work have been in our discipline. Even those who may eschew the "Bultmannian" or "post-Bultmannian" points of view will admit both his deep influence and the character of his work as a turning point in postwar NT studies.

This list of significant contributors, long as it is, represents only a small portion of the highly influential scholars who have shaped NT studies over the centuries. It does, however, bring us to the beginning of World War II, where the present volume again takes up the narrative of the ongoing development of NT studies.

It will be obvious that the essays that follow have at least two significant omissions, for there are neither separate chapters nor substantive discussions of either the social world of the NT or feminist perspectives on NT scholarship. Perhaps the editors were remiss in not assigning separate contributions on these subjects, but in the late 1970s, when this trilogy on The Bible and Its Modern Interpreters was planned, investigations of the NT social world were only beginning and a distinctive feminist perspective on NT studies was even less well articulated than were such perspectives on the study of religion generally, or on theology, or even on the OT—from which NT studies has so often taken its cue—for in that field also only a modicum of work had been done prior to the present decade. It will be the responsibility, therefore, of the next generation to assess NT scholarship in these two areas, for surely during the coming decades NT social world and anthropological studies will demonstrate their vital significance for interpreting the NT, and all along feminist perspectives will continue to correct the male-dominated biblical scholarship of the past eighteen centuries and more. It is important to recognize, however, that the same editorial board of the SBL Centennial Publications series that authorized the trilogy of which this volume is a part also commissioned the work edited by Adela Yarbro Collins entitled *Feminist Perspectives on Biblical Scholarship* (1985), to which the reader is referred.

Finally, those who read the contributions in the present volume with critical care will note that there is variation in their points of closure, for some chapters cover their fields of scholarship up to the period of 1980, while others carry their coverage to that date or even well beyond it. This ragged-edge effect is the result of a protracted—and frequently delayed—editorial process, and the responsibility for it must rest primarily with this editor rather than with the authors. The trilogy The Bible and Its Modern Interpreters was originally planned for publication during the Society of Biblical Literature's centennial year—1980—or shortly thereafter, and most of our assignments were made and accepted by mid-1978, with submission of contributions requested for late 1979. Most authors complied with this schedule and all have been exceedingly patient as the three collaborative volumes have moved through the press. Several contributors have requested, however, that the volume take note of the fact that their portions were completed prior to 1980, so that readers will understand that the cut-off point for the assessment of scholarship in some cases precedes by several years the actual publication date. In the long run, this is not a matter of great concern, for the volume's intent is to provide perspective on that significant period of scholarship that has brought us to the present, rather than to offer quick reference to the latest views or fads. After all, the proper distinction between the prosaic or fadish and that which constitutes significant scholarly contribution often can be made only when the appropriate distance has been established between the achievement and the evaluation.

It remains, then, to thank these patient contributors and to assure them that their efforts will be richly rewarded as this volume—and its two companion works — are employed by scholars, students, and the clergy over the next generation. Additional thanks are extended to the general editor of the trilogy, Professor Douglas A. Knight of Vanderbilt University; to Ms. Paula McNutt, a graduate student at Vanderbilt, who prepared the maps; to Drs. Maurya Horgan and Paul Kobelski of The Scriptorium for copyediting and typesetting that are fully informed by scholarly expertise; and to Scholars Press and Fortress Press and to the National Endowment for the Humanities for their support of the project.

As this volume was in the final stages of editorial preparation, my esteemed and distinguished co-editor, George W. MacRae, died suddenly and most unexpectedly on 6 September 1985.

> George W. MacRae, S.J., was the first permanent Charles Chauncey Stillman Professor of Roman Catholic Theological Studies at Harvard Divinity School. He was a person of wide and deep learning with fine analytic and synthetic skills, a masterful writer and articulate speaker, an extraordinary diplomat, a totally unselfish mentor and colleague, a loyal friend wholly without guile, a serious and devoted churchman, and the finest of human beings.

It has been an honor for all of us to work with him on the present project and in so many other ways both in and beyond the Society of Biblical Literature, and it is fitting that this volume be dedicated to his memory.

Eldon Jay Epp

BIBLIOGRAPHY

Bentley, Jerry H.
  1983   *Humanists and Holy Writ: New Testament Scholarship in the Renaissance.* Princeton: Princeton University Press.
Brown, Raymond E., S.S.
  1981   *The Critical Meaning of the Bible.* New York and Ramsey, NJ: Paulist.
Cobb, James Harrel
  1947   "Current Trends in Catholic Biblical Research." Pp. 116–28 in *The Study of the Bible Today and Tomorrow.* Ed. H. R. Willoughby. Chicago: University of Chicago Press.
Kümmel, Werner Georg
  1972   *The New Testament: The History of the Investigation of Its Problems.* Tr. S. McLean Gilmour and Howard C. Kee. Nashville and New York: Abingdon.
Saunders, Ernest W.
  1982   *Searching the Scriptures: A History of the Society of Biblical Literature, 1880–1980.* SBL Biblical Scholarship in North America 8. Chico, CA: Scholars Press.
Yarbro Collins, Adela, ed.
  1985   *Feminist Perspectives on Biblical Scholarship.* SBL Biblical Scholarship in North America 10. Chico, CA: Scholars Press.

ABBREVIATIONS

AB	Anchor Bible
ACW	Ancient Christian Writers
AGJU	Arbeiten zur Geschichte des antiken Judentums und des Urchristentums
ALGHJ	Arbeiten zur Literatur und Geschichte des hellenistischen Judentums
ALW	*Archiv für Liturgiewissenschaft*
AnBib	Analecta Biblica
ANRW	*Aufstieg und Niedergang der römischen Welt: Geschichte und Kultur Roms im Spiegel der neueren Forschung.* Ed. H. Temporini and W. Haase. Berlin and New York: de Gruyter.
ArOr	*Archiv orientální*
ASNU	Acta seminarii neotestamentici upsaliensis
ASTI	*Annual of the Swedish Theological Institute*
ATANT	Abhandlungen zur Theologie des Alten und Neuen Testaments
ATR	*Anglican Theological Review*
AusBR	*Australian Biblical Review*
AUSS	*Andrews University Seminary Studies*
BA	*Biblical Archaeologist*
BAC	Biblioteca de autores cristianos
BAG	W. Bauer, W. F. Arndt, and F. W. Gingrich, *A Greek-English Lexicon of the New Testament and Other Early Christian Literature.* 2d ed. rev. by Gingrich and F. W. Danker. Chicago: University of Chicago Press, 1979.
BBB	Bonner biblische Beiträge
BETL	Bibliotheca ephemeridum theologicarum lovaniensium
BEvT	Beiträge zur evangelischen Theologie
BFCT	Beiträge zur Förderung christlicher Theologie
BG	Codex Berolinensis Gnosticus (P. Berol. Copt. 8502)
BGBE	Beiträge zur Geschichte der biblischen Exegese
BHT	Beiträge zur historischen Theologie
Bib	*Biblica*
BibLeb	*Bibel und Leben*
BibOr	Biblica et orientalia
BJRL	*Bulletin of the John Rylands Library*
BJS	Brown Judaic Studies
BK	*Bibel und Kirche*
BLit	*Bibel und Liturgie*
BO	Bibliotheca orientalis
BR	*Biblical Research*
BSac	*Bibliotheca Sacra*
BT	*The Bible Translator*
BTB	*Biblical Theology Bulletin*
BU	Biblische Untersuchungen
BWANT	Beiträge zur Wissenschaft vom Alten und Neuen Testament
BZ	*Biblische Zeitschrift*
BZNW	Beihefte zur ZNW
CB	*Cultura biblica*

CBQ	Catholic Biblical Quarterly
CBQMS	CBQ Monograph Series
CH	Church History
CJT	Canadian Journal of Theology
CNT	Commentaire du Nouveau Testament
ConBNT	Coniectanea biblica, New Testament
ConNT	Coniectanea neotestamentica
CQR	Church Quarterly Review
CRB	Cahiers de la Revue biblique
CSCO	Corpus scriptorum christianorum orientalium
CTM	Concordia Theological Monthly
DBSup	Dictionnaire de la Bible, Supplément. Ed. H. Cazelles and A. Feuillet. Paris: Letouzey et Ané, 1928–.
DTT	Dansk teologisk tidsskrift
EBib	Études bibliques
EJMI	Early Judaism and Its Modern Interpreters. Ed. Robert Kraft and G. W. E. Nickelsburg. Philadelphia: Fortress; Atlanta, GA: Scholars Press, 1986.
EKKNT	Evangelisch-katholischer Kommentar zum Neuen Testament
EPRO	Études préliminaires aux religions orientales dans l'empire romain
EstBib	Estudios bíblicos
ETS	Erfurter theologische Studien
EvQ	Evangelical Quarterly
EvT	Evangelische Theologie
EWNT	Exegetisches Wörterbuch zum Neuen Testament. Ed. H. Balz and G. Schneider. 2 vols. Stuttgart: Kohlhammer, 1978–.
ExpTim	Expository Times
FBBS	Facet Books, Biblical Series
FGLP	Forschungen zur Geschichte und Lehre des Protestantismus
FRLANT	Forschungen zur Religion und Literatur des Alten und Neuen Testaments
GCS	Die griechischen christlichen Schriftsteller der ersten drei Jahrhunderte
GRBS	Greek, Roman, and Byzantine Studies
Greg	Gregorianum
GNT	Grundrisse zum Neuen Testament
HAW	Handbuch der Altertumswissenschaft
HDR	Harvard Dissertations in Religion
HeyJ	Heythrop Journal
HibJ	Hibbert Journal
HNT	Handbuch zum Neuen Testament
HNTC	Harper's NT Commentaries
HNTSup	Supplements to HNT
HR	History of Religions
HTKNT	Herders theologischer Kommentar zum Neuen Testament
HTR	Harvard Theological Review
HTS	Harvard Theological Studies
HUT	Hermeneutische Untersuchungen zur Theologie
IB	The Interpreter's Bible. Ed. G. A. Buttrick. Nashville: Abingdon, 1952–57.
ICC	International Critical Commentary
IDBSup	Interpreter's Dictionary of the Bible, Supplementary Volume. Ed. K. Crim. Nashville: Abingdon, 1976.
IEJ	Israel Exploration Journal
IGNTP	International Greek New Testament Project

Int	*Interpretation*
JA	*Journal asiatique*
JAAR	*Journal of the American Academy of Religion*
JAC	*Jahrbuch für Antike und Christentum*
JACSup	Supplements to *JAC*
JBC	*Jerome Biblical Commentary.* Ed. R. E. Brown, J. A. Fitzmyer, and R. Murphy. Englewood Cliffs, NJ: Prentice-Hall, 1968.
JBL	*Journal of Biblical Literature*
JBR	*Journal of Bible and Religion*
JEA	*Journal of Egyptian Archaeology*
JEH	*Journal of Ecclesiastical History*
JES	*Journal of Ecumenical Studies*
JJS	*Journal of Jewish Studies*
JQR	*Jewish Quarterly Review*
JR	*Journal of Religion*
JSJ	*Journal for the Study of Judaism*
JSNT	*Journal for the Study of the New Testament*
JSS	*Journal of Semitic Studies*
JTC	*Journal for Theology and the Church*
JTS	*Journal of Theological Studies*
KD	*Kerygma und Dogma*
LD	Lectio divina
LTK	*Lexikon für Theologie und Kirche.* Ed. J. Höfer and K. Rahner. 11 vols. 2d ed. Freiburg im B.: Herder, 1957–67.
MeyerK	H. A. W. Meyer, Kritisch-exegetischer Kommentar über das Neue Testament
MScRel	*Mélanges de science religieuse*
MTS	Marburger theologische Studien
MTZ	*Münchener theologische Zeitschrift*
NCB	New Century Bible
NedTTs	*Nederlands theologisch tijdschrift*
Neot	*Neotestamentica*
NHS	Nag Hammadi Studies
NICNT	New International Commentary on the New Testament
NorTT	*Norsk Teologisk Tidsskrift*
NovT	*Novum Testamentum*
NovTSup	Supplements to *Novum Testamentum*
NRT	*La nouvelle revue théologique*
NTAbh	Neutestamentliche Abhandlungen
NTD	Das Neue Testament Deutsch
NTS	*New Testament Studies*
NTTS	New Testament Tools and Studies
NZSysTh	*Neue Zeitschrift für systematische Theologie*
OBO	Orbis biblicus et orientalis
OLP	Orientalia lovaniensia periodica
OLZ	*Orientalische Literaturzeitung*
Or	*Orientalia*
OrAnt	*Oriens antiquus*
OTS	*Oudtestamentische Studiën*
PCB	*Peake's Commentary on the Bible.* Ed. M. Black and H. H. Rowley. London: Nelson, 1962.
PIRS	*Perspectives in Religious Studies*
PO	Patrologia orientalis
PSTJ	*Perkins School of Theology Journal*
PTMS	Pittsburgh Theological Monograph Series

PTS   Patristische Texte und Studien
PW   *Paulys Real-Encyclopädie der klassischen Altertumswissenschaft.* Ed.
          G. Wissowa. Stuttgart: Metzler, 1893.
QD   Quaestiones disputatae
RAC   *Reallexikon für Antike und Christentum*
RB   *Revue biblique*
RBén   *Revue bénedictine*
RCB   *Revista de cultura bíblica*
RechBib   Recherches bibliques
RevExp   *Review and Expositor*
RevistB   *Revista biblica*
RevQ   *Revue de Qumran*
RevScRel *Revue des sciences religieuses*
RevThom   *Revue thomiste*
RGG   *Die Religion in Geschichte und Gegenwart.* Ed. K. Galling. 3d ed.
          7 vols. Tübingen: Mohr-Siebeck, 1957–65.
RHPR   *Revue d'histoire et de philosophie religieuses*
RHR   *Revue de l'histoire des religions*
RivB   *Rivista biblica*
RivBSup   Supplements to *RivB*
RNT   Regensburger Neues Testament
RSR   *Recherches de science religieuse*
RTL   *Revue théologique de Louvain*
RTP   *Revue de théologie et de philosophie*
RVV   Religionsgeschichtliche Versuche und Vorarbeiten
SB   Sources bibliques
SBJ   *La sainte bible de Jérusalem*
SBL   Society of Biblical Literature
SBLDS   SBL Dissertation Series
SBLMS   SBL Monograph Series
SBLSBS   SBL Sources for Biblical Study
SBLTT   SBL Texts and Translations
SBM   Stuttgarter biblische Monographien
SBS   Stuttgarter Bibelstudien
SBT   Studies in Biblical Theology
SC   Sources chrétiennes
SCHNT   Studia ad corpus hellenisticum Novi Testamenti
SD   Studies and Documents
SE   *Studia Evangelica*
SEÅ   *Svensk exegetisk årsbok*
SEAJournTheol *South East Asia Journal of Theology*
Sem   *Semitica*
SHAW   Sitzungsberichte der Heidelberger Akademie der Wissenschaften
SJLA   Studies in Judaism in Late Antiquity
SJT   *Scottish Journal of Theology*
SNT   Studien zum Neuen Testament
SNTSMS   Society for New Testament Studies Monograph Series
SPap   *Studia papyrologica*
SPAW   Sitzungsberichte der preussischen Akademie der Wissenschaften
SPB   Studia post-biblica
SR   *Studies in Religion/Sciences religieuses*
ST   *Studia theologica*
StudHell Studia Hellenistica
SUNT   Studien zur Umwelt des Neuen Testaments

SWGFrankfurt	Sitzungsberichte der Wissenschaftlichen Gesellschaft an der Johann
Wolfgang Goethe-Universität Frankfurt am Main
TBl	*Theologische Blätter*
TBT	*The Bible Today*
TBü	*Theologische Bücherei*
TDNT	*Theological Dictionary of the New Testament.* Ed. G. Kittel and G.
Friedrich. Trans. G. W. Bromiley. 10 vols. Grand Rapids: Eerd-
mans, 1964–76.
TextS	Texts and Studies
TF	*Theologische Forschung*
TGl	*Theologie und Glaube*
THKNT	Theologischer Handkommentar zum Neuen Testament
ThStud	Theologische Studien
TLZ	*Theologische Literaturzeitung*
TP	*Theologie und Philosophie*
TPQ	*Theologisch-Praktische Quartalschrift*
TQ	*Theologische Quartalschrift*
TRE	*Theologische Real-enzyklopädie*
TRev	*Theologische Revue*
TRu	*Theologische Rundschau*
TS	*Theological Studies*
TTKi	*Tidsskrift for Teologi og Kirke*
TToday	*Theology Today*
TU	Texte und Untersuchungen
TuK	Texte und Kommentare
TWNT	*Theologisches Wörterbuch zum Neuen Testament.* Ed. G. Kittel. 10
vols. Stuttgart: Kohlhammer, 1933–73.
TynBul	*Tyndale Bulletin*
TZ	*Theologische Zeitschrift*
UNT	Untersuchungen zum Neuen Testament
USQR	*Union Seminary Quarterly Review*
VC	*Vigiliae christianae*
VF	*Verkündigung und Forschung*
WMANT	Wissenschaftliche Monographien zum Alten und Neuen Testament
WO	*Die Welt des Orients*
WTJ	*Westminster Theological Journal*
WUNT	Wissenschaftliche Untersuchungen zum Neuen Testament
ZKG	*Zeitschrift für Kirchengeschichte*
ZKT	*Zeitschrift für katholische Theologie*
ZNW	*Zeitschrift für die neutestamentliche Wissenschaft*
ZRGG	*Zeitschrift für Religions- und Geistesgeschichte*
ZTK	*Zeitschrift für Theologie und Kirche*
ZWT	*Zeitschrift für wissenschaftliche Theologie*

Part One

The World of
the New Testament

1

GRECO-ROMAN RELIGION AND PHILOSOPHY AND THE NEW TESTAMENT

Abraham J. Malherbe

The last fifty years have not witnessed intense effort to situate the NT in its Greco-Roman context. The reason for this neglect is not simply the oft-repeated lament that students no longer come to advanced study of early Christianity with a sound knowledge of Greek and Latin. Rather, the desuetude into which the enterprise has fallen appears to be due to a combination of factors: the absence of dramatic new discoveries; the parochialism of classical scholarship, which has neglected the Hellenistic period and excluded Christianity from its purview; inadequate classical education of students of early Christianity, and—after the history-of-religions school's fall into disfavor—no new, commanding hypothesis to serve as an interpretative framework. That this peculiar mix of elements does not exist today in the same way or degree that it did seventy years ago does not mean, however, that work in the area has ceased (Judge, 1979; Hommel, 1966:3–4; Malherbe, 1988: nn. 21–27). The following survey of major developments in the field will identify some recent accomplishments as well as methodological issues that demand attention.

I. GRECO-ROMAN RELIGION AND PHILOSOPHY

Investigation of ancient religion and philosophy has proceeded with renewed intensity during the last two decades (Beaujeu).[1] With few exceptions, however, no major works of synthesis have been produced. Attention has been given instead to the collection and interpretation of new materials, to reevaluation of classic works in the field in the light of new discoveries and ongoing research, and to the development and application of new methodologies.

Reference Works and Handbooks

Work on the major reference books has continued, and some new ones have been published. Pauly-Wissowa-Kroll, *Realencyclopädie der classischen*

---

[1] *ANRW*, Part 2, vols. 16, 17, and 18 will contain numerous important essays, some of which have already appeared.

Altertumswissenschaft (ed. G. Wissowa et al.; Munich: A. Druckenmüller, 1893–), except for the indexes, was completed in 1972, and the *Supplements,* to which John P. Murphey and Hans Gärtner and Albert Wünsch have provided useful indexes, reached volume 15 in 1978. An updated five-volume edition, *Der kleine Pauly,* was published from 1964 to 1975 (Stuttgart: A. Druckenmüller). On a less pretentious scale, the *Oxford Classical Dictionary* (Oxford: Clarendon Press) has gone through two editions (1948 and 1970), and the *Lexikon der Alten Welt* (ed. C. Andresen; Tübingen and Zurich: Bertels and Huber, 1965) has joined the ranks of excellent reference works. The monumental *Aufstieg und Niedergang der römischen Welt* (ed. H. Temporini and W. Haase; Berlin and New York: de Gruyter, 1972–) promises to become one of the major sources of information on research in the field.

The most impressive of the handbooks on Greek religion is that of Martin P. Nilsson, who thought that a history of the religions of late antiquity should include Christianity but considered the time not yet ripe for such a study of syncretism and presented his work only as a *Vorarbeit* (5). Kurt Latte, on Roman religion, has been criticized for inaccuracy and narrowness of viewpoint and is less useful to the student of early Christianity. For the philosophy of the period, *The Cambridge History of Later Greek and Early Medieval Philosophy* (ed. A. H. Armstrong; Cambridge: University Press, 1970) is dominated and skewed by an interest in Plotinus and therefore is of limited value to students of the NT, who still benefit most from Zeller and Praechter.

Collections of material, especially dealing with the cults, have been made and are listed by Jean Beaujeu, who does not, however, take note of E. J. and L. E. Edelstein's work on Asclepius or L. Vidman's on Isis and Sarapis. The scores of volumes published by E. J. Brill under the editorship of M. J. Vermaseren since 1961 in the series *Études préliminaires aux religions orientales dans l'empire romain,* as well as those planned for future publication, have underlined the preliminary nature of much of the current activity. Similar collections of philosophical material have been published. The Neopythagoreans have been well served by Holger Thesleff and Maria Timpanaro Cardini and the Epicureans by G. Arrighetti; a new edition of the Cynic letters has made these neglected documents available to a larger public.[2] Collections of the fragments from individual authors, too, have appeared, for example the editions of Aristippus by Erich Mannebach, Antisthenes by F. Decleva Caizzi, Bion of Borysthenes by Jan Fredrik Kindstrand, Teles by Edward N. O'Neil, Posidonius by L. Edelstein and I. G. Kidd and another by Willy Theiler, Demetrius the Cynic by Margarethe Billerbeck, and both Atticus and Numenius by Edouard Des Places. In addition, a new edition of the *Tabula of Cebes* has been published by J. T.

---

[2] Malherbe, 1977a. See pp. 1–5 for information on other Cynic collections.

Fitzgerald and L. M. White, and a collection of Hellenistic moral instruction of interest to students of early Christianity has been edited by A. Malherbe (1986). Finally, a most useful collection of the fragments of various Socratics, including Aristippus, Antisthenes, Diogenes, and Crates, has been provided by Gabriele Giannantoni.

Studies

The studies of particular cults, phenomena, or persons reveal an ongoing assessment of old presuppositions and a testing of new approaches. This is less the case with philosophy, where the approaches and interests tend to be the traditional ones, yet with an increasing awareness of the diversity and development within the different schools and thus a diminishing emphasis on the homogenized "philosophical Koine." Studies of the oriental cults have for the most part stressed particularities. Thus, they have begun to treat systematically for particular cults the language, rituals, religious functionaries, and individual and collective forms of cultic participation with the aim of identifying the constants and variants within particular cults and the resemblances and differences between various religions. They also insist on more precise chronological and geographical differentiation of the data than has been customary and have shown a special interest in the expansion of these religions and in the routes and circumstances of their diffusion. In addition, there has been a growing interest in the social dimension of these religions. The sociological approach, particularly as it has dealt with specific cults, problems, or regions, has further contributed to the critical assessment of older hypotheses and the growing reluctance to generalize (Gordon; Brown; Petit: 227–32). Especially valuable in this regard is an extensive canvass of methodological issues by C. R. Phillips. Attention has not, however, been confined to the oriental religious influx, which has been of major interest to NT scholars (MacMullen). Latte, for instance, deals primarily with the earlier period of Roman religion. Both he and Jean Bayet draw a contrast between it and the waves of foreign cults that engulfed it during the empire (Latte: 25–35, 251–93, 327–59; Bayet: 144–69), but an interest in the native cults (Petit: 230–31; J. Z. Smith, 1971, 1978:ix–xvi) and the continuing influence of traditional Roman religion (Brown: 35ff.; H. Weiss; Nock, 1964:xi; Liebeschuetz) can be detected.

The issue of definition has been raised anew in connection with the phenomenon of syncretism, which has loomed large in the study of ancient religion during the last seventy years. Always fraught with ambiguity, syncretism has been the subject in the last decade of a number of conferences that have aimed at greater precision,[3] and Ulrich Berner has devoted a major

---

[3] In the Bibliography see Hartman (Abo), Dunand and Lévêque (Besançon), Dietrich (Göttingen), Pearson (Santa Barbara), Strassburg.

study to the use of the concept. The term has generally been used to describe either the mixture of elements from several religions which influence each other mutually, or the acceptance of elements from one religion by another without any basic change occurring in the character of the receiving religion. There have been two tendencies in approaching syncretism. The one utilized the broad concept to explain particular phenomena; the other placed emphasis on treating things in their concreteness, particularity, and specificity and moved to synthesis, if at all, with great caution and reluctance. The latter approach has characterized especially, but not exclusively, the so-called Uppsala school[4] and some British scholars such as A. D. Nock.[5]

In the earliest of the recent conferences, Helmer Ringgren identified certain problems of syncretism that have also come up for discussion in the succeeding ones. His opinion that neither the etymology of the term nor a historical analysis of its use appears to be particularly illuminating has evidently not been shared by some (Wikander), but others have moved on to present typologies of syncretisms (Lévêque) or to more philosophical considerations of the phenomenon (Pannikar; Nouailhat) or to apply concepts from fields such as linguistics to it (Segert). It has also been argued that a preliminary consideration in gaining a firmer grasp on syncretism should be that a latent inclination to independence in a religion should be seen as counterbalancing the tendency to merge with the new and that the combination should have the capacity for continuing its existence (Colpe: 19). The conferees, however, have not laid stress on abstract definition but have preferred to start from the empirical fact of the encounter of religions and to examine the various types, conditions, and results of such an encounter (Ringgren: 7; Wiessner: 11). Whereas the approach to syncretism in the past has been largely historical and philological, the call has been made to learn from sociology, psychology, and social anthropology (Ringgren: 9). The probes made in the conferences have been hesitant to undertake this task on a large scale but have focused on particularities and have thus shared in the general concerns of the discipline.

The present status of the discipline therefore suggests that the time for synthesis, however desirable it might be, has not yet come. Until it does, one has to make do with contributions that are essentially preliminary but are not the less valuable for that.

---

[4] See Capps, esp. 36–37, 39 for the emphasis of the Uppsala school. Geo Widengren, as a major example, hesitates to use the word syncretism and confesses, after four decades of studying Syrian Christianity, not to have come to a synthesis.

[5] See Zeph Stewart's description of Nock's work (Nock, 1972:1–5) and Nock's own statement, "A fact is a holy thing, and its life should never be laid down on the altar of a generalization" (333).

II. THE NEW TESTAMENT

Writing on Paul and Hellenism more than twenty years ago, Helmut Koester correctly observed that the Hellenistic background of Paul had been brought into ill repute (1965:187). There has been no general improvement in the situation since then. The history-of-religions approach is frequently dismissed or viewed with suspicion on the grounds that it fails to do justice to the historical singularity of Christianity (Judge, 1972:23), and there is still a tendency on dogmatic grounds to deny any real Hellenistic influence on Paul and to speak rather of analogies and verbal borrowings. Paul's indebtedness to Jewish traditions, however, is accepted as somehow preserving his theological integrity. This assessment does not escape the apologetic view of the *Dictionnaire Apologétique de la Foi Catholique* (Paris: Beauchesne) that syncretism compromises the unique, revealed, true religion by reducing it to a simple residue of diverse religions (d'Ales; cf. Nouailhat: 214–16), and it is as evident among conservative Protestants as it is among certain Roman Catholics.[6] The same state of affairs exists with respect to the rest of the NT, yet the effort to place the NT in its Greco-Roman environment has not been abandoned.

Reference Works, Handbooks, and Interpretations

On the most elementary level, the relevance of the Greco-Roman world for the study of the NT is paid lip service by the sourcebooks, which provide texts illuminating the "Background," "*Umwelt*," or "origins" of the NT or early Christianity, and by its treatment in introductory handbooks. Of much greater significance, but of general interest, is the fact that the Corpus Hellenisticum project has experienced new life during the last two decades as a result of the work and influence of W. C. van Unnik (e.g., 1973) and H. D. Betz (e.g., 1975, 1978). The excellent indexes in vol. 10 of the German edition of the *TWNT* further show that the Greco-Roman side to early Christianity has not been neglected completely.

A number of reference works containing articles of *religionsgeschichtliche* interest are in production. The eleventh volume of the supplements to the *Dictionnaire de la Bible* (*DBSup*; Paris: Letouzey et Ané) is currently appearing in fascicles and reached "Salut" in 1987. Frequently very thorough in its treatment, it tends to be conservative in its interpretations. The same is also true of the *Dictionnaire de spiritualité, ascétique et mystique* (Paris:

---

[6] For Catholic views, see Jacquier, and Cambier. For an approach seemingly characteristic of British and evangelical scholarship, F. F. Bruce is illustrative. In his work on NT history (1972) the Jewish background receives extensive treatment, but only a short account is given of the philosophical schools and none of pagan religion; his SNTS presidential address (1976) equally fails to engage the subject.

Beauchesne) of which volume 12 is appearing in fascicles (up to "Quodvult-
deus" in 1983). Much more impressive and useful is the *Reallexikon für
Antike und Christentum* (Stuttgart: Hiersemann), which began publication in
1950 and reached volume 13 ("Hekate") in 1987. The entries, especially in
the later volumes, are frequently comprehensive and for the most part well
balanced, but they tend to treat the NT too cursorily. Publication of a series
of supplements began in 1985 and reached "Athen 2" in 1986. The companion *Jahrbuch für Antike und Christentum*, of which volume 29 appeared
in 1987, publishes material supplementary to the *Reallexikon* entries, as well
as substantial book reviews. Yet another supplementary series, the *Ergänz-
ungsbände*, reached volume 13 in 1987.

As in the case of the pagan material, very few attempts at synthesis have
been made from the Christian side, but a few should be mentioned. The
most valuable handbook is that of Karl Prümm (1954), recognized by Rudolf
Bultmann as a model of the genre (1950:482). Written for theological
students, it belongs to a long tradition not confined to Roman Catholics.
Prümm holds to the view that, beginning with a primitive monotheism, the
history of pagan religion is that of a decline into a condition from which
Christianity rescued it. Although exception has been taken to this and to
what has been viewed as Prümm's apologetic treatment of certain points of
detail, the book has been widely received, especially for its thoroughness and
the information it provides on the individual characteristics of the cults,
particularly in the provinces.

In sharp contrast is the book by Carl Schneider, written in the tradition
of the history-of-religions school. Schneider holds to the conviction that
despite many regional and individual details, there remains a uniform
stratum that can be referred to as "Hellenistic religion." Ancient religion,
which culminated for him in mystery theology, and ancient philosophy are
considered a "geistesgeschichtliche" entity that ultimately found its form in
Christianity after essentially foreign Jewish elements had been rejected. The
book has been severely criticized, not least of all by Hermann Langerbeck,
for its overall conception, generalizations, factual errors and arbitrary
interpretations.

One of the few broadly interpretative contributions in English is that of
F. C. Grant. The most impressive attempt to utilize Greco-Roman religion
and philosophy in interpreting the NT has been that of Bultmann. In his
Primitive Christianity in Its Contemporary Setting (1956), which probably
overstresses the intellectualism of Greek life, he formulates a question
(p. 179) whose answer is worked out at great length in his *Theology of the
New Testament*, namely, whether Christianity is really a syncretistic religion
or whether there is a fundamental unity behind all its diversity.[7] In the latter

---

[7] For the earlier debate in the history-of-religions school on the syncretistic nature of Christianity, see Ittel: 30–33.

work especially, Bultmann makes use of insights derived from the master-piece of the history-of-religions schools, Wilhelm Bousset's *Kyrios Christos*. Bousset had sharply distinguished between Hellenistic Christianity and the primitive Palestinian community and had described the influence especially of the pagan mystery religions and the Kyrios cult on the former. Bultmann accepted this basic, two-stage religious history and, with a greater emphasis on gnosticism as an influence on syncretistic Hellenistic Christianity, sought to make it theologically fruitful. His acceptance of Bousset's construction has frequently met with opposition for its overall conception (e.g., Marshall) as well as for its presentation of details (e.g., Hengel, 1972, 1976), but his work is unequalled for its independence and coherence and for its achievement in theologically interpreting the data.

A New Approach: James M. Robinson and Helmut Koester

With renewed appreciation for Walter Bauer's *Orthodoxy and Heresy in Early Christianity*, James M. Robinson and Helmut Koester have recently proposed a way out of the impasse. Sketching the development of early Christianity in certain geographical areas, Bauer had argued that orthodoxy, as traditionally perceived, was a late development. Initially Christianity was characterized by a rich diversity and in some areas assumed forms that would later be deemed heretical after the Roman view became dominant. Bauer's view has met with various criticisms—by Roman Catholics, among others—that he had failed to deal with the theological aspect of church history, but he has nevertheless come to exert a major influence on German and American NT scholarship.[8] In the new approach proposed by Robinson and Koester, the theological and historical approaches cannot be simply distinguished, and the enterprise they promote, governed by their view of a dynamic, developing Christianity, includes the Greco-Roman environment within its perspective.

Robinson decries what he calls the static, monolithic, immobile view of the history-of-religions research of the NT "environment" or "background" through which early Christianity moved. He warns that this background cannot be mastered by reducing it to a mass of disorganized parallels to the NT (cf. Koester 1965:191); it must be conceptualized in terms of move-ments, "trajectories" through the Hellenistic world (Robinson: 1–19). Departing from an assumption of the history-of-religions school, Robinson and Koester stress the cultural and religious pluralism of the Hellenistic and Roman eras in general, and of contemporary Judaism in particular, and claim that the diversity of early Christianity corresponded to that of its pagan context.

[5] See Bauer, 1971:286–316 for an account of the reception and influence of the book.

In a number of programmatic essays, Koester has demonstrated his perception of the task. Walter Bauer was right, Koester claims, and it is necessary to examine particular situations in limited geographical areas in order to understand the interplay between Christianity and ancient culture (1971:273–77), and he has therefore extended Bauer's investigations back into the first century (1971:114–57). Koester's demand for precision seems to have heightened his sense of the importance of the particular. Writing on Paul, he had called for precision in dealing with "Hellenistic Judaism, a syncretistic religion," and with the syncretism of Paul's environment and of his theology (1965:191–92). Six years later, having had the benefit of the important work of A. Thomas Kraabel, he could say that the Jewish population of western Asia Minor was Hellenized but not necessarily syncretistic, and he affirmed the existence of regional distinctions within Judaism in both Palestine and the Diaspora.[9] It is also natural that such an approach should discover the need for detailed sociological analysis of religions within particular areas (1971:274).

Koester has also found the history-of-religions material theologically important. Impressed by the diversity of early Christianity and the confrontations to which it is thought to have led, Koester correctly claims that what is important in such confrontations is not the mere occurrence of certain terms or concepts from the environment but the modifications of them and the criteria used in the debates (1965:192ff.; 1971:205–31). "The investigation of this history and the analysis of the structures of these conflicts and of the tendencies of its language is the place where the endeavors of the historian, the theologian and the interpreter are identical" (1971:279). The approach thus conceived escapes the charge of positivism.

Clearly, this approach is methodologically more responsible than the generalizations of the history-of-religions school and is in line with the current emphases in the study of Greco-Roman religion. In addition, it has the not inconsiderable value of once again providing a hypothesis that offers a framework within which disparate data may be viewed. Nevertheless, further clarification is necessary, not least of all of the way syncretism is viewed. In the first place, as Kraabel has demonstrated, in the case of Jews in Sardis physical proximity did not lead to syncretism or "religious creativity," but produced clarity in their understanding of their Judaism and contributed to a conservatism that reinforced the piety of the past (1978:31–32). This must be entertained as a possibility in each case considered. Second, there is cause for uneasiness about the importance attributed to confrontation as the knothole through which the phenomenon is viewed. One should reckon with the likelihood that NT writers were as

---

[9] Of major importance are the following works of Kraabel: "The Diaspora Synagogue: Archaeological and Epigraphic Evidence since Sukenik," in *ANRW* 2.19.1; and *Judaism in Western Asia Minor under the Roman Empire* (SPB; Leiden: Brill [forthcoming]).

concerned with what they considered dangerous developments due to their readers' pagan traditions and environment as they were with competing theologies (Walter). Special care should be exercised not to impose the confrontational model of Christianity on its milieu, substituting Bauer's theory for the generalizations of the history-of-religions school. The whole range of possible ways in which religions react when they meet, extending from opposition or rejection through amelioration to assimilation, conscious and unconscious, should be taken into consideration. This will require the type of empirical investigation that is uncongenial to generalization, and should be pursued despite the bogeyman of "positivism." Koester's recent *Introduction to the New Testament* (1982), impressive as it is for its comprehensiveness and brilliance, witnesses to the fact that the problems he has helped to identify demand still more attention, and the program he has set forth has still to be carried out with precision.

III. INDIVIDUAL TOPICS

Mystery Religions

The mystery religions have occupied an important place in the study of Greco-Roman religion as well as early Christianity. The concern of the history-of-religions school, as represented by Richard Reitzenstein, was with the religiousness or piety of an entire state in the development of Hellenistic religion. The method followed was to compare as many disconnected written works as possible to arrive at an understanding of the general features of the missionary mystery religions, with only secondary interest in particular cults and none in chronological sequence. Paul was thought to have undertaken a systematic study of the mysteries' language and their conception of the world in preparation for his own mission (113–14, 536). Bousset was equally concerned with the form of the mysteries' piety, and not with analogies or parallels, and attempted to demonstrate the broad intellectual connections Christians like Paul had with this atmosphere in which Christianity grew. It was not a question of whether Paul was dependent on one or another particular mystery religion. The Hellenistic church had already unconsciously appropriated categories from the environment in developing its sacramentalism and Christology, and Paul built further on those foundations. Bousset knew that the high point of the mysteries came only in the second century, but he insisted that that was true of the upper classes, whereas Christians generally came from the lower. He argued further that the cults had an earlier history in the East, where Christianity also began (15, 18, 188–89).

Enthusiasm for the mysteries has cooled over the years, and Reitzenstein and Bousset have come in for severe criticism from classicists, liberal and conservative Protestants, and Roman Catholics alike, although not always for the same reasons.[10] Continuing investigation has shown that the degree of diffusion and the influence of the cults had been vastly overestimated (Prümm, 1954:281–82; 1960:160ff.; Nilsson: 670, 699–700; Nock, 1972:81; Wiens), and it has been questioned whether they can even be described as missionary religions (Nilsson: 700). Nock was reluctant to accept the mysteries as the prime expression of something as indeterminate as a "spirit of paganism" (1972:72), but Nilsson granted that they were at least one representative of a certain "religious atmosphere" (699–700). There is now widespread agreement that it is erroneous to think that one, general mystery theology existed (e.g., Nilsson: 664, 685; Grant: 18, 39, 77). Nilsson has charged that in a certain way modern researchers have continued the practice of the church fathers, who interpreted the mysteries in the light of Christian practices and that this emphasis on ideas rather than practices has caused them to overlook or undervalue the distinctions between the cults (685). Recent study has tended to trace these differences (Prümm, 1954:255–307; Nilsson: 679–701) and to stress the different stages of development of both the cults and Christianity during the period when they were thought to or did interact (Rahner). Great pains have been taken to explain apparent similarities between Christianity and the mysteries (e.g., Prümm, 1954:327–35), frequently by affirming different significance to the language they shared (e.g., Metzger). This has been especially so in the examination of the terminology Reitzenstein had thought to have been derived from the mysteries (Prümm, 1960:173–225). Despite occasional acceptance of such dependence (e.g., Casel), Nock's conclusion, that the mystery language had acquired a generic quality and an almost universal appeal and that its use in no way shows direct dependence on specific mysteries (1972:796ff.), seems to have carried the day. But the opinion that the mysteries influenced Paul's view of the sacraments and his Christology has continued to receive support, for example, from Bultmann, who may be taken as representative.

Bultmann held that the Hellenistic church understood baptism on analogy to the initiation sacraments of the mystery religions. He carefully specified that this was a secondary interpretation of the church's traditions, which Paul in turn received and united with his own view (1951:140–44, 311–12; cf. Schoeps: 114–15). This has been rejected by Nock and others who have laid greater stress on Jewish and Christian traditions (Nock, 1972:803–11), but the major response has come from Günther Wagner, who rejected the global view of the history-of-religions school and convincingly demonstrated that the mystery model presumably behind Romans 6 is found in no known cult. He claimed that there is an unbridgeable gap between Paul's view of baptism and mystery piety. Ethics has been an important element in the debate (Gäumann). It is frequently claimed that the moral

---

[10] For surveys of the reactions, see Rahner: 148–55; Metzger; Wagner: 1–57.

imperative in Christianity, especially as it is related to baptism, sharply distinguished Christianity from Greco-Roman religion in general and the mysteries in particular, with the possible exceptions of Mithraism and the cult of Isis (Nock, 1972:63ff.; Prümm, 1954:322–27; Rahner: 169–70; Wagner: 12). This is surely an overstatement and smacks of special pleading.[11] Closer to the truth about what set Christianity off is that it claimed to offer the power to live the moral life in addition to the motive for it (Nock, 1933:218–20; Wagner: 48), but the matter deserves more careful treatment than it has received (Wedderburn).

Bultmann also held that in a similar way the Hellenistic church before Paul had understood the Lord's Supper as a sacrament in the sense of the mystery religions and that Paul united his own view with theirs (1951:114–51; cf. Schoeps: 115–17). This view has likewise been rejected (e.g., Nock, 1972:803–11), but Hans-Josef Klauck has suggested that, although the Lord's Supper was not derived from the meals of the Hellenistic cults and mysteries, it would not have developed in the way it did without Hellenistic influence.

Bousset's interpretation of Paul's Christology (188–89) was developed further by Bultmann, who explained that it was possible for Paul to describe Christ's death as the means of release from the powers of this age because he appropriated a similar idea from the mysteries and expanded it by simultaneously integrating Christ's death with categories of gnostic myth (298). This construction, including the existence of the pre-Pauline Hellenistic church as conceived by Bousset and Bultmann, continues to find qualified acceptance (see Boers), but has also been rejected—for example by Hengel—who on chronological and other grounds argues for the importance of Jesus and the Jewish Christian traditions in the development of Christology (1972; 1976). H. J. Schoeps, however, accepted Bultmann's basic view and suggested that Paul undertook his development of Christology in order to have a point of contact in his preaching with people who were familiar with the cults (112, 153, 158). Nock reacted with the overstatement that he could not find in Paul's epistles any knowledge of paganism save in the most general terms, and expressed the opinion that, in view of the horror Paul had of paganism, such accommodation to it on his part was psychologically unthinkable (1972:930). His review of Schoeps's book closes with this advice: "We must at times admit the existence of originality in authors and movements that have survived" (1972:939; cf. Nilsson: 685).

The Divine Man

In recent years there has been a resurgence of interest in the *theios anēr* or "divine man" of earlier scholarship. Whereas the category had generally

---

[11] The distinction is frequently extended to include all Greek and Roman religion. Liebeschuetz provides a corrective by stressing the relation between Roman religion and morality.

been brought to bear on NT Christology, now its use was extended to clarify the dialectic between various competing Christian groups. The literature on the subject has burgeoned beyond manageable proportions (M. Smith, 1971; Kee; Tiede: 242–92; Holladay: 1–45), which is due in no small measure to the imaginative dissertation by Dieter Georgi on Paul's opponents in 2 Corinthians.

Georgi accepted the broadly sketched picture of "the divine man" and described what he thought to have been its importance in the propaganda of philosophers and cultists of various sorts. In their preaching, these wandering individuals were thought to have described their ancient heroes as well as themselves as "divine men," to have supported these claims by performing miracles, and to have emphasized in theory and practice the importance of rhetorical finesse. Hellenistic Judaism was advanced as the medium through which the phenomenon was made available to Christianity. The interpretation of biblical heroes and "divine men" would facilitate the later development of "divine man" Christologies. Furthermore, the charismatic, miracle-working propagandist or apologist who, in his interpretation of the Scripture experienced the divine presence, becoming a "divine man" himself, reflected the self-understanding shared by Paul's opponents in Corinth. These opponents, in Georgi's argument, held to a "divine man" Christology that Paul regarded as heretical, and they performed with a self-consciousness of themselves as "divine men." Georgi's provocative presentation has been enthusiastically received but has also met with some reservation, particularly from David Tiede and Carl Holladay.

Analysis of the term *theios anēr* and related language, as they are applied by Hellenistic Jewish authors to their biblical heroes, leads Holladay to the conclusion that, contrary to widespread opinion, these authors did not, in their interpretation of the ancient worthies, bridge the gap between the human and divine for propagandistic reasons. Rather, they more strenuously preserved the distinction. The strength of Holladay's study lies in the treatment of the Jewish texts, which had formed an important part of Georgi's argument, and it therefore challenges the substance of one part of that argument. However, although Holladay correctly questions the freedom with which a broad category derived from the history of ideas has been used in historical study, he does not subject the pagan traditions from which the model had been abstracted in the first place to detailed investigation.

It is to Tiede's credit that in an earlier study he had raised methodological questions about the construction of the model. His critique of the *theios anēr* hypothesis ends with a "negative evaluation of the interpretative significance of the generalized portrait of the *theios anēr* . . ." (238). He convincingly shows the need for greater precision in dealing with the phenomena which in the past have been lumped together in the discussion of "divine men" and "aretalogies." An examination of pagan texts dealing with the divine sage and of Hellenistic Jewish texts dealing with Moses leads him to the view that two propagandistic, aretalogical traditions can be differentiated, viz., that of the divine wise man and that of the miracle worker, and that the forms their propaganda took were discrete, corresponding to originally discrete aretalogies. The need for clearer differentiation had been recognized before (245–46), and Tiede's point is well taken.

In response to Tiede, Morton Smith has argued that there is no adequate evidence for originally discrete aretalogies and that intellectual as well as popular traditions knew of men who were at once sages and miracle workers (1978). That may very well be so, but methodological rigor is of prime importance. The construction of the divine figure has frequently proceeded in an uncritical manner. Disparate, to say nothing of opposing, traditions have sometimes been blended, and convincing evidence still has to be presented that propagandists who regarded *themselves* as divine men were as well recognized a phenomenon as has been supposed. To be sure, the difficulties confronting attempts to clarify the picture by sharper differentiation are formidable (M. Smith, 1971:186–88), but they should not be allowed to justify easy acceptance of generalizations that become unstable foundations for massive superstructures. Differentiation may not be possible in every case, especially when dealing with "popular" traditions, but the effort should be made if we are to attain any degree of certainty on the matter.[12]

Philosophy

In recent decades NT scholars have not shown the same ardor to place their literature in its philosophical context that patristic scholars have with regard to theirs. Given the current interest in Middle Platonism, for example, one could expect that Hebrews would by now have been examined in the light of roughly contemporary Platonists, but no thoroughgoing effort to do so has yet been published. Two volumes edited by Betz (1975, 1978) do indeed deal with Plutarch and the NT, but they paint with a broad brush, and the Platonism of Plutarch does not stand out clearly. The Epicureans have fared even less well. Instead of opening a new window on the NT as he had hoped they would, N. W. De Witt's two books on Epicurus and the NT seem to have bricked it up (1954a, 1954b). His excesses should not be allowed to disqualify more responsible attempts. In the light of the demonstrated importance of the Epicureans for the study of the fathers (e.g., Schmid), it would be strange if serious investigation were to show them to be completely irrelevant for an earlier period. The Neopythagoreans, especially Apollonius of Tyana, have come in for some discussion in connection with the "divine man," but with the exception of David L. Balch's work, which utilizes nonbiographical Neopythagorean material, they have otherwise not received much

---

[12] For differences between Stoic and Cynic divinization of the sage, see Malherbe, 1978.

attention. Stoicism is still taken up primarily in treatments of Paul's view of freedom (Niederwimmer; Nestle: 12–35), of ethics, and of natural theology (Pohlenz).[13]

There are many reasons for the neglect of the philosophers. Admittedly, the material, frequently preserved only in fragments, is difficult to work with. The major studies on the various authors or schools to which one might look for guidance into the material are frequently too specialized and devoted to subjects not of immediately obvious relevance to the NT. But the way in which the material has most frequently been approached has contributed both to the limitation to certain schools and authors and to the failure to stimulate interest. The enterprise is frequently conceived by some of its representatives and certainly by many in the scholarly community as a hunting for "parallels." This has had two results. First, those pagan authors have been studied who are likely to offer obvious points for comparison. This has meant that the emphasis has remained where Johannes Weiss placed it in 1908 (see Malherbe, 1985), on the Stoic moralists (Seneca, Musonius Rufus, Epictetus, Dio Chrysostom), and in addition on Plutarch and Lucian—those gold mines of information on popular culture in the early empire. Second, the lists of parallels have disintegrated both the pagan materials and the NT and have consequently become a curiosity that in practice is used, if at all, in lexical study. The most valuable contributions have been those which treat particular, limited topics at some depth and without prejudice (e.g., Pohlenz). More attention should be given to entire traditions, traced in some detail, with which Christianity might have come in contact. But the net should be cast even wider. The concern not only should be to find points of contact but also should include traditions that offered dissimilar or even antithetic views of God, humanity , and the world. Only when we are fully aware of all the options that were available, including those Christianity did not assimilate, shall we attain a firm grasp on the place of early Christianity in its intellectual environment. Thus conceived, the enterprise may theoretically even include the Peripatetics and the Skeptics.

Nevertheless, there are signs that we are entering a new stage. The importance of the Socratic traditions has again been affirmed. Hildebrecht Hommel (1966) has argued that traces of the tradition can be discerned in the Gospel traditions of Jesus' teaching. Betz (1972), whose recent work has included the study of ancient rhetoric, has offered the thesis that in his apology in 2 Corinthians 10–13 Paul refuses to make a rhetorical apology but instead continues a tradition going back to Socrates, which had been mediated to him by contemporary philosophers. Reflecting the current interest in sociological inquiry into early Christianity (see Malherbe, 1977b;

[13] Instead of pagan philosophy as the background of the Areopagus speech, Bertil Gärtner and W. Nauck have pointed to Hellenistic Jewish apologetic and mission propaganda; but see Hommel, 1955; and Des Places, 1969.

Meeks, 1983), Ronald F. Hock has demonstrated that a differentiation between Stoics and Cynics, and among Cynics themselves, allows us to place Paul's missionary practice more securely in its social (1978) and intellectual contexts (1979). Similarly, attention has been drawn to the way Paul's pastoral practice in forming Christian communities is similar to the "psychagogy" of his philosophic contemporaries (Malherbe, 1987).

Work has also progressed on the philosophical literary forms introduced into the discussion more than half a century ago by Bultmann and Martin Dibelius.[14]

The Haustafeln ("Household Rules")

Until recently, Dibelius's view of the *Haustafel* prevailed (1953; Weidinger). Stressing their Stoic background, he had suggested that Christians adopted and modifed the *Haustafeln* as their expectation of the parousia waned and they found it necessary to come to terms with the world. Both the origin of the *Haustafeln* and the functions to which they were put in the NT have now come to be viewed differently. David Schroeder has argued for OT apodictic law as the ultimate origin of their form and the teaching of Jesus as the source of their ethical conception. James E. Crouch, still worrying about the problem of Stoic influence, suggested that Christians took the material from which they formed their *Haustafeln* from Hellenistic Judaism and that they used the device to provide stability in a context of tension between enthusiastic and nomistic elements in the church. This preoccupation with Stoicism is unjustified,[15] and Balch has broadened the investigation by examining other philosophical traditions and aiming at greater precision in establishing the social function the *Haustafel* in 1 Peter is made to serve. He finds some similarities between the NT *Haustafeln* and Neopythagorean ideas on household management (1977; 1988) and argues that both are dependent on a topos "On the Constitution," which goes back to Aristotle. The function in 1 Peter is taken to be apologetic (1981). The discussion will continue as it takes up new data and new questions.

The Diatribe

In his 1910 dissertation, Bultmann compared Paul's preaching style with the Cynic-Stoic diatribe. The diatribe, which he thought of as a *Gattung*, represented for him the public oral preaching of the moralists. The same style is found also in Paul's method of preaching. Very little original work on the subject has been done by students of Christianity since Bultmann, and his book has become the major authority for NT scholars despite the questions that have insistently been raised about it, as well as the

---

[14] For greater detail on what follows, see Malherbe, 1987, 1988. See also Fiore; Fitzgerald, 1988.

[15] See Thraede for other philosophical traditions dealing with the subject matter.

Gattung he studied. Bultmann's student, Hartwig Thyen, failed to make any substantial advance in his study of what he thought to be Hellenistic Jewish homilies. His work is flawed by methodological naïvete and lack of originality in treating the nature of the diatribe. Stanley K. Stowers's study is the first major effort since Bultmann's. By bringing the discussion up to date, addressing the most important methodological issues, studying the most characteristic diatribal feature — its dialogical element — and proposing the schoolroom rather than the street corner as the social context for the diatribe, he has provided material for further discussion.

IV. CONCLUSION

Attempts to place the NT in its Greco-Roman environment seem to share the directions, emphases, and methodological concerns of the larger field of Greco-Roman religion and philosophy. In addition, the importance of Hellenistic Judaism, not simply as a conduit for pagan influences into Christianity but also as an illustration of resistance in a syncretistic context, is increasingly recognized. Investigation is steadily moving beyond past reconstructions by testing new hypotheses and focusing on particulars and the differences that may have characterized them. The atomization to which uneasiness with generalization can lead is at least partially offset by a tendency to stress traditions and functions instead of concentrating exclusively on isolated data. The present state of the discipline does not suggest that a satisfactory synthesis will soon be attained, but it does show that at last NT scholars may be prepared to move beyond the brilliant work of an earlier generation on which they have far too long been dependent.

BIBLIOGRAPHY

Arrighetti, G.
   1973   *Epicuro. Opere.* Biblioteca di cultura filosofica 41. Turin: Einaudi.

Balch, David L.
   1977   "Household Ethical Codes in Peripatetic, Neopythagorean and Early Christian Moralists." Pp. 397–404 in *Society of Biblical Literature 1977 Seminar papers.* Ed. P. J. Achtemeier. Missoula, MT: Scholars Press.
   1981   *Let Wives Be Submissive: The Domestic Code in 1 Peter.* SBLMS 26. Chico, CA: Scholars Press.
   1988   "The Neopythagorean Moralists and the New Testament." In *ANRW* 2.26.1. Ed. W. Haase. Berlin and New York: de Gruyter, in press.

Bauer, Walter
   1971   *Orthodoxy and Heresy in Earliest Christianity.* Trans. Philadelphia Seminar on Christian Origins. Ed. Robert Kraft and Gerhard Krodel (from 2d German edition by G. Strecker). Philadelphia: Fortress.

Bayet, Jean
   1969   *Histoire politique et psychologique de la religion romaine.* 2d ed. Paris: Payot.

Beaujeu, Jean
   1978   "Le paganisme romain sous le Haut Empire." Pp. 3–26 in *ANRW* 2.16.1. Ed. W. Haase. Berlin: de Gruyter.

Berner, Ulrich
   1982   *Untersuchungen zur Verwendung des Synkretismus-Begriffes.* Wiesbaden: Harrassowitz.

Betz, Hans Dieter
   1972   *Der Apostel Paulus und die sokratische Tradition.* BHT 45. Tübingen: Mohr-Siebeck.
   1975, ed. *Plutarch's Theological Writings and Early Christian Literature.* SCHNT 3. Leiden: Brill.
   1978, ed. *Plutarch's Ethical Writings and Early Christian Literature.* SCHNT 4. Leiden: Brill.

Bianchi, U., and M. J. Vermaseren
   1982   *La soteriologia dei culti orientali nell' Impero Romano.* EPRO 92. Leiden: Brill.

Billerbeck, Margarethe
   1979   *Der Kyniker Demetrius.* Philosophia Antiqua 36. Leiden: Brill.

Boers, Hendrikus
   1970   "Jesus and the Christian Faith: New Testament Christology since Bousset's *Kyrios Christos.*" *JBL* 89: 450–56.

Bousset, Wilhelm
   1970   *Kyrios Christos.* Trans. John E. Steely. Nashville: Abingdon.

Brown, Peter
   1978   *The Making of Late Antiquity.* Cambridge, MA: Harvard University Press.

Bruce, Frederick Fyvie
   1972   *New Testament History.* Garden City, NY: Doubleday.
   1976   "The New Testament and Classical Studies." *NTS* 22: 229–42.

Bultmann, Rudolf
   1910   *Der Stil der paulinischen Predigt und die kynisch-stoische Diatribe.* FRLANT 13. Göttingen: Vandenhoeck & Ruprecht.
   1950   Review of Karl Prümm, *Religionsgeschichtliches Handbuch für den Raum der altchristlichen Umwelt.* TLZ 75: 482–84.
   1951   *Theology of the New Testament,* 1. Trans. Kendrick Grobel. New York: Scribner.
   1956   *Primitive Christianity in Its Contemporary Setting.* Trans. R. H. Fuller. New York: Meridian.

Caizzi, Fernanda Decleva
   1966   *Antisthenis Fragmenta.* Milan: Cesalpino.

Cambier, J.
   1966   "Paul." *DBSup* 7: 279–387.

Capps, Walter H.
   1975   "Uppsala Methodology and the Problem of Religious Syncretism: An Afterword on Prolegomena." Pp. 21–45 in Pearson.

Cardini, Maria Timpanaro
  1958–1964   *Pitagorici: Testimonianze e frammenti*, 1–3. Biblioteca di studi
              superiori 28, 41, 45. Florence: Nuova Italia Editrice.
Casel, Odo
  1950   "Zur Kultsprache des Heiligen Paulus." *ALW* 1: 1–64.
Colpe, Carsten
  1975   "Die Vereinbarkeit historischer und struktureller Bestimmungen des
              Synkretismus." Pp. 15–37 in Dietrich.
Crouch, James E.
  1972   *The Origin and Intention of the Colossian Haustafel.* FRLANT 109.
              Göttingen: Vandenhoeck & Ruprecht.
d'Alés, A.
  1922   "Syncrétisme." *Dictionnaire Apologétique de la foi Catholique* 4:
              1582–83. Paris: Beauchesne.
Des Places, Edouard
  1969   *La Religion Grecque.* Paris: Picard.
  1973   *Numenius: Fragments.* Collection des Universités de France. Paris:
              Belles Lettres.
  1977   *Atticus: Fragments.* Collection des Universités de France. Paris:
              Belles Lettres.
De Witt, Norman Wentworth
  1954a   *Epicurus and His Philosophy.* Minneapolis: University of Minnesota
              Press.
  1954b   *St. Paul and Epicurus.* Minneapolis: University of Minnesota Press.
Dibelius, Martin
  1953   *An die Kolosser, Epheser, an Philemon.* 3d ed. Ed. H. Greeven. HNT
              12. Tübingen: Mohr-Siebeck.
Dietrich, Albert, ed.
  1975   *Synkretismus im syrisch-persischen Kulturgebiet: Bericht über ein
              Symposion in Reinhausen bei Göttingen in der Zeit vom 4. bis 8.
              Oktober 1971.* Göttingen: Vandenhoeck & Ruprecht.
Dunand, F., and P. Lévêque, eds.
  1975   *Les syncrétismes dans les religions de l'antiquité: Colloque de Besançon
              (22–23 Octobre 1973).* EPRO 46. Leiden: Brill.
Edelstein, E. J., and L. E. Edelstein
  1945   *Asclepius: A Collection and Interpretation of the Fragments.*
              Baltimore, MD: Johns Hopkins University Press.
Edelstein, L., and I. G. Kidd
  1972   *Posidonius I: The Fragments.* Cambridge Classical Texts and Com-
              mentaries, 13. Cambridge: University Press.
Fiore, Benjamin
  1986   *The Function of Personal Example in the Socratic and Pastoral Epistles.*
              AnBib 105. Rome: Biblical Institute Press.
Fitzgerald, J. T.
  1988   "*Cracks in an Earthen Vessel*": An Examination of the Catalogues of
              Hardships in the Corinthian Correspondence. SBLDS 99. Atlanta:
              Scholars Press.
Fitzgerald, J. T., and L. M. White
  1983   *The Tabula of Cebes.* SBLTT 24, Graeco-Roman Religion Series 7.
              Chico, CA: Scholars Press.

Gärtner, Bertil
    1955   *The Areopagus Speech and Natural Revelation.* ASNU 21. Uppsala:
              Almqvist & Wiksell.

Gärtner, Hans, and Albert Wünsch
    1980   *Paulys Realencyclopädie der classischen Altertumswissenschaft:*
              Register der Nachträge und Supplemente. Munich: A. Druckenmüller.

Gäumann, Niklaus
    1968   *Taufe und Ethik: Studien zu Römer 6.* BEvT 47. Munich: Kaiser.

Georgi, Dieter
    1964   *Die Gegner des Paulus im 2. Korintherbrief: Studien zur religiösen*
              Propaganda in der Spätantike. WMANT 11. Neukirchen-Vluyn:
              Neukirchener Verlag. Eng. trans.: *The Opponents of Paul in Second*
              Corinthians. Philadelphia: Fortress, 1986.

Giannantoni, Gabriele
    1983–1985 *Socraticorum Reliquiae.* 4 vols. Naples: Edizione dell'Ateneo.

Gordon, R. L.
    1972   "Mithraism and Roman Society." *Religion* 2: 92–121.

Grant, Frederick C.
    1962   *Roman Hellenism and the New Testament.* Edinburgh: Oliver & Boyd.

Hartman, Sven S., ed.
    1969   *Syncretism: Based on Papers read at the Symposium on Cultural*
              Contact, Meeting of Religions, Syncretism held at Abo on the 8th–10th
              of September, 1966. Ed. S. S. Hartman. Uppsala: Almqvist & Wiksell.

Hengel, Martin
    1972   "Christologie und neutestamentliche Chronologie. Pp. 43–68 in
              Neues Testament und Geschichte: Historischen Geschehen und
              Bedeutung im Neuen Testament: Oscar Cullmann zum 70. Geburtstag.
              Ed. H. Baltensweiler and B. Reicke. Zurich: Theologischer Verlag.
    1976   *The Son of God: The Origin of Christology and the History of Jewish-*
              Hellenistic Religion. Philadelphia: Fortress.

Hock, Ronald F.
    1978   "Paul's Tentmaking and the Problem of His Social Class." *JBL* 97:
              555–64.
    1979   *The Social Context of Paul's Ministry: Tentmaking and Apostleship.*
              Philadelphia: Fortress.

Holladay, Carl R.
    1977   *THEIOS ANER in Hellenistic Judaism: A Critique of the Use of This*
              Category in New Testament Christology. SBLDS 40. Missoula, MT:
              Scholars Press.

Hommel, Hildebrecht
    1955   "Neue Forschungen zur Areopagrede Acta 17." *ZNW* 46: 145–78.
    1966   "Herrenworte im Lichte sokratischer Ueberlieferung." *ZNW* 57:
              1–23.

Ittel, Gerhard Wolfgang
    1956   "Urchristentum und Fremdreligionen im Urteil der Religions-
              geschichtliche Schule." Inaugural Dissertation, Erlangen.

Jacquier, E.
    1922   "Mystères paiens (les) et Saint Paul." *Dictionnaire Apologétique de la*
              Foi Catholique 3: 964–1014.

Judge, Edwin A.
 1972   "St. Paul and Classical Society." *JAC* 15: 19–36.
 1979   "'Antike und Christentum': Towards a Definition of the Field.—A
           Bibliographical Survey." Pp. 3–58 in *ANRW* 2.23.1. Ed. W. Haase.
           Berlin and New York: de Gruyter.

Kee, Howard C.
 1973   "Aretalogy and Gospel." *JBL* 92: 402–22.

Kindstrand, Jan Fredrik
 1976   *Bion of Borysthenes: A Collection of the Fragments with Introduction
           and Commentary.* Acta Universitatis Upsaliensis: Studia Graeca
           Upsaliensis 11. Stockholm: Almqvist & Wiksell.

Klauck, Hans-Josef
 1982   *Herrenmahl und hellenistischer Kult.* NTAbh ns 15. Münster:
           Aschendorff.

Koester, Helmut
 1965   "Paul and Hellenism." Pp. 187–95 in *The Bible in Modern Scholar-
           ship: Papers Read at the 100th Meeting of the Society of Biblical
           Literature.* Ed. J. P. Hyatt. Nashville: Abingdon.
 1971   (with James M. Robinson) *Trajectories through Early Christianity.*
           Philadelphia: Fortress.
 1982   *Introduction to the New Testament.* 2 vols. Foundations and Facets.
           Philadelphia: Fortress.

Kraabel, Alf Thomas
 1978   "Paganism and Judaism: The Sardis Evidence." Pp. 13–33 in
           *Mélanges offerts à Marcel Simon: Paganisme, Judaisme, Christianisme:
           Influences et affrontements dans le monde antique.* Ed. A. Benoit, M.
           Philonenko, and C. Vogel. Paris: Boccard.
 1979   "The Diaspora Synagogue: Archaeological and Epigraphic Evidence
           since Sukenik." Pp. 477–510 in *ANRW* 2.19.1. Ed. W. Haase. Berlin
           and New York: de Gruyter.

Langerbeck, Hermann
 1956   Review of Carl Schneider, *Geistesgeschichte des antiken Christen-
           tums.* *Gnomon* 28: 481–501.

Latte, Kurt
 1960   *Römische Religionsgeschichte.* HAW 5.4. Munich: Beck.

Lévêque, Pierre
 1973   "Essai de typologie des syncrétismes." Pp. 179–87 in *Les syncrétismes
           dans les religions grecque et romaine: Colloque de Strasbourg (9–11
           juin 1971).* Paris: Presses universitaires de France.

Liebeschuetz, J. H. W. G.
 1979   *Continuity and Change in Roman Religion.* Oxford: Clarendon Press.

MacMullen, Ramsay
 1981   *Paganism in the Roman Empire.* New Haven, CT: Yale University
           Press.

Malherbe, Abraham J.
 1977a   *The Cynic Epistles: A Study Edition.* SBLSBS 12. Missoula, MT:
           Scholars Press.
 1977b   *Social Aspects of Early Christianity.* Baton Rouge: Louisiana State
           University Press. 2d enlarged ed.; Philadelphia: Fortress, 1983.

1978   "Pseudo Heraclitus, Epistle 4: The Divinization of the Wise Man."
            JAC 21: 42–64.
1986   *Moral Exhortation: A Greco-Roman Sourcebook.* Philadelphia:
            Westminster.
1987   *Paul and the Thessalonians: The Philosophic Tradition of Pastoral
            Care.* Philadelphia: Fortress.
1988   "Hellenistic Moralists and the New Testament." In *ANRW* 2.26.1. Ed.
            W. Haase. Berlin and New York: de Gruyter, in press.

Mannebach, Erich
1961   *Aristippi et Cyrenaicorum fragmenta.* Leiden: Brill.

Marshall, I. Howard
1973   "Palestinian and Hellenistic Christianity: Some Critical Comments."
            NTS 19: 271–87.

Meeks, Wayne A.
1983   *The First Urban Christians: The Social World of the Apostle Paul.* New
            Haven, CT: Yale University Press.

Metzger, Bruce M.
1955   "Considerations of Methodology in the Study of the Mystery
            Religions and Early Christianity." *HTR* 48: 1–20.

Murphey, John P.
1976   *Index to the Supplements and Supplementary Volumes of Pauly-
            Wissowa's R.E.: Index to the Nachträge and Berichtungen in Vols. I-
            XXIV of the first series, Vols. I-X of the second series, and Supplemen-
            tary Volumes I-XIV of Pauly-Wissowa-Kroll's Realenzyklopädie.*
            Chicago: Ares.

Nauck, W.
1956   "Die Tradition und Komposition der Areopagrede." *ZTK* 53: 11–52.

Nestle, Dieter
1967   *Eleutheria: Studien zum Wesen der Freiheit bei den Griechen und im
            Neuen Testament. Teil I: Die Griechen.* Hermeneutische Unter-
            suchungen zur Theologie 6. Tübingen: Mohr-Siebeck.

Niederwimmer, Kurt
1966   *Der Begriff der Freiheit im Neuen Testament.* Berlin: Töpelmann.

Nilsson, Martin P.
1961   *Geschichte der griechischen Religion.* 2d ed. HAW 5.2. Munich: Beck.

Nock, Arthur Darby
1933   *Conversion: The Old and the New in Religion from Alexander the Great
            to Augustine of Hippo.* Oxford: Clarendon Press.
1964   *Early Gentile Christianity and Its Hellenistic Background.* New York:
            Harper.
1972   *Essays on Religion and the Ancient World 1-2.* Ed. Zeph Stewart.
            Cambridge, MA: Harvard University Press.

Nouailhat, René
1975   "Remarques méthodologiques à propos de la question de 'l'hellénisa-
            tion du christianisme': Syncrétisme, herméneutique et politique." Pp.
            212–34 in Dunand and Lévêque.

O'Neil, Edward N.
1977   *Teles (The Cynic Teacher).* SBLTT 11, Graeco-Roman Religion Series
            3. Missoula, MT: Scholars Press.

Pannikar, Raimundo
1975   "Some Notes on Syncretism and Eclecticism Related to the Growth of Human Consciousness." Pp. 47–62 in Pearson.

Pearson, Birger A., ed.
1975   *Religious Syncretism in Antiquity: Essays in Conversation with Geo Widengren.* Series on Formative Contemporary Thinkers 1. Missoula, MT: Scholars Press.

Petit, Paul
1967   *Pax Romana.* Trans. James Willis. Berkeley and Los Angeles: University of California Press.

Phillips, Charles Robert
1986   "The Sociology of Religious Knowledge in the Roman Empire to A.D. 284." Pp. 2677–2773 in *ANRW* 2.16.3. Ed. W. Haase. Berlin and New York: de Gruyter.

Philonenko, M., and M. Simon, eds.
1975   *Mystères et Syncrétismes.* Etudes d'histoire des religions 2. Paris: Geuthner.

Pohlenz, Max
1949   "Paulus und die Stoa." *ZNW* 42: 69–104.

Praechter, Karl
1926   *Die Philosophie des Altertums.* In F. Ueberweg, *Grundriss der Geschichte der Philosophie,* vol. 1. Berlin: Mittler.

Prümm, Karl
1954   *Religionsgeschichtliches Handbuch für den Raum der altchristlichen Umwelt.* 2d ed. Rome: Päpstliches Bibelinstitut.
1960   "Mysterès." *DBSup* 6: 1–225.

Rahner, Hugo
1963   "Christian Mystery and the Pagan Mysteries." Pp. 148–78 in *Pagan and Christian Mysteries: Papers from the Eranos Yearbooks.* Ed. Joseph Campbell. New York: Harper.

Reitzenstein, Richard
1978   *Hellenistic Mystery Religions: Their Basic Ideas and Significance.* Trans. John E. Steely. PTMS 18. Pittsburgh: Pickwick Press. [German original 1910; 3d ed. 1927.]

Ringgren, Helmer
1969   "The Problems of Syncretism." Pp. 7–14 in Hartman.

Robinson, James M.
1971   (with Helmut Koester) *Trajectories through Early Christianity.* Philadelphia: Fortress.

Schmid, W.
1962   "Epikur." *RAC* 5: 681–819.

Schneider, Carl
1954   *Geistesgeschichte des antiken Christentums,* 2 vols. Munich: Beck.

Schoeps, Hans Joachim
1961   *Paul: The Theology of the Apostle in the Light of Jewish Religious History.* Trans. Harold Knight. Philadelphia: Westminster.

Schroeder, David
1959   "Die Haustafeln des Neuen Testaments: Ihre Herkunft und ihr theologischer Sinn." Dissertation, Hamburg.

Segert, Stanislav
    1975   "Some Remarks concerning Syncretism." Pp. 63–66 in Pearson.
Smith, Jonathan Z.
    1971   "Native Cults in the Hellenistic Period." *HR* 11: 236–49.
    1978   *Map Is Not Territory: Studies in the History of Religions.* SJLA 23.
            Leiden: Brill.
Smith, Morton
    1971   "Prolegomena to a Discussion of Aretalogies, Divine Men, the
            Gospels and Jesus." *JBL* 90: 174–99.
    1978   "On the History of the 'Divine Man.'" Pp. 335–45 in *Mélanges Offerts
            à Marcel Simon: Paganisme, Judaisme, Christianisme: Influences et
            affrontements dans le monde antique.* Ed. A. Benoit, M. Philonenko,
            and C. Vogel. Paris: Boccard.
Stowers, Stanley K.
    1981   *The Diatribe and Paul's Letter to the Romans.* SBLDS 57. Chico, CA:
            Scholars Press.
Strassburg
    1973   *Les syncrétismes dans les religions grecque et romaine: Colloque de
            Strasbourg (9–11 juin 1971).* Paris: Presses universitaires de France.
Theiler, Willy
    1982   *Poseidonios: Die Fragmente.* 2 vols. TuK 10.1–2. Berlin: de Gruyter.
Thesleff, Holger
    1961   *An Introduction to the Pythagorean Writings of the Hellenistic Period.*
            Acta Academiae Aboensis: Humaniora 24.3. Abo: Abo Akademi.
    1965   *The Pythagorean Texts of the Hellenistic Period.* Acta Academiae
            Aboensis, Ser. A: Humaniora 30.1. Abo: Abo Akademi.
Thraede, Klaus
    1977   "Aerger mit der Freiheit: Die Bedeutung von Frauen in Theorie und
            Praxis der alten Kirche." Pp. 31–182 in *Freunde in Christus
            Werden . . .: Die Beziehung von Mann und Frau als Frage an Theologie
            und Kirche.* Ed. G. Scharffenorth and K. Thraede. Gelnhausen and
            Berlin: Burckhardthaus.
Thyen, Hartwig
    1955   *Der Stil der jüdisch-hellenistischen Homilie.* FRLANT 47. Göttingen:
            Vandenhoeck & Ruprecht.
Tiede, David Lenz
    1972   *The Charismatic Figure as Miracle Worker.* SBLDS 1. Missoula, MT:
            Scholars Press.
Unnik, Willem C. van
    1973   *Sparsa Collecta: Collected Essays. Part I.* NovTSup 29. Leiden: Brill.
Vidman, L.
    1969   *Sylloge inscriptionum religionis Isiacae et Sarapiacae.* RVV 28. Berlin:
            de Gruyter.
Wagner, Günther
    1967   *Pauline Baptism and the Pagan Mysteries.* Edinburgh and London:
            Oliver & Boyd.
Walter, Nikolaus
    1979   "Christusglaube und heidnische Religiosität in paulinischen
            Gemeinden." *NTS* 25: 422–42.

Wedderburn, A. J. M.
    1982   "Paul and the Hellenistic Mystery Cults: On Posing the Right Questions." Pp. 817–33 in Bianchi and Vermaseren.
Weidinger, Karl
    1928   *Die Haustafeln: Ein Stück urchristlicher Paränese.* UNT 14. Leipzig: Hinrichs.
Weiss, Herold
    1967   "The *Pagani* among the Contemporaries of the First Christians." *JBL* 86: 42–52.
Weiss, Johannes
    1908   *Die Aufgaben der neutestamentlichen Wissenschaft in der Gegenwart.* Göttingen: Vandenhoeck & Ruprecht.
Wiens, Devon H.
    1980   "Mystery Concepts in Primitive Christianity and in its Environment." Pp. 1248–84 in *ANRW* 2.23.2. Ed. W. Haase. Berlin and New York: de Gruyter.
Wiessner, Gernort
    1975   "Vorwort." Pp. 9–13 in Dietrich.
Wikander, Stig
    1973   "Les '-ismes' dans la terminologie historico-religieuse." Pp. 9–14 in *Les syncrétismes dans les religions grecque et romaine: Colloque de Strasbourg (9–11 juin 1971).* Paris: Presses universitaires de France.
Zeller, Eduard
    1963   *Die Philosophie der Griechen in ihrer geschichtlichen Entwicklung dargestellt.* 6 vols. Reprint, Darmstadt: Wissenschaftliche Buchgesellschaft.

2

JUDAISM AND THE NEW TESTAMENT

Anthony J. Saldarini

This essay will review the literature that uses some aspect of Judaism as a major tool for interpreting the NT. The Dead Sea Scrolls will be treated separately below, and works concerned with Judaism alone, including attempts to describe the Pharisees, are treated in *EJMI*, volume 2 of the present series. Since many of the books written on the NT in recent years have referred to Judaism, preference will be given to works that have been influential or are illustrative of an important point and make extensive use of primary sources. Attention will be focused on the many problems of method that have arisen in relating Christian and Jewish sources and on the more secure results that have been achieved in major studies up to 1980, the year of the Society of Biblical Literature's centennial.[1]

Judaism itself has been "redefined" in the past three decades. Judaism has often meant rabbinic Judaism, represented by the classic talmudic and midrashic texts dating from the third century C.E. to the Middle Ages. P. Billerbeck (1924–28) collected his texts from these sources, and G. F. Moore (1927–30) made these texts central to his often-criticized concept of "normative" Judaism. This Judaism was often contrasted with Hellenism, Diaspora Judaism, and sectarian Judaism. Studies by S. Lieberman and others have shown that Palestinian Judaism was influenced in important ways by Hellenism. Diaspora Judaism has many links with traditions found in Palestinian Judaism. The Dead Sea Scrolls and G. Scholem's many studies in mysticism have demonstrated that Judaism in the first century was very diverse and that "halakic" interests and sectarian, mystical, and apocalyptic trends all overlapped. The most successful studies now take into account all varieties of Judaism along with the many movements in Christianity and

---

[1] In the eight years since this chapter originally was written the study of the NT in its Jewish context has depended less on rabbinic texts and broadened its scope to include diverse forms of Judaism and the wider social context of the Greco-Roman empire. Evaluation of new trends would require a new chapter covering a wider range of material.

Many useful studies that impinge on Judaism and the NT can be found in the massive volumes of the series *Aufstieg und Niedergang der römischen Welt*, edited by H. Temporini and W. Haase (Berlin and New York: de Gruyter). Some of the studies in *Jewish and Christian Self-Definition*, edited by E. P. Sanders et al. (Philadelphia: Fortress, 1980–81) help clarify the relationships between early Christianity and Judaism.

related phenomena in the Greco-Roman world. Broader-based studies also help to control the most intractable problem to beset those who would relate rabbinic literature to the NT—the dating of rabbinic traditions.

I. CHRISTIANITY AND JUDAISM

Since most of the works on Judaism and the NT are by Christians, special heed must be given to the prejudices that have often deformed statements made about Judaism by Christians. Leaving aside anti-Semitism, which has misguided a minority of scholars, theological assumptions that Christianity is better than Judaism, a replacement for Judaism, a corrective for the deficiencies of Judaism or a fulfillment of a seriously incomplete Judaism have often prevented Christian scholars from fairly describing and evaluating Judaism. Moore, in his classic article, "Christian Writers on Judaism" (1921), reviewed the fundamental works influential in his day, and E. P. Sanders (1977) has shown that many of the misperceptions of Judaism have endured from Moore to the present. C. Klein (1978) quotes extensively from continental NT and systematic theologians who evaluate Judaism as "late," decadent, and legalistic. In a chapter added to the English translation, she notes that prejudicial attitudes are less common in Anglo-American literature, probably through the influence of Moore and R. T. Herford. Recent years have seen a more sensitive and unbiased discussion of Jewish-Christian relations and of the passages in the NT that have often been used to evaluate Judaism unfairly. S. Sandmel (1978) has recently provided a good overview of the anti-Jewish passages in the NT. He uses the generally accepted conclusions of NT scholarship to explain the meaning of passages that deal with the Jews. Essays on the NT and later periods can be found in A. T. Davies (1979). Further data for this problem is contained in redactional studies of NT documents, studies of the Christian social milieu, and studies of anti-Semitism in the ancient world. Many NT statements about the Jews reflect the authors' own situations and literary purposes. Numerous recent studies of the passion narratives are pertinent, as are more explicit studies such as that by R. Leistner (1974) on John. Leistner finds that John's passion narrative stresses political motives rather than religious ones and is less anti-Jewish than those of Matthew or Mark. D. Hare uses Matthew to determine the extent of antagonism between Jews and Christians in Matthew's social situation and traces Matthew's replacement of Israel by the church to this antagonism. Further light is shed on the NT by recent studies of anti-Semitism in the Greco-Roman world by J. N. Sevenster (1975) and J. L. Daniel (1979), which show how pervasive and enduring was the contempt and distrust for Jewish strangeness, exclusivity, and "superstition." J. Gager (1983) argued for the persistence of Judaism as a positive force in the Roman Empire and in relation to the early church; he has concluded that Paul accepted Judaism as the way of salvation for Jews and addressed his critique of law and defense of justification only to Gentile Christians for whom the law was inappropriate.

A major point of controversy has been the trial of Jesus. A series of studies have examined the Gospel and Greco-Roman evidence from every angle without reaching firm conclusions. P. Winter (1961; rev. ed. 1974) provoked 150 responses, reviews, and notices which appreciated his critical work on the Gospels but generally disputed his conclusions that the Jews had the *jus gladii* (which they did not use) and that the Romans alone executed Jesus for political reasons. The state of research after Winter and a number of other authors has been ably summarized by D. Catchpole (1971, 1976), who concludes that the dispute over the legality of the trial is insoluble, that Jewish and Christian sources must be used very critically, and that the political theory cannot totally explain Jesus' downfall. Recently, A. Strobel concluded that the legal data pertinent to the trial of Jesus contain historically reliable material.

Method

Billerbeck's collection of rabbinic parallels (see Strack and Billerbeck) has initiated many NT scholars into Judaism with the good result that they became convinced that Jewish literature was crucial for the interpretation of the NT. Billerbeck's negative evaluation of Judaism, however, misled many scholars who lacked the expertise to consult the sources for the context, genre, and relevance of the parallels adduced to illuminate the NT. Because of the inaccessibility of rabbinic literature, Billerbeck is often used today, but it should be supplemented by reference to the texts and attention to the criticisms of M. Smith (1951:49–54), Sandmel (1962), and E. P. Sanders (1977:42–43, 234–35).

The dangers of "parallelomania" were pointed out most effectively by Sandmel (1962). A rigorous method for avoiding these dangers was already present in M. Smith's *Tannaitic Parallels to the Gospels* (1951), a study that has been of limited influence—probably because it reached few positive conclusions. Given the proliferation of exaggerated theses concerning rabbinic literature and the NT, Smith's caution and extensive analysis of the data merit careful study. Analyses of parallels of words, idioms, forms, and genres clearly show the difficulty in establishing influence between the two literatures. Other problems of method are reviewed by G. W. Buchanan (1977).

E. P. Sanders (1977) has made a methodological initiative through a holistic analysis of Paul and Judaism according to their "pattern of religion." A pattern of religion is a functional definition of a religion, as perceived by its adherents, with respect to how one gets in and stays in the religion (1977:17). Thus defined, a pattern of religion covers part of the area called

soteriology in systematic theology. Though Sanders's effort has been criticized by J. Neusner (1978) and A. Saldarini (1979), the direction in which
he has moved and some of his results point the way for subsequent study of
Judaism and the NT.

The most consistent teacher of method, as well as of substance, has
been W. D. Davies, whose *Paul and Rabbinic Judaism* (1948; 2d ed. 1955)
has been the most influential book in the English-speaking world on Judaism
and the NT. In a series of studies of Pauline motifs, Davies, who is first a NT
exegete, draws from a wide range of Jewish sources (far wider than the
rabbinic literature he claims as his main topic) to establish the links between
ideas and images in Judaism and Paul. Davies is judicious and restrained in
interpreting and relating his sources. He uses datable sources whenever
possible and does not fly toward the improbable. When he argues for direct
influence, he marshals detailed data, and when he cannot discern the history
of a tradition, he limits himself to showing the general cultural background
of Paul. His key conclusion is that Paul and Judaism are in harmony, rather
than antithetical. Put a bit more sharply, his conclusion is that for Paul
Christianity was the advent of the true and final form of Judaism, not a new
religion (324), a view that enjoys growing acceptance. See a further extensive statement in Davies, 1977–78. Though both NT studies and Jewish
studies have advanced in the last thirty years, Davies anticipated many of the
advances and avoided many errors embraced by others. He interpreted
rabbinic sources in context and did not force them to early dates. He drew
from a broad range of sources and did not succumb to "parallelomania." He
studied major themes rather than isolated passages. Davies's agenda is set
by the NT, so he does not treat the whole "pattern of religion" found in
Judaism, but his respect for and sensitivity to Judaism guides him well in a
majority of interpretations.

Davies's major books show the many sides of his approach. *Torah in the
Messianic Age and/or the Age to Come* (1952) is a careful examination of
Jewish teaching on a topic of interest to Christians. Though the idea of a
"new Torah" is late, vague, and inchoate in Judaism, Davies argues cautiously for its presence in first-century Judaism. His major evidence for an
early date is drawn from the NT, a mode of argument that has become
common only in the past decade. In *The Setting of the Sermon on the Mount*
(1963), Davies presented extensive parts of the Jewish social and thought
world in order to interpret the most "Jewish" part of the most "Jewish"
Gospel. As K. Stendahl suggests (2d ed. 1968:xii, n. 1), Davies sees too direct
a Palestinian influence on a document written in Greek and based on Greek
sources, but he does bring together a central Christian document with a
broad sweep of Judaism. Finally, in *The Gospel and the Land* (1974), Davies
has taken a theme that is central to Judaism, rather than to Christianity, and
examined its influence and decline in the successive strata of the NT,
probably because of the influx of Gentiles into Christianity and the stress on

cosmic eschatology which modified the land-based messianic framework of Judaism. Recently, Davies (1982) continued his study of the land by tracing the importance of the land to Jews throughout their tradition and distinguishing a relationship to Palestine from a symbolic understanding of the land. A number of Davies's recent essays have been collected under the title *Jewish and Pauline Studies* (1984).

Paul and Judaism

Both Paul's own relationship to Judaism and subsequent scholarship on that subject have been stormy. Paul claims to be a Jew, converted to Christ, but he polemicizes against practices and positions associated with Judaism. He uses Jewish categories in his writings but claims to be teaching something radically new. These tensions in Paul contribute to the later contrast of law and Gospel, works and grace, and Judaism and Christianity. A voluminous literature has grown up concerning the meaning and importance of justification in Paul's thought. We shall not address this critical issue, but rather single out a few writers who have interpreted Paul as strongly Jewish. J. Munck (1954) attacked F. C. Baur's thesis, perpetuated in several forms, that Paul's career was a constant struggle against Judaism. Munck found an essential unity between Paul and the Jerusalem community on the nature of Christianity (a thesis accepted by few) and located Paul's center in eschatology rather than justification. Munck does not use a diversity of sources and levels both Judaism and Paul by a single-minded stress on eschatology.

H. J. Schoeps (1959) accepted eschatology as central to Paul, and his study of Paul against Judaism is rich and nuanced. His presentation is marred, however, by too strong a contrast between Judaism and Hellenism and the use of the "savior myth" to explain the non-Jewish elements in Paul. Schoeps uses rabbinic sources from the first few centuries with some attention to dates, but often the relevance of a rabbinic text to Paul is questionable. A. T. Hanson (1974) turned to Paul's interpretation of scripture as the source of his theology. His work is generally valuable for relating exegesis to Paul's thought, but when he argues for a (possibly direct) relationship between parts of Romans 12–13 and the traditions in *m. 'Abot* 2, he fails to deal with complete passages in context and adduces very tenuous verbal parallels. Stendahl (1976) has attacked the classic view that justification is the key to Paul's theology because it is an analysis of the human predicament. Justification in Paul is a missionary teaching to explain how Gentiles are saved along with Jews. Consequently, Romans 9–11 on the place of Israel in God's plan is the climax of Paul's argument in Romans, not an appendix to it.

Most recently E. P. Sanders (1977) has argued that the center of Paul's theology is a participationist eschatology which stresses union with Christ as salvific. Paul's position is contrasted with Judaism's covenantal nomism, though both agree in stressing that one must stay in the salvation community by obedience to God's law. Sanders consciously relates his position to A. Schweitzer and W. D. Davies and with them relegates justification to a secondary place in Paul's thought. Very recently Sanders (1983) has continued his work on Paul and Judaism with a more detailed treatment of Paul's positions toward law and Judaism. Though many questions remain concerning Paul's relationship to Judaism, progress has been made. The trends pointed out by Davies (1965) continue to have their effect: the study of Judaism in relation to Paul must include the substantial influence of Hellenism; Jewish mysticism and apocalyptic thought must be valued like rabbinic thought; and eschatology must occupy a central place in Pauline thought.

II. THE NEW TESTAMENT AND ITS JEWISH MILIEU

General Background

David Daube and J. Duncan M. Derrett, British legal historians with immense erudition and fertile minds, have both written numerous articles and books filled with novel and suggestive insights into individual pericopae of the NT. Neither enters into extensive dialogue with current NT scholarship, and neither articulates an overall interpretation of the NT or any of its books. Rather, they compare text with text, seeking to illuminate the NT from the Jewish milieu in which it was born. Daube's *The New Testament and Rabbinic Judaism* (1956) has been very influential and its many chapters are often quoted. His studies are gathered under three headings: "Messianic Types," "Legislative and Narrative Forms," and "Concepts and Conventions." Some chapters, like his comparison of the four questions asked by the four types of sons in the Passover Haggadah with the succession of questions in Mark 12, have received constant attention and have contributed to an ongoing discussion. Many others of his suggestions are weakened by three difficulties: (1) Daube claims that many of the literary parallels he finds are forms common to Christianity and Judaism, but the "forms" are often so loose and general that they prove nothing. His whole analysis lacks any attempt to provide a history of traditions. As a result, very diverse examples are gathered under the heading "Tripartite Forms" (175–95) and the six antitheses in Matthew 5 ("You have heard that it was said . . . , but I say to you . . .") are inexactly and incorrectly paralleled with the rabbinic formula, "You might read/understand . . . , but you must say. . . ."; (2) Daube uses the full range of rabbinic literature without serious attention to the dating problem. For example, "Blessed is he who comes in the name of the Lord" (Matthew 21) is compared with a similar greeting found in the circumcision rite. Without any attempt to date the parts of this rite to the first century, Daube refers to the "Chair of Elijah" in the rite and infers that Matthew 21 implies an expectation of Elijah; (3) Daube is often led by overlapping meanings to improbable associations (27–51) of the kind criticized by James Barr. Though Daube is too quick in asserting relationships between forms and texts, his juxtaposing of materials is often suggestive and opens paths for new research.

In *Law and the New Testament* (1970), Derrett published eighteen studies written during the 1960s. Paying close attention to expressions and details of Gospel parables and narratives, Derrett works out the laws, customs, attitudes, and socioeconomic situations implied by the narratives. His goal, as an Orientalist, is to reveal to the Western mind Oriental presuppositions of which it is not conscious. Derrett's more recent work (1973, 1977, 1978) continues this line of research. Like Daube, Derrett does not illumine the development of traditions, but rather assumes that laws and customs endure virtually unchanged. Though this is true in many cases, it cannot be assumed, especially concerning the details given in literary sources. Derrett does not give sufficient attention to the purposes and redaction of the whole Gospel narrative. This is especially clear in his explanation of parables, where he tries to make sense of conflicts or shocking details in relation to Eastern customs, but fails to explain their effect and purpose in the Gospels. He justifies the conduct of the vineyard owner toward his workers by the concept of a minimum wage, but removes the pungency of the parable (1977:48–75). The same may be said of his treatment of the prodigal son (1970:100–125). Often his perspective is too narrow, the parallels he adduces too tenuous to be convincing, and secondary developments not taken into account. In his book on the NT world, he deduces some strange conclusions from NT texts (1973:81 nn. 37, 39, 40, and esp. 41). Yet Derrett is at his best when tackling difficult texts and obscure passages. His wide erudition produces materials and ideas of some help to the exegete, and his concrete treatment of laws and customs sometimes gives a sound basis for understanding the world presumed by the NT.

Two other works have drawn on a broad range of evidence from the Jewish tradition to provide a general setting for understanding Gospel traditions. B. Gerhardsson (1961) has tried to derive from rabbinic literature a picture of how Jewish traditions were passed on from master to disciple and to use this model to explain the relation of Jesus to his disciples and the passing on of Jesus-traditions in Acts and elsewhere. His thesis has been effectively attacked by M. Smith (1963) and W. D. Davies (1962). (See his response, 1964.) Generally, Gerhardsson may be faulted for an uncritical use of later talmudic materials to speak about the first century and for an underemphasis on the place of written texts in Jewish and Christian tradition. Moreover, even were his sketch of Judaism accurate, he must press Acts beyond endurance to find these same phenomena in Christianity. Later

Gerhardsson (1979) affirmed his earlier position on the exact oral transmission of Jesus' teachings, but his position has been undercut by W. Kelber (1983), who explains the unique characteristics of oral transmission and distinguishes sharply the flexibility of oral transmission from the exactitude of written transmission.

The heavily Greek context of much of early Christianity gives much room for other models of learning and transmission. G. Vermes (1973) makes his greatest contribution by locating Jesus within Galilean, charismatic Judaism. Though some of his data are suspect, he tries to draw on traditions that contrast Galilee with other Judaisms, and he does shed light on Jesus as a healer, exorcist, and holy man. These holy men, such as Honi and Hanina ben Dosa, were of great influence but often in conflict with the authorities and other groups. Even though some interpretations of NT data and of Jesus' titles are controversial and need modification from other NT methods, Vermes does outline a stream of Judaism useful for understanding the origins of the NT.

Mention should also be made of two other books that present Jesus against a Palestinian background. D. Flusser's *Jesus* (1968) uses a wide range of Jewish sources to show Jesus within a Jewish milieu. Flusser accepts rabbinic sources as generally trustworthy for describing first-century Judaism. M. Smith (1978) presents a wealth of evidence concerning magic in Syria and Palestine, but he fails in his attempt to derive from anti-Christian polemical writings and general magical works a probable case for identifying Jesus as a typical magician.

Midrash in the New Testament

Many authors have found midrash in various parts of the NT (see Miller for a survey). The key studies that have controlled the definition of midrash used by NT scholars are by R. Bloch (1957; Eng. trans. 1978), A. Wright (1967), and R. Le Déaut (1969; Eng. trans. 1971). Bloch and Le Déaut have stressed midrash as a process in contrast to Wright, who used a literary approach. In general, the literary approach is more controlled and useful for comparative analysis. However, Wright draws his definitions from rabbinic collections dated long after the NT and imposes them on earlier, more varied and fluid forms. He is correct to insist on rigorous definitions, but by failing to describe the origins, developments, and concrete purposes of different forms he fails to complete the critical task. Bloch and Le Déaut include any interpretation of scripture under the term midrash, as well as techniques and attitudes that lead to this activity. Their broad descriptions sketch the total area to be covered, but midrash, pesher, formula quotation, targumizing, and other phenomena must each be given a precise description and placed within the social and religious world of their origin.

One of the early, influential studies of midrash in the NT was J. W. Doeve, *Jewish Hermeneutics in the Synoptic Gospels and Acts* (1954). Doeve correctly recognized the need for a general comparative method between midrash and the NT's interpretation of the OT. In chapter 2 he enumerates the difficulties that impede the use of rabbinic literature in comparison with the NT, especially dating, textual problems, the great changes in Judaism after 70 C.E., the historical unreliability of the sources, and their sectarian nature. Despite these obstacles, Doeve thought that one could make cautious and moderate use of these sources. In the light of subsequent scholarship, he was too optimistic. Chapter 3 reviews Jewish interpretation of scripture from Hillel to Akiba, using Hillel's seven rules of exegesis and the usual anecdotes from rabbinic literature, but such a presentation can no longer claim to inform us about the situation in the first century. Many sources and exegeses cited by Doeve come from a later period or were modified by subsequent redaction. He has similar problems with the NT in attributing some interpretations to Jesus himself and to his messianic self-consciousness, conclusions that are treated with great skepticism by NT scholars.

Doeve begins with the OT quotations used in the NT, but then attempts to account for related NT ideas by other OT passages not quoted in the NT. The use of a word in the NT causes Doeve to cite several passages from the OT as influential on the New because of the same word and, more improbably, to hypothesize connections with further ideas associated with the OT passages, but not even hinted at in the New. For example, reference to the glory of the Son of man (Matt 25:31) quite properly recalls Dan 7:14, but then Doeve (151ff.) says that glory and Shekina (divine presence) are associated in *Tg. Isa* 6:5 and that, consequently, Jesus' closeness to God is implied in Matthew. This closeness then explains the title Son of God and the power of the Son of man to forgive sins. Such associative linking of words and merging of fields of meaning is not a sound basis for scholarship, as noted by J. Barr and others. The presence of certain thought patterns and tendencies of the NT may be explained by the general fund of thoughts and expressions available to anyone in contact with Judaism; specific verses need be cited only when a substantial influence can be demonstrated.

M. Gertner (1962) in an often quoted article follows a method similar to Doeve's. He also uses a web of conceptual allusions and refers to rabbinic parallels that are from later collections. For example, Luke 1:76–79 is often thought to be an addition to the Benedictus, but Gertner says that it is a midrash on the Priestly Blessing in Num 6:24–26. He cites a number of verbal and conceptual links between the two texts, though he notes (181) that the order is not the same. The first part of the Benedictus is said to be a psalmistic poem, but no strong evidence is offered for this contention. Gertner calls this kind of midrash "covert," as opposed to overt midrash, where text and commentary are clearly present. Covert midrash involves "a religious idea or a legal principle (which) is midrashically interpreted into, or derived from, a given text; this is done by means of various midrashic techniques. Yet none of them, neither the text nor the idea nor the technique, are named, defined or mentioned" (269). He further theorizes that some of the covert midrashim were originally overt interpretations of a biblical text but were subsequently shorn of their text and technical language. Other midrashim that were always covert are the targums, the Septuagint, and the *Genesis Apocryphon*. Gertner is attempting to get at the attitudes and mental processes used in the composition of NT texts which have a relationship to the Hebrew Bible, but his definition of covert midrash is too loose and uncontrolled to be of much use, and his hypothesis of early Christian midrashim is unproved. Some of his suggestions, however, are helpful. He explains the structure of Mark 4 satisfactorily on the basis of a wordplay involving Jer 4:3. In this case his explanation fits the text tightly and does not involve many loosely associated texts or doubtful conceptual nexuses.

E. Earle Ellis has adopted Gertner's basic hypothesis in a number of articles now published in a collection (1978). Ellis changes Gertner's terminology to explicit and implicit midrash, and he expands on the idea of early Christian midrash. He locates midrashic activity among charismatic prophets teaching in both Greek and Semitic languages. Their inspired and authoritative teachings were based on the Hebrew Bible, itself inspired and authoritative, and the midrashic forms have some similarities to Jewish forms. Ellis analyzes numerous NT texts to discover the presence of midrashic forms. He suggests that the proem, known from late midrashic collections, can be found in the NT (154–57). But most of his examples here and elsewhere diverge from the norm sufficiently to render his whole comparison suspect. Moreover, Ellis does not answer the formidable difficulties opposed to dating the proem before the third century (Heinemann, 1971). The evidence adduced by A. Finkel (1964:155–69) for proems in the NT, as well as his general presentation of Judaism in the first century, is not convincing. Neither Ellis nor Finkel squarely faces the difficulty in using late sources for a period centuries earlier. Ellis also finds the pesher type of midrash in the NT, though in his earlier *St. Paul's Use of the Old Testament* (1957) he made a firm distinction between early Christian pesher and Jewish exegesis from Palestine and Alexandria. In a number of places Ellis suggests that NT writers have drawn on midrashim now lost, but neither he nor others have been able to establish firmly the existence or form of these works. Ellis's whole thesis is intriguing, but close analysis of texts does not provide the probability necessary for this thesis of midrashic activity by Christian prophets as the origin of Christian reflection on Jesus. Ellis himself recognizes the difficulty in defining, dating, and identifying midrash, and he suggests that the NT scholar "can only be grateful for the progress achieved and seek to apply it judiciously to problems within his own discipline" (192). Developments in the study of rabbinic literature during the past ten years have placed the type of analysis that undergirds Ellis's position more and more in doubt.

Midrash in Matthew

The other early and basic study which raised many of the central problems dealt with by subsequent authors and still under investigation today is K. Stendahl's *The School of St. Matthew and Its Use of the Old Testament* (1954; 2d ed. 1968). Stendahl found that the formula quotations were of a mixed text type, as opposed to the other quotations in Matthew, which are close to the Septuagint. He theorized that the interpreter modified OT texts and consulted different versions for exegetical purposes in a manner similar to that found in the Qumran pesharim. He located this exegetical activity in a school where formal and communal study of scripture was undertaken. Few have accepted Stendahl's school hypothesis, and the data supporting it are slim. But no one else has successfully sketched a generally acceptable setting for the origin of Matthew's Gospel. B. Gärtner (1954) suggests that the formula quotations originated in missionary preaching; M. D. Goulder (1974) proposes midrashic activity in a liturgical setting; R. H. Gundry (1967) argues for a composition of the apostle Matthew with the aid of a collection of notes in several languages; W. D. Davies (1963) derives Matthew from post-Jamnia polemics. Several have disputed whether Matthew's audience is Jewish-Christian or Gentile-Christian. Stendahl's original investigation must be worked out in a larger context and, as Stendahl notes in the preface to his second edition (1968:x–xiv), the job has not been completed. Similarities between Matthew and the pesharim must be accepted, but striking differences require a more nuanced explanation of their origin than the school hypothesis, In addition, recent research into the many OT text types extant in the first century has cast doubt on the theory of modification of the text (Stendahl, 1968:vi). Finally, further study of the biblical quotations in Matthew by Gundry (1967) and of the formula quotations by G. M. Soares-Prabhu (1976) and others shows that the affinities of Matthew's text are mixed and difficult to draw conclusions from. Much of their meaning comes from redactional activity, but little of their precise setting is known beyond a general connection with Jewish modes of interpretation.

Several subsequent studies written on Matthew show clearly the difficulties of relating the NT to Judaism and midrash. Gundry's theory (1967) of a collection of notes in Aramaic, Syriac, Hebrew, and Greek behind the quotations in all the Synoptics suggests the trilingual milieu of Syria and a targumizing activity exercised on a number of textual traditions, including the Hellenistic Septuagint strain embedded in Mark. Gundry supports his hypothesis by reference to the widespread use of notebooks in the Hellenistic school setting. But the data in the Synoptics are so varied that they do not impart compelling probability to his theory. The synoptic traditions could have derived from preaching, teaching, or a school just as easily as from a single tradent using a collection of notes. Goulder (1974) proposes a more controlled, literary hypothesis that Matthew used only Mark as his source, expounding him with standard Jewish exegetical methods. Matthew was pursuing one of the goals of midrash, to reconcile conflicting traditions, in this case Jewish and Gentile. Though Goulder makes a generally accepted point, that Matthew is in some sense a rewriting of Mark, and brings out some of Matthew's originality in imagery and construction of parables, he does no more than show that the midrashic activity excludes other traditions and sources, and he must strain unconvincingly to relate everything in Matthew to midrashic activity on Mark. He presents scribal activity as a setting for Matthew, but he does not address the dating problems associated with Hillel's hermeneutical rules and with the data concerning ancient Jewish education.

B. Gerhardsson and O. Lamar Cope see midrashic activity at work in certain sections of Matthew. Gerhardsson (1966) interprets the temptation as a haggadic midrash. He correctly elucidates the rich world of OT theme and allusion behind the story. He finds the complex of ideas in the temptation present in Deuteronomy 6–8, the chapters from which Jesus' replies to Satan are drawn. Gerhardsson does not show that the author is proceeding through Deuteronomy 6–8 in any systematic way. Certainly Deut 8:2–3 contains crucial information for the temptation narrative, but it is not clear that the story is created as an interpretation of Deuteronomy 6–8; it may as easily have been expanded and developed by exodus themes found there and elsewhere in the OT. In chapter 4 Gerhardsson argues that Deut 6:5, as interpreted in *m. Ber.* 9:5, triggers the order of temptations in Matthew, but this theory is weakened by dating problems and the strained paralleling of key words. His characterization of Matthew's temptation narrative as midrash is not founded on a broad comparison of midrash and the narrative in regard to form, style, and exegetical method. Further, Gerhardsson's theory of midrash here tends to contradict his earlier hypothesis (1961) of Christian tradents passing on Jesus' words and works in a way similar to the later Jewish memorization of Mishna. His study of Jewish oral tradition and its relation to Christianity is open to the same objections as his study of midrash: evidence from later periods is applied to the first century and disparate data are marshaled into hypotheses that lack support in extant historical sources.

Cope (1976) is more complete in his exegesis of whole Matthean passages in which he sees the OT quotation as a central and controlling factor. He does a broad exegesis of whole passages and takes into account other approaches to Matthew in a very satisfactory way. His analyses of Matthew 12, 13, and 15 show the integral relation of OT text and NT development, and he recognizes that his cases for Matthew 9, 10, and 11 are weaker. Yet even in Matthew 12 Cope's claim that Isa 42:1–4 (Matt 12:17–21) explains the presence of the initial two stories and diverse elements following depends on some slim associations of words and connotations. Cope shows more successfully than others how OT quotations are integrated into Matthew, but he does not prove that they are the organizing key to whole sections. In a further chapter, Cope analyzes four passages modeled on OT passages through the use of allusions. Cope draws conclusions with admirable restraint, noting that the presence of allusions must be judged by their cumulative relationship to the structure of the passage. Again, his examples are not thoroughly convincing, though his case for Psalm 22 in the passion narrative is strong. Cope's conclusion, that the author of Matthew is a scribe, like Gerhardsson's that he is a learned Pharisee, lacks detailed development. Their studies do elucidate the text of Matthew and show its general relation to Jewish traditions, but no precise setting or relationship is proved.

Targumic Research

Targumic research has been a major stimulus to study of midrash in the NT. The discovery of *Neofiti* in the Vatican Library by A. Díez Macho and basic research emanating from P. Kahle and others have merged with comparative midrashic studies to trace early exegetical traditions, some of which are found in the NT. An annotated bibliography by J. T. Forestell (1979) has correlated literature on the Targums with individual NT passages for the convenient study of alleged targumic influence on the NT. J. A. Fitzmyer (1979) collected a series of his essays, several of which treat Aramaic influence on the NT. A review of recent work may also be found in an article by R. Le Déaut (1974). R. Bloch (1955; Eng. trans. 1978) studied the targums and other Jewish sources in an attempt to trace traditions of biblical interpretation. She established some initial definitions and guidelines which stimulated subsequent research. G. Vermes has carried on this task in a variety of essays (1961; 2d ed. 1973; 1975), some of which treat major NT themes in a Jewish context (for example, the Akedah in 1961:193–227). Vermes typifies several healthy trends in targumic and midrashic study. He makes cautious use of the targums and their traditions, using all available evidence to distinguish earlier and later traditions. Datable sources in Philo, Josephus, Pseudo-Philo, and the NT are used to the fullest. The NT is studied as part of a total picture, and its traditions and exegetical moves are seen within a larger complex.

R. Le Déaut has been another leader in this field, but has concentrated more exclusively on targums and especially *Neofiti*. In *La Nuit Pascale* (1963) he sought to discover Jewish religious thought concerning Passover in the first century. He is properly cautious in the use of rabbinic materials, and he depends upon a comparative analysis of targumic traditions to discern the traditions underlying all the extant versions of the Palestinian targums (63). He examines the tradition concerning the four nights (targum to Exod. 12:42) of creation, the sacrifice of Isaac, the first Passover, and the end of the world as they developed and interacted within the tradition. Though his argument that the core of the traditions, and especially of the Akedah, is early has been generally accepted (Daly, 1977), the consensus has been strongly challenged by P. R. Davies and B. D. Chilton (1978). Le Déaut uses his sources carefully but gives too much weight to the targums. The tendency to treat targumic traditions as a unified whole must be adjusted to allow for multiple traditions influencing one another. The problem of dating traditions to the first century cannot be overcome by an appeal to targums, as can be seen even more clearly in the work of M. McNamara (1966; rev. ed. 1978; 1972), who has studied numerous parallels between the targums and the NT. He is less restrained than previous authors in his claim to find significant parallels, and he assumes the early date of the targumic traditions too readily. Many of his hypotheses are too imprecise and associative to be probative; for example, a reference to the Great Sea in *Neofiti* supposedly shows the source for the reference to Abyss in Rom 10:6–8 (1966:74–76). His work does provide an overview of the targums and some useful aids to NT, but Fitzmyer's skepticism about early dating of the targums must be heeded (1968a; 1968b).

B. Malina (1968) has studied a single tradition and has produced much more controlled and usable results. Malina spends forty pages on different versions of OT manna traditions, fifty on targums to those traditions, and then correlates these results with three passages in the NT (1 Cor 10:3; Rev 2:17; and John 6:31ff.). He wishes to discover what Judaism was teaching about manna during the first century and also to show the continuity of interpretation over time. He generally succeeds, and he is sensitive to the need to date the targums by external sources. Some of his conclusions are questionable, for example, that the lamb without blemish destined before the foundation of the world (1 Pet 1:19–20) is the lamb of the Akedah mentioned in rabbinic lists of ten things created on the evening of the first sabbath. On the whole, Malina presents his data accurately and marshals his arguments cautiously.

New Testament Books as Midrashim

Some authors have claimed that whole books of the NT can be characterized as midrashim, but usually with little success. J. Bowman (1965) reads Mark as a Christian haggadah, modeled on Exodus, which was meant to replace (but was not directly built upon) the Passover Haggadah. Bowman adduces many parallels to rabbinic thought and makes loose compositional comments, but nowhere does he define haggadic midrash in any sophisticated way or present a coherent analysis of Mark's genre as midrash in detailed comparison with known models. G. W. Buchanan's commentary on Hebrews (1972) claims that Hebrews is a homiletical midrash, yet it lacks all but a general definition of a homiletical midrash as a work built around a central text. Some scattered comments purport to show that Psalm 110 is the central text for Hebrews, but thematic texts in rabbinic homiletical midrashim are treated differently from Psalm 110 in Hebrews, and overall organization and development proceed along different courses. As D. M. Hay (1973) has observed in his study of Psalm 110, Hebrews is a christological argument; analogies for its genre are still best sought among more Hellenistic works. Psalm 110 does not control the whole of Hebrew's structure.

Goulder (1974) interprets Matthew as a midrashic rewriting of Mark on the analogy of *Jubilees* or *Genesis Apocryphon*. J. Drury (1976) has been influenced by Goulder in proposing that Luke is a midrashic interpretation of Mark and Matthew. Both make some valuable comments on the composition of the Gospels, and Drury develops partial control through comparison of Luke with OT theological storytelling. Neither Drury nor Goulder defines midrash in a sophisticated way, nor assembles a detailed group of comparative characteristics, nor offers a convincing hypothesis for the setting and goals of the author. Though they refer to Judaism and midrash, they do not investigate them thoroughly.

Many suggestions have been made that parts of the NT are midrashic or are based on earlier Jewish and Christian midrashim, which have been transformed and incorporated into the NT. Two examples must suffice. R. E. Brown (1977) exhaustively reviews the many articles and books on the infancy narratives, many of which suggest that the relationship of these narratives to the extensive OT material in them should be characterized as midrash. Brown correctly concludes (Appendix 6) that the infancy narratives are influenced by midrashic methods and materials but are not of the literary genre midrash. Throughout his commentary he wrestles with highly difficult hypotheses that earlier Jewish midrashim may have influenced Christian composition of the infancy narratives. Similarly, L. Hartman (1966) proposes that the eschatological discourse in Mark 13 is built upon a midrash on Daniel that has been stripped of its explicit association with biblical texts and expanded by other OT texts and by paraenesis. In attempting to discern the history of traditions that leads to the Gospels, both Brown and Hartman demonstrate the rich web of OT allusions that underlie these passages. Both note that hypotheses of earlier midrashim and their exact shapes vary greatly in probability but are useful in interpretation.

In summary, the comparison of the NT with Jewish midrash is beset with difficulties. Appeal to a midrashic mind or way of thought is too general and vague to settle intractable exegetical problems. No comprehensive genre linking together the many forms of midrash has been convincingly expounded. Rabbinic and NT materials are separated by problems of dating and modes of transmission. Yet the Christian tradition of interpreting the Hebrew scriptures grew out of the Jewish tradition and retains so many similarities to it that the struggle to develop a reliable method and to clarify the relationship must proceed. The most stable base for scholarship will be found in two types of cases: (1) those in which both traditions use very similar formal structures and exegetical techniques or draw upon common exegetical traditions; (2) those in which a passage has been used in a variety of situations so that a history of interpretation can be traced to show how the traditions manifest continuity with one another along with great variety (see J. A. Sanders, 1975). Analysis must be carried out with great rigor, and care must be taken to avoid facile identification of forms with one another under vague headings. It is to be hoped that such work may give us some insight into the goals of the ancient interpreters and allow us to place them in their social context.

The Old Testament in the New

A number of studies examine the use of the OT in the New (see D. M. Smith, 1972), using form and redaction criticism as controlling methods, rather than a comparison with Jewish midrash. Because they are complementary or alternatives to midrashic hypotheses, a few will be mentioned. A. Suhl (1965) denies that the OT texts in Mark shaped individual passages in Mark and argues, in conjunction with W. Marxsen's thesis, that Mark does not use the scheme of prophecy and fulfillment. Rather Mark simply uses OT phraseology to present the story of Jesus. Suhl's thesis has been correctly attacked as narrowly tendentious; M. Miller (1971:72) questions how one distinguishes precisely between just presenting and actually shaping Gospel traditions using the OT. The studies of E. Freed (1965) and G. Reim (1974) examine the OT in John, and Reim especially contributes to the knowledge of Johannine sources and composition but not to John's relation to Judaism. Rendel Harris's testimony book hypothesis, as modified by C. H. Dodd (1952) and B. Lindars (1961), has been influential in NT study. Both argue for a coherent and limited oral collection of OT passages intensively used in early Christian preaching and teaching. Lindars uses form criticism to trace three early stages in the development of these traditions and locates their origin in an apologetic defense of the resurrection. Lindars has certainly moved in the right direction by examining carefully different uses of key passages, but his total picture is very hypothetical and controversial. D. M. Hay (1973) has done a precise and nuanced study of Psalm 110 which shows the varied impulses emanating from early Christology through Psalm 110. Though his hypothesis of a pre-Christian Jewish interpretation of Psalm 110 as messianic is weak, his work is a good complement to studies of Jewish exegesis and is a foundation for wider study.

Lectionary and Calendar

P. Carrington (1952) gave impetus to this approach to the Gospels through his theory that Mark is structured as a series of lectionary readings for Sundays and the Easter period. A liturgical setting has also been proposed for Matthew (Kilpatrick, 1946). Carrington's thesis is simplified because he must deal only with Christian sources, but a significant number of NT studies have tried to relate portions of the NT to the Jewish lectionary cycle of sabbath and festival readings. Jewish sources show evidence of at least two cycles, a yearly (in use today) and a triennial (probably in use in the first century). A. Guilding (1960) argued that John is organized according to the triennial cycle and was meant to be read in large sections on major feasts. Guilding's work is often quoted or imitated, but her thesis is beset with problems. Most important, the reconstructions of the reading cycle by Adolf Büchler and Jacob Mann are highly hypothetical and have been effectively undermined by J. Heinemann (1968), who showed that they were not fixed until the sixth–seventh century C.E., contrary to Guilding's claim that evidence for the cycle can be found in the Bible as early as 400 B.C.E. Heinemann (1977) and R. Sarason (1978) have made abundantly clear that Jewish liturgical texts and practices varied from place to place and century to century until a late date. Guilding's attempts to parallel John and the lectionary cycle are often forced, consisting of one thematic word or a few verses. Many correspondences are questionable: for example, that John 11 refers to the deaths of Jacob and Moses, and not to Passover, and that John 12 refers to Passover. Finally, the highly organized literary and thematic structure of John becomes obscured in Guilding's analysis. The same problems dog Goulder (1974), half of whose book tries to relate Matthew to the lectionary cycle as a *lectio continua*. For example, the Day of Atonement is connected to Matt 12:38, the sign of Jonah, because both have the theme of judgment. Goulder (1978) has again marshaled the evidence for this theory that the lectionary forms the backbone of the Gospels and has applied it to Luke and Mark. More cautious use has been made of lectionary evidence by C. Perrot (1973a, 1973b) in a study of Luke 4:16–30 and other texts. Perrot substantiates his work with a critical study of the whole lectionary question.

A. Jaubert (1957; Eng. trans. 1965) tried to reconcile conflicting evidence for the day of the Last Supper by placing Jesus' paschal meal on Tuesday, which was the Passover according to a sectarian calendar based on *Jubilees*. She amassed a complex of evidence from Jewish sources to show that a 364-day solar calendar was in use in the postexilic period, but her evidence does not show that this calendar was in use beyond the Maccabean crisis, (VanderKam, 1979). The redaction of the Gospels and the desire to associate Jesus' death with the Passover sacrifice better explain conflicts in

Gospel evidence concerning the Last Supper, since we can connect Jesus with no sect using this calendar.

Diverse Forms of Judaism

Because John embraces so many streams of thought and imagery, Johannine scholars have been more and more forced to integrate diverse forms of Judaism, gnosticism, and Greco-Roman religion into their studies. C. H. Dodd (1953) gave direction to this approach by showing that Alexandrian Judaism (Philo) and the Hermetic literature have ideas in common with John. He also showed that the rabbinic notions of Torah and messiah differ widely from those ideas in John. P. Borgen (1965) followed up on Dodd's suggestions and used the manna traditions in Philo, John, and rabbinic literature to isolate a rudimentary homily built on (1) a major verse and a secondary verse; (2) an inclusion at the end, using one of the verses; and (3) a paraphrase of the text, using the text's language. He shows the many details of the manna traditions shared by all the sources. By doing a comparative study of several traditions and controlling his data carefully, Borgen is more successful than some scholars who make extravagant claims for midrash. But even Borgen's thesis fails, for the similarities among the texts are too general and limited, and the variations and peculiarities too many for him to establish the existence of a common oral or literary pattern.

W. Meeks (1967) drew upon many Jewish sources (Qumran, apocrypha, pseudepigrapha, Josephus, Philo, rabbinic literature, Samaritans, and Mandaeans) without an artificial split between Palestinian and Diaspora Judaism or "orthodox" and sectarian traditions. He traced the affinities of the prophet-king and postulated a Johannine polemic against a Jewish group that gave great importance to Moses. The comprehensive history of a tradition yields more probable results than concentration on a few, often late, rabbinic sources.

C. K. Barrett (1970; Eng. trans. 1975) found many Jewish and non-Jewish influences in John. In an attempt to identify the type of Judaism implied in John, he stressed caution in drawing historical conclusions, but found evidence for a nonapocalyptic, institutional Judaism of the type developed after the Temple was destroyed. At the same time he acknowledged strong affinities with gnostic and other Hellenistic movements found inside and outside Judaism. J. L. Martyn (1968) and R. E. Brown (1979) have analyzed Johannine and related data and have established the existence of several groups related to and in conflict with the Johannine community. The researches of these scholars have shown that careful exegesis of the NT material must be combined with a broad review of related phenomena in the Greco-Roman empire.

The attempt to find Paul's opponents within the Jewish and Hellenistic world has led to a plethora of studies and hypotheses (see the discussion of

W. D. Davies and E. P. Sanders above). J. J. Gunther (1973) summarized a long series of Jewish texts gathered under the headings legalism, asceticism, sacerdotal separatism, angelology, messianism and pneumatology, apocalyptic, mystic gnosticism, and apostolic authority. He has drawn material from rabbinic literature, Qumran, apocrypha, pseudepigrapha, and early Christian literature and is certainly correct in attempting to correlate these many forms of Judaism. However, Gunther achieves little because he does not subject the texts to sophisticated analysis and has only a four-page synthesis at the end. D. Georgi (1964) has been more successful in correlating 2 Corinthians with the social and religious phenomena of the Hellenistic world, both Jewish and Gentile. Though his reconstruction of the situation in Corinth is hypothetical and subject to various criticisms, both his methods and conclusions have encouraged a broader type of research into the whole Hellenistic-Jewish milieu of the early church. The studies of Colossians collected by F. Francis and W. A. Meeks (1973) are another example of sophisticated analysis using a wide range of phenomena to explain the NT in its Hellenistic and Jewish setting. Both D. L. Tiede (1972) and C. R. Holladay (1977) have examined the *theios anēr* in Hellenistic Judaism (especially with reference to the figure of Moses) in order to test various hypotheses concerning the use of this concept in the NT. They found that the concept lacks a single, technical meaning, and Holladay undermines the hypothesis that Jewish Hellenistic writers transmitted this figure or type into the early Christian tradition. He also questions our ability to reconstruct the whole social and religious milieu of Hellenistic Judaism in any detail. Nevertheless, Hellenistic Judaism remains an important part of the discussion of early Christianity in its relation to Judaism.

The unique theology of Hebrews has been attributed to a variety of influences. Both S. Sowers (1965) and R. Williamson (1970) have examined the relationship of Hebrews to Philo and rejected C. Spicq's thesis (1952–53) that the author of Hebrews had direct contact with Philo. Sowers showed that Hebrews and Philo have many terms, arguments, and ideas in common and suggested that the author of Hebrews knew the conclusions of allegorical exegesis, but practiced an original typological exegesis based on Christology. Williamson took an even stronger position that the author of Hebrews had no contact with Alexandrian exegesis, but used a common fund of Greek ideas and works drawn from the Septuagint in a Jewish Christian context. Williamson's thesis was accepted by Buchanan (1972), who saw Hebrews as a homiletical midrash under Jewish influence. Sowers's study is most adequate in that he demonstrated a nuanced relationship between Alexandrian traditions and Hebrews and elucidated the extremely complex interactions between Palestinian and Diaspora Judaism, interactions that were weighed too little by Williamson. Most recently, G. W. MacRae (1978) affirmed Palestinian and Hellenistic influences in Hebrews.

Finally, research into the apocrypha and pseudepigrapha has intensified in recent years (see bibliographies in Charlesworth, 1976). The new awareness of diversity within Judaism and the discovery of the Dead Sea Scrolls have ended the assignment of various works to the Sadducees and Pharisees and freed scholars to correlate these works with the traditions, characteristics, and experiences of other groups in Jewish history. These works and others, such as Pseudo-Philo, are valuable and often datable sources for Judaism before and during the NT period. Imagery, exegetical traditions, literary forms, and perspectives on God and humans are shared by this literature. The studies emanating from the SBL Pseudepigrapha Seminar are especially valuable, as is the study of afterlife by G. W. E. Nickelsburg (1972). Nickelsburg does a tradition history of certain literary forms and exegetical complexes, a study that provides a sure foundation for work in the NT and later Jewish literature. An example of this kind of work is his study of the poor in Luke and in the last chapters of *1 Enoch* (1979). M. Philonenko (1973) has also gathered some helpful general and particular observations on NT and intertestamental literature.

Three recent books have rendered nonrabbinic Judaism of the NT period much more accessible to nonspecialists. Nickelsburg (1981) wrote an excellent introduction to the intertestamental Jewish literature. J. J. Collins (1983) has reviewed the Hellenistic Jewish materials with attention to the various movements and trends in Judaism outside Palestine. The appearance of the two-volume Doubleday *Old Testament Pseudepigrapha* edited by J. H. Charlesworth (1983, 1985) has provided ample material for scholars engaged in comparative work between Judaism and the NT.

III. CONCLUSION

Some may object that this review has been overly critical and negative; certainly it has been more negative than the reviewer anticipated. Though the NT's roots in Judaism and continuity with Jewish traditions have been established, concrete theses concerning direct dependence and literary influence have generally failed to gather firm support. A wealth of allusions, parallels, and suggestions firmly relate the two literatures to each other and demand that the historian and the interpreter see the one in the light of the other. But the sectarian history of the first century, the development of religious genres of literature, and the interplay of theological debate remain obscure and hypothetical in the extreme with little agreement on "assured results." Consequently, the very different dates and worlds of various documents have prevented rigorous analysis and comparison of these documents leading to convincing conclusions. NT documents have generally benefited from sophisticated form and redaction criticism with close attention to Jewish sources rather than from wholesale assertions that Jewish techniques and traditions are the central hermeneutical key to the NT.

Further progress will be made. The rabbinic midrashic collections and the parts of the NT strongly influenced by the Bible, as well as other contemporary interpretations of the Bible, must be subjected to a detailed literary, historical, and structural analysis. This work is already in progress, and, as individual documents are understood, comparative analysis can be more fruitfully undertaken. Precise and comprehensive descriptions of texts will lead to the recognition of genres, some of them common to diverse literatures and others unique to particular groups. Whether the Jewish and Christian imperative to relate everything to scripture can be understood as one complex and comprehensive genre is as yet unknown; more likely a fundamental cultural tendency found expression in a series of independent creations. In either case Judaism and Christianity must be seen as a complex world composed of rich and varied modes of life and belief that will be understood only as we understand their rich and difficult literature. Investigation of significant texts and traditions must be undertaken with attention to the many forms of Judaism and Christianity interacting within the larger Greco-Roman world. The history of traditions must be worked out on the basis of whatever texts can be firmly dated, and hypotheses must be cautiously generated which fill out the social situation in which Christianity and Judaism developed during the first century.

BIBLIOGRAPHY

Barrett, Charles Kingsley
  1970   *Das Johannesevangelium und das Judentum.* Stuttgart/Berlin: Kohlhammer. Eng. trans.: *The Gospel of John and Judaism.* Philadelphia: Fortress, 1975.

Bloch, R.
  1955   "Note méthodologique pour l'étude de la littérature rabbinique." *RSR* 43: 194–227. Eng. trans. by W. S. Green and W. J. Sullivan: "Methodological Note for the Study of Rabbinic Literature." Pp. 51–75 in *Approaches to Ancient Judaism: Theory and Practice.* Ed. W. S. Green. BJS 1. Missoula, MT: Scholars Press, 1978.
  1957   "Midrash." *DBSup* 5, cols. 1263–1281. Eng. trans. by M. H. Callaway: "Midrash." Pp. 29–50 in *Approaches to Ancient Judaism: Theory and Practice.* Ed. W. S. Green. Missoula, MT: Scholars Press, 1978.

Borgen, Peder
  1965   *Bread from Heaven: An Exegetical Study of the Concept of Manna in the Gospel of John and the Writings of Philo.* NovTSup 10. Leiden: Brill.

Bowman, J.
  1965   *The Gospel of Mark: The New Christian Jewish Passover Haggadah.* SPB 8. Leiden: Brill.

Brown, Raymond E.
    1977   *The Birth of the Messiah: A Commentary on the Infancy Narratives in
                Matthew and Luke.* Garden City, NY: Doubleday.
    1979   *The Community of the Beloved Disciple.* Paramus, NJ: Paulist.

Buchanan, George Wesley
    1972   *To the Hebrews.* AB 36. Garden City, NY: Doubleday.
    1977   "The Use of Rabbinic Literature for New Testament Research." *BTB*
                7: 110–22.

Carrington, Philip
    1952   *The Primitive Christian Calendar: A Study in the Making of the
                Marcan Gospel.* Vol. 1, *Introduction and Text.* Cambridge: University
                Press.

Catchpole, David R.
    1971   *The Trial of Jesus: A Study in the Gospels and in Jewish Historiography
                from 1770 to the Present Day.* SPB 18. Leiden: Brill.
    1976   "Trial of Jesus." In *IDBSup,* 917–19.

Charlesworth, James H.
    1976   *The Pseudepigrapha and Modern Research.* Missoula, MT: Scholars
                Press.
    1983,   *The Old Testament Pseudepigrapha.* 2 vols. Garden City, NY:
    1985, ed.   Doubleday.

Collins, John J.
    1983   *Between Athens and Jerusalem: Jewish Identity in the Hellenistic
                Diaspora.* New York: Crossroad.

Cope, O. Lamar
    1976   *Matthew: A Scribe for the Kingdom of Heaven.* CBQMS 5. Washing-
                ton, DC: Catholic Biblical Association.

Daly, Robert J.
    1977   "The Soteriological Significance of the Sacrifice of Isaac." *CBQ* 39:
                45–75.

Daniel, Jerry L.
    1979   "Anti-Semitism in the Hellenistic-Roman Period." *JBL* 98: 45–65.

Daube, David
    1956   *The New Testament and Rabbinic Judaism.* London: Athlone.

Davies, Alan T., ed.
    1979   *Anti-Semitism and the Foundations of Christianity.* New York,
                Ramsey, NJ, and Toronto: Paulist.

Davies, P. R., and B. D. Chilton
    1978   "The Aqedah: A Revised Tradition History." *CBQ* 40: 514–46.

Davies, William D.
    1948   *Paul and Rabbinic Judaism: Some Rabbinic Elements in Pauline
                Theology.* London: SPCK. 2d ed. 1955.
    1952   *Torah in the Messianic Age and/or the Age to Come.* SBLMS 7.
                Philadelphia: Society of Biblical Literature.
    1962   "Reflections on a Scandinavian Approach to 'the Gospel Tradition.' "
                Pp. 14–34 in *Neotestamentica et Patristica: Eine Freundesgabe Herrn
                Professor Dr. Oscar Cullmann zu seinem 60. Geburtstag.* NovTSup 6.
                Leiden: Brill. Reprinted in Davies, 1963.

1963 *The Setting of the Sermon on the Mount.* Cambridge: University Press.
1965 "Paul and Judaism." Pp. 178–86 in *The Bible in Modern Scholarship: Papers Read at the 100th Meeting of the Society of Biblical Literature.* Ed. J. Philip Hyatt. Nashville: Abingdon.
1974 *The Gospel and the Land: Early Christianity and Jewish Territorial Doctrine.* Berkeley and Los Angeles: University of California Press.
1977–78 "Paul and the People of Israel." *NTS* 24: 4–39.
1982 *The Territorial Dimension of Judaism.* Berkeley and Los Angeles: University of California Press.
1984 *Jewish and Pauline Studies.* Philadelphia: Fortress.

Derrett, J. Duncan M.
1970 *Law and the New Testament.* London: Darton, Longman & Todd.
1973 *Jesus' Audience: The Social and Psychological Environment in which He Worked.* Crossroad Book. New York: Seabury.
1977 *Studies in the New Testament.* Vol. 1, *Glimpses of the Legal and Social Presuppositions of the Authors.* Leiden: Brill.
1978 *Studies in the New Testament.* Vol. 2, *Midrash in Action and as a Literary Device.* Leiden: Brill.

Dodd, Charles H.
1952 *According to the Scriptures: The Substructure of New Testament Theology.* London: Nisbet.
1953 *The Interpretation of the Fourth Gospel.* Cambridge: University Press.

Doeve, J. W.
1954 *Jewish Hermeneutics in the Synoptic Gospels and Acts.* Assen: van Gorcum.

Drury, John
1976 *Tradition and Design in Luke's Gospel.* London: Darton, Longman & Todd.

Ellis, E. Earle
1957 *St. Paul's Use of the Old Testament.* Edinburgh: T. & T. Clark.
1978 *Prophecy and Hermeneutic in Early Christianity: New Testament Essays.* WUNT 18. Tübingen: Mohr-Siebeck. Reprinted, Grand Rapids: Eerdmans.

Finkel, Asher
1964 *The Pharisees and the Teacher of Nazareth: A Study of Their Background, Their Halachic and Midrashic Teachings, the Similarities and Differences.* AGJU 4. Leiden: Brill.

Fitzmyer, Joseph A.
1968a Review of M. Black, *An Aramaic Approach to the Gospels and Acts.* *CBQ* 30: 417–28.
1968b Review of M. McNamara, *The New Testament and the Palestinian Targum to the Pentateuch.* *TS* 29: 322–26.
1979 *A Wandering Aramean: Collected Aramaic Essays.* SBLMS 25. Missoula, MT: Scholars Press.

Flusser, David
1968 *Jesus in Selbstzeugnissen und Bilddokumenten.* Hamburg: Rowohlt. Eng. trans. by R. Walls: *Jesus.* New York: Herder, 1969.

Forestell, J. T.
1979 *Targumic Traditions and the New Testament: An Annotated Bibliography with a New Testament Index.* SBL Aramaic Studies 4. Chico, CA: Scholars Press.

Francis, Fred O., and Wayne A. Meeks
1973   *Conflict at Colossae*. Missoula, MT: Scholars Press.

Freed, Edwin
1965   *Old Testament Quotations in the Gospel of John*. NovTSup 11. Leiden: Brill.

Gager, John
1983   *The Origins of Anti-Semitism: Attitudes toward Judaism in Pagan and Christian Antiquity*. New York: Oxford University Press.

Gärtner, Bertil
1954   "The Habakkuk Commentary and the Gospel of St. Matthew." *ST* 8: 1–24.

Georgi, Dieter
1964   *Die Gegner des Paulus im 2. Korintherbrief: Studien zur religiösen Propaganda in der Spätantike*. WMANT 11. Neukirchen-Vluyn: Neukirchener Verlag. Eng. trans.: *The Opponents of Paul in Second Corinthians*. Philadelphia: Fortress, 1986.

Gerhardsson, Birger
1961   *Memory and Manuscript: Oral Tradition and Written Transmission in Rabbinic Judaism and Early Christianity*. ASNU 22. Lund: Gleerup.
1964   *Tradition and Transmission in Early Christianity*. ConNT 20. Lund: Gleerup.
1966   *The Testing of God's Son (Matt. 4:1–11 and Par.): An Analysis of an Early Christian Midrash*. ConBNT 2:1. Lund: Gleerup.
1979   *The Origins of the Gospel Traditions*. Philadelphia: Fortress.

Gertner, M.
1962   "Midrashim in the New Testament." *JSS* 7: 267–92.

Goulder, M. D.
1974   *Midrash and Lection in Matthew*. London: SPCK.
1978   *The Evangelists' Calendar: A Lectionary Explanation of the Development of Scripture*. London: SPCK.

Guilding, A.
1960   *The Fourth Gospel and Jewish Worship: A Study of the Relation of St. John's Gospel to the Ancient Jewish Lectionary System*. Oxford: Clarendon Press.

Gundry, Robert H.
1967   *The Use of the Old Testament in St. Matthew's Gospel*. Leiden: Brill.

Gunther, John J.
1973   *St. Paul's Opponents and Their Background: A Study of Apocalyptic and Jewish Sectarian Teachings*. NovTSup 35. Leiden: Brill.

Hanson, Anthony T.
1974   *Studies in Paul's Technique and Theology*. Grand Rapids: Eerdmans.

Hare, Douglas R. A.
1967   *The Theme of Jewish Persecution in the Gospel According to St Matthew*. SNTSMS 6. Cambridge: University Press.

Hartman, Lars
1966   *Prophecy Interpreted: The Formation of Some Jewish Apocalyptic Texts and of the Eschatological Discourse Mark 13 par.* ConBNT 1. Lund: Gleerup.

Hay, David M.
  1973   *Glory at the Right Hand: Psalm 110 in Early Christianity.* SBLMS 18. Nashville: Abingdon.

Heinemann, J.
  1968   "The Triennial Lectionary Cycle." *JJS* 19: 41–48.
  1977   *Prayer in the Talmud: Forms and Patterns.* Trans. R. Sarason. Berlin and New York: de Gruyter. Revision of *Ha-tefilla bitequfat ha-tannaim we-ha-'amoraim.* Jerusalem: Magnes Press, 1964.

Holladay, Carl R.
  1977   *THEIOS ANER in Hellenistic-Judaism: A Critique of the Use of This Category in New Testament Christology.* SBLDS 40. Missoula, MT: Scholars Press.

Jaubert, A.
  1957   *La Date de la Cène: Calendrier biblique et liturgie chrétienne.* EBib. Paris: Gabalda. Eng. trans.: *The Date of the Last Supper.* Staten Island, NY: Alba House, 1965.

Kelber, W.
  1983   *The Oral and the Written Gospel: The Hermeneutics of Speaking and Writing in the Synoptic Tradition, Mark, Paul and Q.* Philadelphia: Fortress.

Kilpatrick, George D.
  1946   *The Origins of the Gospel According to St. Matthew.* Oxford: Clarendon Press.

Klein, Charlotte
  1978   *Anti-Judaism in Christian Theology.* Trans. E. Quinn. Philadelphia: Fortress. With additions from *Theologie und Anti-Judaismus.* Munich: Kaiser, 1975.

Le Déaut, R.
  1969   "A propos d'une définition du midrash." *Bib* 50: 395–413. Eng. trans. by Mary Howard: "Apropos a Definition of Midrash." *Int* 25 (1971) 259–82.
  1963   *La Nuit Pascale: Essai sur la signification de la Pâque juive à partir du Targum d'Exode xii, 42.* AnBib 22. Rome: Pontifical Biblical Institute. Reprint 1975.
  1974   "Targumic Literature and New Testament Interpretation." *BTB* 4: 243–89.

Leistner, R.
  1974   *Anti-Judaismus im Johannes-Evangelium? Darstellung des Problem in der neueren Auslegungsgeschichte und Untersuchung der Leidensgeschichte.* Bern and Frankfurt: Lang.

Lindars, Barnabas
  1961   *New Testament Apologetic: The Doctrinal Significance of the Old Testament Quotations.* London: SCM; Philadelphia: Westminster.

McNamara, Martin
  1966   *The New Testament and the Palestinian Targum to the Pentateuch.* AnBib 27. Rome: Pontifical Biblical Institute. [Additions 1978.]
  1972   *Targum and Testament: Aramaic Paraphrases of the Hebrew Bible: A Light on the New Testament.* Grand Rapids: Eerdmans; Shannon: Irish University Press.

MacRae, George W.
1978 "Heavenly Temple and Eschatology in the Letter to the Hebrews."
Semeia 12: 179–99.

Malina, Bruce
1968 *The Palestinian Manna Tradition: The Manna Tradition in the Palestinian Targums and Its Relationship to the New Testament Writings.*
AGJU 7. Leiden: Brill.

Martyn, J. Louis
1968 *History and Theology in the Fourth Gospel.* New York: Harper. Rev.
ed. Nashville: Abingdon, 1979.

Meeks, Wayne A.
1967 *The Prophet-King: Moses Traditions and the Johannine Christology.*
NovTSup 14. Leiden: Brill.

Miller, M.
1971 "Targum, Midrash and the Use of the Old Testament in the New
Testament." *JSJ* 2: 29–82.

Moore, George Foot
1921 "Christian Writers on Judaism." *HTR* 14: 197–254.
1927–30 *Judaism in the First Three Centuries of the Christian Era: The Age of
the Tannaim.* 3 vols. Cambridge, MA: Harvard University Press.

Munck, Johannes
1954 *Paulus und die Heilsgeschichte.* Copenhagen: Universitets-forlaget.
Eng. trans. by F. Clarke: *Paul and the Salvation of Mankind.* London:
SCM, 1959.

Neusner, Jacob
1978 "Comparing Judaisms." *HR* 18: 177–91.

Nickelsburg, George W. E.
1972 *Resurrection, Immortality and Afterlife in Intertestamental Literature.*
HTS 26. Cambridge, MA: Harvard University Press.
1979 "Riches, the Rich and God's Judgment in 1 Enoch 92–105 and the
Gospel According to Luke." *NTS* 25: 324–44.
1981 *Jewish Literature between the Bible and the Mishnah: A Historical and
Literary Introduction.* Philadelphia: Fortress.

Perrot, C.
1973a *La lecture de la Bible dans la synagogue: Les anciennes lectures palestiniennes du Shabbat et des fêtes.* Hildesheim: Gerstenberg.
1973b "Luc 4, 16–20 et la lecture biblique dans l'ancienne synagogue."
Pp. 170–86 in *Exégèse biblique et judaïsme.* Ed. J. E. Ménard.
Strasbourg: Université.

Philonenko, Marc
1973 "La Littérature intertestamentaire et le Nouveau Testament."
Pp. 116–25 in *Exégèse biblique et judaïsme.* Ed. J. E. Ménard.
Strasbourg: Université.

Reim, Günther
1974 *Studien zum alttestamentlichen Hintergrund des Johannesevangelium.*
SNTSMS 22. Cambridge: University Press.

Saldarini, Anthony J.
1979 Review of E. P. Sanders, 1977. *JBL* 98: 299–303.

Sanders, E. P.
1977   *Paul and Palestinian Judaism: A Comparison of Patterns of Religion.*
            Philadelphia: Fortress.
1980–81   *Jewish and Christian Self-Definition.* Vols. 1–2. Philadelphia:
            Fortress.
1983   *Paul, the Law, and the Jewish People.* Philadelphia: Fortress.

Sanders, J. A.
1975   "From Isaiah 61 to Luke 4." Pp. 75–106 in *Christianity, Judaism and
            Other Greco-Roman Cults: Studies for Morton Smith at Sixty,* vol. 1.
            Ed. J. Neusner. SJLA 12. Leiden: Brill.

Sandmel, Samuel
1962   "Parallelomania." *JBL* 81: 1–13.
1978   *Anti-Semitism in the New Testament.* Philadelphia: Fortress.

Sarason, R.
1978   "On the Use of Method in the Modern Study of Jewish Liturgy."
            Pp. 97–172 in *Approaches to Ancient Judaism: Theory and Practice.*
            Ed. W. S. Green. BJS 1. Missoula, MT: Scholars Press.

Schoeps, Hans Joachim
1959   *Paulus: Die Theologie des Apostels im Lichte der jüdischen Religions-
            geschichte.* Tübingen: Mohr-Siebeck. Eng. trans. by H. Knight, with
            revisions: *Paul: The Theology of the Apostle in the Light of Jewish
            Religious History.* London: Lutterworth, 1961.

Sevenster, J. N.
1975   *The Roots of Pagan Anti-Semitism in the Ancient World.* NovTSup 41.
            Leiden: Brill.

Smith, D. Moody
1972   "The Use of the Old Testament in the New." Pp. 3–65 in *The Use of
            the Old Testament in the New and Other Essays.* Ed. J. M. Efird.
            Durham, NC: Duke University Press.

Smith, Morton
1951   *Tannaitic Parallels to the Gospels.* SBLMS 6. Philadelphia: SBL.
1963   "A Comparison of Early Christian and Early Rabbinic Tradition." *JBL*
            82: 169–76.
1978   *Jesus the Magician.* San Francisco: Harper & Row.

Soares-Prabhu, G. M.
1976   *The Formula Quotations in the Infancy Narrative of Matthew.* AnBib
            63. Rome: Biblical Institute Press.

Sowers, S.
1965   *The Hermeneutics of Philo and Hebrews.* Basel Studies of Theology 1.
            Zurich: EVZ.

Spicq, Ceslas
1952–53   *L'Epitre aux Hebreux.* 3d ed. 2 vols. EBib. Paris: Gabalda.

Stendahl, Krister
1954   *The School of St. Matthew and Its Use of the Old Testament.* Phila-
            delphia: Fortress. 2d ed. 1968.
1976   *Paul among Jews and Gentiles and Other Essays.* Philadelphia:
            Fortress.

Strack, H., and P. Billerbeck
1924–1928   *Kommentar zum Neuen Testament aus Talmud und Midrasch.* 6 vols.
            Munich: Beck.

Strobel, A.
1980   *Die Stunde der Wahrheit: Untersuchungen zum Strafverfahren gegen Jesus.* WUNT 21. Tübingen: Mohr-Siebeck.

Suhl, A.
1965   *Die Funktion der alttestamentliche Zitate und Ausspielungen im Markusevangelium.* Gütersloh: Mohn.

Tiede, David L.
1972   *The Charismatic Figure as Miracle Worker.* SBLDS 1. Missoula, MT: SBL.

VanderKam, James C.
1979   "The Origin, Character, and Early History of the 364-Day Calendar: A Reassessment of Jaubert's Hypothesis." *CBQ* 41: 390–411.

Vermes, Geza
1961   *Scripture and Tradition in Judaism: Haggadic Studies.* SPB 4. Leiden: Brill. 2d ed. 1973.
1973   *Jesus the Jew: A Historian's Reading of the Gospels.* London: Collins.
1975   *Post Biblical Jewish Studies.* SJLA 8. Leiden: Brill.

Williamson, Ronald
1970   *Philo and the Epistle to the Hebrews.* ALGHJ 4. Leiden: Brill.

Winter, Paul
1974   *On the Trial of Jesus.* 2d ed. rev. and ed. T. A. Burkill and G. Vermes. Berlin and New York: de Gruyter. Original 1961.

Wright, A.
1967   *The Literary Genre Midrash.* Staten Island, NY: Alba House.

3

QUMRAN AND THE NEW TESTAMENT

Jerome Murphy-O'Connor, O.P.

Once paleography (Wright) and archaeology (de Vaux) confirmed the date of the scrolls, scholars realized that they belonged to a unique category with regard to NT studies. They were documents that revealed the inner life of a Palestinian Jewish community contemporary with Jesus and the early church, and they presented none of the dating problems that bedeviled the critical use of rabbinic materials. The 1950s saw the beginning of a stream of comparisons that quickly assumed the proportions of a flood; it diminished somewhat in the 1960s and became a tiny trickle in the 1970s.

This survey of the scholarly productions of the past thirty years will concentrate on the most important areas of the NT which are thought to have been illuminated by the scrolls. It is divided into two parts because authors have detected Essene influence both on personages and groups who lived in Palestine and on documents composed outside of Palestine. By way of conclusion I shall offer a number of methological observations that will reflect a general assessment of this area of research.

I. PALESTINE

The contributions touching this domain cover the following topics: Palestinian Aramaic, John the Baptist, Jesus, and the early church.

Palestinian Aramaic

Aramaic, Greek, and Hebrew were used in Palestine during the NT period, but Aramaic was the tongue most commonly spoken (Fitzmyer, 1970; Lapide). Apart from a number of inscriptions and one ostracon, all the Aramaic texts dated between 150 B.C. and A.D. 70 come from Qumran and have made extremely important contributions to the study of the NT.

On the negative side, the Qumran texts call into question a number of commonly accepted assumptions in the famous "Son of Man" debate. The Parables of Enoch (*1 Enoch* 37–71) were frequently used as evidence for pre-Christian Jewish use of "Son of Man" in an individual titular sense, but this section of *Enoch* was not among the many fragments found at Qumran; it seems to be a later substitution for the Book of the Giants, which does appear at Qumran (Milik, 1976). The date and provenance of the Parables are now open questions.

Further, Fitzmyer (1975a:92–94; 1979a:143–60) has pointed out that "Son of Man" is not attested as a form of direct address, as a title for an expected or apocalyptic figure, or as a surrogate for "I," and that the first-century form is always *bar 'enaš* (or in the Hebraized form *'ĕnoš*) — that is, with the initial aleph — and always means either "someone" (indefinite sense) or "a human being" (generic sense). Such evidence obviously has methodological priority over texts whose late date is betrayed by the forms *bar naš* or *bar naša*.

The silence of Qumran is also significant in another respect. It has been claimed that the use of *memra* ("command," "word") in the targumim prepared the way for the Johannine *logos* ("word") (McNamara: 101–6). Qumran furnishes a targum that is indisputably pre-Christian, and though *memra* appears twice it is never used in a personified sense (Fitzmyer, 1973:394–96).

On the positive side, the most significant contribution of Qumran is to provide evidence for the absolute use of *mare'* ("Lord"). This is the missing link between the construct and suffixal forms in Aramaic and the absolute Greek usage of *kyrios* ("Lord") as applied to Jesus in the NT (Fitzmyer, 1975b).

Another Aramaic text (4Q243) combines the titles "Son of God" and "Son of the Most High" with phrases parallel to Luke 1:32, 35. Though the text is dated to the last third of the first century B.C., its fragmentary nature permits it to be interpreted either in a historical or an apocalyptic sense (Fitzmyer, 1973:391–94). This uncertainty necessitates extreme prudence in any discussion of the relationship of 4Q243 to Luke 1–2, but its importance is undeniable, particularly since the *anthrōpoi eudokias* ("people of good will") of Luke 2:14 also has an Aramaic parallel at Qumran (Fitzmyer, 1958).

Qumran also throws light on the Matthean infancy narrative, because the doubt of Joseph is paralleled by the doubt of Lamech in 1QapGen 2:1–27. In the end Noah proves to have been born of a normal union, but J. A. Fitzmyer is certainly correct in underlining that "the idea of another sort of conception is at least entertained" (1973:400).

Even though the text is in Hebrew, this seems the most appropriate place to mention 1QSa 2:11–12, which speaks of the begetting of the messiah. The subject of the verb is missing, but many authors accept the editor's restoration of "God" (Michel and Betz). R. E. Brown claims that this provides Palestinian evidence for "the figurative use of the divine begetting of the Messiah" (1977:137 n. 14), but even if the restoration is correct, the text does not ambiguously suggest direct causality; the hiphil can equally well express indirect causality, in which case the text would be concerned with the providential moment of the messiah's birth and not with its mode.

John the Baptist

Long before the discovery of the scrolls, scholars had postulated a relationship between John the Baptist and the Essenes on the basis of the proximity of John's preaching area to the Essene base by the Dead Sea. H. Graetz (III/1, 277–78) claimed that John was an Essene and that his baptism implied adhesion to the Essene movement. The discussions that followed the appearance of the scrolls never went so far as to affirm the second point, but initially there was a strong tendency to suggest that John had been adopted by the Essenes as a child (Brownlee, 1950:70–72; 1957:35; O. Betz, 1958:222), or at least that he had close affinities with the Essenes (Daniélou: 22). John and the Essenes were seen to share common ground on a number of points: asceticism, eschatological vision, and the importance given to bathing in water.

However, as the debate developed, these analogies were subjected to more intense scrutiny, and it became progressively clearer that what was genuinely specific in John's vision and practice could not be explained as due to Essene influence. The unconscious shift from possibility to probability was highlighted by H. H. Rowley as a major methodological flaw in many contributions. H. Braun (2:24) and E. Cothenet echo his skepticism regarding any real relationship between John and Qumran.

In the light of this conclusion, it becomes difficult to maintain, as many have done, that John and his disciples were the medium through which Essene influence touched Jesus himself (Cullmann: 217–19), the Hellenists of Acts and the epistle to the Hebrews (Spicq, 1959:366), or the Johannine church (Brown, 1955:574).

Jesus

At least fifty scholars have dealt with various aspects of the relationship between Jesus and the Essene movement (H. Braun: 2:85). Every possible similarity has been explored at length, but only five points seem deserving of serious consideration.

1. *Eschatology.* Earlier comparisons of Jesus' eschatological vision with that of the Essenes concentrated on the expectation of an imminent end (H. Braun: 2:90), but this has now been shown to be inadequate with regard to both Jesus and the Essenes. The eschatological perspective of Jesus is revealed by a combination of present and future statements; salvation is both hoped for and already experienced (Kümmel: 147). Precisely the same combination appears in the *Hymns of the Community* and is found nowhere else in Jewish literature of the period (H.-W. Kuhn: 203).

It is uncertain whether this realized eschatology was current in the wider Essene movement. The documents that certainly antedate the foundation of Qumran exhibit a purely futurist eschatology, but this may be due to their intended purpose. The point may not be relevant because H.-W. Kuhn (204) maintains that there is in reality no connection between the eschatological vision of these hymns and that of Jesus; for the Essenes, future salvation is present in the community, whereas for Jesus it is present in his actions. Other differences inevitably flow from this.

The real parallel to the Essene perspective is in the Pauline and Johannine churches, where the community is the place of salvation, but, since this can be explained as a consequence of their understanding of Jesus, Essene influence appears an unnecessary hypothesis.

2. *Attitudes toward riches.* A close analogy is seen between Jesus' warnings regarding the dangers of wealth and the Essene avoidance of private property. Direct dependence, however, is not claimed, because both attitudes stand in the mainstream of OT prophetic teaching. A more specific point of contact is found in Jesus' directive that his missionaries should not carry money and should be confident of the hospitality of the communities to which they come (Matt 10:9). This parallels Essene practice (Josephus *J.W.* 2.8.4 §§142–26) and is not attested elsewhere (Carmignac: 83). Jesus may have adopted an Essene custom because he saw its witness potential, but it is equally possible that he simply instructed his disciples to do as he did (Matt 8:20).

3. *Laying on of hands.* The laying on of hands to cure an illness or to exorcise an unclean spirit, a gesture occurring frequently in miracles performed by Jesus, is not attested in any Jewish writings with the exception of 1QapGen 20:22, 29 (Flusser). This document may have been composed at Qumran, but the laying on of hands as part of a healing rite is attested in the literature of Assyro-Babylonian magic (Dupont-Sommer: 252 n. 1). Since the Essene movement began in Babylon (Murphy-O'Connor, 1974:219–23), the gesture may have been in use outside Qumran; Essene interest in medicine is stressed by Josephus (*J.W.* 2.8.6 §136).

4. *Marriage and divorce.* One of the most generally accepted *ipsissima verba Jesu* is the absolute prohibition of divorce. An identical prohibition appears in 11QTemple 57:17–19. Fitzmyer (1976) was the first to point out that this passage destroyed the consensus that Jesus' attitude toward divorce was unique in a Jewish Palestinian setting. Since divorce is essentially the right to marry again (*m. Giṭ.* 9.3), this prohibition accords with the literal sense of CD 4:20–21, which forbids any second marriage even after the death of a spouse (Davies, 1987:73–85). Since both 11QTemple and this portion of CD antedate the foundation of Qumran, the prohibition of divorce belongs to general Essene teaching and must have been widely known, even though neither Philo nor Josephus mentions it.

Fitzmyer does not raise the question of Jesus' dependence on Essene teaching, even though both CD 4:20–21 and Mark 10:6//Matt 19:4 base the prohibition of divorce on the order of creation expressed in Gen 1:27. Already committed to the priority of Mark, his concern is to reinforce this hypothesis by underlining that the form of the Marcan question (10:2) is now perfectly at home in a Palestinian setting. This, of course, is correct, but so is the Matthean question (19:3), and the Matthean use of "permit" and "command" is rabbinically accurate whereas Mark's use is not. The problem needs further investigation.

5. *The Last Supper.* A. Jaubert (1954) first proposed that the date of the Last Supper was fixed according to the Essene calendar, a hypothesis that she refined and supported by new arguments in subsequent studies (1957, 1960, 1966a, 1966b, 1967, 1968, 1972, 1975, 1978). The existence of the solar calendar attested at Qumran is confirmed by *Jubilees* and indirectly by CD 6:19; both of these texts antedate the foundation of Qumran. It would appear, therefore, that the calendar was common to the whole Essene movement, though the silence of Philo and Josephus is a little disconcerting.

If it is possible that Jesus knew the Essene calendar, is it likely that he followed it? In her affirmative answer, Jaubert argues that it clears up certain difficulties in the Gospels and that it was in use by Christians in the patristic period. The extreme fragility of Jaubert's argumentation regarding this second point has been pointed out by J. Blinzler, who questions the antiquity of the patristic tradition highlighting Wednesday. Jaubert's subsequent studies have not furnished a satisfactory reply to Blinzler's objection that no reliance can be placed in a tradition first clearly attested in the third century A.D. There is more than a hint of despair in Jaubert's evocation of "an unconscious liturgical 'memory'" (1972:75).

Jaubert's treatment of the Gospels also fails to inspire confidence because she shows little awareness of the complexity of the Gospel tradition, particularly in the passion narrative. Her starting point is the paschal character of the Last Supper. That it is so presented by the Gospels in their present form is beyond question, but this may be for theological and liturgical reasons and cannot decide the historical question. There are good arguments to sustain the hypothesis that the Last Supper was not in fact a paschal meal (Haag: 121–29). If this is correct, Jaubert's thesis has no foundation.

K. G. Kuhn (1950a), who denied that Jesus celebrated a Passover meal, was also the first to point out that features of the Last Supper that were unexplainable by Passover customs had close analogies in Essene community meals. These parallels were much debated in the 1950s (H. Braun: 2:30), but these studies contributed little of significance to Kuhn's analysis, whose insight and prudence make it a model of its genre. As the debate progressed, authors became much more cautious regarding any dependence of the Last Supper on Essene customs because, as M. Black (115) pointed out, "The main difficulty . . . lies in our ignorance of other forms of such a meal in Judaism itself apart from the Passover meal. The Pharisees also had their religious meals in their Guilds or *Haburoth*; and, in any case, every meal in Judaism was, in some sense, a religious meal."

The Early Church

Many analogies have been seen between the vocabulary, practices, and organization of the church in Palestine and those of the Essenes (Johnson; Reicke; Mowry). Few, if any, stand up to close examination, and scholars have become progressively more prudent regarding the affirmation of any direct Essene influence on the early church (H. Braun: 2:144–65; LaSor: 154–67; Schmitt).

II. OUTSIDE PALESTINE

Contrary to what might have been expected, the closest analogies to Essene doctrines have been found in Christian documents composed outside Palestine. Very soon after comparisons began to be made, this was pointed out for the Pauline and Johannine literature (K. G. Kuhn, 1950b:209–10) and not long afterwards for the Epistle to the Hebrews (F.-M. Braun: 35–38), a document whose affinities with both Paul and John are well known (Spicq, 1952, 1:109–38, 144–68).

Pauline Literature

It is generally agreed that the scrolls have significantly amplified the linguistic background of such Pauline terms as "mystery" (Coppens, 1960), "flesh" and "spirit" (K. G. Kuhn, 1952; W. D. Davies), "power" (Murphy), "perfect" (Rigaux), "truth" (Murphy-O'Connor, 1965a), and "holy" (H.-W. Kuhn: 90–93). In such detailed studies, the question of dependence is rarely, if ever, raised, presumably because it is rightly recognized that an adequate answer can be given only in the context of more far-reaching studies devoted to major parallel themes in Paul and Qumran. Justification is certainly one such topic, but the studies devoted to it (Grundmann; Starcky) are vitiated by the uncritical way in which they combine data from disparate Essene documents.

An unusually high proportion of Essene traits appears in 2 Cor 6:14–7:1 (K. G. Kuhn, 1951:74–75). Despite the fact that a better series of parallels can be found in Philo, Fitzmyer (1961) and J. Gnilka admit direct Essene influence but consider it a post-Pauline interpolation. G. Klinzing (179–82) argues that it was originally a baptismal exhortation, and this hypothesis finds some confirmation in R. Deichgräber's (78–84) stress on the Essene coloring of such baptismal texts as Acts 26:18 and Col 1:12–14. The "hymns of the community" also reflect such key elements of Paul's baptismal synthesis as the anticipation of the end in "resurrection" and "new creation" (H.-W. Kuhn: 44–112).

Alternatively it has been suggested that 2 Cor 6:14–7:1 reflects the theology of Paul's opponents in Galatia (H. D. Betz). If correct, this view (which is not incompatible with Klinzing's) would link up with another plausible hypothesis, viz., that the Colossian heresy had its roots in an Essene-type theology (Saunders; Kehl). No Essene traits appear in Paul's response to the Colossians. This makes it all the more surprising that, of all the NT writings, Ephesians exhibits the closest linguistic, stylistic, and thematic parallels to the Essene documents (K. G. Kuhn, 1960; Mussner; Murphy-O'Connor, 1965b; Deichgräber: 65–76).

In order to explain this influence, it has been suggested that Essenes were among the two thousand Jewish families transported from Babylon to the Lycus Valley by Antiochus III (Murphy-O'Connor, 1974:225); from the vicinity of Colossae their influence could have spread east to Galatia and west to Ephesus. Many of the contacts between Ephesians and the scrolls come from the liturgical "hymns of the community," which may antedate the return of the Essenes to Palestine. A significant number, however, come from documents composed at Qumran. A closer analysis of the possibility that the style of these hymns influenced the Teacher of Righteousness and the authors of other Qumran texts needs to be undertaken as a control of the above hypothesis. Should the result be negative, serious attention will have to be given to the proposal that, after the destruction of Qumran, some members of the community fled to Asia Minor (F.-M. Braun: 35).

Johannine Literature

Some two hundred studies have been devoted to different facets of the relationship between John and the scrolls (Charlesworth: 195–204).

> John's pervading ethical and eschatological dualism with its contrasts between light and darkness, truth and falsehood, finds a very plausible background in Qumran dualism; and in our judgement the Scrolls consistently offer better parallels to John than do any of the non-Christian elements in the Mandaean documents emphasized by Bultmann or the examples in Philo and the Hermetica offered by Dodd. The angelic figure in the Scrolls, who as prince of lights and spirit of truth leads the sons of light, has been adapted in John to the figure of Jesus (the light of the world, the truth) and to the Paraclete (the Spirit of truth). The Christian community is constituted, not by faith in an interpretation of the Law which is truth for Qumran, but by faith in Jesus who embodies truth." (Brown, 1966b:21–22).

To this admirable summary we must add the common priestly-ritual dimension and belief in a realized eschatology.

Brown's summary also hints at an important shift in the critical assessment of the Fourth Gospel. Prior to the discovery of the scrolls, the dominant opinion saw John as heavily dependent on a hellenized gnosis; thereafter many proclaimed the Gospel to be firmly rooted in a Palestinian milieu (H. Braun: 2:140–42). From this they naturally drew conclusions regarding the date of John and the value of its historical information, which differed significantly from the current consensus.

When viewed from the perspective of contemporary Johannine research, the comparative studies of John and the scrolls reveal a surprising phenomenon; all the authors proceed as if there had never been any debate about the sources and composition of the Fourth Gospel! Presumably this was due in some measure to skepticism regarding Bultmann's hypothesis and to the vagueness of other solutions. W. Wilkens and R. Schnackenburg (59–60) distinguish three levels in John, whereas Brown (1966a:xxxiv) finds five; these authors rarely, if ever, say to which level a particular text belongs. M.-É. Boismard and A. Lamouille are the only commentators to assign each text to a specific level; they find the contacts with Qumran to be concentrated in the third level, whose style corresponds to that of 1 John and which was probably composed at Ephesus (66).

Whatever one thinks of the Boismard-Lamouille hypothesis, it is certain that the Fourth Gospel can no longer be regarded as a literary unity, and comparisons with the scrolls must take this into account. The value of older studies which fail to do so must henceforth be considered highly dubious.

Regarding the source of Essene influence on Johannine circles, it should be noted that a great many of the parallels come from the Treatise on the Two Spirits (1QS 3:13–4:26), a text which is not a literary unity (von der Osten-Sacken; Duhaime) and whose older portions enjoyed an independent existence before being incorporated into the *Rule* (Murphy-O'Connor, 1969:541–43). They may have been current among the wider Essene community, not only within Palestine but outside. Here we rejoin the problem of Essenism in Asia Minor noted apropos of the Pauline literature.

The Epistle to the Hebrews

Three major studies have been devoted to the relationship between Hebrews and the scrolls (Yadin; Spicq, 1959; Kosmala). It is curious that the thrust of all three is not to furnish information that might help to identify the author, but rather to characterize the recipients of the letter; they are presented as being, wholly or in part, converts from Qumran. The stress on the priestly character of Christ, on his superiority to Moses and angels, and the theme of the new tabernacle are all seen as an approach that would be particularly appropriate to those formed by Essene theology, a theology in which the figure of Melchizedek played a role (Milik, 1972; Delcor).

Criticism of this hypothesis has come from Coppens (1962) and H. Braun (2:182–83), but their arguments miss the point; they prove only that the author of Hebrews was not an Essene. The problem needs further investigation, and in this research the possibility of Essene influence in Asia Minor must receive adequate attention.

III. METHODOLOGY

Despite the variety of conflicting opinions of the relationship between the scrolls and the NT, in the early part of the debate no attention was paid to the methodology of assessing the dependence of one set of documents on another. P. Benoit and S. Sandmel made an important contribution by insisting that many parallels were without significance because both Qumran and the NT were influenced by the OT. Thus, throughout H. Braun's magisterial study, "allgemein jüdisch" ("generally Jewish") is consistently used to dismiss irrelevant analogies. This had the effect, however, of making "nicht allgemein jüdisch" ("not generally Jewish") appear to be a valid argument for the dependence of the NT on Qumran, since the scrolls antedated the NT writings.

Authors such as K. G. Kuhn (1954:203), B. Gärtner (139), H. Braun (1:190), and G. Klinzing (210) take it for granted that Paul must have borrowed the idea of the community as a spiritual temple from the Essenes, even though Klinzing points out that the key component in the Pauline concept is not found in the Qumran texts. The one voice raised against this consensus was that of Schüssler Fiorenza, but she contents herself with showing that the concept could have developed independently among Christians and Essenes.

These studies illustrate a methodological error that flaws virtually all comparisons of Qumran and the NT; plausibility is assumed to be probability. A single hypothesis is never anything more than a possible explanation. Real probability demands the demonstration that one hypothesis is more likely than all the alternative explanations of the same phenomenon. Few, if any, of the studies under review undertake such a demonstration. Their conclusions may be correct but a nagging doubt remains.

This error in procedure is compounded by a widespread assumption that is typified by the most recent book devoted to the whole spectrum of relations between Qumran and the NT, that of W. S. LaSor. The scrolls are treated as a homogeneous body of literature, devoid of any internal tensions and showing no trace of development. Phrases from different documents are presumed to have the same meaning. Texts from documents differing in date and intention are strung together in a way highly reminiscent of precritical theologies of the NT which conflated Pauline and Johannine texts without any respect for their divergent points of view.

The validity of this assumption was called into question very early. I. Rabinowitz (1953) argued for an internal development within the Qumran sect, and both he (1954) and C. Rabin disputed the literary unity of CD. These studies, however, received no more attention than subsequent efforts to lay bare the evolution of the sect (Denis, 1964) or to demonstrate the composite character of 1QS (Murphy-O'Connor, 1969; Pouilly), 1QH (Jeremias; H.-W. Kuhn), CD (Denis; Stegemann; Murphy-O'Connor, 1972), and 1QM (Hunzinger; Becker; von der Osten-Sacken; P. R. Davies; Duhaime, 1977a). The lack of any real consensus in the conclusions of these literary analyses cannot be permitted to obscure the genuine difficulties that they try to explain. The scrolls are neither a literary nor a theological unity, and any approach that treats them as such is automatically invalidated. This, of course, means that much of the work done on comparative syntheses (e.g., justification, anthropology) will have to be redone because the presentation of the Qumran material is critically unreliable. One conspicuous example of rigorous methodology is J. Becker's *Das Heil Gottes*, where each block of material, after literary-critical analysis, is permitted to speak for itself, and facile unfounded syntheses are avoided.

In general, scholars who postulate borrowing from the scrolls on the part of the NT have been concerned with suggesting how information could have passed from Essenes to Christians. This, of course, is crucial to the credibility of any hypothesis of dependence, but the complexity of the problem does not seem to have been perceived.

There is wide agreement now that the group at Qumran were Essenes, but it is equally well known that the information on the Essenes furnished by Philo, Josephus, and Pliny the Elder does not harmonize perfectly with that provided by the scrolls. The evidence available at present tends to show that the Qumranians were the far right wing of a much larger Essene movement from which they broke off about the middle of the second century B.C. (Murphy-O'Connor, 1974). The Qumranians lived in a very isolated area, advocated stringent separation from outsiders (1QS 5:1, 10; 9:8, 20), prohibited revelation of the sect's doctrines to nonmembers (1QS 9:16–17), and reinforced secrecy by writing certain documents in code (e.g., 4Q186). The non-Qumran Essenes, on the other hand, were both more numerous and more accessible. Though they were under the same obligation of secrecy (Josephus, *J.W.* 2.8.7 §141), it seems likely that their neighbors knew much of their doctrines and practices. A priori, therefore, it is much more probable that Christians acquired information regarding the Essenes who lived in the towns and villages rather than about those who insulated themselves at Qumran.

This probability raises another methodological question: To what extent can the scrolls be taken as representative of the Essene movement as a whole? In the present state of our knowledge one thing is clear: certain elements in the scrolls were not acceptable to the Essene movement as a whole. The split in the movement was occasioned by the rejection of certain proposals put forward by the Teacher of Righteousness (Stegemann: 225–56; Murphy-O'Connor, 1974:233–38). These went beyond the suggestion to move to the desert, because at Qumran traditional Essene teaching, known as "the former ordinances," was completed by "the latter ordinances" deriving from the Teacher of Righteousness (Laperrousaz). The scrolls, therefore, contain elements that were particular to Qumran. Given the conservative character of the Qumranians, it is equally clear that the scrolls must contain elements shared with the wider Essene movement (Weinert). Hence, unless the probability of contact is to be robbed of all meaning, the information found in the scrolls must be carefully evaluated, since direct dependence of the NT on teachings proper to Qumran is as unlikely as contact between Christians and the wider Essene movement is possible.

This once again underlines the importance of literary criticism of the scrolls; material that antedates the split in the Essene movement may be incorporated in documents that acquired their final form at Qumran. A much closer literary analysis of references to the Essenes (Philo, Josephus, Pliny, Hippolytus, Solinus, Porphyrius, Josippus) is also imperative. Until something approaching a consensus is achieved in these areas, comparisons between the scrolls and the NT are likely to be at best superficial and at worst misleading.

BIBLIOGRAPHY

Becker, Jürgen
    1964   *Das Heil Gottes: Heils- und Sündenbegriffe in den Qumrantexten und im Neuen Testament.* SUNT 3. Göttingen: Vandenhoeck & Ruprecht.

Benoit, Pierre
    1960   "Qumran et le Nouveau Testament." *NTS* 7: 276–96. [= Murphy-O'Connor, 1968:1–30.]

Betz, Hans Dieter
    1973   "2 Cor 6:14–7:1: An Anti-Pauline Fragment." *JBL* 92: 88–108.

Betz, Otto
    1958   "Die Proselytentaufe der Qumransekte und die Taufe im Neuen Testament." *RevQ* 1: 213–34.

Black, Matthew
    1961   *The Scrolls and Christian Origins: Studies in the Jewish Background of the New Testament.* London: Nelson.

Blinzler, Josef
    1958   "Qumran-kalendar und Passionschronologie." *ZNW* 49: 238–51.

Boismard, Marie-Émile, and Arnaud Lamouille
    1977   *Synopse des Quatre Évangiles en Français III: L'évangile de Jean.* Paris: Cerf.

Braun, François-Marie
    1955   "L'arrière-fond judaïque du quatrième évangile et la communauté de l'alliance." *RB* 62: 5–44.

Braun, Herbert
    1966   *Qumran und das Neue Testament, I-II.* Tübingen: Mohr-Siebeck.

Brown, Raymond E.
1955   "The Qumran Scrolls and the Johannine Gospel and Epistles." *CBQ*
            17: 403–19, 559–74. [= Stendahl: 183–207.]
1966a   *The Gospel according to John I-XII.* AB 29. Garden City, NY:
            Doubleday.
1966b   "Second Thoughts X: The Dead Sea Scrolls and the New Testament."
            ExpTim 78: 19–23. [= Charlesworth: 1–8.]
1977   *The Birth of the Messiah: A Commentary on the Infancy Narratives in
            Matthew and Luke.* Garden City, NY: Doubleday.

Brownlee, William H.
1950   "A Comparison of the Covenanters of the Dead Sea Scrolls with Pre-
            Christian Jewish Sects." *BA* 13: 50–72.
1957   "John the Baptist in the New Light of Ancient Scrolls." Pp. 33–53 in
            Stendahl.

Carmignac, Jean
1957   *Le Docteur de Justice et Jésus-Christ.* Paris: Orante.

Charlesworth, James H., ed.
1972   *John and Qumran.* London: Chapman.

Coppens, Joseph
1960   "Le 'mystère' dans la théologie paulinienne et ses parallèles qumrân-
            iens." Pp. 142–65 in *Littérature et théologie pauliniennes.* RechBib 5.
            Bruges: Desclée de Brouwer. [= Murphy-O'Connor, 1968:132–59.]
1962   "Les affinités qumrâniennes de l'Epître aux Hébreux." *NRT* 84:
            128–41, 257–82.

Cothenet, E.
1978   "Qumran et le Nouveau Testament. A. Jean-Baptiste." *DBSup* 9, cols.
            981–96.

Cullmann, Oscar
1955   "The Significance of the Qumran Texts for Research into the Begin-
            nings of Christianity." *JBL* 74: 213–26. [= Stendahl: 18–32.]

Daniélou, Jean
1957   *Les manuscrits de la mer Morte et les origines du christianisme.* Paris:
            Orante.

Davies, Philip R.
1977   *1QM, the War Scroll from Qumran: Its Structure and History.* BibOr
            32. Rome: Biblical Institute Press.
1987   *Behind the Essenes: History and Ideology in the Dead Sea Scrolls.* BJS
            94. Atlanta: Scholars Press.

Davies, William D.
1957   "Paul and the Dead Sea Scrolls: Flesh and Spirit." Pp. 157–82 in
            Stendahl.

Deichgräber, Reinhard
1967   *Gotteshymnus und Christushymnus in der frühen Christenheit: Unter-
            suchungen zu Form, Sprache und Stil der frühchristlichen Hymnen.*
            SUNT 5. Göttingen: Vandenhoeck & Ruprecht.

Delcor, Mathias
1971   "Melchisedech from Genesis to the Qumran Texts and the Epistle to
            the Hebrews." *JSJ* 2: 115–35.

Denis, Albert-Marie
1964 "Evolution de structures dans la secte de Qumran." Pp. 23–49 in *Aux origines de l'Eglise.* RechBib 7. Bruges: Desclée de Brouwer.
1967 *Les thèmes de connaissance dans le Document de Damas.* StudHell 15. Louvain: Publications Universitaires.

Duhaime, Jean
1977a "La rédaction de 1QM xiii et l'évolution du dualisme à Qumrân." *RB* 84: 210–38.
1977b "L'instruction sur les deux esprits et les interpolations dualistes à Qumrân (1QS iii,13–iv,26)." *RB* 84: 566–94.

Dupont-Sommer, André
1960 "Exorcismes et guérisons dans les écrits de Qoumrân." Pp. 246–61 in *Congress Volume: Oxford, 1959.* VTSup 7. Leiden: Brill.

Fitzmyer, Joseph A.
1958 " 'Peace upon Earth among Men of His Good Will' (Lk 2:14)." *TS* 19: 225–27. [= Fitzmyer, 1974:101–4.]
1961 "Qumran and the Interpolated Paragraph in 2 Cor 6:14–7:1." *CBQ* 23: 271–80. [= Fitzmyer, 1974:205–20.]
1970 "The Languages of Palestine in the First Century A.D." *CBQ* 32: 501–31. [= Fitzmyer, 1979a:29–56.]
1973 "The Contribution of Qumran Aramaic to the Study of the New Testament." *NTS* 20: 382–407. [= Fitzmyer, 1979a:85–114.]
1974 *Essays on the Semitic Background of the New Testament.* SBLSBS 5. Missoula, MT: Scholars Press.
1975a "Methodology in the Study of the Aramaic Substratum of Jesus' Sayings in the New Testament." Pp. 73–102 in *Jésus aux origines de la christologie.* Ed. J. Dupont. BETL 40. Gembloux: Duculot. [= Fitzmyer, 1979a:1–28.]
1975b "Der semitische Hintergrund des neutestamentlichen Kyriostitels." Pp. 267–98 in *Jesus Christus in Historie und Theologie: Neutestamentliche Festschrift für Hans Conzelmann zum 60. Geburtstag.* Ed. G. Strecker. Tübingen: Mohr-Siebeck. [= Fitzmyer, 1979a:115–42.]
1976 "The Matthean Divorce Texts and Some New Palestinian Evidence." *TS* 37: 197–226.
1979a *A Wandering Aramean: Collected Aramaic Essays.* SBLMS 25. Missoula, MT: Scholars Press.
1979b "The New Testament Title 'Son of Man' Philologically Considered." Pp. 143–60 in Fitzmyer, 1979a.

Flusser, David
1957 "Healing through the Laying-on of Hands in a Dead Sea Scroll." *IEJ* 7: 107–8.

Gärtner, Bertil
1965 *The Temple and the Community in Qumran and the New Testament.* SNTSMS 1. Cambridge: University Press.

Gnilka, Joachim
1963 "2 Cor 6:14–7:1 in the Light of the Qumran Texts and the Testaments of the Twelve Patriarchs." Pp. 48–68 in Murphy-O'Connor, 1968.

Graetz, Heinrich
1888 *Geschichte der Juden,* vol. 3, 4th ed. 11 vols. in 13, 1853–76 with subsequent editions. Leipzig: Leiner.

Grundmann, Walter
1960 "Der Lehrer der Gerechtigkeit von Qumran und die Frage nach der Glaubensgerechtigkeit in der Theologie des Apostels Paulus." *RevQ* 2: 237–59. [= Murphy-O'Connor, 1968:85–114.]

Haag, Herbert
1971 *Vom alten zum neuen Pascha: Geschichte und Theologie des Osterfestes.* SBS 49. Stuttgart: Katholisches Bibelwerk.

Hunzinger, Claus-Hunno
1957 "Fragmente einer älteren Fassung des Buches Milhama aus Höhle 4 von Qumran." *ZAW* 69: 131–51.

Jaubert, Annie
1954 "La date de la dernière Cène." *RHR* 146: 140–73.
1957 *La date de la Cène.* Paris: Cerf.
1960 "Jésus et le calendrier de Qumran." *NTS* 7: 1–30.
1966a "Une lecture du lavement des pieds au mardi/mercredi sainte." *Museon* 79: 264–70.
1966b "Une discussion patristique sur la chronologie de la Passion." *RSR* 54: 407–10.
1967 "Le mercredi où Jesus fut livré." *NTS* 14: 145–64.
1968 "Le mercredi de Nouvel An chez les Yezidis." *Bib* 49: 244–48.
1972 "The Calendar of Qumran and the Passion Narrative in John." Pp. 62–75 in Charlesworth.
1975 "Un nouveau calendrier liturgique à la lumière de l'archéologie." *Dossiers de l'archéologie* 10: 82–86.
1978 "Fiches de calendrier." Pp. 305–11 in *Qoumran: Sa théologie, sa piété, son milieu.* BETL 46. Gembloux: Duculot.

Jeremias, Gert
1963 *Der Lehrer der Gerechtigkeit.* SUNT 2. Göttingen: Vandenhoeck & Ruprecht.

Johnson, Sherman E.
1954 "The Dead Sea Manual of Discipline and the Jerusalem Church of Acts." *ZAW* 66: 106–20. [= Stendahl: 129–42.]

Kehl, N.
1969 "Erniedrigung und Erhöhung in Qumran und Kolossä." *ZKT* 91: 364–94.

Klinzing, Georg
1971 *Die Umdeutung des Kultus in der Qumrangemeinde und im Neuen Testament.* SUNT 7. Göttingen: Vandenhoeck & Ruprecht.

Kosmala, Hans
1961 *Hebräer-Essener-Christen: Studien zur Vorgeschichte der frühchristlichen Verkündigung.* SPB 1. Leiden: Brill.

Kuhn, Heinz-Wolfgang
1966 *Enderwartung und gegenwärtiges Heil: Untersuchungen zu den Gemeindeliedern von Qumran.* SUNT 4. Göttingen: Vandenhoeck & Ruprecht.

Kuhn, Karl Georg
1950a "Ueber den ursprünglichen Sinn des Abendmahles und sein Verhältnis zu den Gemeinschaftsmahlen der Sektenschrift." *EvT* 10: 508–27. [Revised substantially in Stendahl: 65–93.]

| 1950b | "Die in Palästina gefundenen hebräischen Texte und das Neue Testament." *ZTK* 47: 192–211. |

1950b "Die in Palästina gefundenen hebräischen Texte und das Neue Testament." *ZTK* 47: 192–211.

1951 "Die Schriftrollen vom Toten Meer: Zum heutigen Stand ihrer Veröffentlichung." *EvT* 11: 72–75.

1952 "*Peirasmos-hamartia-sarx* im Neuen Testament und die damit zusammenhängenden Vorstellung." *ZTK* 49: 200–22. [= Stendahl: 94–113.]

1954 "Les rouleaux de cuivre de Qumran." *RB* 61: 193–205.

1960 "Der Epheserbrief im Lichte der Qumrantexte." *NTS* 7: 334–46. [= Murphy-O'Connor, 1968:115–31.]

Kümmel, Werner Georg
1956 *Verheissung und Erfüllung: Untersuchungen zur eschatologischen Verkündigung Jesus.* ATANT 6. Zurich: Zwingli.

Laperrousaz, E. M.
1971 "Les 'ordonnances premières' et les 'ordonnances dernières' dans les manuscrits de la mer Morte." Pp. 405–19 in *Homages à André Dupont-Sommer.* Paris: Maisonneuve.

Lapide, P.
1975 "Insights from Qumran into the Languages of Jesus." *RevQ* 8: 483–501.

LaSor, William Sanford
1972 *The Dead Sea Scrolls and the New Testament.* Grand Rapids: Eerdmans.

McNamara, Martin
1972 *Targum and Testament: Aramaic Paraphrases of the Hebrew Bible: A Light on the New Testament.* Shannon: Irish University Press.

Michel, Otto, and Otto Betz
1960 "Von Gott gezeugt." Pp. 3–23 in *Judentum, Urchristentum, Kirche: Festschrift für Joachim Jeremias.* Ed. W. Eltester. BZNW 26. Berlin: Töpelmann.

Milik, Josef
1972 "Milkî-sedeq et Milkî-reša dans les anciens écrits juifs et chrétiens." *JJS* 23: 95–144.

Milik, Josef, with M. Black
1976 *The Books of Enoch: Aramaic Fragments of Qumran Cave 4.* Oxford: Clarendon Press.

Mowry, Lucetta
1962 *The Dead Sea Scrolls and the Early Church.* Chicago: University of Chicago Press.

Murphy, Roland E.
1961 "GBR and GBWRH in the Qumran Writings." Pp. 137–43 in *Lex Tua Veritas: Festschrift für H. Junker.* Trier: Paulinus.

Murphy-O'Connor, Jerome
1965a "La 'verite' chez saint Paul et à Qumran." *RB* 72: 29–76. [= 1968: 179–230.]
1965b "Who wrote Ephesians?" *TBT* 1: 1201–9.
1968, ed. *Paul and Qumran: Studies in New Testament Exegesis.* London: Chapman.
1969 "La genèse littéraire de la Règle de la Communauté." *RB* 76: 528–49.

1972   "A Literary Analysis of Damascus Document xix, 33–xx,34." *RB* 79:
            544–64.
1974   "The Essenes and their History." *RB* 81: 215–44.

Mussner, Franz
1963   "Beiträge aus Qumran zum Verständnis des Epheserbriefs." Pp. 185–
            98 in *Neutestamentliche Aufsätze: Festschrift für Josef Schmid zum 70.
            Geburtstag.* Ed. J. Blinzler, O. Kuss, and F. Mussner. Regensburg:
            Pustet. [= Murphy-O'Connor, 1968: 159–78.]

Osten-Sacken, Peter von der
1969   *Gott und Belial: Traditionsgeschichtliche Untersuchungen zum
            Dualismus in den Texten aus Qumran.* SUNT 6. Göttingen: Vanden-
            hoeck & Ruprecht.

Pouilly, Jean
1976   *La Règle de la Communauté de Qumran: Son évolution littéraire.* CRB
            17. Paris: Gabalda.

Rabin, Chaim
1954   *The Zadokite Documents.* Oxford: Clarendon Press.

Rabinowitz, I.
1953   "Sequence and Date of the Extra-Biblical Dead Sea Scrolls and
            'Damascus' Fragments." *VT* 3: 175–85.
1954   "A Reconsideration of 'Damascus' and '390 Years' in the 'Damascus'
            ('Zadokite') Fragments." *JBL* 73: 11–35.

Reicke, Bo
1954   "Die Verfassung der Urgemeinde im Lichte jüdischer Dokumente."
            TZ 10: 95–112. [= Stendahl: 143–56.]

Rigaux, Beda
1957   "Révélation des mystères et perfection à Qumran et dans le Nouveau
            Testament." *NTS* 4: 237–62.

Rowley, H. H.
1959   "The Baptism of John and the Qumran Sect." Pp. 218–29 in *New
            Testament Essays: Studies in Memory of Thomas Walter Manson.* Ed.
            A. J. B. Higgins. Manchester: Manchester University Press.

Sandmel, Samuel
1962   "Parallelomania." *JBL* 81: 1–13.

Saunders, E. W.
1967   "The Colossian Heresy and Qumran Theology." Pp. 133–45 in
            *Studies in the History and Text of the New Testament in Honor of
            Kenneth Willis Clark.* Ed. B. L. Daniels and M. J. Suggs. SD 29. Salt
            Lake City, UT: University of Utah Press.

Schmitt, J.
1978   "Qumran et le Nouveau Testament: C. La communauté primitive."
            DBSup 9, cols. 1007–11.

Schnackenburg, Rudolf
1965   *Das Johannesevangelium.* HTKNT 4/1. Freiburg: Herder.

Schüssler Fiorenza, Elisabeth
1976   "Cultic Language in Qumran and in the New Testament." *CBQ* 38:
            159–77.

Spicq, Ceslaus
    1952   *L'épître aux Hebreux:* Vol. 1, *Introduction.* EBib. Paris: Gabalda.
    1959   "L'épître aux Hebreux: Apollos, Jean-Baptiste, les Hellénistes et Qumran." *RevQ* 1: 365–90.

Starcky, Jean
    1978   "Qumran et le Nouveau Testament: B/II. La justification." *DBSup* 9, cols. 999–1003.

Stegemann, Hartmut
    1971   *Die Entstehung der Qumrangemeinde.* Bonn: privately published.

Stendahl, Krister, ed.
    1957   *The Scrolls and the New Testament.* New York: Harper.

Vaux, Roland de
    1949   "La grotte des manuscrits hébreux." *RB* 56: 586–609.

Weinert, F. D.
    1977   "A Note on 4Q159 and a New Theory of Essene Origins." *RevQ* 9: 223–30.

Wilkens, Wilhelm
    1958   *Die Entstehungsgeschichte des vierten Evangeliums.* Zollikon: Evangelisher Verlag.

Wright, G. Ernest
    1948   "A Phenomenal Discovery." *BA* 11: 21–23.

Yadin, Yigael
    1958   "The Scrolls and the Epistle to the Hebrews." Pp. 36–55 in *Aspects of the Dead Sea Scrolls.* Ed. C. Rabin and Y. Yadin. Scripta Hierosolymitana 4. Jerusalem: Magnes Press.

Part Two

Methods of
New Testament Scholarship

4

TEXTUAL CRITICISM

Eldon Jay Epp

New Testament textual criticism, like every other area of academic inquiry, is always in process. Its history is a record of various discoveries, insights, methods, and distinctive achievements that provide the basis for further investigation, but with fewer definitive conclusions or final resolutions than might be expected. A periodic assessment of the "state of the discipline," or of one segment in its long history, can be enlightening both with respect to understanding those accomplishments of the past and in facing the tasks of the future. Though history is eminently instructive, obviously it is more urgent for us to understand the unfinished tasks and to seek ways to accomplish them. Any assessment of such decision points in *current* NT textual criticism, however, almost of necessity requires at least a brief review of decision points in *past* NT textual criticism. If the "past is prologue," such a review will provide, at the very least, the necessary perspective for understanding the current and future issues, and at best will contain the basis for their resolution. This chapter,[1] therefore, includes those two aspects — past turning points in NT text-critical study and decision points in the current discipline of NT textual criticism — with an intervening section on specific developments since World War II that assists us in grasping those current issues that require our attention.

I. PAST DECISION POINTS IN
NEW TESTAMENT TEXTUAL CRITICISM

It is a curious but intriguing fact that if the past is divided roughly into fifty-year periods, starting in 1980 and moving backward through time, many of the major landmarks or turning points in NT textual criticism appear or find their impetus at such fifty-year intervals — give or take a few years — and most of them are landmarks in text-critical methodology. This will provide

---

[1] Sections I and III of this paper draw upon presentations at the annual meetings of the Society of Biblical Literature in 1980 and 1981 and of the Eastern Great Lakes Biblical Society in 1983, though with much revision. Some portions utilize material from *HTR* 73 (1980) 131–51, and others overlap with material presented in the Kenneth W. Clark Memorial Lectures at Duke University in 1986.

a convenient framework for our quick review of the major factors in the development of the discipline as we know it today.

One should begin at the beginning—1750 years ago—with Origen of Caesarea, who undoubtedly was the first to apply critical canons to the NT text. His *Commentary on John* was written in the few years before and after A.D. 230, followed by commentaries on Matthew and Romans, and these works contain most of his references to variant readings in the NT that have the support of "few," "many," or "most" manuscripts accessible to him, as well as applications of such canons as suitability to context and harmony with parallel passages (Metzger, 1963:81–92; Pack, 1960:144–45; cf. Epp, 1976:216). Origen's lack of sophistication and consistency in applying such "rules" hardly qualifies him as a model of text-critical method, but his use of these embryonic guidelines does suggest that he was the discipline's founder. One hundred and fifty years later, beginning with his *Commentary on Galatians* in the late 380s, Jerome noted variant readings and was employing canons such as an older manuscript carries more weight than a recent one and a reading is preferable that fits the grammar or context of its passage (Hulley, 1944:91–93 *et passim;* Metzger, 1980:199–208).

These first, rudimentary "landmarks" of text-critical method bore little fruit prior to modern times, though 1050 years later Lorenzo Valla, in his "Neopolitan period" (1435–1448) produced two editions of his *Collatio novi testamenti,* for which he collated several Greek manuscripts of the NT and in which he pointed out both involuntary and conscious scribal alterations, including variants due to homonyms and assimilation (Bentley, 1983:34–46). Though these early efforts were but adumbrations of modern critical approaches, the modern period does begin somewhere in the century between Valla's work on the NT text and Erasmus's final edition of his *Annotations* in 1535, which—in a much less developed form—had accompanied his 1516 *editio princeps* of the Greek NT and which rather fully explained the use of manuscripts and methods employed in his NT text. Of interest in this transition to modernity is the fact that Erasmus published Valla's second edition of the *Collatio* (which Erasmus called *Adnotationes*) in the very year (1505) that Erasmus himself began studying and collating NT manuscripts and observing thousands of variant readings in preparation for his own edition (Bentley, 1983:35, 138). In the middle of this transitional century, that is, in 1481 (500 years ago), the first publication of any portion of the NT in Greek took place, the Magnificat and the Benedictus, printed in Milan and appended to a Greek Psalter (Darlow and Moule: 2:574)—not a methodological landmark, of course, but the very beginning point of a stream of editions of the NT in its original language.

As the development of the new discipline of textual criticism continued, a few other early milestones can be identified in that formative period before variant readings in NT manuscripts were systematically sought and published. One such event occurred 400 years ago, when around 1582 the

Reformation theologian Theodore Beza presented two important uncial manuscripts to Cambridge University, Codex Bezae and Codex Claromontanus. Beza himself apparently made little, perhaps no, use of these in his own editions of the Greek NT, nor did other editors until Brian Walton some seventy-five years later, but Beza's gift meant that these important and early codices became part of the accessible sources for critical study.

Similarly, one could look back 350 years to a pair of more noteworthy landmarks in the period of the 1630s, the first of which also consisted of the placing of an important manuscript in the public domain, when the fourth-century Codex Alexandrinus was presented in 1627 to King Charles I by the patriarch of Constantinople. The variant readings of Alexandrinus first appeared at the foot of the pages of the Greek NT portion of Brian Walton's *Polyglot Bible* (1655–1657), and his was the first report of these variants; in addition, Walton was the first to use a capital letter as a siglum for an uncial manuscript, employing "A" for Alexandrinus. More important, however, is the fact that the availability of the very ancient Codex Alexandrinus around 1630 and the recognition and use of this fourth-century manuscript by Walton represented, as K. W. Clark described it (1962:666), "the beginning of a fundamental critical process." This was not the beginning of genuinely modern or scientific NT textual criticism, for that is more likely to be identified at our next fifty-year interval with John Mill, but it is of more than passing interest to note that Codex Alexandrinus figured prominently in Mill's work.

The second milestone of the 1630s is the occurrence in the second edition of Elzevir's Greek NT (1633) of the instantly famous phrase, *textus receptus*, in the declaration "You have the text, now received by all," a marker not particularly noteworthy in itself, but one that two centuries later was to have special significance in the pivotal work of Karl Lachmann and the great modern textual critics who followed. Indeed, without this arrogant — though not unrealistic — generalization, challenges to this sweeping claim might have been even slower in coming.

Looking back 300 years to the period around 1680 brings into view two important figures from the beginning of a very lengthy period during which textual critics collected variant readings and printed them in various editions of the *textus receptus*. The two figures are John Fell and John Mill. In 1675 Fell produced the first Greek NT printed at Oxford, an elegant octavo volume that presented variants (so he claimed) from more than one hundred manuscripts and versions and provided an important stimulus for seeking and assembling additional variants. Edward Miller (1894: 2:200) refers to Fell's small Greek NT as "the legitimate parent of one of the noblest works" of this type, John Mill's large Greek NT. It was Mill, our second figure, who began almost precisely at this time (1677) his thirty years of "labours nearly Herculean" (as Mill himself describes them; see A. Fox: 60, cf. 61–64) that were to lead to the publication of his impressive Greek NT of 1707, which was important not for its text (since he printed the 1550 text of Stephanus) but for its extensive apparatus (containing evidence on more than 21,000 variation-units and comprising more than 30,000 various readings; (A. Fox: 64, 105) and for its prolegomena, where some interesting principles of textual criticism were enunciated and where "a foreshadowing of the genealogical method in noting relationships between manuscripts" appears (Vincent: 68). Mill, of course, was not without his opponents (see A. Fox: 105–15; Parvis, 1962:604), yet both his innovative, massive apparatus (which, by its very presence and its size, raised disturbing questions about the *textus receptus*) and his rudimentary canons of criticism were to affect all succeeding work. As a matter of fact, M. R. Vincent, in his 1903 *History of the Textual Criticism of the New Testament* (67), asserts—not unjustly—that John Mill "marked the foundation of textual criticism," that is, of the genuinely modern discipline.

The next fifty-year stopping place, around the 1730s—250 years ago—brings to light an event that is more a curious and fortunate occurrence than a methodological marker, for in October 1731 Richard Bentley, at the age of sixty-nine, rescued the four-volume Codex Alexandrinus (so important in this early period of textual criticism) from a fire in the Cottonian Library (A. Fox: 125). For much of the twenty years prior to this event, Bentley had been planning and collecting materials for an edition of the Greek and Latin NT that would present the text of the time of Origen ("the true exemplar of Origen") and thereby supplant the *textus receptus* (A. Fox: 118–19; Ellis: xvii), a project never brought to completion but one significant nonetheless for the very fact of its proposal and for the text-critical principles that were intended to form its basis.

Another event of 1730, however, was more properly a milestone, though it too had its curious aspect. In that year, one of Bentley's collators, J. J. Wettstein, published (anonymously) the *Prolegomena* for his proposed edition of the Greek NT, an edition that was only to make its appearance twenty-one years later in 1751–1752. Wettstein's *Prolegomena* listed nineteen principles of textual criticism, including such items as the more ample reading is not preferable to the shorter (no. 9), the Greek reading more in accord with the ancient versions is preferable (no. 13), and the more ancient reading is preferable (no. 17) (see Epp, 1976:224), principles (especially the last two) closely akin to those of Bentley before him (which is not surprising) and to those of J. A. Bengel, who was shortly to follow. What is curious, however, is that Wettstein backed away from these canons in the interval before his edition appeared, and the text he printed was the *textus receptus* of Elzevir, rather than a text based on Codex Alexandrinus, as had been his original intention. Hence, neither did the methodological breakthrough that Bentley might have made come to fruition, nor did Wettstein put into practice his stated principles of 1730.

It is for these reasons that we take notice, next, of the genuine landmark of 250 years ago, the publication of J. A. Bengel's Greek NT in 1734. His printed text was still the *textus receptus*, but in at least three respects his work was to have far-reaching effects nonetheless. One was his pioneering division of the extant manuscripts into groups; another was his system of signs in the text, showing how close or far from the original he judged variants to be; and the third involved the canons of criticism that he enunciated and practiced, including his insistence that textual witnesses must be weighed and not merely counted. In these and other ways Bengel greatly accelerated the notion that the oldest manuscripts—rather than the most numerous or smoothest—were the best manuscripts, and the negative impact of this principle upon the *textus receptus* would show itself increasingly as time passed.

These developments by Bentley (A. Fox: 122–24), Wettstein (Epp, 1976:223–25), and Bengel (Metzger, 1968a:113) were to bear fruit roughly at the next fifty-year landmark, namely, J. J. Griesbach's Greek NT of 1775–1777, which—along with its subsequent editions and his influential canons of criticism—constituted the first daring though measured departure at numerous points from the *textus receptus*. Thus, it was with Griesbach that a decisive break with the *textus receptus* had arrived in theory—but only in theory—for by no means had it yet been achieved in clear and thorough practice. In fact, however, the preceding one hundred years (from Mill's work in 1677 until Griesbach in 1777) and the fifty years following Griesbach comprised that lengthy period of exploration and experimentation in text-critical method that effectually laid the foundation for the final overthrow of the *textus receptus*—which so long had dominated the field.

The decisive departure from the *textus receptus* in actual accomplishment and practice arrived with the next fifty-year landmark, now 150 years ago: Karl Lachmann's Greek NT of 1831. A classical scholar like many editors of the Greek NT before him, Lachmann made a proposal that actually was quite modest, for he sought only to establish the text as it had existed in Eastern Christianity just prior to A.D. 400. Lachmann's method of achieving his goal, however, was anything but modest or reserved. Rather, it was both innovative and bold, for he relied for his NT text on no previous printed edition, but, laying aside the whole established traditional text, he devised a text entirely from the most ancient witnesses known to him, including, of course, the oldest Greek uncials (though no minuscules), but also the Old Latin and Vulgate versions and some early fathers, such as Origen, Irenaeus, and Cyprian (see Kenyon, 1926:286–88; Metzger, 1968a:125–26). Lachmann's 1831 edition contained fewer than one hundred words describing his principles for selecting the readings of his text; his first principle of selection was that he followed "nowhere his own judgment," but "the usage of the most ancient eastern churches"; when this evidence was not consistent, he preferred the reading on which the "Italian and

African" witnesses agreed. Worth emphasis again is the fact that he gave no
consideration to the "received readings," and in this respect Lachmann, the
first scholar to make such a clean break with the *textus receptus,* had taken
a giant step forward by backing away 1200 years from the "received text" of
the sixteenth century and seeking to establish that of the fourth.

The period from Lachmann to Westcott-Hort, 1831–1881, undoubtedly constitutes the single most significant fifty-year period in the history of
NT textual criticism, for important new materials appeared and significant
new methodologies were implemented. Together these would bring us fully
into the modern period. This fifty-year period opened with the beachhead
by Lachmann against the *textus receptus*—a beachhead that was fiercely
resisted, just as were the earlier assualts upon the *textus receptus* by Bentley
and Bengel. But Lachmann represents more than a beachhead; his edition
stands for the decisive battle—it was D-Day—and now it was only a matter
of time until the territory hitherto held by the *textus receptus* would be fully
occupied by the triumphant forces led by a vanguard of the earliest NT
witnesses. If this military imagery can be tolerated a bit longer, one of the
leading "generals," soon on the scene, was Constantine Tischendorf, whose
eight editions of the Greek NT between 1841 and 1872 and whose nearly
two dozen volumes publishing new manuscripts were major factors in the
occupation of the newly won territory. Codex Sinaiticus was, of course, the
most prominent of these discoveries.

Tischendorf's second edition in 1849 provided the rationale for his
text—a basic principle similar to Lachmann's:

> The text should be sought solely from ancient witnesses, and chiefly
> from Greek codices, but by no means neglecting the testimonies of
> the fathers and versions. Thus, the whole arrangement of the text is
> bound by necessity to arise from the witnesses themselves. . . , not
> from the edition of Elzevir, which is called "received"; however, to
> be placed first among disagreeing witnsses are those regarded as the
> oldest Greek codices, i.e., written from the fourth to about the ninth
> century. Again, among these those that excel in antiquity prevail in
> authority, and this authority increases if testimonies of the versions
> and fathers are added, nor is this authority surmounted by the
> disagreement of most or even of all the recent codices, i.e., those
> written from the ninth to the sixteenth centuries. (Quoted in
> Gregory's *Prolegomena* to Tischendorf's 8th ed., 1894:3.47–48)

Tischendorf's terse and quotable dictum, witnesses "that excel in antiquity
prevail in authority," no longer required defense, for Lachmann had already
firmly established the point.

Another "officer" in the campaign—perhaps a brigadier general—was
S. P. Tregelles, who announced his text-critical principles in 1854, unaware
of Lachmann's similar principles. Tregelles's aim was "to form a text on the
authority of ancient copies without allowing the 'received text' any prescrip-
tive rights" (152; see Epp, 1976:233). The occupation of the ground formerly

held by the *textus receptus* was occurring at an increasing pace.

If D-Day belonged to Lachmann, V-Day—fifty years later at our next landmark—belonged to the undisputed "general of the army," F. J. A. Hort, and his "first officer," B. F. Westcott. The Westcott-Hort text of 1881—just about one hundred years ago—resulted from a skillful plan of attack and a sophisticated strategy for undermining the validity of the *textus receptus*. Hort, the strategic expert, outlined in the introductory volume to the edition certain guidelines that were crucial in the plan. Some of these were old, others new, such as:

1. Older readings, manuscripts, or groups are to be preferred.
2. Readings are approved or rejected by reason of the quality, and not the number of their supporting witnesses.
3. A reading combining two simple, alternative readings is later than the two readings comprising the conflation, and manuscripts rarely or never supporting conflate readings are texts antecedent of mixture and are of special value.
4. The reading is to be preferred that most fitly explains the existence of the others.
5. The reading is less likely to be original that shows a disposition to smooth away difficulties.
6. Readings are to be preferred that are found in a manuscript that habitually contains superior readings as determined by intrinsic and transcriptional probability.

(Westcott-Hort: 2:55, 44, 49–50, 22–23, 28, 32–33, respectively)

The application of these (and other) principles effected a thorough and dramatic rout of the *textus receptus* (which Westcott-Hort called the "Syrian" text), for its chief witnesses could not withstand the charges concerning (1) their recent date, (2) their conflated readings and smoothening of difficulties, (3) the inability of their readings to explain the other readings, and (4) the fact that they kept company with numerous other manuscripts sharing these same characteristics. This strategy pushed to the forefront the oldest and "best" manuscripts and the "best" groups of manuscripts, those witnesses which—they said—had virtually escaped corruption and contamination, and which they called—understandably—the "Neutral" text. Accordingly, this Neutral text was acclaimed by Westcott-Hort and accepted by many others as "The New Testament in the Original Greek," as the title of their edition reads.

What was most surprising in this final campaign in the overthrow of the *textus receptus* was the last point, the audacious move by Westcott-Hort radically beyond the kind of modest proposal of Lachmann—to establish the text of the fourth century—to the unqualified claim to have established the text of the NT "in the original Greek." Would it not have been adequate for Westcott-Hort to have sought the text of the second century, for they were able with some assurance (based primarily on patristic quotations) to trace important portions of the text to that period? As it turned out, their final daring thrust—to identify the Neutral text with the original—represented an overkill (something not uncommon in a final military drive). It is the more understandable, then, that the strategy that had led to this result was itself quickly attacked at its vulnerable points. Some of these vulnerable points, as is well known, concern (1) Westcott-Hort's overly negative valuation of both the Byzantine text and the so-called Western text; (2) questions about their assessment of the components of the Western text and of what they termed the "Alexandrian" text; and, of course, (3) whether the Neutral text was really as pure and neutral and stood in so close and direct a relationship to the original as they claimed. The discussion of these and other questions was quick to be undertaken and ranged from the measured criticism of F. H. A. Scrivener and George Salmon (see Metzger, 1968a:137) to the vehement attacks by J. W. Burgon.

What was far more significant than such immediate responses, however, was the fact that Westcott-Hort's edition and the hypotheses behind it provided an incentive for text-critical investigations that led directly to many of the major opportunities and problems that face us currently in the discipline. Such discussions occupied the succeeding fifty-year period until the next landmark was reached in the 1930s and when an unexpected development at that point infused new life and new directions into the older discussions and brought fresh issues into view. These developments will occupy our attention momentarily, but some of the investigations most obviously stimulated by Westcott-Hort deserve mention. For example, Hort's staunch defense of the three most prominent text-types of their theory (Syrian, Western, and Neutral) evoked two major branches of studies. One concerned the Syrian or Byzantine text, and investigations took at least two directions: efforts were made to redeem Byzantine readings (if not the entire text-type) from the low status accorded them by Westcott-Hort, and attempts—most notably by H. von Soden—were made to classify the massive body of Byzantine manuscripts into manageable groups and to assess their respective character. Another major branch of studies concerned the so-called Western text. Here Hort's judgment—that Western readings, though very ancient, evidenced extensive corruption—provided a challenge to defend their originality at many points and, for example, encouraged Friedrich Blass to develop fully the view that Luke wrote two versions of his canonical books, one represented by the Neutral and the other by the Western text. (Such a view had been mentioned and rejected by Hort himself, but is now being revived—in the 1980s—by E. Delebecque, 1980, 1982a, 1982b, 1982c, 1983, 1986; Boismard and Lamouille). In addition, Hort's assignment to the Western text-type of witnesses soon recognized to be disparate and divergent rather than homogeneous converged with a series of new manuscript discoveries (such as codices Washingtonianus and Koridethi and the Sinaitic Syriac) to quicken studies that would lead to the identification of a separate text-type, the Caesarean. All of these developments are well known to us, and numerous analyses of the Western, Byzantine, and Caesarean text-types occupied textual critics for fifty years and longer.

It was, as a matter of fact, just fifty years after the Westcott-Hort edition that the next landmark appeared, for in 1930–1931 Chester Beatty acquired the famous papyri that bear his name, notably—for our purposes—P[45], P[46], and P[47], and the London *Times* of 19 November 1931 carried the first public announcement of the discovery. These were the first early and extensive NT papyri to come to light, and a whole new era of NT textual criticism suddenly unfolded. This discovery is a landmark not because NT papyri had not been found before but because the Chester Beatty papyri effected not merely a *quantitative change in the materials* available, but a *qualitative change in the discipline*. The Oxyrhynchus papyri, of course, had been discovered and published already beginning in 1898, providing many fragments of NT text, and the Bodmer papyri from 1956 and following were in some significant ways to overshadow the Chester Beatty, yet the Chester Beatty papyri were so extensive and so early in date that they rightly demanded a restructuring of NT text-critical theory and practice. Such a restructuring, of course, did not actually take place; for example, when P[45] in the Gospels was aligned with the Caesarean text, critics still called that text Caesarean rather than the P[45] text or the Chester Beatty text (either of which would have been an appropriate and natural designation). Nevertheless, the ultimate effects of these papyri upon critical editions—both text and apparatus—and as stimuli to studies across the entire discipline were enormous and lasting, and the landmark quality of the discovery is indisputable. When the Bodmer papyri, most notably P[66] and P[75], are recognized also as ingredients of the period since 1930, it is quite appropriate to refer to the fifty-year period from 1930 to 1980 as the "Period of the Papyri," for, given the high valuation placed upon these and the other papyri, we seem to have reached a new stage— perhaps "plateau" is the word—which provides a new and refreshing vantage point for viewing the NT text, but a plateau from which, for the moment at least, we have not been led to an obvious higher plane.

All of us share this high valuation of these extraordinarily early and significant NT witnesses that have rightly received such close attention during the fifty-year "Period of the Papyri," and perhaps our newest fifty-year landmark—that of the 1980s—has now made its appearance in the "Intro-duction" to the twenty-sixth edition of the Nestle-Aland Greek NT (1979), where the editors affirm that for this new "Standard Text" of the NT the forty earliest papyri (and the four earliest but fragmentary uncials) are "of automatic [*automatisch*] significance, because they were written before the III/IV century, and therefore belong to the period before the rise of the major text types" (K. Aland, 1979:12*, cf. 49*; see Epp, 1980:144–50). Whether this is a legitimate claim, or a plausible claim, or a claim much over-drawn is a highly complex question to which we shall return, yet—unless significant new papyrus discoveries are made—it seems clear that the fifty-year "Period of the Papyri" from 1930 to 1980, that period of the discovery, analysis, and utilization of the earliest and most substantial papyri, may have to give way to a fresh period of the *re*assessment of the papyri and perhaps of their *re*application to the history and theory of the NT text. This, however, brings us up to date and leads directly to that part of our discussion concerned with current challenges in the discipline. Before joining those issues, the post–World War II period requires finer scrutiny.

II. THE POST–WORLD WAR II SETTING

New Testament textual criticism was a quiet discipline as the scholarly community regrouped and reemerged following World War II. How textual critics viewed themselves and their work can be garnered from any of the numerous "state-of-the-discipline" reports that appeared in the first decade of the period. An interesting contrast appears, however, when one takes a prewar status report from one of the most prominent textual critics and compares it with the postwar reports. Sir Frederic Kenyon, when asked in 1938 to contribute an article on "The Text of the Greek New Testament" for the *Expository Times* series "After Fifty Years," describes in glowing terms the astounding manuscript discoveries since 1888, refers to "much progress" in textual theory, and, with reference to the confidence of scholars in the Alexandrian text [Hort's Neutral], concludes with a statement, which—while cautious and modest on the surface—exudes that same high confidence in what has been achieved: "We shall," he said, "do well to recognize that complete certainty in details is not obtainable, and that there may be something yet to be learned from discoveries still to be made" (71). In contrast, Merrill Parvis, in *The Study of the Bible Today and Tomorrow*—a 1947 collaborative volume like the present one—affirmed that "no great advance has been made in the method of textual study since the days of Westcott and Hort" (58); several years later K. W. Clark, in a 1956 status report, echoed the same sentiments in referring to "how little, and how tentatively, textual criticism since 1930—and much earlier—has altered the New Testament text we study" and in positing that "any substantial effort to improve the basic critical text must 'mark time' until the whole complex of textual studies reveals a new integrating pattern" (41–42); and—as a third example—in 1962 H. H. Oliver's status report indicated that "so far, the 20th century has been a period characterized by general pessimism about the possibility of recovering the original text by objective criteria. This pessimism has persisted despite the appearance of new materials" (308). The change in mood is of more than passing interest, for this same lack of progress—attributed to an even broader portion of the discipline—could be claimed by at least one person in the field as recently as 1973 (Epp, 1974).

We shall return to these issues after a brief survey of post–World War II efforts under three categories: critical editions, discoveries, and methods.

Critical Editions and Studies

Editions of the Greek NT

The critical apparatuses of Mark and Matthew produced by S. C. E. Legg just prior to and during the war (1935, 1940) were not highly acclaimed either for their conception, accuracy, or usefulness. One by one, however, the various hand-editions of the Greek NT reappeared after the war. That of H. J. Vogels first appeared in 1920, with a fourth edition in 1955; A. Merk's originated in 1933, with a third edition in 1938, followed by a postwar sixth edition completed in 1948, and a current ninth edition, 1964. J. M. Bover's was a wartime product, appearing in 1943, with several postwar editions through the fifth of 1968, and revised by J. O'Callaghan for inclusion in the 1977 *Nuevo Testamento Trilingüe* (Bover and O'Callaghan). A. Souter's Greek NT (original, 1910) made a postwar appearance in a revised form in 1947. G. D. Kilpatrick revised the 1904 *British and Foreign Bible Societies Greek New Testament* to produce its second edition in 1958. In 1964 R. V. G. Tasker published "the actual Greek text, of which *The New English Bible* is a translation" (ix). In the same year K. Aland (1964) issued his *Synopsis quattuor evangeliorum*, with text and apparatus of the four gospels, and in 1981 H. Greeven produced a new critical text of the four Gospels (with apparatus) for his *Synopsis*. Finally, in 1982, Z. C. Hodges and A. L. Farstad edited a "majority text" NT, based on the Byzantine manuscripts. (For earlier attempts to rehabilitate the *textus receptus*, see Hills; Fuller, 1972, 1973, 1975; Pickering).

But the most widely used hand-edition of the Greek NT, at least in Europe, was that of Eberhard Nestle, which had passed through sixteen editions prior to the war (by 1936) and made its first reappearance after the war in a photographic reproduction by the American Bible Society in New York sometime prior to 1948 (when I purchased my copy), though it bears no publication date. The Nestle edition had been edited, beginning with the thirteenth edition of 1927, by Nestle's son, Erwin, but Kurt Aland appears as coeditor after the twenty-first edition of 1952, and later as sole editor until Barbara Aland became the second editor of the twenty-sixth edition of 1979. The text of this latest edition is, by agreement, identical with that of the third edition of the United Bible Societies' *Greek New Testament* (*UBSGNT*) of 1975, and this Greek NT text (contained in these two hand-editions) has recently been designated the "Standard Text" by Kurt Aland. As the most readily available and most widely used Greek NT text, it may justly be called the "Standard Text," though claims made for it as a text universally accepted as the "best" or "original" NT text continue to be debated (e.g., Moir, 1981; Elliott, 1983b; Bartsch, and K. Aland's reply, 1982).

The Westcott-Hort text of 1881, some three or four generations in the past by the outbreak of the war, perhaps retained more status as a modern *textus receptus* than any other critical text, at least in English-speaking scholarship. The ground swell, however, for a new major critical edition or apparatus was beginning to form in the period between the wars, prompted more than anything else by the new manuscript discoveries of the twentieth century. A push for a "new Tischendorf" based on the Nestle text had emerged already in the mid-1920s in a British-German group, but the German group withdrew when no agreement could be reached on the textual base to be utilized; it was at this point that the British group carried on, producing the ill-fated Legg volumes. Recognition of their inadequacy led to a British-American undertaking, the so-called International Greek New Testament Project (IGNTP), whose goal was a new critical apparatus of the NT — that is, the provision of the *data* essential for a new critical text of the NT, though not proposing to create that *critical text* itself. This project was conceived on a large scale but began where Legg left off — with the Gospel of Luke — though envisioning a vastly enlarged manuscript coverage as compared with Legg. Its collation base was the *textus receptus,* employed on the correct assumption that the most economical way in which to display the variants in the apparatus was against this "fullest" of texts. The choice of the *textus receptus* was misunderstood and, indeed, ridiculed by Kurt Aland (1966b; see the replies by Suggs [in Duplacy and Suggs: 197–98, 204–6] and Epp, 1974:402–3), but the British-American project persisted through nearly forty years of cooperative efforts and discouraging delays until the first — and perhaps only — results appeared in 1984 and 1987, an apparatus to the text of Luke's Gospel (*The New Testament in Greek: The Gospel according to St. Luke, Part One: Chapters 1–12* [1984]; *Part Two: Chapters 13–24* [1987]). Users and critics will have to judge its usefulness, but the economical display of vast amounts of material seems to be a self-justification for the principles on which this critical apparatus of the Greek NT [it is not really an edition] was constructed.

The IGNTP's long history began in 1948 with a large British committee, chaired successively by R. H. Lightfoot, H. I. Bell, G. H. C. McGregor, and J. M. Plumley; J. N. Birdsall served as executive editor from 1968 to 1977 and was succeeded by J. K. Elliott. A somewhat smaller American committee was organized, chaired from 1949 to 1970 by E. C. Colwell, who was succeeded by B. M. Metzger. K. W. Clark served as executive editor of the materials prepared by the American committee. (Parvis, 1950; Colwell et al., 1968; Robinson et al., 1970; Elliott, 1983a.)

The current British committee (now a committee of the British Academy) consists of H. F. D. Sparks, G. D. Kilpatrick, J. M. Plumley (chm.), S. P. Brock, M. Black, T. S. Pattie, J. L. North, J. K. Elliott, and W. J. Elliott, and the present American committee consists of B. M. Metzger (chm.), A. P. Wikgren, M. J. Suggs, E. J. Epp, G. D. Fee, I. A. Sparks, and P. R.

McReynolds (American and British Committees: 1:xiv-xv). Whether the IGNTP will carry forward its original plan to provide next a critical apparatus for the Fourth Gospel is unclear at this time.

The division of work provided that the British committee assemble most of the patristic and versional evidence, while the American committee was to oversee the collation of the Greek manuscripts and Greek lectionaries and obtain the textual evidence for most of the Greek fathers and for the Armenian, Ethiopic, Georgian, Gothic, and Old Church Slavonic versions. Two hundred and eighty-three scholars, mostly from North America, participated in the collection of data from the Greek manuscripts and Greek fathers, and many other scholars from Great Britain, America, and other countries assisted in collecting the versional evidence (American and British Committees: 1:v, xiv-xvi).

Several methodological issues were faced in connection with the American assignments, resulting in the Claremont Profile Method for quickly assessing the character of minuscule manuscripts—permitting the selection of a relatively small number of manuscripts for inclusion in the apparatus that would adequately represent the various manuscript types in the minuscule mass (Colwell et al.: 191–97; Epp, 1967:27–38; Wisse and McReynolds: 67–75; McReynolds; now esp. Wisse). A considerable literature is developing around this Profile Method (e.g., Richards, 1977a, 1977b, 1979, 1980). In addition, criteria were devised for choosing appropriate representatives of the complex lectionary text (Colwell et al.: 188–91; cf. Duplacy, 1970), and, finally, precision was introduced into the process of differentiating patristic "citations," "allusions," and "adaptations" (Colwell et al.: 187–88; Suggs; Metzger, 1980:167–88; but esp. Fee, 1971a, 1971b; cf. R. M. Grant in Parvis and Wikgren: 117–24; P. Prigent in K. Aland, 1972:436–54; H. J. Frede in Aland, 1972:455–78).

The Greek text that appears in Nestle-Aland[26], which seems to have replaced all the hand-editions and which (as indicated above) has been proclaimed recently as the "Standard Text" by Kurt Aland, was produced, beginning in 1955, by an international team working under the sponsorship of the United Bible Societies. Titled simply *The Greek New Testament*, it is referred to as the *UBSGNT*. Eugene A. Nida of the American Bible Society initiated and administered the project, and the editorial committee for the first edition was composed of K. Aland, M. Black, B. M. Metzger, A. Wikgren, and A. Vööbus; for the second and third editions, C. M. Martini replaced Vööbus. The first edition appeared in 1966, the second in 1968, and a more thorough revision in 1975, which—by design—is identical in text to that of Nestle-Aland[26]. A revised fourth edition is in preparation; meanwhile, in 1983 an interim corrected third edition was issued. Assistance was provided all along by the Münster Institut für neutestamentliche Textforschung. An accompanying *Textual Commentary*, written for the committee by Bruce M. Metzger and published in 1971, comments on hundreds of variation units in the NT and provides explanations for the choice of one reading over others. A torrent of reviews and assessments of both the *UBSGNT* and the companion *Commentary* have been published since these volumes appeared, and the flow has resumed as each new edition has been issued.

Finally, it was the leading critic of the International Greek New Testament Project, Kurt Aland, who spearheaded several projects involving NT editions and other text-critical work at his Institut für neutestamentliche Textforschung (just mentioned above). The Nestle-Aland hand-edition and the cooperative *UBSGNT* have already been described. In addition, Aland and his Institut produced the monograph series, Arbeiten zur neutestamentlichen Textforschung (see K. Aland, 1963, 1967, 1969, 1972, and 1975–83). The first volume (1963) is the *Kurzgefasste Liste der griechischen Handschriften des Neuen Testaments*, which, with a supplement in volume 3 (1969:1–53), provides the official list of the Greek manuscripts of the NT, covering the papyri, uncials, minuscules, and lectionaries. The numerous essays in volumes 2, 3, and 5 (1967, 1969, 1972) are of great importance for the study and research of the NT text, with volume 5 devoted to NT versions, patristic citations, and lectionaries. Volume 4 of the series is the now standard *Vollständige Konkordanz zum griechischen Neuen Testament* (K. Aland, 1975–83), an indispensable tool for NT exegetes as well as textual critics (see the reviews, e.g., by Fitzmyer, 1976–85; and Epp, 1979–84). The Institut continues to work toward its *editio maior critica*—its major critical edition of the Greek NT, which began with the Catholic Epistles (see K. Aland, 1970). All of these projects are carried through with meticulous care and thoroughness, and the discipline owes much to Professor Aland and his Institut. (For reports on the status of various projects, see Kunst.)

Critical Editions of Versions and Fathers

Limitation of space permits reference only to post–World War II monographic works and not to periodical literature. (Editions of versions are listed in a separate section of the bibliography.)

The study of the Latin NT has been greatly assisted by two projects. The first is *Itala*, an edition of the Old Latin Gospels begun by A. Jülicher but later edited by W. Matzkow and K. Aland. The second is the *Vetus Latina*, a large-format edition of the Old Latin Bible with a detailed critical apparatus, carried out at the Beuron monastery under the supervision of Alban Dold until his death in 1960 and then directed by Bonifatius Fischer under the auspices of the Vetus Latina Institut. Currently Walter Thiele oversees the work, and, to date, the Catholic Epistles have been completed (Thiele, 1956–69), as well as Ephesians, Philippians, Colossians (Frede, 1962–69), and 1–2 Thessalonians, 1–2 Timothy, Titus, and Philemon (Frede, 1975–83). In addition, an index of the fathers has been compiled by Frede

(1981, 1984), and an accompanying monograph series provides specialized studies (Frede, 1961, 1964, 1973; Thiele, 1965; Fischer, 1985; Hammond Bammel, 1985). On both projects, see Metzger, 1977:320–22.

The Old Georgian version of the Gospels has been edited for Mark and Matthew by Robert P. Blake (1974, 1976), for John by Blake and Maurice Brière (1950), and for Luke by Brière (1955). The Georgian version of Acts was edited by Gérard Garitte in 1955. The Ethiopic of the Apocalypse was edited by Josef Hofmann in 1967, and the Coptic of John by Rodolphe Kasser in 1966.

Among numerous studies of the versions are the comprehensive manuals by Vööbus (1954) and Metzger (1977) and the masterful survey edited by Aland (1972), which contains studies by B. Fischer and W. Thiele on the Latin, M. Black on the Syriac, G. Mink on the Coptic, L. Leloir on the Armenian, J. Molitor on the Georgian, J. Hofmann on the Ethiopic, E. Stutz on the Gothic, and C. Hannick on the Old Church Slavonic, as well as chapters on NT citations in Greek fathers by P. Prigent and in Latin fathers by H. J. Frede. Lists of versional manuscripts are provided by Metzger (1977), by Clemons for the Syriac of the epistles and the Apocalypse, and by Rhodes for the Armenian. Monographs on the Latin versions have been authored by Zimmermann (1960), Tinnefeld (1963), Frede (1964), Nellessen (1965), Thiele (1965), and Fischer (1985); on the Old Syriac Gospels by Vööbus (1951a) and on the Old Syriac Paul by Kerschensteiner (1970), on the Syriac of the Gospels by Vööbus (1951c) and Strothmann (1971), on the Harclean Syriac by Zuntz (1945; see now Brock), and on the Peshitta by Vööbus (1948); on the Diatessaron by Lyonnet (1950), Messina (1951), Leloir (1962), Henss (1967), Ortiz de Urbina (1967), Quispel (1975), and Petersen (1985); on the Coptic Acts by Joussen (1969); on the Ethiopic Gospels by Vööbus (1951b) and the Apocalypse by Hofmann (1969); on the Armenian by Lyonnet (1950) and Leloir (1967); on the Old Georgian Gospels by Vööbus (1953) and Molitor (1965); and on the Gothic by Friedrichsen (1961).

Regarding patristic quotations of the NT text, the postwar period has provided us with a four-volume index of citations (Allenbach, 1975–87) and a number of studies: Muncey (1959) on Ambrose (but see the warning in Metzger, 1980:172); Baarda (1975) on Aphrahat; Mees (1970) and Zaphiris (1970) on Clement of Alexandria; Greenlee (1955) on Cyril of Jerusalem; Ehrman (1986) on Didymus the Blind; Leloir (1953–54, 1958, 1962, 1967) and Petersen (1985) on Ephrem; Eldridge (1969) on Epiphanius of Salamis; Blackman (1948) on Marcion; Frede (1961) and Borse (1966) on Pelagius; D. J. Fox (1979) on Philoxenus; Hammond Bammel (1985) on Rufinus; Vogels (1955b, 1957) on Rufinus and Ambrosiaster; Quispel (1975) on Tatian; and Lo Bue (1963) on Tyconius.

Discoveries

New materials are the "grist" of the text-critical "mill," and the premier discoveries of the post–World War II period are the Bodmer papyri, notably

P[66], P[72], P[74], and P[75] (Martin, 1956, 1962; Testuz; Kasser, 1961; Martin and Kasser, 1961a, 1961b). These discoveries brought the Chester Beatty papyri into renewed discussion, and a large literature developed on the NT papyrus manuscripts. In addition to the three Bodmer papyri mentioned above, the other papyri numbered from P[55] through P[88] came to light after World War II. P[58] was found to belong to P[33]; P[64] and P[67] were parts of the same manuscript; and P[73], P[83], P[84], and P[87] remain unedited. Places of publication may be found in the handbooks by Metzger (1968a:247–56) and by Aland and Aland (1982:106–11; Eng. 96–101).

This is not the place to attempt a summary of other manuscript discoveries since World War II, but the following texts were published in monograph form: a Greek fragment of 1 Peter by Daris (1967); the Greek portions (with parts of the Gospels) of Codex Climaci Rescriptus by Moir (1956); a Greek papyrus of Matthew by Roca-Puig (1962). Latin texts were published by Vogels (1953) and Frede (1973); Syriac by Vööbus (1978); Coptic by Browne (1979), Hintze and Schenke (1970), Husselman (1962), Kasser (1958, 1962), Orlandi (1974), Quecke (1972, 1977, 1984), and Schenke (1981); and an Arabic manuscript of Paul by Staal. Publication of other texts can be found, for instance, in K. Aland, 1969 (ten items by various editors); Birdsall and Thomson (33–63); Elliott, 1976 (235–38, 262–75, 301–12); in *New Documents Illustrating Early Christianity,* treating papyri and inscriptions (Horsley, 1981–87), and in other scholarly volumes and periodicals too numerous to record here.

Additional studies of Greek manuscripts were contributed by Davies (1968), Elliott (1968) and Fee (1968a); studies of the Greek lectionary text by Bray (1959), Buck (1958), and Harms (1966) were provided in the Chicago series on Studies in the Lectionary Text of the Greek New Testament, and another by Cocroft (1968) in Studies and Documents, and chapters by Metzger and Junack can be found in K. Aland, 1972; monographs appeared on Greek uncials by Cavallo (1967), on Greek catena by Reuss (1957, 1966, 1984); Treu (1966) published a list of NT manuscripts in the U.S.S.R.; and Voicu and D'Alisera furnished an index of facsimiles of Greek NT manuscripts. Current lists of all uncials and important minuscules can be found in Aland and Aland (1982:113–66; Eng. 106–55). Surveys of discoveries, not only of Greek manuscripts but also of versional materials have been offered by Metzger in various articles (1955b, 1959, 1963:145–62; 1965:347–69).

Methods

The postwar period was a rich one for text-critical methodology. This evaluation may be placed in context by recalling the basic (though not the only) task of NT textual criticism — recovery of the original text — and by reviewing the fundamental methods employed to accomplish that task. In view of our earlier survey of its history, NT textual criticism obviously is a highly complex discipline, yet in conception it really is relatively simple. Actually, the same circumstance accounts for both descriptions—both its complexity and its simplicity—and that circumstance is the vast quantity of raw material available to us: For the NT—a rather small volume of writings —we possess some 5,355 Greek manuscripts alone (86 different papyri, 274 uncials, 2,795 minuscules, and about 2,200 lectionaries [Aland and Aland, 1982:106–11, 113, 137, 172 Eng. 96–105, 128, 160]), plus thousands of versional documents and an untold number of patristic citations. The point is that we have so many manuscripts of the NT and that these manuscripts contain so many variant readings that surely the original reading in every case is somewhere present in our vast store of material. In theory, then, that should make the task of recovering the original text relatively simple. Incidentally, this vast number of manuscripts is the reason that conjectures— which play so large a role in the textual criticism of classical literature, and also in that of the OT—are rare and almost nonexistent in NT textual studies (see, e.g., Elliott, 1974:352; Kilpatrick, 1981; Rhodes, 1981; but to the contrary, see, e.g., Strugnell).

We have, therefore, a genuine embarrassment of riches in the quantity of manuscripts that we possess, and this accounts, on the one hand, for the optimism in the discipline and for the promise of solid results, but also, on the other hand, for the extreme complexity in the study of the NT text. The writings of no Greek classical author are preserved on this scale. Among the most popular ancient authors, Homer's *Iliad* is found in fewer than 700 Greek manuscripts, Euripides' tragedies in somewhat more than 300, but other ancient writings, such as the first six books of the Latin *Annals* of Tacitus, are preserved only in a single manuscript (see Metzger, 1968a:34–35).

The riches in NT manuscripts, however, are not only in their *quantity* but also in their *quality*. Here I refer primarily to age. As is well known, the interval between the author and the earliest extant manuscripts for most classical writings is commonly hundreds—sometimes many hundreds—of years, and a thousand-year interval is not uncommon. In the examples given a moment ago, that single manuscript of Tacitus dates from the ninth century, and most of Euripides' manuscripts are from the Byzantine period (Metzger, 1968a:34–35). Of course, most of the NT manuscripts are also of late date, but what is striking is that so many others are early and that the interval between the NT authors' times and the transmission dates of a sizable number of extensive manuscripts is only a century, more or less. In at least one case, P[52] of John's Gospel, the interval may be as brief as twenty-five years. In addition, we have two elegant parchment manuscripts from about the year 350, codices Vaticanus and Sinaiticus. This aspect of quality stands in sharp contrast to much other ancient literature. By the way, for the most part the oldest manuscripts of the NT have been found most recently, for the Chester Beatty and Bodmer papyri turned up in the 1930s and 1950s, respectively.

We must not exaggerate the NT manuscript materials, however, for the vast majority of the early papyri are highly fragmentary, and among the earliest uncial manuscripts only Codex Sinaiticus contains the entire NT — though about fifty later manuscripts also provide complete coverage (see Aland and Aland, 1982:91; Eng. 78). The Apocalypse of John is the least well preserved, being found in only 287 Greek manuscripts (Aland and Aland, 1982:91; Eng. 79) — still a rather lavish scale of preservation for a writing of such modest size. Far more numerous are the witnesses to the Gospel of Luke, for which the International Greek New Testament Project's elaborate apparatus has recently been published (as referred to earlier). The new apparatus presents the textual evidence from the 8 papyri that contain portions of Luke; from 62 uncial manuscripts (out of 69 that contain Luke); from 128 minuscules (scientifically selected from the nearly 1700 exant minuscule manuscripts of Luke); and from 41 lectionary manuscripts (scientifically selected to represent the hundreds that contain Luke); as well as evidence from the Latin, Syriac, Coptic, Armenian, Georgian, Ethiopic, Gothic, and Old Church Slavonic versions, from the Arabic and Persian Diatessaron; and from all Greek and Latin church fathers up to A.D. 500, as well as evidence from selected Syriac church fathers. And that is just the Gospel of Luke as it has come down to us in the process of transmission!

These are some indications of the riches in manuscripts that we possess for determining the original text of the NT; the embarrassment is that we have not often been able to agree on solutions or, in fact, to find satisfactory solutions at all for some of our leading problems.

If, then, the original reading in virtually every case is somewhere present in our raw material, the only problem is how to find that original reading — and, by extension, how to find the original text of the Greek NT as a whole. There are essentially three ways to identify the most likely original reading:

1. *Historical-documentary method.* A first method attempts to reconstruct the history of the NT text by tracing the lines of transmission back through our extant manuscripts to the very earliest stages and then choosing the reading that represents the earliest attainable level of the textual tradition.

It is not, of course, that simple, but the theory is that we should be able to organize all of our extant manuscripts into groups or clusters, each of which has a very similar type of text. Then, as a result of this process of reconstruction, we would or should be able to identify some clusters of manuscripts — or ideally one such cluster — that represent the earliest known group, and therefore to identify other groups that fall into an identifiable chronological succession — groups, that is, that are later. Further, this method attempts to reconstruct the streams of textual transmission that have brought our extant manuscripts to us, conceiving of each manuscript as a point on a trajectory of textual transmission. If these clusters and streams can be reconstructed with any measure of certainty, then we shall have isolated the earliest stages of those streams or the earliest points on those trajectories, and we shall have isolated also the earliest clusters, that is, the earliest types of text in the transmission process. If this were to result in the identification of only one very early cluster, succeeded by one or more later clusters, then readings belonging to that earliest cluster might legitimately be identified as those closest to the original and as most plausibly the original readings.

Ideally, then, when faced with a variation unit—that is, a NT passage in which the manuscript tradition presents two or more differing textual readings—the reading would be chosen that comes from the earliest cluster or stream of textual tradition. This is the traditional method of external or documentary textual criticism, so-called because it emphasizes external criteria—such as the age and provenance of a document or manuscript, as well as the general quality of its scribe and its text (on scribal habits, see Colwell, 1967:9–11; 1969:106–24; Fee, 1968a; Royse; Junack, 1981). It might, therefore, be called the "historical-documentary" (or even the "historical-genealogical" method, though strict genealogical method has never been feasible in NT textual criticism, for there is too much textual mixture in the complex array of manuscripts—Colwell, 1969:63–83; Birdsall, 1970:317; cf. Zuntz).

The earliest papyri, as well as the early uncial manuscripts, play a significant role in this historical-documentary method. These early manuscripts have the highest possible value, which is even more greatly enhanced in proportion to their age, and the reason for this high value is just as obvious: the early papyri offer for the first time a realistic hope of reconstructing the history of the NT text in the 150- to 200-year period preceding the great parchment codices Vaticanus and Sinaiticus and the other great landmarks of textual history, such as codices Alexandrinus, Bezae, Washingtonianus, and a grand host of others. We shall explore these possibilities in Section III, below.

There are, of course, complications of enormous complexity in pursuing this historical-documentary model, some of which will be discussed later (see also Birdsall, 1970:309–17). Yet many textual critics, particularly those in this country who were inspired by recent scholars like Kenneth Clark (see 1980) and Ernest Colwell (see 1967, 1969), are convinced that this is the path that must be followed and that the isolation of the earliest text-types must be our goal. We are convinced that only in this way can a solid foundation be laid for understanding the history of our NT text and that only in this way can we secure a large measure of confidence that we are genuinely in touch with the actual, historical origin of the NT writings. It was in this spirit and with these goals that the International Greek New Testament Project was developed and that much postwar text-critical work was pursued, including the extensive studies in quantitative measurements of manuscript relationships.

The development of quantitative measures to establish relationships between and among manuscripts by comparing the extent to which they share significant readings has an extended history, as demonstrated by Duplacy (1975), but E. C. Colwell, with E. W. Tune, provided (in 1963) the recent inspiration for the methods currently in use (reprinted in Colwell, 1969:56–62). Important refinements were provided by Fee (1968a, 1968b, 1971b); see also Hurtado, McReynolds, Griffith (1969, 1973), Wisse (1982), the discussion above on the Claremont Profile Method, and cf. Zuntz, Dearing (1959, 1974). For surveys of such methods, see Wisse (1982:19–32), Epp (1974:407–10), but above all the comprehensive treatment of the entire history of quantitative methods by Duplacy (1975).

Even the assessment of textual variation for theological motivation arose out of this approach, for the aim of the historical-documentary method has always been the better understanding of manuscripts (à la Hort). If theological or ideological bias could be identified in any manuscript, that would aid in placing it in its proper position in the textual streams or clusters — or in identifying it as an aberrant member of a cluster. The postwar period witnessed much discussion and some controversy in this area, primarily related to the Western text: see Menoud; Fascher; Epp (1966, 1981); Barrett; Martini (1980:103–13, 165–79, 181–88); Rice (1980a, 1980b, 1984, 1985); Eshbaugh; Globe; Black (1974, 1981); Pervo; Witherington; Delobel; also Williams; Clark (1980:90–103, 104–19).

E. C. Colwell (1967:5) referred to the working out of this external method of textual criticism as "the task of the next generation," and some of its leading problems and possible ways toward solutions will be explored in Section III, below.

2. *Rigorous eclectic method.* At the opposite extreme stands a second method, which examines all the variants available to us in a given variation unit and selects the reading that makes the best sense in terms of the internal criteria. That is, we select the variant reading that best suits the context of the passage, the author's style and vocabulary, or the author's theology, while taking into account such factors as scribal habits, including their tendency of conformity to Koine or Attic Greek style (Kilpatrick, 1963a; see the caution by Martini, 1980:145–52), to Semitic forms of expression, to parallel passages, to OT passages, or to liturgical forms and usage. This method, therefore, emphasizes internal evidence and is called "rigorous" or "thoroughgoing" eclecticism, and also "rational" or "impartial criticism" by its proponents (Elliott, 1978:95; Epp, 1976a:251–55; Fee, 1976:174–76).

Actually, this is a method of recent vintage that is practiced primarily by two fine and persistent British scholars, George D. Kilpatrick and J. Keith Elliott. It stems largely, however, from C. H. Turner's famous "Notes" on

Marcan usage published during the 1920s, on the first page of which Turner altered Westcott-Hort's famous dictum "Knowledge of documents should precede final judgement upon readings" to "Knowledge of an author's usage should precede final judgement" (see Epp, 1976a:250). Kilpatrick's views appeared during the war, beginning in 1943 and 1944, and a few phrases quoted from him and Elliott will clarify the method further. Kilpatrick says: "the decision rests ultimately with the criteria as distinct from the manuscripts, and . . . our evaluation of the manuscripts must be determined by the criteria" (1943:25–26); or "each reading has to be judged on its merits and not on its [manuscript] supports"; or "readings must be considered severally on their intrinsic character. Further, contrary to what Hort maintained, decisions about readings must precede decisions about the value or weight of manuscripts" (1965:205–6). Elliott says: "the cult of the best manuscripts gives way to the cult of the best reading"; and the method "devotes its main attention to the individual variants themselves and very little attention to external evidence" (1972:340), for "we are concerned with which reading is likely to represent what our original author wrote. We are not concerned with the age, prestige or popularity of the manuscripts supporting the readings we would adopt as original" (1974:352); or "the thoroughgoing eclectic would accept the reading which best suited the context and would base his reasons on exclusively internal criteria" (Elliott, 1978:99); or, finally, "it seems to be more constructive to discuss as a priority the worth of readings rather than the worth of manuscripts" (1978:115).

From these quotations it is at once apparent that to these rigorous eclectics the NT manuscripts are repositories of raw material and have independent importance only to the extent that they may furnish textual variants or readings that may commend themselves as original by the application of internal criteria: Does a new reading conform to the author's style and vocabulary, to his theology, to the context? Can it explain the origin of the other readings? If so, it may well be judged the original reading. The fact that many of the papyri and the great fourth-century uncials are extremely early does not, in this method, lend to them any special consideration or authority, nor does it account them as possessing any special character or value. It is well known that rigorous eclectics diligently search the late Byzantine manuscripts for readings that might be original and that they have accredited scores of such readings, for—as Kilpatrick put it—"the outright condemnation of the Byzantine text by Westcott and Hort was one of the main errors in practice of their work"(1963b:76). So, for "rigorous" eclectics, readings are readings are readings, whether early or late.

The challenge of this view is discussed in Section III below.

3. *Reasoned eclectic method.* A third approach combines these two procedures. It is essential to have this third method if—as is realistically the case—the criteria for making decisions on the basis of the first method (the

historical-documentary) are not obvious or clear, and if—as many textual critics think—the second method (rigorous eclecticism), though valuable for its numerous insights, is—in isolation—a one-sided and less than adequate method. On this third procedure, when faced with any variation-unit, we would choose the variant reading that appears to be in the earliest chronological group *and* that also makes the best sense when the internal criteria are applied. Moreover, if no one cluster or type of text can be identified unambiguously as the earliest, then we would choose the variant reading in any given case that is in *one* of the earliest clusters *and* that best fits the relevant internal considerations. This method, therefore, utilizes both external and internal criteria and is called "reasoned eclecticism" or "moderate" or "genuine" eclecticism, or simply the "eclectic" method (Fee, 1976:174–76; Epp, 1976a:212–14, 244–45), for it utilizes the best available methods from across the methodological spectrum. In this method it is recognized that no single criterion or invariable combination of criteria will resolve all cases of textual variation, and it attempts, therefore, to apply evenly and without prejudice any and all criteria—external and internal— appropriate to a given case, arriving at an answer based on the relative probabilities among those applicable criteria. (Birdsall [1970:316–18] in his masterly survey of NT textual criticism in *The Cambridge History of the Bible* uses the original term "rational criticism," from M.-J. Lagrange, for this method, but the co-opting of this term by "rigorous eclectics" suggests that a more specific term, such as "reasoned eclecticism," is now preferable to the less precise, generic term.) As Kenneth Clark said of the method in 1956:

> It is the only procedure available to us at this stage, but it is very important to recognize that it is a secondary and tentative method. It is not a new method nor a permanent one. The eclectic method cannot by itself create a text to displace Westcott-Hort and its off-spring. It is suitable only for exploration and experimentation. . . . The eclectic method, by its very nature, belongs to an age like ours in which we know only that the traditional theory of the text is faulty but cannot yet see clearly to correct the fault. (1956:37–38)

This is to say that if we had worked out the early history of the text, as prescribed under the first method, neither rigorous nor reasoned eclecticism would be necessary. Until that is accomplished, however, most textual critics will rely upon the latter—a genuinely eclectic method that pays careful attention both to the documentary evidence from the history of the manuscript tradition and also to the internal criteria of readings. Together they can help us with the urgent textual decisions that we must make until the time when the historical-documentary method has been fully worked out. And, if the reconstruction of the early textual history cannot be achieved, the eclectic method will continue to be the method of choice— and of necessity.

The text common to the Nestle-Aland twenty-sixth edition and to the third edition of the *UBSGNT* was formed in accordance with this kind of eclectic method, though placing emphasis, wherever possible, on the reading that explains the other readings and treating that as the most likely original. This latter procedure is what Kurt Aland calls the "local-genealogical method" (Aland and Aland, 1979:42*-43*), which is discussed further in Section III below.

It will already be recognized from the very mention of these several optional methods that the situation in NT textual criticism is not ideal and that neither automatic formulas nor easy decisions are readily forthcoming. The challenges emerging from the postwar discussions of method will be treated in Section III below.

Regrettably, our survey of editions, discoveries, and methods cannot begin to cover the hundreds of contributions made by scholars worldwide to these important areas of research.

III. CURRENT AND FUTURE DECISION POINTS IN NEW TESTAMENT TEXTUAL CRITICISM

The decision points in current and future NT textual criticism all arise out of this lengthy, productive, and yet largely inconclusive past history, and they present us with a degree of difficulty and with a measure of urgency that are disquieting. I wish to focus on three turning points or issues currently under investigation. Certainly there are others, but these seem to me the most critical. The three items have a common characteristic: each constitutes a distinct "battleground" in the discipline; that is, they represent disputed areas that recently have been or shortly will be contested not only with vigor but even with some vehemence. The three conflicts that face us are the following.

The Struggle over the Text-Type

Perhaps the word "struggle" is too strong, yet there is a continuing and genuine disagreement, if not contention, as to whether or not "text-types" existed in the earliest centuries of the transmission of the NT text. That question in itself may not seem to involve a significant issue, but the answer to it does affect rather directly the obviously important issue of whether or not—and if so, how—we can trace the history of the earliest NT text, which—in turn—is related directly to the ultimate goal of recovering the original text. The validity of these steps is, at any rate, the conviction of many of us, with the result that the question of early text-types deserves close attention.

When J. A. Bengel long ago placed manuscripts into classes or groups, the development of text-types was under way in the textual critic's mind, reaching its classical formulation in the system of Westcott-Hort, though the more elaborate classifications of von Soden were still to come. As new manuscripts were analyzed, they were placed into a Westcott-Hort or a von Soden framework; this was appropriate enough if the manuscripts in question were generally later in time than the cornerstone manuscripts of each text-type. When, however, much earlier manuscripts — primarily papyri — began to appear (particularly those well beyond the fragmentary stage), we began to recognize the anachronism of placing these earlier manuscripts into groups whose nature had been determined on the basis only of the complexion of later manuscripts (see Birdsall, 1960:8–9, 17; Klijn, 1969:33–38, 50).

The identification of text-types and of the manuscripts comprising them was a controversial matter for two centuries from Bengel to the discussions about the Caesarean text (roughly 1735 to 1935), but it was the analysis of papyri like P[45], P[46], P[66], and P[75] that brought a new dimension to the controversy, namely, whether the established text-type categories any longer made sense or were even useful for the earliest period, or — to push the question even farther — whether there were, in fact, any identifiable text-types at all in that period.

Discussions of the papyri in relation to text-types during the 1950s and 1960s led to statements like that of E. C. Colwell in 1961 that "very few, if any, text-types were established" by A.D. 200 (Colwell, 1969:55), or the more radical statement of Kurt Aland in 1964 that one can speak of an Alexandrian [or Egyptian] and of an Antiochian [or Byzantine] text-type, but:

> These are, it seems to me, the only text-types which may be regarded as certain, and that only since the fourth century. Everything else is extremely doubtful. It is impossible to fit the papyri, from the time prior to the fourth century, into these two text-types, to say nothing of trying to fit them into other types, as frequently happens. The simple fact that all these papyri . . . did exist side by side . . . in Egypt . . . is the best argument against the existence of any text-types, including the Alexandrian [Egyptian] and the Antiochian [Byzantine]. (1965)

P[75] had been published when these statements were made, and perhaps its close affinity with Codex Vaticanus (B), pointed out in 1966 by (the now archbishop of Milan) Carlo Martini (see Fee, 1974), should have acted as a restraint on this all-too-rapidly developed view that there were no entities in the first centuries that can be called "text-types." Yet it is clear enough that the study of the early and extensive papyri constitutes the turning point from confidence to skepticism about early text-types. (It is one thing, of course, to say that the traditional text-types are not useful as pigeonholes into which the early papyri may be placed, which — as his context shows — is the force of Colwell's statement and something quite different to affirm that no text-types existed in the earliest period, which seems clearly to be what Aland means.)

These varying skeptical opinions about early text-types were not, however, the only judgments on the subject in the 1950s and 1960s. A. F. J. Klijn, for example, argued that two text-types existed side by side in Egypt, a Western text and a Neutral text (to use Hort's terms) (1969:39–49). It seems to me, therefore, that we should not yet withdraw from this battle-field, as though the matter were settled or as though we ought to abandon hope that the early papyri can be classified according to varying textual complexions ("individual manuscripts can be characterized" – Colwell, 1967:5) or that they can be linked with later manuscripts that can be said to possess a similar textual character ("manuscripts can still be grouped and the group characterized" – Colwell, 1967:5).

I am reluctant to repeat suggestions that I have made over the past several years and which still await development, but it seems clear to me, first, that differing *textual complexions can be identified* in the various papyri, even in the fragmentary ones – and many textual critics assign them to textual categories, including Aland himself. Second, if this is so, it seems clear to me that the *grouping of early witnesses is possible* (and such groups or clusters might very well be designated "text-types"). Third, it seems clear to me that lines of connection or *trajectories can be traced* from early to later witnesses of similar textual character or complexion. When such an exercise is carried out, we may find that a text-type labeled "P⁷⁵" appears for the Gospels in the earliest period (third century) and has later representatives in Codex B in the fourth century, in Codex L in the eighth century, in Codex 33 in the ninth century, in MS 1739 in the tenth, and so on. In addition, we may find that a less well documented but still adequate trajectory can be traced for Acts from a type of text found in P²⁹ and P⁴⁸ in the third century, with later representatives in P³⁸ around A.D. 300, in Codex D of the fourth or fifth century, and in MSS 614 and 383 in the thirteenth century; or that another type of text of the Gospels (and Acts), to be named for P⁴⁵, appears in the third century and follows a line to Codex W in the fifth century, though it seems to stop there (see Hurtado: 63–66; Epp, 1974:395–98; on manuscript trajectories, Epp, 1974:397–400; 1980:147–49).

Much more work, admittedly, is required in this area, but we should not so easily capitulate to those forces that contend that no text-types existed or can be identified in the pre-fourth-century period of NT textual transmission. We need answers; we need them soon; and I think that – by diligent effort – they can be found for this important issue. As will be obvious, it is precisely the papyri that can lead the way, for they extend the textual streams or trajectories much farther back than was previously possible, and they assist us in identifying the earliest textual clusters.

Reference to a debate over the text-types, however, is only another way of saying that we face a crisis over *methodology* in NT textual criticism. Identifying early text-types is one means – or at least one aspect – of reconstructing the earliest history of the transmission of the NT text. Such a history of the text — if indeed it could be written for the earliest period — would provide a rather firm methodological track back to a point very close to the original text. Thus, to the extent that all Greek manuscripts of the NT can be classified according to types of text, or at least placed on a continuum in accordance with their differing textual complexion, and to the extent that a history of the text can be reconstructed, to that extent we can speak of having formulated a theory of the NT text (or at least a portion of such a theory). To state it differently, we need to devise a plausible and defensible hypothesis that explains how the original NT text issued in our thousands of extant manuscripts, with their varying textual complexions. We seem not to have such a theory, though most of the great figures of the past ventured to formulate one. Westcott-Hort surmised that two early text-types were in competition in the second-century church, one corrupted by paraphrastic expansions (the Western) and the other virtually untouched in its course of transmission from the original (the Neutral) (see Epp, 1974:392). Von Soden and B. H. Streeter and a host of others announced and defended their theories of the NT text, but none has stood the tests of criticism or of time. Yet the task is not to be abandoned, for it is a correct and proper task if significant progress is to be made in NT textual criticism. Though a hundred years have passed, it is still prudent to keep in mind the two — and the only two — principles that Hort printed in large type in his chapter on method: "Knowledge of documents should precede final judgement upon readings" and "All trustworthy restoration of corrupted texts is founded on the study of their history" (Westcott-Hort: 2:31, 40). So the decision point over text-types becomes a broader and more significant decision point about basic textual history and theory and about fundamental methodology in the discipline of NT textual criticism. To resolve the issue of early text-types, therefore, would have far-reaching theoretical implications. For one thing, it would fulfill the hope implied in K. W. Clark's 1956 statement that "we know only that the traditional theory of the text is faulty but cannot yet see clearly to correct the fault" (1956:37–38).

The Crisis of the Criteria

The second area of conflict is the present crisis over the criteria for determining the originality of readings, or the "canons of criticism," as they were known in earlier times. This is a significant decision point, for NT text-critical methodology — though more on the practical level now than the theoretical — in its essence and at its very heart is concerned with the criteria employed to choose the most likely original reading wherever the textual tradition presents two or more readings at a given point in the text. To be quite blunt — if also a bit cynical — it is this simple-sounding matter of how to choose the "right" or "best" reading that is not only the major interest, but (I fear) often the *only* interest that exegetes have in textual criticism. Yet this attitude—whether widespread or not—is actually a compliment to textual criticism, for it points to the important practical application and utility that the discipline has, as well as to the high expectations that our colleagues hold for it and for us. They may care little for our theories and disputations, but they do care greatly about how they shall make those decisions between and among competing readings that exegesis so regularly demands.

These critical canons or criteria have been of concern to NT textual critics since Origen and Jerome in ancient times, since Gerhard von Mastricht's formal list—the first such attempt—in his Greek NT of 1711, and particularly since they were given prominence by such notables as J. A. Bengel, J. J. Wettstein, J. J. Griesbach, Karl Lachmann, C. Tischendorf, S. P. Tregelles, and Westcott-Hort. Throughout this lengthy period, during which the criteria were evolving, the clash (as is well known) was between reliance on the numerous later manuscripts or on the growing—but still relatively small—number of older manuscripts, or, to put it differently, the struggle was between *quantity* of the manuscripts and "weight" or *quality* of the manuscripts supporting a reading, culminating in the triumph of the few earlier manuscripts over the many that represented the *textus receptus*. Though this period concluded with bitter conflict, complete with the acrimonious language of J. W. Burgon, it is not this skirmish that interests us (in spite of the present-day revival of the *textus receptus* by some who take Burgon's side against the rest of us—e.g., the recent edition by Hodges and Farstad; see their introduction: ix-xiii). Rather, what does interest us is that, following Westcott-Hort but beginning particularly with C. H. Turner (1923ff.), M.-J. Lagrange (1935), G. D. Kilpatrick (1943ff.), A. F. J. Klijn (1949), and J. K. Elliott (1968ff.), a new crisis of the criteria became prominent and is very much with us today: a duel between external and internal criteria and the widespread uncertainty as to precisely what kind of compromise ought to or can be worked out between them. The temporary "cease-fire" that most—but certainly not all—textual critics have agreed upon is called "moderate" or "reasoned" eclecticism (for the terminology, see Fee, 1976:174-77, and the discussion above) or what I have designated the "eclectic generalist" approach (Epp, 1976a:244-48), in which it is recognized that no single criterion or invariable combination of criteria will resolve all cases of textual variation and which, therefore, attempts to apply evenly and without prejudice any and all criteria—external and internal—appropriate to a given case, arriving then at an answer based on the relative probabilities among those applicable criteria (Epp, 1976a:244-48). We are all familiar with this method, for we all—or nearly all—employ it, as did the committee who prepared the *UBSGNT*, and abundant examples of the method at work can be observed in the pages of that edition's *Textual Commentary*. This "reasoned" eclecticism is not recognized as appropriate by those "eclectic specialists" who practice a "rigorous" or "thoroughgoing" eclecticism that emphasizes the internal criteria, notably (as described earlier) George D. Kilpatrick and J. Keith Elliott. Even a "reasoned" eclecticism is accorded only a temporary "victory" by many of us who feel strongly that it is indeed a method for our time but not the ultimate method. As J. Neville Birdsall put it already a quarter of a century ago:

> Although for the present we must utilize these diverse criteria and establish a text by an eclectic method, it is impossible to stifle the hope that, at some future time, we shall find our methods and our resultant text justified by manuscript discoveries and by the classical methods ... which Hort exemplified so brilliantly in his work. (1957:199)

Many of us share this hope that the eclectic method can be replaced by something more permanent — a confidently reconstructed history and a persuasive theory of the text — and we are working actively toward that goal. In the meantime, all of us need to recognize, first, that the crisis of the criteria is real; second, that the literature of the past two or three decades is replete with controversy over the eclectic method, or at least is abundant with evidence of the frustration that accompanies its use; and, third, that we must devote our best and most serious efforts to refining the eclectic method in any and all appropriate ways, for it is likely to be our only guide for some time to come.

How can we refine the eclectic method? An important first step (which will not be necessary for all) is to understand the criteria themselves, their history, development, and use; I attempted such an assessment in some fifty pages in the *Harvard Theological Review* for 1977 that proved to be instructive for me. Second, we need to analyze critically each of the fifteen or so external and internal criteria as to their validity and relative worth. Is it really incontrovertible that the shorter or harder reading is to be preferred? Does wide geographical distribution of a reading or its attestation by several established groups give it added weight? Does antiquity of documentary evidence outweigh everything else? Is fitness to the context or with the author's style or theology automatically decisive? As a matter of fact, can our various criteria be placed in some hierarchic order, so that some are consistently more decisive than others? These and many other questions require continued and conscientious attention, and they need to be addressed both at the theoretical level and at the level of practice. Naturally, the trial and error of the laboratory and the give-and-take of everyday application can lead to significant insights and subsequent refinements in method. In addition, we can learn much from those who elevate one category of criteria or even a single criterion to a dominant position, as have those, for example, who practice "rigorous" eclecticism. Very recently a new challenge of this kind has come from Kurt Aland through the published definition of his "local-genealogical" method, which appears to be a refinement or a very special form of eclecticism, though he vigorously denies that it can properly be called "eclectic" (Aland and Aland, 1979:43*; 1982:44; Eng. 34). This method arrives at the most likely original text by selecting that variant that best explains all the other variants in the variation unit, and in the process Aland employs the various criteria or canons of criticism as possible ways of explaining how each secondary reading might have arisen. Professor Aland will surprise some — perhaps many — by his forthright statement that "from the perspective of our recent knowledge, this local-genealogical method . . . is the only one which meets the requirements of the New Testament textual tradition" (Aland and Aland, 1979:43*) and it is, he claims further, the method that produced the new "Standard Text" (as he calls it) in the third edition of the *UBSGNT* and the twenty-sixth edition of the Nestle-Aland Greek NT (see also K. Aland, 1979:10). Testing his claim that this local-genealogical procedure has exclusive validity can be a further avenue for refining the eclectic method — an urgent decision point for current NT textual criticism. All the while, however, many of us will continue to hope — but more than that, to work — toward those more objective methods (like the historical-documentary method), based on better knowledge of the history of the NT text and its transmission, which will enable us to surmount the "crisis of the criteria."

The Coming Battle over the Papyri

I referred earlier to three fields of conflict, and the third is the coming battle over the papyri. This represents our final, but doubtless most critical, decision point in current text-critical discussion. I emphasize the word "coming" for good reason. Since the discovery of the early NT papyri, but particularly since the nonfragmentary P[45], P[46], P[66], P[75], and others have come to light, there has hardly been anything that one could call strife or conflict in this area, for each new papyrus, whether extensive or fragmentary, has been welcomed with rejoicing and analyzed in anticipation of positive and constructive results. When, for example, P[75] was shown to possess a text virtually identical to that of Codex B (Martini, 1966; Fee, 1974), yet two centuries or so earlier in date, the long-standing conviction of a fourth century recension of what had been called the B-text was freely given up — no struggle, no strife.

My suggestion of a *coming battle* over the papyri refers to something else: it concerns primarily two issues. The first of these is the *worth* of the papyri as textual witnesses, though this — as all will recognize — is merely a question of *relative* worth, for it goes without saying that the NT papyri are of exceptionally high value and will be thus esteemed by all textual critics (with the possible exception of the few "rigorous eclectics," who tend to view even the earliest manuscripts — along with all others — merely as sources for potentially original readings). The question, rather, is whether these papyri, or at least the earliest ones — those dating up to about A.D. 300 — are to be accorded what might be characterized as a rightful status one or two rungs above that of our great uncials of the fourth century, or are to be accorded a considerably or even vastly higher status than that, one that raises them in significance far above our other eminent witnesses and that elevates them to a position somewhat akin to that accorded the relics of the saints. I am alluding here, of course, to the extraordinary status afforded these earliest papyri by Kurt Aland, who (in his "Introduction" to the twenty-sixth edition of Nestle-Aland: 12*,49*) not only affirms their "automatic significance" as textual witnesses, but in a later article makes the astounding claim that in the forty papyri (and uncials) prior to about A.D. 300 the early history of the NT text "can be studied in the original," and that all other efforts to get a glimpse of the early text "must remain reconstructed theories" (K. Aland, 1979:11).

Such an exceptionally high valuation of the earliest papyri has its problems, and included among these is the second issue over which conflict is inevitable, namely, the question of how *representative* of the earliest history of the text these early papyri are? If his statement means what it seems to mean, Professor Aland is virtually identifying the text of the pre-fourth-century papyri with the "original" text. If this seems incredible or unlikely, it may be added that, in a still more recent article on "the new 'Standard Text' in its relation to the early papyri and uncials," Aland employs these pre-fourth-century papyri and uncials as the "touchstone" of original-ity, for he states that the common text of the twenty-sixth edition of Nestle-Aland and the third edition of the *UBSGNT* "has passed the test of the early papyri and uncials. It corresponds, in fact, to the text of the early time," and he then goes on to a more startling conclusion. Speaking of the text of Nestle-Aland (26th ed.), he asserts: "A hundred years after Westcott-Hort, the goal of an edition of the New Testament 'in the original Greek' seems to have been reached" (1981:274–75). It is, of course, the unique value ascribed to the papyri that is the key to this remarkable claim.

It seems clear to me that a struggle over the papyri — about their relative worth as textual evidence and about their representative nature — has in fact begun, will increase in intensity and is a crucial decision point requiring our serious attention. Can such high claims as Aland makes be sustained? I for one wish that they could be readily accepted and be as easily substantiated, for that would constitute a breakthrough in both method and practice that would be highly significant and warmly welcomed. Yet some disturbing questions arise and call for answers before we rush to embrace such claims about the papyri.

To begin with an obvious question — yet one too rarely discussed or even raised — how representative, really, of the earliest history of the NT text are these earliest papyri? What assurance do we have that these randomly surviving manuscripts represent in any real sense the entire earliest period of the text? Subsidiary questions appear: First, all of these documents come from one region, Egypt. Can we be satisfied with Egypt as the exclusive locale for viewing this earliest history of the text? Was Egypt in the third century A.D. representative of the NT text for *all* of Christianity at that period? Was any NT book written in Egypt? Probably not. Does not Egypt then represent at best a secondary and derivative stage in the history of the NT text? After all, is it not merely an accident of history (though a most fortunate one) that papyrus almost exclusively survives only in the dry sands of Egypt?

If textual witnesses, then, are to have "automatic significance" (to use Aland's phrase), should there not be a basis for so significant a role that is more substantive than merely their early age? And, before we claim that in these papyri the history of the NT text "can be studied in the original" (again to use Aland's words), should we not assure ourselves either that these earliest witnesses present a unitary text (which, of course, they do not), or — lacking that assurance — should we not require a guarantee (or at least some persuasive evidence) that they are genuinely representative of the earliest history of the text, representative, that is, of the various textual complexions that existed in the earliest period? As a matter of fact, as suggested earlier, certain "types" of text or textual complexions do seem to be represented by various of the early papyri, including (1) the Alexandrian or Egyptian (Hort's Neutral) text, (2) the so-called Western text, and (3) a text somewhere in between (now usually designated pre-Caesarean) (see Epp, 1974:393–96; cf. 1980:146–47; Hurtado: 88–89).

We are faced, then, with a puzzle, for there is one rather clear sense in which the early papyri seem *not* to be representative — and that is their restriction to a single geographical segment of Christianity — and another sense in which they *may* be representative — and that is their presentation of textual complexions characteristic of what have previously been identified as the major early text-types. For these reasons, it seems that we have been thrust into a period of the *reassessment* of the papyri. Certainly it is more than mere curiosity or coincidence to find that fifty years ago, after his preliminary analysis of the Chester Beatty papyri, Sir Frederic Kenyon made the following provocative statement in his Schweich Lectures of the British Academy for 1932: "There remains what is perhaps the most perplexing problem of all, the problem of the Biblical text in Egypt" (Kenyon, 1933:80). And in 1949, before the Bodmer papyri came to light, A. F. J. Klijn said, "Egypt appears to be more and more important for the history of the text" (Klijn, 1949: 145). How much closer to solving that puzzle have the past fifty years brought us? Certainly we have more abundant materials for the task than Kenyon and Klijn had — notably the Bodmer papyri — and we may hope that we will not have to wait for another fifty-year landmark to see these questions about the significance of the papyri resolved. After all, there is virtually unanimous agreement that the NT papyri not only are textual criticism's greatest treasure but also its best hope for "cracking" the textual "code" and breaking through to the original text.

Despite confident claims to the contrary, however, we have not yet reached the point of readily and assuredly identifying any manuscript, any group of manuscripts, or any critical text with that elusive "original," but the papyri most certainly will be the instruments that we shall use to settle the struggle over the text-type, to resolve the crisis of the criteria, and to push toward a "standard text" acknowledged by all. The difficult question that remains, of course, is exactly *how* we are to use them to achieve these urgent goals.

IV. CONCLUSION

New Testament textual criticism is a vigorous and stimulating discipline, in which—as history demonstrates—new discoveries are always possible (though not assured) and in which many theoretical decisions—fundamental to the discipline—remain to be made on the basis of the materials we have. Since World War II new discoveries have come to light and new methods have been devised (or old ones refined), and there has been much progress. On the other hand, as we have noted, major issues still require resolution. In these cases textual critics and not the discoveries or theories themselves will lead to further progress, and in this connection the words of Georg Luck (166), a prominent classical textual critic, are discomfiting but nonetheless true: "Part of the problem is that our critical texts are no better than our textual critics." If competent textual critics can be rallied in NT studies, our new materials and refined methods can be utilized to solve the critical problems, and the discipline can move toward that ideal of a critical text that closely approximates the "original" NT text.

BIBLIOGRAPHY

Editions of the Greek New Testament

Aland, Kurt, and Barbara Aland, eds.
    1979   *Novum Testamentum Graece post Eberhard Nestle et Erwin Nestle, communiter ediderunt Kurt Aland, Matthew Black, Carlo M. Martini, Bruce M. Metzger, Allen Wikgren.* 26th ed. Stuttgart: Deutsche Bibelstiftung. 4th rev. printing, 1981.

Aland, Kurt, Matthew Black, Carlo M. Martini, Bruce M. Metzger,
  and Allen Wikgren, eds.
    1975   *The Greek New Testament.* 3d ed. New York, London, Edinburgh, Amsterdam, and Stuttgart: United Bible Societies.

American and British Committees of the International Greek New Testament Project
    1984–87   *The New Testament in Greek: The Gospel according to St. Luke: Part One: Chapters 1–12. Part Two: Chapters 13–24.* 2 vols. Oxford: Clarendon Press.

Boismard, M.-É., and A. Lamouille
    1984   *Le texte occidental des Actes des Apôtres: Reconstitution et réhabilitation: Tome I: Introduction et textes; Tome II: Apparat critique, Index des caractéristiques stylistiques, Index des citations patristiques.* Synthèse, 17. Paris: Editions Recherche sur le Civilisations.

Bover, Joseph M., S.J., ed.
    1968   *Novi Testamenti biblia graeca et latina.* 5th ed. Madrid: Consejo superior de investigaciones científicas.

Bover, Joseph M., and José O'Callaghan, eds.
    1977   *Nuevo Testamento trilingüe.* BAC 400. Madrid: La editorial católica.

Hodges, Zane C., and Arthur L. Farstad, eds.
    1982   *The Greek New Testament according to the Majority Text.* Nashville, Camden, and New York: Thomas Nelson.

Kilpatrick, George D., ed.
    1958   Η ΚΑΙΝΗ ΔΙΑΘΗΚΗ. 2d ed., with revised critical apparatus. London: British and Foreign Bible Society.

Legg, S. C. E., ed.
    1935   *Nouum Testamentum graece secundum textum Westcotto-Hortianum: Euangelium secundum Marcum.* Oxford: Clarendon Press.
    1940   *Nouum Testamentum graece secundum textum Westcotto-Hortianum: Euangelium secundum Matthaeum.* Oxford: Clarendon Press.

Merk, Augustinus, S.J., ed.
    1964   *Novum Testamentum graece et latine.* 9th ed. Rome: Biblical Institute Press.

Souter, Alexander, ed.
    1947   *Novvm Testamentvm Graece: Textvi retractatoribvs anglis adhibito brevem adnotationem criticam svbiectit.* 2d ed. Oxford: Clarendon Press.

Tasker, R. V. G., ed.
    1964   *The Greek New Testament, Being the Text Translated in the New English Bible.* Oxford: Oxford University Press; Cambridge: University Press.

Westcott, Brooke Foss, and Fenton J. A. Hort
    1881–82   *The New Testament in the Original Greek.* 2 vols. Cambridge and London: Macmillan. 2d ed. 1896.

Editions of Ancient Versions of the New Testament

Blake, Robert P., ed.
    1974   *The Old Georgian Version of the Gospel of Mark from the Adysh Gospels with the Variants of the Opiza and Tbet' Gospels.* Patrologia Orientalis 20:3. Turnhout, Belgium: Brepols.
    1976   *The Old Georgian Version of the Gospel of Matthew from the Adysh Gospels with the Variants of the Opiza and Tbet' Gospels.* Patrologia Orientalis 24:1. Turnhout, Belgium: Brepols.

Blake, Robert P., and Maurice Brière, eds.
1950   *The Old Georgian Version of the Gospel of John from the Adysh
        Gospels with the Variants of the Opiza and Tbet' Gospels.* Patrologia
        Orientalis 26:4. Paris: Firmin-Didot.

Brière, Maurice, ed.
1955   *La version géorgienne ancienne de l'Evangile de Luc d'après les
        Evangiles d'Adich avec les variantes des Evangiles d'Opiza et de Tbet'.*
        Patrologia Orientalis 28:3. Paris: Firmin-Didot.

Frede, Hermann Josef
1962–   *Vetus Latina: Die Reste der altlateinischen Bibel.* Vol. 24, *Epistula ad
1969, ed. Ephesios; Epistulae ad Philippenses et ad Colossenses.* Freiburg:
        Herder.
1973   *Ein neuer Paulustext und Kommentar.* 2 vols. Vetus Latina: Aus der
        Geschichte der lateinischen Bibel 7. Freiburg: Herder.
1975–   *Vetus Latina: Die Reste der altlateinischen Bibel.* Vol. 25, *Epistulae ad
1983, ed. Thessalonicenses, Timotheum, Titum, Philemonem, Hebraeos.* Frei-
        burg: Herder. [1–2 Thessalonians, 1–2 Timothy, Titus, and Philemon
        completed to date, Hebrews in progress, 1987ff.; see also Thiele.]

Garitte, Gérard
1955   *L'ancienne version géorgienne des Actes des Apôtres d'après deux
        manuscrits du Sinaï.* Bibliothèque du Muséon 38. Louvain: Publica-
        tions Universitaires.

Hofmann, Josef, ed.
1967   *Die äthiopische Übersetzung der Johannes-Apokalypse.* 2 vols. CSCO
        281–82, Scriptores Aethiopici 55–56. Louvain: CSCO.

Jülicher, Adolf
1954–72 *Itala: Das Neue Testament in altlateinischer Überlieferung.* Ed. Walter
        Matzkow and Kurt Aland. *Matthäus-Evangelium,* 2d ed. 1972;
        Markus-Evangelium, 2d ed. 1970; *Lucas-Evangelium,* 1954; *Johannes-
        Evangelium,* 1963. Berlin: de Gruyter.

Kasser, Rodolphe
1966   *L'Evangile selon Saint Jean et les Versions coptes de la Bible.* Biblio-
        theque théologique. Neuchâtel: Delachaux et Niestlé.

Thiele, Walter
1956–   *Vetus Latina: Die Reste der altlateinischen Bibel.* Vol. 26, *Epistulae
1969, ed. Catholicae.* Freiburg: Herder. [See also Frede.]

Publications of Texts (in monograph form)

Browne, Gerald M., ed.
1979   *Michigan Coptic Texts.* Studia et textus 7. Barcelona: Papyrologica
        Castroctaviana.
1982   *Griffith's Old Nubian Lectionary.* Studia et textus 8. Rome and
        Barcelona: Papyrologica Castroctaviana.

Casson, Lionel, and Ernest L. Hettich
1950   *Excavations at Nessana.* Vol. 2, *Literary Papyri.* Princeton, NJ:
        Princeton University Press.

Daris, Sergio, ed.
1967   *Un nuovo frammento della prima lettera di Pietro (1 Petr 2,20–3,12).*
        Papyrologica Castroctaviana 2. Barcelona: Papyrologica Castrocta-
        viana.

Greenlee, J. Harold
    1968   *Nine Uncial Palimpsests of the Greek New Testament.* SD 39. Salt Lake
                City, UT: University of Utah Press.

Hintze, Fritz, and Hans-Martin Schenke, eds.
    1970   *Die Berliner Handschrift der Sahidischen Apostelgeschichte (P. 15
                926).* TU 109. Berlin: Akademie-Verlag.

Horsley, G. H. R., ed.
    1981–87   *New Documents Illustrating Early Christianity: A Review of the Greek
                Inscriptions and Papyri Published in 1976. ...1977. ...1978. ...1987.* 4
                vols. to date. North Ryde, N.S.W., Australia: Ancient History
                Documentary Research Centre, Macquarie University.

Husselman, Elinor M., ed.
    1962   *The Gospel of John in Fayumic Coptic (P. Mich. Inv. 3521).* University
                of Michigan, Kelsey Museum of Archaeology Studies 2. Ann Arbor,
                MI: Kelsey Museum of Archaeology.

Kasser, Rodolphe, ed.
    1958   *Papyrus Bodmer III: Evangile de Jean et Genèse I-IV,2 en bohaïrique.*
                2 vols. CSCO 177–78, Scriptores coptici 25–26. Louvain: CSCO.
    1961   *Papyrus Bodmer XVII: Actes des Apôtres, Epîtres de Jacques, Pierre,
                Jean et Jude.* Cologny-Genève: Bibliotheca Bodmeriana.
    1962   *Papyrus Bodmer XIX: Evangile de Matthieu XIV,28–XXVIII,20, Epître
                aux Romains I,1-II,3 en sahidique.* Cologny-Genève: Bibliotheca
                Bodmeriana.

Leloir, Louis, ed.
    1963   *Saint Ephrem: Commentaire de l'Evangile concordant, texte syriaque
                (Manuscrit Chester Beatty 709).* Chester Beatty Monographs 8.
                Dublin: Hodges Figgis.

Lo Bue, Francesco, ed.
    1963   *The Turin Fragments of Tyconius' Commentary on Revelation.* TextsS
                7. Cambridge: University Press.

Martin, Victor, ed.
    1956   *Papyrus Bodmer II: Evangile de Jean chap. 1-14.* Cologny-Genève:
                Bibliotheca Bodmeriana.
    1962   *Papyrus Bodmer II: Supplement: Evangile de Jean chap. 14-21.* New
                ed. (with facsimiles). Cologny-Genève: Bibliotheca Bodmeriana.

Martin, Victor, and Rodolphe Kasser, eds.
    1961a   *Papyrus Bodmer XV: Evangile de Jean chap. 1-15 (P[75]).* Cologny-
                Genève: Bibliotheca Bodmeriana.
    1961b   *Papyrus Bodmer XV: Evangile de Luc chap. 3-24 (P[75]).* Cologny-
                Genève: Bibliotheca Bodmeriana.

Moir, Ian A., ed.
    1956   *'Codex Climaci Rescriptus Graecus': A Study of Portions of the Greek
                New Testament Comprising the Underwriting of Part of a Palimpsest
                in the Library of Westminster College, Cambridge (Ms. Gregory 1561,
                L).* TextsS ns 2. Cambridge: University Press.

Orlandi, Tito, ed.
    1974   *Papiri della Università degli Studi di Milano (P. Mil. Copti), Volume
                Quinto: Lettere di San Paolo in Copto-Ossirinchita.* Milan: Istituto
                Editoriale Cisalpino-La Goliardica.

Quecke, Hans, ed.

1972   *Das Markusevangelium saïdisch: Text der Handschrift PPalau Rib. Inv.-Nr. 182 mit den Varianten der Handschrift M 569.* Studia et textus 4. Barcelona: Papyrologica Castroctaviana.

1977   *Das Lukasevangelium saïdisch: Text der Handschrift PPalau Rib. Inv.-Nr. 181 mit den Varianten der Handschrift M 569.* Studia et textus 6. Barcelona: Papyrologica Castroctaviana.

1984   *Das Johannesevangelium saïdisch: Text der Handschrift PPalau Rib. Inv.-Nr. 183 mit den Varianten der Handschriften 813 und 814 der Chester Beatty Library und der Handschrift M 569.* Studia et textus 11. Barcelona: Papyrologica Castroctaviana.

Roca-Puig, R., ed.

1962   *Un papiro griego del evangelo de san Mateo.* 2d ed., with a note by Colin Roberts. Barcelona: Gremio Sindical de Maestros Impresores.

Sanz, Peter, ed.

1946   *Griechische literarische Papyri christlichen Inhaltes I (Biblica, Väterschriften und Verwandtes).* Mitteilungen aus der Papyrussammlung der Nationalbibliothek in Wein ns 4. Baden bei Wien: Rohrer.

Schenke, Hans-Martin, ed.

1981   *Das Matthäus-Evangelium im mittelägyptischen Dialekt des Koptischen (Codex Scheide).* TU 127. Berlin: Akademie-Verlag.

Staal, Harvey

1969   *Codex Sinai Arabic 151: Pauline Epistles.* 2 vols. SD 40. Salt Lake City, UT: University of Utah Press. Arabic text and English trans.

Testuz, Michel, ed.

1959   *Papyrus Bodmer VII-IX. VII: L'Epître de Jude, VIII: Les deux Epîtres de Pierre, IX: Les Psaumes 33 et 34.* Cologny-Genève: Bibliotheca Bodmeriana.

Vogels, Heinrich Joseph

1953   *Evangelium Colbertinum: Codex Lat. 254 der Bibliothèque Nationale zu Paris.* BBB 4. 2 vols. Bonn: Peter Hanstein.

Vööbus, Arthur, ed.

1978   *The Apocalypse in the Harklean Version: A Facsimile Edition of MS. Mardin Orth. 35, fol. 143r-159v, with an Introduction.* CSCO 400, Subsidia 56. Louvain: CSCO.

Books (and Articles cited)

Aland, Barbara

1976   "Neutestamentliche Textkritik heute." Pp. 3–22 in *Verkündigung und Forschung: Neues Testament.* Beihefte zu *EvT* 2. Munich: Kaiser.

1985   "Die neuen neutestamentlichen Handschriften vom Sinai." Pp. 76–89 in *Kunst.*

Aland, Kurt

1957–76   "Neue neutestamentliche Papyri." *NTS* 3 (1957) 261–86; 9 (1963) 303–16; 10 (1963) 62–79; 11 (1964) 1–21; 20 (1974) 357–81; 22 (1976) 375–96. [Parts 1 and 2 = K. Aland, 1967: 91–136; 137–54.]

1959   "The Present Position of New Testament Textual Criticism." *SE* 1: 717–31.

1963	*Kurzgefasste Liste der griechischen Handschriften des Neuen Testaments. I, Gesamtübersicht.* Arbeiten zur neutestamentlichen Textforschung 1. Berlin: de Gruyter.
1964, ed.	*Synopsis quattuor evangeliorum.* Stuttgart: Württembergische Bibelanstalt. Reissued in 1972 as *Synopsis of the Four Gospels: Greek-English Edition of the Synopsis quattuor evangeliorum with the Text of the Revised Standard Version.* London: United Bible Societies.
1965	"The Significance of the Papyri for Progress in New Testament Research." Pp. 325–46 in Hyatt.
1966a	"Der heutige Text des griechischen Neuen Testament: Eine kritischer Bericht über seine modernen Ausgaben." Pp. 44–71 in *Die Bibel in der Welt: Band 9: Jahrbuch des Verbandes der Evangelischen Bibelgesellschaften in Deutschland 1966.* Ed. Robert Steiner. Halle. Revision, pp. 58–80 in K. Aland, 1967.
1966b	"Bemerkungen zu Probeseiten einer grossen kritischen Ausgabe des Neuen Testaments." *NTS* 12: 176–85. [= K. Aland, 1967:81–90.]
1967	*Studien zur Überlieferung des Neuen Testaments und seines Textes.* Arbeiten zur neutestamentlichen Textforschung 2. Berlin: de Gruyter.
1969, ed.	*Materialien zur neutestamentlichen Handschriftenkunde I.* Arbeiten zur neutestamentlichen Textforschung 3. Berlin: de Gruyter.
1970	"Novi testamenti graeci editio maior critica: Der gegenwärtige Stand der Arbeit an einer neuen grossen kritischen Ausgabe des Neuen Testamentes." *NTS* 16: 163–77.
1972, ed.	*Die alten Übersetzungen des Neuen Testaments, die Kirchenväterzitate und Lektionare: Die gegenwärtige Stand ihrer Erforschung und ihre Bedeutung für die griechische Textgeschichte.* Arbeiten zur neutestamentlichen Textforschung 5. Berlin and New York: de Gruyter.
1975–1983, ed.	*Vollständige Konkordanz zum griechischen Neuen Testament: Unter Zugrundelegung aller modernen kritischen Textausgaben und des Textus Receptus.* 2 vols. in 3. Arbeiten zur neutestamentlichen Textforschung 4. Berlin and New York: de Gruyter.
1976, ed.	Ed. for the Patristischen Arbeitsstelle of Münster: *Repertorium der griechischen christlichen Papyri: I: Biblische Papyri: Altes Testament, Neues Testament, Varia, Apokryphen.* Patristische Texte und Studien 18. Berlin and New York: de Gruyter.
1979	"The Twentieth-Century Interlude in New Testament Textual Criticism." Pp. 1–14 in Best and Wilson.
1981	"Der neue 'Standard Text' in seinem Verhältnis zu den frühen Papyri und Majuskeln." Pp. 257–75 in Epp and Fee.
1982	"Ein neuer Textus Receptus für das griechische Neue Testament?" *NTS* 28: 145–53.
1985	"Die Grundurkunde des Glaubens: Ein Bericht über 40 Jahre Arbeit an ihrem Text." Pp. 9–75 in Kunst.

Aland, Kurt, and Barbara Aland

| 1982 | *Der Text des Neuen Testaments: Einführung in die wissenschaftlichen Ausgaben sowie in Theorie und Praxis der modernen Textkritik.* Stuttgart: Deutsche Bibelgesellschaft. Eng. trans. by E. R. Rhodes: *The Text of the New Testament: An Introduction to the Critical Editions and to the Theory and Practice of Modern Textual Criticism.* Grand Rapids: Eerdmans; Leiden: Brill, 1987. |

Allenbach, J., et al.
1975–   *Biblia patristica: Index des citations et allusions bibliques dans la*
1987   *littérature patristique.* 4 vols. Centre d'analyse et de documentation
         patristiques. Paris: Centre National de la Recherche Scientifique.

Baarda, Tjitze
1975   *The Gospel Quotations of Aphrahat the Persian Sage: I: Aphrahat's
         Text of the Fourth Gospel.* 2 vols. Akademisch Proefschrift, Free
         University. Amsterdam: Krips Repro B.V. Meppel.
1983   *Early Transmission of Words of Jesus: Thomas, Tatian and the Text of
         the New Testament: A Collection of Studies.* Ed. J. Helderman and S. J.
         Noorda. Amsterdam: VU Boekhandel [Free University Press].

Barbour, Ruth
1981   *Greek Literary Hands A.D. 400–1600.* Oxford: Clarendon Press.

Barrett, Charles Kingsley
1979   "Is There a Theological Tendency in Codex Bezae?" Pp. 15–27 in
         Best and Wilson.

Bartsch, Hans-Werner
1981   "Ein neuer Textus Receptus für das griechische Neue Testament?"
         NTS 27: 585–92.

Becker, Ulrich
1963   *Jesus und die Ehebrecherin: Untersuchungen zur Text- und Überliefer-
         ungsgeschichte von Joh. 7,53 – 8,11.* BZNW 28. Berlin: Töpelmann.

Benoit, André, and Pierre Prigent, eds.
1971   *La Bible et les Pères: Colloque de Strasbourg (1er-3 octobre 1969).*
         Bibliothèque des centres d'études supérieures spécialisés. Paris:
         Presses universitaires de France. [Several text-critical studies.]

Bentley, Jerry H.
1983   *Humanists and Holy Writ: New Testament Scholarship in the
         Renaissance.* Princeton, NJ: Princeton University Press.

Best, Ernest, and R. McL. Wilson, eds.
1979   *Text and Interpretation: Studies in the New Testament Presented to
         Matthew Black.* Cambridge and New York: University Press. [Several
         text-critical studies.]

Birdsall, J. Neville
1957   "The Text of the Fourth Gospel: Some Current Questions." *EvQ* 29:
         195–205.
1957–58 "Current Trends and Present Tasks in New Testament Textual
         Criticism." *Baptist Quarterly* 17: 109–14.
1960   *The Bodmer Papyrus of the Gospel of John.* Tyndale New Testament
         Lecture, 1958. London: Tyndale.
1965   "How the New Testament Came to Us." Pp. 121–44 in *Understanding
         the New Testament.* Ed. O. Jessie Lace. Cambridge: University Press.
1970   "The New Testament Text." Chap. 11, pp. 308–77 in *The Cambridge
         History of the Bible.* Vol. 1, *From the Beginnings to Jerome.* Ed. P. R.
         Ackroyd and C. F. Evans. Cambridge: University Press.

Birdsall, J. Neville, and Robert W. Thomson, eds.
1963   *Biblical and Patristic Studies in Memory of Robert Pierce Casey.*
         Freiburg, Basel, and New York: Herder. [Several text-critical
         studies.]

Black, Matthew
1967   *An Aramaic Approach to the Gospels and Acts.* 3d ed. Oxford: Clarendon Press.
1974   "Notes on the Longer and Shorter Text of Acts." Pp. 119–31 in *On Language, Culture, and Religion in Honor of Eugene A. Nida.* Ed. M. Black and W. A. Smalley. The Hague and Paris: Mouton.
1981   "The Holy Spirit in the Western Text of Acts." Pp. 159–70 in Epp and Fee.

Black, Matthew, and Robert Davidson
1981   *Constantin von Tischendorf and the Greek New Testament.* Glasgow: University of Glasgow Press.

Blackman, Edwin Cyril
1948   *Marcion and His Influence.* London: SPCK.

Borse, Udo
1966   "Der Kolosserbrieftext des Pelagius." Inaugural diss., Bonn.

Bray, William D.
1959   *The Weekday Lessons from Luke in the Greek Gospel Lectionary.* Studies in the Lectionary Text of the Greek New Testament 2:5. Chicago: University of Chicago Press.

Brock, Sebastian
1981   "The Resolution of the Philoxenian/Harclean Problem." Pp. 325–43 in Epp and Fee.

Bruce, F. F.
1950   *The Books and the Parchments: Some Chapters on the Transmission of the Bible.* Westwood, NJ: Revell.

Buck, Harry Merwyn
1958   *The Johannine Lessons in the Greek Gospel Lectionary.* Studies in the Lectionary Text of the Greek New Testament 2:4. Chicago: University of Chicago Press.

Cavallo, Guglielmo
1967   *Ricerche sulla maiuscola biblica.* 2 vols. Studi e testi di papirologia 2. Florence: Le Monnier. [Includes 115 pls.]

Champlin, Russell
1966   *Family E and Its Allies in Matthew.* SD 28. Salt Lake City, UT: University of Utah Press.

Clark, Kenneth Willis
1956   "The Effect of Recent Textual Criticism upon New Testament Studies." Pp. 27–51 in *The Background of the New Testament and Its Eschatology.* Ed. W. D. Davies and D. Daube. Cambridge: University Press.
1962   "The Textual Criticism of the New Testament." Pp. 663–70 in *Peake's Commentary on the Bible.* Ed. M. Black and H. H. Rowley. London and New York: Thomas Nelson.
1980   *The Gentile Bias and Other Essays.* Selected by John L. Sharpe III. NovTSup 54. Leiden: Brill. [Many of his text-critical studies.]

Clemons, James T.
1968   *An Index of Syriac Manuscripts Containing the Epistles and the Apocalypse.* SD 33. Salt Lake City, UT: University of Utah Press.

Cocroft, Ronald E.
1968   *A Study of the Pauline Lessons in the Matthean Section of the Greek Lectionary.* SD 32. Salt Lake City, UT: University of Utah Press.

Colwell, Ernest C.
1967   "External Evidence and New Testament Criticism." Pp. 1–12 in Daniels and Suggs.
1969   *Studies in Methodology in Textual Criticism of the New Testament.* NTTS 9. Leiden: Brill. [Many of his text-critical studies.]

Colwell, Ernest C., Irving Alan Sparks, Frederik Wisse, and Paul R. McReynolds
1968   "The International Greek New Testament Project: A Status Report." *JBL* 87: 187–97.

Dain, A.
1964   *Les manuscrits.* Rev. ed. Collection d'études anciennes. Paris: Les Belles Lettres. [lst ed., 1949.]

Daniels, Boyd L., and M. Jack Suggs, eds.
1967   *Studies in the History and Text of the New Testament in Honor of Kenneth Willis Clark, Ph.D.* SD 29. Salt Lake City, UT: University of Utah Press. [Numerous text-critical studies.]

Darlow, T. H., and H. F. Moule
1903   *Historical Catalogue of the Printed Editions of Holy Scripture in the Library of the British and Foreign Bible Society.* 2 vols. in 4. London: Bible House.

Davies, Margaret
1968   *The Text of the Pauline Epistles in Manuscript 2344 and Its Relationship to the Text of Other Known Manuscripts, in Particular to 330, 436 and 462.* SD 38. Salt Lake City, UT: University of Utah Press.

Dearing, Vinton A.
1959   *A Manual of Textual Analysis.* Berkeley and Los Angeles: University of California Press.
1974   *Principles and Practice of Textual Analysis.* Berkeley, Los Angeles, and London: University of California Press.

Delebecque, Edouard
1980   "Les deux prologues des Actes des Apôtres." *RevThom* 80: 628–34.
1982a   "Ascension et Pentecôte dans les Actes des Apôtres selon le *codex Bezae*." *RevThom* 82: 79–89.
1982b   "De Lystres à Philippes (Ac 16) avec le *codex Bezae*." *Bib* 63: 395–405.
1982c   "Paul à Thessalonique et a Bérée selon le texte occidental des Actes (XVII, 4–15)." *RevThom* 82: 605–16.
1983   "Les deux versions du voyage de saint Paul de Corinthe à Troas (Ac 20,3–6)." *Bib* 64: 556–64.
1986   *Les deux Actes des Apôtres.* EBib ns 6. Paris: Gabalda.

Delobel, Joël
1985   "Luke 6,5 in Codex Bezae: The Man Who Worked on Sabbath." Pp. 453–77 in *À cause de l'évangile: Mélanges offerts à Dom Jacques Dupont.* LD 123. Paris: Cerf.

Duplacy, Jean
    1959   *Où en est la critique textuelle du Nouveau Testament?* Paris: Gabalda.
    1970   "Les lectionnaires et l'édition du Nouveau Testament grec."
            Pp. 509-45 in *Mélanges bibliques en hommage au R. P. Béda Rigaux.*
            Ed. A. Descamps and A. de Halleux. Gembloux: Duculot.
    1975   "Classification des états d'un texte, mathématiques et informatique:
            Repères historiques et recherches méthodologiques." *Revue d'His-*
            toire des Textes 5: 249-309. [With a bibliography from 1881 to 1974.]

Duplacy, Jean, and M. Jack Suggs
    1971   "Les citations grecques et la critique du textes du Nouveau Testa-
            ment: Le passé, le présent et l'avenir." Pp. 187-213 in Benoit and
            Prigent.

Ehrman, Bart D.
    1986   *Didymus the Blind and the Text of the Gospels.* SBL: New Testament
            in the Greek Fathers 1. Atlanta, GA: Scholars Press.

Eldridge, Lawrence Allen
    1969   *The Gospel Text of Epiphanius of Salamis.* SD 41. Salt Lake City, UT:
            University of Utah Press.

Elliott, J. Keith
    1968   *The Greek Text of the Epistles to Timothy and Titus.* SD 36. Salt Lake
            City, UT: University of Utah Press.
    1972   "Rational Criticism and the Text of the New Testament." *Theology*
            75: 338-43.
    1974   "Can We Recover the Original New Testament?" *Theology* 77: 338-
            53.
    1976, ed.   *Studies in New Testament Language and Text: Essays in Honour of*
            George D. Kilpatrick on the Occasion of His Sixty-fifth Birthday.
            NovTSup 44. Leiden: Brill. [Numerous text-critical studies.]
    1978   "In Defence of Thoroughgoing Eclecticism in New Testament Tex-
            tual Criticism." *Restoration Quarterly* 21: 95-115.
    1982   *Codex Sinaiticus and the Simonides Affair: Examination of the Nine-*
            teenth Century Claim that the Codex Sinaiticus Was Not an Ancient
            Manuscript. Analecta Vlatadon 33. Thessaloniki: Patriarchal Institute
            for Patristic Studies.
    1983a   "The International Project to Establish a Critical Apparatus to Luke's
            Gospel." *NTS* 29: 531-38.
    1983b   Review of Aland and Aland, 1982. In *TZ* 39: 247-49.

Ellis, Arthur A.
    1862   *Bentleii critica sacra: Notes on the Greek and Latin Text of the New*
            Testament, Extracted from the Bentley MSS. in Trinity College
            Library. Cambridge: Deighton, Bell.

Epp, Eldon Jay
    1966   *The Theological Tendency of Codex Bezae Cantabrigiensis in Acts.*
            SNTSMS 3. Cambridge and New York: Cambridge University Press.
    1967   "The Claremont Profile-Method for Grouping New Testament
            Minuscule Manuscripts." Pp. 27-38 in Daniels and Suggs.
    1974   "The Twentieth Century Interlude in New Testament Textual
            Criticism." *JBL* 93: 386-414.
    1976a   "The Eclectic Method in New Testament Textual Criticism: Solution
            or Symptom?" *HTR* 69: 211-57.

1976b   "Textual Criticism, NT." *IDBSup*, 891–95.

1976c   "Toward the Clarification of the Term 'Textual Variant.' " Pp. 153–73 in Elliott, 1976.

1979–84   Review of Aland, 1975–83. In *CBQ* 41 (1979) 148–51; 42 (1980) 258–61; 46 (1984) 778–80.

1980   "A Continuing Interlude in New Testament Textual Criticism." *HTR* 73: 144–50.

1981   "The Ascension in the Textual Tradition of Luke-Acts." Pp. 131–45 in Epp and Fee.

Epp, Eldon Jay, and Gordon D. Fee, eds.
1981   *New Testament Textual Criticism: Its Significance for Exegesis: Essays in Honour of Bruce M. Metzger.* Oxford: Clarendon Press. [Text-critical studies.]

Eshbaugh, Howard
1979   "Textual Variants and Theology: A Study of the Galatians Text of Papyrus 46." *JSNT* 3: 60–72.

Farmer, William R.
1974   *The Last Twelve Verses of Mark.* SNTSMS 25. Cambridge and New York: Cambridge University Press.

Fascher, Erich
1953   *Textgeschichte als hermeneutisches Problem.* Halle (Salle): Niemeyer.

Fee, Gordon D.
1968a   *Papyrus Bodmer II (P66): Its Textual Relationships and Scribal Characteristics.* SD 34. Salt Lake City, UT: University of Utah Press.

1968b   "Codex Sinaiticus in the Gospel of John: A Contribution to Methodology in Establishing Textual Relationships." *NTS* 15: 23–44.

1971a   "The Text of John in *The Jerusalem Bible*: A Critique of the Use of Patristic Citations in New Testament Textual Criticism." *JBL* 90: 163–73.

1971b   "The Text of John in Origen and Cyril of Alexandria: A Contribution to Methodology in the Recovery and Analysis of Patristic Citations." *Bib* 52: 357–94.

1974   "P75, P66, and Origen: The Myth of Early Textual Recension in Alexandria." Pp. 19–45 in *New Dimensions in New Testament Study.* Ed. R. N. Longenecker and M. C. Tenney. Grand Rapids: Zondervan.

1976   "Rigorous or Reasoned Eclecticism — Which?" Pp. 174–97 in Elliott, 1976.

1978   "The Textual Criticism of the New Testament." Pp. 127–55 in R. K. Harrison, B. K. Waltke, D. Guthrie, and G. D. Fee, *Biblical Criticism: Historical, Literary and Textual.* Grand Rapids: Zondervan.

Finegan, Jack
1974   *Encountering New Testament Manuscripts: A Working Introduction to Textual Criticism.* Grand Rapids: Eerdmans.

Fischer, Bonifatius
1985   *Lateinische Bibelhandschriften im frühen Mittelalter.* Vetus Latina: Aus der Geschichte der lateinischen Bibel 11. Freiburg: Herder.

Fitzmyer, Joseph A., S.J.
1976–85   Review of Aland, 1975–83. In *JBL* 95 (1976) 679–81; 97 (1978) 604–6; 100 (1981) 147–49; 102 (1983) 639–40; 104 (1985) 360–62.

Fox, Adam
 1954 *John Mill and Richard Bentley: A Study of the Textual Criticism of the New Testament 1675-1729.* Oxford: Blackwell.

Fox, Douglas J.
 1979 *The "Matthew-Luke Commentary" of Philoxenus: Text, Translation and Critical Analysis.* SBLDS 43. Missoula, MT: Scholars Press.

Frede, Hermann Josef
 1961 *Pelagius der irische Paulustext Sedulius Scottus.* Vetus Latina: Aus der Geschichte der lateinischen Bibel 3. Freiburg: Herder.
 1964 *Altlateinische Paulus-Handschriften.* Vetus Latina: Aus der Geschichte der lateinischen Bibel 4. Freiburg: Herder.
 1981 *Kirchenschriftsteller: Verzeichnis und Sigel.* 3d ed. Vetus Latina 1/1. Freiburg: Herder. [3d ed. of *Verzeichnis der Sigel für Kirchenschriftsteller* by Bonifatius Fischer, 1949, ²1963.]
 1984 *Kirchenschriftsteller: Aktualisierungsheft 1984.* Vetus Latina 1/1A. Freiburg: Herder.

Friedrichsen, G. W. S.
 1961 *Gothic Studies.* Medium Aevum Monographs 6. Oxford: Blackwell.

Froger, J.
 1968 *La critique des texts et son automatisation.* Initiation aux nouveautés de la science 7. Paris: Dunod.

Fuller, David Otis, ed.
 1972 *Which Bible?* 3d ed. Grand Rapids: Grand Rapids International Publications.
 1973 *True or False? The Westcott-Hort Textual Theory Examined.* Grand Rapids: Grand Rapids International Publications.
 1975 *Counterfeit or Genuine: Mark 16? John 8?.* Grand Rapids: Grand Rapids International Publications.

Gamble, Harry, Jr.
 1977 *The Textual History of the Letter to the Romans: A Study in Textual and Literary Criticism.* SD 42. Grand Rapids: Eerdmans.

Geerlings, Jacob
 1961a *Family 13—The Ferrar Group: The Text according to Matthew.* SD 19. Salt Lake City, UT: University of Utah Press.
 1961b *Family 13—The Ferrar Group: The Text according to Luke.* SD 20. Salt Lake City, UT: University of Utah Press.
 1962a *Family 13—The Ferrar Group: The Text according to John.* SD 21. Salt Lake City, UT: University of Utah Press.
 1962b *Family Π in Luke.* SD 22. Salt Lake City, UT: University of Utah Press.
 1963 *Family Π in John.* SD 23. Salt Lake City, UT: University of Utah Press.
 1964 *Family Π in Matthew.* SD 24. Salt Lake City, UT: University of Utah Press.
 1968a *Family E and Its Allies in Mark.* SD 31. Salt Lake City, UT: University of Utah Press.
 1968b *Family E and Its Allies in Luke.* SD 35. Salt Lake City, UT: University of Utah Press.

Globe, Alexander
 1980 "Some Doctrinal Variants in Matthew 1 and Luke 2, and the Authority of the Neutral Text." *CBQ* 42: 52–72.

Greenlee, J. Harold
1955　　*The Gospel Text of Cyril of Jerusalem.* SD 17. Copenhagen: Munksgaard.
1964　　*Introduction to New Testament Textual Criticism.* Grand Rapids: Eerdmans.

Greeven, Heinrich
1981　　*Synopse der drei ersten Evangelien mit Beigabe der johanneischen Parallelstellen/Synopsis of the First Three Gospels with the Addition of the Johannine Parallels.* 13th rev. ed. of Albert Huck, *Synopse.* Tübingen: Mohr-Siebeck.

Griffith, John G.
1969　　"Numerical Taxonomy and Some Primary Manuscripts of the Gospels." *JTS* 20: 389–406.
1973　　"The Interrelations of Some Primary MSS of the Gospels in the Light of Numerical Analysis." *SE* 6: 221–38.

Hammond Bammel, Caroline P.
1985　　*Der Römerbrieftext des Rufin und seine Origenes-Übersetzung.* Vetus Latina: Aus der Geschichte der lateinischen Bibel 10. Freiburg: Herder.

Harms, Ray
1966　　*The Matthean Weekday Lessons in the Greek Gospel Lectionary.* Studies in the Lectionary Text of the Greek New Testament 2:6. Chicago: University of Chicago Press.

Hatch, William Henry Paine
1951　　*Facsimiles and Descriptions of Minuscule Manuscripts of the New Testament.* Cambridge, MA: Harvard University Press.

Henss, Walter
1967　　*Das Verhältnis zwischen Diatessaron, christlicher Gnosis und "Western Text."* BZNW 33. Berlin: Töpelmann.

Hills, Edward F.
1973　　*The King James Version Defended! A Space-Age Defense of the Historic Christian Faith.* Des Moines, IA: Christian Research Press.

Hofmann, Josef, ed.
1969　　*Die äthiopische Johannes-Apokalypse kritisch untersucht.* CSCO 297, Subsidia 33. Louvain: CSCO.

Howard, Wilbert Francis
1949　　*The Romance of New Testament Scholarship.* London: Epworth.

Hug, Joseph
1978　　*La finale de l'evangile de Marc (Mc 16, 9–20).* EBib. Paris: Gabalda.

Hulley, K. K.
1944　　*Principles of Textual Criticism Known to St. Jerome.* Harvard Studies of Classical Philology 55. Cambridge, MA: Harvard University Press.

Hurtado, Larry W.
1981　　*Text-Critical Methodology and the Pre-Caesarean Text: Codex W in the Gospel of Mark.* SD 43. Grand Rapids: Eerdmans.

Hyatt, J. Philip
1965　　*The Bible in Modern Scholarship: Papers Read at the 100th Meeting of the Society of Biblical Literature, December 28–30, 1964.* Nashville and New York: Abingdon. [Several text-critical studies.]

Joussen, Anton
1969   *Die Koptischen Versionen der Apostelgeschichte (Kritik und Wertung).*
        BBB 34. Bonn: Peter Hanstein.

Junack, Klaus
1981   "Abschreibpraktiken und Schreibergewohnheiten in ihrer Auswir-
        kung auf die Textüberlieferung." Pp. 277–95 in Epp and Fee.

Kenyon, Frederic G.
1926   *Handbook to the Textual Criticism of the New Testament.* 2d ed. Lon-
        don: Macmillan.
1933   *Recent Developments in the Textual Criticism of the Greek Bible.*
        Schweich Lectures, 1932. London: British Academy.
1938–39 "The Text of the Greek New Testament." *ExpTim* 50: 68–71.
1958   *Our Bible and the Ancient Manuscripts.* Rev. by A. W. Adams. New
        York and Evanston, IL: Harper & Row.

Kerschensteiner, Josef
1970   *Der altsyrische Paulustext.* CSCO 315, Subsidia 37. Louvain: CSCO.

Kieffer, René
1968   *Au delà des recensions? L'evolution de la tradition textuelle dans Jean
        VI,52–71.* ConBNT 3. Lund: Gleerup.

Kilpatrick, George Dunbar
1943   "Western Text and Original Text in the Gospels and Acts." *JTS* 44:
        24–36.
1963a   "Atticism and the Text of the Greek New Testament." Pp. 125–37
        in *Neutestamentliche Aufsätze: Festschrift für Prof. Josef Schmid zum
        70. Geburtstag.* Ed. J. Blinzler, O. Kuss, and F. Mussner. Regensburg:
        Pustet.
1963b   "An Eclectic Study of the Text of Acts." Pp. 64–77 in Birdsall and
        Thomson.
1965   "The Greek New Testament Text of Today and the *Textus Receptus.*"
        Pp. 189–208 in *The New Testament in Historical and Contemporary
        Perspective: Essays in Memory of G. H. C. MacGregor.* Ed. H.
        Anderson and W. Barclay. Oxford: Blackwell.
1981   "Conjectural Emendation in the New Testament." Pp. 349–60 in Epp
        and Fee.

Klijn, A. F. J.
1949   *A Survey of the Researches into the Western Text of the Gospels and
        Acts.* Utrecht: Kemink.
1969   *A Survey of the Researches into the Western Text of the Gospels and
        Acts: Part Two 1949–1969.* NovTSup 21. Leiden: Brill.

Kubo, Sakae
1965   *P⁷² and the Codex Vaticanus.* SD 27. Salt Lake City, UT: University
        of Utah Press.

Kümmel, Werner Georg
1972   *The New Testament: The History of the Investigation of Its Problems.*
        Trans. S. McLean Gilmour and Howard C. Kee. Nashville and New
        York: Abingdon.

Kunst, Hermann, ed.
1985   *Bericht der Hermann Kunst-Stiftung zur Förderung die neutestament-
        lichen Textforschung für die Jahre 1982 bis 1984.* Ed. Hermann
        Kunst. Münster: Hermann Kunst-Stiftung.

Lagrange, M.-J.
1935   *Critique textuelle. II: La critique rationelle.* EBib. Paris: Gabalda.

Leloir, Louis
1953–54   *Saint Ephrem : Commentaire de l'Evangile concordant, version armé-
            nienne.* 2 vols. CSCO 137, 145, Scriptores armeniaci 1–2. Louvain:
            CSCO.
1958   *L'Evangile d'Ephrem d'après les oeuvres éditées: Recueil des textes.*
            CSCO 180, Subsidia 12. Louvain: CSCO.
1962   *Le Témoignage d'Ephrem sur le Diatessaron.* CSCO 227, Subsidia 19.
            Louvain: CSCO.
1967   *Citations du Nouveau Testament dans l'ancienne tradition arménienne.*
            2 vols. CSCO 283–84, Subsidia 31–32. Louvain: CSCO.

Lewis, Naphtali
1974   *Papyrus in Classical Antiquity.* Oxford: Clarendon Press.

Luck, Georg
1981   "Textual Criticism Today." *American Journal of Philology* 102:
            164–94.

Lyonnet, S., S.J.
1950   *Les origines de la version arménienne et le Diatessaron.* BibOr 13.
            Rome: Biblical Institute Press.

McReynolds, Paul R.
1979   "Establishing Text Families." Pp. 97–113 in O'Flaherty.

Martini, Carlo M.
1976   "Text, NT." *IDBSup,* 884–86.
1966   *Il problema della recensionalità del codice B alla luca del papiro
            Bodmer XIV.* AnBib 26. Rome: Biblical Institute Press.
1980   *La parola di Dio alle origini della Chiesa.* AnBib 93. Rome: Biblical
            Institute Press. [Numerous text-critical studies.]

Mees, Michael
1970   *Die Zitate aus dem Neuen Testament bei Clemons von Alexandrien.*
            Quaderni di "Vetera Christianorum" 2. Bari: Istituto di Letteratura
            Cristiana Antica.
1975   *Ausserkanonische Parallelstellen zu den Herrenworten und ihre
            Bedeutung.* Quaderni di "Vetera Christianorum" 10. Bari: Istituto di
            Letteratura Cristiana Antica.

Menoud, Philippe Henri
1951   "The Western Text and the Theology of Acts." In *Studiorum Novi
            Testamenti Societas, Bulletin* 2:19–32. Reprinted in *Bulletin of the
            Studiorum Novi Testamenti Societas* I–III. Cambridge: University
            Press, 1963. Also pp. 61–83 in Menoud, *Jesus Christ and the Faith:
            A Collection of Studies.* Trans. E. M. Paul. PTMS 18. Pittsburgh:
            Pickwick, 1978.

Messina, Giuseppe, S.J.
1951   *Diatessaron Persiano.* BibOr 14. Rome: Biblical Institute Press.

Metzger, Bruce M.
1955a   *Annotated Bibliography of the Textual Criticism of the New Testament
            1914–1939.* SD 16. Copenhagen: Munksgaard.
1955b   "A Survey of Recent Research on the Ancient Versions of the New
            Testament." *NTS* 2: 1–16.

1959   "Recent Discoveries and Investigations of New Testament Manu-
            scripts." *JBL* 78: 13–20.
1963   *Chapters in the History of New Testament Textual Criticism.* NTTS 4.
            Leiden: Brill. [Text-critical studies.]
1965   "Recent Contributions to the Study of the Ancient Versions of the
            New Testament." Pp. 347–69 in Hyatt.
1968a   *The Text of the New Testament: Its Transmission, Corruption, and
            Restoration.* 2d ed. Oxford and New York: Oxford University Press.
            German trans. of 1st ed. (1964) by Wolfram Lohse. Stuttgart:
            Kohlhammer, 1966.
1968b   *Historical and Literary Studies: Pagan, Jewish, and Christian.* NTTS
            8. Leiden: Brill. [Several text-critical studies.]
1977   *The Early Versions of the New Testament: Their Origin, Transmission,
            and Limitations.* Oxford: Clarendon Press.
1980   *New Testament Studies: Philological, Versional, and Patristic.* NTTS
            10. Leiden: Brill. [Numerous text-critical studies.]
1981   *Manuscripts of the Greek Bible: An Introduction to Greek Palaeog-
            raphy.* New York and Oxford: Oxford University Press.

Miller, Edward, ed.
1894   *A Plain Introduction to the Criticism of the New Testament,* by F. H. A.
            Scrivener. 4th ed. 2 vols. New York: Bell.

Moir, Ian A.
1981   "Can We Risk Another 'Textus Receptus'?" *JBL* 100: 614–18.

Molitor, Joseph
1965   *Synopsis latina evangeliorum Ibericorum antiquissimorum secundum
            Matthaeum, Marcum, Lucam desumpta e codicibus Adysh, Opiza,
            Tbeth necnon e fragmentis biblicis et patristicis quae dicuntur
            Chanmeti et Haemeti.* CSCO 256, Subsidia 24. Louvain: CSCO.
1968   *Grundbegriffe der Jesusüberlieferung im Lichte ihrer orientalischen
            Sprachgeschichte.* Kommentare und Beiträge zum Alten und Neuen
            Testament. Düsseldorf: Patmos.

Muncey, R. W.
1959   *The New Testament of Saint Ambrose.* TextsS 4. Cambridge: Univer-
            sity Press.

Nellessen, Ernst
1965   *Untersuchungen zur altlateinischen Überlieferung des ersten Thessalo-
            nicherbriefes.* BBB 22. Bonn: Peter Hanstein.

O'Callaghan, José, S.J.
1970   *"Nomina sacra" in papyris graecis saeculi III neotestamentariis.* AnBib
            46. Rome: Biblical Institute Press.

O'Flaherty, Wendy Doniger, ed.
1979   *The Critical Study of Sacred Texts.* Berkeley, CA: Berkeley Religious
            Studies Series. [Several text-critical studies.]

Oliver, Harold H.
1962   "Present Trends in the Textual Criticism of the New Testament." *JBR*
            30: 308–20.

Orchard, Bernard, and Thomas R. W. Longstaff, eds.
1978   *J. J. Griesbach: Synoptic and Text-Critical Studies 1776–1976.*
            SNTSMS 34. Cambridge and New York: Cambridge University Press.
            [Two text-critical studies.]

Ortiz de Urbina, Ignatius, S.J., ed.
1967   *Vetus Evangeliorum Syrorum et exinde excerptum Diatessaron Tatiani.* Biblia Polyglotta Matritensia, 6. Madrid: Consejo superior de investigaciones científicas.

Palmer, Humphrey
1968   *The Logic of Gospel Criticism: An Account of the Methods and Arguments Used by Textual, Documentary, Source, and Form Critics of the New Testament.* London: Macmillan; New York: St. Martin's Press. Pp. 55–111 on text-criticism.

Parvis, Merrill M.
1947   "New Testament Criticism in the World-Wars Period." Pp. 52–73 in *The Study of the Bible Today and Tomorrow.* Ed. H. R. Willoughby. Chicago: University of Chicago Press.
1950   "The International Project to Establish a New Critical Apparatus of the Greek New Testament." *Crozer Quarterly* 27: 301–8.
1962   "Text, NT." *IDB* 4. 594–614.

Parvis, Merrill M., and Allen P. Wikgren, eds.
1950   *New Testament Manuscript Studies: The Materials and the Making of a Critical Apparatus.* Chicago: University of Chicago Press. [Text-critical studies.]

Pervo, Richard I.
1985   "Social and Religious Aspects of the 'Western' Text." Pp. 229–41 in *The Living Text: Essays in Honor of Ernest W. Saunders.* Ed. D. E. Groh and R. Jewett. Lanham, New York, and London: University Press of America.

Petersen, William Lawrence
1985   *The Diatessaron and Ephrem Syrus as Sources of Romanos the Melodist.* CSCO 475, Subsidia 74. Louvain: CSCO and Peeters.

Pickering, Wilbur N.
1977   *The Identity of the New Testament Text.* Nashville and New York: Thomas Nelson.

Quispel, Gilles
1975   *Tatian and the Gospel of Thomas: Studies in the History of the Western Diatessaron.* Leiden: Brill.

Reuss, Joseph
1957   *Matthäus-Kommentare aus der griechischen Kirche aus Katenenhand-schriften.* TU 61. Berlin: Akademie-Verlag.
1966   *Johannes-Kommentare aus der griechischen Kirche aus Katenenhand-schriften.* TU 89. Berlin: Akademie-Verlag.
1984   *Lukas-Kommentare aus der griechischen Kirche aus Katenenhand-schriften.* TU 130. Berlin: Akademie-Verlag.

Rhodes, Erroll F.
1959   *An Annotated List of Armenian New Testament Manuscripts.* Annual Report of Theology, Monograph Series, 1. Tokyo: Rikkyo (St. Paul's) University.
1981   "Conjectural Emendations in Modern Translations." Pp. 361–74 in Epp and Fee.

Rice, George E.
1980a   "The Anti-Judaic Bias of the Western Text in the Gospel of Luke."
          AUSS 18: 51–57.
1980b   "Some Further Examples of Anti-Judaic Bias in the Western Text of
          the Gospel of Luke." *AUSS* 18: 149–56.
1984   "Western Non-Interpolations: A Defense of the Apostolate." Pp. 1–16
          in *Luke-Acts: New Perspectives from the Society of Biblical Literature
          Seminar*. Ed. C. H. Talbert. New York: Crossroad.
1985   "Is Bezae a Homogeneous Codex?" Pp. 39–54 in *Perspectives on the
          New Testament: Essays in Honor of Frank Stagg*. Ed. C. H. Talbert.
          Macon, GA: Mercer University Press.

Richards, William Larry
1974   "Textual Criticism on the Greek Text of the Catholic Epistles: A
          Bibliography." *AUSS* 12: 103–11.
1977a   *The Classification of the Greek Manuscripts of the Johannine Epistles*.
          SBLDS 35. Missoula, MT: Scholars Press.
1977b   "A Critique of a New Testament Text-Critical Methodology—The
          Claremont Profile Method." *JBL* 96: 555–66.
1979   "Manuscript Grouping in Luke 10 by Quantitative Analysis." *JBL* 98:
          379–91.
1980   "An Examination of the Claremont Profile Method in the Gospel of
          Luke: A Study in Text-Critical Methodology." *NTS* 27: 52–63.

Roberts, Colin H.
1979   *Manuscript, Society and Belief in Early Christian Egypt*. Schweich
          Lectures, 1977. London: Oxford University Press.
1956   *Greek Literary Hands 350 B.C. – A.D. 400*. Oxford: Clarendon Press.

Roberts, Colin H., and T. C. Skeat
1983   *The Birth of the Codex*. London: Oxford University Press.

Robinson, James M., et al.
1970   "The Institute for Antiquity and Christianity: International Greek
          New Testament Project." *NTS* 16: 180–82.

Royse, James R.
1979   "Scribal Habits in the Transmission of New Testament Texts."
          Pp. 139–61 in O'Flaherty.

Sacchi, Paolo
1956   *Alle origini del Nuovo Testamento: Saggio per la storia della tradizione
          e la critica del testo*. Pubblicazioni della Università degli studi di
          Firenze Facoltà di Lettere e Filosofia 4 ser.: 2. Florence: Felice Le
          Monnier.

Salmon, Victor
1976   *The Fourth Gospel: A History of the Textual Tradition of the Original
          Greek Gospel*. Trans. M. J. O'Connell. Collegeville, MN: Liturgical
          Press. French orig., 1969.

Sanders, E. P.
1969   *The Tendencies of the Synoptic Tradition*. SNTSMS 9. Cambridge and
          New York: Cambridge University Press.

Schmid, Josef
1955–56   *Studien zur Geschichte des griechischen Apokalypse-Textes*. Mün-
          chener Theologische Studien, Historische Abteilung 1. Ergänzungs-
          band. 3 vols. Munich: Karl Zink.

Strothmann, Werner
1971   *Das Wolfenbütteler Tetraevangelium syriacum: Lesarten und Lesungen.* Göttinger Orientforschungen 1st series: Syriaca 2. Wiesbaden: Harrassowitz.

Strugnell, John
1974   "A Plea for Conjectural Emendation in the New Testament, with a Coda on 1 Cor 4:6." *CBQ* 36: 543–58.

Suggs, M. Jack
1958   "The Use of Patristic Evidence in the Search for a Primitive New Testament Text." *NTS* 4: 139–47.

Taylor, Vincent
1963   *The Text of the New Testament: A Short Introduction.* 2d ed. London: Macmillan; New York: St. Martin's Press.

Thiele, Walter
1965   *Die lateinischen Texte des 1. Petrusbriefes.* Vetus Latina: Aus der Geschichte der lateinischen Bibel 5. Freiburg: Herder.

Timpanaro, Sebastiano
1963   *La genesi del metodo del Lachmann.* Bibliotechina del saggiatore 18. Florence: Felice Le Monnier. German ed, trans. D. Irmer: *Die Enstehung der Lachmannschen Methode.* 2d rev. ed., Hamburg: Helmut Buske, 1971.

Tinnefeld, Franz Hermann
1963   *Untersuchungen zur altlateinischen Überlieferung des 1. Timotheusbriefes.* Klassisch-philologische Studien 26. Wiesbaden: Harrassowitz.

Tregelles, Samuel P.
1854   *An Account of the Printed Text of the Greek New Testament.* London: Bagster.

Treu, Kurt
1966   *Die griechischen Handschriften des Neuen Testaments in der UdSSR.* TU 91. Berlin: Akademie-Verlag.

Turner, C. H.
1923–28 "Marcan Usage: Notes, Critical and Exegetical on the Second Gospel." *JTS* 25 (1923–24) 377–86; 26 (1924–25) 12–20, 145–56, 225–40, 337–46; 27 (1925–26) 58–62; 28 (1926–27) 9–30, 349–62; 29 (1927–28) 275–89, 346–61.

Turner, Eric G.
1968   *Greek Papyri: An Introduction.* Oxford: Clarendon Press.
1971   *Greek Manuscripts of the Ancient World.* Oxford: Clarendon Press.
1973   *The Papyrologist at Work.* J. H. Gray Lectures, University of Cambridge, 1971. Greek, Roman and Byzantine Monograph 6. Durham, NC: Duke University Press.
1977   *The Typology of the Early Codex.* Haney Foundation Series 18. Philadelphia: University of Pennsylvania Press.

Vincent, Marvin R.
1903   *A History of the Textual Criticism of the New Testament.* New Testament Handbooks. New York: Macmillan.

Vogels, Heinrich Joseph
1955a   *Handbuch der Textkritik des Neuen Testaments.* 2d ed. Bonn: Peter Hanstein.

1955b   Untersuchungen zum Text paulinischer Briefe bei Rufin und Ambro-
         siaster. BBB 9. Bonn: Peter Hanstein.
1957, ed. Das Corpus Paulinum des Ambrosiaster. BBB 13. Bonn: Peter
         Hanstein.

Voicu, Sever J., and Serenella D'Alisera
1981   I.MA.G.E.S.: Index in manuscriptorum graecorum edita specimina.
         Rome: Borla.

Vööbus, Arthur
1948   Researches on the Circulation of the Peshitta in the Middle of the Fifth
         Century. Contributions of Baltic University 64. Pinneburg: Baltic
         University.
1951a   Neue Angaben über die textgeschichtlichen Zustände in Edessa in den
         Jahren ca 326–340: Eine Beitrag zur Geschichte des altsyrischen
         Tetraevangeliums. Papers of the Estonian Theological Society in
         Exile 3. Stockholm: n.p.
1951b   Die Spuren eines älteren äthiopischen Evangelientextes im Lichte der
         literarischen Monumente. Papers of the Estonian Theological Society
         in Exile 2. Stockholm: n.p.
1951c   Studies in the History of the Gospel Text in Syriac. CSCO 128,
         Subsidia 3. Louvain: Durbecq.
1953   Zur Geschichte des altgeorgischen Evangelientextes. Papers of the
         Estonian Theological Society in Exile 4. Stockholm: n.p.
1954   Early Versions of the New Testament: Manuscript Studies. Papers of
         the Estonian Theological Society in Exile 6. Stockholm: n.p.

Wikenhauser, Alfred, and Josef Schmid
1973   Einleitung in das Neuen Testament. 6th ed. Freiburg, Basel, and
         Vienna: Herder. "Der Text des Neuen Testaments," pp. 65–186.

Wilcox, Max
1965   The Semitisms of Acts. Oxford: Clarendon Press.

Williams, C. S. C.
1951   Alterations to the Text of the Synoptic Gospels and Acts. Oxford:
         Blackwell.

Wisse, Frederik
1982   The Profile Method for the Classification and Evaluation of Manuscript
         Evidence as Applied to the Continuous Greek Text of the Gospel of
         Luke. SD 44. Grand Rapids: Eerdmans.

Wisse, Frederik, and Paul R. McReynolds
1970   "Family E and the Profile Method." Bib 51: 67–75.

Witherington, Ben
1984   "The Anti-Feminist Tendencies of the 'Western' Text in Acts." JBL
         103: 82–84.

Wright, Leon E.
1952   Alterations of the Words of Jesus as Quoted in the Literature of the
         Second Century. Harvard Historical Monographs 25. Cambridge,
         MA: Harvard University Press.

Yoder, James D.
1961   Concordance to the Distinctive Greek Text of Codex Bezae. NTTS 2.
         Leiden: Brill.

Zaphiris, Gérassime
    1970   *Le texte de l'Evangile selon saint Matthieu d'après les citations de Clément d'Alexandrie comparées aux citations des Pères et des Théologiens grecs du IIe au XVe siecle.* Gembloux: Duculot.

Zimmermann, Heinrich
    1960   *Untersuchungen zur Geschichte der altlateinischen Überlieferung des zweiten Korintherbriefes.* BBB 16. Bonn: Peter Hanstein.

Zuntz, Gunther
    1945   *The Ancestry of the Harklean New Testament.* British Academy Supplemental Papers 7. London: Oxford University Press.
    1953   *The Text of the Epistles: A Disquisition upon the Corpus Paulinum.* Schweich Lectures, 1946. London: British Academy.

5

PHILOLOGY

Schuyler Brown

I. THE PROBLEM OF DEFINITION

The word "philology" has been used both for the scientific study of literature (*Literaturwissenschaft*) and for the scientific study of language (*Sprachwissenschaft*). The former understanding of the word was prevalent in the eighteenth century; the latter in the nineteenth (Albright: 42). Philology in the eighteenth-century sense is the subject of all the contributions to this volume, and we must therefore take our task to be the narrower one of treating the major issues raised by the scientific study of language, as they relate to the interpretation of the NT. Our *terminus a quo* will be the year 1946, which marked the *terminus ad quem* of our earlier survey (Brown, 1964:334).

Understood in the narrower sense, philology might appear to be synonymous with linguistics. The distinction mentioned in the previous paragraph would then coincide with F. de Saussure's distinction between *parole* and *langue*. *Langue*, the subject matter of linguistics, is a supra-individual system or institution, consisting of interpersonal rules and norms of communication. *Parole* is the manifestation of this system of linguistic competence in speech and writing. Greek and Semitic philology, the two main areas to be surveyed here, could then be regarded as falling under the heading of "historical linguistics," which deals with language diachronically, that is, with reference to the changes that language undergoes in time.

But, if the subject matter of philology and linguistics appears to be the same (language/*langue*), the different designations betray a significant difference in approach. The concern for language as system directs the linguist first of all to *spoken* language. Only with the help of a native speaker can the linguist describe the internal structure of a language with such comprehensiveness as to explain every *possible* linguistic phenomenon. In contrast, the glimpse of linguistic structure afforded solely by literary remains is necessarily fragmentary and incomplete.

On the other hand, the use of the same word, "philology," to designate both *Literaturwissenschaft* and *Sprachwissenschaft* reflects the fact that philology in the narrow sense derives not from the study of spoken language (in our case, Modern Greek, Modern Hebrew, and Modern Aramaic) but from the study of literary remains (the NT, together with Greek and Semitic documents considered relevant for linguistic comparison).

Nor does the distinction between synchronic and diachronic approaches to language correspond to the distinction between the study of spoken language as system and the study of language through literary remains. Although the diachronic approach, by definition, has no application to the study of spoken language, it *is* possible to apply synchronic description to ancient literary texts (Sawyer: 60–88), as well as to contemporary speech.

Furthermore, the linguist gives a priority to the synchronic approach that the philologist may be reluctant to accept. Some linguists go so far as to state that the synchronic approach is the *only* one congenial to the subject matter, since only synchronic linguistics deals with language *systems* (Ullmann: 142). But the limitation of the diachronic approach, which can deal only with *elements* of language, may not be felt so acutely by the philologist, whose primary interest is literature. It is possible, with only a very fragmentary knowledge of the *system* of an ancient language, to attain the surface meaning of its literary remains, and this, after all, is the philologist's purpose. For philology in the narrow sense is ordered to philology in the broad sense, just as linguistics is ordered to anthropology and translation science.

The sort of linguistic description that may seem entirely adequate for purposes of translating ancient texts may be totally inadequate for the linguist, whereas the subordinate role of historical linguistics may be problematic for the philologist, who is interested in literary remains from various historical periods. The use of etymology, for example, is often the only means of recovering the lost meaning of a word not sufficiently attested to make possible a synchronic description. But when biblical scholars, whose primary training is in theology, make use of etymological interpretations, the door is opened for forcing upon the lexical stock of biblical Hebrew and NT Greek theological nuances which cannot be verified by sound linguistic method.

Philology and linguistics are therefore not only distinct but also in tension. This fact reflects the altered position of philology in biblical studies today, contrasted with thirty years ago. First of all, decreasing standards in secondary and university schooling in languages generally and a decline in interest in ancient languages in particular have contributed to a decrease in purely philological research. But the present uncertainty concerning the role of philology in biblical studies derives more fundamentally from the fact that many people today are questioning whether the historical-critical method, of which philology is the heart, is really the most appropriate method for studying the Bible (Stuhlmacher).

II. THE LIMITATIONS OF PHILOLOGY
AS *SPRACHWISSENSCHAFT*

Undoubtedly the most imposing single accomplishment in NT philology since World War II has been the completion of Gerhard Kittel's

Theologisches Wörterbuch zum Neuen Testament and its translation into English. This monumental work is a gold mine of information and will remain an indispensable tool for students of the NT for the foreseeable future. Nevertheless, the criticism of the dictionary's methodology (Barr, 1961:206–62) exemplifies the problematical relationship between philology as *Literaturwissenschaft*, philology as *Sprachwissenschaft* (study of the elements of language), and linguistics (study of language as system).

The basic criticism of Kittel's dictionary is that a study of the lexical stock of NT Greek is not a suitable way to expound the religious thought of the NT authors. For it is not possible to establish anything more than a haphazard connection between the Greek words used in the NT and the distinctive features of NT thought. The lexical stock in the NT is not, on the whole, *proper* to the NT. Some Greek words are found only in Christian writers or have become so specialized in Christian usage that they are virtually technical terms. But most Greek words used in the NT acquire theological significance only from the context in which they occur. For example, "the Spirit of God" and "the Holy Spirit" are important concepts in NT thought. But the Greek word *pneuma* is not distinctive or theologically significant in many of its uses: as physical event ("wind"), physiological event ("breath"), "spirit of a person," or "evil spirit." For the most part, the lexical stock of the NT acquires theological significance only from the context in which it occurs. In other words, the very notion of a "theological dictionary" that is not limited to technical theological vocabulary is highly questionable.

The prospectus for the forthcoming *Exegetisches Wörterbuch zum Neuen Testament,* while acknowledging a debt to Kittel (*"EWNT* steht in der Tradition der weltweit verbreiteten und anerkannten *ThWNT"*), declares that "the main emphasis [of the new work] lies in understanding the individual word *in the textual context"* (emphasis added). Nevertheless, the attempt to cast light on NT theology through word studies still goes on. In such studies the underlying assumption is that in each word there is a hard core of meaning that is relatively stable and can only be modified by the text within certain limits. Such an assumption runs counter to the fundamental insight of modern linguistics that linguistic signifiers are purely differential, that is, they do not correspond to ideas given in advance, nor do they have any positive content. They are defined only negatively by their relations with other signifiers within the system (Saussure: 117). The word-study approach to NT theology not only illustrates a confusion between philology as *Sprachwissenschaft* and philology as *Literaturwissenschaft*; it also illustrates the conflict between two approaches to language, one of which focuses on elements of language (in this case, vocabulary) while the other studies language as system.

The criticism of Kittel's attempt to illuminate NT theology by the study of words extends to *any* attempt to establish a connection between linguistic signs, of which words are but one example, and NT thought. The differential nature of linguistic units ("brown" is what is not "red," "black," "grey," "yellow," etc.) applies to the whole of language, which is an arbitrary system of semantic signs. Any attempt to establish a direct connection between language and thought founders on the obvious fact that the same language can be used to express diametrically opposed views. The historical accident that the literary remains of ancient Hebrew come from worshipers of Yahweh rather than of Baal should not mislead us into seeking connections between the Hebrew language and biblical theology. Thought is revealed in the particular, contingent utterance of an individual (*parole*), not in the system of semantic signs that the individual uses to make it (*langue*). As the scholastic adage puts it, truth is in the judgment.

III. THE PROBLEM OF NEW TESTAMENT GREEK

The proper task of philology (*Sprachwissenschaft*) is to describe and classify the language of the NT. It is not always clear in the discussion of NT Greek whether "language" is being understood as spoken language, written language, or both. This ambiguity is evident in the common characterization of NT Greek as *Volkssprache* (Schmid and Wikenhauser: 187), a term whose precise meaning was already queried by L. Radermacher (6).

Obviously, changes in spoken language are reflected in literary documents, and the study of the orthography of the papyri of the Roman and Byzantine periods (Gignac: 1977) contributes greatly to our knowledge of the historical development of Greek phonology. However, in modern language, where it is possible to compare the written and spoken forms, the relationship between the two appears to be quite complex (Gleason: 437). Therefore, inferences concerning the language spoken by the NT authors are bound to be hypothetical, particularly since the linguistic features of a particular author may be the result of a number of factors, of which the author's spoken Greek is only one.

Therefore, despite the undeniable interconnection between written and spoken language, there is an advantage in defining "the language of the NT" as the system or systems of written signs in terms of which the NT books have meaning. If this is done, then the frequent practice of referring to the Greek of a particular NT author as "good" or "bad" is quite meaningless. If the Greek of Mark's Gospel is understood to be a semantic system, then it could be called "bad" only if it failed to communicate meaning.

Of course, value judgments on the Greek of NT authors usually imply a comparison with other Greek writers. When opponents of Christianity such as Celsus, Porphyry, and Julian make the language of the NT an object of polemic, their criticism seems to be based on a comparison with the fashionable Atticism of the day (Schmid and Wikenhauser: 188). Today the question of what kind of Greek literature is most appropriate for purposes of comparison is very much a live issue. It is now generally agreed that only writings that are roughly contemporaneous may be used. The comparison of a NT book with works of classical or modern Greek is methodologically invalid. But this still leaves a vast amount of material from which to choose.

For A. Deissmann the nonliterary papyri served as the basis for comparison, and the similarity between these documents and the language of the NT led him to the conclusion that NT Greek was the common daily speech of the mass of the people in the late Hellenistic period. BAG suggest in addition "a number of authors who were more or less able to avoid the spell of antiquarianism which we know as 'Atticism'" (x). L. Rydbeck (1967) has called our attention to popular philosophic literature and technical writings (*Fachprosa*), such as the Corpus Hippocraticum.

This last suggestion serves to remind us of the influence of genre on written language. Origen explained the language of the NT by the fact that Jesus chose simple, uneducated men to be his disciples (*Contra Celsum* 1.62), but, quite apart from his presumption of apostolic authorship, such an inference from written language to the social and educational level of the author is hazardous. A writer's language depends not only on the writer's education but also on the kind of audience that is being addressed and the kind of work that the author wishes to write. In Luke-Acts we see an author deliberately varying his language in different parts of the same work in order to achieve a literary effect.

The description of NT Greek should restrict itself to the linguistic phenomena and avoid the use of terms that imply a causal explanation for these phenomena. This descriptive task has the best chance for success if it focuses on individual books or authors, for the NT is a collection of quite different kinds of writings. If we grant the haphazard correspondence between language and thought, we cannot assume that the common concern of all NT authors for Jesus Christ has produced a unity on the strictly linguistic level.

It is significant that the fourth and final volume of J. H. Moulton's *Grammar of New Testament Greek* (Turner, 1976b) is devoted to style. For style is something personal and individual ("le style c'est l'homme") that emerges from "a contrasting of linguistic facts among various authors" (1). But stylistic analysis must also include a contrasting of linguistic facts within the same work or corpus, since an author may sacrifice his individual style either in order to incorporate earlier materials, with their own stylistic characteristics, or as an exercise of *imitatio* ("imitation"), which was such a prevalent feature of Greek and Roman literature in the first century C.E. (Brown, 1974).

An author's style includes not only syntax, the subject of Turner's earlier volume (1963), but also the author's preferences in the choice of words and in the use of forms. Even if we exclude elements of literary style, such as the patterns revealed by architecture analysis (Talbert), the question of linguistic style is extremely comprehensive: out of the total linguistic inventory of Hellenistic Greek—that is, the available linguistic units and the possible morphological and syntactical combinations—which linguistic units and which rules for combining them does a particular author employ, and with what regularity?

From a linguistic point of view, it is disputed whether style belongs to *parole* or to *langue*. According to one of Saussure's criteria—the distinction between "social" and "individual"—style, as something individual, would come under *parole* and therefore would not be the concern of linguistics. However, style may be contrasted with its concrete manifestation in writing; that is, it may be defined as an individual author's literary competence, as distinct from literary production. In terms of such a distinction, style would belong to *langue*. L. Hjelmslev has, in fact, replaced Saussure's twofold distinction with a fourfold one: schema, norm, usage, and *parole* (Culler, 1976:81). "Usage" corresponds to style, since it is the statistically regular exercise of individual freedom in the use of linguistic elements, within the limitations determined by "norm."

It is not easy at present to define these limitations precisely, since a comprehensive grammar of Hellenistic Greek has yet to be written. Nevertheless, though the last thirty-five years have produced nothing to compare, in its impact on Greek philology, with the discovery of the papyri in the earlier part of the century, there are, nonetheless, a number of scholarly projects that are steadily advancing our knowledge of Koine Greek. Of particular importance for our subject are the studies in Jewish Greek literature (Septuagint, intertestamental apocrypha, and Josephus) and the Corpus Hellenisticum project. The study of Greco-Roman religious texts will not only help free NT studies from parochialism but will also serve, through increased cooperation between NT and classics scholars, to integrate "NT philology" into the scientific study of the Greek language during the Greco-Roman period.

Just as the stylistic analysis of NT Greek is best done in terms of individual authors, so too the comparison of these authors, whether among themselves or with other Hellenistic writers, should be carried out on a one-to-one basis. Since the nonliterary papyri exhibit as much stylistic diversity as the books of the NT, general statements about the relationship of NT Greek to the rest of Koine are suspect as long as they fail to provide the necessary statistical data.

N. Turner concludes his book on style with this statement: "The range of NT styles, in fact, is too extensive for their classification together as one category of contemporary Greek, while their varying distinction from all contemporary styles is too great to be passed over" (1976b:159). The first part of this sentence is demonstrated by the book itself, but the very fact that the index of textual references is limited to the NT makes one wonder about the latter part of the assertion.

Can it be demonstrated that, when allowance is made for the common use of specialized theological vocabulary, NT writings as stylistically diverse as Hebrews and Revelation are more similar to each other than either one of them is to any other contemporary Greek document? When Turner relates "the remarkable unity" of biblical Greek to its "strongly Semitic character" and to "the old question of a 'Holy Ghost language' " (1963:9), it is hard to avoid the suspicion that the distinctiveness of the language of the NT may be only a theologoumenon.

Indeed, it is hardly to be expected that writings ranging from 50 C.E. (1 Thessalonians) to 130 C.E. (2 Peter) and coming from an indeterminately broad geographical area will manifest a stylistic homogeneity that separates them from all other writings of the period. At the present time "NT Greek" must be understood as a *Sammelbegriff* ("collective term"), not as a single linguistic system, and still less as a "dialect" of Koine Greek.

IV. THE DIACHRONIC PERSPECTIVE

The historical development of the Greek language is marked not only by orthographic changes, reflecting changes in pronunciation, but also by changes in morphology, syntax, and vocabulary. When a linguistic phenomenon is comparatively rare in the Greek literature of the period, and when it has an analogy in another language that the writer is thought to have spoken, then bilingual interference may be inferred to have reinforced, at least, a tendency within the Greek language itself.

Instances of such bilingual interference in the NT are called "Semitisms." They are not "un-Greek elements" (Rehkopf: 4). Indeed, they are not observable linguistic elements of any one language. The ambiguity of the term "Semitisms" enables it to cover linguistic phenomena in Greek that could have been caused by either Hebrew or Aramaic (the two Semitic languages whose influence is suspected), since both have analogies to the Greek phenomena in question. Such bilingual interference is proved only when the Greek phenomenon is truly rare in the language of the period. Therefore, the study of this question requires not only a knowledge of NT Greek and of the Semitic languages involved but also a firm grounding in the language of the "control literature."

K. Beyer asserts that the frequency of the conditional relative clause in the Gospels and Johannine epistles is certainly caused by Semitic influence (145). But in Mark's Gospel, which, after Matthew, shows the greatest frequency of this construction, we find twenty-eight instances (Beyer: 230), compared with ten indefinite conditional clauses. A simple count of the same two types of clauses in the first two books of Epictetus shows twenty-six conditional relative clauses and ten indefinite clauses (Maloney: 99–104). These statistics do not support Beyer's assertion.

If bilingual interference in a NT book can be proved, then this finding may cast light on problems of text composition, authorship, or date and place of origin (Mussies: 350–52). However, the causes of linguistic phenomena pertain to the diachronic study of language and are therefore irrelevant to the synchronic task of reconstructing the system as a functional whole (Culler, 1975:12).

The evidence for bilingual interference usually does not permit us to determine whether the writer's peculiar Greek is the result of dependence on a non-Greek source or simply the consequence of the unconscious influence of his mother tongue. However, there is one written source which, beyond all question, has influenced the language of the NT, and that is the Greek Bible. Its influence is seen not only in "Septuagintisms" (constructions which, because they use elements of Hebrew grammar incorrectly, cannot be Hebraisms [Beyer: 11]) but also in the use of Greek vocabulary to express religious conceptions of the OT (Hill).

Here again we must be careful not to confuse the diachronic and synchronic perspectives of language study. The origin of a vocabulary item does not determine its meaning. Readers of the Septuagint, if they knew no Hebrew, would perceive that a particular Greek word was being used in a new and unusual way only if this was made clear by the Greek text. Consequently, the Hebrew Bible, particularly as interpreted by modern scholars, does not determine the meaning of Septuagintal vocabulary in the NT. We must look both to the literary context in which these words appear and to their paradigmatic and syntagmatic relations with the inventory of Hellenistic Greek. These relations, of course, are themselves affected by the Septuagintal and NT usages of the words in question.

The distinction between diachronic and synchronic perspectives has a definite bearing on NT interpretation. Even if one could accept the hazardous generalization that "the NT was not written by Greeks but by Jews, whose native idiom interfered with their Greek extensively," would it follow that therefore "NT Greek . . . must be read in light of Semitic language patterns" (Gignac, 1973:171)?

When we attempt to communicate with foreigners, we use our knowledge of their native idioms to guess at the meaning of their curious English. But is this procedure appropriate in interpreting written documents? Particularly when the writer is no longer available for consultation, the practice of reading the work in the light of something that is not in it makes interpretation a subjective act. It is precisely in reaction to such subjectivism that semiotic analysis relies on the semantic organization that is immanent in the text (Aletti: 199).

An illustration of this problem is found in the current debate over "the Son of man" in the NT. Granting G. Vermes's attractive suggestion that *bar (e)nasha* is an Aramaic form of veiled self-designation, must we accept his conclusion that the bottom falls out of the titular interpretation of ὁ υἱὸς τοῦ ἀνθρώπου? Precisely *because* the latter is an obscure expression, which Hellenistic Greek fails to clarify, one would expect a Greek reader to understand it as a *Hoheitstitel* ("title of sovereignty/majesty") when it is used of someone "sitting at the right hand of Power and coming with the clouds of heaven" (Mark 14:62 par.).

V. THE PALESTINIAN TARGUMS, QUMRAN, AND THE LANGUAGE OF THE NEW TESTAMENT

Most of the recent literature on the languages spoken in the Near East during the first century C.E. concentrates on Palestine. And yet there is scarcely a book in the NT that is likely to have been written in Palestine, and evidence for bilingual interference will hardly ever pinpoint the precise geographical area where the language responsible for the Semitic interference would have been spoken.

The emphasis on Palestine is explained by the special interest in Jesus' homeland and in Jerusalem as the center of the earliest Christian community. But this emphasis also reflects the growing importance for NT interpretation of the Palestinian targums, which may contain an exegetical tradition held in common by Jews and Christians (Wilcox: 1979).

The date of the Palestinian targums is a subject of much recent debate. M. McNamara's arguments for a pre-Christian dating of Codex *Neofiti* are based on matters of content, such as the nature of the paraphrase, the geographical terms used, and the form of the halakah (1972: 86–88). J. A. Fitzmyer appeals mainly to linguistic considerations in support of his view that Qumran Aramaic "should certainly be used in preference to the later form of the language that is found in the targums for the study of New Testament and its Aramaic background" (1971b:25).

The linguistic evidence is complex and cannot be summarized here. As far as orthography, phonetics, and syntax are concerned, the antiquity of the Qumran manuscripts is certainly a factor in considering them to be a more reliable representative of the literary language of the first century C.E. (Delcor: 254). However, A. Díez Macho distinguishes between the "literary" language of Qumran and the "spoken Aramaic" reflected in the Palestinian targums, which he considers to have existed simultaneously (1973:189). He therefore rejects Fitzmyer's distinction between the "middle Aramaic" of Qumran and the "late Aramaic" of the targums as "a simplistic diachronic presentation which does not seem to take sufficient account of the arguments in favor of the synchronic solution of the problem" (1973:180–81). Fitzmyer replies that "until we get real evidence about the form of the spoken Aramaic of the first century—which is presently more postulated than attested—this mode of argument is wistful" (1975:87). Indeed such an appeal to the influence of *Volkssprache* ("vernacular language") on the targums is similar to the theory that the language of the Septuagint has its origin in a Jewish Greek used in religious circles (Hill: 17), or to the contention that the matrix of NT Greek is the language of the Greek-speaking synagogue (Black, 1965–66:23). In all three cases the influence of an extinct dialect is postulated to account for the phenomena of written language.

Unfortunately, "the Aramaic background of the NT" is an ambiguous expression. It could refer to Aramaic writings that cast light on the exegetical methods found in the NT. This concerns the executive side of language (*parole*), where strictly linguistic distinctions (*langue*) are not necessarily determinative. Documents written in a later stage of a language can contain early material.

Even if we restrict our consideration to the purely philological question, it is not always clear just what it is for which comparative material is being sought: "the language of Jesus," the language of Aramaic Q, or the Semitic mother tongue of certain NT writers?

Since Hebrew, Aramaic, and Greek were all spoken during the first century C.E., it is important to keep in mind that "semitism in content or form is no evidence whatever of relative antiquity *vis-à-vis* Greek material" (Smith: 309).

Finally, though all would agree on the principle that, in any discussion of the Semitic background of NT Greek, contemporary material should be used, Vermes has insisted that this principle applies only "when the proper kind of contemporaneous documents are available in sufficient quantity" (24). Is this condition fulfilled with the recent publication of *A Manual of Palestinian Aramaic Texts* (Fitzmyer and Harrington)?

VI. CONCLUSION

It would have been impossible within the limits of this article to discuss or evaluate a representative selection of the scholarly publications on Greek and Semitic philology that have appeared during the last thirty-five years and have had a bearing on NT interpretation.

We have therefore chosen to discuss some of the issues that have been raised by the scientific study of language during this period. Once we have distinguished between the synchronic and diachronic levels, we see that the questions related to the two perspectives show considerable similarity. Is it meaningful or possible to compare "NT Greek" with "the rest of Koine," or should one focus on the style of individual NT authors? If one adopts the latter approach, which extrabiblical writings are most suitable for purposes of comparison?

What precisely is included under "the Semitic background of the NT"? For purposes of comparison must we limit ourselves to Aramaic writings that are certifiably contemporaneous with the NT, or does the paucity of material from the first century C.E. justify the admission of later Aramaic evidence? On both levels the confusion between spoken and written language, expressed by the imprecise term *Volkssprache,* often complicates the task of descriptive analysis. The distinction between two levels of language study has nothing to do with the distinction so often made between Greek and Hebrew thought. This latter distinction has been the basis both for the contrast between NT Greek and "pure" Greek made by classicists, and for the emphasis on the "Semitic" character of the language of the NT, in which theologians have seen the philological expression of its distinctiveness. Today NT Greek appears rather as the linguistic expression of an age marked by a unique cultural symbiosis between Hellenism and Judaism (Friedrich, 1978:44–50).

In our judgment, the most important linguistic development since the end of World War II has been the introduction into NT studies of an approach to language quite different from the one in which most exegetes — the present writer included — have been trained. Modern linguistics not only provides the model for the structuralist interpretation of the Bible, which is rapidly gaining ground, but also is the area in which many Bible translators have received their training. And yet the first introduction to NT Greek that utilized the principles of modern linguistics did not appear until 1965 (Goetchius).

The distinctions made by modern linguistics (*parole/langue;* synchronic/ diachronic; paradigmatic/syntagmatic) have put certain problems of NT philology in a new perspective. Moreover, Saussure's insistence on the arbitrary character of linguistic signs has helped us realize how an old-fashioned approach to language can be the occasion of giving linguistic phenomena a theological significance.

Nevertheless, the science of modern linguistics has its origin in spoken language and cannot be transferred without adaptation to the study of ancient writings. The emphasis of modern linguists on synchronicity may make them prone to a theological *Tendenz* ("tendency") of their own. To ignore the diachronic relationship between the NT and the modern reader could promote a fundamentalism that makes the biblical writers converse with readers as simply and unambiguously as if the writers were at the other end of a telephone. Such an "actualization" of the biblical text would be influenced by the translator's own theological convictions, as the "updating" of the Bible in the targums and the NT so clearly demonstrates.

BIBLIOGRAPHY

Aland, Kurt, ed.
    1975–83   *Vollständige Konkordanz zum griechischen Neuen Testament: Unter Zugrundelegung aller modernen kritischen Textausgaben und des Textus Receptus.* Arbeiten zur neutestamentlichen Textforschung 4. Berlin and New York: de Gruyter.

Albright, William Foxwell
1957   *From the Stone Age to Christianity*. Anchor Book. Garden City, NY: Doubleday. [Original, 1940]

Aletti, Jean Noël
1977   "Une lecture en questions." Pp. 189–208 in *Les miracles de Jésus*. Ed. Xavier Léon-Dufour. Paris: Seuil.

Altheim, Franz, and Ruth Stiehl
1966   "Jesus der Galiläer." Pp. 74–97 in *Die Araber in der alten Welt*, Vol. 3. Berlin: de Gruyter.

Argyle, Aubrey William
1953   "The Theory of an Aramaic Source in Acts 2, 14–40." *JTS* 4: 213–14.
1955–56 "Did Jesus Speak Greek?" *ExpTim* 67: 92–93, 383.
1974   "Greek among the Jews of Palestine in New Testament Times." *NTS* 20: 87–89.

Bardy, Gustave
1948   *La question des langues dans l'église ancienne*. Paris: Beauchesne.

Barr, James
1961   *The Semantics of Biblical Language*. London: Oxford University Press.
1968   "Common Sense and Biblical Language." *Bib* 49: 377–87.
1969   *Biblical Words for Time*. London: SCM.
1971   "Which Language Did Jesus Speak?—Some Remarks of a Semitist." *BJRL* 53: 9–29.
1972   "Semantics and Biblical Theology—A Contribution to the Discussion." Pp. 11–19 in *Congress Volume: Uppsala, 1971*. VTSup 22. Leiden: Brill.
1975   "The Nature of Linguistic Evidence in the Text of the Bible." Pp. 35–57 in *Language and Texts: The Nature of Linguistic Evidence*. Ed. Herbert H. Paper. Ann Arbor, MI: Center for Coordination of Ancient and Modern Studies, University of Michigan.

Barrett, Charles Kingsley
1975   *The Gospel of John and Judaism*. London: SPCK.

Bauer, Walter, William F. Arndt, and F. Wilbur Gingrich
1957   *A Greek-English Lexicon of the New Testament and Other Early Christian Literature*. Chicago: University of Chicago Press. [2d ed., revised and augmented by F. W. Gingrich and F. W. Danker, 1979.]

Beyer, Klaus
1968   *Semitische Syntax im Neuen Testament: 1. Satzlehre, Teil 1*. Göttingen: Vandenhoeck & Ruprecht.

Birkeland, Harris
1964   *The Language of Jesus*. Oslo: Dybwad.

Black, Matthew
1947–48 "Unresolved New Testament Problems. The Problem of the Aramaic Element in the Gospels." *ExpTim* 59: 171–76.
1948   "Aramaic Studies and the New Testament: The Unpublished Work of the Late A. J. Wensinck of Leyden." *JTS* 49: 157–65. [= Black, 1967:296–304.]
1956–57 "The Recovery of the Language of Jesus." *NTS* 3: 305–13.
1957   "Die Erforschung der Muttersprache Jesu." *TLZ* 82: 654–67.

1963-65 "Semitismos del Nuevo Testamento." *Enciclopedia de la Biblia* 6. 594-96.
1965-66 "Second Thoughts: IX. The Semitic Element in the New Testament." *ExpTim* 77: 20-23.
1967 *An Aramaic Approach to the Gospels and Acts.* 3d ed. Oxford: Clarendon Press.
1968 "Aramaic Studies and the Language of Jesus." BZAW 103: 17-28.

Boismard, M.-É.
1958 "Importance de la critique textuelle pour établir l'origine araméenne du quatrième évangile." Pp. 41-57 in *L'Evangile de Jean: Etudes et problèmes.* Louvain: Desclée de Brouwer.

Boman, Thorlief
1962 "Hebrew and Greek Thought-Forms in the New Testament." Pp. 1-22 in *Current Issues in New Testament Interpretation: Essays in Honor of Otto A. Piper.* Ed. W. Klassen and G. F. Snyder. London: SCM; New York: Harper.

Bonsirven, Joseph
1949 "Les aramaïsmes de S. Jean l'Evangéliste?" *Bib* 30: 405-32.

Bowker, John
1969 *The Targums and Rabbinic Literature.* Cambridge: University Press.

Bratsiotis, Nikolaus P.
1966 "Nepeš—psychē: Ein Beitrag zur Erforschung der Sprache und der Theologie der Septuaginta." Pp. 58-89 in *Volume du Congrès: Genève, 1965.* VTSup 15. Leiden: Brill.

Brockelmann, Carl
1954 *Das Aramäische, einschliesslich des Syrischen.* Leiden.

Brown, Schuyler
1964 "From Burney to Black: The Fourth Gospel and the Aramaic Question." *CBQ* 26: 323-39.
1974 "Précis of Eckhard Plümacher, *Lukas als hellenistischer Schriftsteller.*" Pp. 103-13 in *Society of Biblical Literature 1974 Seminar Papers.* Vol. 2. Ed. G. W. MacRae. Missoula, MT: Scholars Press.

Bujard, W.
1973 *Stilanalytische Untersuchungen zum Kolosserbrief als Beitrag zur Methodik von Sprachvergleichen.* SUNT 11. Göttingen: Vandenhoeck & Ruprecht.

Burchard, Christoph
1970 "Fussnoten zum neutestamentlichen Griechisch." ZNW 61: 157-71.
1978 "Fussnoten zum neutestamentlichen Griechisch." ZNW 69: 143-57.

Burrows, Millar
1951 "The Semitic Background of the New Testament." *BT* 2: 67-73.

Cadbury, Henry Joel
1951 "The Vocabulary and Grammar of New Testament Greek." *BT* 2: 153-59.

Cantineau, Jean
1955 "Quelle langue parlait le peuple en Palestine au 1er siècle de notre ère?" *Sem* 5: 99-101.

Chomsky, William
1951-52 "What Was the Jewish Vernacular during the Second Commonwealth?" *JQR* 42: 193-212.

Connolly, Hugh
1948 "The Appeal to Aramaic Sources of our Gospels." *Downside Review* 66: 25–37.

Culler, Jonathan
1975 *Structuralist Poetics: Structuralism, Linguistics, and the Study of Literature.* Ithaca, NY: Cornell University Press.
1976 *Saussure.* Glasgow: Fontana Modern Masters.

Daube, David
1959 "The Earliest Structure of the Gospels." *NTS* 5: 174–87.

Debrunner, Albert
1954 *Grundfragen und Grundzüge des nachklassischen Griechisch.* Sammlung Göschen. Berlin: de Gruyter.

Delcor, M.
1973 "Le Targum de Job et l'Araméen du temps de Jésus." *RevScRel* 47: 232–61.

Dey, Joseph
1960 "Von der Sprache des Neuen Testaments." *BibLeb* 1: 39–50.
1961 " 'Ad graecam originem revertentes': Literatur zur neutestamentlichen Philologie." *BibLeb* 2: 120–31.

Díez Macho, Alexandro
1960 "The recently discovered Palestinian Targum: Its Antiquity and Relationship with the other Targums." Pp. 222–45 in *Congress Volume: Oxford, 1959.* VTSup 7. Leiden: Brill.
1963 "La lengua hablada por Jesucristo." *OrAnt* 2: 95–132.
1973 "Le Targum Palestinien." *RevScRel* 47: 169–231.

Doubles, Malcolm C.
1965 "Toward the Publication of the Extant Texts of the Palestinian Targum(s)." *VT* 15: 16–27.
1968 "Indications of Antiquity in the Orthography and Morphology of the Fragment Targum." BZAW 103: 79–89.

Doudna, John Charles
1961 *The Greek of the Gospel of Mark.* SBLMS 12. Philadelphia: SBL.

Draper, H. M.
1956 "Did Jesus Speak Greek?" *ExpTim* 67: 317.

Emerton, John Adney
1961 "Did Jesus Speak Hebrew?" *JTS* 12: 189–202.
1973 "The Problem of Vernacular Hebrew in the First Century A.D. and the Language of Jesus." *JTS* 24: 1–23.

Fitzmyer, Joseph A.
1970 "The Languages of Palestine in the First Century A.D." *CBQ* 32: 501–31.
1971a *Essays on the Semitic Background of the New Testament.* London: Chapman. [Reprinted, SBLSBS 5; Missoula, MT: Scholars Press, 1974.]
1971b *The Genesis Apocryphon of Qumran Cave I: A Commentary.* Rev. ed. BibOr 18A. Rome: Biblical Institute Press.
1974a "Some Observations on the Targum of Job from Qumran Cave XI." *CBQ* 36: 503–24.

1974b   "The Contribution of Qumran Aramaic to the Study of the New Testament." *NTS* 20: 382–407.

1975   "Methodology in the Study of the Aramaic Substratum of Jesus' Sayings in the New Testament." Pp. 73–102 in *Jésus aux origines de la christologie*. Ed. J. Dupont. BETL 40. Louvain: Leuven University.

1979   *A Wandering Aramean: Collected Aramaic Essays*. SBLMS 25. Missoula, MT: Scholars Press.

Fitzmyer, Joseph A., and Daniel J. Harrington
1978   *A Manual of Palestinian Aramaic Texts (Second Century B.C. – Second Century A.D.)* BibOr 34. Rome: Biblical Institute Press.

Fletcher, Basil
1967   *The Aramaic Sayings of Jesus*. London: Hodder & Stoughton.

Frankemölle. H.
1975   "Exegese und Linguistik – Methodenprobleme neuerer exegetischer Veröffentlichungen." *TRev* 71: 1–11.

Friedrich, Gerhard
1959   "Die Problematik eines Theologischen Wörterbuchs zum Neuen Testament." *SE* I: 481–86. [= TU 73.]

1969   "Semasiologie und Lexikologie." *TLZ* 94: 801–16.

1978   "Zur Vorgeschichte des Theologischen Wörterbuchs zum Neuen Testament." *TWNT* 10/1. 1–52.

Frösen, J.
1974   "Prolegomena to a Study of the Greek Language in the First Centuries A.D.: The Problem of Koine and Atticism." Diss., Helsinki.

Funk, Robert W., Friedrich Blass, and Albert Debrunner
1961   *A Greek Grammar of the New Testament and Other Early Christian Literature*. Chicago: University of Chicago Press.

Gehman, Henry S.
1951   "The Hebraic Character of Septuagint Greek." *VT* 1: 81–90.

Gignac, Francis T.
1973   *An Introductory New Testament Greek Course*. Chicago: Loyola University.

1977–81   *A Grammar of the Greek Papyri of the Roman and Byzantine Periods*. Vol. 1, *Phonology*. Vol. 2, *Morphology*. Testi e documenti per lo studio dell'antichità 55:1–2. Milan: Istituto editoriale Cisalpino-La Goliardica.

Gingrich, F. Wilbur
1954   "The Greek New Testament in the Course of Semantic Change." *JBL* 73: 189–93.

Gleason, H. A.
1961   *An Introduction to Descriptive Linguistics*. New York: Holt, Rinehart & Winston.

Goetchius, Eugene van Ness
1965   *The Language of the New Testament*. New York: Scribner.

Grant, E. L.
1951   "Hebrew, Aramaic and the Greek in the Gospels." *Greece and Rome* 20: 115–22.

Grelot, Pierre
1959   "Les Targums du Pentateuque: Etude comparative d'après Gen. 4, 3–16." *Sem* 9: 59–88.

Grintz, Jehoshua M.
1960   "Hebrew as the Spoken and Written Language in the Last Days of the Second Temple." *JBL* 79: 32–47.

Gundry, Robert H.
1964   "The Language Milieu of First-Century Palestine: Its Bearing on the Authenticity of the Gospel Tradition." *JBL* 83: 404–8.

Hilhorst, A.
1976   *Sémitismes et latinismes dans le Pasteur d'Hermas.* Graecitas Christianorum Primaeva 5. Nijmegen: Dekker & van de Vegt.

Hill, David
1967   *Greek Words and Hebrew Meanings: Studies in the Semantics of Soteriological Terms.* Cambridge: University Press.

Irmscher, Johannes
1959   "Der Streit um das Bibelgriechisch." *Acta antiquae academiae hungaricae* 7: 127–34.

Jeremias, Joachim
1949   "Zur aramäischen Vorgeschichte unserer Evangelien." *TLZ* 74: 527–32.
1959   "Die Muttersprache des Evangelisten Matthäus." *ZNW* 50: 270–74.

Kahle, Paul
1958   "Das Palästinische Pentateuchtargum und das zur Zeit Jesu gesprochene Aramäisch." *ZNW* 49: 100–16.

Katz (Walters), Peter
1954–56   "Zur Übersetzungstechnik der Septuaginta." *WO* 2: 267–73.
1973   *The Text of the Septuagint: Its Corruptions and their Emendations.* Cambridge: University Press.

Kilpatrick, George Dunbar
1963   "Atticism and the Text of the Greek New Testament." Pp. 125–37 in *Neutestamentliche Aufsätze: Festschrift für Prof. Josef Schmid zum 70. Geburtstag.* Ed. J. Blinzler, O. Kuss, and F. Mussner. Regensburg: Pustet.
1967   "Style and Text in the Greek New Testament." Pp. 153–60 in *Studies in the History and Text of the New Testament in Honor of Kenneth Willis Clark Ph.D.* Ed. B. L. Daniels and M. Jack Suggs. SD 29. Salt Lake City, UT: University of Utah Press.
1969   "Some Problems in the New Testament Text and Language." Pp. 198–208 in *Neotestamentica et Semitica: Studies in Honor of Matthew Black.* Ed. E. E. Ellis and M. Wilcox. Edinburgh: T. & T. Clark.
1970   "Language and Text in the Gospels and Acts." *VC* 24: 161–71.

Kittel, Gerhard, and Gerhard Friedrich, eds.
1964–76   *TDNT.* 10 vols. Grand Rapids: Eerdmans.

Koch, Klaus
1973   "Reichen die formgeschichtlichen Methoden für die Gegenwartsaufgaben der Bibelwissenschaft zu?" *TLZ* 98: 801–14.

Kuiper, G. J.
1968   "A Study of the Relationship between *A Genesis Apocryphon* and the Pentateuchal Targumim in Genesis 14:1–12." *BZAW* 103: 149–61.

Kutscher, Eduard Yechezkel
1959   "The Language of the Genesis Apocryphon: A Preliminary Survey."
        Pp. 1–35 in *Aspects of the Dead Sea Scrolls*. Ed. C. Rabin and Y.
        Yadin. Scripta Hierosolymitana 4. Jerusalem: Magnes Press.
1960   "Das zur Zeit Jesu gesprochene Aramäisch im neuen Köhler-
        Baumgartner." Pp. 158–75 in *Hebräische Wortforschung: Festschrift
        zum 80. Geburtstag von Walter Baumgartner*. VTSup 16. Leiden:
        Brill.

Lampe, Geoffrey William Hugo
1961–70 *A Patristic Greek Lexicon*. Oxford: Clarendon Press.

Le Déaut, Roger
1968   "Le substrat araméen des évangiles: Scolies en marge de l'*Aramaic
        Approach* de Matthew Black." *Bib* 49: 388–99.
1978–81 *Targum du Pentateuque*. 5 vols. Paris: Cerf.

Lejeune, M.
1955   *Traité de phonétique grecque*. Paris.

Liddell, H. G., Robert Scott, and H. Stuart Jones
1968   *A Greek-English Lexicon: A Supplement*. Oxford: Clarendon Press.

Lieberman, Saul
1963   *How Much Greek in Jewish Palestine?* Waltham, MA: Brandeis Univer-
        sity Press.

Ljungvik, Herman
1968   "Aus der Sprache des Neuen Testaments." *Eranos* 66: 24–51.

McKnight, Edgar V.
1965   "Is the New Testament Written in 'Holy Ghost' Greek?" *BT* 16:
        87–93.
1966   "The New Testament and 'Biblical Greek.'" *JBR* 34: 36–42.

McNamara, Martin
1966   *The New Testament and the Palestinian Targum to the Pentateuch*.
        Rome: Biblical Institute Press.
1972   *Targum and Testament: Aramaic Paraphrases of the Hebrew Bible: A
        Light on the New Testament*. Shannon: Irish University Press; Grand
        Rapids: Eerdmans.

Maloney, Elliott C.
1981   *Semitic Interference in Marcan Syntax*. SBLDS 51. Chico, CA:
        Scholars Press.

Mandilaras, Basil G.
1973   *The Verb in the Greek Non-literary Papyri*. Athens: Hellenic Ministry
        of Culture and Sciences.

Martin, Raymond A.
1960   "Some Syntactical Criteria of Translation Greek." *VT* 10: 295–310.
1964–65 "Syntactical Evidence of Aramaic Sources in Acts i-xv." *NTS* 11:
        38–59.
1974   *Syntactical Evidence of Semitic Sources in Greek Documents*.
        Missoula, MT: SBL.

Mayer, Günter
1974   *Index Philoneus*. Berlin: de Gruyter.

Mohrmann, Christine
1957   "Linguistic Problems in the Early Christian Church." *VC* 11: 11–36.

Morag, Solomon
    1956   "Until When Was Hebrew Spoken?" *Leshonenu* 7–8: 3–10. (Hebrew)
Morgenthaler, Robert
    1958   *Statistik des neutestamentlichen Wortschatzes*. Zurich: Gotthelf-
                Verlag.
Moule, Charles Francis Digby
    1952   *The Language of the New Testament*. Cambridge: University Press.
    1959   *An Idiom Book of New Testament Greek*. Cambridge: University Press.
Mussies, G.
    1971   *The Morphology of Koine Greek as Used in the Apocalypse of St. John:
                A Study in Bilingualism*. NovTSup 27. Leiden: Brill.
Nida, Eugene A., and Charles R. Taber
    1969   *The Theory and Practice of Translation*. Helps for Bible Translators
                8. Leiden: Brill. [Original, 1964.]
Olsson, Birger
    1974   *Structure and Meaning in the Fourth Gospel: A Text-Linguistic
                Analysis of John 2:1–11 and 4:1–42*. ConBNT 6. Lund: Gleerup.
Ott, H.
    1967   "Um die Muttersprache Jesu: Forschungen seit Gustaf Dalman."
                NovT 9: 1–25.
Patterson, Samuel W.
    1946   "What Language Did Jesus Speak?" *Classical Outlook* 23: 65–67.
Pax, Elpidius
    1972   "Probleme des neutestamentlichen Griechisch." *Bib* 53: 557–64.
Poythress, Vern S.
    1979   "Analysing a Biblical Text: Some Important Distinctions." *SJT* 32:
                113–37.
Rabin, Chaim
    1968   "The Translation Process and the Character of the Septuagint."
                Textus 6: 1–26.
Rabinowitz, I.
    1962   " 'Be Opened' = 'Εφφαθά (Mark 7. 34): Did Jesus Speak Hebrew?"
                ZNW 53: 229–38.
    1971   "'Εφφαθά (Mark VII. 34): Certainly Hebrew, not Aramaic." *JSS* 16:
                151–56.
Radermacher, Ludwig
    1925   *Neutestamentliche Grammatik: Das Griechisch des Neuen Testaments
                im Zusammenhang mit der Volkssprache*. Tübingen: Mohr-Siebeck.
Rehkopf, Friedrich, Friedrich Blass, and Albert Debrunner
    1976   *Grammatik des neutestamentlichen Griechisch*. 14th ed. rev. by
                Rehkopf. Göttingen: Vandenhoeck & Ruprecht.
Rengstorf, Karl H.
    1973–75   *A Complete Concordance to Flavius Josephus*. Leiden: Brill.
Richter, Wolfgang
    1971   *Exegese als Literaturwissenschaft: Entwurf einer alttestamentlichen
                Literaturtheorie und Methodologie*. Göttingen: Vandenhoeck &
                Ruprecht.

Roberts, J. W.
1961   "The Language Background of the New Testament." *Restoration Quarterly* 5: 193-204.

Rood, L.
1949   "Heeft Jezus Grieks gesproken?" *Streven* 2: 1026-35.

Rowley, Harold Henry
1963   "Notes on the Aramaic of the Genesis Apocryphon." Pp. 116-29 in *Hebrew and Semitic Studies Presented to G. R. Driver.* Ed. D. Winton Thomas and W. D. McHardy. Oxford: Clarendon Press.

Rydbeck, Lars
1967   *Fachprosa, vermeintliche Volkssprache und Neues Testament.* Stockholm: Almqvist & Wiksell.
1974-75   "What Happened to New Testament Greek Grammar after Albert Debrunner?" *NTS* 21: 557-64.

Saussure, Ferdinand de
1960   *Course in General Linguistics.* Trans. W. Baskin. London: Peter Owen.

Sawyer, John F. A.
1972   *Semantics in Biblical Research: New Methods of Defining Hebrew Words for Salvation.* London: SCM.

Schenk, Wolfgang
1973   "Die Aufgaben der Exegese und die Mittel der Linguistik." *TLZ* 98: 881-94.

Schmid, Josef, and Alfred Wikenhauser
1973   "Die Sprache des NT." Pp. 186-202 in *Einleitung in das Neue Testament.* Freiburg: Herder.

Schürmann, Heinz
1951   "Die Semitismen im Einsetzungsbericht bei Markus und bei Lukas (Mk 14, 22-24/Lk 22, 19-20)." *ZKT* 73: 72-77.
1958   "Die Sprache des Christus: Sprachliche Beobachtungen an den synoptischen Herrenworten." *BZ* 2: 54-84.
1959-60   "Sprachliche Reminiszensen an abgeänderte oder ausgelassene Bestandteile der Spruchsammlung im Lukas- und Matthäusevangelium." *NTS* 6: 193-210.

Schwyzer, Eduard
1953   *Griechische Grammatik: Im Anschluss an Karl Brugmans "Griechische Grammatik" bearbeitet.* Munich.

Segert, Stanislav
1957   "Aramäische Studien: II. Zur Verbreitung des Aramäischen in Palästina zur Zeit Jesu." *ArOr* 25: 21-37.
1963a   "Zur Orthographie und Sprache der aramäischen Texte von Wadi Murabba'at." *ArOr* 31: 122-37.
1963b   "Die Sprachenfrage in der Qumrangemeinschaft," *Qumranprobleme*: 315-39. Berlin.
1963c   "Klassische Philologie und Orientalistik." (German summary). *Listy filologické* 86, 1:17-18.

Sevenster, Jan N.
1968   *Do You Know Greek? How Much Greek Could the First Jewish Christians Have Known?* NovTSup 19. Leiden: Brill.

Silva, M.
1972   "Semantic Change and Semitic Influence in the Greek Bible." Diss., Manchester.
1975-76   "Semantic Borrowing in the New Testament." *NTS* 22: 104-10.
1978   "New Lexical Semitisms?" *ZNW* 69: 253-57.

Smith, Morton
1958   "Aramaic Studies and the Study of the New Testament." *JBR* 26: 304-13.

Sparks, Hedley Frederick Davis
1950   "The Semitisms of Acts." *JTS* 1: 16-28.

Springhetti, Emilio
1966   *Introductio historica-grammatica in graecitatem Novi Testamenti.* Rome: Gregorian University.

Steyer, Gottfried
1968   PROS PĒGĒN ODOS: *Handbuch für das Studium des neutestamentlichen Griechisch: II. Satzlehre.* Berlin: Evangelische Verlagsanstalt.

Stuhlmacher, Peter
1979   *Historical Criticism and Theological Interpretation of Scripture: Towards a Hermeneutics of Consent.* Trans. R. A. Harrisville. London: SPCK; Philadelphia: Fortress.

Tabachovitz, David
1956   *Die Septuaginta und das Neue Testament: Stilstudien.* Lund: Gleerup.

Talbert, Charles H.
1974   *Literary Patterns, Theological Themes, and the Genre of Luke-Acts.* SBLMS 20. Missoula, MT: Scholars Press.

Torrey, Charles Cutler
1953   "Studies in the Aramaic of the First Century A.D." *ZAW* 65: 228-47.
1958   *The Apocalypse of John.* New Haven, CT: Yale University Press.

Treu, Kurt
1973   "Die Bedeutung des Griechischen für die Juden im Römischen Reich." *Kairos* 1-2: 123-44.

Turner, Nigel
1954-55   "The 'Testament of Abraham': Problems in Biblical Greek." *NTS* 1: 219-23.
1955   "The Unique Character of Biblical Greek." *VT* 5: 208-13.
1955-56   "The Relation of Luke i and ii to the Hebraic Sources and to the Rest of Luke-Acts." *NTS* 2: 100-109.
1957   "The Style of St. Mark's Eucharistic Words." *JTS* 8: 108-11.
1959-60   "Philology in New Testament Studies." *ExpTim* 71: 104-7.
1963   *A Grammar of New Testament Greek by James Hope Moulton: Vol. III. Syntax.* Edinburgh: T. & T. Clark.
1966   *Grammatical Insights into the New Testament.* Edinburgh: T. & T. Clark.
1976a   "The Quality of the Greek of Luke-Acts." Pp. 387-400 in *Studies in New Testament Language and Text: Essays in Honour of George D. Kilpatrick on the Occasion of His Sixth-fifth Birthday.* Ed. J. K. Elliott. NovTSup 44. Leiden: Brill.
1976b   *A Grammar of New Testament Greek by James Hope Moulton: Vol. IV. Style.* Edinburgh: T. & T. Clark.

Ullmann, Stephen
  1957   *The Principles of Semantics: A Linguistic Approach to Meaning.*
              Oxford: Blackwell.
Unnik, Willem Cornelis van
  1973   "Aramaisms in Paul." Pp. 129–43 in *Sparsa collecta: Collected Essays:
              Part 1. Evangelia, Paulina, Acta.* NovTSup 29. Leiden: Brill.
Vermes, Geza
  1978   " 'The Son of Man' Debate." *JSNT* (Issue 1): 19–32.
Watson, M.
  1967   "The Semitic Element in New Testament Greek." *Restoration
              Quarterly* 10: 225–30.
Wifstrand, Albert
  1948   "Stylistic Problems in the Epistles of James and Peter." *ST* 1: 170–82.
  1949   "A Problem Concerning the Word Order in the New Testament." *ST*
              3: 172–84.
Wilcox, Max
  1965   *The Semitisms of Acts.* Oxford: Clarendon Press.
  1979   "On Investigating the Use of the Old Testament in the New Testa-
              ment." Pp. 231–43 in *Text and Interpretation: Studies in the New
              Testament Presented to Matthew Black.* Ed. Ernest Best and R. McL.
              Wilson. Cambridge: University Press.
Winter, P.
  1954–55   "Some Observations on the Language in the Birth and Infancy Stories
              of the Third Gospel." *NTS* 1: 111–21.
York, A. D.
  1974   "The Dating of Targumic Literature." *JSJ* 5: 49–62.
Zerwick, Maximilian
  1963   *Biblical Greek Illustrated by Examples* Trans. Joseph Smith. Rome:
              Biblical Institute Press.

6

FORM AND REDACTION CRITICISM

Edgar V. McKnight

I. INTRODUCTION

Relationship of Form and Redaction Criticism

Form and redaction criticism of the NT have paralleled one another in their origin and development. Each of the disciplines was inaugurated following the literary inactivity of a world war by young scholars who were beginning their careers. Both methods are historically oriented, form criticism giving attention to the history of the units that were transmitted orally in the early church and redaction criticism concerned with the end of the historical process, the situation and theology of the evangelist and his church, which can be ascertained by the editorial activity of the evangelist.

Redaction Criticism: A New Discipline?

The relationship of form and redaction criticism has led to the question of whether redaction criticism ought to be considered simply a further application of form criticism. Willi Marxsen is responsible not only for the name "redaction criticism" but also for the clear distinction between redaction criticism and form criticism. Rudolf Bultmann had maintained that the composition of the Gospels "involves nothing in principle new, but only completes what was begun in the oral tradition" (1921:321). Marxsen denies that the anti-individualistic sociological orientation of the study of the tradition can be maintained in the study of the Gospels as wholes. The redaction counteracts the fragmentation that takes place in the anonymous transmission of material, and this counteraction of redaction "cannot be explained without taking into account an individual, an author personality who pursues a definite goal with his work" (18).

Redaction critics after Marxsen do not agree unanimously with his evaluation. Georg Strecker, for example, denies to the evangelist both an individual dogmatic conception and individual creativity on the literary level. The evangelists are exponents of their congregations, not authors who want to compose literary works that express their individuality (10). The question of the relationship of form and redaction criticism is a key to the contemporary use of both methods.

149

This essay will sketch some recent development in form-critical studies; trace the history of redaction-critical studies, with particular attention to shifts in the definitions of the situation and the theology of the various evangelists and their churches and to the need to develop a reliable methodology; and present contemporary linguistic challenges and contributions to both form and redaction criticism.

II. FORM CRITICISM

Development into a Classical Method of Study

Within a generation of its founding, form criticism had crossed confessional and geographical boundaries and had developed into a classical method of synoptic study. As it crossed these boundaries, however, modifications were made in the method to make it more compatible with the presuppositions and purposes of those who utilized it, particularly with source criticism and the study of the history of the events recounted in the tradition. (For the cautious evaluation and acceptance by Roman Catholic scholars, see Schick and Benoit. For English scholarship, see Taylor and Redlich. For American scholarship, see Grant, Riddle, and Scott.)

Form criticism, in spite of its name, was never limited to literary-formal questions. Along with study of primitive Christian literature and the communities responsible for its formation, form criticism has been used for a variety of historical and theological purposes: to complete the task of source criticism, to distinguish between "primary" and "secondary" materials in the tradition, to determine the most basic content of faith's witness, and to carry out satisfying theological interpretation. William G. Doty has given a broad definition that provides a framework for a myriad of uses: "Form criticism is a systematic, scientific, historical and theological methodology for analyzing the genres and, to some extent, the content, of the primitive Christian literature, with special reference to the history of the early Christian movement in its reflective and creative theological activity" (293).

The "Forms" of Form Criticism

Nomenclature

The different names of the forms result from particular conceptualizations of the formation of the tradition that continue to be influential. Dibelius's constructive method emphasized preaching and the effect on the hearers. The name he gave to the narratives of Jesus' deeds that conclude with a statement of Jesus, therefore, was "paradigm" (example). "Tales" existed for the pleasure of the narrative itself. "Legends" satisfied the desire of Christians to know more about the holy men and women in the story of Jesus as well as about Jesus himself. Bultmann's analytic approach resulted in more neutral names derived from the content: apophthegm, saying, miracle story, historical story, and legend.

Vincent Taylor's nomenclature has been popular with English and American scholars. Taylor proposed "pronouncement story" for Martin Dibelius's "paradigm," and Bultmann's "miracle story" rather than Dibelius's "tale." For the remaining stories about Jesus, Taylor chose to use the general expression "stories about Jesus" rather than to distinguish other forms. In terms of the saying material, Taylor found only the "parable" to be a proper form.

Suggestions of New Forms

The continuing domination of Bultmann's classification of form and his general approach to form criticism, along with the introduction of redaction criticism, have discouraged concentrated work on additional forms of the synoptic tradition. Nevertheless, some new suggestions have been made. Günther Bornkamm, for example, has suggested a division of the synoptic stories about Jesus into two groups. The first is "Jesus stories," which tell of his miracles and are designed to awaken faith in him. The second group is "Christ stories," which have the same aim to an even higher degree but which are stamped from the outset by faith and express this faith often with legendary motifs. Such stories include the infancy narratives of Matthew and Luke, baptism, temptation, confession of Peter, transfiguration, entry into Jerusalem, the Lord's supper, and the resurrection narrative (1958a:752; 1958b:1001).

Ernst Käsemann has also proposed a form that he calls "sentences of holy law," which is a pronouncement of God's judgment in terms of the offense. For example: "If anyone destroys God's temple, God will destroy him" (1 Cor 3:17). Käsemann sees the original setting of these sentences in proclamation of NT prophets who carried over the form of certain OT utterances.

The Passion Narrative

The passion narrative was seen by the early form critics as the longest and most traditional block of pre-gospel material and as an exception to the rule that the pre-gospel tradition circulated in independent units. In 1970, Eta Linnemann inaugurated a new stage in the study of the Marcan passion narrative by a rejection of the thesis of a pre-Marcan narrative. She attempted to show that the narrative is a collection of reports and not simply the rewording of a connected account.

Recent American studies support Linnemann's rejection of a pre-Marcan narrative. However, these studies begin with the premise that Mark is not simply a collector of reports but a creative author, and they study the narrative as a composition that owes its final form and coherent structure and meaning to Mark (see essays in Kelber, 1976).

Sitz-im-Leben

The assumption of the earliest form critics was that the form of the units coalesced out of the institutional life of the Christian communities. For Dibelius, preaching was the specific and all-inclusive setting for the formation of the tradition. Bultmann specified more carefully both the items of the tradition and the settings. He placed apologetics, polemics, edification, discipline, and scribal activity alongside preaching (1921:60–61).

The concept of *Sitz-im-Leben* ("life-setting") was adopted from OT study, particularly the work of Hermann Gunkel on the stories of Genesis. The fact that forms such as hymns and psalms of complaint often arise and become standardized in institutional contexts led some OT scholars to push in the direction of "sociological determination." Other scholars suggest that forms are determined not only by a setting understood in terms of particular institutions; Gene M. Tucker would broaden "setting" to include such matters as tradition, the prelinguistic activity of the human mind, the spirit of an age, particular literary concerns, actual performances, and specific creative occasions (343).

NT form criticism may continue to emphasize the sociological *Sitz-im-Leben*, expanding the range of possible settings in light of the work done by redaction criticism on the possible situations and theologies of the various Gospels. Form criticism, however, may broaden its understanding of "setting," not ignoring the possibility of typical institutional settings but concerning itself, in addition, with the variety of sociocultural and intellectual matrices which can account for texts (see Doty: 295, 304–5, 318–19).

Resistance to Form Criticism

The emphasis on the creativity of the early church has been seen by some as a denigration of the role of Jesus as a teacher and the place of eyewitnesses. The work of C. H. Dodd (1955) and T. W. Manson allowed some students to integrate form-critical insights with the view that "in broad lines the Marcan order does represent a genuine succession of events within which movement and development can be traced" (Dodd, 1955:11) and that the Gospel tradition may be used as respectable historical material (Manson: 6).

A Scandinavian school, represented by Harald Riesenfeld and Birger Gerhardsson, has attempted to prove false the postulate that the synoptic tradition was formed in the later Christian community. The analogy offered by Riesenfeld and Gerhardsson, that the oral Torah in the rabbinic tradition explains the transmission of the Gospel tradition, has not been generally accepted by scholarship, but the concern to trace the formation of the material behind the early church has continued. Heinz Schürmann has argued for a collection of sayings used by the disciples of Jesus during Jesus' lifetime. He has used form-critical principles to support the preaching mission of the disciples as the setting for the formation of these teachings.

E. Earle Ellis has extended the work of Schürmann to try to show that some gospel traditions were probably transmitted in written form during Jesus' earthly ministry and that biblical exposition (like Luke 10:25–37 and Matt 21:33–46) must be reckoned as a form, the setting for which is probably Jesus' earthly life.

III. REDACTION CRITICISM

Origins

Günther Bornkamm

Bornkamm's 1948 article on the pericope of the Stilling of the Storm in Matt 8:23–27 is credited with being the first work in the new method of study, which six years later would be given the title "redaction criticism" by Willi Marxsen. Bornkamm uses contemporary form-critical principles to make clear the evangelist's method of working. The redactional activity emphasized by Bornkamm is Matthew's reordering of the material. The nature miracle is taken out of the biographical context of Mark and placed in a series in Matthew consisting primarily of healing miracles which are designed to show Jesus as Messiah of deed and which parallel the presentation of Jesus as Messiah of the word in Matthew 5–7. The two sayings of Jesus about discipleship which precede the miracle actually give the story its meaning. Matthew interprets "the journey of the disciples with Jesus in the storm and the stilling of the storm with reference to discipleship, and that means with reference to the little ship of the Church" (55).

Bornkamm continued his investigation into the redactional activity of Matthew with a 1954 paper, "Matthew as Interpreter of the Words of the Lord," which was expanded and published in 1960 as "End-Expectation and Church in Matthew." The complete study sets out to examine Matthew's theological peculiarities and the theme of his Gospel and to show the extent to which the first evangelist is an interpreter of his tradition (49).

In the analysis of Matthew's discourses which begins the work, Bornkamm uncovers a union of end-expectation and conception of the church that is peculiar to Matthew. The discourse of John the Baptist shows this unique union, particularly as it is related to the message of Jesus. By having John as well as Jesus preach the message "Repent for the kingdom of heaven is at hand" (3:2 and 4:17), Matthew makes the Baptist into a preacher of the Christian congregation. John's call for repentance rejects the appeal of his hearers that they are the children of Abraham. Jesus' call (in 3:2 and chap. 7, where false prophets replace the Pharisees and Sadducees) rejects the conception of the church held by the false prophets who appeal to their discipleship and charismatic miracles. The false prophets are not willing to admit that membership in the messianic community is decided according to the standard of bringing forth the "fruits of repentance" and doing the will of the heavenly father.

The understanding of the law is the link between the church and end-expectation in Matthew and is the key to Matthew's interpretation of the tradition. In this light, Matthew's indication that the law is binding down to the jot and tittle (Matt 5:17–19) is seen by Bornkamm as having been given a representative place and a programmatic meaning by the evangelist. The passage is a clue to the situation of Matthew and his church in that it stems from a Jewish-Christian congregation and is directed against a tendency to abandon the law. Bornkamm confirms the conclusion of G. D. Kilpatrick that the Jewish opposition in Matthew's Gospel is that of the Judaism between 70 and 135, when Jewish sects and Christians are being accused of heresy and excommunicated (22 n. 2). In Matthew, a Jewish-Christian congregation is pictured "which holds fast to the law and which has not yet broken away from union with Judaism but rather stands in sharp contrast to a doctrine and mission set free from the law (which Matthew would regard as lawless) . . ." (22; for a later view, see Bornkamm, 1964).

Hans Conzelmann

Redaction criticism is possible with Luke-Acts, according to Conzelmann, because it is with the work of Luke that the distinction between the period of Jesus and the period of the church becomes fully conscious. In the first phase of the development of the tradition—up to Mark and Q—the problems and answers of the community are somewhat unreflectively projected back into reports of Jesus' life. In the second phase, the kerygma is not simply passed down and received; the kerygma is itself the subject of reflection (1954:12). The theological reflection and the fundamental motif of Luke result, according to Conzelmann, from the delay of the parousia. This defines the Christology and ecclesiology of Luke and causes him to transform eschatology into a broad scheme of the history of salvation.

The view of eschatology as the key to Luke's reflection on the kerygma and salvation history as the result of Luke's reflection do not simply flow from a redaction critical study of Luke-Acts. Earlier scholars had noted these matters (see Baer: 108, 111–12; Bultmann, 1955; Vielhauer); Conzelmann's contribution was to show how Luke's editing of his sources may be related to the postulated historical and theological situation. Conzelmann's article of 1952, "Zur Lukas Analyse," summarizes the purpose, method, and major results of his study on Luke-Acts. He utilizes source and form criticism to deal with the composition, individuality, and purpose of the Gospel of Luke. His study shows that Luke's reaction to the delay of the parousia resulted in a reconstruction so radical that a timeless message was resounded and the length of the interim period no longer constituted a problem.

Conzelmann amplified and substantiated his interpretation of the work of Luke in *Die Mitte der Zeit,* and a typical picture of Conzelmann's method may be obtained by an examination of his treatment of "Luke's Eschatology." Mark contains evidence of a change of attitude toward eschatology, but this is an unconscious modification, and Mark himself retains the early expectation. With Luke, however, a new outline is provided: "A solution which will not demand further revision in the course of time" (120). At the beginning of the Gospel, this revision is evident in the elimination of the apocalyptic idea of a forerunner and the placing of John in the line of all the other prophets. Jesus, then, is understood not by reference to the eschatological idea of a forerunner but in light of the preparation for his coming in the whole period of the law and prophets (1954:101). The account of the rejection at Nazareth (4:16–30) gives evidence of the process of placing eschatology within the course of history. Jesus' statement that "today the scripture has been fulfilled in your hearing" is thought of as belonging to past history. It is "at that time," when Jesus was still living and active on earth, that the fulfillment which is described came about (1954:103).

A comparison of Luke 9:27 with Mark 9:1 shows how Luke interpreted the tradition so as to provide a permanent solution to the problem of the delay of the parousia. Luke omits "come with power" because it is a realistic description of the parousia, and Luke wishes to replace the idea of the coming by a timeless concept of the kingdom. The reference to "those standing here" means "those who are standing by 'at the time,' " and "to see the kingdom" means the perception of the kingdom in the life of Jesus. From the life of Jesus we can see what the kingdom is like. But the time of the appearance of the kingdom is not disclosed. The coming of the kingdom, then, is proclaimed as a future fact, the nature of which can be seen now (1954:104).

Willi Marxsen

Bornkamm and Conzelmann were not fully conscious of the fact that they were pioneering a new method of study. Willi Marxsen, however, is fully conscious of the novelty of the new approach and emphasizes that the change of orientation from individual units to the completed Gospels makes of redaction criticism something different from form criticism and something not essentially dependent upon form criticism (22).

Marxsen suggests that a redaction-critical study of Mark will follow two procedures: (1) a separation of tradition from redaction so that the composition of Mark may be illuminated, and (2) attention to the altered points of view of Matthew and Luke in order to get a clearer grasp of what is typically Marcan. This procedure is used in studies on John the Baptist, the geographical outline of Mark, the concept of "gospel," and Mark 13.

The key to Mark's composition in general and to the John the Baptist material in particular is seen as Mark's "backward composition." The passion narrative is primary. To this Mark prefixes first of all the Jesus tradition and then the tradition of John the Baptist. The story of the Baptist, therefore, must be read with Jesus as the point of reference. The principle of backward composition governs not only the relationship of larger complexes to one another but also the relationship of the units within the larger complexes. Moreover, the same relationship that exists between Jesus and John the Baptist exists between John the Baptist and the OT (30–31).

By means of analysis on the basis of backward composition, Marxsen shows the theological significance of John's location by Mark "in the wilderness" and Jesus' appearance after John was "delivered up." A "backward directed prophecy" with the expression "in the wilderness" is prefaced by Mark to his Baptist tradition, and the tradition is adjusted to the prophecy by repeating "in the wilderness" in v 4. "In the wilderness," then, qualifies the Baptist as the one who fulfilled OT prophecy. "Put in exaggerated form, the Baptist would still be the one who appears 'in the wilderness' even if he had never been there in all his life" (37–38). The historical concept of "delivered up" is also emptied of historical content. Mark prefixes the Jesus complex with the Baptist complex and records that Jesus made his first public appearance after John had been "delivered up" because the Baptist belongs to the topical "prehistory" of Jesus. The connection of John and Jesus is made not from a temporal but from a theological or christological point of view (38–43).

Marxsen sees the geographical outline with the beginning in Galilee and the ending in Jerusalem as the result of Marcan redaction and a key to Mark's situation. The pre-Marcan passion narrative contained references that could have been used for an outline similar to that in the Gospel of John. But Mark composes an outline that emphasizes Galilee. The real stimulus for Mark's Galilean emphasis is a community situation prevailing in the time of Mark himself. "To overstate the case, Mark does not intend to say: Jesus worked in Galilee, but rather: Where Jesus worked there is Galilee" (93–94). Mark's use of the term "Galilee," nevertheless, is seen by Marxsen as implying either the existence of a community in Galilee or movement toward Galilee. He believes that "the reason for the communities' sojourn in Galilee, or the reason for their journey to Galilee might be seen in the fact that the Parousia was expected there. This makes clear the problem of locale" (107).

Marxsen's study of Mark 13 is seen as a validation of the hypothesis that Mark wrote with a view to the imminent parousia. Although the chapter results from the unification of various materials, Mark understood the chapter as a unity the meaning of which is to be deduced by Mark's connection of v 2 to v 3, which weaves the saying on the destruction of the temple into the discourse on last things. The destruction, then, is a part of the end event. Mark is the transformation of apocalyptic into eschatology. The several acts of apocalyptic eschatology are replaced with one last act, and "for Mark this act has already begun and . . . only the finale remains" (189).

Early Redactional Studies

Although redaction criticism seems to be a rather simple and objective method, the practice of the method is not so simple. A distinction must be made between the tradition and the redacted material, but the changes made in the sources do not necessarily reflect conscious theological decisions by the author. How can distinction be made between (1) the unconscious modifications resulting from the tradition and the community within which the evangelist works and (2) the conscious modification of the evangelist himself for theological purposes? When conscious redaction is presupposed, the meaning is not obvious from the redaction itself. Some larger historical and theological framework must be presupposed, accepted, or created by the critic in which the redaction can make sense. In general, redaction-critical studies immediately following the pioneers maintained their historical and theological presuppositions.

Matthean Studies

Gerhard Barth and Heinz Joachim Held were the earliest successors of Bornkamm. They were his students, whose dissertations were accepted by the theological faculty of Heidelberg in 1955 and 1957, respectively, and Bornkamm indicates that it was the work of these men which confirmed and made fully clear to him the value of the study of Matthew's theology and method of composition. Bornkamm's view that an understanding of law links Matthew's eschatology, ecclesiology, and Christology would indicate that the work of Barth on Matthew's understanding of the law is actually an extension of Bornkamm's interest and study. In an initial section, "Expectation of the Judgment and Exhortation to Do the Will of God," Barth shows that Matthew even displaces the proclamation of Jesus in order to make these emphases. In Matt 24:42 and 25:13 the original point was "behavior in face of the immediately imminent irruption of the rule of God." In the work of Matthew, this expectation recedes so that exhortation may come to the fore (61). Barth is convinced that these emphases are related to the situation of the author and his congregation, which is reflected also in such factors as Matthew's emphasis upon the law's abiding validity (62–75); the contrast between Matthew and the rabbinate, which centers in the fact that for Matthew the love commandment is made the principle of interpretation (75–105); and Matthew's placing of the understanding of the disciples in opposition to the obduracy of the greater part of the Jewish nation (111–12).

Barth attempts to sketch as precisely as possible the antinomians who were opposed (along with the rabbinate) by Matthew. They held that "in the past the law and the prophets rightly held, but Christ has abolished the law and the prophets; since the coming of Christ their validity is ended" (159). The antinomians were not a Pauline group or in the area of Jewish-Christianity at all. They must have been in the area of Hellenistic Christianity, even though gnostic influences are not present among them. Barth cannot be more specific in his determination of the life setting of Matthew and his congregation, but he is convinced that the picture he has painted of the battlefront is important for an understanding of the Gospel of Matthew (159–64).

Heinz Joachim Held's work on Matthew as interpreter of the miracle stories takes the work of Bornkamm on the Stilling of the Storm in Matthew as its beginning point. Matthew was an exegete of the tradition. Matthew's characteristic abbreviation of the healing miracles was a result of his interpretation and shows that he attached no importance to details or to the pictorial nature of the events described. Rather he was concerned with bringing to the fore the essential theological content of the statements for the instruction of the church (211). The fact that the miracle stories of Matthew correspond more closely to the paradigm of Dibelius also emphasized the instructional nature of the stories (211–13).

The meaning of Jesus for Matthew is shown by his collection of the miracle cycle of Matthew 8–9 and his placing of it into the framework of 4:17–11:16. Jesus is the one who fulfills OT prophecy and is in particular God's servant who acts with authority, the Lord and helper of his congregation, and the one who brings the congregation to participate in the authority of her Lord (246–75). The representation of the disciples as those of little faith (in those passages where Mark had spoken of unbelief or lack of understanding or inability) links the history of Jesus and his disciples with the later history of the church with its conflicts and challenges (275–96).

Held concludes that in his interpretation Matthew is still the transmitter, for "he does not really introduce a new thought into the tradition, but rather reveals himself as its exegete in the exact sense of the word: he elucidates what it contains" (296).

Wolfgang Trilling (1959), Georg Strecker (1962), and Reinhart Hummel (1963) come to views of the situation in Matthew's church which are in opposition to those of Bornkamm, Barth, and Held. Trilling begins his study with O. Michel's view that Matthew's Gospel is to be understood with hindsight, from the missionary command of Matt 28:18–20, which teaches an unqualified universality of the Christian faith (21). Trilling does not deny the existence of Jewish-Christian tradition in Matthew, but he makes a distinction between Matthew's material and the final redaction. The Jewish-Christian traditions preserved in Matthew were not to end in a Gospel teaching a Jewish-Christian heresy; they were to be used in the development of a universal Christianity which cannot be called typically Jewish-Christian or typically Gentile-Christian.

Strecker explains the separatist Jewish-Christian and the universalist Gentile-Christian features in Matthew as does Trilling: the Jewish-Christian features are to be traced to the period of transmisson and the Gentile-Christian features to the final redaction. The setting of the final redaction is

Hellenistic-Jewish Christian. As noted earlier, Strecker emphasizes that the redactor is in a dialectical relationship with his community. Strecker also sees a dialectical relationship between history and eschatology in the Gospel, for Matthew, just as Luke (and even Mark), has adjusted to the delay of the parousia by coordinating the historical with the eschatological and by dividing the history of salvation into epochs.

Hummel determined Matthew's place in early Christianity by a redactional study of the passages in which a controversy with Judaism appears, and he did so on the assumption that the debates of Jesus with his Jewish opponents reflect the circumstances of Matthew's day as well as Matthew's theology. Hummel mediates between the view of Bornkamm and that of Trilling and Strecker. Matthew's church has actually not yet parted from the Jewish community; it has not yet been excluded from the society of Judaism. Nevertheless, Matthew's church is something fundamentally new compared with the Israelite national community.

Lucan Studies

The view that Luke's work must be understood as a response to the problem of the delay of the parousia and as a theology of a history of salvation was quickly accepted as an "assured result" of Lucan studies. The framework provided by Conzelmann was a powerful way of understanding and presenting the material of Luke-Acts as a whole and of dealing with particular passages and themes in the books.

Eduard Lohse applied Conzelmann's programmatic ideas (independently of Conzelmann's book) in articles in 1953 and 1954. Lohse relates the work of Luke to the OT and makes a positive evaluation of Luke's theology. For Luke, the life of Jesus is evidence of the faithfulness of God in regard to his people Israel. The events are recounted by Luke to show what God has accomplished. The work of Luke is also related to OT historiography, particularly that of the Deuteronomist. Conzelmann had concluded that in Luke's development of his idea of redemptive history his attitude to history "represents something entirely new compared with that of Judaism" (1954:167). In Lohse's view, however, Luke has joined the story of past salvation to his day, just as the Deuteronomist telescoped the past of Moses and the present of Israel (1954a:271 n. 60).

Ulrich Wilckens's study of the six missionary speeches in the first thirteen chapters of Acts (1961) advances the work of Conzelmann by the thesis that these speeches result from Luke's creative ability and theology and not from primitive Christian theology. However, for the speeches of Paul in Lystra and Athens, Luke used a Hellenistic-Christian pattern that was known to him from the tradition. The difference in the form of the two types of sermons is due to Luke's theology. The mission to the Jews is reflected in the sermons to the Jews, which refer to their place in salvation history. When the Jews are dropped out of salvation history, the mission to the Gentiles is reflected in sermons that refer to their situation.

Marcan Studies

Although Marxsen established redaction criticism as a new study, his work did not meet with the same degree of critical acclaim as did Conzelmann's work on Luke and the work of Bornkamm, Barth, and Held on Matthew. Scholars in general found the work of W. Wrede on the messianic secret more basic. Alfred Suhl's study of OT citations and allusions in Mark (1965), however, does contrast Mark's use of the OT with the prophecy-and-fulfillment pattern of Matthew and Luke. This supports the view that Mark had a heightened expectation of the end and that the Gospel is to be understood as an address to Mark's church.

Johannes Schreiber (1967) may be considered an adherent of Marxsen's method of backward composition and analysis in that he begins with the account of the crucifixion, which is seen as the high point of the passion narrative. But Schreiber comes to conclusions that are different from those of Marxsen. Mark taught that salvation and judgment are already included in the cross and, hence, the eschaton is present. Mark, then, is not concerned with anxious awaiting of the parousia, as Marxsen held. The parousia is for unbelievers to whom it will make clear the judgment and salvation already present for believers in the cross. Behind the Gospel of Mark, Schreiber sees a Gentile-Christian Hellenistic theology that is stamped with gnostic elements that determine Mark's concepts.

Shifting Sands

In early redactional studies it became increasingly clear that a dialectical relationship exists between detailed redactional studies and the understanding of the larger historical and theological context. Of course, other factors extending from textual criticism and source analysis to the situation of the interpreter are inevitably included. Recent redactional studies have related the various elements of redaction criticism in ways that result in radically different conclusions about the situation and theology of the Synoptic Gospels.

Shifting Sands in Matthean Studies

Alongside Matthew's relationship to Judaism and to the law, salvation history, covenant, and Christology are themes that have become important in the study of Matthew.

Rolf Walker (1967) sees Matthew in terms of the history of salvation, which begins with Abraham and runs till the parousia. The situation of the author of Matthew is that of the last time, and from this perspective the evangelist composes a "life of Jesus," which is also an "acts of the apostles" in that the story of the post-Easter mission of the church is depicted in the story of Jesus (see also Thompson).

For Kenzo Tagawa (1970), "Matthew's undifferentiated community consciousness" (162) is the key to understanding the thought of the Gospel. The confusion between Israel and the church occurs because both of these are in Matthew's milieu. Insofar as the church is identified with Israel, the apostles are not to go beyond Israel (10:5). Insofar as the church is a community distinct from the Jewish nation, the command to make disciples of all nations (28:19) makes sense.

According to Hubert Frankemölle (1974), Matthew's Gospel is an answer to the question of God's faithfulness, which arose because of Israel's rejection of Jesus as Messiah and the destruction of Jerusalem. To answer the question, Matthew employs covenant theology and develops a theology of God's activity in history. The church has taken the place of unfaithful Israel, and God, in the person of Jesus, has come to be with his own and to renew his covenant.

Jack Dean Kingsbury defines Matthew's purpose as christological on the basis of Matthew's main threefold structure, which sets forth the person of Jesus Messiah (1:1–4:16); the proclamation of Jesus (4:17–16:20); and the suffering, death, and resurrection of Jesus Messiah (16:20–28:20) (1975:9–25). In a second organization, Matthew operated with a design of the history of salvation. He differentiates between the time of Israel and the time of Jesus, of which Matthew's own age is a subdivision (37).

Shifting Sands in Lucan Studies

Over a quarter century after publication of Conzelmann's work, there is widespread agreement only "on the point that Conzelmann's synthesis is inadequate" (Talbert, 1976:395).

Günter Klein (1961) finds the Lucan emphasis upon apostolic succession to be related to the problem of gnostic heretics, and Charles H. Talbert (1966, 1970) has shown how Luke's work as a totality may be understood as a reaction to gnosticism. Hans-Werner Bartsch (1963) declares that instead of a historicizing of eschatology, Luke urged constant readiness for the end! G. Schneider (1975), following J. Dupont (1972), finds that in material unique to Luke there is an individualization of eschatology so that Luke is able to say that the kingdom is near for believers without contradicting his conception of the delay of the parousia. Luke anticipated the parousia as an event of immediate relevance for himself and his contemporaries, according to Eric Franklin (1975). The event that Franklin sees as central, however, is the ascension, and the value of Luke is that he was able to see the significance of continuing history without abandoning the traditional eschatology.

Luke's use of complementary, climactic, and antithetic parallelism convinced Helmut Flender (1965) that Luke's work is more subtle than

Conzelmann and other interpeters have discerned, and he finds a kerygmatic emphasis within the historical aspects of Luke's work. W. C. Robinson
(1964) sees a travel plan in the work of Luke that is the result of Luke's
transformation of temporal eschatology into historical geography. K. Löning
(1969) explains the salvation motif as a result of the apologetic nature of the
work. I. H. Marshall (1970, 1978) has defended the thesis that "Luke was
primarily an evangelist or preacher, concerned to lead men to Christian
belief on the basis of a reliable record of the historical facts" (1970:9).

Shifting Sands in Marcan Studies

Since the work of Marxsen, there has developed "general scholarly
agreement that henceforth Mark must be read as a theological book." But
at the present time "there is a bewildering diversity of opinion as to the
theological needs this gospel was designed to meet" (Martin, 1978:23).

Quentin Quesnell (1969) interprets Mark from Mark 6:52 and finds that
lack of comprehension, mystery, and the emphasis on bread are keys to
Mark's message. The message is that the Christian faith is a mystery to be
understood only through faith in the resurrection but which is symbolically
expressed and experientially known in the celebration of the Eucharist
(276).

Theodore J. Weeden (1971) suggests that Mark is confronting heretics
who follow a "divine-man" theology by dramatizing the christological dispute
between Mark and his opponents in a historical drama, with Jesus serving
as a surrogate for Mark and the disciples for the opponents of Mark.

Werner H. Kelber (1974) sees Mark as addressed to displaced Christians who are without hope after the fall of Jerusalem in 70. The fundamental
purpose of the Gospel is to affirm the realization of the kingdom in Galilee.
"This manifesto is truly gospel message for a people who had suffered the
loss of the kingdom and were bereft of orientation in space and time. It
reaffirms the Kingdom in a new spatio-temporal configuration" (139).

Howard Clark Kee (1977) concludes that Mark is the product of an
apocalyptic community just prior to the fall of Jerusalem. The Gospel was
designed to serve as a guidebook for the community as it awaited God's
vindication of Jesus as the triumphant Son of Man.

In the past decade some scholars have defended Mark as a "conservative" redactor. Jürgen Roloff declares that Mark "will not simply be a presentation of the risen lord in the historicized garb; it understands itself as a
presentation of a past history to be contrasted fundamentally from the
present" (1969:93). Heine Simonsen (1972) sees the evangelist as standing
in the midst of a living tradition which possessed authority for him and which
he served through the formation of a gospel. There is, then, continuity from
Jesus' own view of his work through the process of tradition to the redaction
of the Gospel (22–23).

Rudolf Pesch's commentary on Mark is based on the thesis that Mark took a conservative attitude toward the material at his disposal, arranging traditional material for the instruction of his community in Rome to convey the fundamentals of the gospel and the challenge of the mission to the Gentiles (12–13, 48–63).

Development of Method

Redaction-critical studies have shown that the evangelists' editorial activities may be used to explain different situations and theologies. Perhaps no method will be able to prove that one particular situation and theological message is to be associated with a Gospel. However, reliable principles and methods are needed to guide the discipline and guard against purely idiosyncratic reconstructions.

Comprehensiveness of Redaction

In 1961, Johannes Schreiber gave principles for the study of Mark that may be considered to have been implicit in the work of Marxsen. The first principle is applicable to study of the three Synoptic Gospels and may be called the principle of comprehensiveness: "All verses of Mark that are to be ascribed to the redaction of Mark with the help of the methods of analytical research provide the point of departure for establishing his theology, to the extent that in these verses scattered over the whole gospel a unified theological conception becomes visible" (1961:154). This principle, of course, will not prove a particular hypothesis, but it will rule out certain proposals built upon limited data. The application of this principle (perhaps unconsciously) has called into question the one-sided views of Conzelmann on Luke's treatment of eschatology and of Bornkamm on the Jewish character of Matthew's church.

Composition as Structure

The third principle of Schreiber supports the need for coordinating the results of redaction with the structuring of the Gospel: "The selection and arrangement of the tradition in the gospel of Mark also allows inferences as to Mark's redaction" (1961:155). Leander Keck suggests that the abandonment of the idea that the outline of Mark accurately sketches developments in the life of Jesus should be replaced with the insight that "the architecture of the text" expresses the concern of the evangelist (96; see also Edwards: 394; Perrin, 1969:66; and Talbert, 1974:1–10). This principle has been applied by Jack Dean Kingsbury, who sees Matthew as "the penetration of a carefully developed topical outline by a precise conception of history" (1975:37).

Composition in a Broad Sense

In 1969, Norman Perrin emphasized not only that redaction criticism must go beyond redaction in the limited sense to include the arrangement of the material and narrative development but also that the "whole range of creative activities which we can detect in an evangelist" ought to be used in determining the theology of the evangelist (1969:66). Attention to the product of the author as "literature" has inaugurated a phase of Gospel study which emphasizes the "text of the gospel as a coherent text with its own internal dynamics" (Perrin, 1976:120; see Perrin, 1972:5–18; Talbert, 1974; Petersen).

The Gospel Genre

Charles Talbert has forcefully reintroduced the possibility of viewing the Gospel genre not only as the result of tradition but in light of the genre of Greco-Roman biographies. The methods of composition and the sociological settings of such works provide suggestive parallels for studying the Gospels and Acts (1974, 1977).

Coordination of Elements

The attempt to discern the situation and theology of the evangelists today seems to require a system of study which coordinates various elements in a fashion that no one element can determine the final outcome but no one element can be ignored. In such a situation, it is important that the appropriate elements be related in a proper way. For Mark, Kee suggests a triangular method, the coordination of social, literary, and conceptual modes (1–13). For Luke, Schneider suggests that analysis and correlation of four elements will result in determination of the intention and goal of Luke-Acts: (1) the explicit statement of the intention of the author, (2) details that confirm the statement of intention and illuminate the accomplishment, (3) themes and problems that are to be seen in Luke-Acts, and (4) the genre of the work as suggested by Talbert.

The view of the Gospels as literary products to be studied in light of such factors as plot and character yields a system that can be coordinated with the system of form and redaction criticism. The material of the Gospels may be studied from the form-redaction perspective and the theological interests of the churches and their evangelists traced out. At the same time, the material has literary functions that are more affective in nature. The two systems may be used to guide and correct each other.

IV. LINGUISTIC CHALLENGES AND CONTRIBUTIONS TO FORM AND REDACTION CRITICISM

"Candid Questions" of Erhardt Güttgemanns

Erhardt Güttgemanns raised a series of questions concerning form and redaction criticism in a 1970 volume, and in later writings he has attempted to develop a theological program on the basis of contemporary studies in linguistics and literature. Güttgemanns (1970) attempted to show that Bultmann's assumption of continuity between the oral form and the written form of the tradition cannot be maintained. The process of formation is a dialectical interlacing of collectively transmitted "material" and individual intentional "act." The result is that the "material" of the tradition is transformed into a new linguistic *Gestalt* ("form") and serves the meaning-structure of this new form with its meaning-horizon. The model which has been used in form criticism is thereby destroyed (1970:189).

In later works Güttgemanns has made use of Noam Chomsky's generative transformational grammar to distinguish between the "performance" level of the Gospel material and the "competence" that lies behind the performance. Güttgemanns explains the origin of individual forms and the form of the Gospel on the basis of a "competence" that may be quantified scientifically. He refers to this "competence" as a "text grammar" and emphasizes that the meaning of a "text" is not the result of the configuration on the surface level but of the "grammar" or the relations on a deeper linguistic level. Traditional exegesis is a rudiment of historical positivism that must be repudiated in light of modern linguistics (1973:69).

Linguistic Contributions

The "crucial questions" raised by Güttgemanns challenged the entire NT establishment and were not immediately taken up. Nevertheless, Güttgemanns did raise pertinent questions, and some scholars have seen help in the variety of linguistic and literary tools to which Güttgemanns introduced them.

The Redactor and His Church from the Perspective of Information Theory

Hubert Frankemölle (1979) seeks to relate the tradition to the redaction by viewing the relationship of the evangelist to his church in terms of a model based on information theory and oriented toward human relationships. Such a model shows that the formation of tradition is a dialectical process involving the evangelist and his church. The religious practices and traditions of the evangelist and his church provide a repertoire of oral and written linguistic patterns for the process. In a model oriented toward human communication, the evangelist and the church are both seen as speakers and hearers, and the factors related to both are in continual flux. Hence, the Gospels (just as the NT letters) are to be seen as a "snapshot" out of a continuous linguistic communication between the evangelist and his church.

The Sitz im Leben of the Written Gospel

Werner H. Kelber agrees with Güttgemanns that there was no tendency in the oral tradition that resulted in the written Gospels, and he attempts to find a setting that will explain the creation of the new meaning-*Gestalt*. The "law of social identification" (1979:27) and not verbal memory directed the oral tradition; many social interests resulted in many traditions. The written Gospel is seen by Kelber as a reduction of social interests to one and as "a crucial alternative to the oral way of being" (1979:51). The written form resulted from the crisis mirrored in Mark 13. The event of 70 brought the primitive prophets' proclamation of the real presence of Christ in the logia more and more into disrepute. A crisis of trust developed, and the Gospel text was developed to set a new basis of trust and stability. "The text guaranteed as text a measure of permanence that was completely out of reach in the world of oral uncertainty" (1979:50).

Mediation through Structural Insights

Gerd Theissen has attempted to further (rather than destroy) classical form criticism by a structural approach to the miracle stories. Theissen asks if the individual units could have been taken up into a broader composition without the destruction of their narrative integrity. If so, form criticism is possible. "The solution rests in the fact that the small units were not only integrated in a totality external to them but that this totality was structured through them" (211). Theissen suggests that this mutuality is conceivable because of the existence of different levels of linguistic phenomena. The Saussurean dichotomy, *langue/parole* (paralleled by the competence/performance dichotomy of Chomsky), is translated by Theissen into potential form structure/realization. With this distinction, Theissen is able to reconcile Bultmann's view to that of Marxsen and even that of Güttgemanns: "Continuity reigns above all on the level of potential form structure. Each actualization of this form structure in concrete texts may be understood as a new creation. When one compares different actualizations as they follow one another, one can confirm either a further development or a recoinage" (227). Theissen studies the miracle stories in terms of form (the synchronic moment), history (the diachronic moment), and function (the comprehensive structure of constraints and acts and intentions of social life). Theissen sees that the function (and *Sitz im Leben*) is not to be limited to typical narrative situations. A broader definition will include social constraints and anthropological data which help us understand why one seizes upon and utilizes particular literary forms (12).

Robert W. Funk has approached the miracle stories from the perspective of structuralism (discourse analysis) in order to move from the surface level of the narrative to deeper structures and to discover the formal narrative composition of the NT healing miracle stories.

Hermeneutic-oriented Form and Redaction Criticism

Klaus Berger agrees with Güttgemanns that the Gospel form does not result from the simple accumulation of smaller units, that analysis must proceed from the view that the Gospel text was a meaningful totality for the final redactor (64–65). This does not mean that the individual units cannot be analyzed linguistically and that their historical-sociological aspects cannot be clarified. Berger does not relate the different phases of development by means of an abstract linguistic level underlying the surface level, which can explain a wide variety of surface-level forms. He uses the concept of "semantic field" to mediate between the individual units and the completed Gospels. "Texts are not enclosed systems. Semantic fields mediate between texts on the linguistic level. These semantic fields are 'intertextual,' that is, they do not exist isolated but only in a number of texts" (166).

The most important insight of Berger has to do with the centrality of hermeneutics in form and redaction study. The origin and each later reception of a text is to be understood in terms of the same hermeneutic principles. The formation of tradition and understanding are inextricably related. Considering origin and reception as coparticipants results in a vision of the unification of the linguistic process in linguistic forms and semantic fields and the unification of essential significance of interest and the fundamentally sociological dimensions of the linguistic process (268–69).

V. CONCLUSION

The future of form and redaction criticism will involve attempts to integrate traditional historical approaches with nonhistorical linguistic and literary methods of study. The expansion of the concept of *Sitz im Leben* ("life-setting") is a strategy that would allow conventional criticism to embrace newer approaches. The individual units and Gospels as wholes would be seen not only in the light of institutional settings but also in the light of linguistic, literary, and other cultural settings. The tradition and completed Gospels will not be explained by any one *Sitz im Leben* (historical or nonhistorical) but in the light of a plurality of settings.

BIBLIOGRAPHY

Baer, H. von
    1926   *Der Heilige Geist in den Lukasschriften.* BWANT 39. Stuttgart: Kohlhammer.

Barth, Gerhard
    1960   "Das Gesetzesverständnis des Evangelisten Matthäus." Pp. 54–154 in Bornkamm, Barth, and Held. Quotations from Eng. trans., "Matthew's Understanding of the Law," pp. 58–164.

Bartsch, Hans-Werner
    1963   *Wachet aber zu jeder Zeit! Entwurf einer Auslegung des Lukasevangeliums.* Hamburg-Bergstedt: Herbert Reich.

Benoit, Pierre
1946   "Réflexions sur la 'Formgeschichtliche Methode.' " *RB* 53: 481–512.
               Reprinted in his *Exégèse et théologie*, 1. 25–61. 3 vols. Paris: Cerf,
               1961–68. Eng. trans. "Reflections on 'Formgeschichtliche Methode.' "
               Pp. 11–45 in *Jesus and the Gospel*, vol. 1. 2 vols. New York: Herder
               and Herder/Seabury, 1973–75.

Berger, Klaus
1977   *Exegese des Neuen Testaments: Neue Wege vom Text zur Auslegung.*
               Heidelberg: Quelle & Meyer.

Bertram, Georg
1922   *Die Leidensgeschichte Jesu und der Christuskult.* Göttingen: Vanden-
               hoeck & Ruprecht.

Bornkamm, Günther
1948   "Die Sturmstillung im Matthäusevangelium." *Wort und Dienst:*
               Jahrbuch der Theologischen Schule Bethel n.s. 1: 49–54. Eng. trans.,
               "The Stilling of the Storm in Matthew." Pp. 52–57 in Bornkamm,
               Barth, and Held.
1954   "Matthäus als Interpret der Herrenworte." *TLZ* 79: 341–46.
1958a   "Evangelien, formgeschichtlich." *RGG*³ 2. 749–53.
1958b   "Formen und Gattungen im Neuen Testament." *RGG*³ 2. 999–1005.
1960   "Enderwartung und Kirche in Matthäusevangelium." Pp. 13–47 in
               Bornkamm, Barth, and Held. Quotations from Eng. trans., "End-
               Expectation and Church in Matthew," pp. 15–51.
1964   "Der Auferstandene und der Irdische: Mt 28, 16–20." Pp. 171–91 in
               Zeit und Geschichte: Dankesgabe an Rudolf Bultmann zum 80.
               Geburtstag. Ed. E. Dinkler. Tübingen: Mohr-Siebeck.

Bornkamm, Günther, G. Barth, and H. J. Held
1960   *Überlieferung und Auslegung im Mattäusevangelium.* Neukirchen-
               Vluyn: Neukirchener-Verlag. Eng. trans., *Tradition and Interpreta-*
               tion in Matthew. Philadelphia: Westminster, 1963.

Bovon, François
1976   "Orientations actuelles des études lucaniennes." *RTP* 26: 161–90.
1978   *Luc le théologien: Vingt-cinq ans de recherches (1950–1975).* Le
               monde de la Bible. Neuchâtel and Paris: Delachaux and Niestlé.

Bultmann, Rudolf
1921   *Die Geschichte der synoptischen Tradition.* Göttingen: Vanden-
               hoeck & Ruprecht. Eng. trans. of 3d ed. (1958), *History of the Synop-*
               tic Tradition. New York: Harper, 1963.
1955   "The Transformation of the Idea of the Church in the History of Early
               Christianity." *CJT* 1: 73–81.

Cadbury, Henry J.
1923   "Between Jesus and the Gospels." *HTR* 16: 81–92.

Conzelmann, Hans
1952   "Zur Lukas-Analyse." *ZTK* 49: 16–33.
1954   *Die Mitte der Zeit: Studien zur Theologie des Lukas.* BHT 17. Tübin-
               gen: Mohr-Siebeck. 4th ed., 1962. Quotations from Eng. trans. of 2d
               ed. (1957), *The Theology of St Luke.* New York: Harper, 1960.
1956   "Formen und Gattungen: II. Im NT." Pp. 1310–15 in *Evangelisches*
               Kirchenlexicon, vol. 1. Ed. Heinz Brunotte and Otto Weber. Göttin-
               gen: Vandenhoeck & Ruprecht.

Dibelius, Martin
     1919   *Die Formgeschichte des Evangeliums.* Tübingen: Mohr. Eng. trans. of
               2d ed. (1933): *From Tradition to Gospel.* New York: Scribner, 1934.
               Reprinted Greenwood, SC: Attic, 1972.

Dodd, Charles H.
     1935   *The Apostolic Preaching and Its Developments.* New York: Harper.
     1952   "The Framework of the Gospel Narrative." In his *New Testament
               Studies.* Manchester: Manchester University Press; New York:
               Scribner.

Doty, William G.
     1969   "The Discipline and Literature of New Testament Form Criticism."
               ATR 51: 257–321.

Dupont, Jacques
     1972   "L'après-mort dans l'oeuvre de Luc." *RTL* 3: 3–21.

Easton, Burton Scott
     1928   *The Gospel Before the Gospels.* New York: Scribner.

Edwards, Richard A.
     1969   "The Redaction of Luke." *JR* 49: 392–405.

Ellis, E. Earle
     1975   "New Directions in Form Criticism." Pp. 299–315 in *Jesus Christus
               in Historie und Theologie: Neutestamentliche Festschrift für Hans
               Conzelmann zum 60. Geburtstag.* Ed. Georg Strecker. Tübingen:
               Mohr-Siebeck. Reprinted in his *Prophecy and Hermeneutic in Early
               Christianity,* 237–53. Grand Rapids: Eerdmans, 1978.

Flender, Helmut
     1965   *Heil und Geschichte in der Theologie des Lukas.* Munich: Kaiser.
               Quotations from Eng. trans., *St Luke: Theologian of Redemptive
               History.* London: SPCK; Philadelphia: Fortress, 1967.

Frankemölle, Hubert
     1974   *Jahwebund und Kirche Christi.* Münster: Aschendorff.
     1979   "Evangelist und Gemeinde: Eine methodenkritische Besinnung (mit
               Beispielen aus dem Mattäusevangelium)." *Bib* 60: 153–90.

Franklin, Eric
     1975   *Christ the Lord: A Study in the Purpose and Theology of Luke-Acts.*
               Philadelphia: Westminster.

Funk, Robert W.
     1978   "The Form of the New Testament Healing Miracle Story." *Semeia* 12:
               57–96.

Gerhardsson, Birger
     1961   *Memory and Manuscript: Oral Tradition and Written Transmission in
               Rabbinic Judaism and Early Christianity.* ASNU 22. Lund: Gleerup.

Grant, Frederick C.
     1933   *The Growth of the Gospels.* New York: Abingdon.

Grobel, Kendrick
     1937   *Formgeschichte und Synoptische Quellenanalyse.* Göttingen: Vanden-
               hoeck & Ruprecht.

Güttgemanns, Erhardt
1970   *Offene Fragen zur Formgeschichte des Evangeliums: Eine methodologische Skizze der Grundlagenproblematik der Form- und Redaktionsgeschichte.* BEvT 54. Munich: Kaiser. Eng. trans.: *Candid Questions
concerning Gospel Form Criticism.* PTMS 26. Pittsburgh: Pickwick,
1979.
1972   "Linguistisch-literatur-wissenschaftliche Grundlegung einer neutestamentlichen Theologie." *Linguistica Biblica* 13/14: 2–18.
1973   "Narrative Analyse synoptischer Texte." *Linguistica Biblica* 25/26:
50–73.

Haenchen, Ernst
1955   "Tradition und Komposition in der Apostelgeschichte." *ZTK* 52:
205–25.
1956   *Die Apostelgeschichte neu übersetzt und erklärt.* MeyerK 3. Göttingen: Vandenhoeck & Ruprecht. Eng. trans. of 14th ed. (1965): *The
Acts of the Apostles: A Commentary.* Philadelphia: Westminster,
1971.

Harrington, Daniel J.
1975   "Matthean Studies since Joachim Rohde." *HeyJ* 16: 375–88.

Held, Heinz Joachim
1960   "Matthäus als Interpret der Wundergeschichten." Pp. 155–287 in
Bornkamm, Barth, and Held. Quotations from Eng. trans., "Matthew
as Interpreter of the Miracle Stories," pp. 165–299.

Hooker, Morna D.
1972   "On Using the Wrong Tool." *Theology* 75: 570–81.

Hummel, Reinhart
1963   *Die Auseinandersetzung zwischen Kirche und Judentum im Matthäusevangelium.* BEvT 33. Munich: Kaiser.

Iber, G.
1957–58 "Zur Formgeschichte der Evangelien." *TRu* n.s. 24: 283–338.
1961   "Neuere Literatur zur Formgeschichte." "Nachwort" to 4th ed. of
Dibelius, *Die Formgeschichte des Evangeliums,* 302–12. Tübingen:
Mohr-Siebeck.

Jervell, Jacob
1972   *Luke and the People of God: A New Look at Luke-Acts.* Minneapolis:
Augsburg.

Käsemann, Ernst
1954–55 "Sätze heiligen Rechtes im NT." *NTS* 1: 248–60. Eng. trans.:
"Sentences of Holy Law in the New Testament." Pp. 66–81 in his
New Testament Questions of Today. Philadelphia: Fortress, 1969.

Keck, Leander E.
1968   "Review of John the Baptist in the Gospel Tradition." *USQR* 24: 96.

Kee, Howard Clark
1977   *Community of the New Age: Studies in Mark's Gospel.* Philadelphia:
Westminster.
1978   "Mark's Gospel in Recent Research." *Int* 32: 353–68.

Kelber, Werner H.
1974   *The Kingdom in Mark: A New Place and a New Time.* Philadelphia:
Westminster.

1979   "Markus und die mündliche Tradition." *Linguistica Biblica* 45: 5–58.
1983   *The Oral and the Written Gospel: The Hermeneutics of Speaking and Writing in the Synoptic Tradition, Mark, Paul and Q.* Philadelphia: Fortress.

Kingsbury, Jack Dean
1975   *Matthew: Structure, Christology, Kingdom.* Philadelphia: Fortress.
1977   *Matthew.* Proclamation Commentaries. Philadelphia: Fortress.

Klein, Günter
1961   *Die zwölf Apostel: Ursprung und Gestalt einer Idee.* FRLANT 77. Göttingen: Vandenhoeck & Ruprecht.

Lightfoot, Robert H.
1934   *History and Interpretation in the Gospels.* Bampton Lectures. London: Hodder & Stoughton; New York: Harper.

Linnemann, Eta
1970   *Studien zur Passionsgeschichte.* Göttingen: Vandenhoeck & Ruprecht.

Lohse, Eduard
1953   "Die Bedeutung des Pfingstberichtes im Rahmen des lukanischen Geschichtswerkes." *EvT* 13: 422–36.
1954a   "Lukas als Theologe der Heilsgeschichte." *EvT* 14: 256–75.
1954b   "Missionarisches Handeln Jesu nach dem Evangelium des Lukas." *TZ* 10: 1–13.

Löning, K.
1969   "Lukas-Theologe der von Gott geführten Heilsgeschichte." Pp. 200–28 in *Gestalt und Anspruch des Neuen Testaments.* Ed. J. Schreiner. Würzburg: Echter-Verlag.

McArthur, Harvey K.
1967   "A Survey of Recent Gospel Research." *Int* 18: 39–55.

McKnight, Edgar V.
1969   *What Is Form Criticism?* Guides to Biblical Scholarship. Philadelphia: Fortress.
1978   *Meaning in Texts: The Historical Shaping of a Narrative Hermeneutics.* Philadelphia: Fortress.

Manson, Thomas W.
1962   *Studies in the Gospels and Epistles.* Ed. M. Black. Manchester: Manchester University Press; Philadelphia: Westminster.

Marshall, I. H.
1970   *Luke: Historian and Theologian.* Exeter: Paternoster.
1978   *The Gospel of Luke: A Commentary on the Greek Text.* NICNT. Grand Rapids: Eerdmans.

Martin, Ralph P.
1978   "The Theology of Mark's Gospel." *Southwestern Journal of Theology* 21: 23–36.

Marxsen, Willi
1956   *Der Evangelist Markus: Studien zur Redaktionsgeschichte des Evangeliums.* FRLANT 67. Göttingen: Vandenhoeck & Ruprecht. Quotations from Eng. trans.: *Mark the Evangelist: Studies on the Redaction History of the Gospel.* New York and Nashville: Abingdon, 1969.

Perrin, Norman
1967   *Rediscovering the Teaching of Jesus.* New York: Harper & Row.
1969   *What Is Redaction Criticism?* Guides to Biblical Scholarship. Philadelphia: Fortress.
1972   "The Evangelist as Author: Reflections on Method in the Study and Interpretation of the Synoptic Gospels and Acts." *BR* 17: 5–18.
1976   "The Interpretation of the Gospel of Mark." *Int* 30: 115–24.

Pesch, Rudolf
1976   *Das Markusevangelium: I. Teil: Einleitung und Kommentar zu Kap. 1,1–8,26.* HTKNT 2:1. Freiburg, Basel, and Vienna: Herder.

Petersen, Norman R.
1978   *Literary Criticism for New Testament Critics.* Guides to Biblical Scholarship. Philadelphia: Fortress.

Quesnell, Quentin
1969   *The Mind of Mark: Interpretation and Method through the Exegesis of Mk 6,52.* AnBib 38. Rome: Pontifical Biblical Institute.

Redlich, E. B.
1939   *Form Criticism: Its Value and Limitations.* London: Duckworth.

Riddle, Donald W.
1939   *The Gospels: Their Origin and Growth.* Chicago: University of Chicago Press.

Riesenfeld, Harald
1957   *The Gospel Tradition and Its Beginnings: A Study in the Limits of "Formgeschichte."* London: Mowbray.

Robinson, William C.
1964   *Der Weg des Herrn: Studien zur Geschichte und Eschatologie im Lukas-Evangelium: Ein Gesprach mit Hans Conzelmann.* TF 36. Hamburg-Bergstedt: Herbert Reich.

Rohde, J.
1966   *Die redaktionsgeschichtliche Methode.* Hamburg: Furche-Verlag. Eng. trans., *Rediscovering the Teaching of the Evangelists.* Philadelphia: Westminster, 1968.

Roloff, Jürgen
1969   "Das Markusevangelium als Geschichtsdarstellung." *EvT* 29: 73–93.
1970   *Das Kerygma und der irdische Jesus: Historische Motive in den Jesus-Erzählungen der Evangelien.* Göttingen: Vandenhoeck & Ruprecht.

Schick, E.
1940   *Formgeschichte und Synoptikerexegese: Eine kritische Untersuchung über die Möglichkeit und die Grenzen der formgeschichtliche Methode.* NTAbh. Bd. 18, Heft 203. Münster: Aschendorff.

Schmidt, Karl Ludwig
1919   *Der Rahmen der Geschichte Jesu: Literarkritische Untersuchungen zur ältesten Jesusüberlieferung.* Berlin: Trowitzsch. Reprint Darmstadt: Wissenschaftliche Buchgesellschaft, 1964.

Schneider, Gerhard
1975   *Parusiegleichnisse im Lukas-Evangelium.* SBS 74. Stuttgart: Katholisches Biblewerk.
1977   "Der Zweck des lukanischen Doppelwerke." *BZ* n.s. 21: 45–66.

Schreiber, Johannes
    1961   "Die Christologie des Markusevangeliums: Beobachtungen zur
              Theologie und Komposition des zweiten Evangeliums." *ZTK* 58:
              154–83.
    1967   *Theologie des Vertrauens: Eine redaktionsgeschichtliche Untersuchung
              des Markusevangeliums.* Hamburg: Furche-Verlag.

Schürmann, Heinz
    1962   "Die vorösterlichen Anfänge der Logientradition: Versuch eines
              formgeschichtlichen Zugangs zum Leben Jesu." Pp. 342–70 in *Der
              historische Jesus und der Kerygmatische Christus.* Ed. H. Ristow and
              K. Matthiae. East Berlin: Evangelische Verlagsanstalt.

Scott, Ernest F.
    1938   *The Validity of the Gospel Record.* New York: Scribner.

Simonsen, Heine
    1972   "Zur Frage der grundlegenden Problematik in form und redaktions-
              geschichtlicher Evangelienforschung." *ST* 27: 1–23.

Strecker, Georg
    1962   *Der Weg der Gerechtigkeit: Untersuchung zur Theologie des Matthäus.*
              FRLANT 82. Göttingen: Vandenhoeck & Ruprecht.

Suhl, Alfred
    1965   *Die Funktion der alttestamentlichen Zitate und Anspielungen im
              Markusevangelium.* Gütersloh: Mohn.

Tagawa, Kenzo
    1970   "People and Community in the Gospel of Matthew." *NTS* 16: 149–62.

Talbert, Charles H.
    1966   *Luke and the Gnostics.* Nashville and New York: Abingdon.
    1970   "The Redaction Critical Quest for Luke the Theologian." Pp. 171–
              222 in *Jesus and Man's Hope,* vol. 1. 2 vols. Pittsburgh: Pittsburgh
              Theological Seminary.
    1974   *Literary Patterns, Theological Themes, and the Genre of Luke-Acts.*
              SBLMS 20. Missoula, MT: Scholars Press.
    1976   "Shifting Sands: The Recent Study of the Gospel of Luke." *Int* 30:
              381–95.
    1977   *What Is a Gospel? The Genre of the Canonical Gospels.* Philadelphia:
              Fortress.

Taylor, Vincent
    1933   *The Formation of the Gospel Tradition.* London: Macmillan.

Theissen, Gerd
    1974   *Urchristliche Wundergeschichten: Ein Beitrag zur formgeschichtlichen
              Erforschung der Synoptischen Evangelien.* Gütersloh: Mohn.

Thompson, William G.
    1974   "An Historical Perspective in the Gospel of Matthew." *JBL* 93:
              243–62.

Trilling, Wolfgang
    1959   *Das wahre Israel: Studien zur Theologie des Matthäusevangeliums.*
              Erfurter Theologische Studien. Leipzig: St. Benno-Verlag. Quota-
              tions from 3d ed. Munich: Kösel, 1964.

1969   "Matthäus, das kirchliche Evangelium: Überlieferungsgeschichte
          und Theologie." Pp. 186–99 in *Gestalt und Anspruch des Neuen
          Testaments*. Ed. J. Schreiner and G. Dautzenberg. Würzburg:
          Echter-Verlag.

Tucker, Gene M.
1976   "Form Criticism, OT." *IDBSup*, 342–45.

Vielhauer, P.
1950   "Zum 'Paulinismus' der Apostelgeschichte." *EvT* 10: 1–15. Eng.
          trans.: "On the 'Paulinism' of Acts." Pp. 33–50 in *Studies in Luke-Acts*.
          Ed. L. E. Keck and J. L. Martyn. New York and Nashville: Abingdon,
          1966.

Walker, Rolf
1967   *Die Heilsgeschichte im ersten Evangelium*. Göttingen: Vandenhoeck &
          Ruprecht.

Walker, William O.
1969   "The Quest for the Historical Jesus: A Discussion of Methodology."
          ATR 51: 38–56.

Weeden, Theodore J.
1971   *Mark — Traditions in Conflict*. Philadelphia: Fortress.

Wilckens, Ulrich
1961   *Die Missionsreden der Apostelgeschichte: Form- und traditions-
          geschichtliche Untersuchungen*. WMANT 5. Neukirchen-Vluyn:
          Neukirchener Verlag.
1966   "Interpreting Luke-Acts in a Period of Existentialist Theology."
          Pp. 60–83 in *Studies in Luke-Acts*. Ed. L. E. Keck and J. L. Martyn.
          Nashville and New York: Abingdon.

7

RECENT LITERARY CRITICISM

William A. Beardslee

I. THE BACKGROUND OF RECENT LITERARY CRITICISM

The most comprehensive work on NT literary criticism is still that of Paul Wendland, dating from 1912. It is still extremely useful. That this book has never been replaced is a sign both of the neglect of literary criticism in NT studies, and, more recently, of the diversity of approaches that has made a comprehensive treatment difficult.

Wendland's work could be described, as Eduard Norden described his work on ancient artistic prose—written not long before—as a "history of development" (1:vii). Historical literary criticism, the effort to trace the development of forms and to locate specific forms in specific settings, was the usual understanding of the field as a discipline of NT study in its "classic" period early in this century. Wendland and others, such as Adolf Jülicher, drew heavily on comparative studies and on ancient rhetoric, but with the aim of emphasizing the distinctiveness of separate phenomena, the historical concreteness of particular forms. At the same time, it was assumed that historical development was a process that supplied meaningful connections between the discrete phenomena.

The function of historical literary criticism was paradigmatically illustrated by the two-document hypothesis of synoptic relationships. Both the historical concreteness of the separate sources and the lines of developmental connection functioned to make this hypothesis a satisfying one, so much so that for decades it was simply presupposed without question. At the same time, the concern for history tended to overpower attention to formal literary features, which were studied for their value in establishing the historical development.

It is not too much to say that classical historical literary criticism was absorbed into the discipline of "Introduction," so that today one turns to works like those of Philipp Vielhauer and Helmut Koester for the fruits of research on literary history. From the literary criticism of sources developed the discipline of form criticism, treated elsewhere in this volume by Edgar McKnight.

The period in which form criticism developed was marked by a loss of confidence in the meaning of continuities in history, so that interpretive schemes other than historical development were necessary to provide theological or humanistic meaning. Of literary criticism in this period, the work of Bultmann is particularly notable, because he continued to give close attention to form, as in his study of the synoptic tradition (1963), while concurrently developing a hermeneutical position in which a stance toward existence prior to language was seen as fundamental (1958), so that a recent discussion of Bultmann as a literary critic (Detweiler, 1978:63–72) can analyze his view of how a text makes its impact without even mentioning any of his formal studies (see also Tannehill, 1975:8).

It should be noted that a traditional literary perspective in the interpretation of the Bible was kept alive in the "Bible as literature" movement, even though these works usually concentrated on the Hebrew scriptures. Older examples like Chase contain, along with studies of form, a good deal of historical scholarship. More recent works of this type often put almost total stress on formal analysis, as in Gros Louis. A useful review of this movement, with bibliography, is provided by Wilder (1971:xii-xxi). Not unrelated, but without the anti-theological presuppositions, has been the tradition of teaching English Bible in seminaries, which has often provided an introduction to the study of literary structure (Traina). The linguistic side of literary criticism was introduced into NT studies by Bible translators (see Nida, 1964).

II. AESTHETIC-RHETORICAL CRITICISM: AMOS N. WILDER

Through the long period from World War I to the present, no one has been more important in NT scholarship than Amos N. Wilder in calling attention to the formal, literary, and aesthetic qualities of the NT. Being himself both a poet and literary critic and a NT scholar, he was able to see the limitations of an often too-rationalistic tradition of scholarship and to call for attention to the role of imagination and symbolism.

Though Wilder's concerns for aesthetic-rhetorical criticism and for an appreciation of the role of imagination in faith were of long standing, his *Early Christian Rhetoric* (1964; reissue with new preface, 1971) came at a time when many scholars in the discipline were ready to hear these emphases, and the book marked a turning point in the work of both established scholars and younger ones; Norman Perrin is an example (1976:131).

Particularly important for the development of NT literary criticism was Wilder's emphasis on the power of metaphorical language (1971:118–28). He turned attention away from the effort to find a fixed conceptual equivalent for the text, stimulating a series of inquiries that are still under way. In relation to the "new hermeneutic," which similarly emphasized the creative power of language, Wilder insisted on "meaning" as well as "address" (1964). His more recent work on imagination and faith (1976) stresses the potential for recovery of biblical symbols. For further interpretation of Wilder's perspective, see Beardslee, 1978a; and Crossan, 1981; for his bibliography see Dewey.

III. THE INTERPRETATION OF THE PARABLES

We can best move toward more recent developments in literary criticism by focusing on the interpretation of the parables, which has been central in the effort to develop new approaches. (See also the review of this subject in Perrin, 1976:89–193.) The base line is provided by the work of C. H. Dodd and J. Jeremias, who drew in turn from Adolf Jülicher. Both Dodd and Jeremias attended to form primarily for the purpose of finding an original form located in an original historical situation. They manifested the interest in historical concreteness mentioned above and were in fact reacting against interpretations of the parables in more general terms, whether through allegory or through Jülicher's general truths. But both Dodd and Jeremias assumed, as did the interpreters they criticized, that the parables are communications *about* something (mainly but not wholly the kingdom). Their criterion that simplicity of form indicates originality was what generated their close attention to form.

The effort to reconstruct an original form of a parable is still central to much parable research (e.g., Crossan, 1973, with the subtitle *The Challenge of the Historical Jesus;* Weeden) and still proceeds by the same attention to formal structure. But two different moves have supplemented or even displaced this interest. They may be termed the phenomenological and the aesthetic-rhetorical types of interpretation. In practice they often overlap, but the following discussion will separate them for the sake of methodological clarity.

Phenomenological Interpretation of the Parables

Phenomenological literary criticism, best known in NT studies under the rubric of the "new hermeneutic," shifts attention away from form as a vehicle of communication about something. It concentrates on the process of reading or hearing and is in fact a phenomenology of reading. A severe reduction that strips away "unessential" detail to become open to the intentionality of what is heard, discovered by close attention to the essential elements in the reader's response, is at the heart of the method. Instead of language being a perhaps neutral vehicle for content, it is itself the reality that creates what happens in the reader's response: the well-known "language-event." The particular form of phenomenological literary criticism that became effective in NT studies was a Heideggerian one mediated by Bultmann and the new hermeneutic; for a placing of this group in phenomenological literary criticism generally, see Detweiler: 31–102.

A first example of this approach, Robert W. Funk's first major discussion of the parables (1966:124–222), does not depend wholly on the phenomenology of the "new hermeneutic," but is enriched by the study of metaphor by Philip Wheelwright, Owen Barfield, and others as well. Nevertheless, it will serve well to illustrate the style of interpretation.

It is the definition of parable as metaphor (from Dodd: 16; see also Wilder, 1971:71–88) that structured Funk's move away from parable as direct communication about something to parable as language-event which reshapes the (linguistically shaped) world of the hearer. The phenomenological reduction harmonizes well with the secularity of the parables stressed by Funk (1966:153) following Wilder (1971:73). That is, for Funk the everydayness of parable imagery makes it easier to bracket the question of God and the kingdom of God as known elsewhere, in order to concentrate on the linguistic work of the parable itself. Characteristic of much of the phenomenological work on the parables is Funk's emphasis on the incommensurability of derived, discursive language with the metaphorical speech of the parable (1966:149–52; 1974:80). His interest is in affirming the creative power of metaphor and its work, in the case of the parable, of inviting the hearer to participate in the world opened up by the parable. The question of the communication between the parabolic, metaphorical speech and discursive speech has remained a central one in NT literary criticism. Other dimensions of Funk's literary criticism, some of which will be referred to below, can be seen in a collection of his essays (1982).

Much of John Dominic Crossan's work on the parables springs from an analogous phenomenological perspective. Again the reader's response is the key to the interpretation, though Crossan, like Funk, retains a strong sense of the value of historical construction in order to filter out what is perceived as an inadequate reader's response, namely, the early church's interpretation of the parables. Though he recognizes real variety among them, the distinctive function of the parables is to reverse the hearer's expectation, to bring an end not to a specific world, but to world—that is, structured expectation (1973:27). In contrast to C. H. Dodd and J. Jeremias, who held that it was possible both in parables and otherwise to speak of God, for Crossan the transcendent cannot be spoken of as such, but can only be glimpsed when "world" is broken as it is in the real hearing of parable (1975:121–22). Though Perrin (1976:168) thought of Crossan as a historical interpreter of the parables, this level of interpretation does not disclose Crossan's deepest intention, as can be seen in his further works, which uncover the disconcerting, seriously playful quality of the parables by comparing the parables of Jesus with those of Franz Kafka (Crossan, 1975:78–80) and J. L. Borges (Crossan, 1976).

In a more recent work (1979), a whole volume on a single verse (Matt 13:44), Crossan draws on structural studies of folklore materials (buried treasure stories) to define what is special about Jesus' treasure parable. It turns out that Jesus' move in comparison to traditional treasure stories is so radical that Jesus calls for giving up the parable itself, that is, casting oneself on life totally without protecting structure. For Crossan's later work, see below on post-structuralist interpretation of the parables (section III).

Aesthetic-Rhetorical Interpretation of the Parables

A very different emphasis came into parable study with the work of Dan O. Via, Jr. (1967). He drew heavily on existentialist interpretation, supplemented, however, by a study of what British students of ordinary language were saying about religious statements. But his distinctive emphasis was on studying the parables as aesthetic objects; here he drew heavily on such critics as Murray Krieger, Northrop Frye, and Philip Wheelwright. He viewed the parables as having an internal pattern that was the clue to their meaning in any situation. Specifically, Via turned to Aristotle's distinction between comic and tragic plots, and he classified the parables into comic parables, with rising plot line, and tragic parables, with falling plot line.

Though Via gave some weight to historical reconstruction of the earlier stages of parables, his rhetorical-aesthetic analysis (which notes the earlier approaches to this dimension by G. V. Jones and by A. N. Wilder [1971]) enabled him to consider the parables apart from any specific setting. This was a fundamental alteration of perspective. Via was also more moderate than some of the phenomenological interpreters in that he did not try to find a single gesture that represented the proper response to parable, but allowed for variety. A significant indicator is that he let the less intense exemplary stories stand as a distinct category (1967:12–13; 1974), rather than reinterpreting them as truly metaphorical parables in their original use by Jesus, as Funk had done for the Good Samaritan (1966:210–22; 1974), followed by Crossan (1974:63–104).

Aesthetic-rhetorical perspectives are presupposed in the work of Sallie McFague TeSelle, Mary Ann Tolbert, and James Breech, though each takes a distinctive direction. Sallie McFague TeSelle [now Sallie McFague] emphasizes the nontransferability of the parabolic metaphor, but she seeks analogies between the metaphorical work of the parable and that of the story of Jesus.

Mary Ann Tolbert turns particularly to the theory of signs in semiotics for an analysis of the inevitable polyvalence of parabolic communication, but she also presents a rhetorical analysis of the polyvalence of metaphor. This approach turns away from the quest for the original historical meaning (51–66; so also Wittig: 75–103; see the other articles on polyvalence in *Semeia* 9; *contra* Weeden: 118 n 10). The structure of the parable does not generate "a meaning," but it does provide basic constraints and possibilities within which a variety of meanings may be perceived. Tolbert thus emphasizes the profoundly metaphorical nature of the parables, but she distances herself from that view of metaphor which claims that it cannot be analogously represented in another frame of reference. Rather, the basic language structure of the parable provides a standard for evaluating various interpretive possibilities. The emphasis on polyvalence opens the way for Tolbert to offer a Freudian interpretation and indeed to test two such interpretations and choose one as superior because it is in consonance with the narrative structure of the parable under consideration (note also Via's Jungian parable interpretation, 1977:21–44). As against the interpretations of Funk and Crossan, Tolbert's view does not stress limit or total transformation of world, but parable as opening insight into continuing everyday realities.

The work of James Breech (1983; see also 1979) has affinities with that of Crossan and Funk as well as with the perspective of Via. Breech's effort is cast in the form of the recovery of the original Jesus, but he has tried to break as sharply as possible with the criterion of appropriateness to the historical and social setting of Jesus. He finds that which is distinctive in the sayings and parables of Jesus by perceiving a structural similarity to the recognition of the "actual other" in works by Dostoievski, Gerard Manley Hopkins, and J. D. Salinger, among others. He draws on the category "story," but reduces its implications of social interaction to the minimum of encounter between two persons.

Structural Analysis of the Parables

A natural step beyond the interpretation of parables as aesthetic objects was the move to subject them to what intends to be a more rigorous analysis of form: structural analysis. The move to structuralism in literary criticism generally is a move toward greater rigor in control of the categories of study.

Structuralism is derived in part from aesthetic-rhetorical criticism, in its attention to form, and in part from phenomenology, in its attention to the process of reading. It differs from the former in seeking structures that are not apparent on the surface, and from the latter in that phenomenology's concern with a concrete, deciding self disappears in favor of the structure of language itself.

Structuralism does not concern itself with "what" a text means (its content), nor with "why" it means (ontological or theological perspectives on a text), but with "how" it means. It views meaning not as an intuitive whole but as a construct, and it aims to deconstruct the "meaning effect" of a text and show how it is produced. Thus, it searches for very general properties in different types of speech or writing, "deep structures," which are properties not in the first place of a specific text, but which are general possibilities, competences that generate specific texts.

Since most NT structural interpretation, including of course that of the parables, has dealt with narrative, it is not surprising that the most common model has been that of A. J. Greimas, based on the work of V. Propp, and sometimes applied in the further version of Claude Bremond. Structural criticism of this type requires a special vocabulary and a diagramming system that make it forbidding to the nonspecialist. More important, it is not a form of interpretation, but an analysis of what lies prior to interpretation. This can be seen in Daniel Patte's analysis of the Parable of the Good Samaritan (1974:1–26), which casts the narrative into Greimas's system, as well as in Crossan's account, which emphasizes the conflict of deep structures (1974:82–112). Güttgemanns's brief treatment of the same parable (1976c: 164–65) is in consonance with Patte's, though cast in a different terminology.

Patte's study of the parable of the Prodigal Son (1976b:71–149) illustrates the strengths and the one-sidedness of the method. He analyzes the syntagmatic (sequential) aspect of the story in its subunits in terms of Greimas's actantial model, then offers a paradigmatic (deep structure) mythical model, which shows how the story articulates oppositions, then generalizes these oppositions in a semiotic square, a diagram of logical oppositions. It is a demonstration of how narrative springs from nonnarrative, logical oppositions, and expresses one of the many contemporary relativizations of the narrative sense. Meaning, in this perspective, is not an intuitive whole but a "meaning effect" (1976a:21–24), which is analyzed into its separate elements.

Probably even more revealing of the function of structural analysis is the discussion of the parables of the Good Samaritan and the Prodigal Son by the Entrevernes Group.[1] They bypass the actantial (syntagmatic) schematizing of narrative action and proceed directly to a study of the system of oppositions in each parable, offering a clear presentation of how the very general model of oppositions is filled with specific narrative possibilities in each case.

Structuralism is one form of the modern hermeneutic of suspicion, which holds that what transpires in the encounter with a text is very different from what is immediately perceived and consciously articulated. Structuralism attempts a more radical reduction than phenomenology, by directing attention away from the scrutiny of consciousness toward general patterns of language. To give these patterns of tension concrete form, one has to look at the surface features of the text—in Patte's terms, to the cultural codes. Structuralism offers little guidance at this point. But it has shown itself a powerful tool in making clear the multiple possibilities of meaning in any text and in clarifying the basically conflictual nature of narrative. It has raised fundamental questions about the ontological reality of the narrative sense by showing how narrative is composed of nonnarrative oppositions.

---

[1] The Entrevernes Group of French biblical scholars and semioticists is made up of Jean Calloud, Georges Combet, Jean Delorme, Corina Galland-Combet, François Génuyt, Jean-Claude Giroud, Louis Panier, and Annie Perrin. In the present volume they are joined by Jacques Geninasca and A. J. Greimas.

Post-Structuralist Interpretation of the Parables

The interpreter who finds structuralism arid for hermeneutic purposes but who wishes to remain in the scientific stance that structuralism affirms may move beyond this restricted methodology to work in a wider frame of linguistics (see below, section V). Another move is to radicalize structuralism into the deconstruction associated particularly with the name of Jacques Derrida (on Derrida, see Detweiler, 1982). Crossan's later work has close affinities with deconstruction, in its emphasis on play, on polyvalence, and on indeterminacy (see Crossan, 1980).

The British literary critic Frank Kermode is also to be classified here. Kermode's work on narrative, focused on the Gospel of Mark, deals also with the parables. Kermode takes Mark 4:10–12 very seriously and faults traditional exegetes for explaining it away. Parables are intended to be enigmatic, and in this way they are emblematic of the Gospels as a whole (especially Mark); the Gospels, in turn, are emblematic of narrative as a whole: "The apparently perspicuous narrative yields up latent senses to interpretation; we are never inside it, and from the outside may never experience anything more than some radiant intimation of the source of all these senses" (45). The "inside" and the "outside" come from Mark 4; the radiance from a parable in Kafka's *The Trial*. The parable is an opening not to clarification but to a sharper confrontation with the permanent obscurity of our existence.

Trends in Parable Interpretation

This survey of trends in parable interpretation discloses most of the moves that can be seen in other literary-critical studies of the NT. They can be summarized under three heads. First, there has come to be a strong difference of opinion about the value of the older historical literary criticism. Some critics see it as of little value in the face of the radical plurality of meaning evoked by a text (Tolbert, Wittig, Kermode), whereas others find it useful as a propaedeutic to formal or structural analysis, or hold that historical and structural methods supplement each other in the total task of interpretation (Crossan, Funk, Patte). Second, the introduction of aesthetic-rhetorical criticism in NT studies was quickly followed by a move away from this criticism grounded in a tradition from Aristotle to the new critics (Wilder, 1971; Via, 1967) toward more recent methods that intend to be less intuitive and more rigorous (Patte and other structuralists; Via's later work has shared this move to some degree [1975]). Yet some interpreters who do make use of the more recent methods also insist that actual interpretation comes only at a later stage, by "divination" (Kermode); thus they maintain a long-standing cleft between interpretation and understanding. Third, somewhat in contrast to the former trend, there has been a dissolution of the distinction between literary criticism and hermeneutics; no longer are there clearly defined formal methods of analysis that can be used without engaging in reflection about general theory of interpretation.

IV. LITERARY CRITICISM AND HISTORICAL STUDY

The first of these trends, that which makes an issue of the relation between formal and historical study, comes to the fore in connection with a shift of cultural sensitivity. As Martin J. Buss observes (1–2; see also 3–44), in a discussion oriented toward the Hebrew scriptures, the shift from historical to formal methods reflects a turn away from individualism toward an interest in community and generality. To see the matter in this light is an aid in resisting the more strident calls for emphasis on one or the other type of method. What is needed is more thoughtful interaction between them.

The gap between historical and formal studies has been narrowed by renewed attention to the study of NT books and forms in relation to ancient literary forms and genres and to ancient rhetoric. One topic that has received fresh attention after a long period of dormancy is the question of the genre of the Gospels. Challenging a fairly extensive consensus that the Gospels were a unique Christian literary type (Bultmann, 1963:374), Moses Hadas and Morton Smith renewed an older affirmation that the Gospels are to be understood as a Hellenistic form. Fixing on the demonstration of unusual power as a common feature, they classified the Gospels as aretalogies (Hadas and Smith; Smith). H. Koester and J. M. Robinson drew attention to the aretalogical features especially in Mark and John (see Koester's chapter 5 in Robinson and Koester; and Robinson, 1970).

Challenging the appropriateness of "aretalogy" for the Gospel form as a whole, Kee claimed that the Gospels are derived from the apocalypse, though not narrowly apocalyptic in genre (1973, 1977a, 1977b). Similarly, Perrin (1974) classified Mark as an apocalyptic drama.

The broader category of biography has been defended by C. H. Talbert (1977), who developed a typology of ancient biographies and located the Gospels within it. Talbert countered Bultmann's rejection of this affiliation by contending that some ancient biographies showed mythic patterns as the Gospels do and that some were related in the broad sense to cult. Talbert also showed affinities between the literary structures of Luke-Acts and Hellenistic patterns (1974).

A contrasting way of relating the Gospels to the wider culture was chosen by Via (1975), who described Mark as a "tragi-comedy." Although he drew his parallels between Mark and classic Greek dramatic works, he was not concerned with the literary traditions of the concrete historical environment, as were those mentioned above, but with very general patterns of human response. His approach was formal and structural rather than historical.

The discussion of Gospel form has been inconclusive, since the Gospels, as least the Synoptics, do have affinities both with biography/aretalogy and with apocalypse. One is left with the questions, How broadly is the circle to be drawn? How relevant are content and function in determining genre, or are formal considerations to prevail? For a useful summary of the Gospel genre question and for a mediating conclusion that the Gospels are "eschatological memorabilia," see Robbins, 1980. On genre in general, see Doty, 1972b.

In a parallel way, the letters of Paul have been studied with a renewed appreciation for their affinities with Hellenistic rhetoric and literary criticism. Again Funk was a pathbreaker. He reviewed the history of this inquiry and made a fresh contribution to the study of Pauline form and style (1966: chap. 10); he then set a particular feature of the Pauline letter—the references to Paul's coming—in the framework of the wider tradition of Greek letter writing (1967). More recently, the study of the Greek letter tradition has been carried forward in the SBL; see the work of John L. White and of the SBL Ancient Epistolography Group (White, 1982). Doty (1973) offers an introduction to literary criticism of the letter form.

Rhetorical dimensions of the Pauline letters have been pursued in other ways. Abraham J. Malherbe compared Paul's rhetoric with that of Dio Chrysostom. In particular, H. D. Betz has pressed the connection with ancient conventions of writing in his study of Galatians, which he defined as an apologetic letter (1975; 1979a: *passim* and esp. 14–26). Although it may be questioned whether the apologetic theme and structure really unify the whole letter, Betz's thorough knowledge of ancient rhetoric and literary criticism, both in their concrete instances and in the ancient works that theorize about them, has shown the importance of continuing this type of investigation in other connections. Parenthetically, we may note that Betz has followed a similar approach with the Sermon on the Mount, which he has classified as an epitome, or summary of a master's teaching (1979b).

A different approach was taken by Wilhelm Wuellner, who directed attention, in the study of Romans, away from literary structure toward the type of rhetorical argumentation. He proposed that Romans is epideictic rather than forensic or deliberative, but his basic point was that rhetorical rather than logical argumentation would be the proper framework for understanding this letter. Thus, in addition to the resources of H. Lausberg's handbook (also used by the scholars referred to above), Wuellner drew from C. Perelman and L. Olbrechts-Tyteca. These latter explicitly attack the Cartesian emphasis on the sole importance of logical proof and attempt to reinstate probabilistic knowledge as basic, and not just a vaguer form of logical argument.

Other NT texts are also being studied in the context of ancient rhetoric, for example, the pronouncement stories (Tannehill, 1980, 1981; Robbins, 1982). We may expect this field to be an active one in the near future.

In the broader interpretive problems raised by the interaction of the two types of literary approach, the formal and the historical, there are two separate issues: the issue of the value of the concrete and definite as against the general (one of the great values of fiction is its definiteness of imagery), and the issue of the importance of historical factuality, happenedness. Even the descriptively historical has often actually made its effect by the concreteness of its imagery.

The call by some literary critics to recognize the kerygma as fiction (Kermode: 121–23; cf. Schneidau; Hoy) is a claim for the priority of language over history and an effort to encourage imaginative encounter with the kerygma by dissociating it from what is perceived as an institutionalized interpretation. This call correctly affirms that there could be no history as we traditionally know it unless the teller and the hearer could perceive and imagine reality in a narrative way. Thus, the Entrevernes Group (290) affirm that "an immanent analysis does not reflect history, it produces it."

Recognizing this situation does not necessarily lead to the conclusion that history is fiction in the sense that historical existence means directionlessness or that any reach for an organizing principle or teleology amounts to "transcendental narcissism" (Hoy: 94). Rather, the relativization of ontological and empirical or historical language, which results from the recognition of the linguistic production of meaning, is balanced by the relativity of linguistic structures to the referential dimension which they express. This mutual relativity need not result in skepticism. It is this writer's judgment, however, that historical factuality can only be regarded as important in a perspective that affirms that our access to reality is not totally shaped by language.

V. AESTHETIC-RHETORICAL CRITICISM AND LINGUISTIC-STRUCTURAL CRITICISM

Aesthetic-Rhetorical Criticism

The effort to find greater rigor in method will be carried further, as in general literary criticism. Various forms of traditional aesthetic-rhetorical criticism will maintain themselves as well, because of their ability to join imagination and disciplined method. The appearance of Northrop Frye's *The Great Code*, with its subtitle, *The Bible and Literature*, is a sign of the vitality of this type of interpretation as well as a reminder of a factor not dealt with in this review, that is, the literary heritage of the Hebrew scriptures as a factor in literary criticism of the NT. Frye works with myth as well as with metaphor and typology as interpretive categories. The work of Erich Auerbach and that of Wilder continue to be influential, as can be seen in the reissue of a group of classic articles by Wilder with an introduction by Breech (Wilder, 1982). Tannehill's book on forceful and imaginative sayings in the Gospels (1975) has been followed by other literary-critical studies, for example, on Mark's Christology (1979) and on the pronouncement story (1980, 1981). The present writer's brief introduction to literary criticism of the NT (1970a), as well as articles on the rhetorical function of the proverb (1970b, 1978b, 1979b), the work of Perrin on the language of the kingdom (1976), and George W. MacRae on the distinction of literary styles in Hebrews may also be mentioned. David Rhoads and Donald Michie have ably summarized much of the recent research on the literary features of Mark and have integrated these specialized studies into a careful study of Mark's narrative techniques. See also Doty (1972a) for a general introduction to literary study of the NT.

From the phenomenological side, the more intuitive criticism is well represented by Funk (1975) on Jesus as precursor of such figures as Henry David Thoreau, Franz Kafka, and J. L. Borges; like much literary criticism, this work broadens the trajectory within which the NT is to be considered. Funk's Jesus as ironist (a not-surprising result of the phenomenology of reading, which uncovers the indirectness of metaphorical speech) is a reminder that there is no thorough study of irony in the NT, though such a work exists for the Hebrew scriptures (Good). Such a study will have to pay attention to Wayne C. Booth's distinction between stable and unstable irony; Jesus or a NT writer as an "unstable" ironist could be a powerful reading for a modern interpreter, but would not be appropriate as a historical reconstruction.

Further, there is no hard and fast line to be drawn between rhetorical criticism and linguistic-structural criticism. Via (1975) has carried forward his comic-and-tragic analysis of NT plot structures with a careful use of phenomenological and structural methods. Norman R. Petersen (1978a) has given an analysis of the plot structure of Mark that is modeled on Roman Jakobson's communication theory as expanded by a rhetorical study of the interweaving of plotted elements. Petersen has also studied authorial point of view in Mark with an eye to making a judgment about the unity of the narrative (1978b).

We may expect aesthetic-rhetorical criticism to continue, increasingly in interaction with linguistic-structural studies, as well as with studies of ancient rhetoric, for it deals with the impact of meaning as a whole, and it opens the way for imaginative encounter with the text.

Structural Criticism

The more rigorous, sometimes quantified modes of criticism attempt to reduce the intuitive element in traditional literary criticism. They are still in process of development. French structuralism, discussed above under the parables, has been extensively applied to other NT texts (see *Semeia* 1, 2, 6, 9, 10; Barthes; Marin; Patte, 1976a, 1976b; Calloud; Patte and Patte; Entrevernes Group). The nonspecialist cannot do better than begin with

Jean Starobinski's study of the demoniac of Gerasa. A model of clarity and comprehensibility, the article shows how a study of the dynamics of opposition in the story and of shifts in narrative attention can uncover a dimension missed in traditional exegesis.

Patte and Patte have carried structural analysis further into actual interpretation of NT texts and into dialogue with hermeneutics. The Entrevernes Group has offered a thorough discussion of this method, enriched by a contribution by Greimas.

No NT scholar has made stronger claims for a rigorous linguistic approach than Erhardt Güttgemanns. He merits great thanks for forcing attention to new methods upon a highly traditional discipline. Nevertheless, his claim that now for the first time the NT can be accurately "translated" into contemporary preaching is an oversimplification. Güttgemanns's project of "generative poetics" draws on Noam Chomsky and a wide range of linguists. His journal, *Linguistica Biblica*, and such writings as Gerber and Güttgemanns, and Güttgemanns, 1978, present a wide range of linguistic options. But his actual procedures for analyzing a text are very similar to those of structuralism, being drawn from Propp as modified by Alan Dundes (Güttgemanns, 1976b). The modern principle that "grammar ontologically and logically precedes history" (1976c:169) is basic. Specifically, Güttgemanns discovers sixteen pairs of binary opposites in the narrative lexicon of the Gospels; the choice of combinations of these pairs determines genre (1976c:129).

The shift in attention represented by this work is well indicated by Güttgemanns's remark that A. Jülicher's parable interpretation was on the right lines (1976c:173). Analogously, Starobinski spoke appreciatively of allegorical interpretation, which likewise expressed very general patterns. Of importance for the theological interpreter is the clarity with which Güttgemanns shows that narrative is built on conflict. Most narrative is a zero-sum game; someone has to lose (Güttgemanns, 1976a:9; he modifies this for God, 1976b:81). Correct as the emphasis on conflict is, it need not be asserted in so unqualified a way. In part, this judgment arises from taking Propp's folktales as the corpus from which a narrative model is developed; contrast Greimas (in Entrevernes Group: 309) on the difference between folktales, which return to their original table of values, and the Gospel narratives, which move toward founding a new table of values. For an extended discussion of Güttgemanns's work, see *Semeia* 10.

These comments make clear that structuralism, which can be presented simply as a technique of rigorous analysis, is heavy with implications for interpretation (on structuralism and hermeneutics, see especially Patte and Patte; Entrevernes Group; Detweiler 1978; McKnight; Jobling; Kovacs). The central issue is the question of the relation between the deconstructed elements which compose meaning, and meaning itself. If the deconstruction is taken to show the illusoriness of meaning as immediately encountered in the text, one reaches a post-structuralist position like that of Derrida, who proposes "the joyous affirmation of the freeplay of the world and without truth, without origin" (cited in West: 79). Much literary criticism of the NT has been pushing toward such an interpretation of its subversive impact on our securities (see Crossan above). But there are other alternatives, which recognize the relativity of our knowledge, but, by recourse to the analogy of deconstruction of language with the deconstruction of experience (e.g., Ricoeur, drawing on the phenomenological tradition; McKnight, in a thorough study drawing on Wilhelm Dilthey, or, very briefly sketched, Beardslee, 1979a, drawing on A. N. Whitehead) affirm that the dialectic between meaning and its deconstructed elements enables us to make ontological affirmations.

Discourse Analysis and Linguistics

It may well turn out to be the case that another type of linguistic interpretation, making much less extensive hermeneutical claims, will come to be even more fruitful for actual exegesis than structuralism or Güttgemanns's generative poetics. Another group of linguists, appreciative of the work of Propp, Greimas, and others in the structuralist school, nevertheless take a different approach, studying the interplay of surface patterns as their clue to the organization of meaning. "Discourse analysis," unknown to most NT scholars, has been influential in the interpretation of the Bible for some years in the practical and theoretical work of Bible translators. (Nida, 1964, can serve as a useful introduction to much of modern linguistics.) Like the structuralists, these linguists look for regularities in patterns greater than the sentence and for general theories to account for them. But they find the patterns in linguistic clues by which the discourse is articulated, the clues that enable the speaker to put a discourse together and the hearer to follow its organization. For the theory behind this practice, see Grimes, 1975a; and see van Dijk for the theory of the macrostructures underlying discourse. J. Beekman and J. Callow, and K. Callow offer a useful survey of discourse analysis. Application to the NT is not yet far advanced, except in connection with translation, but see Nida, 1972; Louw; Grimes, 1975b. Perhaps the most accessible study of NT texts is Funk's essay on the NT miracle stories (1978).

The schemes exposing the linkages of discourse may be as forbidding at first sight as structuralist diagrams, but their content is much closer to the surface structure and is aimed at disclosing the organization of discourse. There are several reasons why this type of analysis may prove to be useful. First, the method focuses on language as communication, surely central for NT interpretation. Second, although the models are generated by study of a large body of materials, they do not focus as structuralism does on abstract features of language. Rather, by noting the particular network of relations in a specific text, discourse analysis can go far to clarifying the combination of the general and particular in that text, while structuralism concentrates on general features. Finally, the inward turn toward language structure in structuralism contrasts with the openness of discourse analysis to socio-linguistics, which could lead to the drawing of connections between linguistic studies and the sociological studies of early Christianity, which constitute an active research front today.

Discourse analysis has presupposed a setting in general linguistics. To articulate the full dimensions of the implications of modern linguistics for the interpretation of biblical texts is the task that lies beyond discourse analysis. As they appear in most of the treatments noted below, the linguistic approaches stand in contrast to structuralism in putting emphasis on the "pragmatics" of the text, that is, how it affects the reader. (Structuralists too are reaching toward a fuller linguistic setting; see Delorme.) Study of the NT and related texts in terms of linguistics is more fully advanced in European scholarship than in the United States. For an extensive discussion of method, in the context of a study of Hermas, see Hellholm. Convenient statements of linguistic theory can be found in Baldinger, and Plett. Olsson is a fully developed treatment of John 4 from a linguistic point of view; for a parallel interpretation of the same text, see Boers. Further theory and a preliminary setting of traditional types of parable interpretation in a linguistic framework can be seen in Frankemölle. Linguistic approaches are increasingly being used by scholars whose primary interests are historical (e.g., Zeller).

Structuralism, discourse analysis, and linguistics are supplemented by other probes toward rigor in literary analysis, such as J. Arthur Baird's computer study of the audience of Jesus' sayings and John J. Collins's inventory approach to the genre of apocalyptic.

VI. LITERARY CRITICISM AND HERMENEUTICS

A discussion of recent hermeneutics lies beyond the scope of this paper. (For background, see Robinson and Cobb; for recent discussion, see *New Literary History* 10 [1978] 1; and *USQR* 34 [1979] 2 and 3). Four areas where the literary criticism discussed here impinges on hermeneutics can, however, be noted. Two of these have already been sketched above: the question of the relation between fiction and history in narrative, and the question of the relation between meaning and its deconstructed elements. A third issue, that of metaphor and symbol, has received an important discussion by Paul Ricoeur in relation to NT texts (1975; see also for symbol, 1967; for metaphor, 1976, 1977). Here it can only be noted that Ricoeur has insisted that metaphor does have an aspect of reference, even as it breaks the limits of existing meaning to redescribe reality. He has resisted, in other words, a completely inward turn in the interpretation of metaphor.

Finally, a central hermeneutic issue is that of language for the transcendent. The question of the transcendent is very much at issue also among secular critics, who avoid traditional theological language. Three approaches to the question can be seen in recent discussion.

First, there are those who discount the element of reference in language and who see the play of ambiguity as subjected, indeed, to linguistic constraints, but not in such a way as to allow communication either about a dependable world or about an element of constancy in value. From this point of view, the transcendent is radically beyond language. In Kermode's terms, the world is unfollowable, and the most that can be hoped for is "the perception of a momentary radiance, before the door of disappointment is finally shut upon us" (145) — the conclusion of his book on Mark. Crossan, with his emphasis on the transcendent as end of world, represents a related position. This view is directed against a false possessiveness of the transcendent, which is attributed both to Western philosophy and to traditional theology.

A second way of locating language for the transcendent is represented by Hans W. Frei (cf. also Mallard). In a program analogous to that of Martin Kähler, but strictly focused on literary issues, Frei examines the Gospel narratives with an eye to their techniques of identity description. He comes to the conclusion that the structure of the narrative itself demands the recognition of its own claims if it is taken seriously. Frei's literary criticism is a protest against the dissection of meaning in much traditional NT scholarship and a strong reaffirmation of a particular locus for transcendence language.

A third path is to reaffirm the view that transcendence is present in all communication, even though often obscured. Such a view can affirm much of the tradition both of hermeneutics and literary criticism, while at the same time remaining sensitive to the criticisms of static views of transcendence. What was wrong in the older theories was not their claim to knowledge, but their claim to certainty. In this perspective, it is possible to speak about the transcendent or God, even if very imperfectly.

This survey shows the need both for the vigorous continuation of a plurality of methods (well sketched in Berger) and for a series of fresh attempts at reconstruction of overall theories of interpretation. Here again there are options. The present writer (1979a) and Barry A. Woodbridge have sketched the beginnings of a theory based on Whitehead. Buss works from communication theory. McKnight orients his discussion from the work of Dilthey. Most comprehensive at present is the work of Ricoeur, referred to above.

The rapid development of the field and the variety of work being done have required the presentation above to be selective rather than comprehensive. Richard A. Spencer offers a collection that probes many of the actual issues in the field. For current work, beyond the journals that focus on this field—such as *Semeia, Linguistica Biblica,* and *Sémiotique et Bible,*—see *SBL Seminar Papers,* and, increasingly, the standard journals in the field of NT.

BIBLIOGRAPHY

Auerbach, Erich
  1953   *Mimesis: The Representation of Reality in Western Literature.* Garden City, NY: Doubleday, Anchor.

Baird, J. Arthur
  1969   *Audience Criticism and the Historical Jesus.* Philadelphia: Westminster.
  1976   "Content-Analysis and the Computer: A Case Study in the Application of the Scientific Method to Biblical Research." *JBL* 95: 255–76.

Baldinger, Kurt
  1980   *Semantic Theory: Toward a Modern Semiotics.* Ed. Roger Wright. Trans. William C. Brown. New York: St. Martin's.

Barthes, Roland, et al.
  1974   *Structural Analysis and Biblical Exegesis: Interpretational Essays.* PTMS 3. Pittsburgh: Pickwick.

Beardslee, William A.
  1970a   *Literary Criticism of the New Testament.* Philadelphia: Fortress.
  1970b   "Uses of the Proverb in the Synoptic Gospels." *Int* 24: 61–73.
  1978a   "Amos Niven Wilder: Poet and Scholar." *Semeia* 12: 1–14.
  1978b   "Parable, Proverb, and Koan." *Semeia* 12: 153–77.
  1979a   "Whitehead and Hermeneutic." *JAAR* 47: 31–37.
  1979b   "Saving One's Life by Losing It." *JAAR* 47: 57–72.

Beekman, John, and John Callow
  1974   *Translating the Word of God: Semantic Features and Semantic Structures.* Grand Rapids: Zondervan.

Berger, Klaus
  1977   *Exegese des Neuen Testaments: Neue Wege vom Text zum Auslegung.* Heidelberg: Quelle & Meyer.

Betz, Hans Dieter
  1975   "The Literary Composition and Function of Paul's Letter to the Galatians." *NTS* 21: 353–79.
  1979a   *Galatians.* Hermeneia. Philadelphia: Fortress.
  1979b   "The Sermon on the Mount: Its Literary Genre and Function." *JR* 59: 285–97.

Boers, Hendrikus W.
  1980   "Discourse Structure and Macro-Structure in the Interpretation of Texts: John 4:1–42 as an Example." Pp. 159–82 in *Society of Biblical Literature 1980 Seminar Papers.* Ed. Paul J. Achtemeier. Chico, CA: Scholars Press.

Booth, Wayne C.
  1974   *A Rhetoric of Irony.* Chicago: University of Chicago Press.

Breech, (Earl) James
1979   "Kingdom of God and the Parables of Jesus." *Semeia* 12: 15–40.
1983   *The Silence of Jesus: The Authentic Voice of the Historical Man.*
        Philadelphia: Fortress.

Bultmann, Rudolf
1958   *Jesus Christ and Mythology.* New York: Scribner.
1963   *History of the Synoptic Tradition.* New York: Harper & Row. 2d ed.
        [corrected], 1968. German original, 1921.

Buss, Martin J.
1979   "Introduction," and "Understanding Communication." Pp. 1–2, 3–44
        in *Encounter with the Text: Form and History in the Hebrew Bible.* Ed.
        M. J. Buss. Philadelphia: Fortress; Missoula, MT: Scholars Press.

Calloud, Jean
1976   *Structural Analysis of Narrative.* SBL Semeia Supplements 4.
        Philadelphia: Fortress; Missoula, MT: Scholars Press.

Callow, Kathleen
1974   *Discourse Considerations in Translating the Word of God.* Grand
        Rapids: Zondervan.

Chase, Mary Ellen
1944   *The Bible and the Common Reader.* New York: Macmillan.

Collins, John J., ed.
1979   *Semeia 14: Apocalypse: The Morphology of a Genre.* Missoula, MT:
        Scholars Press.

Crossan, John Dominic
1973   *In Parables: The Challenge of the Historical Jesus.* New York:
        Harper & Row.
1974   "Parable and Example in the Teaching of Jesus." *Semeia* 1: 63–104.
1975   *The Dark Interval: Toward a Theology of Story.* Niles, IL: Argus.
1976   *Raid On the Articulate: Comic Eschatology in Jesus and Borges.* New
        York: Harper & Row.
1979   *Finding Is the First Act: Trove Folktales and Jesus' Treasure Parable.*
        SBL Semeia Supplements 9. Philadelphia: Fortress; Missoula, MT:
        Scholars Press.
1980   *Cliffs of Fall: Paradox and Polyvalence in the Parables of Jesus.* New
        York: Seabury.
1981   *A Fragile Craft: The Work of Amos Niven Wilder.* SBL Biblical
        Scholarship in North America 3. Chico, CA: Scholars Press.

Delorme, Jean
1979   "L'intégration des petits unités littéraires dans l'Evangile de Marc du
        point de vue de la sémiotique structurale." *NTS* 25: 469–91.

Detweiler, Robert
1978   *Story, Sign, and Self: Phenomenology and Structuralism as Literary
        Critical Methods.* SBL Semeia Supplements 6. Philadelphia: Fortress;
        Missoula, MT: Scholars Press.
1982, ed. *Semeia 23: Derrida and Biblical Studies.* Chico, CA: Scholars Press.

Dewey, Arthur J.
1978   "Bibliography and Vita of Amos Niven Wilder." *Semeia* 13: 263–87.

Dijk, Teun A. van
1972   *Some Aspects of Text Grammars: A Study in Theoretical Linguistics
        and Poetics.* Janua Linguarum, Series maior 63. The Hague: Mouton.

Dodd, Charles Harold
    1935   *The Parables of the Kingdom.* Shaffer Lectures, 1935. New York: Scribner.

Doty, William G.
    1972a   *Contemporary New Testament Interpretation.* Englewood Cliffs, NJ: Prentice-Hall.
    1972b   "The Concept of Genre in Literary Analysis." Pp. 413–48 in *Society of Biblical Literature 1972 Seminar Papers,* vol. 2. Ed. Lane C. McGaughy. Missoula, MT: SBL.
    1973   *Letters in Primitive Christianity.* Philadelphia: Fortress.

Entrevernes Group, The
    1978   *Signs and Parables: Semiotics and Gospel Texts.* PTMS 23. Pittsburgh: Pickwick.

Frankemölle, H.
    1982   "Kommunikatives Haldeln in Gleichnissen Jesu. Historisch-kritische und pragmatische Exegese. Eine kritische Sichtung." *NTS* 28: 61–90.

Frei, Hans W.
    1975   *The Identity of Jesus Christ: The Hermeneutical Bases of Dogmatic Theology.* Philadelphia: Fortress.

Frye, Northrop
    1982   *The Great Code: The Bible and Literature.* New York: Harcourt Brace Jovanovich.

Funk, Robert W.
    1966   *Language, Hermeneutic, and Word of God: The Problem of Language in the New Testament and Contemporary Theology.* New York: Harper & Row.
    1967   "The Apostolic Parousia: Form and Significance." Pp. 246–68 in *Christian History and Interpretation: Studies Presented to John Knox.* Ed. W. R. Farmer, C. F. D. Moule, and R. R. Niebuhr. Cambridge: University Press.
    1974   "The Good Samaritan as Metaphor." *Semeia* 2: 74–81.
    1975   *Jesus as Precursor.* SBL Semeia Supplements 2. Philadelphia: Fortress; Missoula, MT: Scholars Press.
    1978   "The Form of the New Testament Healing Miracle Story." *Semeia* 12: 57–96.
    1982   *Parables and Presence: Forms of the New Testament Tradition.* Philadelphia: Fortress.

Gerber, Uwe, and Erhardt Güttgemanns, eds.
    1973   *Glauben und Grammatik: Theologisches "Verstehen" als grammatischer Textprozess.* Bonn: Linguistica Biblica.

Good, Edwin M.
    1965   *Irony in the Old Testament.* Philadelphia: Westminster.

Grimes, Joseph E.
    1975a   *The Thread of Discourse.* Janua Linguarum, Series minor 207. The Hague: Mouton.
    1975b   "Signals of Discourse Structure in the Koine." Pp. 151–66 in *Society of Biblical Literature Seminar Papers,* vol. 1. Ed. George W. MacRae. Missoula, MT: Scholars Press.

Gros Louis, Kenneth R. R., ed.
1974 *Literary Interpretation of Biblical Narratives.* Nashville: Abingdon.

Güttgemanns, Erhardt
1976a "What Is 'Generative Poetics'? Theses and Reflections Concerning a New Exegetical Method." *Semeia* 6: 1–21.
1976b "Introductory Remarks Concerning the Structural Study of Narrative." *Semeia* 6: 23–125.
1976c "Narrative Analysis of Synoptic Texts." *Semeia* 6: 127–79.
1978 *Einführung in die Linguistik für Textwissenschaftler.* Bonn: Linguistica Biblica.

Hadas, Moses, and Morton Smith
1965 *Heroes and Gods.* New York: Harper & Row.

Hellholm, David
1980 *Das Visionenbuch des Hermas als Apokalypse. I. Methodologische Vorüberlegungen und makrostrukturelle Textanalyse.* Lund: Gleerup.

Hoy, David C.
1979 "Taking History Seriously: Foucault, Gadamer, Habermas." *USQR* 34: 85–95.

Jeremias, Joachim
1963 *The Parables of Jesus.* Rev. ed. New York: Scribner.

Jobling, David K.
1979 "Structuralism, Hermeneutics, and Exegesis: Three Recent Contributions to the Discussion." *USQR* 34: 135–47.

Jones, Geraint Vaughan
1964 *The Art and Truth of the Parables: A Study of Their Literary Form and Modern Interpretation.* London: SPCK.

Jülicher, Adolf
1899 *Die Gleichnisreden Jesu.* 2 vols. Tübingen: Mohr-Siebeck.

Kähler, Martin
1964 *The So-Called Historical Jesus and the Historic, Biblical Christ.* Philadelphia: Fortress. German original, 1892.

Kee, Howard Clark
1973 "Aretalogy and Gospel." *JBL* 92: 402–22.
1977a *Jesus in History: An Approach to the Study of the Gospels.* 2d ed. New York: Harcourt Brace Jovanovich.
1977b *Community of the New Age: Studies in Mark's Gospel.* Philadelphia: Westminster.

Kermode, Frank
1979 *The Genesis of Secrecy: On the Interpretation of Narrative.* Cambridge, MA: Harvard University Press.

Koester, Helmut
1982 *Introduction to the New Testament.* 2 vols. Philadelphia: Fortress.

Kovacs, Brian W.
1979 "Philosophical Issues in Sociological Structuralism: A Bridge from Social Science to Hermeneutics." *USQR* 34: 149–57.

Lausberg, H.
1967 *Elemente der literarischen Rhetorik.* 3d ed. Munich: Huebner.

Louw, Johannes P.
1973   "Discourse Analysis and the Greek New Testament." *BT* 24: 101–18.

McKnight, Edgar V.
1978   *Meaning in Texts: The Historical Shaping of a Narrative Hermeneutic.*
        Philadelphia: Fortress.

MacRae, George W., S.J.
1978   "Heavenly Temple and Eschatology in the Letter to the Hebrews."
        Semeia 12: 179–99.

Malherbe, Abraham J.
1970   "Gentle as a Nurse: The Cynic Background of I Thess. ii." *NovT* 12:
        203–17.

Mallard, William
1977   *The Reflection of Theology in Literature.* San Antonio, TX: Trinity
        University Press.

Marin, Louis
1971   *Sémiotique de la Passion: Topiques et Figures.* Paris: Bibliothèque des
        Sciences Religieuses.

Nida, Eugene A.
1964   *Toward a Science of Translating.* Leiden: Brill.
1972   "Implications of Contemporary Linguistics for Biblical Scholarship."
        JBL 91: 73–89.

Norden, Eduard
1958   *Die antike Kunstprosa.* 2 vols. Darmstadt: Wissenschaftliche Buch-
        gesellschaft. Original, 1898.

Olsson, Birger
1974   *Structure and Meaning in the Fourth Gospel: A Text-Linguistic
        Analysis of John 2:1–11 and 4:1–42.* ConBNT 6. Lund: Gleerup.

Patte, Daniel
1974   "An Analysis of Narrative Structure and the Good Samaritan." *Semeia*
        2: 1–26.
1976a   *What Is Structural Exegesis?* Guides to Biblical Scholarship.
        Philadelphia: Fortress.
1976b, *Semiology and Parables: Exploration of the Possibilities Offered by
ed.   Structuralism for Exegesis.* PTMS 9. Pittsburgh: Pickwick.

Patte, Daniel, and Aline Patte
1978   *Structural Exegesis: From Theory to Practice: Exegesis of Mark 15 and
        16; Hermeneutical Implications.* Philadelphia: Fortress.

Perelman, Chaim, and L. Olbrechts-Tyteca
1971   *The New Rhetoric: A Treatise on Argumentation.* Notre Dame, IN:
        University of Notre Dame Press.

Perrin, Norman O.
1974   *The New Testament: An Introduction.* New York: Harcourt Brace
        Jovanovich.
1976   *Jesus and the Language of the Kingdom: Symbol and Metaphor in New
        Testament Interpretation.* Philadelphia: Fortress.

Petersen, Norman R.
1978a   *Literary Criticism for New Testament Critics.* Guides to Biblical
        Scholarship. Philadelphia: Fortress.
1978b   " 'Point of View' in Mark's Narrative." *Semeia* 12: 97–121.

Plett, Heinrich F.
  1979   *Textwissenschaft und Textanalyse: Semiotik, Linguistik, Rhetorik.* 2d
              ed. Heidelberg: Quelle & Meyer.

Rhoads, David, and Donald Michie
  1982   *Mark as Story: An Introduction to the Narrative of a Gospel.*
              Philadelphia: Fortress.

Ricoeur, Paul
  1967   *The Symbolism of Evil.* Boston: Beacon.
  1975   "Biblical Hermeneutics." *Semeia* 4: 29–148.
  1976   *Interpretation Theory: Discourse and the Surplus of Meaning.* Fort
              Worth: Texas Christian University Press.
  1977   *The Rule of Metaphor.* Toronto: University of Toronto Press.

Robbins, Vernon K.
  1980   "Mark as Genre." Pp. 371–99 in *Society of Biblical Literature 1980
              Seminar Papers.* Ed. Paul J. Achtemeier. Chico, CA: Scholars Press.
  1982   "Pronouncement Stories and Jesus' Blessing of Children: A Rhetor-
              ical Approach." Pp. 407–30 in *Society of Biblical Literature 1982
              Seminar Papers.* Ed. Kent Harold Richards. Chico, CA: Scholars
              Press.

Robinson, James M.
  1970   "On the *Gattung* of Mark (and John)," Pp. 99–129 in *Jesus and Man's
              Hope,* vol. 1. Ed. David G. Buttrick. Pittsburgh: Pittsburgh Theo-
              logical Seminary.

Robinson, James M., and John B. Cobb, Jr., eds.
  1964   *The New Hermeneutic.* New Frontiers in Theology 2. New York:
              Harper & Row.

Robinson, James M., and Helmut Koester
  1971   *Trajectories through Early Christianity.* Philadelphia: Fortress.

Schneidau, Herbert N.
  1976   *Sacred Discontent: The Bible and the Western Tradition.* Baton Rouge,
              LA: Louisiana State University Press.

Smith, Morton
  1971   "Prolegomena to a Discussion of Aretalogies, Divine Men, the
              Gospels and Jesus." *JBL* 90: 174–99.

Spencer, Richard A., ed.
  1980   *Orientation by Disorientation: Studies in Literary Criticism and Bib-
              lical Literary Criticism Presented in Honor of William A. Beardslee.*
              PTMS 35. Pittsburgh: Pickwick.

Starobinski, Jean
  1974   "The Gerasene Demoniac: A Literary Analysis of Mark 5:1–20."
              Pp. 57–84 in *Structural Analysis and Biblical Exegesis,* by Roland
              Barthes et al. PTMS 3. Pittsburgh: Pickwick.

Talbert, Charles H.
  1974   *Literary Patterns, Theological Themes, and the Genre of Luke-Acts.*
              SBLMS 20. Missoula, MT: Scholars Press.
  1977   *What Is a Gospel? The Genre of the Canonical Gospels.* Philadelphia:
              Fortress.

Tannehill, Robert C.
1975   *The Sword of His Mouth: Forceful and Imaginative Language in
            Synoptic Sayings.* SBL Semeia Supplements 1. Philadelphia: Fortress;
            Missoula, MT: Scholars Press.
1979   "The Gospel of Mark as Narrative Christology." *Semeia* 16: 57–95.
1980   "Synoptic Pronouncement Stories: Form and Function." Pp. 51–56
            in *Society of Biblical Literature 1980 Seminar Papers.* Ed. Paul J.
            Achtemeier. Chico, CA: Scholars Press.
1981, ed.   *Semeia 20: Pronouncement Stories.* Chico, CA: Scholars Press.

TeSelle, Sallie McFague [now Sallie McFague]
1975   *Speaking in Parables: A Study of Metaphor and Theology.* Philadel-
            phia: Fortress.

Tolbert, Mary Ann
1979   *Perspectives on the Parables: An Approach to Multiple Interpretations.*
            Philadelphia: Fortress.

Traina, Robert A.
1952   *Methodical Bible Study: A New Approach to Hermeneutics.* Wilmore,
            KY: privately published.

Via, Dan O., Jr.
1967   *The Parables: Their Literary and Existential Dimension.* Philadelphia:
            Fortress.
1974   "Parable and Example Story: A Literary-Structuralist Approach."
            Semeia 1: 105–33.
1975   *Kerygma and Comedy in the New Testament: A Structuralist Approach
            to Hermeneutics.* Philadelphia: Fortress.
1977   "The Prodigal Son: A Jungian Reading." *Semeia* 9: 21–43.

Vielhauer, Phillip
1975   *Geschichte der urchristlichen Literatur.* Berlin: de Gruyter.

Weeden, Theodore J., Sr.
1979   "Recovering the Parabolic Intent in the Parable of the Sower." *JAAR*
            47: 97–120.

Wendland, Paul
1912   *Die urchristlichen Literaturformen.* 3d ed. Tübingen: Mohr.

West, Cornel
1979   "Schleiermacher's Hermeneutics and the Myth of the Given." *USQR*
            34: 71–84.

White, John L.
1972   *The Form and Function of the Body of the Greek Letter.* SBLDS 2.
            Missoula, MT: Scholars Press.
1982, ed.   *Semeia 22: Studies in Ancient Letter Writing.* Chico, CA: Scholars
            Press.

Wilder, Amos Niven
1964   "The Word as Address and the Word as Meaning." Pp. 198–218 in
            Robinson and Cobb, eds.
1971   *Early Christian Rhetoric: The Language of the Gospel.* Cambridge,
            MA: Harvard University Press. Reissue of *The Language of the
            Gospel: Early Christian Rhetoric.* New York: Harper & Row, 1964,
            with a new introduction.

1976   *Theopoetic: Theology and the Religious Imagination.* Philadelphia:
            Fortress.
1982   *Jesus' Parables and the War of Myths.* Ed. James Breech. Philadel-
            phia: Fortress.

Wittig, Susan
1977   "A Theory of Multiple Meanings." *Semeia* 9: 75–103.

Woodbridge, Barry A.
1979   "An Assessment and Prospectus for a Process Hermeneutic." *JAAR*
            47: 121–28.

Wuellner, Wilhelm
1977   "Paul's Rhetoric of Argumentation in Romans: An Alternative to the
            Donfried-Karris Debate over Romans." Pp. 152–74 in *The Romans
            Debate.* Ed. Karl P. Donfried. Minneapolis: Augsburg.

Zeller, Dieter
1977   *Die weisheitlichen Mahnsprüche bei den Synoptikern.* Würzburg:
            Echter-Verlag.

Part Three

The Literature of
the New Testament

8

THE CANON OF THE NEW TESTAMENT

Harry Y. Gamble

I. INTRODUCTION

Although the discipline of NT studies presupposes the phenomenon of the canon and has traditionally been pursued on the presumption of the theological authority of the canon, the study of the formation and significance of the canon has rarely been a prominent item on the agenda of NT studies. Although the student of the NT has at least an obligatory interest in the subject, both the resources and the results of the study of the canon have seemed to belong more properly to the disciplines of church history and historical theology, an impression that has been unfortunately furthered by the increasing specialization of the theological disciplines since the turn of the century. This has served to limit the attention given to the question by NT scholars. Moreover, the enormous productivity of canon studies in the late nineteenth and early twentieth centuries, including the rich accumulation of evidence by T. Zahn (1888–1892, 1881–1929) and the impressive interpretations of it by Adolf Harnack (1889, 1925), H. Leitzmann (1907) and J. Leipoldt (1907), gave rise to a strong consensus which seemed to make further inquiries almost superfluous, and the few subsequent studies prior to World War II, such as those of E. J. Goodspeed (1926) and M.-J. Lagrange (1933), added little. The years since the war, however, have witnessed a dramatic resurgence in the study of the canon, and today one may say without exaggeration that the canon has become a leading concern of NT scholarship.

The reasons for this renewed attention to the canon are many. Just as the discovery of the Qumran library reopened the question of the OT canon by showing just how indeterminate were the authoritative scriptures of Judaism at the time of Christian beginnings—an insight indirectly relevant also for the history of the NT canon—so likewise has recently discovered early Christian literature, and not least the Nag Hammadi library, stimulated the study of the NT canon, partly by providing new evidence and partly by giving fresh illustration to the theological and literary variegation of early Christianity. A heightened sense of this diversity, especially as it has been influentially interpreted by W. Bauer (1971), has enhanced the appreciation of apocryphal materials and has made the NT canon seem less a natural product of consensus than a contrived instrument of controversy. Still more important has been the ever more rigorously historical interpretation of the NT literature itself, which has fractured the presumed unity of the NT by revealing that perhaps the most salient feature of the canon is its diversity, which is not only chronological and situational, but theological as well. This recognition has rendered all the more intriguing the question, on the one hand, how this collection came to be formed, and, on the other hand, what sort of theological authority can belong to a collection with little apparent internal coherence. Ironically, then, exegesis itself has helped to reopen the problems of the history of the canon and its theological value.

If for such reasons the NT canon has become a more pressing concern than at any time since early in this century, it has also become a more complex and far-reaching concern. Along with traditional historical questions it now incorporates controversial theological issues of broadly ecumenical importance. The historical and theological aspects of the problem of the canon are intimately related and cannot finally be separated. But it is helpful to distinguish them initially for purposes of discussion.

II. THE CANON AS A HISTORICAL PROBLEM

General Conceptions of the History of the Canon

In his broad sketch of the history of the canon W. Schneemelcher (1963:29) commented that "most points in the history of the canon are now so fully clarified that one can almost speak of a *communis opinio.*" This was an overstatement even twenty years ago, and today such a claim can certainly not be made. It is true that many particular facts of the history of the canon are adequately certified. Yet many important matters of fact remain undecided, and on some points the absence or ambiguity of evidence frustrates all inquiries, and this is especially true for the second century. In addition to the difficulty of acquiring sufficient data, there is the larger problem of how known facts should be coordinated and interpreted to yield an accurate and comprehensive understanding of the history of the canon, and about this there is little agreement. But for the current situation to stand out clearly it is necessary to summarize the consensus to which Scheemelcher referred.

The work of Harnack, Lietzmann, and Leipoldt made it clear that the formation of the canon was a protracted process extending over the first four centuries and into the fifth. However, the second century appeared to embrace the most crucial developments, for during that period, and especially in its second half, various Christian literature came into wide use and began to be cited alongside the (already) canonical OT scriptures. Toward the end of the second century this resulted in the availability of a "core NT" consisting of the four Gospels, the thirteen letters of Paul, Acts, 1 Peter and 1 John. This result was found to be attested by the Muratorian Fragment and the major fathers of the late second and early third centuries, despite minor variations. The idea, basic substance, and shape of the NT having been achieved, only marginal issues remained to be decided, and the consensus of the church gradually acknowledged or rejected a few other books until the NT reached final form. The commonly cited completion of this process is Athanasius's Easter Letter of 367, which offers a list of NT books exactly like our own.

As to the causes of the emergence of the canon, a strong emphasis has usually been laid on the ecclesiastical reactions to heterodox groups: the Marcionites with their reductionistic, ultra-Pauline scriptures; the Gnostics with their esoteric traditions, and the Montanists with their claims to new prophetic revelations. Indeed, these movements have often been viewed as the *sine qua non* of canon formation, even if other factors have not been entirely discounted, such as the disappearance of apostles and "apostolic men," the decline of oral tradition, the liturgical use of Christian writings, and the difficulty of sustaining Christian teaching on the basis of the OT alone.

The consensus very broadly sketched here relies heavily but often unwittingly on the work of Harnack, at least for the general course of canon history and the basic factors at work in it, even though the emphasis may be differently placed in the matter of formative influences. A large number of encyclopedia and dictionary treatments provide basically the same picture (Beare, 1962; Brown, 1968; Grant, 1970; Metzger, 1963; Sanders, 1962), as do the somewhat lengthier treatments of Souter (1954) and Grant (1965). In its basic features it is also represented in the only full-scale and detailed study of the history of the canon to be written in the postwar period, the magisterial work of Hans von Campenhausen (1972).

Von Campenhausen's study is valuable and provocative, precisely because he rightly disavows the idea that the history of the canon consists simply in the history of the citation of individual documents. He seeks instead to identify the dynamic forces that conspired to produce the NT and define its contents. Like Harnack, he views the history of the canon not as an isolated literary phenomenon but as an integral feature of the complex theological and institutional history of the ancient church. This approach, together with a wealth of documentation, sets his work decisively apart from the comparatively modest and superficial surveys of Souter and Grant. Still, von Campenhausen moves wholly within the general framework of the consensus outlined above, maintaining that the concept and fundamental content of the NT canon had fully emerged by about A.D. 200, so that for him too the second century has critical importance. For all practical purposes, the formation of the canon occurred in the period between Marcion and the Muratorian Fragment—and preeminently in reaction to heterodox movements of that period. Hence, little or no importance is attached to the disputations of the third century or to the official decisions of the fourth and fifth centuries.

This long-standing point of view has come under direct challenge by A. C. Sundberg, who has argued programmatically for a revised conception of the history of the canon (1968a). In his study of the development of the history of the OT canon (1964a; see 1958 for a summary), Sundberg refuted the idea that the early church inherited from Judaism a closed collection of Jewish scriptures. By the time the OT canon was closed in Judaism, the church had already gone its independent way, and so had to arrive on its own at a decision about the scope of its OT canon. When it did, the church's OT canon was not the same as Judaism's (1964, 1968b). The absence of a strictly defined canon of Jewish scriptures means that the early church's concept of scripture was open-ended and that the citation of Christian writings alongside Jewish scriptures, even when the same formulas are employed, does not signify their "canonical" status (1968a). Sundberg argues that a clear distinction must be maintained between the terms "scripture" and "canon," the former designating authoritative religious writings, but the latter being reserved for a strictly delimited collection held to be exclusively authoritative (1968a; 1971; see also Knox, 1942:19–25). Since uncertainties about the number of authoritative writings persisted well into the fourth century, and since Sundberg (1973) rejects the traditional date and provenance of the Muratorian Canon, he protests speaking about a "canon" in the strict sense at this time. The process of canonization proper, Sundberg insists, belongs to the later period when lists of exclusively authoritative Christian writings began to be drawn up. The effect of Sundberg's thesis is to throw the decisive period of canon formation forward from the second to the fourth century.

Although Sundberg appears to propose a dramatic departure from earlier views, the differences should not be overestimated. To some extent we have to do only with a problem of definition. General usage has customarily employed the terms "canon" and "canonical" rather loosely to designate documents widely held in authority, without regard to a definitive and exclusive determination of a group of such documents. On this basis, writings that were authoritative in the second and third centuries are sometimes said to constitute an "open" or "developing" canon, the stress falling on their normative use or function. Sundberg considers it inappropriate to speak of a "canon" of any sort until there exist definitive lists of authoritative writings, for a canon is by definition "closed." When this difference of definition (which might be characterized as "functional" versus "formal") is taken into account, Sundberg's departure from the common view seems less radical, for he also recognizes that by the late second century the Gospels and the Pauline letters had acquired a commanding authority, just as it has always been noted that the status of most other writings varied widely through the third and fourth centuries. Still, a scrupulousness about terminology is needed in order not to blur real distinctions, and Sundberg properly maintains that the history of the canon is not concerned simply with the normative use of Christian writings but with the delimitation of a specific group of such writings and with its meaning and function *as a collection*. Thus, there are significant differences beyond the merely semantic. Not the least of these is seen in the fact that Sundberg is led to regard the NT canon as the result of conscious discussion and official decision, and thus fully as a product of the church, a perspective that has otherwise been characteristic of Roman Catholic interpreters of the history of the canon (e.g., Appel, 1964). Von Campenhausen, on the other hand, represents the typically Protestant viewpoint, which prefers to see in the official lists and decisions of the fourth and fifth centuries hardly more than a *pro forma* "recognition" or "confirmation" of a much earlier and natural consensus of the church, which owed nothing to ecclesiastical authority. Here the theological ramifications of different concepts of the history of the canon begin to be evident.

The adequacy of such programmatic efforts to comprehend the history of the canon can be evaluated only by a continuing assessment of the historical evidence itself, and in the last several decades many studies have been devoted to particular questions that bear on the formation of the NT. A survey of these will suggest the points at issue and their relation to the larger conceptual problems.

The History of Component Collections

It is commonly recognized that the formation of the NT was less a matter of selective discrimination among individual documents than a "collection of collections." The four-Gospel collection and the Pauline corpus each had a prehistory that was largely independent of the shaping of the NT as a whole. Only Acts, the Catholic Epistles and Revelation seem not to have belonged to any larger grouping before being taken up into a comprehensive collection. The origins and early histories of these component collections are, at least by extension, part of the whole history of the canon.

The Pauline Corpus

The letters of Paul are not only the earliest extant Christian literature but also the earliest *collected* Christian literature. Yet the origins of the Pauline corpus are obscure and have been quite variously explained. That the Pauline letters were early valued and circulated outside the particular communities to which they were addressed (Harnack, 1926; Mowry, 1944) is clear both from the generalizing emendations of the addresses of some of them (Dahl, 1962; Gamble, 1977) and from the production and character of early Pauline pseudepigrapha (Colossians, Ephesians, 2 Thessalonians), which presuppose the currency of "Pauline" letters. Thus, at least some of the apostle's letters must have become widely known and used at an early time (*contra* Goodspeed, 1926, 1945, 1951, etc.). The silence of Acts about Paul's letters, though persistently puzzling, need not impede this conclusion (Knox, 1942:132–36; 1966:280; Klein: 190–92; Enslin; Barrett; Schenke; Walker). It is a long-standing view that the Pauline corpus emerged, more or less haphazardly, simply by a gradual process of accretion attending the exchange of his letters among various communities (e.g., Lake; see now Aland, 1979b). Plausible as this may be, there is little that could demonstrate such an assumption, and more particular hypotheses have often been preferred.

Two hypotheses have been widely publicized but rarely adopted. Goodspeed (1926, 1933, 1945, 1951, 1956) argued that the letters of Paul, neglected and forgotten, were "rediscovered" after the publication of Acts, which prompted a person already acquainted with two of the letters (Colossians and Philemon) to search out other letters of Paul among the communities mentioned in Acts. Finding these, this person composed Ephesians as a commendatory summary of Pauline thought and issued a collection of ten letters, including Ephesians as a preface. This theory has been variously supported and elaborated, mainly by Goodspeed's students. A. E. Barnett (1941) argued that near the end of the first century Paul's letters suddenly became widely known, and that this supported Goodspeed's conjecture. J. Knox (1935; repr. 1959) tried to prove that the collector was Onesimus, but rejected the publication of Acts as the occasion of the collection. C. L. Mitton both analyzed Ephesians on Goodspeed's assumptions (1951) and later provided a full statement of the theory·(1955). Otherwise this conception of the origin of the corpus has found little favor and has been rightly criticized for an excess of ingenuity, an inadequate comprehension of Ephesians, and incompatibility with the documentary evidence. Very different and no less ingenious is the theory of W. Schmithals (1972), who supposes that the corpus was produced by an individual whose set purpose was to create an effective weapon for the church in its struggle with Gnosticism. The distinctive feature of Schmithals's thesis is to represent the collector as a thoroughgoing editor who freely recast a large number of smaller Pauline letters and letter fragments in order to create an (ecumenical) collection of seven letters, each of which was made to contain anti-Gnostic elements. This theory of the occasion and purpose of the collection stands or falls with Schmithals's many conjectures about the redaction of individual letters, and to many these have seemed arbitrary and in some cases indefensible. Besides, the theory does not cohere well with the external evidence (Gamble, 1975). Notably, however, both Goodspeed and Schmithals have sought clues to the origin of the collection in the character of the corpus itself and have offered specific occasions and agents for its emergence. These are attractive features of their theories. The same concerns are also to be seen in the more recent theory sketched by H.-M. Schenke (1975), who regards the redaction of various letters, the production of Pauline pseudepigrapha, and the gathering of Paul's literary legacy as the work of a "Pauline school" whose aim was to preserve and propagate Pauline Christianity in the historic mission field of Paul after the apostle's death. This suggestion of a concrete sociological and theological setting for the post-Pauline history of the letters is particularly attractive. It properly assumes that the development of the corpus should be seen in terms of theological as well as literary history; it comprehends together the phenomena of redaction, pseudonymity, and collection as different aspects of a coherent endeavor; it is not hampered by the notion of a single agent; and it gains plausibility from continuities with the methods and agents associated with the missionary activity of Paul himself (see Conzelmann, 1965; Ellis; Ollrog). Each of these theories illustrates the tendency of modern studies, lacking clear external evidence about the collection of Paul's letters, to look to the substance and shape of the corpus for insights into its origin and to give special attention to its redactional and pseudepigraphical features. In light of these, an adequate theory of the post-Pauline history of the letters and the formation of the collection cannot be altogether simple.

The external evidence for the Pauline corpus prior to the late second century has remained difficult to define and to interpret (see Aland, 1979a). That Clement, Ignatius, Polycarp, and 2 Peter were acquainted with letters of Paul is beyond doubt, but it remains uncertain how many letters each knew and whether any of them had the letters in an actual "edition," in spite of claims that Ignatius (Rathke), Clement (Hagner), and Polycarp (Nielsen) knew a majority of Paul's letters and perhaps a full corpus (see Zahn, 1888–92, I/2:811–29). The alleged allusions do not support this (Lindemann: 201–16; Rensberger: 41–64; Schneemelcher, 1964). It is only with Marcion that we gain any detailed knowledge of an early edition of Paul's letters, but there is nothing to favor the surmise that he was "the first systematic collector of the Pauline heritage" (Bauer: 221). Rather, it now appears that Marcion merely took over an existing edition and reworked it to his own purpose (Frede, 1969:295–96; Finegan: 88; Dahl, 1978: 252–57; Clabeaux).

Good progress has been made, however, in delineating the shape of early editions of the corpus that reach back before the middle of the second century. Analyses of the early orders of the letters (Buck; Finegan; and esp. Frede, 1969) have revealed two very old arrangements, both based on the principle of decreasing length—but one counting letters to the same community (Corinthians, Thessalonians) as single units, the other counting them separately. This provides one order beginning with Corinthians, Romans, Ephesians, Thessalonians, and another with the "standard" order, Romans, Corinthians, Galatians, etc. Frede regards the former as the more primitive order and as governed by the "seven churches" concept (though he thinks it contained the Pastorals also), and he sees the standard order and the order of Marcion (which is thought to be chronological) as early derivations from it (1969:290–92). But the idea of a single, early, and archetypal edition seems untenable in view of the textual evidence (Gamble, 1977:121; Aland, 1979b; *contra* Zuntz; Harnack, 1926; Lietzmann, 1933). This makes all the more appealing the conjecture that there were two independent early editions of the corpus (Dahl, 1978:253–54), one containing Paul's letters to seven churches (lacking the Pastorals), the other containing thirteen letters of Paul (including the Pastorals), both of which must have antedated Marcion. The edition attested for Marcion may be derivative from the seven churches edition or may constitute yet a third independent edition, but in any case it is probably built on a chronological theory of the composition of the letters and need not be seen as a distinctively Marcionite creation (Frede, 1964:165–66). In spite of the early use of Hebrews by Clement of Rome and its presence in P^{46} among Paul's letters, there is no good warrant for the claim that Hebrews had a place in the earliest editions of the corpus (*contra* Anderson; Quinn; Aland, 1979b).

Apart from the appeals to Paul by Marcion and the Gnostics, which were sufficient for Tertullian to dub Paul *hereticorum apostolus*, a broad indifference to Paul's letters by many Christian writers of the second century cannot be gainsaid (Schneemelcher, 1964; Bauer). From this observation the conclusion has often been drawn that the church abandoned Paul on account of the heterodox appropriation of his letters and that he was only tardily reclaimed and domesticated with the aid of the Pastorals and/or Acts (Schneemelcher, 1964; Bauer: 226–28; von Campenhausen, 1972:144–45, 177–78; Carroll, 1953; Knox, 1942:113–39; 1966:285–86; Barrett; Strecker). But this is an argument from silence, and not a very good one, since outside Jewish-Christian circles there is no explicit antipathy toward Paul to be discovered in any writer, since the number of sources is small, and since the nature of the sources is not such as to encourage capitalization on Paul (Lindemann; Rensberger; Dassmann). While various factors may have limited appeals to Paul, it is not clear that the heterodox use of his letters was one of them. By the late second century the letters of Paul had come to be fully and universally established in Christian esteem.

The Gospels

The prehistory of the four-Gospel collection is, if anything, even more obscure than the formation of the Pauline corpus. The old view, represented by Zahn and Harnack among others, that a four-Gospel collection was already current near the beginning of the second century has been almost universally rejected (but cf. Crehan). The form-critical emphasis on oral tradition in the formation of Gospel literature and the recognition that oral tradition persisted alongside written Gospels well into the second century have undermined the basis of this opinion. Koester (1957) has made a strong case that the primary contact of the apostolic fathers with Gospel traditions was through free oral tradition rather than written Gospels. In this light, Papias's explicit preference for oral tradition over documents (*Hist. eccl.* 3.39.4) should probably be regarded as typical for the early second century.

Of course, Papias also offers testimony about written Gospels, and this has been much discussed in recent study, yet remains opaque (the Papias fragments are conveniently collected and carefully discussed by Schoedel: 89–130; and Kürzinger, 1983). While Papias is the first to refer to written Gospels by name, there is no clear evidence for Papias's reliance on any of our Gospels (Heard, 1954b). It has generally been taken for granted that he knew our Mark, but even this has been questioned by G. Kennedy (147–49), who has suggested that Papias referred only to "notes" preliminary to the composition of Mark and not the Gospel itself, a suggestion that gains some support from the fragmentary letter of Clement of Alexandria recently discovered and published by M. Smith (1973; cf. Meeks: 167–69). What other Gospels Papias may have known remains uncertain, whether Matthew (Schoedel; Petrie; [the designation *logia* does not preclude this according to Gryson; Robinson, 1971b:74–75]), Luke (Munck), or John (Grant, 1965; Merkel, 1971:48–49). But whatever Gospels Papias knew, he apparently did not value them as "scripture" or consider them beyond criticism. However, his defense of such documents and his interest in their sources presage a transition toward a higher regard for them.

It is only with Justin about the middle of the second century that we first meet with a knowledge and appreciation of several Gospels. Justin never names any of these but typically refers to them as "memoirs" (*apomnēmoneumata*) of the apostles or their followers. In this it appears both that he thought the Gospels were of apostolic origin and that he viewed them as historical records rather than as inspired scripture (Grant, 1961:15–18; Cosgrove). The designation *apomnēmoneumata* may have been used to emphasize especially the written character of the traditions about Jesus (Hyldahl; Abramowski) and may originally have been employed in anti-Gnostic argumentation (Abramowski). Nevertheless, it cannot be claimed that Justin was acquainted with a four-Gospel collection, for even if he knew the Fourth Gospel he made only the most tentative use of it (Sanders, 1943), and on the whole it is doubtful that he knew it at all (Hillmer, 1966:51–73). Besides the question of what Gospels Justin knew, there is the problem of how he may have used them. The characteristic differences between Justin's citations of Gospel traditions (both narrative and sayings material) and our Synoptic Gospels have long been noted and have been variously explained as due to faulty memory, the use of some other written Gospel, or the use of a Gospel harmony. Refining Koester's work (1957), A. J. Bellinzoni has argued that Justin did not quote dominical *logia* ("sayings") from written Gospels but relied instead on a post-synoptic harmonizing compilation of sayings which was widely used for catechetical and apologetic purposes (see Osborn: 120–34), and Kline supposes that the same harmony was employed by Justin and the Pseudo-Clementine Homilies. This thesis has been severely criticized by Strecker, and for good reasons, so that the character of Justin's citations of Gospel traditions remains a puzzle to which no really adequate and demonstrable solution has been found.

Tatian's *Diatessaron,* the best known and most influential—though certainly not the only—instance of harmonizing Gospel materials (von Campenhausen, 1972:174–75; cf. Leipoldt: 132–39), has always figured prominently in assessing the history of the fourfold Gospel because Tatian is the earliest witness to all four of our canonical Gospels. Earlier scholarship readily took this to show that the four-Gospel collection existed by Tatian's time. Recent studies, however, have rightly retreated from this conclusion. It is still asserted that Tatian's joint usage of these four Gospels "confirms that there already existed a collection of the four Gospels" (Kümmel, 1975:488), or shows that the church "recognized the primacy and unique-ness of only four Gospels" (Grant, 1965:138), or even that Tatian was the creator of the fourfold Gospel (Carroll, 1967:64–67; cf. 1954), but all such judgments are untenable. Tatian also made at least some use of other materials (Messina: xxxv-lii; Baarda; Charlesworth), regardless of whether he actually drew on a fifth Gospel (Quispel argues that he used the Gospel according to the Hebrews; for discussion see Klijn: 7–16). Hence, he scarcely viewed the four Gospels as unique or exclusively authoritative. Moreover, Tatian's free handling of the texts, including substantial omissions along with consistent conflation and transposition, indicates that he valued the Gospels for their contents but accorded them no special status as individual, let alone sacrosanct, texts. Whatever Tatian's precise purposes may have been, the *Diatessaron* symptomizes the persistent preference for a single and self-consistent Gospel which is elsewhere evident in the second century (Cullmann, 1956), and by its very existence contradicts any general acknowledgment of four separate Gospels. Indeed, the facts that Tatian encountered no criticism and that the *Diatessaron* enjoyed a very broad popularity in the ancient church (for a survey, see Metzger, 1977:10–36) indicate that Tatian hit on an appealing alternative to multiple Gospels.

The discovery of Papyrus Egerton 2 (portions of the "Unknown Gos-pel"), first-hand acquaintance with the *Gospel of Thomas* and other docu-ments from Nag Hammadi, and a renewed appreciation of the large number and various forms of Gospel-type literature in the early church have only complicated the problem of the emergence of the four-Gospel collection. It has been urged that the "Unknown Gospel," often dated to the early second century, shows a knowledge of all four of our canonical Gospels (e.g., Jere-mias, 1963:95), but a very strong case has been made for its independence (Mayeda). Similarly, some have thought that the *Gospel of Truth* (which is not itself actually a gospel) proves the existence not only of a four-Gospel canon but also of virtually the whole later canon by the middle of the second century (van Unnik, 1955; Crehan; Schelkle), but this is very doubtful because the alleged allusions are so subtle. On the other hand, it is widely agreed that the *Gospel of Thomas* represents an independent redaction of old tradition, and this has been maintained also for other apocryphal Gospels, for example, the *Gospel of Peter*, and the *Dialogue of the Savior* and the *Apocryphon of John* from Nag Hammadi (Koester, 1980; cf. Crossan). Thus, the older view that the apocryphal Gospels can be dismissed as secondary, imitative developments that are dependent on our canonical Gospels and attest their early popularity is now mentioned only with caution (Schneemelcher, 1963b) or completely rejected (Koester, 1971, 1980). The modern emphasis on the free and diverse oral transmission of gospel traditions has severely limited the possibility of making general or persuasive claims that apocryphal gospels depend in either form or content on the Gospels which finally became canonical. This means that the apocryphal Gospels cannot be offered in evidence for the early use or collection of the canonical Gospels.

Oscar Cullmann's helpful discussion (1956) of the theological problematic posed for the early church by a multiplicity of Gospels points to what was undoubtedly a factor in the shaping of a four-Gospel collection, namely, the desire on the one hand for a Gospel that was comprehensive enough to be theologically adequate, which led to the proliferation of Gospel writings, and the idea on the other hand that there should be one self-consistent Gospel, which prompted efforts to reduce the number of Gospels. This tension allows the four-Gospel collection to be seen as a compromise. But his claim that the use of a single Gospel was a gnostic-docetic proclivity should be viewed with skepticism. Actually there are excellent textual and paleographic indications that when written Gospels came into wide use they circulated individually for a long time (Moule: 253–55, and cf. p^{52}, P^{66}) and were variously subject to revision or expansion (beyond the longer ending of Mark, the interpolation of John 8:1–11 and the addition of chap. 21 to the Fourth Gospel, see Linton, and M. Smith). Originally it seems to have been typical for a given community (or region) to employ only one Gospel document, so that the use of multiple Gospels was an innovation. The preference for a single Gospel would in that case only be a traditional tendency, not a symptom of theological perversity. Moreover, although theological interests ought not be discounted in this connection, a plurality of Gospels also posed exegetical and historical problems on account of the differences among the Gospels, a fact to which the early church was by no means insensitive (Grant, 1961; Merkel, 1971; and for a useful collection of relevant texts, Merkel, 1978). It must have been largely for this reason that the Gospel of John was so tardy in gaining general recognition alongside the Synoptics.

It has often been claimed that by the time of Irenaeus "the four Gospel canon is already an established entity" (von Campenhausen, 1972:172), but this is surely an overstatement. Irenaeus had to argue vigorously and inventively for its legitimacy; the *Gospel of Peter* was still being read in Syria; Clement of Alexandria continued to grant a fair measure of authority to the *Gospel according to the Hebrews* and the *Gospel of the Egyptians;* the *Diatessaron* was in broad use; the Gospel of John was still liable to criticism and rejection in Rome itself (see J. Smith; and on the shifting fortunes of this Gospel in the second century, see Sanders, 1943; Hillmer), and there are signs of hesitancy about Luke (Sundberg, 1964b). Thus, the conviction of earlier scholarship that the four-Gospel collection had already taken shape early in the second century, or at any rate near mid-century, is no longer persuasive to most. The tendency of recent study has been to find a highly fluid situation in the production and use of Gospel literature almost throughout the second century and to locate an emerging but not yet absolute preeminence of our canonical Gospels only near the end of the second century.

Apart from the four Gospels and the letters of Paul, collections that had acquired full shape and broad authority by the early third century, there is no evidence that other writings eventually to be included in the canon ever belonged to early, independent collections, in spite of the close affinities among the Johannine letters or the fact that the Catholic Epistles are seven in number. The Catholic Epistles had diverse individual histories, and came finally to be grouped and ranged alongside the letters of Paul, perhaps in order to document the common witness of the primitive apostles, and especially of Paul and the "pillar apostles," on the basis of Gal 2:9 (Lührmann). The varying attitudes toward the Catholic Epistles suggest earlier usages of a local and regional sort. Only 1 Peter and 1 John seem to have had much currency in the second century (hence it is odd that the Muratorian Fragment knows only of Jude and two Johannine letters). As for the other documents, it is well known that Revelation was much used in the west but little in the east, and that Hebrews had exactly the opposite fate. Thus, the usage of Christian literature in the second century was highly diverse and did not clearly foreshadow the final substance of the canon. An inclination toward a more precise definition of the fund of authoritative documents can be seen in Irenaeus and also in the Muratorian Fragment, to which some attention may now be given.

The Muratorian Fragment

Since its publication in 1740 the fragmentary Muratorian list of Christian scriptures has been discussed again and again. On the basis of early studies it became the common view that this list is a late second-century product, probably of Roman origin. As such, it has had a special significance for the history of the NT canon, showing that the growth of the NT canon was well on its way by the end of the second century and had already eventuated in a collection whose basic elements were fixed. But the question of the date and provenance of the Muratorian Fragment has been reopened by A. C. Sundberg (1973, cf. 1968a), who proposes with interesting arguments that the list should be assigned a fourth-century date and an Eastern setting. He has shown that certain terms and phrases that have been crucial to the Roman location and second-century dating of the Fragment are susceptible of a different interpretation, but the weight of his argument rests on the treatment given by the Fragment to various documents, especially the listing of the Wisdom of Solomon among Christian books, the rejection of the *Shepherd* of Hermas, and the ambivalence toward the apocalypses of John and Peter. In all of these features Sundberg finds close affinities with Eusebius and other Syro-Palestinian witnesses of a later period. Furthermore, it is only with the fourth century that lists of NT books began to be drawn up, so that the Muratorian Fragment seems anomalous at the end of the second century, the moreso since R. P. C. Hanson (1954:133–45) has shown that a list of NT books should not be attributed to Origen on the basis of Eusebius.

It is surprising that Sundberg's thesis has not yet evoked much response (but see Ferguson). Yet it seems unlikely to displace the traditional view, for there are as many features of the Fragment that intimate an early date and a western, if not specifically Roman, origin as might seem to militate against them. We might mention among these the absence of Hebrews, the actually positive regard for the *Apocalypse of John*, allusions to heterodox movements of the second century (Ferguson: 680–81), the embryonic attitude toward the Catholic Epistles — not to mention the admittedly debatable interpretation of particular words and phrases. That similar lists do not emerge until the fourth century is certainly a point to be considered, but this is an argument from silence (Ferguson: 680), and the fortuitous preservation of the evidence, of which the Muratorian Fragment is itself a vivid instance, ought to caution against making too much of such a circumstance. Yet Sundberg has usefully called attention to some problematical points and has made it clear that not all the important questions about the Fragment have been definitively answered.

More particular aspects of the Muratorian Fragment have been illuminated by other studies. A. A. T. Ehrhardt (1953), one of few to persist in thinking that the document was composed in Latin, has focused on the statements about the Gospels, arguing that the compiler relied on Papias not only for his information about Mark but also for his remarks on the Fourth Gospel and finding various signs in the Fragment of the theological disputes in which the Roman church was involved near the end of the second century. He suggests that the Fragment reflects special considerations extended by the Roman church to the churches of Asia Minor. K. Stendahl (1962) has noted the Fragment's emphasis on catholicity as a criterion of canonicity, observing that the particularity of Paul's letters was problematical in this respect (see also Dahl, 1962), even though Paul's apostolic status was undoubted: Paul's catholicity is established by the Fragment through an appeal to the Apocalypse, whose author was inspired and so addressed the church as a whole, but did so by means of letters to seven churches. Other criteria of canonicity that figure in the Fragment have been helpfully sorted out by C. Burkhardt (1974), who also urges that their variety and unsystematic use should not lead to an underestimation of responsible reflection in the formation of the canon. The order of the Pauline letters in the Fragment, which has often been taken to reflect a corpus beginning with the Corinthian letters, has been thought by N. A. Dahl (1961) to presuppose instead our canonical order and thus to reflect a corpus beginning with Romans. Then the first but partial enumeration of letters in the Fragment would be explained as the compiler's effort to set out a chronological sequence. And the supposition of P. Katz (1957) that originally the Fragment mentioned all three Johannine letters rather than just two has proved attractive to some but must remain merely conjectural.

As interesting as the Muratorian Fragment is, our comprehension of the general course of the recognition of various books as authoritative would not be very different in its absence (Ferguson: 677). Evidence is ample that near the end of the second century the four Gospels and the letters of Paul, along with Acts, 1 Peter, and 1 John, had secured wide and exceptional esteem. Irenaeus, Tertullian, and Clement appeal chiefly to these. However, this does not mean that the same situation prevailed everywhere. Even among these witnesses there are notable divergencies in the authority attached to other writings, and such differences persisted broadly through the third century and well into the fourth. Even if the Muratorian Fragment is to be dated to the late second or early third century, not much interest is otherwise apparent at that time in drawing a firm line between authoritative and non-authoritative documents. There were not many who knew the usages of the churches or pondered them as carefully as Origen (Ruwet, 1942; Hanson, 1954:127–56), yet he provided only graded classifications and not two clear-cut categories. Certainly it is fair to say that a discriminatory instinct was already at work in the late second century, but it was not systematic and had yielded no sharp results. To this extent, the date and provenance of the Muratorian Fragment are not crucial considerations. But they obviously do gain in importance once the concept of canonization is strictly defined as a matter of creating lists (with Sundberg, 1968a), for then a document like the Muratorian Fragment can affect the basic understanding of the formation of the canon.

Factors in the Formation of the Canon

The prehistory of its constituent parts, like the history of the citation of individual documents, is not to be confused with the formation of the NT as such. The question of how and why just these materials were brought together in a normative, bipartite collection to be set alongside the Jewish scriptures as a "New" Testament has no obvious or simple answer, and a variety of factors call for notice. But, in assessing the concept of a NT and the motives leading to its creation, attention has centered especially on the heterodox movements of the second century—Marcionism, Gnosticism, and Montanism.

The influence of Marcion on the history of the NT canon is a particularly fascinating problem, for he undertook to base his theological program on authoritative documents, constituted a critically edited collection comprising a version of Luke's Gospel and ten letters of Paul, and thus created the first fixed collection of theologically normative Christian literature. Harnack (1924:210–15, 441–44; 1925a:30–35, 57–60) therefore credited Marcion with conceiving the idea of a Christian canon and with developing the first such reality, and he argued that the catholic NT came into being as "an anti-marcionite creation on a marcionite basis" (1924:444). Many recent interpreters have not only concurred in this opinion but have carried it somewhat further. Knox (1942) rightly challenged Harnack's belief that a four-Gospel collection antedated Marcion, and at the same time he emphasized that since it is the essence of canon to be closed, Marcion created the first NT canon in the strict sense, which makes Marcion's work more drastic and definitive. Hans von Campenhausen represents Marcion as the decisive factor in the formation of the canon: "The idea and the reality of a Christian Bible were the work of Marcion, and the church which rejected his work, so far from being ahead of him in this field, from a formal point of view simply followed his example" (1972:148; see also 1966).

The evidence for this popular view is mostly circumstantial. The chronological priority of Marcion's canon is indisputable, but if he was the first to set up a particular group of writings as exclusively authoritative, the concept of authoritative Christian literature scarcely originated with him. He must have found Paul's letters already in use and probably simply took over and then revised an existing edition of the Pauline corpus that had been worked up on the assumption, surely, of their relevance and authority. And the delineation of Marcion's canon was a function of his peculiar theological presuppositions: even if his rejection of the Jewish scriptures did not of itself require him to fashion a substitute, his conception of the gospel—and his theory of the theological and literary history of earlier Christianity as one of progressive adulteration—required him both to fix the number of authoritative books and to expurgate their contents. But the chronological precedence of Marcion's canon must be distinguished from the question of its actual influence. This influence has been seen at various points: in posing an inescapable necessity for the church to formulate its own canon in opposition to Marcion; in providing the structural principle of gospel–apostle on which the catholic canon was built; in the prominence accruing to Paul's letters; and in the need to balance and contextualize Paul's letters by incorporating further literature. But in none of these particulars is it really possible to show that Marcion's canon provided the cause, or even exercised any influence. Therefore, the evidence for Marcion's influence on the formation of the NT, so far as it is merely circumstantial, is not very strong.

The argument for Marcion's impact on the history of the canon has, however, usually entailed appeal to documentary evidence as well, particularly to the so-called Marcionite prologues to the Pauline epistles and the so-called anti-Marcionite prologues to the Gospels. The old prologues to the Pauline letters found in many Vulgate manuscripts have been commonly regarded as Marcionite products since this claim was first made by D. de Bruyne (1907) and P. Corssen (1909), on the grounds that they presume a Marcionite order of the letters and reflect a Marcionite ideology. Following Harnack (1924:127–34; 1925:59–60, 165–68), both Knox (1942) and von Campenhausen (1972), along with many others, affirm their Marcionite origin, which has been forcefully reargued by K. T. Schäfer (1973a, 1973b), and take their presence in catholic manuscripts as a clear indication of Marcion's influence. Recent investigations have made this argument increasingly suspect. H. J. Frede (1964:171–78; 1969:292) has shown that the order of the letters attested for Marcion and presupposed by the prologues is not exclusively Marcionite but is an adaptation of an earlier order and that the placement of Galatians at the beginning, instead of betraying a Marcionite dogmatic preference, probably results from an effort to make a chronological sequence. Although the theological scheme of the prologues (especially to Corinthians and Romans) seems to reveal some typically Marcionite ideas, Dahl (1978:257–62) has demonstrated that it is easily possible to understand the prologues as the product of a catholic editor who had, to be sure, an anti-Judaizing attitude but not a Marcionite ideology and that both the attestation and the history of transmission of the prologues make the theory of their Marcionite origin quite implausible. Similarly, the so-called anti-Marcionite prologues to the Gospels, which de Bruyne (1928) and others (esp. Harnack, 1928) thought were composed in the second century to counter Marcion, have been cited in support of the claim that the NT canon was constructed in deliberate opposition to Marcion. But more recent studies have called various aspects of this estimate into question (Gutwenger, 1946; Heard, 1955), and it has been systematically discredited by J. Regul (1969: esp. 75–94), who proves that these prologues do not constitute a unified set, betray no particular animus toward Marcion, and are probably not to be dated before the fourth century.

Thus, the documentary evidence that has long served to symptomize Marcion's impact on the formation of the NT canon has been deeply eroded and now seems inadequate to sustain the argument. Those who have not found reason to see in Marcion the *sine qua non* of the canon have usually been willing to allow that he in some way hastened its development.

Although this may be true, it is hardly demonstrable, and for the same reason it cannot be categorically denied. Still, in spite of the great importance attached to Marcion by von Campenhausen, there is a growing and well-justified conviction that Marcion's influence and the evidence for it have been exaggerated (Blackman: 23–41; Grant, 1965:125–26; H. E. W. Turner: 252–56; Sundberg, 1968a:459–60; Balas: 102–5).

In spite of the Nag Hammadi discovery and the modern ferment in Gnostic studies generally, relatively little light has so far been shed from this angle on the history of the canon, and what is to be learned will more likely pertain to the history of the individual writings than to the formation of the canon as a whole. The question here is about the role of Gnosticism in general as a factor in the shaping of the canon. Since it is evident that Gnostic circles produced literature unambiguously expressing their own conception of Christianity and characteristically appealed to esoteric traditions, it may be supposed that the formation of the NT canon was, at least in part, a calculated effort to counter these tendencies. On the other hand, it is also clear, and has been confirmed by recent discoveries, that Gnostic groups made full and free use of the Christian literature that enjoyed a general esteem (Grant, 1965:121–30; H. E. W. Turner: 180–86, 232–38; Hanson, 1962:197–201). Whether or not it was among Gnostics that Christian writings first came to be viewed as "scripture" (Grant, 1965:121–24), it does seem that this literature, particularly the Gospels and the Pauline letters, became theologically significant at an earlier time to Gnostic groups than to the church at large, and systematic exegesis of Christian writings first made its appearance among Gnostics (Pagels, 1973, 1975). The difference between the Gnostics and other Christian groups consisted less in appeals to different writings than in a different hermeneutical approach to much of the same literature. In that case, the formation of the NT canon would not in itself have been a very effective anti-Gnostic stratagem, except as it furnished a means of disenfranchising specifically Gnostic literary products.

Just as Marcion has been credited with conceiving the idea of a Christian canon and forcing the church to respond with its own enlarged canon of scriptures, the Montanist movement has often been thought to have evoked in the church a heightened emphasis on written authority, a determined effort to limit the number of authoritative writings, and an insistence that revelation is confined to the apostolic past (esp. Harnack, 1925:34–39). Hence it is claimed that in the responses to Marcionism and Montanism we may see the two main forces in the canon-building process—the first expansive and the second restrictive. Great importance has continued to be attached to Montanism in more recent studies (von Campenhausen, 1972:211–43; Ehrhardt, 1962:107; van Unnik, 1949; Blackman: 33–34; Paulsen). But the influence of Montanism on the history of the canon, if any, is immensely difficult to determine because so little is known with certainty about the character, chronology, and development of Montanism itself. The evidence for the production of specifically Montanist books or for any interest in expanding the number of authoritative writings is slight and questionable (Vokes, 1968; Paulsen: 28–32); and, far from a simple juxtaposition of prophetic revelation and written tradition, the Montanist controversy reveals little or no dispute about the authority of generally acknowledged Christian scriptures, which the Montanists freely received and employed in their own behalf (Paulsen: 22–28; Ash: 243; Groh: 340; von Campenhausen, 1972:222). Hence, Montanism cannot be accorded much importance in connection with the normative status of Christian writings. Of course, it cannot be denied that the Montanist controversy posed fundamental questions about "the function and meaning of historical tradition, its definitive nature and its relation to present revelation," and it may be that an emphasis on selected aspects of written tradition and the need of its authoritative interpretation were heightened by the dispute (Paulsen: 32–52). But as E. Kalin (1967; cf. 1971) has shown, the church did not, as a result of the Montanist crisis, confine inspiration to the apostolic past, and J. L. Ash (1976) has pointed out that even anti-Montanists affirmed the necessary persistence of the prophetic charisma in the church, and so did not view ecstatic prophecy and canon as antithetical phenomena. In that case it is doubtful whether Montanism ought to be regarded as a significant factor in the development of the canon. If perhaps it helped to promote the conception of a closed canon, it certainly did not bring such a thing about. That happened only later, and then without any reference to Montanism. In this connection, van Unnik (1961:217–18) has withdrawn his earlier claim (1949) that the anti-Montanist quoted by Eusebius (*Hist. eccl.* 5.16.3) spoke of a closed collection of authoritative books.

Although it ought not be denied that the heterodox movements of the second century perhaps furnished some constructive impulses toward the formation of the canon, it is difficult to identify what these may have been. In any case, these movements cannot be persuasively represented as the determinative forces either for the conception of a Christian canon or for the shape it ultimately assumed. In general, it may be said that on the one hand these variant types of Christianity reflect in themselves the same sorts of tendencies in regard to authoritative writings as are visible elsewhere in second-century Christianity, and that on the other hand the confrontation with these heterodox movements posed rather sharply the problem of identifying the loci of authoritative tradition and controlling its interpretation. Only in this general way is the history of the canon clarified by reference to Marcionism, the Gnostics, and Montanism.

Various other factors have occasionally been proposed as important. I. Frank (1971) has developed the thesis that the aim of the construction of the canon was to ensure the unity of the church and that this objective had as its basis Logos-Christology and the Fourth Gospel in particular, so that the latter should be regarded as the foundation stone of the NT canon. But in view of the marginal and tardy regard for the Fourth Gospel in the second century, such a claim is hardly tenable. Farmer (1982:177–259; 1983:7–95) has given special emphasis to the influence of persecution and martyrdom in bringing into esteem certain books and leading finally to the fixing of their number in what he calls a "martyr's canon." It is hardly convincing that the books that became canonical did so because of their appeal specifically to communities experiencing persecution, even if this theme is recurrent in the literature of the NT. But it is probably worth considering to what extent the proscription, requisition, and destruction of Christian books in times of persecution may have contributed to the drawing up of lists specifying which books were sacred and might not be surrendered to the authorities. Of course, the influence of the attitudes of leading theologians in the ancient church cannot be overlooked (Aland, 1962:20–21); for the fate of some books this was decisive, though in the whole process of canon formation it had no thoroughgoing effect. And if, with Sundberg (1968a), a decided stress is placed on the creation of definitive lists, then the official decisions of bishops and synods which began to be issued in the last half of the fourth century will take on a larger importance than has usually been assigned to them. It does appear that without these decisions the content of the NT canon would not be exactly what it is today. D. Groh (342–43) has raised the interesting question whether the broad tendency in the Greco-Roman world during this period toward summarization, regularization, and canonization must not be thought of as a background factor in the shaping of a canon of Christian scriptures.

But amid these diverse recent suggestions it is essential not to lose sight of internal and circumstantial factors in the emergence of the canon. The traditional reading of certain early Christian texts in a liturgical setting, which may well go back to the first century, was a very powerful considera- tion which is explicitly acknowledged as such in the deliberations of Origen and Eusebius about the authority of various documents. The increasing distance of the church from its point of historical origins threw into ever greater relief the value of documents that belonged to its earliest stages and constituted its ancestral records, and the dissipation of reliable oral tradition led to the same result. In addition, the practical needs of catechesis and apologetics must have played a role. In summary, it is probably misguided to seek for a single cause or a small number of explanatory factors, just as it is to look for a crucial moment, in a process so protracted and complex as the formation of a canon of Christian scriptures.

Principles of Canonicity

Beyond the question of historical forces that contributed to the shaping of the canon, increasing attention has been given also to the principles or criteria that may have informed the attitudes of the early church toward its literature. Since a rather large number of criteria are found in the evidence, and since they were apparently not applied with great rigor or consistency, it is not surprising that there is little agreement among modern scholars about their meaning or importance. For example, E. Flesseman-van Leer (1964:418) maintains that the most important principle (at least in the West) was "apostolicity as a historical fact." H. Diem (1952:5) thinks that no definite principles can be discovered, though apostolic authorship was early an effective norm; von Campenhausen (1972:330) can perceive only the principle of chronological limitation, such that "normative testimonies must derive from the period closest to Christ, namely that of Christian origins, the age of the apostles and their disciples," and considers apostolic authorship to have been no factor at all, with content playing the more decisive role. Aland (1962:14–15) contends that in the formation of the canon "one can speak only of the principle of having no principles." Amid the variety of the criteria themselves and of scholarly evaluations of them, it is still clear that in the formation of the canon the church did engage from time to time in conscious reflection on the grounds for accepting or rejecting the authority of particular documents and that the most prominent among these were apostolicity, catholicity, traditional usage, and conformity with the faith of the church. Yet even of these fundamental considerations, none was applied in every case or with absolute value.

A very thorough and useful study of the principles of canonicity has been made by K.-H. Ohlig (1972), who has also made an effort to draw out from them a "theology of the canon" (1970), in the belief that the canon as we have it cannot be recognized as normative nor its substance defended on any grounds other than those which actually led to its formation (see Flesseman-van Leer, 1964). Leaving the latter question aside for the moment, Ohlig has rightly seen the importance even on historical grounds of determining just what the ancient church meant when it spoke of such matters as apostolicity, age, agreement with the (OT) scriptures, reception by the oldest churches, etc. Especially instructive is his discussion of the central criterion of apostolicity, which he shows to have been a much broader, more flexible, and historically less specific category than modern usage has generally granted: the designation of a document as "apostolic" affirms the correspondence of its content with the early time of the church, and only rarely signifies apostolic authorship in any strict sense. Therefore "apostolicity" has as its controlling meaning *Urkirchlichkeit* ("early church-ness"), a concept that embraces all the other particular criteria but has little to do with literary authenticity. Generally, it appears that the "theoretical" criteria such as apostolicity and catholicity were less decisive than the more "practical" criteria of established usage and dogmatic correctness. Of these last two, however, it was established usage that constituted the most powerful commendation of a writing, whereas judgments about dogmatic correctness operated mainly in a negative way, that is, to exclude certain writings.

"Inspiration" was not early invoked as a distinguishing mark of author-itative Christian writings, except, naturally, in the case of prophetic-apocalyptic documents (see Windisch), even though it was regularly asserted of Jewish writings. Only after the end of the second century did it become common to speak of authoritative Christian writings as inspired (Hanson, 1962:211–13), and in this development Origen played an impor-tant role (von Campenhausen, 1972:315–26). Recent studies have amply demonstrated that inspiration did not constitute a criterion of discrimination in the formation of the canon (Stendahl, 1962:243–45; and very fully, Kalin, 1967, 1971; see also Sundberg, 1975; Ohlig, 1972:244–68). So far as inspira-tion came into play at all, it served to differentiate orthodox from heretical writings, but not canonical from noncanonical. The reason for this is simply that inspiration was considered a property of the church as a whole, and not peculiarly of specific writings within the church. Thus, the concept of inspiration was much broader than the concept of scripture, and the inspira-tion of the authors of scripture was not believed to be different in degree or kind from that of other Christians. So, far from sharply limiting the number of authoritative writings, a strong emphasis on inspiration tended rather to expand their number (see Ruwet, 1948, on Clement of Alexandria).

The formulation and application of various principles of canonicity show that the formation of the canon was not entirely an uncritical process. But their importance must not be overstressed, for they were not early formulated, narrowly defined, or systematically applied. Certainly they represent the *desiderata* of the church and tell us something about the theological basis for the authority of certain writings within the church. But it must remain doubtful how fully such criteria really serve to explain the history of the canon. Usually they were less the effective reasons for canonical recognition than means of rationalizing usages that had come about on other grounds. Estimates of the importance of these principles will vary to some extent with larger conceptions of the formation of the NT. If the canon is regarded as the product of a developing consensus and delibera-tive judgments of the church, then principles of canonicity will be respected as providing a basis for the church's reflections. But if the canon appears to have emerged rather unreflectively on the basis of usage, then the criteria will have little explanatory value. But, of course, it is neither necessary nor realistic to stipulate an exclusive alternative between historical contingen-cies and deliberative decisions (Ohlig, 1972:34–53). Certainly, for example, apostolicity was a powerful factor almost from the first in the commendation of a writing, as the production of Pauline and other apostolic pseudepigrapha shows (Brox, 1975:81–129), even though a reflective application of apos-tolicity as a criterion of discrimination among documents appears only later. On the other hand, to abstract the history of the canon from circumstantial exigencies would risk oversimplification and dogmatic naïveté. Cogent inter-pretation must reckon with the interplay of both aspects.

Concluding Observations

What has been said will have indicated that the history of the canon has not yet become lucid to NT scholarship. Many particular points of evidence remain in dispute, as does the vantage point from which all the evidence can be coherently and convincingly interpreted. Still other questions that bear on the history of the canon are deserving of greater attention than they have traditionally received.

The history of the canon, for example, is linked up in various ways with the history of book production in antiquity, the study of which has already yielded some interesting insights and promises more. That already by the mid-second century Christians transcribed the Jewish scriptures in codices rather than rolls, as Jewish tradition dictated, is probably due to the fact that specifically Christian writings, which were for the most part circulated in codex form, provided the format for all the sacred scriptures of the church, including those taken over from Judaism. This implies that some Christian writings had become quite authoritative in content (thus also in format) at an earlier time, probably before the end of the first century (Roberts, 1949; 1954:187–91; 1970:57–60; and now Roberts and Skeat, 1983), and the convention of the *nomina sacra* in second-century Christian manuscripts points in the same direction (Roberts, 1970:60–61; 1979:26–48). Ultimately the transcription of various Christian scriptures within a single codex gave concrete form and expression to the idea of a Christian canon, but so long as codices remained small this was impossible; apparently only discrete collections (the four Gospels, the Pauline epistles, etc.) could be gathered up in this way before the fourth century. Perhaps it is not merely coincidental that the NT canon began to achieve a high degree of fixity only in the period when codices became available which could encompass the whole (cf. E. G. Turner, 1977).

Further, a greater emphasis needs to be given to the fact that the history of the text of the NT is part and parcel of the history of the NT canon. The close correlation of textual criticism and the history of the canon could once be taken for granted, but no longer. The increasing specialization and mutual isolation of these disciplines have been detrimental to both, especially in a period characterized by many manuscript finds. Too often, historians of the canon have been content to speak only about documents, without attending to the question of what *texts* of those documents were employed in a given region and period, and without sufficient concern for the manuscripts in which those texts were preserved and transmitted. But types of texts, families of manuscripts, individual manuscripts and their prehistories, and early editions of scriptural texts are all matters of moment for the history of the canon. The modern preoccupation of textual criticism with statistical and eclectic methods has limited the attention devoted to such problems and to that extent has reduced the value of *Textgeschichte* ("textual criticism" or "the history of the text") for *Kanongeschichte* ("the history of the canon"). But there is much to be learned about the history of the canon from the data of textual criticism (e.g., Gamble, 1977; Aland, 1979a; Clabeaux) and manuscript studies (e.g., Wiefel; Dahl, 1979), and it is to be hoped that the future will bring a closer working relationship between these disciplines.

Finally, a comprehension of the history of the canon involves an understanding of how Christian writings actually functioned in the life of the ancient church. This includes, of course, questions about the use of scripture in liturgy, dogmatics, apologetics, etc., and about the relation of the authority of scripture to other authorities acknowledged by the ancient church, especially tradition (Flesseman-van Leer; Cullmann, 1956b; Hanson, 1962, among others). But it also includes the question of private, informal uses of scripture by ordinary believers, a subject scarcely touched since Harnack (1912), in spite of more recent relevant data. And in connection with all uses of scripture in the early church, it remains necessary to inquire into the hermeneutical assumptions and methods that were brought to it and into their consequences for its valuation and authority. Because the religious authority that accrued to these writings was inevitably a function of interpretation, that is, of what they were taken to mean by their readers, the history of the canon cannot be understood independently of the history of interpretation.

Since the history of the canon must summon together such a wide range of concerns and many different sorts of data, future progress will necessarily depend on the cooperative efforts of scholars with diverse expertise.

III. THE CANON AS A THEOLOGICAL PROBLEM

This essay has emphasized the history of the canon, but it would create a false impression if its focus were entirely historical, since, in fact, the canon has engaged modern scholarship just as much in theological as in historical terms, and perhaps more so. When H. Strathmann (1941) spoke of the problem of the canon as a "lingering illness" of Protestant churches and theology, he could not foresee that exactly this issue would become the topic of energetic debate in the postwar years—and not merely in Protestant circles but in ecumenical discussion as well. Therefore, I. Lønning rightly remarks that "anyone who today takes up the problem of the biblical canon finds himself immediately at the center of the entire field of theological problems" (12). Nevertheless, the discussion of the theological problematic of the canon has so far been carried on mainly in German scholarship and has not elicited many contributions outside the Continent, although this situation is changing. Even so, the volume of literature pertaining to this issue has already become almost unmanageable. It is helpful that some of the most seminal studies have been collected and evaluated by E. Käsemann

(1970), whose own contributions have been instrumental in provoking the debate and setting its agenda, and that general assessments of the most important issues have been provided by N. Appel (1964), representing a Catholic viewpoint, and Lønning, speaking from a Protestant position. To raise the question of the canon as a theological problem is to be drawn quickly out of the field of NT studies and into the concerns of historical and systematic theology. In the present context it is possible only to sketch the lineaments of some major questions, and these mainly in their relationship to NT studies proper.

The Limits of the Canon and Its Unity

The history of the canon makes it evident that the canon is not a primordial or even a particularly early feature of Christianity; it is the final product, rather, of a long and gradual development conditioned by a variety of historical circumstances, theological controversies, and ecclesiastical decisions. Therefore, it has to be asked whether, to what extent, and on what basis it is possible to attach normative value to the canon, if it is not to be regarded merely as the upshot of historical contingencies (Kümmel, 1965:231; Braun: 310–13; Sand, 1973). From a critical point of view it is no longer possible to legitimize the canon simply on the basis of the explicit criteria invoked by the ancient church in setting these writings apart from all the others. This is especially true of the long-standing assumption that these are apostolic documents, all the more if this is taken to be a matter strictly of apostolic authorship. Modern scholarship lodges little or no confidence in the ancient traditions associating these writings directly with apostles (and here the authentic letters of Paul are the exceptions that prove the rule). The other old criteria of canonicity, especially of the "theoretical" sort, are likewise questionable. If it is insisted that the authority of the canon can be defended today only on the basis of the criteria that contributed to its formation (Flessemann-van Leer, 1964), that can only be done by a broader and more flexible understanding of those criteria (see Ohlig, 1970, 1972).

If judgments based on the traditional principles of canonicity are left aside as having been ineffectual or as being too tenuous, then the normative status of the canon is usually asserted by claiming either that this literature possesses an intrinsic and self-authenticating authority, or that it derives its authority from its official recognition by the church. This alternative takes another and slightly more historical form in the question whether the canon evolved more or less spontaneously on the basis of the religious experience and intuition of the various communities, or was deliberately and carefully constructed by the church. Actually, neither view is fully adequate as an interpretation of the history of the canon (Flessemann-van Leer, 1964:418; Kümmel, 1965:243–44; Ebeling, 1968:114; von Campenhausen, 1972:331).

That in its official decisions of the fourth and fifth centuries the church merely ratified and made *de jure* a status that these writings had already secured for themselves (Aland, 1962:18–24; Diem, 1952:6–7; Hahn, 1980:462–63; Murray, among others) is simply not true for the canon as a whole or as such, since a number of writings then adjudged canonical had not been widely used or everywhere received as authoritative. Hence, as a closed and definitive collection the canon must be seen as a product of the church. On the other hand, the high regard enjoyed from an early time and almost everywhere by the Synoptic Gospels and the letters of Paul owed nothing to official fiat, and the later church was scarcely in a position to render a decision about their authority. Authoritative scripture, though not formalized as a definitive collection, was functionally prior to the church, insofar as the church is grounded in the primitive witness to the Christ-event (Kümmel, 1965:243–44).

The burden of recent Protestant reflection has been to acknowledge that the canon is "factually" or "historically" closed and yet to insist that the limits of the canon defined by the ancient church are not themselves binding, so that "in principle" the canon remains open to revision (Kümmel, 1965:249–59; Diem, 1952:15–16; 1953:389; Schweizer: 350; Marxsen, 1972:14–29; 1968a; 1968b; Filson: 37–42; Ebeling, 1967:62–64; 1968a:113–21; Lønning: 263–68). Of course, this stance does not actually envision an alteration of the traditional boundaries of the canon; rather, it aims to meet the problem of the untenability of the ancient formal criteria of canonicity—and, even more, to avoid making the canon hostage to ecclesiastical authority by preserving its critical independence over against the church. For when the canon is regarded as a "strictly dogmatic reality, that is, when not only the boundaries of the canon but also the meaning of its canonicity are considered as beyond all discussion, Protestantism has already become Catholic in principle, for it is then founded upon the infallibility of a doctrinal decision of early Catholicism" (Ebeling, 1967:63). Without an infallible teaching office, there is no attainable certainty about the limits of the canon (Lønning: 264). Nevertheless, it can be said that the canon at least theoretically must have limits since a historical revelation is inaccessible apart from immediate, chronologically limited testimony (Kümmel, 1965:247–49). Catholic interpreters are not at all reticent to admit as final and binding the canonical boundaries set by the ancient church. Even if it is conceded that the formal criteria of canonicity have been undercut by historical criticism, the canon is nevertheless respected as the work of the church, acting in accordance with established usage, the tradition of faith, and the guidance of the Spirit within it (Appel, 1964:115–20; Horst: 177–80; Brown: 533). Here canon and church constitute an indissoluble unity.

Independently of the history of the canon, the limits of the canon have also been drawn into question by exegesis itself. Historical criticism entails an investigation of the religio-historical context of the canonical literature and an understanding of its interconnections with extracanonical literature. The interpreter of the NT is thus driven outside the canon precisely in order to make sense of the canonical materials and so must ignore, or at least temporarily suspend, the concept of canon. For this reason it has been suggested that "the classical 'Introduction to the New Testament' has lost its scientific justification. One can only speak of a 'history of early Christian literature' " (Koester, 1971b:270; 1975). Although the premise behind this claim ought not be disputed, "it is important that we distinguish a formal and methodological suspension of the canon from a material dissolution of it; otherwise we make precisely the historiographical task even more difficult," since it is the canon that reveals what literature was most significant and influential in early Christianity and is really the basis of modern historical interest in early Christianity (Keck).

But the impact of exegesis on the understanding of the canon goes deeper than this and poses more difficult and specifically theological problems in making clear that the canon of the NT embraces an astonishing range of theologically divergent positions (Käsemann, 1964:95–102; Braun: 314–20; and very fully, Dunn). The range and character of this diversity may be somewhat differently estimated, but it is not reducible simply to varying idioms or situations. Rather it relates to fundamental theological positions that appear to stand in tension and even in contradiction. To this extent, the canon as such cannot serve as à decisive theological norm: far from securing the unity of the church, the canon as a formal entity only legitimizes the multiplicity of confessions (Käsemann, 1964a:103; 1964b:54–58; 1970:402), even if it is true that confessional differences also have a broader basis (Ebeling, 1968b). By throwing into sharp relief the remarkable profusion of theological positions within the canon, historical criticism has made untenable the traditional legal understanding of the canon, widely prevalent in Protestantism and Catholicism alike, according to which the canon is a dogmatic unity possessing equal authority in all its parts, with theological discrepancies and contradictions being ruled out in principle (Käsemann, 1964a; Ebeling, 1968a:142–44; 1968b). It is no longer possible to appeal simply to the canon of scripture as a "formal principle." Thus, exegesis has in its own way made the limits of the canon a matter of dispute and has shown that the function of the canon as a theological norm cannot be grasped in connection with its outer boundaries.

The Question of a Canon in the Canon

Once a formal, legal, and dogmatic concept of the canon is given up in recognition of the historical evolution and internal diversity of the canon, it becomes an open question how it is possible for the canon to play a genuinely normative role. This question is usually answered in Protestant (and especially Lutheran) circles by appealing to a material principle or center (*Sachkriterium, Sachmitte*), often designated as a "canon in the canon." Here, of course, it is not a matter of any literary reduction of the formal canon, but of the discovery of a hermeneutical criterion by which to discern the "gospel" in the canon.

While the necessity of such a material principle — an actual canon (norm) within the formal canon (list) — is widely acknowledged in Protestant scholarship, efforts to formulate it are various (see Schrage for a survey): the justification of the ungodly, christologically interpreted (Käsemann, 1970:368–71, 404–8; 1971:138–66, etc.); humanity radically challenged and called into question (Braun: 321–22); the central message of Christ as found in the earliest witnesses (Kümmel, 1965:255–59); the irreducible primitive preaching (Marxsen, 1968:98–103); the earthly Jesus (Jeremias, 1960:24–25), or, in the venerable formula of Luther, *was Christum prediget und treibet* ("that which preaches and promotes Christ"). In spite of these different phrasings, however, the fundamental principle is generally understood (especially in Lutheran circles) as justification by grace through faith (Schrage: 437–42). Most such formulations are not meant to be construed in literary terms, as though the canon in the canon could or should be located in particular documents, nor are they to be construed historically, as if historical research could identify and certify an essential hermeneutical principle. Rather, the question What is the gospel? can be answered "only by the believer who is led by the Spirit and listens obediently to the Scripture" (Käsemann, 1964a:106; 1964b:54–58; 1971) — that is, in a dialectic of scripture and gospel, of "letter and Spirit."

Catholic scholars have been predictably critical of the effort to adduce a canon within the canon and regard it as a symptom of the basic inadequacy of the *sola scriptura* ("scripture alone") principle (which indeed is true so long as *sola scriptura* is understood in a merely formal way). They have objected to the reductionism, selectivity, and arbitrary subjectivity that it seems to involve and have emphasized to the contrary the need to affirm the unity and normative character of the canon as a whole (Küng, 1963; 1964:151–69; Lengsfeld: 146–47; Elliott; Mussner, 1961, 1964; Appel, 1964:253–65, 332–44; for an overview, see Kümmel, 1968). Such criticisms are understandable, but it remains questionable how pertinent such reservations are, for generally they fail to take account of the dialectical relationship between scripture and gospel posited by Protestant interpreters and neglect the fact that it is not a matter of the whole and its parts but a question of the proper interpretation of the whole, that is, a hermeneutical question (Käsemann, 1970:376). Furthermore, Catholic criticisms fail to indicate just how it is possible, once the theological diversity of the canon is granted, to give equal authority to all the canonical literature, for this must mean either that historical results are not taken seriously or that a perspective is discovered *outside* the canon which determines how scripture is to be understood, in which case the authority of the canon is effectively given up.

Nevertheless, on this issue one cannot speak simply of a Protestant/ Catholic division, since there are Catholic scholars who admit the necessity of some form of intracanonical discrimination (Kuss; Horst: 180–83; Trilling; Ohlig, 1973; Murray; and to some extent even Küng, 1963:186–87, Mussner, 1961:290), and likewise Protestant scholars who, for various reasons, oppose the idea of a canon in the canon (Diem, 1959:224–39; Cullmann, 1967:297– 98; Schweizer: 355–56; Barr: 160–62; Ebeling, 1968a:143–44). It should also be mentioned that some have found in the theological variety of the NT not a need for a canon in the canon but a positive endorsement of broad confessional pluralism, albeit within the perimeters of canonical diversity (Filson: 133–34; Dunn: 374–82), a perspective that falls outside the terms of the Continental debate and is responsive, obviously, to the Anglo-American setting.

Lønning (268) correctly observes that the issue of a canon in the canon is at bottom the issue of whether there can be any opposition between canon and church, that is, whether and how the canon of scripture can exercise a critical function over against the church and thus actually serve as a norm in itself. It is clear enough that the concerns about the external limits of the canon on the one hand and about the "center" of the canon on the other are closely related: when the outer boundary of the canon is understood to be absolutely fixed, the theologically normative function of the canon is correspondingly relativized; and when the critical function of the canon is the primary theological concern, the significance of the external limits of the canon is relativized. If the formal canon is to be effectively canonical, that is, truly normative, the question of a canon within the canon can hardly be avoided. At the same time, "as little as the program of a canon in the canon can be accomplished by a revision of the external limits of the canon, just as little can it be carried out once and for all by a theological formula" (Lønning: 271).

Scripture and Tradition

Another aspect of the theological problem of the canon in modern study lies in the relationship between scripture and tradition. The fixed and facile distinction between "scripture" and "tradition," as well as the simple juxtaposition of the Protestant principle of *sola scriptura* to the Catholic conjunction of *scriptura et traditio* ("scripture and tradition"), has been deprived of any clear basis or application. Both the history of the canon and of exegesis have played a role in this.

The history of the canon shows that the ultimate determination of the content of the NT was made by the church in accordance with tradition (i.e., the tradition of ecclesiastical usage, traditional ideas about authorship, and traditional conceptions and formulations of the faith). Therefore, to acknowledge the authority of the canon is *eo ipso* to acknowledge the authority of tradition. This point has often been made by Catholic scholars (e.g., Lengsfeld: 102–4) against the Protestant tendency to oppose scripture and tradition, and it is a point that is now increasingly admitted by Protestant scholars (Ebeling, 1967:62–63; 1968a:113–14; Marxsen, 1972:16–20; Cullmann, 1956b:87–98), albeit with certain reservations, such as that it is an oversimplification to regard canonization simply as a matter of ecclesiastical decisions (Ebeling), or that by affirming the canonicity of certain writings the church deliberately subordinated itself and its tradition to scripture or, more precisely, to the apostolic norm (Cullmann). Nevertheless, it cannot be disputed that the canon of scripture is ultimately rooted in tradition.

Exegesis has done its part to erode the standing distinction between scripture and tradition by showing the extent to which individual documents of the canon are themselves products of tradition. This is preeminently true of the Gospels, as form criticism has shown, but a consistent reliance upon and deference to tradition (confessional, liturgical, paraenetic, and exegetical) is everywhere evident in the rest of the NT literature. That tradition precedes scripture and is presumed by scripture is simply a statement of historical fact. As a result, the problem of scripture and tradition, which has usually been a concern of church history and dogmatic theology, has become the province of exegesis as well. Therefore, it is increasingly common for Protestant scholars to characterize the canonical literature as "a specific form of tradition" (Ebeling, 1968a:108), a "freezing" or "transcription" of tradition at a particular stage (Best: 264–67; Evans, 1971:18–19), "the oldest Christian tradition" (Hahn, 1980) or "apostolic tradition" (Cullmann, 1956b). Here one may perhaps see an approximation of the Catholic distinction between scripture and tradition in terms of written and unwritten tradition.

The recognition of the historical importance of tradition for determining the shape and substance of the canon of scriptures, however, does not necessarily confirm the Catholic principle of tradition or discredit the Protestant principle of *sola scriptura* (Ebeling, 1968a). But it does require a thorough reconsideration of the nature and basis of the authority of the canon in order to take full account of the actual, historical relationship between scripture and tradition. Among Protestant interpreters the normative status of scripture is now often defended precisely by means of an appeal to tradition, though this is done in different ways. For example, Cullmann (1956b) regards the canon as constituting apostolic tradition but differentiates apostolic tradition (= scripture) from ecclesiastical tradition, maintaining that the former is normative for the latter because the apostolic office is unique and incapable of succession and because in canonizing apostolic tradition the church deliberately and permanently submitted itself to this norm (see Lønning: 253–63 for criticism). Hahn (1970, 1980) views the composition and valuation of the NT literature as an effort to collect and fix oral tradition deriving from the apostolic period, the result of which is a scriptural witness having unique value because it is historically closely related to the once-for-allness of the Christ-event. Ebeling (1968a) attributes an exclusive validity to the original tradition, which, because its immediate subject is Jesus, has a unique and irreplaceable significance. According to this view, the principle of *sola scriptura* "represents the struggle for genuine tradition." Clearly, none of these formulations concedes anything to tradition as a source of authoritative teaching independently of scripture. Rather, they comprehend scripture as the only resource of authoritative tradition and represent the task of subsequent ecclesiastical tradition as the critical interpretation and faithful exposition of scripture. This does not mean that tradition brings anything to scripture such that without tradition scripture could not be rightly understood, but only that tradition is the process of allowing that text of scripture to speak for itself (Ebeling, 1968a:126–40; Hahn, 1970:466–68). In the end, the problem of scripture and tradition is a hermeneutical question — that is, whether and how scripture serves adequately as its own interpreter, which is the burden of *sola scriptura,* or whether the interpretation of scripture requires supplementation by an external principle, which is the burden of *scriptura et traditio.* This question in turn is finally reducible to the problem of what canonicity really means and how it takes effect.

That recent years have witnessed a renewed appreciation in Protestant circles of the importance of tradition, and in Catholic circles of the importance of scripture, and that on both sides there is a recognition of the need to reassess old positions in a critical and constructive way, are promising signs. But it is still too early to speak of any genuine rapprochement, still less of any fundamental agreement, on the intricate problem of scripture and tradition. Historical studies have made it clear that in the ancient church scripture and tradition were not two separate categories but were coinherent realities (Flesseman-van Leer, 1954; Hanson, 1962; Tavard). The study of the history of the canon and of the meaning of canonicity may point the way toward their reintegration in modern Christianity.

BIBLIOGRAPHY

This bibliography is necessarily selective, but an effort has been made to include the most important materials of the last three decades. When English translations of foreign works are available, the dates of the translations have been cited in the text and bibliography, but in the bibliography the original date of publication has been provided in parentheses.

Abramowski, L.
    1983   "Die 'Erinnerungen der Apostel' bei Justin." Pp. 341–53 in *Das Evangelium und die Evangelien.* Ed. P. Stuhlmacher. Tübingen: Mohr-Siebeck.

Aland, K.
1962   *The Problem of the New Testament Canon*. London: Mowbray.
1967   "Das Neue Testament in der frühen Kirche." Pp. 90–111 in *Ein anderes Evangelium? Wissenschaftliche Theologie und Christliche Gemeinde*. Ed. K. Aland. Witten: Luther-Verlag. Reprinted, pp. 9–25 in his *Neutestamentliche Entwürfe*. TBü 63. Munich: Kaiser.
1979a   "Methodische Bemerkungen zum Corpus Paulinum bei den Kirchenvätern des zweiten Jahrhunderts." Pp. 29–48 in *Kerygma und Logos: Beiträge zu den geistesgeschichtlichen Beziehungen zwischen Antike und Christentum: Festschrift für Carl Andresen*. Ed. A. M. Ritter. Göttingen: Vandenhoeck & Ruprecht.
1979b   "Die Entstehung des Corpus Paulinum." Pp. 302–50 in his *Neutestamentliche Entwürfe*. TBü 63. Munich: Kaiser.

Andersen, W.
1960   "Die Verbindlichkeit des Kanons." Pp. 25–46 in *Die Verbindlichkeit des Kanons*. Ed. F. Hübner. Fuldaer Hefte 12. Berlin: Lutherisches Verlagshaus.

Anderson, C. P.
1966   "The Epistle to the Hebrews and the Pauline Letter Collection." *HTR* 59: 429–38.

Appel, N.
1964   *Kanon und Kirche: Die Kanonkrise im heutigen Protestantismus als kontroverstheologisches Problem*. Konfessionskundliche und kontroverstheologische Studien 9. Paderborn: Bonifacius.
1971   "The New Testament Canon: Historical Canon and Spirit's Witness." *TS* 32: 627–46.

Ash, J. L.
1976   "The Decline of Ecstatic Prophecy in the Early Church." *TS* 37: 227–52.

Baarda, T.
1969   *Vier = Een: Enkele bladzijden uit de geschiedenis van de harmonistiek der Evangeliën*. Kampen: Kok.

Balas, D. L.
1980   "Marcion Revisited: A 'Post-Harnack' Perspective." In *Texts and Testaments*. Ed. W. E. March. San Antonio, TX: Trinity University Press.

Barnett, A. E.
1941   *Paul Becomes a Literary Influence*. Chicago: University of Chicago Press.

Barr, J.
1973   *The Bible in the Modern World*. New York: Harper & Row.

Barrett, C. K.
1976   "Acts and the Pauline Corpus." *ExpTim* 88: 2–5.

Bauer, W.
1971   *Orthodoxy and Heresy in Earliest Christianity*. Trans. Philadelphia
(1934)   Seminar on Christian Origins. Ed. Robert Kraft and Gerhard Krodel (from 2d German edition by G. Strecker). Philadelphia: Fortress.

Beare, F. W.
1962   "Canon of the New Testament." *IDB* 1. 520–32.

Bellinzoni, A. J.
1967   *The Sayings of Jesus in the Writings of Justin Martyr.* NovTSup 17. Leiden: Brill.

Best, E.
1979   "Scripture, Tradition and the Canon of the New Testament." *BJRL* 61: 258–89.

Blackman, E. C.
1948   *Marcion and His Influence.* London: SPCK.

Braun, Herbert
1962   "Hebt die heutige neutestamentlich-exegetische Forschung den Kanon auf?" Pp. 219–32 in his *Gesammelte Studien zum Neuen Testament und seiner Umwelt.* Tübingen: Mohr-Siebeck.

Brown, R. E.
1968   "Canonicity." *JBC* 2. 515–34.

Brox, N.
1975   *Falsche Verfasserangaben: Zur Erklärung der frühchristlichen Pseudepigraphie.* SBS 79. Stuttgart: Katholisches Bibelwerk.

Bruyne, D. de
1907   "Prologues bibliques d'origin marcionite." *RBén* 24: 1–14.
1928   "Les plus anciens prologues latines des évangiles." *RBén* 40: 193–214.

Buck, C. H.
1949   "The Early Order of the Pauline Corpus." *JBL* 68: 351–57.

Burkhardt, C.
1974   "Motive und Masstäbe der Kanonbildung nach dem Canon Muratori." *TZ* 30: 207–11.

Campenhausen, H. von
1965   "Irenäus und das Neue Testament." *TLZ* 90: 1–8.
1966   "Marcion et les origines du canon néotestamentaire," *RHPR* 46: 213–26.
1972   *The Formation of the Christian Bible.* Philadelphia: Fortress.
(1968)

Carroll, K. L.
1953   "The Expansion of the Pauline Corpus." *JBL* 72: 230–37.
1954   "The Creation of the Fourfold Gospel." *BJRL* 37: 68–77.
1955   "The Earliest New Testament." *BJRL* 38: 45–57.
1962   "Toward a Commonly Received New Testament." *BJRL* 44: 327–49.
1967   "Tatian's Influence on the Developing New Testament." Pp. 59–70 in *Studies in the History and Text of the New Testament in Honor of Kenneth Willis Clark, Ph.D.* Ed. B. L. Daniels and M. J. Suggs. SD 29. Salt Lake City: University of Utah Press.

Chapman, G. C.
1968   "Ernst Käsemann, Hermann Diem, and the New Testament Canon." *JAAR* 36: 3–12.

Charlesworth, J. H.
1974   "Tatian's Dependence upon Apocryphal Traditions." *HeyJ* 14: 5–17.

Clabeaux, J. J.
1983   "The Pauline Corpus which Marcion Used: The Text of the Letters
            of Paul in the Early Second Century." Diss., Harvard.

Conzelmann, H.
1965   "Paulus und die Weisheit." *NTS* 12: 321–44.

Corssen, P.
1909   "Zur Überlieferungsgeschichte des Römerbriefes." *ZNW* 10: 1–45,
            97–102.

Cosgrove, C. H.
1982   "Justin Martyr and the Emerging Christian Canon: Observations on
            the Purpose and Destination of the Dialogue with Trypho." *VC* 36:
            209–32.

Crehan, J. H.
1959   "The Fourfold Character of the Gospel." *SE* I [= TU 73] 3–13.

Cullmann, O.
1956   "The Plurality of the Gospels as a Theological Problem in Antiquity."
(1945)   Pp. 39–54 in his *The Early Church*. Philadelphia: Westminster.
1956b   "The Tradition." Pp. 59–99 in his *The Early Church*. Philadelphia:
(1953)   Westminster.
1967   *Salvation in History*. London: SCM.
(1965)

Dahl, N. A.
1961   "Welche Ordnung der Paulusbriefe wird vom muratorischen Kanon
            vorausgesetzt?" *ZNW* 52: 39–48.
1962   "The Particularity of the Pauline Epistles as a Problem in the Ancient
            Church." Pp. 261–71 in *Neotestamentica et Patristica: Eine Freundes-
            gabe Herrn Prof. Dr. Oscar Cullmann zu seinem 60. Geburtstag*.
            NovTSup 6. Leiden: Brill.
1978   "The Origin of the Earliest Prologues to the Pauline Letters."
            Pp. 233–77 in *The Poetics of Faith: Essays offered to A.N. Wilder*. Ed.
            W. A. Beardslee. *Semeia* 12. Missoula, MT: Scholars Press.
1979   "0230 (= PSI 1306) and the Fourth-Century Greek-Latin Edition of
            the Letters of Paul." Pp. 79–98 in *Text and Interpretation: Studies in
            the New Testament Presented to Matthew Black*. Ed. E. Best and
            R. McL. Wilson. Cambridge: University Press.

Dassmann, E.
1979   *Der Stachel im Fleisch: Paulus in frühchristlichen Literatur bis
            Irenäus*. Münster: Aschendorff.

Diem, H.
1952   *Das Problem des Schriftkanons*. ThStud 32. Zollikon-Zurich:
            Evangelischer Verlag.
1953   "Die Einheit der Schrift." *EvT* 13: 385–405.
1959   *Dogmatics*. Edinburgh: Oliver & Boyd.
(1955)

Dungan, D. L.
1975   "The New Testament Canon in Recent Study." *Int* 29: 339–51.

Dunn, J. D. G.
1977   *Unity and Diversity in the New Testament*. Philadelphia: Westmin-
            ster.

Ebeling, G.
    1967   *The Problem of Historicity in the Church and Its Proclamation.*
    (1954)   Philadelphia: Fortress.
    1968a   "'Sola Scriptura' and Tradition." Pp. 102–47 in his *The Word of God*
    (1963)   *and Tradition.* Philadelphia: Fortress.
    1968b   "The New Testament and the Multiplicity of Confessions." Pp. 148–
             59 in his *Word of God and Tradition.* Philadelphia: Fortress.

Ehrhardt, A. A. T.
    1953   "The Gospels in the Muratorian Fragment." *Ostkirchliche Studien* 2:
             121–38.
    1962   "Christianity Before the Apostles' Creed." *HTR* 55: 74–119.

Elliott, J. K.
    1966   "The New Testament is Catholic: A Re-evaluation of *sola scriptura*."
             Una Sancta 23: 3–18.

Ellis, E. E.
    1971   "Paul and His Co-Workers." *NTS* 17: 437–52.

Enslin, M. S.
    1970   "Once Again, Luke and Paul." *ZNW* 61: 253–71.

Evans, C. F.
    1971   *Is Holy Scripture Christian?* London: SCM.

Farmer, W. R.
    1982   *Jesus and the Gospel: Tradition, Scripture and Canon.* Philadelphia:
             Fortress.
    1983   *The Formation of the New Testament Canon* (with D. M. Farkasfakvy).
             New York: Paulist. Pp. 7–95.

Ferguson, E.
    1982   "Canon Muratori: Date and Provenance." Pp. 677–83 in *Studia*
             Patristica 18. New York: Pergamon.

Filson, F. V.
    1957   *Which Books Belong to the Bible? A Study of the Canon.* Philadelphia:
             Westminster.

Finegan, J.
    1956   "The Original Form of the Pauline Collection," *HTR* 49: 85–103.

Flesseman-van Leer, E.
    1954   *Tradition and Scripture in the Early Church.* Assen: van Gorcum.
    1964   "Prinzipien der Sammlung und Ausscheidung bei der Bildung des
             Kanons." *ZTK* 61: 404–20.
    1968   "Present-day Frontiers in the Discussion about Tradition." Pp. 154–
             70 in *Holy Book and Holy Tradition.* Ed. F. F. Bruce and E. G. Rupp.
             Manchester: Manchester University Press.

Frank, I.
    1971   *Der Sinn der Kanonbildung: Eine historisch-theologische Untersuch-*
             ung der Zeit vom 1. Clemensbrief bis Irenäus von Lyon. Freiburger
             Theologische Studien 90. Freiburg: Herder.

Frede, H. J.
    1964   *Altlateinische Paulus-Handschriften.* Vetus Latina: Aus der
             Geschichte der lateinischen Bibel 4. Freiburg: Herder.

1969   "Die Ordnung der Paulusbriefe und der Platz des Kolosserbriefs im Corpus Paulinum." Pp. 290–303 in *Vetus Latina: Die Reste der altlateinischen Bibel.* Vol. 24/2, *Epistulae ad Philippenses et ad Colossenses.* Freiburg: Herder.

Gamble, H. Y.
1975   "The Redaction of the Pauline Letters and the Formation of the Pauline Corpus." *JBL* 94: 403–18.
1977   *The Textual History of the Letter to the Romans.* SD 42. Grand Rapids: Eerdmans.
1985   *The New Testament Canon: Its Making and Meaning.* Guides to Biblical Scholarship. Philadelphia: Fortress.

Goodspeed, E. J.
1926   *The Formation of the New Testament.* Chicago: University of Chicago Press.
1933   *The Meaning of Ephesians.* Chicago: University of Chicago Press.
1945   "Editio princeps of Paul." *JBL* 64: 193–204.
1951   "Ephesians and the First Edition of Paul." *JBL* 70: 285–91.
1956   *The Key to Ephesians.* Chicago: University of Chicago Press.

Grant, R. M.
1961   *The Earliest Lives of Jesus.* New York: Harper.
1965   *The Formation of the New Testament.* New York: Harper & Row.
1970   "The New Testament Canon." Pp. 284–308 in *The Cambridge History of the Bible,* vol. 1. Ed. P. R. Ackroyd and C. F. Evans. Cambridge: University Press.

Groh, D.
1974   "Hans von Campenhausen on Canon: Positions and Problems." *Int* 28: 331–43.

Gryson, R.
1965   "A propos du témoignage de Papias sur Matthieu: Le sens du mot *logion* chez les Pères de IIe siècle." *ETL* 41: 530–47.

Gutwenger, E.
1946   "The Anti-Marcionite Prologues," *TS* 7: 393–409.

Hagner, D. A.
1973   *The Use of the Old and New Testaments in Clement of Rome.* NovTSup 34. Leiden: Brill.

Hahn, F.
1970   "Das Problem 'Schrift und Tradition' im Urchristentum." *EvT* 30: 449–68.
1980   "Die Heilige Schrift als älteste christliche Tradition und als Kanon." *EvT* 40: 456–66.

Hanson, R. P. C.
1954   *Origen's Doctrine of Tradition.* London: SPCK.
1962   *Tradition in the Early Church.* Philadelphia: Westminster.

Harnack, Adolf
1889   *Das Neue Testament um das Jahr 200.* Freiburg.
1912   *Bible Reading in the Early Church.* New York: Putnam.
1924   *Marcion: Das Evangelium vom fremden Gott.* 2d ed. Leipzig: Hinrichs.
1925a   *The Origin of the New Testament and the Most Important Conse-*
(1914)   *quences of the New Creation.* London: Williams & Norgate.

| 1925b | "Über den Verfasser und den literarischen Charakter des muratorischen Fragments." *ZNW* 24: 1–16. |

1925b   "Über den Verfasser und den literarischen Charakter des muratorischen Fragments." *ZNW* 24: 1–16.

1926   *Die Briefsammlung des Apostels Paulus und die anderen vorkonstantinischen Briefsammlungen.* Leipzig: Hinrichs.

1928   "Die ältesten Evangelien-Prologe und die Bildung des Neuen Testaments." SPAW, Phil.-hist. Kl. 24: 322–41.

Heard, R.

1954a   "The *Apomnemoneumata* in Papias, Justin, and Irenaeus." *NTS* 1: 122–29.

1954b   "Papias' Quotations from the New Testament." *NTS* 1: 130–34.

1955   "The Old Gospel Prologues." *JTS* n.s. 6: 1–16.

Hillmer, M. R.

1966   "The Gospel of John in the Second Century." Diss., Harvard.

Horst, U.

1968   "Die Divergenzen im neutestamentlichen Kanon als theologisches Problem." *Communio* 1: 161–84.

Hyldahl, N.

1960   "Hegesipps Hypomnemata." *ST* 14: 70–113.

Jeremias, J.

1960   "Der gegenwärtige Stand der Debatte um das Problem des historischen Jesus." Pp. 12–25 in *Der historischen Jesus und der kerygmatische Christus.* Ed. H. Ristow and K. Matthiae. Berlin: Evangelische Verlagsanstalt.

1963   "An Unknown Gospel with Johannine Elements." Pp. 94–97 in *New Testament Apocrypha*, vol. 1. Ed. E. Hennecke and W. Schneemelcher. Philadelphia: Westminster.

Joest, W.

1966   "Erwägungen zur kanonischen Bedeutung des Neuen Testaments." *KD* 12: 27–47.

Kalin, E.

1967   "Argument from Inspiration in the Canonization of the New Testament." Diss., Harvard.

1971   "The Inspired Community: A Glance at Canon History." *CTM* 42: 541–49.

Käsemann, E.

1964a   "The Canon of the New Testament and the Unity of the Church."
(1951)   Pp. 95–107 in his *Essays on New Testament Themes.* London: SCM.

1964b   "Is the Gospel Objective?" Pp. 48–62 in his *Essays on New Testament*
(1952–53)   *Themes.* London. SCM.

1970   *Das Neue Testament als Kanon: Dokumentation und kritische Analyse zur gegenwärtigen Diskussion.* Göttingen: Vandenhoeck & Ruprecht.

1971   "The Spirit and the Letter." Pp. 138–66 in his *Perspectives on Paul.* Philadelphia: Fortress.

Katz, P.

1957   "The Johannine Epistles in the Muratorian Canon." *JTS* n.s. 8: 273–74.

Keck, L. E.

1980   "Is the NT a Field of Study? Or, From Outler to Overbeck and Back." *Second Century* 1: 19–35.

Kennedy, G.
1978   "Classical and Christian Source Criticism." Pp. 125–55 in *The Relationships Among the Gospels*. Ed. W. O. Walker. San Antonio, TX: Trinity University Press.

Klein, G.
1961   *Die zwölf Apostel: Ursprung und Gestalt einer Idee*. FRLANT 77. Göttingen: Vandenhoeck & Ruprecht.

Klijn, A. F. J.
1969   *A Survey of the Researches into the Western Text of the Gospels and Acts: Part Two, 1949–1969*. Leiden: Brill.

Kline, L. L.
1975   "Harmonized Sayings of Jesus in the Pseudo-Clementine Homilies and Justin Martyr." *ZNW* 66: 223–41.

Knox, J.
1935   *Philemon Among the Letters of Paul*. Rev. ed. Nashville: Abingdon. Reprinted, 1959.
1942   *Marcion and the New Testament*. Chicago: University of Chicago Press.
1966   "Acts and the Pauline Letter Corpus." Pp. 279–87 in *Studies in Luke-Acts*. Ed. L. E. Keck and J. L. Martyn. New York and Nashville: Abingdon.

Koester, H.
1957   *Synoptische Überlieferung bei den apostolischen Vätern*. TU 65. Berlin: Akademie.
1971a   "One Jesus and Four Primitive Gospels." Pp. 158–204 in Robinson, 1971a.
1971b   "The Intention and Scope of Trajectories." Pp. 269–79 in Robinson, 1971a.
1975   "New Testament Introduction: A Critique of a Discipline." Pp. 1–20 in *Christianity, Judaism and Other Greco-Roman Cults: Studies for Morton Smith at Sixty*, vol. 1. Ed. J. Neusner. SJLA 12. Leiden: Brill.
1980   "Apocryphal and Canonical Gospels." *HTR* 73: 105–30.

Kümmel, W. G.
1957   "Sammlung und Kanonisierung des NT." *RGG*[3] 1: 1136–38.
1965   "Notwendigkeit und Grenze des neutestamentlichen Kanons." Pp. 230–59 in his *Heilsgeschehen und Geschichte: Gesammelte Aufsätze 1933–1964*. Ed. E. Grässer, O. Merk, and A. Fritz. Marburger Theologische Studien 3. Marburg: Elwert. [= *ZTK* 47 (1950) 277–313.]
1968   "Das Problem der 'Mitte' des Neuen Testaments." Pp. 71–85 in *L'évangile hier et aujourd'hui: Mélanges offerts F.J. Leenhardt*. Geneva: Labor et Fides.
1975   *Introduction to the New Testament*. Rev. ed. Nashville: Abingdon.

Küng, H.
1963   " 'Early Catholicism' in the New Testament as a Problem in Controversial Theology." Pp. 159–95 in *The Council in Action: Theological Reflections on the Second Vatican Council*. New York: Sheed & Ward.
1964   *Structures of the Church*. New York: Nelson.
(1962)

Kürzinger, J.
1960   "Das Papiaszeugnis und die Endgestalt des Matthäusevangeliums."
        BZ 4: 19–38.
1977   "Die Aussage des Papias von Hieropolis zu literarischen Form des
        Markusevangeliums." BZ 21: 245–64.
1983   Papias von Hieropolis und die Evangelien des Neuen Testaments.
        Regensburg: Pustet

Kuss, O.
1967   "Die Schrift und die Einheit der Christen," MTZ 18: 292–307.

Lagrange, M.-J.
1933   Introduction a l'étude du Nouveau Testament. Vol. 1. Histoire ancienne
        du canon du Nouveau Testament. Paris.

Lake, K.
1911   The Earlier Epistles of St. Paul. London: Williams & Norgate.

Leipoldt, J.
1907   Geschichte des neutestamentlichen Kanons. Vol. 1. Die Entstehung.
        Leipzig: Hinrichs.

Lengsfeld, P.
1960   Überlieferung: Tradition und Schrift in der evangelischen und katho-
        lischen Theologie der Gegenwart. Konfessionskundliche und kontro-
        verstheologische Studien 3. Paderborn: Bonifacius.

Lietzmann, H.
1907   "Wie wurden die Bücher des Neuen Testaments Heilige Schrift?"
        Pp. 15–98 in Kleine Schriften, 2. Ed. K. Aland. TU 68. Berlin:
        Akademie, 1958.
1933   "Einführung in die Textgeschichte der Paulusbriefe." Pp. 138–59 in
        Kleine Schriften, 2. Ed. K. Aland. TU 68. Berlin: Akademie, 1958.

Lindemann, A.
1979   Paulus im ältesten Christentum: Das Bild des Apostels und die
        Rezeption der paulinischen Theologie in der frühchristlichen Literatur
        bis Marcion. BHT 58. Tübingen: Mohr-Siebeck.

Linton, O.
1967   "Evidences of a Second-Century Revised Edition of St. Mark's
        Gospel." NTS 13: 321–55.

Lønning, I.
1972   Kanon im Kanon: Zum dogmatischen Grundlagen-Problem des neu-
        testamentlichen Kanons. FGLP 43. Oslo: Universitetsforlaget.

Lührmann, D.
1981   "Gal. 2.9 und die katholischen Briefe." ZNW 72: 65–87.

Marxsen, W.
1968a   "Das Problem des neutestamentlichen Kanons aus der Sicht des
        Exegeten." Pp. 91–103 in Der Exeget als Theologe. Gütersloh: Mohn.
        [= NZSysTh 2 (1960) 137–50.]
1968b   "Kontingenz der Offenbarung oder (und?) Kontingenz des Kanons?"
        Pp. 129–38 in Der Exeget als Theologe. Gütersloh: Mohn. [=
        NZSysTh 2 (1960) 355–64.]
1972   The New Testament as the Church's Book. Philadelphia: Fortress.
(1966)

Mayeda, G.
1946   *Das Leben-Jesu-Fragment Papyrus Egerton 2 und seine Stellung in der urchristlichen Literaturgeschichte.* Bern: Haupt.

Meeks, W. A.
1978   "Hypomnemata from an Untamed Sceptic: A Response to George Kennedy." Pp. 157–72 in *The Relationships Among the Gospels.* Ed. W. O. Walker. San Antonio, TX: Trinity University Press.

Merkel, H.
1971   *Die Widersprüche zwischen den Evangelien: Ihre polemische und apologetische Behandlung in der alten Kirche bis zu Augustin.* WUNT 13. Tübingen: Mohr-Siebeck.

1978   *Die Pluralität der Evangelien als theologisches und exegetisches Problem in der alten Kirche.* Bern: Lang.

Messina, Giuseppe
1951   *Diatessaron Persiano.* BibOr 14. Rome: Pontifical Biblical Institute.

Metzger, B. M.
1963   "Canon of the New Testament." Pp. 123–26 in *Hastings Dictionary of the Bible.* Ed. F. C. Grant and H. H. Rowley. New York: Scribner.

1977   *The Early Versions of the New Testament: Their Origin, Transmission, and Limitations.* Oxford: Clarendon Press.

Mitton, C. L.
1951   *The Epistle to the Ephesians: Its Authorship, Origin and Purpose.* Oxford: Clarendon Press.

1955   *The Formation of the Pauline Corpus of Letters.* London: Epworth.

Moule, C. F. D.
1982   *The Birth of the New Testament.* 3d ed. rev. HNTC. New York: Harper.

Mowry, L.
1944   "The Early Circulation of Paul's Letters." *JBL* 63: 73–86.

Munck, J.
1962   "Die Tradition über das Matthäusevangelium bei Papias." Pp. 249–60 in *Neotestamentica et Patristica: Eine Freundesgabe Herrn Dr. Oscar Cullmann zu seinem 60. Geburtstag.* NovTSup 6. Leiden: Brill.

Murray, R.
1970   "How Did the Church Determine the Canon of Scripture?" *HeyJ* 11: 115–26.

Mussner, F.
1961   "Die Mitte des Evangeliums in neutestamentlicher Sicht," *Catholica* 15: 271–92.

1964   " 'Evangelium' und 'Mitte des Evangeliums.' " Pp. 492–514 in *Gott in Welt: Festschrift K. Rahner,* vol. 1. Freiburg: Herder.

Nielsen, C. M.
1965   "Polycarp, Paul and the Scriptures." *ATR* 47: 199–216.

Ohlig, K.-H.
1970   *Woher nimmt die Bibel ihre Autorität? Zum Verhältnis von Schrift-kanon, Kirche und Jesus.* Düsseldorf: Patmos.

1972   *Die theologische Begründung des neutestamentlichen Kanons in der alten Kirche.* Düsseldorf: Patmos.

1973   "Zur Theologie des Kanons der Heiligen Schrift Überlegungen anhand des Geschichte des Kanons." *Theologie der Gegenwart in Auswahl* 16: 74–83.

Ollrog, W.-H.
1979   *Paulus und seine Mitarbeiter*. WMANT 50. Neukirchen-Vluyn: Neukirchener Verlag.

Osborn, E. F.
1973   *Justin Martyr*. BHT 47. Tübingen: Mohr-Siebeck.

Pagels, E. H.
1973   *The Johannine Gospel in Gnostic Exegesis*. Nashville: Abingdon.
1975   *The Gnostic Paul: Gnostic Exegesis of the Pauline Letters*. Philadelphia: Fortress.

Paulsen, H.
1978   "Die Bedeutung des Montanismus für die Herausbildung des Kanons," *VC* 32: 19–52.

Pedersen, S.
1977   "Die Kanonfrage als historisches und theologisches Problem." *ST* 31: 83–136.

Petrie. C. S.
1968   "The Authorship of 'the Gospel according to Matthew': A Reconsideration of the External Evidence." *NTS* 14: 15–33.

Quinn, J. D.
1974   "P46 —The Pauline Canon?" *CBQ* 36: 379–85.

Quispel, G.
1959   "L'évangile selon Thomas et le Diatessaron." *VC* 13: 87–117.

Rathke, H.
1967   *Ignatius von Antiochien und die Paulusbriefe*. TU 99. Berlin: Akademie-Verlag.

Regul, J.
1969   *Die antimarcionitischen Evangelienprologe*. Vetus Latina: Aus der Geschichte der lateinischen Bibel 6. Freiburg: Herder.

Rensberger, D.
1981   "As the Apostle Teaches: The Development of the Use of Paul's Letters in Second Century Christianity." Diss., Yale University.

Roberts, C. H.
1949   "The Christian Book and the Greek Papyri." *JTS* 50: 155–68.
1954   "The Codex." *Proceedings of the British Academy* 40: 169–204.
1970   "Books in the Graeco-Roman World and in the New Testament." Pp. 48–66 in *Cambridge History of the Bible*, vol. 1. Ed. P. R. Ackroyd and C. F. Evans. Cambridge: University Press.
1979   *Manuscript, Society and Belief in Early Christian Egypt*. Schweich Lectures, 1977. London: Oxford University Press.

Roberts, C. H., and T. C. Skeat
1983   *The Birth of the Codex*. London: Oxford University Press.

Robinson, J. M.
1971a   (with Helmut Koester). *Trajectories through Early Christianity*. Philadelphia: Fortress.
1971b   "Logoi Sophon. On the Gattung of Q." Pp. 71–113 in Robinson, 1971a.

Ruwet, J.
1942   "Les 'antilegomena' dans les oeuvres d'Origène." *Bib* 23: 18–42.
1948   "Clement d'Alexandrie: Canon des écritures et apocryphes." *Bib* 29: 77–99, 240–68, 391–408.

Sand, A.
1973   "Die Diskrepanz zwischen historischer Zufälligkeit und normativem Charakter des neutestamentlichen Kanons als hermeneutisches Problem." *MTZ* 24: 147–60.
1974   "Kanon: Von den Anfängen bis zum Fragmentum Muratorianum." Pp. 3–58 in *Handbuch der Dogmengeschichte*, I.3a.I. Freiburg: Herder.

Sanders, J. N.
1943   *The Fourth Gospel in the Early Church*. Cambridge: University Press.
1962   "The Literature and Canon of the New Testament." *PCB* 676–82.

Schäfer, K. T.
1973a   "Marcion und die ältesten Prologe zu den Paulusbriefen." Pp. 135–50 in *Kyriakon: Festschrift Johannes Quasten*. 2 vols. Ed. P. Granfeld and J. A. Jungmann. Münster: Aschendorff.
1973b   "Marius Victorinus und die marcionitischen Prologe zu den Paulusbriefen." *RBén* 80: 7–16.

Schelkle, K. H.
1961   "Das Evangelium Veritatis als kanonsgeschichtliche Quelle." *BZ* n.s. 5: 90–91.

Schenke, H.-M.
1975   "Das Weiterwirken des Paulus und die Pflege seines Erbs durch die Paulusschule." *NTS* 21: 505–18.

Schmithals, W.
1972   "On the Composition and Earliest Collection of the Major Epistles
(1960)   of Paul." Pp. 239–74 in *Paul and the Gnostics*. Nashville: Abingdon.

Schneemelcher, W.
1963a   "The History of the New Testament Canon." Pp. 28–60 in *New Testament Apocrypha*, vol. 1. Ed. E. Hennecke and W. Schneemelcher. Philadelphia: Westminster.
1963b   "Types of Apocryphal Gospels." Pp. 80–84 in *New Testament Apocrypha*, vol. 1.
1964   "Paulus in der griechischen Kirche des 2. Jahrhunderts." *ZKG* 75: 1–20.

Schoedel, W. R.
1967   *Polycarp, Martyrdom of Polycarp, Fragments of Papias*. Apostolic Fathers. Camden, NJ: Nelson.

Schrage, W.
1976   "Die Frage nach der Mitte und dem Kanon im Kanon des Neuen Testaments in der neueren Diskussion." Pp. 415–42 in *Rechtfertigung: Festschrift für Ernst Käsemann zum 70. Geburtstag*. Ed. J. Friedrich, W. Pöhlmann, and P. Stuhlmacher. Tübingen: Mohr-Siebeck.

Schweizer, E.
1971   "Kanon?" *EvT* 31: 339–57.

Smith, J. D.
1979   "Gaius and the Controversy over the Johannine Literature." Diss.,
            Yale University.

Smith, Morton
1973   *Clement of Alexandria and a Secret Gospel of Mark.* Cambridge, MA:
            Harvard University Press.

Souter, A.
1954   *The Text and Canon of the New Testament.* Revised by C. S. C.
            Williams. London: Duckworth.

Stendahl, K.
1962   "The Apocalypse of John and the Epistles of Paul in the Muratorian
            Fragment." Pp. 239–45 in *Current Issues in New Testament Interpre-
            tation: Essays in Honor of Otto A. Piper.* Ed. W. Klassen and G. F.
            Snyder. New York: Harper.

Strathmann, H.
1941   "Die Krise des Kanons der Kirche." *ThBl* 20: 295–310.

Strecker, G.
1978   "Eine Evangelien-Harmonie bei Justin und Pseudoklemens?" *NTS*
            24: 297–316.

Sundberg, A. C.
1958   "The Old Testament of the Early Church." *HTR* 51: 205–26.
1964a   *The Old Testament of the Early Church.* HTS 20. Cambridge, MA:
            Harvard University Press.
1964b   "Dependent Canonicity in Irenaeus and Tertullian." *SE* 3: 403–9.
1968a   "Toward a Revised History of the New Testament Canon." *SE* 4:
            452–61.
1968b   "The Old Testament: A Christian Canon." *CBQ* 30: 143–65.
1971   "The Making of the New Testament Canon." Pp. 1216–24 in *The
            Interpreter's One-Volume Commentary on the Bible.* Ed. C. M.
            Laymon. Nashville: Abingdon.
1973   "Canon Muratori: A Fourth Century List." *HTR* 66: 1–41.
1975   "The Bible Canon and the Christian Doctrine of Inspiration." *Int* 29:
            352–71.

Tavard, G.
1959   *Holy Writ or Holy Church; The Crisis of the Protestant Reformation.*
            New York: Harper.

Trilling, W.
1969   " 'Sola scriptura' und 'Selbstauslegung der Schrift' im Licht der Exe-
            gese." Pp. 49–72 in *Sapienter Ordinare: Festgabe E. Kleineidam.* ETS
            24. Leipzig: St. Benno.

Turner, E. G.
1977   *The Typology of the Early Codex.* Haney Foundation Series 18.
            Philadelphia: University of Pennsylvania Press.

Turner, H. E. W.
1954   *The Pattern of Christian Truth: A Study in the Relations between
            Orthodoxy and Heresy in the Early Church.* London: Mowbray.

Unnik, W. C. van
1949   "De la règle μήτη προσθεῖναι μήτη ἀφελεῖν dans l'histoire du canon." *VC*
            3: 1–36.

1955   "The Gospel of Truth and the New Testament." Pp. 79–131 in *The Jung Codex*. Ed. F. L. Cross. New York.

1961   "'Η Καίνη Διαθήκη—a Problem in the Early History of the Canon." Pp. 212–27 in *Studia Patristica* 4. TU 79. Berlin: Akademie.

Vogels, H.
1953   "Der Einfluss Marcions und Tatians auf Text und Kanon des Neuen Testaments." Pp. 278–89 in *Synoptische Studien Alfred Wikenhauser . . . dargebracht*. Munich: Zink.

Vokes, F. E.
1964   "The Didache and the Canon of the New Testament." *SE* 3: 427–36.
1968   "The Use of Scripture in the Montanist Controversy." *SE* 4: 317–20.

Wainwright, G.
1975   "The New Testament as Canon." *SJT* 28: 551–71.

Walker, W. O., Jr.
1985   "Acts and the Pauline Corpus Reconsidered." *JSNT* 24: 3–23.

Wiefel, W.
1974   "Kanongeschichtliche Erwägungen zu Papyrus Bodmer vii/viii (P⁷²)." *Archiv für Papyrusforschung* 22/23: 289–303.

Windisch, H.
1909   "Der Apokalyptiker Johannes als Begründer des neutestamentlichen Kanons." *ZNW* 10: 148–74.

Zahn, T.
1881–   *Forschungen zur Geschichte des neutestamentlichen Kanons*.
1929   Erlangen: Deichert.
1888–92   *Geschichte des neutestamentlichen Kanons*, vols. 1–2. Erlangen.
1904   *Grundriss der Geschichte des neutestamentlichen Kanons*. Leipzig.

Zuntz, G.
1953   *The Text of the Epistles: A Disquisition upon the Corpus Paulinum*. Schweich Lectures, 1946. London: Oxford University Press.

9

SYNOPTIC STUDIES

Howard Clark Kee

I. CHALLENGES TO COMMON ASSUMPTIONS

By 1950, NT scholars on the North American continent, in Britain, and in Western Europe were largely in agreement on a major set of assumptions regarding the synoptic gospels. By 1980, every one of those assumptions was challenged, and some were overturned.

The Two-Source Hypothesis and Form Criticism

By the midpoint of this century, a widespread assumption was the Two-Source hypothesis, which affirmed that Mark was the earliest of our Gospels and that Matthew and Luke drew on a second source, usually designated as Q, for the non-Marcan material that they share. It was also widely assumed that form criticism had made its point: Our written Gospels were the end products of a process of oral transmission of Jesus tradition, including sayings and narrative material, which had circulated orally in the early church for purposes of preaching and instruction. Careful reading of the Gospels made possible distinguishing the smoothed-off units of tradition from the connective tissue by which the editorial enterprise of the evangelists had linked it together in order to provide the reader a sense of sequence in the Gospel accounts of Jesus. This process was presupposed both by those who attributed the Jesus traditions to the post-Easter Christian community (Bultmann, 1963; Dibelius) and by those who thought all or most of it went back to Jesus himself (Taylor).

A corollary of this assessment of the Gospels as loose collections of traditional material (apart from the passion narrative, which was thought to be the sole sequential feature of the pre-Gospel tradition) was the assumption that the evangelists were "principally collectors of tradition, editors" and "only to the smallest extent authors" (Dibelius: 27). Among the German form critics and those directly influenced by them, the passion narrative was considered to be a pre-Marcan body of tradition (Dibelius: 23, 181–85). It took the form it now has in the Gospels in the process of the proclamation of the kerygma that was normal for Pauline Hellenistic Christianity (Bultmann, 1963:347).

245

Aims of the Evangelists

Unlike Luke's Gospel, which together with Acts was recognized as
having a distinctive and clearly defined purpose (Cadbury; see Section III
below), Matthew was thought to be different from Mark, largely because he
included more material than did Mark. Studies of Matthew were more
concerned with that Gospel's structure (so Bacon), or its original language
(Torrey), or its kinship with rabbinic ethics and exegesis (Strack-Billerbeck)
than with the specific aims of the evangelist.

K. L. Schmidt's brilliant analysis of the editorial work by which Mark
had bound together the tradition found Mark's specific aim to be "not
immediately clear" (317). And the form critics seemed uniformly to share
Martin Kähler's passing remark that Mark was a passion story with an
extended introduction (Kähler: 275), a suggestion that offered no clue to why
Mark had included the material that occupied the first five-sixths of his
writing.

Historical Value of the Gospels

Among conservative scholars, Mark's priority was understood to confirm the historicity of his material, or at least they were confident that his
account stood relatively closer to the events it described. The link between
Jesus and the Gospel tradition was thought to be demonstrated as even
closer by linguistic evidence of Aramaic speech underlying the Greek of the
Gospels (Torrey; Black; Parker). The 1950s saw a resurgence of interest in
the historical Jesus question, but for the most part the aims and methods of
the so-called "New Quest" differed significantly from those of scholars
concerned with demonstrating the continuity of the tradition from Jesus to
the Gospels, as we shall note below.

Basic Theological Shifts

Two quite different factors contributed to the mid-century shifts in NT
studies in general and in synoptic studies in particular. The first was the
impact of basic changes in theological climate. Instead of the Barthian
dogmatics that dominated systematic theology immediately following World
War II, NT study was increasingly attracted by approaches that offered hope
of discovering unity behind the outward diversity of the early Christian
writings. In English-speaking circles, a widely appealing option was that of
C. H. Dodd, whose study of the apostolic kerygma sought to demonstrate
a common message underlying all the NT. At first in Germany, and then on
both sides of the Atlantic, the most powerful voice was that of Rudolf
Bultmann, whose combination of brilliant analytical insights and unifying
existentialist theological formulation provided a rational picture of the
historical development of the NT and an appealing theological center for

faith. Among Roman Catholics, the publication in 1943 of Pius XII's *Divino Afflante Spiritu* opened the doors for full participation by scholars of that tradition in critical biblical study.

New Sources for the New Testament Background

A second factor was the discovery of new documents and the spur that the new finds gave to reexamination of texts contemporary with the NT or potentially relevant for study of it. Most notable, of course, were the manuscripts from Qumran, the so-called Dead Sea Scrolls, which demonstrated in depth the existence, the outlook, the methods of scriptural interpretation, the messianic hopes, and the community self-understanding of a group of Jews living near Jerusalem in the first century of our era, who claimed to be the people of the new covenant. The other major discoveries were the Coptic-gnostic writings found in Upper Egypt, known as the Nag Hammadi Gnostic Library. As a result of these finds, fresh perspectives on synoptic texts and especially on synoptic interpretation of the OT were made possible. Both Jewish and Christian scholars undertook new studies of the rabbinic sources and of the history of both Jewish and non-Jewish religious thought, practices, and institutions during the Hellenistic and early Roman periods, which shed light on Christian origins and called for reappraisal of the historical background of the synoptic material. M. Hengel's (1974) masterful historical reconstruction of Judaism in the Hellenistic period showed the inappropriateness of the neat distinctions common to NT scholarship: Palestinian/Hellenistic. Jacob Neusner's careful study of the Pharisees (1973) demonstrated the evolution of that movement and how distorted is the image of the Pharisees derived from polemical features in the Gospels alone or from extrapolation backward based on the later rabbinic traditions.

Eschatology as a Persistent Theological Problem

A pervasive theme and perennial problem in synoptic studies of the post-1950 period was eschatology. The theologically intractable outcomes of the turn-of-the-century work of Albert Schweitzer and Johannes Weiss were brought to remembrance by such widely used studies as that of Rudolf Otto on Jesus' message of the kingdom of God and his identity as Son of Man (1938). Events during and after World War II — the near apocalypse of the atomic warfare, the holocaust, the fierce world-wide ideological conflicts and utopian programs — made eschatological hope both more nearly credible and more appealing. The hard question was how to interpret critically the fundamentally eschatological claims underlying Jesus' message and mission in the Synoptics. The critical presuppositions, the historical assumptions, and the theological predilections were all subject to change without notice

as NT scholarship resumed synoptic studies following the end of World
War II.

II. ATTACKS ON AND ALTERNATIVES TO
THE TWO-SOURCE THEORY

Griesbach redivivus

The attacks on the Two-Source hypothesis have varied in strategy, in
style, and in stance. The target initially was the method and conclusions of
B. H. Streeter's classic study of the four Gospels. B. C. Butler developed his
case for the priority of Matthew, and W. R. Farmer launched his international enterprise in behalf of the Griesbach theory of Matthean priority in
the form of a frontal assault on the dominant stronghold of the Two-Source
theory. Farmer's strategy of showing that defenders of Marcan priority were
often motivated by values or commitments that had no bearing on the
literary source questions found an ally in H.-H. Stoldt, who exposed the
fears, fantasies, and inflated egos that affected the discussion of the synoptic
problem from Griesbach down to the present. After insisting that any theory
is false that does not account for all the phenomena of synoptic relationships
without remainder, Stoldt rejected the Griesbach hypothesis, leaving the
problem an unsolved riddle. As a result, his historical sketch of the synoptic
problem brings us no nearer a solution (Stoldt: 235). The weapons of others
who have assaulted the Two-Source theory include ancient analogy (Longstaff) and statistics (Sanders), though the results are likewise inconclusive.
D. Dungan (1970) dismisses scholars who prefer the Two-Source hypothesis
as those who "have no clear idea of the correct way to use [evidence]" (68).

   T. R. Longstaff has developed concretely the hypothesis that Mark has
conflated Matthew and Luke, reasoning on the basis of analogies with
medieval and more ancient documents, such as Tatian's *Diatessaron*. His
conclusions are that the pattern of agreements and disagreements in the
selected pericopae he has analyzed does not rule out Mark's having conflated
Matthew and Luke and that the phenomena are in some cases more readily
explained by the Griesbach hypothesis than by the Two-Source theory. He
acknowledges, however, that there is no solid proof that the Griesbach
solution is correct, and he relies largely on the analogies with the conflation
process as observed in the documents he has chosen for comparison. We
shall comment on the plausibility of the Griesbach theory below, but it
should be noted that the appropriateness of the texts adduced as analogies
for the conflation by Mark is debatable. Tatian, for example, was weaving
together Gospel narratives that had already been assigned canonical status
by the time he was at work. But evangelists obviously thought that the
Gospel traditions and the Gospel accounts already known to them were wide
open for extensive editorial modification. The processes of conflation and of
Gospel writing are, therefore, basically dissimilar.

Conflicting Evidence of Tendencies
in the Tradition

The most carefully presented challenge to the Two-Source theory is that of E. P. Sanders, who claims to have shown that the tendencies he traces in the Gospel tradition—changes in length, degree of detail, and use of Semitisms—can never justify the dogmatic statement that one form of a tradition is earlier than another (45, 272). The impressively detailed evidence adduced is, unfortunately, assessed on a largely arithmetic basis: frequency of occurrence rather than specific details of content determines probabilities (275). Sanders refers in passing to the redactional characteristics of the individual evangelists, but the bearing of that crucial factor on matters of detail, length, or Semitisms is never explored systematically. In spite of admirable circumspection and the stance of objectivity, the end result resembles that of Stoldt's work. Sanders demonstrates that literary source questions alone cannot account for the relationships among the Gospels.

Minor Agreements of Matthew and Luke
and the Q Hypothesis

Some scholars attempted to disprove the priority of Mark. Others made the effort to dispense with Q (Farrer). Even among those who espouse the Two-Source hypothesis there have been disagreements as to the extent of Q: whether it is to be defined solely as non-Marcan material common to Matthew and Luke; whether it overlaps Mark; whether it contained a passion narrative. Perhaps the most vulnerable aspect of the Two-Source hypothesis, as acknowledged by champions of the theory and by its opponents as well, is found in the minor agreements of Matthew and Luke against Mark. These were discussed and apparently disposed of by Streeter, but they have continued to reenter the discussion. The most careful analysis of them has been accomplished by F. Neirynck. Quoting with approbation Josef Schmid's observation of a half century ago, he notes that the minor agreements are not—as Streeter suggested—merely alterations that naturally occur to independent editors, but they correspond to what happens in other passages where Matthew or Luke is drawing on and editing Mark. Neirynck concludes that the influence of Q in a limited number of passages and the pervasive impact of the editorial work of Matthew and Luke in their respective Gospels can account for the minor agreements against Mark. R. Morgenthaler's statistical synopsis of the Gospels leads him to the same conclusion.

Arguing from the evidence of agreement of Matthew and Luke in extended passages—the Q material, as understood on the Two-Source hypothesis—Joseph A. Fitzmyer considers "unaccountable" on the theory of Lucan dependence on Matthew the following phenomena in Luke: Luke's unfailing omission of distinctive Matthean material; his breaking up of Matthew's sermons; his failure to locate double tradition in the same context as Matthew; and Luke's complete independence from Matthew whenever he presents non-Marcan material. Although Matthew and Luke frequently agree in identical wording of the double tradition, they place that material in different contexts even while in these double tradition sections there is a common general underlying sequence or order. Without aspiring to a theory that will explain everything, Fitzmyer affirms that the most plausible accounting for the phenomena of similarity and difference between Matthew and Luke is the Q hypothesis. Furthermore, of enduring worth is the careful study on which Fitzmyer here builds: Vincent Taylor's analysis of the original order of Q.

The Credibility of Griesbach's Case

The Griesbach hypothesis, interred for many in academic Latin, could be dismissed or invoked the more readily by those who had never read it. A useful fringe benefit of the fresh raising of the synoptic problem has been the exhumation of Griesbach's essay in the form of a translation into English (Orchard). Many of Griesbach's arguments are simply ludicrous; others are circular; still others are contradicted from within the essay itself. For example, why does Mark write an account that is shorter overall than the other two synoptics, but that included abundant detail that they omit? He supplied details wherever he knew they had been omitted by the other two. Where did he obtain these details? From conversations with Peter and from details he picked up while living with the apostles in Jerusalem. He wanted to write a shorter account, however, so that his friends could have it for a lesser expenditure of time or money than would have been needed to acquire Matthew or Luke. In the next pages, however, Griesbach admits that he has no idea for whom the writing was intended, much less the original readers' economic status. Another example of the reasoning: How can we account for Mark's omission of presumably important Matthean material? Some of it Mark regarded as unsuitable for his readers; other parts he had to omit since at that moment he was following one Gospel and apparently could follow only one at a time. Since we know Mark omitted large sections of Matthew (e.g., the Sermon on the Mount, and especially the long discourses), it should not surprise us that he omitted other sections as well. He observes in a footnote that he cannot recall any instance where there is not some reason or other for Mark's omission of a Matthean or Lucan passage, but the ones he adduces are scarcely persuasive.

Griesbach declares that Mark, through his personal access to the apostles, has the true order of events of the final days of Jesus. Yet he acknowledges on the other hand that elsewhere Mark's account is at certain points in direct conflict with the other two; nevertheless, he is sure that Mark would have corrected those details if he had ever suspected anyone would read his Gospel and compare it with Matthew and Luke. He conjectures that Mark may have used both Greek and Hebrew versions of Matthew, but ignores the fact that we possess no Semitic versions of the Gospels. He is silent on the implications that there was a redactional process, which his proposal implies; he takes no account of the fact that the scriptural base for Mark is the Septuagint, not the Hebrew text. With admirable candor, he acknowledges that if Mark ended at 16:8, his theory could not explain why. Yet that is indeed where not only all the best manuscripts of Mark end, but where Matthew and Luke diverge from Mark. Griesbach claimed he could explain the position of every verse in Mark by his hypothesis, but he had to admit — after repeatedly appealing to Mark's supposedly privileged information — that we know little of the author, or his readers, or the circumstances of the book. Farmer's attempt (1974) to provide an explanation for the ending of Mark is as inconclusive as is the best-attested text of Mark. A theory like Griesbach's, which claims omnicompetence but which must resort to a plea of ignorance to account for its deficiencies, is an unlikely candidate for a firm solution to the synoptic problem.

Theories of Oral Transmission

In despair, some scholars have called for a suspension of judgment on the issue (Sanders: 279), while others have turned back to earlier solutions, especially to the theory of multiple oral or written sources. Thus, W. L. Knox proposed that the Gospel material circulated in the form of tracts; R. H. Gundry suggested that the Synoptics are based on notes that Matthew took during Jesus' life. C. F. D. Moule asked rhetorically if the worshiping Christian community would not from time to time have rehearsed the narratives of Jesus' ministry, taking care to keep within historical limits and to avoid embroidering the tales. Birger Gerhardsson theorized that, like the traditions of the later rabbis, the Jesus tradition was preserved in the memories and notebooks of the disciples, who preserved the narratives and sayings with care and respect. Thorlief Boman thought that the basic pattern of Mark arose in an oral tradition; he claimed to find traces of devices that could still be detected in Mark and on the basis of which Mark had delivered his schematic arrangement of the material. Harald Riesenfeld conceived the locus of preservation of the Gospel tradition as the church's public worship, through which the holy words of and about Jesus were transmitted. He traced them from Jesus via the disciples to the community by means of preaching and instruction, including echoes of the Aramaic original, until they were fixed in written form in the Gospels. The bold claim of an Aramaic origin of all four Gospels has been put forward again by Frank Zimmermann, building on the work of C. C. Torrey, C. F. Burney, and M. Black, and expanding to five hundred the examples of translation phenomena from

252   New Testament

Aramaic into Greek. The fundamental flaw in all these theories of oral transmission of the Gospel tradition is their proponents' ignoring of the overwhelming evidence in the Gospels of verbal identity, of redactional modification, and hence of literary relationships based on Greek documents.

Problems with Oral-Transmission Theory

The form critics all assumed that the Gospel tradition underwent a simple shift from the oral to the written stage. Recent work has shown that this assumption is unwarranted and that the so-called laws of transmission of folk tradition on which form-critical analysis of both OT and NT material were based were irresponsibly formulated. Furthermore, inferences drawn from the oral stage would be inapplicable to the process that lies behind our written Gospels. Tracing the study of oral literature from J. G. Herder and W. Humboldt through Albert Lord, E. Güttgemanns has shown the cavalier manner in which form critics have claimed support for their theories about Gospel origins by appeal to folklorists. Even though Albert Lord asserted that the Gospels display the characteristic features of oral traditional literature and thus express themselves in well-defined genres and forms, his critics (Talbert, 1978; Keck) have shown that his remarks—if at all relevant—may depict only the pre-Gospel stages of the tradition. Ironically, many of the features that Lord describes as characteristic of oral tradition are to be found in Hellenistic and Roman *written* literature, such as the *Aeneid* (Talbert: 98–101). Lord's own work on Slavic oral epics has shown that oral tradition is never reproduced identically but that the rhapsodist varies his account as the circumstances change (Lord: 19). That judgment about the flexibility of oral transmission process is confirmed by Walter Ong, who concludes that it is idle to seek for *the* text of an oral communication. Once the fluidity of the oral is reduced to the controlled organization of a written text, entirely different forces are operative (Ong: 136). The implications of these perceptions about orality are developed by Werner Kelber in his study of the origins of Mark. But the notion that preservation of tradition by memory guarantees precise accuracy is seen to be a delusion. As J. B. Tyson noted, the agreement among the Gospels is so high as to demand a literary relationship.

Attempts such as É. Trocmé's to reconstruct earlier versions of Mark's Gospel seem arbitrary and fruitless. There probably were small collections of written material drawn upon by Mark as he composed his Gospel, as P. J. Achtemeier has shown. The patterns of Marcan adaptation of existing narratives for polemical or paraenetic purposes have been traced by H. C. Kee (1977a:38–41). The evidence, as a whole, when reworked in the light of challenges to the Two-Source hypothesis, continues to point to the priority of Mark and the existence of Q as a source utilized by Luke and Matthew.

III. GOSPEL GENRE AND THE ORIGIN OF GOSPEL

Two closely related questions about the Gospels are these: What are the aims of a Gospel? What are its literary antecedents? Although the responses to those questions about form and function tend to merge, it may be useful to focus in this section on the literary issues before turning in the next section to the factors of social setting for Gospels in the changing circumstances of early Christianity.

The Gospel as Expansion of Kerygma

While the literary approach to Gospel origins represented by Streeter concentrated on linking each Gospel with an apostle and an ancient see, the form critics spoke more broadly of the role played by the tradition and by the Gospels. Specifically, Mark was regarded by Bultmann as an expansion of the Hellenistic kerygma, which consisted of the Christ-myth as we know it from Paul (especially Phil 2:6ff.). The core of the narrative, therefore, was the passion story (Bultmann, 1963:347). Dibelius agreed, adding only that the Gospel dealt incidentally with other data out of the career of Jesus (27). Mark's Gospel, with its indications of private disclosures of Jesus' messiahship to the disciples, Dibelius characterized as a "book of secret epiphanies" (230). Both the thesis of the centrality of the passion and that of Mark as the book of secret epiphanies continue to be affirmed by some scholars down to the present, even though they must leave out of account large portions of Mark's Gospel (Haenchen: 35; Knigge: 68; Koester: 162–64). Apart from the ingenious theory of Riesenfeld that Paul spent the three years in Arabia studying the Gospel tradition (17), few have undertaken to show any links between Paul and Gospel tradition. While Riesenfeld claims that his theory is based on "a large body of evidence," he adduces none. The theory of Mark as an expanded kerygma can offer no explanation of the miracle stories, the parables, the apocalyptic discourse, the controversy stories, and the ethical sections — in short, it cannot account for most of Mark, nor can it explain why the Gospel tradition is largely nonkerygmatic.

Gospel as Aretalogy

Closely linked in recent study of the genre of the Gospels and of Mark have been (a) the theory that there was in the Hellenistic world a fixed literary form, called aretalogy, in which the apotheosis of a miracle-worker was depicted, and (b) the notion that the term divine man (*theios anēr*) was the standard term to designate such a transformed person, Moses Hadas and Morton Smith defined an aretalogy as a biographical writing in which an impressive teacher, endowed with supernatural powers, encounters the hostility of a tyrant and is martyred, but they are forced to contrive a composite example to match their model. Others apparently mean by aretalogy a string of miracle stories. The term, which is relatively rare in antiquity, is used of an account of the deeds of a god, as in the LXX of Sir 36:13; other aretalogies are dedicated to Isis or to a Hellenistic divinity who has come to the aid of the devout followers (Kee, 1973; 1983).

The related term, *theios anēr*, has been shown by D. L. Tiede to have been used for two significantly different types of divinely endowed figures in antiquity: (a) the person who, by reason of superior wisdom, is viewed as in some way akin to the gods; (b) the combination of wonder-worker, shaman, magician, and the wise man. The former has Socrates as its model; the latter is a later development (third to fourth centuries A.D.) and is best exemplified by Philostratus's *Life of Apollonius of Tyana*, which was commissioned by Julia Domna during the reign of Septimius Severus (193–211), but completed in 217 after her death. It can scarcely serve as antecedent or precedent for the Gospels, therefore; nor can its alleged source (the writings of one Damis about Apollonius), which is almost universally recognized as an invention of Philostratus. Within Hellenistic Jewish writings of the first century, Moses is portrayed as a divine man, but with respect to his wisdom and knowledge of God rather than because of the miracles, which are depicted as performed by God through him, as Tiede, Holladay, and Malherbe (1978) have documented.

Some of the scholars who assume that an aretalogy is an account of a miracle worker and that such a person would be designated a divine man have argued that Mark is writing in order to combat a Christology that pictures Jesus as a *theios anēr* and that this Gospel tries to correct that triumphalist view by putting primary stress on the necessity of Jesus' suffering (Weeden). Apart from the terminological difficulties in thus describing Jesus, as noted above, it is by no means clear that Mark wants his readers to view Jesus' miracles negatively. The disciples are unconditionally commissioned to carry forward his work of exorcisms (Mark 6:7), and they are in no way criticized in Mark for their healing and casting out of demons. The Q tradition certainly regards the exorcisms as primary manifestations of the inbreaking of God's reign (Luke 11:20; Matt 12:29), and there is no indication of disagreement on this point between Mark and Q, since this passage occurs in what seems to be an overlap section common to Mark and Q. Viewed positively, therefore, as an ingredient in the hypothetical type of aretalogy, or negatively as a christological model to be eschewed, *theios anēr* is of no aid in perceiving the genre or the intention of a Gospel.

Wisdom Sayings

In spite of attempts to discredit the Q hypothesis by A. Farrer, S. Petrie, and others (Kümmel: 39), it has been studied as a discrete body of Gospel tradition by Perrin (1974:74–77), Kee (1977a:76–120), S. Schulz, and by R. A. Edwards (1976), who has constructed a concordance of Q (1975).

Except for Schulz, these scholars consider Q to have been a thoroughly eschatological document, in which elements of eschatology, prophecy, and wisdom are mingled (Edwards, 1976). Written in confidence that the New Age had begun to dawn with the launching of Jesus' mission and that beyond his suffering and trials were the end of the old order and the arrival of the new, the focus of Q was on prophetic utterance rather than on narrative. Although there was no passion story, there was clear indication of the martyrdom of Jesus as God's messenger and the promise of divine vindication for him and his followers (Luke 11:49–51; 12:4–10, 11–12, 42–46; 13:34–35; 22:28–30). The model that seems to have the closest affinity with Q is that of prophetic-apocalyptic oracles, especially from the postexilic prophets of Israel and the apocalyptic writings of the Hellenistic period. As a loose collection of sayings, Q does not have an overall formal paradigm.

Since the discovery of the gnostic library in Egypt, among which were "gospels" such as the *Gospel of Thomas*, which contained only sayings, the theory has been advanced that we now have evidence of a nonnarrative type of Gospel that antedates the canonical Gospels and has as its archetype the timeless wisdom of the sages of Israel rather than the eschatological wisdom more commonly perceived in Q (Robinson, 1971:71–113). A corollary suggestion is that these noncanonical Gospels may preserve more original versions of the teachings of Jesus than do the Synoptics and John (Koester). Since Q in its commonly accepted form does include eschatological utterances, a subtle analysis is employed that relegates those features to a later stage of redaction of Q and leaves as the pristine core the noneschatological wisdom teaching (Schulz). Quite apart from the lack of control or the peril of circular reasoning (or both) that is represented by redactional analysis of a document that can be reconstructed only hypothetically, the reduction of Q to a wisdom source seems to have an aim unacknowledged by those who advance the theory: to preserve Jesus from eschatology. As a wisdom teacher, he was not involved—so the theory implies—in the later apocalyptic excesses of expectation of an imminent end that overtook the church in the later first century. The evidence as one moves from Pauline to deutero-Pauline literature suggests, however, that the conceptual movement in early Christianity from the late first to the early second century was the reverse of this theory: namely, that the urgency of eschatological expectation became muted and transformed in the postapostolic age. Part of the evidence of that change is to be seen precisely in gnosticized Gospels, which exchange future cosmic hope for timeless, inner renewal.

Gospel as Biography

The proposal advanced in the last century by E. Renan and at the turn of the century by C. W. Votaw, that the Gospels are biographies, has been renewed by C. H. Talbert (1977). Drawing analogies primarily with the

Hellenistic and Roman lives of philosophers, Talbert considers the Gospel genre to be that of the didactic biography, which could have cultic settings, which recounted the life of the hero in such a way as to furnish a myth of the origin of the community that honored him and thereby to give direction for the present life of that community. When the details of the mythology are spelled out, however, they include a miraculous birth, a heavenly ascent, and other features that are suitable for Luke but not for Mark and only partially for Matthew (Talbert, 1977: 41, 93–109). What Talbert has shown, therefore, is that Luke has accommodated the Gospel to the conventions of Hellenistic literature and religion along the lines of the biographical genre, just as he has done with Hellenistic historiography (Cadbury) and romances (Kee, 1980, 1983). But the question of the origin of the Gospel genre remains unanswered by this approach.

Liturgical and Exegetical Origins of the Gospel Genre

Efforts to account for the Gospel as a literary form developed for liturgical ends range from the proposal of P. Carrington that Mark consists of a series of pericopes arranged for reading in successive Sunday worship services, through the attempt to correlate Mark with the Jewish Passover Haggada (Bowman), to the theory that all the Synoptics were written as lectionaries (Goulder). Yet it is by no means evident that the Jewish lectionaries on which the Christians are said to have modeled theirs were in existence at the time the Gospels were written. The fact that the Gospels lent themselves to reading in public worship, as the abundance of lectionary-text manuscripts of the NT attests, does not require us to infer that they originated in that form to serve that purpose.

Gospel as Foundation Document

As we shall consider in subsequent sections, there is a growing scholarly consensus that the matrix out of which early Christianity emerged was Jewish apocalypticism and that, accordingly, the dynamic of the Jesus movement must be assessed against that kind of social background. Once that perspective is accepted, its implications for the Gospel tradition become clear.

Two of the Qumran documents, the *Scroll of the Rule* and the *Damascus Document,* together depict the origins of the Dead Sea sect, how its leader arose, the difficulties he and his followers experienced, how the scriptures are prophetic of the rise of their group and of its destiny, how the community is to obey God in the interim until he vindicates them, and how through ritual they include members in their group and celebrate the final triumph which they await. The fact that the similarities with the early Christian movement as evidenced in the Gospel are so great has led some to conclude that Jesus was a member of the group. That seems unlikely, because his open attitude toward outcasts and outsiders is in complete contrast to the rigid exclusivism of Qumran. What is of paramount importance, however, is that the dynamics by which both groups arose and the aims of some of their basic writings are, sociologically speaking, so similar.

Viewed against this background, the components of the Gospel tradition are a coherent whole, and the Gospel of Mark can be regarded as a unitary document. The rise of the eschatological hope for God's rule appears against the background of disillusionment with established religion and its leadership. A public act of commitment and renewal — baptism — marks the break with the old and the beginning of the community. The conflict is cosmic, involving Satan and the demonic powers, as is evident from the temptation narratives and the importance attached to exorcisms. By sign and parable, the inner group of followers is instructed, warned, encouraged about what its responsibilities and fate will be. The pervasive theme of the interpretation of scripture along unforeseen lines provides insight and assurance of God's present support and future vindication. As is characteristic of apocalyptic groups, of which Daniel and his friends would be the prime example, official opposition and the constant threat of martyrdom are signs of divine favor, not occasions for despair. Visions of ultimate victory are offered in the rich imagery of apocalypticism, but there is no external guarantee apart from confidence in the divine promise. This way of looking at Mark accounts for all its component elements (Kee, 1977b; Perrin, 1974:143–67).

Various studies have contributed to this reconstruction of the apocalyptic setting for the origins of the Gospel. Few have been persuaded by Wilhelm Wrede's effort to show that the secrecy motif in Mark is wholly imposed by the evangelist. Still, exegetical studies have shown that Mark portrays Jesus as disclosing the secret of his messiahship and its ethical implications to a chosen few, even though features of the tradition included by Mark stand in tension with the secrecy theory (Burkill). Detailed analyses of the synoptic apocalypse in Mark 13 have suggested how that material built on the apocalyptic traditions of Judaism, how it went about interpreting scripture as fulfilled in its own time, and how the community behind Mark modified the tradition in the light of its own changing experiences in the years before and after the destruction of Jerusalem (Hartman; Gaston; Lambrecht). Other scholars have demonstrated how early Christian interpretation of scripture helped to shape the Marcan passion narrative (Donahue; Linnemann; Nineham). A case has also been made for the influence of the events connected with the destruction of the temple on the trial scene and the charges leveled against Jesus there (Juel). As K.-G. Reploh has observed with regard to the Marcan narrative as a whole, the evangelist is not concerned with depicting the relationship of the earthly Jesus to the historical disciples so much as to disclose how Jesus is present to the community of Mark's time, whose edification and formation are his primary concern (229).

In explicating the import of Mark's opening phrase, "The beginning of the Gospel," L. E. Keck has noted that Jesus is not merely the chronological beginning of the Gospel but its continuing prototype for the Marcan community, so that Mark's Gospel addresses the church through its own tradition.

IV. HISTORICITY AND
THE GOSPEL TRADITION

D. F. Strauss's insistence that the life of Jesus be studied solely on the basis of natural historical causality tended to force researchers into one of two camps: the positivists, who sought to demonstrate how the life of Jesus "really happened," and the dichotomists, who in one way or another make a sharp distinction between the realms of faith and history. By the 1950s both types of enterprise were flourishing in relation to the study of the Gospel, but the distinction itself was under fire. In what E. Käsemann referred to as the "exchange of fronts," conservatives moved into position to defend the essential historicity of the Gospel accounts; meanwhile, liberals simultaneously carried on critical analysis of the Gospels as an academic exercise while enjoying the safe retreat of an invulnerable theological position. Thus, Bultmann's skepticism about historical reconstruction of the career of Jesus or even of his message in detail is balanced by his existentialist transformation of the Gospel, whereby the resurrection faith is a way of accepting death and eschatological hope is a symbolic statement of openness toward the future. Instead of seeking for Jesus' mission and message concerning God's purpose in history, the existentialist mode advised seeking the meaning of one's own existence through Gospel symbols (Bultmann, 1953; Robinson, 1959).

Once Bultmann's former students had raised anew the question of what could be known historically about Jesus (Käsemann; Bornkamm; Conzelmann; Fuchs), a critical issue appeared: Which criteria are valid for distinguishing authentic Jesus tradition from that which was produced by the early church? Perrin (1967:39–43) developed the principle of dissimilarity, by which he declared that one could attribute to Jesus only those traditions that could not be accounted for as theological creations of the church or mere borrowings from contemporary Judaism. The result of such an undertaking, however, would be to create a new kind of docetic Jesus who would lack any links with the historical circumstances of his life situation. That is, of course, what the interpreters of the Jesus tradition who employ structuralist methods would like to do: to place Jesus and his message above the realm of historical contingency (Via). But that is once more a retreat from rather than a confrontation of the historical issue. N. A. Dahl wisely observed, as the so-called New Quest of the Historical Jesus was getting under way, that the Christian doctrine of the incarnation requires interpreters of the Gospel tradition to deal with the concrete circumstances of a specific human individual whose death is confirmed by nonbiblical sources and whose life and mission demand historical investigation. He acknowledges that we are dealing with approximate results, from which a reasonably clear picture can be drawn of Jesus' mode of life, his teaching, and the impact he made on his followers. The specifics of continuity and discontinuity between Jesus and his contemporary world must be explored openly, not assumed in advance.

V. THE SOCIAL SETTING AND
FUNCTION OF THE GOSPELS

Fruitful has been the recognition that, in addition to whatever the Gospels may tell us about the history of Jesus, they reveal a great deal about the early Christian communities in which that tradition was preserved and for whom it was transmitted in the Gospels as we have them. An important dimension of this growing segment of NT studies has been the attention given to the social and cultural features of early Christianity, including significant diversities. John Gager's study of the correspondences between the origins of Christianity and the sociological analyses of millenarian sects has been especially illuminating, both in methodology and in concrete historical results. Hengel (1968) has noted similarities between the life-style of the disciples as portrayed in the synoptics and that of the itinerant philosopher-teachers of the Cynic-Stoic type from the Hellenistic-Roman texts. Gerd Theissen has analyzed that phenomenon from a sociological viewpoint with illuminating results; Abraham Malherbe has looked afresh at the late classical texts in his attempt to define the social aspects of primitive Christianity. A similar effort has been made specifically to reconstruct the community that is represented in Mark (Kee, 1977b).

What is happening in this new phase of Gospel research is that the term taken over by the NT form critics from their OT predecessors, *Sitz im Leben*, ("life-setting") is being taken seriously as representing the wider socio-cultural setting of the NT writings, rather than a simple classificatory system, as it functioned for Dibelius and Bultmann (kerygmatic, paraenetic, Palestinian, Hellenistic, etc.). The full impact of this methodological shift lies in the future, but in retrospect one can see that in those earlier scholarly endeavors, where attention was given to the cultural setting of the work under scrutiny, the results have often been enduring. This is surely the case in H. J. Cadbury's ever-fresh studies of Luke-Acts, as well as in the monumental *Beginnings of Christianity* in which he collaborated. On a lesser scale, but of no less consequence methodologically, are the studies of E. Lohmeyer and R. H. Lightfoot, in which they sought to reconstruct the community that lies behind Mark and to depict the dynamics of its relationships with other groups within the early Christian church.

VI. RESULTS

For the Study of Mark

The result of the shifts in method and aim of synoptic criticism is more nearly apparent in the monographs and special studies that have been produced in the last three decades than in the commentaries. Those by Vincent Taylor (1952) and by Ernst Haenchen are monuments of learning and filled with important insights into details of the text of Mark, but neither breaks new ground in our understanding of Mark or of his community. Taylor's underlying aim is to defend the tradition; Haenchen identifies himself explicitly with Dibelius's characterization of Mark as a book of secret epiphanies, but implies that he also agrees with the judgment of the earlier form critics that Mark is not fully in control of his material. E. Schweizer's popular commentary treats Mark as a theological tract aimed at offsetting extremist positions (Jesus as wisdom-bringer, as divine man, docetism). Much more aware of the inner dynamics of the Marcan community, especially in relation to the appropriation of the Jesus tradition in light of its own reading of scripture, is D. E. Nineham's popular commentary. W. L. Lane's is learned and filled with valuable philological and exegetical insights, but seems basically concerned with defending the tradition.

Redactional studies of the Gospels are usually said to have begun with the appearance of W. Marxsen's study of Mark, though in fact there were antecedents for this mode of analysis, as we have noted. Marxsen did perform an important service in demonstrating how the evangelist's modification of the tradition (= redaction) is an indispensable avenue to recognition and assessment of his aims. Unfortunately, Marxsen's study of Mark is along almost exclusively theological lines and is accommodated to the dogmatic categories of the Bultmann school. He thinks that Mark was trying to bring the "kerygmatic-visual" tradition into harmony with the Pauline "conceptual theological stream," but to make the case he has to attribute to Mark features that are in fact absent: the preexistence of Jesus and his heavenly exaltation. Idiosyncratic, monothematic analyses of Mark include attempts to subsume all of Mark and all of Christianity under the eucharist, symbolized in the feeding stories of Mark (Quesnell), and the deeschatologized reading of Mark by J. Schreiber, according to which the cry of Jesus from the cross announces that the judgment is past. H. C. Kee's monograph seeks to place all the elements of Mark in a cohesive setting: a Syrian-based apocalyptic community, led by charismatics, regarding itself as the new covenant people, awaiting martyrdom and soon vindication (1977b). A useful, conservative survey of Marcan studies has been prepared by Ralph Martin, though it is marred by a pervasive concern for upholding traditional views. An excellent comprehensive history and analysis of Marcan interpretation, arranged chronologically, is that of S. P. Kealy.

For the Study of Matthew

Analysis of the distinctive features of Matthew goes back to B. W. Bacon (1930), who was concerned with both literary structure and distinctive features of Matthean Christianity. G. D. Kilpatrick (1950) carried forward the study of Matthew along somewhat similar lines. A preponderant influence on the study of this Gospel has been the assembling of alleged parallels to the teachings of Jesus (and especially those in the Sermon on the Mount) from rabbinic sources (Strack-Billerbeck). It is now widely recognized that Billerbeck's parallels are often from a later period of rabbinic tradition than the first century, but a more cautious and sophisticated adducing of rabbinic materials continues to be used as a way of showing both similarities and contrasts between Jesus (or the Matthean Jesus) and the rabbis (Dupont; Davies). The commentaries on Matthew range from competent (Filson; Johnson; Schmid; Gaechter; Fenton) to erratic (Mann—Albright).

Special studies have contributed far more to the interpretation of Matthew than have the commentaries. K. Stendahl's pioneering study of the relationship between scriptural interpretation at Qumran and in Matthew has stood up well under critical attack (1954; new ed., 1968), and the suggestion that there was a school activity has been adapted for the study of other Gospel tradition as well (Culpepper). Significant work on Matthew's restructuring of eschatology, on his interpretation of the law, and his use of the miracle tradition was carried out by G. Bornkamm, G. Barth, and H. J. Held. W. Trilling's reconstruction of the Matthean community as the "True Israel" provides a comprehensive perspective on that Gospel and places it in a persuasive historical context. Important special studies of Matthew from the standpoint of Christology include those of J. D. Kingsbury and M. J. Suggs, although the latter tries to depict Jesus as a proto-gnostic. Georg Strecker's study of Matthean theology produces a convincing picture of a community which is profoundly concerned for ethical responsibility and, therefore, for eschatological judgment, but which awaits the consummation only after the worldwide mission of the church has been completed. (Developments in the study of Luke-Acts are presented in chap. 11, below).

VII. PROSPECTS

Among the "candid questions" addressed to the form critics in E. Güttgemanns's provocative book is the challenge to take with new breadth and seriousness what is implied by *Sitz im Leben* (176–95). The inadequacies of Gospel analysis that centers on kerygma alone have been demonstrated. But the potential for synoptic research which takes into account the social and cultural dimensions of the circles that lie behind our Gospels has also been made evident in some recent Gospel studies, as well as in some earlier studies that have proved to be of enduring worth. As the Society of Biblical

Literature enters its second century, perhaps these are important indicators of fruitful future strategies and subject areas for investigation.

BIBLIOGRAPHY

Achtemeier, Paul J.
1970 "Toward the Isolation of Pre-Markan Miracle Catenae." *JBL* 89: 265–91.

Bacon, Benjamin W.
1930 *Studies in Matthew*. New York: Holt.

Barth, Gerhard
1963 "Matthew's Understanding of the Law." Pp. 58–164 in *Tradition and Interpretation in Matthew*, by G. Bornkamm, G. Barth, and H. J. Held. Philadelphia; Westminster.

Billerbeck, Paul
1922–61 with H. L. Strack. *Kommentar zum Neuen Testament aus Talmud und Midrasch*. 6 vols. Munich: Beck.

Black, Matthew
1967 *An Aramaic Approach to the Gospels and Acts*. 3d ed. Oxford: Clarendon Press.

Boman, Thorlief
1967 *Die Jesus-Überlieferung im Lichte der neueren Volkskunde*. Göttingen: Vandenhoeck & Ruprecht.

Bornkamm, Günther
1960 *Jesus of Nazareth*. Trans. Irene and Fraser McLuskey with J. M. Robinson. New York: Harper.

Bowman, John
1965 *The Gospel of Mark: The New Christian Jewish Passover Haggada*. SPB 8. Leiden: Brill.

Bultmann, Rudolf
1953 *Theologie des Neuen Testament*. Tübingen: Mohr. Eng. trans. by Kendrick Grobel: *Theology of the New Testament*. 2 vols. New York: Scribner, 1951–55.
1963 *History of the Synoptic Tradition*. Trans. John Marsh. New York: Harper & Row.

Burkill, T. A.
1963 *Mysterious Revelation: An Examination of the Philosophy of St. Mark's Gospel*. Ithaca, NY: Cornell University Press.

Burney, C. F.
1922 *The Aramaic Origin of the Fourth Gospel*. Oxford: Clarendon Press.

Butler, B. C.
1951 *The Originality of St. Matthew: A Critique of the Two-Document Hypothesis*. Cambridge: University Press.

Cadbury, Henry Joel
1927 *The Making of Luke-Acts*. London: SPCK.

Carrington, Philip
1952   *The Primitive Christian Calendar: A Study in the Making of the Marcan Gospel.* Cambridge: University Press.

Conzelmann, Hans
1973   *Jesus: The Classic Article from RGG³ Expanded and Updated.* Trans. J. R. Lord. Philadelphia: Fortress.

Culpepper, R. A.
1976   *The Johannine School: An Evaluation of the Johannine School Hypothesis Based on an Investigation of the Nature of Ancient Schools.* SBLDS 26. Missoula, MT: Scholars Press.

Dahl, N. A.
1955   "Der historische Jesus als geschichtswissenschaftliches und theologisches Problem." *KD* 1: 104–32.

Davies, W. D.
1964   *The Setting of the Sermon on the Mount.* Cambridge: University Press.

Dibelius, Martin
1934   *From Tradition to Gospel.* Trans. B. L. Woolf. London: Nicholson & Watson. Reprinted, Greenwood, SC: Attic, 1972.

Dodd, C. H.
1936   *The Apostolic Preaching and Its Developments.* New York: Harper.

Donahue, John R.
1973   *Are You the Christ? The Trial Narrative in the Gospel of Mark.* SBLDS 10. Missoula, MT: SBL.

Dungan, David L.
1970   "Mark — The Abridgement of Matthew and Luke." Pp. 51–97 in *Jesus and Man's Hope,* vol. 1. Ed. D. G. Miller and D. Y. Hadidian. Pittsburgh: Pittsburgh Theological Seminary.

Dupont, J.
1958   *Les Béatitudes: Le problème littéraire — Les deux Versions du Sermon sur la montagne et des Béatitudes.* New ed, Bruges: Abbaye de Saint-André.

Edwards, Richard A.
1975   *A Concordance to Q.* SBLSBS 7. Missoula, MT: Scholars Press.
1976   *A Theology of Q: Eschatology, Prophecy, and Wisdom.* Philadelphia: Fortress.

Farmer, W. R.
1964   *The Synoptic Problem: A Critical Analysis.* New York: Macmillan.
1974   *The Last Twelve Verses of Mark.* SNTSMS 25. London and New York: Cambridge University Press.

Farrer, Austin M.
1955   "On Dispensing with Q." Pp. 55–88 in *Studies in the Gospels: Essays in Memory of R. H. Lightfoot.* Ed. D. E. Nineham. Oxford: Blackwell.

Fenton, John
1964   *The Gospel of St. Matthew.* Pelican. Baltimore: Penguin Books.

Filson, Floyd V.
1950   *A Commentary on the Gospel According to St. Matthew.* New York: Harper.

Fitzmyer, Joseph A.
1970 "The Priority of Mark and the 'Q' Source in Luke." Pp. 131–70 in *Jesus and Man's Hope*, vol. 1. Ed. D. G. Miller and D. Y. Hadidian. Pittsburgh: Pittsburgh Theological Seminary.

Fuchs, Ernst
1964 *Studies of the Historical Jesus*. Trans. Andree Scobie. SBT 42. Naperville, IL: Allenson.

Gaechter, P.
1963 *Das Matthäus-Evangelium: Ein Kommentar*. Innsbruck: Tyrolia.

Gager, John
1975 *Kingdom and Community: The Social World of Early Christianity*. Englewood Cliffs, NJ: Prentice-Hall.

Gaston, Lloyd
1970 *No Stone on Another: Studies in the Significance of the Fall of Jerusalem in the Synoptic Gospels*. NovTSup 23. Leiden: Brill.

Gerhardsson, Birger
1979 *The Origins of the Gospel Tradition*. Philadelphia: Fortress.

Goulder, M. D.
1974 *Midrash and Lection in Matthew*. London: SPCK.

Griesbach, J. J.
1789/90 *Commentatio qua Marci Evangelium totum e Matthaei et Lucae Evangelium totum e Matthaei et Lucae commentariis decerptum esse monstratur*. Reprinted in *J. J. Griesbach: Synoptic and Text-Critical Studies 1776–1976*, 74–102. Ed. B. Orchard and T. R. W. Longstaff. SNTSMS 34. Cambridge: University Press, 1978.

Gundry, Robert H.
1967 *The Use of the Old Testament in St. Matthew's Gospel*. NovTSup 18. Leiden: Brill.

Güttgemanns, Erhardt
1979 *Candid Questions Concerning Gospel Form Criticism: A Methodological Sketch of the Basic Problems of Form and Redaction Criticism*. Trans. W. G. Doty. PTMS 26. Pittsburgh: Pickwick Press.

Hadas, Moses, and Morton Smith
1965 *Heroes and Gods: Spiritual Biographies in Antiquity*. Religious Perspectives 13. New York: Harper & Row.

Haenchen, Ernst
1966 *Der Weg Jesu: Eine Erklärung des Markus-Evangelium und der kanonischen Parallelen*. Berlin: Töpelmann.

Hartman, Lars
1966 *Prophecy Interpreted: The Formation of Some Jewish Apocalyptic Texts and of the Eschatological Discourse Mark 13 par.* ConBNT 1. Lund: Gleerup.

Held, H. J.
See under Barth, Gerhard.

Hengel, Martin
1968 *Nachfolge und Charisma: Eine exegetische-religionsgeschichtliche Studie zu Mt. 8,21f. und Jesu Ruf in die Nachfolge*. BZNW 34. Berlin: Töpelmann. Eng. trans. by James Greig: *The Charismatic Leader and His Followers*. New York: Crossroad, 1981.

1974   *Judaism and Hellenism: Studies in Their Encounter in Palestine during the Early Hellenistic Period.* Trans. John Bowden. 2 vols. Philadelphia: Fortress.

Herder, J. G.
1796   *Christliche Schriften: Vom Erlöser der Menschen: Nach unsern drei ersten Evangelien.* Leipzig: J. F. Hartnoch.

Holladay, Carl
1977   *THEIOS ANER in Hellenistic Judaism: A Critique of the Use of This Category in New Testament Christology.* SBLDS 40. Missoula, MT: Scholars Press.

Humboldt, Wilhelm v.
1963   *Schriften zur Sprachphilosophie.* Stuttgart: Cotta.

Johnson, Sherman E.
1951   Exegesis of Matthew in *IB*, vol. 7.

Juel, Donald
1977   *Messiah and Temple: The Trial of Jesus in the Gospel of Mark.* SBLDS 31. Missoula, MT: Scholars Press.

Kähler, Martin
1964   *The So-Called Historical Jesus and the Historic Biblical Christ.* Trans. C. E. Braaten. Philadelphia: Fortress.

Käsemann, Ernst
1964   "The Problem of the Historical Jesus." Pp. 15–47 in *Essays on New Testament Themes.* SBT 41. London: SCM.

Kealy, Sean P.
1982   *Mark's Gospel: A History of Its Interpretation: From the Beginning until 1979.* New York and Ramsey, NJ: Paulist.

Keck, Leander E.
1978   "Oral Traditional Literature and the Gospels: The Seminar." Pp. 103–22 in *The Relationships among the Gospels: An Interdisciplinary Dialogue.* Trinity University Monograph Series 5. Ed. W. O. Walker, Jr. San Antonio, TX: Trinity University Press.

Kee, H. C.
1973   "Aretalogy and Gospel." *JBL* 92: 402–22.
1977a   *Jesus in History: An Approach to the Study of the Gospels.* 2d ed. New York: Harcourt Brace Jovanovich.
1977b   *Community of the New Age: Studies in Mark's Gospel.* Philadelphia: Westminster.
1980   *Christian Origins in Sociological Perspective: Methods and Resources.* Philadelphia: Westminster.
1983   *Miracle in the Early Christian World: A Study in Socio-historical Method.* New Haven: Yale University Press.

Kelber, Werner H.
1976, ed.   *The Passion in Mark: Studies on Mark 14–16.* Philadelphia: Fortress.
1983   *The Oral and the Written Gospel: The Hermeneutics of Speaking and Writing in the Synoptic Tradition, Mark, Paul and Q.* Philadelphia: Fortress.

Kilpatrick, George D.
1950   *The Origins of the Gospel according to St. Matthew.* 2d ed. Oxford: Clarendon Press.

Kingsbury, Jack Dean
1975   *Matthew: Structure, Christology, Kingdom.* Philadelphia: Fortress.
Knigge, Heinz-Dieter
1968   "The Meaning of Mark." *Int* 22: 53–70.
Knox, W. L.
1953   *The Sources of the Synoptic Gospels: I, St. Mark.* Ed. H. Chadwick.
           Cambridge: University Press.
1957   *The Sources of the Synoptic Gospels: II, St. Luke and St. Matthew.* Ed.
           H. Chadwick. Cambridge: University Press.
Koester, Helmut
1971   "One Jesus and Four Primitive Gospels." Pp. 158–204 in *Trajectories
           through Early Christianity,* by J. M. Robinson and H. Koester. Phila-
           delphia: Fortress. [Orig. in *HTR* 61 (1968) 203–47.]
Kümmel, W. G.
1975   *Introduction to the New Testament.* Rev. ed. Trans. H. C. Kee.
           Nashville and New York: Abingdon.
Lambrecht, Jan
1967   *Die Redaktion der Markus-Apokalypse.* AnBib 28. Rome: Pontifical
           Biblical Institute.
Lane, William L.
1974   *The Gospel according to Mark.* NICNT 2. Grand Rapids: Eerdmans.
Lightfoot, R. H.
1938   *Locality and Doctrine in the Gospels.* London: Hodder & Stoughton.
Linnemann, Eta
1970   *Studien zur Passionsgeschichte.* FRLANT 102. Göttingen: Vanden-
           hoeck & Ruprecht.
Lohmeyer, Ernst
1936   *Galiläa und Jerusalem.* Göttingen: Vandenhoeck & Ruprecht.
Longstaff, Thomas R. W.
1977   *Evidence of Conflation in Mark? A Study in the Synoptic Problem.*
           SBLDS 28. Missoula, MT: Scholars Press.
Lord, Albert B.
1978   "The Gospels as Oral Traditional Literature." Pp. 33–91 in *The
           Relationships among the Gospels: An Interdisciplinary Dialogue.*
           Trinity University Monograph Series 5. Ed. W. O. Walker, Jr. San
           Antonio, TX: Trinity University Press.
Malherbe, Abraham J.
1978a   *Social Aspects of Early Christianity.* Baton Rouge: Louisiana State
           University Press. 2d enlarged ed. Philadelphia: Fortress, 1983.
1978b   "Pseudo Heraclitus, Epistle 4: The Divinization of the Wise Man."
           JAC 21: 42–64.
Mann, C. S., and W. F. Albright
1971   *Gospel of Matthew.* AB 26. Garden City, NY: Doubleday.
Martin, Ralph P.
1973   *Mark: Evangelist and Theologian.* Grand Rapids: Zondervan.
Marxsen, Willi
1969   *Mark the Evangelist: Studies on the Redaction History of the Gospel.*
           Trans. James Boyce et al. Nashville: Abingdon.

Moule, C. F. D.
1959   "The Intention of the Evangelists." Pp. 165–79 in *New Testament Essays: Studies in Memory of Thomas Walter Manson*. Ed. A. J. B. Higgins. Manchester: Manchester University Press.

Neirynck, Frans, ed.
1974   *The Minor Agreements of Matthew and Luke against Mark, with a Cumulative List*. BETL 37. Louvain: Leuven University Press.

Neusner, Jacob
1971   *The Rabbinic Traditions about the Pharisees before 70*. 3 vols. Leiden: Brill.
1984   *The Pharisees*. Hoboken, NJ: Ktav, 1984. [Abridgement of *Rabbinic Traditions*.]

Nineham, D. E.
1964   *The Gospel of St. Mark*. Pelican. Baltimore, MD: Penguin Books.

Ong, Walter J.
1967   *The Presence of the Word: Some Prolegomena for Cultural and Religious History*. New Haven: Yale University Press.

Orchard, Bernard
1978   Eng. trans. of Griesbach's *Commentatio . . .* Pp. 103–35 in *J. J. Griesbach: Synoptic and Text-Critical Studies 1776–1976*. Ed. B. Orchard and T. R. W. Longstaff. SNTSMS 34. Cambridge: University Press.

Otto, Rudolf
1938   *The Kingdom of God and the Son of Man*. London: Lutterworth.

Parker, Pierson
1953   *The Gospel before Mark*. Chicago: University of Chicago Press.

Perrin, Norman
1967   *Rediscovering the Teaching of Jesus*, 39–43. New York: Harper & Row.
1974   *The New Testament: An Introduction: Proclamation and Parenesis, Myth and History*. New York: Harcourt Brace Jovanovich.

Petrie, C. S.
1959   " 'Q' is Only What You Make It." *NovT* 3: 28–33.

Quesnell, Quentin
1969   *The Mind of Mark: Interpretation and Method through the Exegesis of Mark 6,52*. AnBib 38. Rome: Pontifical Biblical Institute.

Renan, Ernst
1864   *Vie de Jesus*. Paris. Eng. trans.: *The Life of Jesus*, 1927.

Reploh, Karl-Georg
1969   *Markus, Lehrer der Gemeinde: Eine redaktionsgeschichtliche Studie zu den Jüngerperikopen des Markus-Evangeliums*. Stuttgart: Katholisches Bibelwerk.

Riesenfeld, Harald
1970   *The Gospel Tradition*. Philadelphia: Fortress.

Robinson, J. M.
1957   *The Problem of History in Mark*. SBT 21. Naperville, IL: Allenson.
1959   *A New Quest of the Historical Jesus*. SBT 25. London: SCM.

1971   *"Logoi Sophon:* On the Gattung of Q." Pp. 71–113 in *Trajectories through Early Christianity,* by J. M. Robinson and H. Koester. Philadelphia: Fortress.

Sanders, E. P.
1969   *The Tendencies of the Synoptic Tradition.* SNTSMS 9. Cambridge: University Press.

Schmid, Josef
1930   *Matthäus und Lukas: Eine Untersuchung des Verhältnisses ihre Evangelien.* Frieburg: Herder.

Schmidt, Karl Ludwig
1919   *Der Rahmen der Geschichte Jesu: Literar-kritische Untersuchungen zur ältesten Jesusüberlieferung.* Berlin: Trowitzsch. Reprinted, Darmstadt: Wissenschaftliche Buchgesellschaft, 1964.

Schreiber, Johannes
1967   *Theologie des Vertrauens: Eine redaktionsgeschichtliche Untersuchung des Markusevangeliums.* Hamburg: Furche-Verlag.

Schulz, Siegfried
1972   *Q, Die Spruchquelle der Evangelisten.* Zurich: Theologischer Verlag.

Schweitzer, Albert
1910   *The Quest of the Historical Jesus.* New York: Macmillan. German original, 1906.

Schweizer, Eduard
1970   *The Good News according to Mark.* Richmond: John Knox.

Smith, Morton
1973   *The Secret Gospel: The Discovery and Interpretation of the Secret Gospel According to Mark.* New York: Harper & Row.

Stendahl, Krister
1968   *The School of St. Matthew and Its Use of the Old Testament.* 2d ed. Philadelphia: Fortress.

Stoldt, Hans-Herbert
1977   *Geschichte und Kritik der Markushypothese.* Göttingen: Vandenhoeck & Ruprecht. Eng. trans. by D. L. Niewyk: *History and Criticism of the Marcan Hypothesis.* Macon, GA: Mercer University Press, 1980.

Strecker, Georg
1962   *Der Weg der Gerechtigkeit: Untersuchung zur Theologie des Matthäus.* FRLANT 82. Göttingen: Vandenhoeck & Ruprecht.

Streeter, B. H.
1924   *The Four Gospels: A Study of Origins.* New York: Macmillan.

Suggs, M. Jack
1970   *Wisdom, Christology, and Law in Matthew's Gospel.* Cambridge, MA: Harvard University Press.

Talbert, Charles H.
1977   *What is a Gospel? The Genre of the Canonical Gospels.* Philadelphia: Fortress.

1978   "Oral and Independent or Literary and Interdependent? A Response to Albert B. Lord." Pp. 93–102 in *The Relationships among the Gospels: An Interdisciplinary Dialogue.* Trinity University Monograph Series 5. Ed. William O. Walker, Jr. San Antonio, TX: Trinity University Press.

Taylor, Vincent
1952   *The Gospel according to St. Mark.* London: Macmillan.
1959   "The Original Order of Q." Pp. 246–69 in *New Testament Essays: Studies in Memory of Thomas Walter Manson.* Ed. A. J. B. Higgins. Manchester: Manchester University Press.

Theissen, Gerd
1975   "Itinerant Radicalism: The Tradition of Jesus Sayings from the Perspective of the Sociology of Religion." *Radical Religion* 2/2 & 3: 84–93.
1978   *Sociology of Early Palestinian Christianity.* Trans. John Bowden. Philadelphia: Fortress.

Tiede, David L.
1972   *The Charismatic Figure as Miracle Worker.* SBLDS 1. Missoula, MT: SBL.

Torrey, Charles C.
1936   *Our Translated Gospels: Some of the Evidence.* New York: Harper.

Trilling, Wolfgang
1959   *Das wahre Israel: Studien zur Theologie des Matthäusevangeliums.* Erfurter Theologische Studien. Leipzig: St. Benno.

Trocmé, Etienne
1975   *The Formation of the Gospel according to Mark.* Trans. P. Gaughan. Philadelphia: Westminster. French original, 1963.

Tyson, J. B.
1976   "Sequential Parallelism in the Synoptic Gospels." *NTS* 22: 276–308.

Via, Dan O., Jr.
1975   *Kerygma and Comedy in the New Testament: A Structuralist Approach to Hermeneutics.* Philadelphia: Fortress.

Votaw, C. W.
1970   *The Gospels and Contemporary Biographies in the Greco-Roman World.* Facet Books: Biblical Series 27. Philadelphia: Fortress.

Weeden, T. J.
1971   *Mark—Traditions in Conflict.* Philadelphia: Fortress.

Weiss, Johannes
1892   *Die Predigt Jesu vom Reiche Gottes.* Göttingen: Vandenhoeck & Ruprecht. Eng. trans. by R. H. Hiers and D. L. Holland: *Jesus' Proclamation of the Kingdom of God.* Lives of Jesus Series. Philadelphia: Fortress, 1971.

Wrede, William
1901   *Das Messiasgeheimnis in den Evangelien: Zugleich ein Beitrag zum Verständnis des Markusevangeliums.* Göttingen: Vandenhoeck & Ruprecht. Eng. trans. by J. C. C. Greig: *The Messianic Secret.* Library of Theological Translations. Greenwood, SC: Attic, 1971.

Zimmermann, Frank
1979   *The Aramaic Origin of the Four Gospels.* New York: Ktav.

10
JOHANNINE STUDIES

D. Moody Smith

I. INTRODUCTION: JOHANNINE STUDIES SINCE 1945

The end of World War II marks a convenient watershed in Johannine research, as in NT scholarship generally.[1] Only after the war did R. Bultmann's commentary (1941) receive attention and scrutiny internationally, in part because of the appearance and translation (1951, 1955) of his *Theology of the New Testament.* Subsequently, C. H. Dodd produced two large and significant works on the Fourth Gospel (1953, 1963), preceded by his commentary on the Johannine epistles (1946). Perhaps as a harbinger of coming works by a new generation of scholars, C. K. Barrett in 1956 published a commentary on the Gospel, a book whose usefulness has been underscored by its appearance more than twenty years later in a revised edition (1978).

Since Barrett, the production of commentaries and other comprehensive works on the Johannine literature has accelerated. There have been commentaries on the Gospel by R. H. Lightfoot (1956), Rudolf Schnackenburg (1965–76; Eng. trans., 3 vols., 1968–82), Raymond E. Brown (1966, 1970), J. N. Sanders (1968), Leon Morris (1971), Barnabas Lindars (1972), M.-É. Boismard (1977), Jürgen Becker (1979–81), and most recently Ernst Haenchen (1981), among others. Meanwhile, about thirty years after its appearance in Germany, Bultmann's commentary was translated into English (1971), the time gap indicating something of the lasting importance of the work. Probably the magnitude of Bultmann's achievement led to the forty-year moratorium on serious critical commentaries on the Fourth Gospel among Continental Protestant scholars, which ended only with the posthumous publication of Haenchen's work. There was during this period, however, no indication of a decline of interest in Johannine matters. A quarter of a century after Bultmann's commentary appeared, his student Ernst Käsemann provoked considerable controversy with a monograph on

---

[1] An earlier version of this essay was read by Professors C. K. Barrett, Raymond E. Brown, Alan Culpepper, Robert Kysar, George W. MacRae, and J. Louis Martyn, each of whom offered valuable criticism and advice for which I am grateful. Of course, I assume full responsibility for its present form.

John 17 (1968)[2] which took issue with fundamental aspects of his teacher's interpretation of that Gospel.

Commentaries on the Johannine epistles have kept pace, beginning with that of Dodd (1946). Schnackenburg produced a commentary on the epistles (5th ed., 1975) prior to his massive commentary on the Gospel. One of Bultmann's last publications was his slim commentary on the epistles (1967), which promptly appeared in English translation (1973). Subsequent to Bultmann, a compact and well-informed commentary by J. L. Houlden (1973) has appeared, as well as a more recent commentary by I. H. Marshall (1978). Finally, Brown's commentary on the epistles was published in 1982, followed by K. Grayston's and S. S. Smalley's in 1984.

The magnitude of publication on the Fourth Gospel and Johannine epistles equals, and probably exceeds, that in any comparable area of NT studies. In addition to scholarly commentaries, monographs, and journal articles, there are numerous books and articles of a popular, semipopular, or inspirational sort, some of which attempt to summarize, condense, disseminate, or apply the results and bearing of research.

Fortunately, in addition to the general bibliographical aids, there exist several extraordinarily helpful and comprehensive guides to the modern scholarly literature in Johannine studies. E. Malatesta's bibliography (1967) thoroughly covers the ground from 1920 to 1965. For subsequent years there is the *Theologische Rundschau Forschungsbericht* of Hartwig Thyen (1974–79) and Jürgen Becker (1982), which begins with a bibliography of nearly fifty pages that contains principally works since Malatesta. (Newer works are cited where relevant as the *Forschungsbericht* progresses.) There is in English a valuable survey of recent scholarship by Robert Kysar (see also Léon-Dufour). The excellent bibliographies in Brown's commentary (1966, 1970), inevitably somewhat dated, may now be supplemented from Haenchen (1981).

Despite the importance of Bultmann's commentary, one could scarcely claim that the viewpoints it represents have gained universal, or even wide, acceptance. But the issues it raised or put into clearer focus have proved to be those that have increasingly dominated subsequent Johannine research. These are, in the order treated here, the literary criticism or literary problem of the Fourth Gospel, the history-of-religions question, the shape and character of the strain of the early Christianity that produced the Fourth Gospel (in relationship to other forms of early Christianity), and finally Johannine theology.

Certain traditional questions of introduction have been more or less settled, while others have attracted less interest. Because of the Rylands

---

[2] In cases where English translations of foreign-language works exist, they are cited in the bibliography, and hence their dates are given in the text. In such cases, dates of original publication are also noted in the bibliography.

Papyrus (P[52]) particularly, John is generally thought to date no later than 110, and probably a decade or two earlier — but not earlier than the publication of the twelfth of the Eighteen Benedictions in the mid-80s (Brown, 1966-70:lxxxv).[3] It is no longer regarded as necessarily later than all the Synoptic Gospels, although few would think it as early or earlier than Mark. (On the problem of dating John, see de Jonge, 1979:112-14.) The question of the geographical provenance of the completed Gospel no longer attracts great interest. Ephesus is by no means ruled out, although a point farther east, for example, in Syria or Palestine, would find many supporters. The discussion of authorship has died down in one form only to arise in another. Inasmuch as the traditional view that the Fourth Gospel is the work of John the Son of Zebedee now has few supporters among critical scholars (but see John A. T. Robinson, 1976:298-311), it is no longer the subject of much controversy or attack. Yet the question of the role of the Beloved Disciple in relation to the origin of the Johannine tradition is very much alive. In writing a commentary without an introduction, Bultmann epitomized a turning away from such traditional introductory questions as largely unsolved and unsolvable. A similar lack of interest in those questions as previously put appears in E. C. Hoskyns's commentary, originally published at about the same time as Bultmann's, and in the work of Dodd. But precisely in the shift to the pursuit of such other issues as are described below, some of the older questions were put in better perspective and even, in the judgment of some, answered.

II. THE LITERARY PROBLEM OF THE FOURTH GOSPEL

By the careful observation of aporias, difficulties in the progress of the text (e.g., 6:1; 14:31), as well as linguistic, stylistic, and even theological characteristics, Bultmann believed he was able to identify five or six major sources or literary strata in the Fourth Gospel: a *sēmeia* ("signs") source, consisting of the miracle stories of the Gospel; a passion source; a collection of revelation discourses so-called; other scattered sources or traditions that could not be assigned to any of the three major sources; the extensive work of the evangelist himself, who wove the sources into a smoother and more consistent whole than now appears even in the traditional text; and an ecclesiastical redaction carried out in order to reestablish the order of the text (after it had undergone some sort of disruption, the cause of which Bultmann does not explain) and to emend it so as to render the Gospel acceptable in a church in which an emerging ecclesiastical orthodoxy prevailed. Bultmann thus posited four stages in the composition of the Gospel: sources,

---

[3] J. A. T. Robinson (1976:254-311) disputes so late a *terminus a quo*, in part because the fall of Jerusalem is not mentioned in John. The date and content of the original form of the Twelfth Benediction are also not undisputed, but on other grounds most Johannine scholars are not inclined to date John earlier.

composition by the evangelist, disruption of the text, and restoration by ecclesiastical redaction. For him the object of exegesis was stage two, the text as composed by the evangelist. The sources in a sense represented the *religionsgeschichtliche* ("history of religions") background of the Gospel (gnostic revelation discourses taken over from the Baptist sect), as well as the earlier Christian tradition on which it was based (*sēmeia* source, used in Christian missionary work among that sect; a passion source; other isolated traditions, e.g., the temple cleansing story). Although Bultmann does not state it in these terms, the original Gospel was the theologically astute response of the evangelist to his situation, as implied by his sources. The ecclesiastical redaction was the key to the survival of this distinctive gospel witness in the light of an emerging ecclesiastical orthodoxy.

Bultmann's literary theory was integrally related to his understanding of the basic issues of Johannine research. We shall comment on the various aspects of Johannine criticism and interpretation as they are raised and focused by this literary theory. But first, How has the theory as such fared? On the one hand, almost no one has accepted it as a whole (see Smith, 1965). In the very nature of the case this might have been expected, since the more complex such a theory, the larger the measure of the sheerly hypothetical that it involves, and by the same token the more idiosyncratic it becomes. On the other hand, certain elements of Bultmann's position have proved quite durable. (By contrast, Bultmann's view of *Grundschrift* [a "basic written source"] and redaction in 1 John has attracted relatively little support.) A large number of scholars of varying points of view have found some form of the *sēmeia* source theory (which admittedly was not Bultmann's invention) useful in coming to terms with the Johannine miracle tradition (e.g., Fortna, 1970; Becker, 1970b; Martyn, 1979:166; Käsemann, 1968:37; Nicol; Schnackenburg, 1968:64–67; James M. Robinson, 1971:238–52; also, even with his reservations, Haenchen, 1981:44). A good many would also agree that John used a passion source independent of the Synoptics, whether written or oral (e.g., Fortna, 1970; Hahn: 23–29; Haenchen, 1968; Dauer; Brown, 1966–70:787–91), a source that had certain relations to, and affinities with, Mark, but was not derived from Mark itself. As for the revelation discourses, neither their integrity as a single source nor their alleged pre-Christian gnostic origin has found much acceptance. Yet the notion that the speeches are constituted in part by some traditional materials or aspects finds fairly wide, if quite varied and diverse, support (e.g., Leroy; Barrett, 1978:21, 26, 133–34; Borgen, 1965; Brown, 1966–70:xxxiv–xxxix; Becker, 1969, 1970a, 1974; Lindars, 1972:51–54; Thyen, 1971, 1974–79). The prologue in particular is widely regarded as based on a tradition, source, or hymn of some sort (Käsemann, 1969; Brown, 1966–70:18–23; Schnackenburg, 1968:224–32), but this view is not uncontested (Barrett, 1971). That certain pieces of synoptic-like tradition (other than the *sēmeia* and passion source) are found in the Fourth Gospel is generally conceded, and most scholars would not insist that they were derived directly from the Synoptic Gospels.

The matter of the roles of evangelist and redactor in composing the Gospel has been the focus of continuing scholarly interest, although Bultmann's hypothesis of the destruction of the text and its reconstitution (i.e., rearrangement) by an ecclesiastical redactor has found little support. Bultmann has sometimes been criticized for relegating the evangelist to a relatively minor role in editing and arranging sources, but a careful reading of his commentary makes it obvious to what a large degree he held the Fourth Evangelist to have been the master of the materials with which he worked. By way of contrast, it is more recent scholarship that has tended to assign less theological creativity to the evangelist and correspondingly more to (Johannine) tradition, while increasingly regarding John as the product of a distinct community or school (Brown, 1979; Martyn, 1978:90–121; Culpepper; Cullmann, 1976; cf. Haenchen, 1981:43–44, 96, 103) in which social and historical influences and conflicts played a seminal role (Meeks, 1972). In view of this emphasis on the role of a community and its concrete historical circumstances in the Gospel's composition, the question of redaction has been seen in a new light. The process of redaction is no longer viewed as an effort to restore order to an accidentally fragmented and disarrayed text and bring it into conformity with an external standard of orthodoxy. Rather, it is typically understood as a process of augmentation and perhaps intentional rearrangement of the Gospel material within a Johannine orbit (Brown, 1966–70:xxxiv–xxxix; Thyen, 1971, 1974–79; Langbrandtner; Richter). Thus, the possibility is frequently contemplated (even as Bultmann proposed, but with a different nuance) that there may have been more than one recension of the Fourth Gospel (Wilkens, 1958; Brown, 1966–70:xxxiv–xxxix; Fortna, 1970; Lindars, 1972:50–51; Richter; Thyen, 1971, 1974–79; Langbrandtner; Haenchen, 1981:43–44). Traces of such an earlier recension may be evidenced by the way in which chap. 21 is appended after a seemingly concluding colophon (20:30–31), by the continuing discourse of chaps. 15–17 after the change of scene anticipated in 14:31, by the apparent advantage gained in reversing the order of chaps. 5 and 6, etc. But whereas Bultmann chose to make such an earlier edition the subject of his exegesis, more recent commentators and other interpreters have agreed on the primary importance of making sense of, or seeing the sense in, the present text, whatever its literary or traditional antecedents may have been.[4]

---

[4] Thyen (1974–79), for example, views the "redactor" as the author who has given the present Gospel its shape and theological direction. Hence he may rightly be called the "evangelist."

III. THE HISTORY-OF-RELIGIONS PROBLEM

Since World War II there has been a notable shift in the weight of scholarly opinion from the Hellenistic to the Jewish, or at least the Near Eastern, side in identifying the milieu of the Fourth Gospel. (Moreover, the view that Hellenism and Judaism were mutually exclusive even in Palestine is now generally repudiated.) John is no longer viewed as the Gospel of the Hellenists, understood as pagan, non-Jewish, non-Semitic. Even this shift was in a sense already prefigured by Bultmann's commentary, in which the principal gnostic background was not pagan or Hellenistic, but Semitic and even Jewish (1971:30–31). The gnosticism of the *Offenbarungsreden* ("revelatory discourse source") was, in his view, mediated through the John the Baptist sect, which, in origin at least, was Jewish. It was closely related to the Mandaean literature and sect, which may have originated in Palestine and Syria as an offshoot of sectarian Judaism (see Rudolph, 1969, and the works cited in that article), and to the *Odes of Solomon* (Charlesworth, 1973), whose Jewish coloration is evident. It is not surprising that Bultmann welcomed the discovery of the Qumran scrolls, with their manifest similarities in terminology and dualism to the Fourth Gospel (1955:13), thinking them a confirmation of his own position rather than its refutation. The discussion of the milieu of Johannine Christianity is not exhausted by the options of Judaism or gnosticism, but it is in these areas that most recent research has been done and new proposals advanced.

No doubt the Qumran scrolls gave the pendulum of scholarly opinion a vigorous push toward the Jewish side. Established scholars, such as W. F. Albright (167–171, acknowledging indebtedness to K. G. Kuhn) and O. Cullmann (1957), as well as emerging leaders of informed opinion such as the young Raymond Brown (1957), were quick to see the importance of the scrolls for understanding the Johannine literature. Some thought John had been directly influenced by the Qumran community or its literature (Charlesworth, 1972:104–5) and the scrolls. The scrolls were sometimes taken as evidence for the early date and Palestinian origin of the Fourth Gospel. Certainly their discovery meant that John could no longer be assumed to be later than the other Gospels or assigned to some non-Palestinian origin simply on the grounds of its allegedly Hellenistic terminology and dualism. Nevertheless, to infer from the scrolls a Palestinian origin and an early date for John, not to mention its historicity, was to strain the evidence beyond what it could reasonably bear. Qumran truly removed the necessity of looking beyond Palestine and beyond the end of the first century for Johannine roots. Yet Qumran alone was not sufficient to prove the Palestinian and early origin of the Fourth Gospel as we presently have it. And even if such an origin and early date were accepted, that in itself would not confirm the Gospel's historicity.

Although the Qumran discoveries understandably gave impetus to the search for Johannine origins within Judaism and within Palestine (see Böcher, 1965; Charlesworth, 1972), the view that the Gospel of John was Hellenistic, in the sense of non-Palestinian and non-Jewish, was not universally held prior to their discovery. In fact, B. W. Bacon, who gave the title *The Gospel of the Hellenists* to his book on the origins of the Fourth Gospel, meant by "Hellenists" the Jewish Christians of that name mentioned in the book of Acts (1933:74–80). In relating the Gospel of John through them to a then largely hypothetical Jewish sectarianism, he actually foreshadowed the discovery of the scrolls, as well as Cullmann's view of Johannine origins.

While the scrolls enormously stimulated research on the Jewish side, not every significant effort to explain the Johannine literature with reference to a Jewish milieu was dependent on them for that purpose. One thinks, for example, of Wayne Meeks's illuminating presentation of the Moses typology in the Fourth Gospel (1967), Peder Borgen's effort to recover or reconstruct an ultimately Palestinian Jewish background and midrashic pattern for the Bread Discourse of John 6 (1965), J. Louis Martyn's interpretation of Johannine origins against the background of a synagogue debate over Jesus' messiahship (1979), the contributions of several scholars (e.g., Meeks, 1967:216–57, 314–19; cf. Purvis) in showing John's relation to Samaritanism, John A. T. Robinson's argument that John's Gospel was addressed to Diaspora Judaism (1960), and S. Pancaro's discussion of the role of the law in the Fourth Gospel. All are relatively independent of Qumran. Obviously, there has been a thoroughgoing reassessment of the possibly Jewish dimensions of the Fourth Gospel. Research in this area, which has covered a wide range of issues, might well have gone on had the Qumran discoveries never been made, but the scrolls certainly stimulated scholars to examine the Johannine literature with a view to isolating evidence pointing to a Jewish ambiance or perspective.

It would be incorrect, however, to leave the impression that Johannine scholarship has settled on a Jewish origin or milieu for the Fourth Gospel to the exclusion of other possibilities. To say "Jewish" is to say at least several things rather than only one, particularly as far as the period with which we are dealing is concerned. Moreover, there is by no means agreement on the extent, character, and direction of Jewish influence on the Fourth Gospel among those who acknowledge such influence. Of course, the history-of-religions quest is at least in theory an infinite regression. To identify something within early Christianity as Jewish, or of Jewish provenance, does not necessarily settle the question of its origin. Thus, for example, the dualism of John may have its origin in Qumran or similar Jewish movements, but that form of sectarian Judaism may have been influenced by Zoroastrianism. To say that some motif is Jewish does not mean that it is necessarily biblical (i.e., *alttestamentlich*, "from the OT"), and even so, that does not mean it could not have originated in the wider world of life and thought outside Israel.

Furthermore, the widely accepted explanation of John in terms of a Jewish origin does not mean that the gnostic option, so strongly represented by Bultmann, is either passé or moribund. Proponents of gnostic antecedents of the Fourth Gospel point to its undeniably dualistic orientation and affinities in language (e.g., *logos,* "word") and conceptuality with gnostic writings. Just as Qumran excited interest in the Jewish background, so the postwar discovery of the Nag Hammadi documents, some of which seem only superficially Christian, has maintained interest in the gnostic. Probably advocacy of a significant relationship of gnosticism to Johannine Christianity remains stronger among German scholars and those influenced by that tradition (e.g., Schottroff, Langbrandtner, and Haenchen, not to mention Cullmann and the standard introduction of Kümmel, 226–28) than in the English-speaking world.

Against the complaint that all extant, datable gnostic writings are later than and therefore could not have influenced the Gospel of John, it is argued that some of these documents embody older traditions or sources that are not identifiably Christian. This is certainly not impossible. An example of the plausibility, but also the difficulty, of such arguments is found in the Mandaean sources, which have been known for some time. They contain some striking terminological and conceptual affinities with John (e.g., *knowledge,* from which the name "Mandaeism" is derived; *truth, life, light;* and imagery such as the shepherd and the vine). The Mandaean writings in their present form are acknowledged to be centuries later than John, but quite likely they contain much older traditional material. If the Mandaean community and traditions originated within or at the fringes of the Palestinian Judaism of the NT period, as some investigators believe (Rudolph, 1969; see also Kümmel: 220), a significant influence of Mandaeism or its antecedents on John or Johannine Christianity would not be inconceivable. But whether in their incipient form those traditions were even gnostic has been contested (Yamauchi, 1970). Difficulties are compounded by the fact that the history of the Mandaean community cannot easily be deduced from the sources.

In the light of recent exploration of the Jewishness of the Johannine literature, the possibility that the Nag Hammadi documents give evidence of a gnostic contact with Judaism prior to any Christian influence is quite intriguing (MacRae, 1966, 1970b; Fallon). If this is the case, gnosticism is not necessarily derived from Christianity, and a Jewish gnosticism in the Johannine milieu becomes a factor to be reckoned with. Actually, several lines of evidence suggest that the Gospel's obvious relationship to Judaism by no means excludes a significant kinship to gnosticism. In addition to the traces of Jewish influence in Nag Hammadi writings and the possible Jewish origins of Mandaeism, there are the apparent intermingling of Jewish and gnostic elements among Ignatius's opponents (Barrett, 1975:53–56) and the sharp dualism of the Qumran scrolls, which led Bultmann to understand them as gnostic. But at best Jewish gnosticism is an elusive phenomenon. The present state of the evidence scarcely permits one to speak with certainty about a gnostic *background* of John. Yet the possibility cannot be dismissed, even if it be granted that the specifically gnostic redeemer myth has not been shown to antedate Christianity. (But, as Talbert has made clear, a myth of a descending redeemer figure was not the sole property of gnostics.) The question still very much subject to further research and discussion is whether such a gnosticism (Jewish or otherwise) as may have existed was a part of the Johannine milieu and influenced directly the development of the Gospel. At present a number of scholars involved in this discussion would at least agree that the Johannine literature developed at some point on a trajectory that led to the gnosticism known to us from second-century and later sources (Meeks, 1972:71–72; cf. Brown, 1979:151–55).

IV. JOHANNINE CHRISTIANITY IN THE CONTEXT OF THE NEW TESTAMENT AND EARLY CHRISTIANITY

In finding it unnecessary to posit John's use of the Synoptic Gospels or Pauline traditions in the composition of the Fourth Gospel, Bultmann prefigured a dominant trend in postwar Johannine studies. Granted the existence of parallel and in some respects similar oral (or written) traditions, the older view that John knew and used the Synoptic Gospels appeared to be an unnecessary, if not unlikely, hypothesis (Gardner-Smith; Goodenough; cf. John A. T. Robinson, 1959:96–97). Dodd turned his attention to the historical tradition of the Fourth Gospel (1963) without presupposing the evangelist's knowledge of the Synoptics, and his intensive investigations confirmed his earlier sense of the correctness of P. Gardner-Smith's position. Moreover, most important commentaries since World War II have been written on the hypothesis of John's relative, if not complete, independence of the Synoptics (e.g., Schnackenburg, 1968:26–43; Brown, 1966–70:xliv–xlvii; Sanders, 1968:8–12; Morris: 49–52; Lindars, 1972:25–28; Haenchen, 1981:79–80, 102)

Johannine-Pauline relations have been the subject of relatively little discussion in recent decades. The older, commonly held assumption (Schweitzer: 349–75; Bacon, 1910:295, 438–39; Bousset: 240) that John knew and built on the Pauline version of Christian theology has, by and large, faded away. Its basis was John's mysticism and explicit Christology, especially the Son of God title put on the lips of Jesus himself. As Bultmann pointed out in his *Theology of the New Testament,* the affinities or agreements between Paul and John can be adequately explained on the basis of common tradition (for Bultmann the kerygma of Hellenistic Christianity) without supposing that John was dependent upon Pauline thought (1955:6–10). He found the characteristically and distinctively Pauline terms and concepts to

be absent from John. Nevertheless, for Bultmann at least, John does constitute, in its substance or thrust, a kind of theological development of Paul,
but one not based on a direct historical relationship. In the English-speaking
world also emphasis on a common kerygma (Dodd, 1936) in early Christianity influenced scholarship to view Paul and John as related primarily through
tradition rather than because of Johannine dependence on the Pauline
letters or on distinctively Pauline Christianity.

The position that John is related to Paul through common or similar
tradition is then analogous to the still widely held view of Johannine–
Synoptic relations. That the latter relationships were indirect and traditional
rather than more direct and literary would also seem to square with the
obvious fact that the closest and most extensive similarities between John
and the Synoptic Gospels are found in their respective passion narratives.
Form and tradition critics have long supposed that the proclamation of
salvation through the death and resurrection of Jesus led to the early
formation of a passion narrative(s). The early oral or literary fixing of such
a passion tradition would suffice to explain the close similarities of content,
order, and occasionally even wording between John and the Synoptics in
that longest of Gospel episodes (Smith, 1980:433; cf. Kümmel: 77 n. 81).
Since in very recent years there has appeared a vigorous, renewed advocacy
of John's knowledge of one or more of the Synoptics (see Teeple: 59–83),
much discussion has appropriately centered on the passion or resurrection
narratives (Kelber, ed: esp. 8–16, 103–5, 153–59; cf. Fortna, 1978:371–83;
on the resurrection narratives, see Neirynck, 1977:95–106; 1984). For good
reason, it has involved the question of whether Mark's passion came to him
as a continuous narration or he himself was the first to compose it out of
isolated units of tradition (Linnemann). In favor of the latter alternative is
the analogy of Mark's apparent composition of the pre-passion part of his
Gospel out of such traditions. Against it is the consideration that much, if not
most, of the passion material finds its reason for being in the context of a
continuous narrative. That is, why preserve and transmit a story of Jesus'
betrayal by Judas unless an account of his arrest, trial, and death is in view?
(Of course, John can be adduced as an example of such a passion narrative
independent of Mark, but here the argument becomes circular.)

The whole question of John's relationship to the Synoptic Gospels may
be more difficult or at least capable of more permutations than at first
appears. Its potential for subtlety and complexity is reflected in the pains-
taking analysis of Boismard, who thinks John was composed of basically
independent although not wholly alien traditions, but drew directly on the
Synoptics in the later stages of its composition history. On the other hand,
Neirynck (1979) in criticizing Boismard deems it more satisfactory simply to
think of the Synoptic Gospels in their present form as known to the Fourth
Evangelist from the beginning. In deciding whether John knew the Marcan
or other synoptic accounts, a crucial consideration may well be whether or

not evidence of Marcan or other synoptic redaction can be found in John. If so, John presumably knew the Gospel of Mark itself (or Matthew or Luke), not merely related tradition. Precisely this is a major question in the discussion of the passion narrative; one asks whether the order of narratives and other elements that John shares with the Synoptics are the result of Mark's or one of the other evangelists' arrangement or are given by tradition. Perrin (227–29) and his students find elements of Marcan redaction in the Fourth Gospel. A. Dauer (developing earlier insights of Dahl, and Borgen, 1959) sees redactional traces of the Matthean and Lucan passion narratives there. But the Perrin school's position has been challenged by Fortna (1978), and Brown (1973) has shown that Dauer's conclusions are at least subject to question. The redaction-critical solution appears only to remove the contest to another arena.

Even if John knew the Synoptics, his relation to them could scarcely have been close or harmonious. In that case one might well suppose that in composing his Gospel the Fourth Evangelist chose, for whatever reason, largely to go his own way. (Given John's knowledge of the Synoptics, H. Windisch's view that he wrote to displace them is not farfetched.) Obviously, the vocabulary, style, and for the most part the theology of the Fourth Gospel are more closely related to the Johannine letters than to any of the other Gospels. A number of factors, taken together, suggest that the Fourth Gospel is the product of a distinct strain of early Christianity: (1) the close affinities with these letters, together with some differences which suggest that the Gospel and epistles may not be the work of the same author; (2) the clear implication of the letters that more than one Christian community or church is in view; (3) the evidence of non-synoptic tradition as well as of redactional activity within the Gospel; (4) the unclear or ambiguous relationship with the Synoptic Gospels or tradition; and (5) the existence of the Apocalypse with its vast differences from the Gospel and letters, together with some apparent points of contact (Smith, 1975:229, 233, 234–35; Böcher, 1981). If John is the product of a distinct circle, school, or sect, the Gospel's divergences from the Synoptics then seem more a function of a different set of historical circumstances and problems than a personal, literary, or theological idiosyncrasy. It is not a matter of chance that in recent years considerable attention from various quarters or perspectives has been devoted to the question of Johannine Christianity and the nature and shape of the community or church that produced the Fourth Gospel; see Culpepper, 1975, 1983; Richter; Cullmann, 1976; Martyn, 1979, 1978:90–121; Brown, 1979; Thyen (e.g., 1977); cf. Meeks, 1972; Smith, 1975.

J. Louis Martyn's seminal and fruitful proposal for understanding the peculiar character of the Johannine community is grounded on the observation that the Fourth Gospel portrays Jesus continually in conflict with Jews, some of whom, while attracted to Jesus, do not confess him for fear of being put out of the synagogue (9:22; 12:42; 16:2). Such features as this, and even the description of those who do not believe in Jesus as "the Jews" (in distinction from Jesus' disciples, who were historically also Jews), as well as the accusation of blasphemy against Jesus for his claims to divine sonship, suggest a situation that evolved after the Roman War and the retrenchment of Judaism represented by Jamnia. Martyn connects this mutual hostility to the formulation of the Twelfth Benediction, aimed at heretics and Nazarenes (Jewish Christians) and traditionally attributed to Samuel the Small (ca. 85 C.E.). His position does not, however, depend entirely on the dating of the Twelfth Benediction, inasmuch as he regards it as symptomatic of a process within the synagogue, and in synagogue–church relations, spanning a period of years. On the other side, Martyn's thesis is anchored in a number of rather explicit Johannine texts that do not fit the time of Jesus, but do fit a later period. The Fourth Gospel is thus seen to reflect in its narratives and dialogues two historical levels, one the (*einmalig*, "unique," "unrepeatable") level of Jesus himself, or at least of the tradition, and the other the recapitulation of Jesus' own struggles and conflicts in the experience of a group of Christian believers that has separated from the synagogue and is now forming its own Christian community or church. Martyn's insights have been adopted, with modifications, by a number of other scholars, particularly Raymond E. Brown (1979:174; cf. Meeks, 1972:69; 1975:183–85), who found in them a way of perceiving developments in the Johannine community compatible with his own perspective. Brown believes, as does Martyn, that the roots of the synagogue conflict antedate the Roman War. But he also argues that the crisis within the synagogue was exacerbated by the introduction of a high Christology with the admission of Samaritan converts. Moreover, Brown emphasizes that the Fourth Gospel as we now have it represents Christian theological interests that go beyond the struggle with Judaism.

Martyn's view is associated with the work of Robert Fortna, who by source-critical analysis has found at the base of the Fourth Gospel a Gospel of Signs (1970), composed entirely of narratives (miracles and passion). In his view this *Grundschrift* ("basic written source") was a missionary document originally employed by Christ-confessing Jews to persuade others within the synagogue to believe in Jesus as Messiah. In the course of ensuing struggles (which evoked the *birkat ha-minim*, "curse on the heretics") this document was heavily redacted (i.e., the discourses were added), finally attaining its present form. The Gospel was now no longer addressed simply to that original missionary purpose, but had become the distinctly Christian theological and even polemical work of Martyn's interpretation. Not all scholars who have found Martyn's thesis illuminating have, however, subscribed to the Sign Gospel. Some are unable to accept the view that a Gospel almost completely without teaching ever existed, finding it more appropriate to think of combinations of narrative and discourse through several stages of the Gospel's development (e.g., Brown, 1966–70:xxxi-xxxii, xxxiv-xxxix; Lindars, 1971: esp. 41-42, 59-60; cf. de Jonge, 1977:117-18). Nevertheless, Fortna's work has proved seminal in continuing the source-critical discussion and in advancing the possibility of redaction criticism of John.

While Martyn has endeavored, perhaps heuristically, to interpret the Fourth Gospel as exhaustively as possible on the basis of the synagogue or Jewish-Christian conflict, others, like Brown (1979), have seen unrelated and distinctly Christian issues emerging at some points (e.g., de Jonge, 1977:99-100), particularly in farewell discourses (Becker, 1970a). More-over, a number of scholars have perceived an identifiable unity of distinctly Christian perspective and purpose in the first epistle (or the epistles) and the final redaction of the Gospel, e.g., Richter; Becker, 1969, 1970a; Segovia; cf. Thyen, 1971:354-56; 1977:277-78, 296-99. Thus, Bultmann's view that an earlier version of the Gospel was subjected to a redactional process has found rather wide support in principle. But that redaction is now perceived as Johannine, or within the Johannine circle or school, rather than extrinsic, that is, the work of a kind of censor representing an external ecclesiastical orthodoxy (Thyen, 1971; Smith, 1975:235; cf. Brown, 1966-70: xxxvi-xxxviii).

Exactly how the Gospel and Epistles and the community that spawned them would have related to the emergence of a developing ecclesiastical authority and organization during the course of the second century is not clear, nor has there been an appreciable consensus on the point. Some scholars (e.g., Braun, 1959) have defended the centrality, apostolicity, or catholicity of John against the view that it early on became the province of gnostics and other heretics (Sanders, 1943; Bauer: 185-87, 206, 209-12, 228; Hillmer), a position based on second-century evidence of John's use and disuse. Ignatius, in the first quarter of the second century, echoes the language of the Fourth Gospel, but does not quote it. Justin Martyr at mid-second century seems to quote the Fourth Gospel, but not as one of the memoirs of the apostles. Only in the last quarter of the century is it attributed to John and cited as scripture by Irenaeus and other orthodox fathers, although knowledge of 1 John (but probably not the Gospel) is attested at mid-century and perhaps earlier in Polycarp's *Letter to the Philippians* (7.1; 1 John 4:2, 3; cf. 2 John 7) and, according to Eusebius, by Papias (*Hist. Eccl.* 3.39.17). At about the same time, however, the Valentinian gnostic Heracleon was writing a commentary on the Gospel (see Pagels). Moreover, many of the recently published Nag Hammadi documents are replete with Johannine language, although how to account for this state of affairs is still a matter of debate.

Contacts with later NT books are as difficult to establish as with earlier. John's cognizance of the church's history and experience and his interest in eschatology in view of the nonoccurrence of the parousia are, for example, shared by Luke. Yet Luke wrote two books of history, one about Jesus and the other about the church, rather than, so to speak, superimposing one on the other; and (at least in the predominant view) he presented the eschaton as postponed rather than in the most significant sense already fulfilled. Because of their obvious interest in establishing right confession, doctrine, and discipline, Conzelmann aptly characterized 1–3 John as Johannine Pastorals. Yet there is little, if any, evidence of knowledge of the Pastorals themselves reflected in the Johannine epistles. An interest in establishing the cosmic role of Christ beyond history and certain linguistic or conceptual tools are shared by John and Hebrews (cf. 1:1–3), as well as Colossians and Ephesians. But clear points of contact are lacking. They are found, however, in Revelation (Smith, 1975:229, 232–33, 234–35). Although both its date and relation to the Fourth Gospel may be problematic (Schüssler Fiorenza; but cf. Brown, 1979:6 n. 5), the possibility of a significant connection cannot be dismissed (Böcher, 1981).

Raymond Brown (1979:145–62; 1982) has recently argued that the evidences of conflict with the epistles, the Johannine literature's relative isolation within the NT, and the rather slow acceptance of the Gospel among orthodox Christians suggest an admittedly hypothetical scenario in which christological conflicts within the community (see 1 John 4:1–6) led to a splitting up of the Johannine group (see also Luz: 103). Part, probably the majority, adopted an increasingly gnostic interpretation of the Fourth Gospel, becoming, or making common cause with, second-century gnostics. Those who produced the epistles or agreed with the polemical stance moved in the direction of the emerging ecclesiastical orthodoxy of the second century. In effect, these two groups introduced two ways of reading the Fourth Gospel, represented in current criticism on the docetic side by Käsemann (1968; cf. Culpepper: 283) and on the orthodox by Raymond Brown and, in a certain sense, Bultmann (1971). The epistles reflect the latter interpretation of the Gospel, that is, the side that finally won out, at a point just before the author and his followers made common cause with the emerging institutional orthodoxy. (In effect, Brown's position accords with Conzelmann's earlier insights about the church-traditional, even pastoral perspective of 1 John.) We do not, of course, have ancient documents supporting the alternative, heretical standpoint!

Two further important questions about Johannine Christianity appear to have reached if not a resolution at least some consensus as to the boundaries within which such a resolution should be sought. First, concerning whether Johannine Christianity was a sect (see Meeks, 1972), the answer seems in large measure to depend on the definition of "sect." Brown, who has tended to see the Gospel and epistles of John lying nearer the center than the periphery of the mainstream of NT Christianity, nevertheless acknowledges the distinctiveness and identifiability of the Christian circles that produced them (1979:14–17). They arose out of a particular set of circumstances that gave rise to a unique configuration of questions and issues. Whether one speaks of a Johannine sect, school, or circles, there is growing agreement on the existence of a concrete and well-defined social reality, distinguishable from the generality of early Christian churches, behind the Johannine literature.

Second, the question of the origin of this group, its relation to Jesus, the circle of eyewitnesses, or the *Urgemeinde* ("earliest church") is now generally agreed to be an important one about which something significant can be said. The growing acknowledgment that the Beloved Disciple was a histor-ical figure (Thyen, 1974–79, 42:223), however much he may have been idealized, is tied to the recognition that he is somehow important for Johan-nine origins and self-definition (Roloff; Lorenzen; Thyen, 1977; Culpepper: 264–70; Haenchen, 1981:601–5). This is the case whether or not he himself was an eyewitness (Brown, 1979:31–34), also the author of the Gospel (Cullmann, 1976:78–85), or even John the Son of Zebedee (John A. T. Robinson, 1976:298–311). The Johannine community conceived of itself as linked directly to Jesus and the original circle of disciples through the Beloved Disciple, however that linkage may have been understood and whatever may be its validity as a historical claim. One finds a wide consensus on this point, a narrower one on whether the Beloved Disciple was an eye-witness, and a small but articulate minority willing to identify him with John the Son of Zebedee in accord with the ancient church tradition.

V. JOHANNINE THEOLOGY

This review of Johannine scholarship has focused primarily on problems and issues that are not ordinarily labeled theological. Yet, in fact, all the matters discussed have direct and significant theological implications. Any presentation of Johannine theology that does not take account of literary questions, the origins of terms and concepts, and their historical significance in a primitive Christian milieu is likely to miss the peculiarly Johannine thrust or emphasis and to read the theological language and intention of the Gospel (or letters) from the perspective of later Christian doctrine and thought, upon which the Johannine literature had a sizable influence. But precisely in gaining that influence the original nuances, relevance, and bear-ing of the distinctly Johannine theology may have been lost from view. Thus, the most significant recent developments in the interpretation of Johannine theology have centered in investigations which set that theology in its literary, historical, or social contexts and, where possible, relate those contexts.

Perhaps the most fundamental and acute problem of Johannine theol-ogy is whether the Gospel was, as has been traditionally assumed, originally intended to assert something approximating the Christian doctrine of the incarnation, or whether it is at bottom naïvely docetic (Käsemann, 1968; cf. Thyen, 1974–79, 42:259–60) or even explicitly gnostic (Schottroff;

Langbrandtner). This discussion is epitomized in the debate over the exegesis of John 1:14. In Bultmann's view (1971) it is intended to assert the paradoxical character of the revelation given in a historical person. Thus, a concept of incarnation congenial with modern and much traditional Christology finds support. But this interpretation of 1:14 and the view of John's Christology consistent with it have not gone undisputed. On Käsemann's reading (1969), the first part of the verse (καὶ ὁ λόγος σὰρξ ἐγένετο καὶ ἐσκήνωσεν ἐν ἡμῖν, "And the Word became flesh and dwelt among us") is only the necessary prolegomenon to the second (καὶ ἐθεασάμεθα τὴν δόξαν αὐτοῦ . . . , "and we have beheld his glory . . ."). In the latter case the Word's becoming flesh is not genuine incarnation but only the necessary presupposition of its appearance on earth.

Generally, the opposing sides on this issue line up according to whether or not a gnostic milieu is espoused. (Yet Bultmann, although accepting the gnostic character of the discourse material with which John worked, maintained that the evangelist intentionally transformed it according to his own theological perspective.) The opposing sides sharply dispute the importance of the death of Jesus in the Gospel. With the view that John's Christology is incarnational goes the position that the death of Jesus is important to it (Forestell). In the view that the Gospel is naïvely docetic and incipiently gnostic, the death is usually held to be narrated only because it is given in the tradition, and it is interpreted as exaltation rather than suffering. In Thyen's understanding of the development of theology within the Gospel and its community, the final redaction was an accommodation of the gnostic *Grundschrift* to the incarnational position by the addition of precisely such passages as 1:14; 6:48–58; and many others (1974–79, esp. 42:218–19; also Langbrandtner: 1–121). Alternatively, Brown (1979) does not take the Gospel itself as basically gnostic (or anti-gnostic), but sees its subsequent interpretation as a battleground between incarnational and docetic elements within the Johannine school. A development in a docetic direction (until the final redaction) from sectarian Jewish roots is proposed by Richter. Meeks (1972) sees the basis of a later gnostic development in the social ostracizing of the Johannine Christians from the Jewish community, which engendered the characteristic dualism, misunderstanding, and irony of the Fourth Gospel (cf. Leroy) and produced a trajectory headed, so to speak, toward gnosticism (Meeks, 1972:71–72). Meeks does not, however, consider the Gospel itself to be gnostic.

Other important questions of miracles, sacraments, eschatology, and church orient themselves around this central issue. The evangelist's affirmation of miracles and sacraments, the espousal of futuristic eschatology, and the view that John emerges from a community not unlike the ones that produced other writings now found in the NT, all tend to accompany the incarnational view. The obverse is true of the gnostic position.

A broader question with more than historical or descriptive theological ramifications is the bearing of exegetical and related findings on the theological appropriation of the burden of the Johannine writings. Admittedly, this is so far-reaching a question as to lie beyond the scope of this essay. Although applicable to any part of scripture, it has particular relevance for the Johannine corpus. If, for example, the significant body of exegetical opinion that now regards the Gospel of John as naïvely docetic is correct, the reservations about it in some quarters of the second-century church were well taken. (Moreover, the people who rejected or suspected the Fourth Gospel were not clearly heterodox by the standards of their time.) Yet that Gospel eventually won a place in the NT canon, and not because it was properly understood, but in this view only because it was misunderstood. Such an assessment may be incorrect, but whether or not it is can scarcely be decided on the basis of theological attractiveness or convenience. Meanwhile, what is to be made of this state of affairs? That is, shall the misinterpretation of the Fourth Gospel be regarded as at once historically inaccurate and theologically advantageous? If so, does this mean that within the church exegesis may proceed from or take as its starting point a view of the Fourth Gospel that is known on historical-exegetical grounds to be infelicitous, if not downright erroneous? It is easier to pose such questions than to address, much less resolve, them. To raise them, however, affords some indication of why the kinds of issues to which Johannine research now addresses itself are fascinating and urgently important, not only for exegesis as a purely literary and historical discipline but also, and particularly, for exegetes whose interest in Johannine criticism and interpretation is also theological.

In retrospect, some lines of agreement in the interpretation of the Fourth Gospel, which render the prospect of having to face the dilemma just posed less likely or less ominous, may now be emerging. Scholars of as diverse interest and perspective as Brown, B. Childs, Culpepper, P. S. Minear, Schnackenburg, and Thyen agree in seeing in the final canonical form of the Gospel the proper object of exegesis and interpretation. On this basis exegetes commit themselves to making positive sense of those elements Bultmann assigned to the ecclesiastical redaction of the Gospel because of their sacramentalism, eschatology, or affinities with the Synoptics, as well as of chap. 21, in which question of pastoral responsibility and the Gospel's authority in the church surface. Although Brown, Schnackenburg, Minear, and Thyen may have different approaches and opinions, they agree in seeing in chap. 21 and other passages such ecclesial interests. These interests, represented in the final redactional layer, provide the framework or perspective for the interpretation of the Gospel as a whole. In the case of Thyen and others (e.g., Richter) the decidedly incarnational elements of the Gospel of John (e.g., 1:14–18) are also ascribed to this latest redaction. This being the case, the final form of the Fourth Gospel has a decidedly orthodox, as well as ecclesial cast, in the light of which the whole is to be understood. For Culpepper and Childs also, although for different reasons, the entire Gospel becomes the basis for interpretation. In the case of Culpepper, literary-critical insights from outside the sphere of biblical criticism per se are employed to make a certain positive sense of the entire Gospel. In the case of Childs, theological principle undergirds the program of canonical criticism or exegesis. The theologically relevant text is the canonical text, not some previous stage that the exegete may by dint of critical ingenuity reconstruct.

Focus on the canonical text as a given for exegesis, however its tradition or redaction history be understood, tends to mollify the severity of the problem posed, precisely because the canonical text includes those perspectives, whether original or added redactionally, which allow the Fourth Gospel to be related positively to the other Gospels (see 20:30–31; 21:25) and to the rest of the NT. If the Fourth Gospel was canonized because it was misunderstood, the misunderstanding began at latest with the final, canonical editing of the text. If Raymond Brown's thesis about the purpose of the letters is correct (1979, 1982), something like this understanding of the Gospel was fixed as the canonical interpretation by their composition and acceptance in the church. Bultmann's conception of ecclesiastical redaction unjustifiably places the final editor in an almost adversarial relationship to the evangelist. Yet he was perhaps correct in seeing this final framing of the Gospel as paving the way for its acceptance in the early catholic church. If, as seems probable, 1 John performed a quite similar function, the proposal that the author of that letter was closely related to the redaction of the Gospel (Segovia), if they were not the work of the same person (Richter, Thyen), embodies a valid insight, even though important aspects of the epistles' polemic are not represented in the Gospel.

BIBLIOGRAPHY

The following bibliography is selective and representative rather than complete. For more extensive bibliographies and bibliographical information, see Malatesta, Thyen, and Kysar (below). English translations of foreign works are cited, where available, with the dates of the original publication included in the entry.

Albright, W. F.
1954   "Recent Discoveries in Palestine and the Gospel of St. John."
        Pp. 153–71 in *The Background of the New Testament and Its
        Eschatology*. Ed. W. D. Davies and D. Daube. Cambridge: University
        Press.

Bacon, Benjamin Wisner
1910   *The Fourth Gospel in Research and Debate*. New York: Moffat, Yard.
1933   *The Gospel of the Hellenists*. Ed. Carl H. Kraeling. New York: Holt.

Barrett, C. K.
1956   *The Gospel According to St. John.* London: SPCK.
1971   *The Prologue of St. John's Gospel.* London: Athlone Press. Reprinted pp. 27–48 in Barrett, *New Testament Essays.* London: SPCK, 1972.
1972   "The Dialectical Theology of St. John." Pp. 49–69 in Barrett, *New Testament Essays.* London: SPCK.
1975   *The Gospel of John and Judaism.* Philadelphia: Fortress.
(1970)
1978   *The Gospel according to St. John,* 2d rev. ed. Philadelphia: Westminster.

Bauer, Walter
1971   *Orthodoxy and Heresy in Earliest Christianity.* Trans. Philadelphia Seminar on Christian Origins. Ed. Robert Kraft and Gerhard Krodel (from 2d German edition by G. Strecker). Philadelphia: Fortress. German original, 1934.

Becker, Jürgen
1969   "Aufbau, Schichtung und theologiegeschichtliche Stellung des Gebetes in Johannes 17." *ZNW* 60: 56–83.
1970a   "Die Abschiedsreden Jesu im Johannesevangelium." *ZNW* 61: 215–46.
1970b   "Wunder und Christologie: Zum literarkritischen und christologischen Problem der Wunder im Johannesevangelium." *NTS* 16: 130–48.
1974   "Beobachtungen zum Dualismus im Johannesevangelium." *ZNW* 65: 71–87.
1979–81 *Das Evangelium nach Johannes.* 2 vols. Ökumenischer Taschenbuch Kommentar zum Neuen Testament 4/1,2. Gütersloh: Mohn.
1982   "Aus der Literatur zum Johannesevangelium (1978–1980)." *TRu* 47: 279–301, 305–47.

Böcher, Otto
1965   *Der johanneische Dualismus im Zusammenhang des nachbiblischen Judentums.* Gütersloh: Mohn.
1981   "Johanneisches in der Apocalypse des Johannes." *NTS* 27: 310–21.

Boismard, M.-É., and A. Lamouille
1977   *Synopse des Quatre Évangiles en Français III: L'evangile de Jean.* Paris: Cerf.

Borgen, Peder
1959   "John and the Synoptics in the Passion Narrative." *NTS* 5: 246–59. Reprinted pp. 67–80 in his *Logos Was the True Light and Other Essays on the Gospel of John.* Relieff 9. Trondheim, Norway: Tapir, 1983.
1965   *Bread from Heaven: An Exegetical Study of the Concept of Manna in the Gospel of John and the Writings of Philo.* NovTSup 10. Leiden: Brill.

Bousset, Wilhelm
1970   *Kyrios Christos.* Trans. John E. Steely. Nashville: Abingdon. German
          original, 1913. 2d ed., 1921.

Braun, François-Marie
1959   *Jean le Théologien et son évangile dans l'église ancienne.* EBib. Paris:
          Gabalda.
1964   *Jean le Théologien: Les grandes Traditions d'Israël: L'Accord des
          Écritures selon le Quatrième Évangile.* Paris: Gabalda.
1966   *Jean le Théologien: Sa Théologie: Le Mystère de Jésus-Christ.* Paris:
          Gabalda.

Brown, Raymond E.
1957   "The Qumran Scrolls and the Johannine Gospel and Epistles."
          Pp. 183–207 in *The Scrolls and the New Testament.* Ed. K. Stendahl.
          New York: Harper.
1966,   *The Gospel according to John.* 2 vols. AB 29, 29A. Garden City, NY:
1970   Doubleday.
1973   Review of Dauer, *Passionsgeschichte, JBL* 92: 608–10.
1979   *The Community of the Beloved Disciple.* Paramus, NJ: Paulist.
1982   *The Epistles of John.* AB 30. Garden City, NY: Doubleday.

Bultmann, Rudolf
1951,   *Theology of the New Testament.* 2 vols. New York: Scribner. German
1955   original, 1948, 1953.
1971   *The Gospel of John: A Commentary.* Philadelphia: Westminster.
          German original, 1941.
1973   *The Johannine Epistles.* Hermeneia. Philadelphia: Fortress. German
          original, 1967.

Charlesworth, James H.
1969   "A Critical Comparison of the Dualism in 1QS iii, 3–iv, 26 and the
          'Dualism' Contained in the Fourth Gospel," *NTS* 15: 389–418.
1972, ed. *John and Qumran.* London: Chapman.
1973   *The Odes of Solomon.* Oxford: Clarendon Press. Rev. ed. issued by
          Scholars Press, 1977.

Childs, Brevard S.
1984   *The New Testament as Canon: An Introduction.* Philadelphia:
          Fortress.

Conzelmann, Hans
1957   " 'Was von Anfang war.' " Pp. 194–201 in *Neutestamentliche Studien
          für Rudolf Bultmann.* Ed. Walter Eltester. BZNW 21. 2d ed. Berlin:
          Töpelmann.

Cullmann, Oscar
1957   "The Significance of the Qumran Texts for Research into the Begin-
          nings of Christianity." Pp. 18–32 in *The Scrolls and the New Testa-
          ment.* Ed. K. Stendahl. New York: Harper.
1976   *The Johannine Circle.* Philadelphia: Westminster. German original,
          1975.

Culpepper, R. Alan
1975   *The Johannine School: An Evaluation of the Johannine-School Hypothesis Based on an Investigation of the Nature of Ancient Schools.* SBLDS 26. Missoula, MT: Scholars Press.
1983   *Anatomy of the Fourth Gospel: A Study in Literary Design.* New Testament Foundations and Facets. Philadelphia: Fortress.

Dahl, Nils A.
1976   "The Passion Narrative in Matthew." In Dahl, *Jesus in the Memory of the Early Church: Essays by Nils Alstrup Dahl.* Minneapolis: Augsburg. Original, 1955.

Dauer, Anton
1972   *Die Passionsgeschichte im Johannesevangelium.* SANT 30. Munich: Kösel.

de Jonge, Marinus
1977   *Jesus: Stranger from Heaven and Son of God: Jesus Christ and the Christians in Johannine Perspective.* SBLSBS 11. Missoula, MT: Scholars Press.
1979   "The Beloved Disciple and the Date of the Gospel of John." Pp. 99–114 in *Text and Interpretation: Studies in the New Testament presented to Matthew Black.* Ed. Ernest Best and R. McL. Wilson. Cambridge: University Press.

de la Potterie, I.
1977   *La Verité dans Saint Jean.* AnBib 73–74. Rome: Biblical Institute Press.

Dodd, C. H.
1936   *The Apostolic Preaching and Its Developments.* London: Hodder & Stoughton.
1946   *The Johannine Epistles.* Moffatt Commentary. London: Hodder & Stoughton.
1953   *The Interpretation of the Fourth Gospel.* Cambridge: University Press.
1963   *Historical Tradition in the Fourth Gospel.* Cambridge: University Press.

Fallon, Francis T.
1978   *The Enthronement of Sabaoth: Jewish Elements in Gnostic Creation Myths.* NHS 10. Leiden: Brill.

Forestell, J. Terence
1974   *The Word of the Cross.* AnBib 57. Rome: Biblical Institute Press.

Fortna, Robert T.
1970   *The Gospel of Signs.* SNTSMS 11. Cambridge: University Press.
1978   "Jesus and Peter at the High Priest's House: A Test Case for the Question of the Relation between Mark's and John's Gospels." *NTS* 24: 371–83.

Gardner-Smith, P.
1938   *Saint John and the Synoptic Gospels.* Cambridge: University Press.

Goodenough, Erwin R.
1945   "John a Primitive Gospel." *JBL* 64: 145–82.

Grayston, Kenneth
1984   *The Johannine Epistles*. NCB. Grand Rapids: Eerdmans.

Haenchen, Ernst
1955   "Aus der Literatur zum Johannesevangelium 1929–56." *TRu* 23:
         295–335.
1968   "Historie und Geschichte in den johanneischen Passionsberichten."
         Pp. 182–207 in *Die Bibel und Wir*. Tübingen: Mohr-Siebeck.
1981   *Das Johannesevangelium: Ein Kommentar*. Ed. Ulrich Busse. Tübin-
         gen: Mohr-Siebeck, 1981. Eng. trans., 2 vols; Hermeneia; Philadel-
         phia: Fortress, 1984.

Hahn, Ferdinand
1970   "Der Prozess Jesu nach dem Johannesevangelium." Pp. 23–96 in
         Evangelisch-Katholischer Kommentar zum Neuen Testament. Vorar-
         beiten Heft 2. Neukirchen-Vluyn: Neukirchener Verlag.

Hillmer, M. R.
1966   "The Gospel of John in the Second Century." Diss., Harvard
         University.

Hoskyns, Edwyn Clement
1947   *The Fourth Gospel*. 2d ed. London: Faber & Faber.

Houlden, James Leslie
1973   *A Commentary on the Johannine Epistles*. HNTC. New York:
         Harper & Row.

Käsemann, Ernst
1968   *The Testament of Jesus: A Study of the Gospel of John in the Light of
         Chapter 17*. Philadelphia: Fortress. [See 1971.] German original,
         1966.
1969   "The Structure and Purpose of the Prologue to John's Gospel." Pp.
         138–67 in his *New Testament Questions of Today*. Philadelphia: For-
         tress. German original, 1957.
1971   *Jesu letzter Wille nach Johannes 17*. Rev. ed. Tübingen: Mohr-
         Siebeck.

Kelber, Werner H., ed.
1976   *The Passion in Mark: Studies on Mark 14–16*. Philadelphia: Fortress.

Kümmel, Werner Georg
1975   *Introduction to the New Testament*. Rev. ed. Trans. H. C. Kee.
         Nashville: Abingdon.

Kysar, Robert
1975   *The Fourth Evangelist and His Gospel: An Examination of Contem-
         porary Scholarship*. Minneapolis: Augsburg.

Langbrandtner, Wolfgang
1977   *Weltferner Gott oder Gott der Liebe: Der Ketzerstreit in der johannei-
         schen Kirche*. BEvT 6. Frankfurt: Peter Lang.

Léon-Dufour, Xavier
1980   "Bulletin de Littérature johannique." *RSR* 68: 271–316.

Leroy, Herbert
1968   *Rätsel und Missverständnis: Ein Beitrag zur Formgeschichte des Johannesevangeliums.* BBB 30. Bonn: Peter Hanstein.

Lightfoot, R. H.
1956   *St. John's Gospel: A Commentary.* Oxford: Clarendon Press.

Lindars, Barnabas
1971   *Behind the Fourth Gospel.* London: SPCK.
1972   *The Gospel of John.* NCB. London: Oliphants.

Linnemann, Eta
1970   *Studien zur Passionsgeschichte.* FRLANT 102. Göttingen: Vandenhoeck & Ruprecht.

Lorenzen, Thorwald
1971   *Der Lieblingsjünger im Johannesevangelium: Eine Redaktionsgeschichtliche Studie.* SBS 55. Stuttgart: Katholisches Bibelwerk.

Luz, Ulrich
1974   "Erwägungen zur Entstehung des 'Frühkatholizismus.'" *ZNW* 65: 88–111.

MacRae, George W.
1966   "Some Elements of Jewish Apocalyptic and Mystical Tradition and their Relation to Gnostic Literature." Ph.D. Diss., Cambridge University.
1970a   "The Fourth Gospel and Religionsgeschichte." *CBQ* 32: 13–24.
1970b   "The Jewish Background of the Gnostic Sophia Myth." *NovT* 12: 86–101.

Macuch, Rudolph, with Kurt Rudolph and Eric Segelberg
1976   *Zur Sprache und Literatur der Mandäer.* Studia Mandaica 1. Berlin: de Gruyter.

Malatesta, Edward
1967   *St. John's Gospel: 1920–1965.* AnBib 32. Rome: Biblical Institute Press.

Marshall, I. Howard
1978   *The Epistles of John.* NICNT. Grand Rapids: Eerdmans.

Martyn, J. Louis
1978   *The Gospel of John in Christian History.* New York: Paulist.
1979   *History and Theology in the Fourth Gospel.* Revised and enlarged ed. Nashville: Abingdon. Original, 1968.

Mattill, A. J.
1977   "Johannine Communities behind the Fourth Gospel: George Richter's Analysis." *TS* 38: 294–315.

Meeks, Wayne A.
1967   *The Prophet-King: Moses Traditions and the Johannine Christology.* NovTSup 14. Leiden: Brill.
1972   "The Man from Heaven in Johannine Sectarianism." *JBL* 91: 44–72.

1975   "'Am I a Jew?' Johannine Christianity and Judaism." Pp. 163–86 in *Christianity, Judaism and Other Greco-Roman Cults: Studies for Morton Smith at Sixty*. Ed. Jacob Neusner. SJLA 12. Part One: New Testament. Leiden: Brill. Pp. 163–86.

Minear, Paul S.
1984   *John: The Martyr's Gospel*. New York: Pilgrim.

Miranda, Juan Peter
1972   *Der Vater der mich gesandt hat: Religionsgeschichtliche Untersuchungen zu den johanneischen Sendungsformeln*. Europäische Hochschulschriften 23, 7. Bern: Herbert Lang.

Morris, Leon
1971   *The Gospel According to John*. NICNT. Grand Rapids: Eerdmans.

Neirynck, Frans
1977   "John and the Synoptics." Pp. 73–106 in *L'Évangile de Jean*. BETL 44. Louvain: Leuven University Press.
1979   *Jean et les Synoptiques: Examen critique de l'exégèse de M.-E. Boismard*. BETL 49. Louvain: Leuven University Press.
1984   "John and the Synotics: The Empty Tomb Stories." *NTS* 30: 161–87.

Nicol, W.
1972   *The Semeia in the Fourth Gospel*. NovTSup 32. Leiden: Brill.

Odeberg, Hugo
1929   *The Fourth Gospel Interpreted in its Relation to Contemporaneous Religious Currents in Palestine and the Hellenistic Oriental World*. Uppsala: Almqvist & Wiksell.

Pagels, Elaine H.
1973   *The Johannine Gospel in Gnostic Exegesis: Heracleon's Commentary on John*. SBLMS 17. Nashville: Abingdon.

Pancaro, Severino
1975   *The Law in the Fourth Gospel*. NovTSup 42. Leiden: Brill.

Perrin, Norman
1974   *The New Testament: An Introduction*. New York: Harcourt, Brace, Jovanovich.

Purvis, James D.
1975   "The Fourth Gospel and the Samaritans." *NovT* 17: 161–98.

Richter, Georg
1975   "Präsentische und futurische Eschatologie im 4. Evangelium." Pp. 117–52 in *Gegenwart und kommendes Reich: Schülergabe Anton Vögtle zum 65. Geburtstag*. Ed. P. Fiedler and D. Zeller. Stuttgart: Katholisches Bibelwerk.

Robinson, James M.
1971   "The Johannine Trajectory." Pp. 232–68 in *Trajectories through Early Christianity*, by J. M. Robinson and H. Koester. Philadelphia: Fortress.
1977, ed. *The Nag Hammadi Library in English*. New York: Harper & Row.

Robinson, John A. T.
1959   "The New Look on the Fourth Gospel." Pp. 338–50 in *Studia Evangelica 1*. TU 73. Berlin: Akademie.
1960   "The Destination and Purpose of St. John's Gospel." *NTS* 6: 117–31.
1976   *Redating the New Testament*. London: SCM.

Roloff, Jürgen
1968   "Der johanneischen 'Lieblingsjünger' und der Lehrer der Gerechtigkeit." *NTS* 15: 129–51.

Rudolph, Kurt
1960–61 *Die Mandäer*. FRLANT 56–57. Göttingen: Vandenhoeck & Ruprecht. Vol. I, *Prolegomena: Das Mandäerproblem;* Vol. II, *Der Kult.*
1969   "Problems of a History of the Development of the Mandaean Religion." *HR* 8: 210–35.
1970   "Die Religion der Mandäer," in *Die Religionen Altsyriens, Altarabiens und der Mandäer*. Die Religionen der Menschheit, 10: 2. Stuttgart: Kohlhammer.

Sanders, J. N.
1943   *The Fourth Gospel in the Early Church: Its Origin and Influence on Christian Theology up to Irenaeus*. Cambridge: University Press.
1968   *A Commentary on the Gospel According to St. John*. HNTC. New York: Harper & Row.

Schlatter, Adolf
1930   *Der Evangelist Johannes: Wie er spricht, denkt und glaubt*. Stuttgart: Calwer.

Schnackenburg, Rudolf
1968–82 *The Gospel According to John*. Vol. 1, New York: Herder and Herder. (Translation of remaining volumes assumed by Seabury and Crossroad; vol. 2, 1980; vol. 3, 1982.) German original: *Das Johannesevangelium*. 3 vols. HTKNT 4, 1–3. Freiburg: Herder, 1965–1976. [Vol. 1 has appeared in a revised edition, 1967.]
1970   "On the Origin of the Fourth Gospel." Pp. 223–46 in *Jesus and Man's Hope*, vol. 1. Ed. D. G. Miller and D. Y. Hadidian. Pittsburgh: Pittsburgh Theological Seminary.
1975   *Die Johannesbriefe*. 5th ed. HTKNT 13, 3. Freiburg: Herder.

Schottroff, Luise
1970   *Der Glaubende und die feindliche Welt: Beobachtungen zum gnostischen Dualismus und seiner Bedeutung für Paulus und das Johannesevangelium*. WMANT 37. Neukirchen-Vluyn: Neukirchener Verlag.

Schüssler Fiorenza, Elisabeth
1977   "The Quest for the Johannine School: The Apocalypse and the Fourth Gospel." *NTS* 23: 402–27.

Schweitzer, Albert
1931   *The Mysticism of Paul the Apostle*. New York: Holt. German original, 1930.

Scobie, C. H. H.
1973   "The Origins and Development of Samaritan Christianity." *NTS* 19: 390–414.

Segovia, Fernando
1982   *Love Relationships in the Johannine Tradition: Agapē/Agapan in 1 John and the Fourth Gospel.* SBLDS 58. Atlanta: Scholars Press.

Smalley, Stephen S.
1978   *John: Evangelist and Interpreter.* Exeter: Paternoster.
1984   *1, 2, 3 John.* Word Biblical Commentary 51. Waco, TX: Word Books.

Smith, D. Moody
1965   *The Composition and Order of the Fourth Gospel: Bultmann's Literary Theory.* Yale Publications in Religion, 10. New Haven: Yale University Press.
1975   "Johannine Christianity: Some Reflections on its Character and Delineation." *NTS* 21: 222–48.
1980   "John and the Synoptics: Some Dimensions of the Problem." *NTS* 27: 425–44.
1984   *Johannine Christianity: Essays on its Setting, Sources, and Theology.* Columbia, SC: University of South Carolina.

Talbert, Charles H.
1976   "The Myth of a Descending-Ascending Redeemer in Mediterranean Antiquity." *NTS* 22: 418–40.

Teeple, Howard
1974   *The Literary Origin of the Gospel of John.* Evanston, IL: Religion and Ethics Institute.

Thyen, Hartwig
1971   "Johannes 13 und die 'kirchliche Redaktion' des vierten Evangeliums." Pp. 343–56 in *Tradition und Glaube: Festgabe für Karl Georg Kuhn.* Ed. G. Jeremias, H.-W. Kuhn, and H. Stegemann. Göttingen: Vandenhoeck & Ruprecht.
1974–79   "Aus der Literatur zum Johannesevangelium." *TRu* 39 (1974) 1–69, 222–52, 289–330; 42 (1977) 211–79; 43 (1978) 328–59; 44 (1979) 97–134.
1977   "Entwicklungen innerhalb der johanneischen Theologie und Kirche im Spiegel von Joh. 21 und der Lieblingsjüngertexte des Evangeliums." Pp. 259–99 in *L'Évangile de Jean.* Ed. M. de Jonge. Leuven: Leuven University Press.

Wilkens, Wilhelm
1958   *Die Entstehungsgeschichte des vierten Evangeliums.* Zollikon: Evangelischer Verlag.

Windisch, Hans
1926   *Johannes und die Synoptiker.* UNT 12. Leipzig: Hinrichs.

Yamauchi, Edwin M.
1970   *Gnostic Ethics and Mandaean Origins.* HTS 24. Cambridge, MA: Harvard University Press.
1973   *Pre-Christian Gnosticism: A Survey of the Proposed Evidences.* Grand Rapids: Eerdmans.

11

LUKE-ACTS*

Charles H. Talbert

I. INTRODUCTION

Prior to the mid-forties Luke was generally viewed as a historian, and research on the Third Gospel and Acts focused on source criticism. By 1966, W. C. van Unnik could speak of the "new look" in Lucan studies that had come from Germany. Since 1950, he said, Luke-Acts has become "one of the great storm centers of New Testament scholarship" (16). As a result, Luke no longer appears "as a somewhat shadowy figure who assembled stray pieces of more or less reliable information, but as a theologian of no mean stature who very consciously and deliberately planned and executed his work" (23).

The roots of this shift from Luke the historian to Luke the self-conscious author and theologian lay in the work of M. Dibelius and R. Bultmann. On the one side, Dibelius's *Aufsätze zur Apostelgeschichte* (1951) collected earlier essays that, taken together, set forth a clear-cut method of studying Acts: style criticism. Unlike the Gospels, which were based on set tradition and were studied by means of form criticism, Acts represents the composition of an author not bound to any fixed sources and must be considered from the point of view of its style. In taking this stance, Dibelius was reflecting the view of H. J. Cadbury, whose assertion that one must first discern the art of the author before seeking the tradition behind the text he had once approvingly cited (Dibelius, 1931:240ff.). Also like Cadbury (1955), Dibelius was sensitive to the degree to which the materials of Acts participated in the literary conventions of Greco-Roman antiquity (e.g., the speeches). Dibelius's legacy to the study of Acts consisted in his attempt to deal with the literary art of the author in relation to the milieu of his time.

On the other side, Bultmann's *Theologie des Neuen Testaments* (1948–53) treated Luke-Acts in the section, "The Development toward the Ancient Church," which focused on the ecclesiastical, doctrinal, and ethical deviations from the early Christian kerygma. Luke, Bultmann said, has lost the original eschatological understanding of Jesus. He has surrendered the

* Some of the material in this article appeared earlier in "An Introduction to Acts." *RevExp* 71 (1974) 437–49, and in "Shifting Sands: The Recent Study of the Gospel of Luke," *Int* 30 (1976) 381–95, and is used with the permission of the editors.

original kerygmatic sense of the Jesus tradition and has historicized it. The author of Luke-Acts endeavors as a historian to describe the life of Jesus. The ecclesiastical office in Acts has become a guarantor of the apostolic tradition (e.g., Acts 20:18ff.). Here one finds already a view of Luke's stance that includes eschatology and early Catholicism as the central points of interest. Bultmann's legacy to the study of Luke-Acts consisted in his attempt to understand the theology of the work in relation to the occasion that prompted it and to evaluate that theology in terms of his content criticism of the canon. From Dibelius and Bultmann came the stimulus for the "new look" in Lucan studies. They attempted to understand Luke as an author who participated in the culture of his time as he gave a theological response to the issues faced by his church.

Ernst Käsemann and Philipp Vielhauer developed Bultmann's view that Luke-Acts belonged to those early Christian writings which reflected a loss of the original kerygmatic sense of the gospel. Käsemann put it: "I can acknowledge as earliest Christianity only that which still has its focus in an eschatology determined by the original imminent expectation in its changing forms. When this focus shifts, a new phase is to be established. That is undoubtedly the case with Luke" (1963:75 n. 1). Luke has replaced primitive Christian eschatology with salvation history. The Third Gospel is the first life of Jesus. When Acts is added, the apostles become guarantors of the gospel tradition (1960:130–31). Although he first became aware that Luke-Acts was not to be read primarily as history but as theology in 1941–1942, Käsemann says that the war and the immediate postwar period prevented his pursuing the literary study of the problem himself (1963:75 n. 1).

It was Hans Conzelmann and Ernst Haenchen who undertook the literary study necessary for the elaboration of the legacy from Dibelius and Bultmann. Conzelmann's *Die Mitte der Zeit* (1954) built on form criticism's contention that the Gospel framework was not a part of the original Jesus tradition but was secondary. As long as the scholar's concern was primarily historical (e.g., the quest for the historical Jesus), the study of the framework would be neglected. It remained for Conzelmann to raise the question about the interpretation of the framework as an entity in its own right. What is the structure of Luke's complete work and what is the essential meaning of that structure? Is it possible to see in the outline of the Gospel the real purpose of Luke's work as an author. The distinctive Lucan perspective, he asserted, can be seen from a comparison of Luke with his primary source, Mark. The door was now open to read Luke-Acts as theology rather than as merely history. Conzelmann believed, moreover, that Luke's position had to be located in the context of the development of the church. That is, the Lucan *tendency* had to be related to the *occasion* of the writing.

Conzelmann contended that an examination of the way the Third Evangelist handled his sources indicates that the Christian tradition has been recast so as to eliminate the primitive Christian expectation of an imminent end of the age. In the place of this expectation, the evangelist substituted a three-stage history of salvation (Israel–Jesus–Church), at the distant end of which lies the hoped-for parousia. The Lucan tendency is the recasting of primitive Christian eschatology into a history of salvation, removing the parousia to a distant future. For Conzelmann, the factor in the Lucan milieu that occasioned such a tendency was the consternation of the church caused by the delay of the parousia. The author of Luke-Acts wrote to deal with the shock experienced by the church of his time over the delay, and he reshaped the primitive tradition so as to eliminate the expectation of an imminent parousia.

Ernst Haenchen's *Die Apostelgeschichte* (1956) and Conzelmann's *Die Apostelgeschichte* (1963) did for Acts what Conzelmann's *Die Mitte der Zeit* had done for the Third Gospel. Haenchen understood Luke as a theologian who composed his work with a distinctive point of view. Faced with two problems arising from the mission to the Gentiles, Acts seeks to establish the continuity between the church and Jewish faith. By forsaking the observance of the law, does Christianity break the continuity of salvation history? By cutting free from Judaism, will Christianity become an object of suspicion to Rome? Luke holds that far from falling away from their Jewish faith, the Christians held fast to it even though God irresistibly steered them into the mission to the Gentiles. Such questions, of course, could only arise if the Lucan community no longer lived in hope of an imminent parousia. Haenchen and Conzelmann, however, are reluctant to place Luke-Acts in an "early Catholic" camp.

In the "new look" in Lucan studies that emerged in Germany after 1950, Luke is a theologian whose distinctive perspective can be discerned by careful attention to his modification of his Marcan source in the Third Gospel and to his style of composition in Acts. The Lucan theological achievement is set in Gentile Christianity's struggle to deal with the problem of the delay of the parousia by substituting the presence of the Holy Spirit in the third stage of a three-stage salvation history. In this group, moreover, some believed that the loss of the original eschatological orientation reduced the kerygmatic Jesus tradition to a historian's life of Jesus and changed the apostles into guarantors for the truth of the tradition. Such changes place Luke-Acts in the early Catholic camp and mark it as a deviation from the true gospel. So compelling did this "new look" appear in the 1960s that C. H. Dodd, in a private letter to J. E. Yates, supposedly said: "I suspect we shall have to give [the Lucan writings] over, so to speak, to Conzelmann" (Williams: 150). Only ten years later, however, Ward Gasque could conclude his exhaustive survey with this assertion: "There is no general agreement among scholars on even the most basic issues of Lucan research" (305). Although overstated, this assertion is generally true. The remainder of this essay will attempt to delineate the main lines of the developments beyond the "new look" in Lucan studies. Our discussion will unfold in terms of four questions.

II. ARE THE LUCAN THEOLOGY AND OCCASION ACCURATELY DESCRIBED BY THE NEW LOOK?

What Is the Text to Be Interpreted?

This question concerns both the matter of textual criticism and that of the unity of Luke 1–2 with the rest of Luke-Acts.

Textual Criticism

By the time of the end of World War II at least four different explanations for the existence of two text types in Luke-Acts had been proposed: the B text is original and the D text is a paraphrase (J. H. Ropes); D is original and B is an abbreviator (A. C. Clark); Luke issued his work in two forms (Blass; Zahn); B was original, was translated into Aramaic by Jewish Christians, then back into Greek as D (C. C. Torrey). In the period under discussion, there have been three main developments in research. (a) A. F. J. Klijn produced a three-part survey of research on the "Western" text (1949, 1959, 1969) and J. D. Yoder a *Concordance to the Distinctive Greek Text of Codex Bezae* (1961), giving us indispensable aids for further study. (b) Eldon Jay Epp, following the limited efforts of P. Menoud and J. Crehan, studied the D texts of Acts without reference to questions of origin and originality and concluded that D in Acts shows a decidedly heightened anti-Judaic attitude. Epp's student George E. Rice attempted to do for the D text of Luke what Epp had done for Acts, with similar results. The theological motivation of the D text seems established. (c) Among the Bodmer collection were a papyrus of Acts, Bodmer XVII (P^{74}) from the sixth or seventh century (Kasser; Prigent); and one containing parts of Luke 3–24, Bodmer XIV (P^{75}), dated between 175 and 225 C.E. (Martin; Fitzmyer, 1962). Because it is our earliest known copy of the Third Gospel, P^{75} has had a significant impact on both the United Bible Societies' Greek NT and the text of Nestle-Aland. Since P^{75} is rarely in agreement with D when this MS stands alone but seems to have an affinity for the B text (Aland: 5–13), P^{75} has had the effect of making the B text's reign supreme in the UBS and 26th Nestle edition. For example, largely as a result of P^{75} Westcott-Hort's so-called Western non-interpolations are widely rejected today as the authoritative readings. The longer readings of B and P^{75} are accepted for Luke 22:19b–20; 24:3, 6, 12, 36, 40, 51 (Snodgrass). Though protests against this procedure have been made by G. D. Kilpatrick, J. K. Elliott, J. M. Ross, and F. Stagg, the preference for the B text over the D text in Luke-Acts seems assured today largely due to the impact of P^{75}.

Luke 1-2

Conzelmann's work on Luke had ignored the first two chapters, treating them as not integral to the Third Gospel. The response to this stance has been uniformly negative. On the one hand, some scholars have accepted Conzelmann's general schema of salvation history and have tried to fit the birth narratives into that view (Oliver; Tatum). On the other hand, others have used the birth narratives to challenge Conzelmann's picture of salvation history (Minear). Today the infancy naratives are taken as integral to Luke-Acts. The text of Luke-Acts that is interpreted today is one that includes Luke 1-2 and is based largely on B and P⁷⁵.

The Occasional Nature of Lucan Theology

This occasional nature is assumed; the author functions in a pastoral way to deal with problems in the life of the church (Maddox: 2). In some ways the "new look's" description of Lucan themes has been sustained; in others it has been reversed.

Salvation History and Eschatology

Conzelmann found a three-stage salvation history in Luke-Acts (Israel–Jesus–Church). He connected it with the supposed elimination of references to an imminent end by the evangelist. Luke, he said, substituted salvation history for the expectation of an imminent end because of the delay of the parousia. Research since Conzelmann has witnessed an unsuccessful attempt to substitute a promise–fulfillment pattern for Conzelmann's three-stage history of salvation (Fitzmyer, 1979; Talbert, 1984). There has been, however, a recognition that for Luke the age of the church was divided into two eras, the apostolic age and the postapostolic age (Talbert, 1974). There is widespread agreement that an expectation of an imminent end is found in Luke-Acts (Kümmel; Geiger; Francis; Talbert, 1970; Mattill, 1972; Hiers; Franklin). This is in no way contradictory to a Lucan salvation history. From the Lucan vantage point, all the stages of holy history have already taken place except the end, that cosmic event which occurs at the end of a series of unfolding stages. Most devastating to Conzelmann's reconstruction is the fact that subsequent scholars have been able to interpret the Lucan effort to write in terms of salvation history as due to a number of different occasions other than a delayed parousia: an over-realized eschatology (Talbert, 1970), acute apocalypticism (Ellis, 1966; Danker), both over-realized eschatology and a loss of hope altogether (Bartsch), both acute apocalypticism and loss of hope altogether (Wilson, 1970, 1973), and the need to establish continuity between the church and Israel (Jervell; Löning). Even if Luke did remove the end into the future, there is no compelling reason to relate this act to the delay of the parousia. Furthermore, alongside Luke's cosmic eschatology there is an individual hope (Flender; Ernst): at death the believer goes to paradise to be with Jesus. Finally, there has been a reluctance on the part of some scholars to regard Lucan eschatology as unique. It is similar to Mark (Geiger) or goes ultimately back to Jesus (Ellis, 1965-66).

Christology and Soteriology

Conzelmann's views on Christology include both a stance on proper method and a certain content. Regarding method, he says that the special elements in Luke's Christology cannot be set out by a statistical analysis of the titles applied to Jesus. Rather Lucan Christology is seen in the context of the total view of salvation history. Regarding content, he sets forth the Lucan Jesus in terms of past, present, and future. The historical Jesus has been relegated to the past as the bearer of the Spirit, preacher of the Kingdom, and gatherer of the witnesses. The exalted Christ of the present is the bestower of the Spirit. Not only is he present to his church as a figure from the past by means of the picture of him presented by tradition; but also he is active through such means as the power of his name, which heals, and appearances to apostles. In the future Jesus will be the eschatological judge.

Research since Conzelmann is divided over the proper way to discern Lucan Christology. Does one concentrate on the titles used for Jesus (Smalley; Jones), or does one look for the overall structure of the Lucan picture of Jesus (Talbert, 1968-69; Kränkl)? On this point Conzelmann seems on target. The question of whether Luke's Christology is adoptionistic has been debated, and some hold the negative (Rese; Jones; Ernst) and others the positive (Lövestam). Though Jesus may proleptically be called Son of God prior to the exaltation in Acts 2 (cf. Acts 13:31-33), it seems impossible to disregard the exaltation as the moment when the sonship is actualized (Marshall, 1970:179-80). There have also been claims that we confront an absentee Christ after the ascension and that Jesus is replaced by the Holy Spirit and is present in history only in the tradition about him (Moule: 179-81; Drury: 176). This has been rightly rejected. Although the relationship with the risen Christ is not a mystical one for Luke-Acts, Christians are by no means restricted to contact with him through the story about him (MacRae; Marshall, 1970:179-82; O'Toole: 119). Attention has been called to the fact that the overall structure of the Lucan picture of Jesus is very much like that found in the myth of immortals in Mediterranean antiquity: (1) miraculous birth; (2) life of virtue; (3) taken to heaven, as evidenced by the facts that his material remains cannot be found, that he appears to friends, that there have been prophecies of the event, and that he is seen ascending into heaven by reliable people; and (4) from heaven he intervenes in behalf of his cause and his people when they are in need (Talbert, 1975).

Conzelmann said that Luke did not develop a positive doctrine of the redemptive significance of the cross. There was for him no connection between Jesus' death and the forgiveness of sins. Further, just as the eschaton for Luke signified no longer present but future circumstances, so also eternal life is removed by Luke into the distant future.

The view that Luke did not connect Jesus' death with the forgiveness of sins has either been sustained or modified only slightly by subsequent research. In Luke-Acts Jesus' death is viewed primarily as part of the divine plan and as a martyrdom of a righteous man, which serves as the dominical basis for Christian suffering (Talbert, 1966:71–82; Schneider, 1973:167; Glöckner). For Luke it is the glorification-exhaltation of Jesus that enables him to be a cause of salvation for people (Zehnle; Marshall, 1970:169). This view of Jesus' death is related to the Lucan understanding of the eucharist not as a remembrance of Christ's death but as an occasion for the exalted Lord to be present in the congregation (Wanke). Conzelmann's judgment that salvation is moved into the distant future for Luke has not been sustained. It has been shown that, whereas in Paul *sōzein* usually refers to final salvation (e.g., Rom 5:9–10), in Luke-Acts it applies almost exclusively to the present. Salvation includes healing as well as forgiveness. It is associated with faith. It comes about not only through hearing the word but also through contact with the miraculous (Throckmorton). Luke has a very positive view of the evangelical benefits of miracle, though he is not so naïve as to reduce one's being saved to being healed (Achtemeier; Busse).

Israel and the Church

Conzelmann's description of the Lucan understanding of the church did not go so far as that of Käsemann and others. The church, he said, is not yet considered a factor in salvation in the sense of its being an object of faith. It appears only as the necessary medium of the message to us. Further, the present office-bearers are authorized by the Spirit, not yet by any particular succession. Haenchen deals in more detail with the relationship between Israel and the church. On the one hand, the Christians held fast to their Jewish faith and only turned exclusively to the Gentiles when the gospel was refused by the Jews. On the other hand, unlike Paul, Luke has abandoned hope of converting Israel. Luke's church directs its mission solely to Gentiles.

Subsequent research has been divided on the issue of a Jewish-Christian succession in Luke-Acts, some favoring it (von Campenhausen; Talbert, 1966, 1974; S. Brown; Schürmann, 1968a), others opposing it (Barrett, 1961; Grässer, 1977:281–82). At present the issue is moot. Jervell has argued that from Luke's perspective the mission to the Gentiles does not arise because Israel has rejected the gospel. Jewish rejection of the missionary message is not the decisive presupposition for the Gentile mission. Rather, for Luke, Israel has not rejected the gospel but has become divided over the issue. Because some in Israel have accepted the gospel, the way can be opened to the Gentiles. The Gentiles have been joined to the Israel that has accepted salvation. In this way the continuity of salvation history has been maintained. In this Jervell is joined by G. Lohfink (1975) and P. Zingg. This explains why there is still an Israel alongside and unrelated to the Christian church, to which the church is not obligated. Only rarely (Wainwright; Karris, 1979) does one find the claim that Luke, like Paul, holds out a hope for the conversion of unrepentant Israel. Most hold that the break with the synagogue is complete (Jervell; R. E. Brown; Lampe).

The Christian Life

Conzelmann's almost total absorption in the interpretation of Luke-Acts from the point of view of an adjustment to a delayed parousia determined that his account of the Christian life in Luke-Acts would be restricted. He was concerned with arguing that for Luke eschatology no longer functioned as a summons but influenced ethics by the idea of judgment.

In subsequent research the emphasis has been more on the content of the ethical stance enjoined by Luke and less on its motive. Two areas deserve comment. *Possessions* are a major concern of Luke. Contrary to Dupont's contention (1973:149–203) that Luke's community consisted only of the poor, Degenhardt (1965) and Karris (1978) establish the fact that the Lucan church was composed of both rich and poor. Much of the evangelist's time is taken up with the rich members, their concerns, and the problems they pose for the community. One of the author's major concerns is to counter the Hellenistic ethic of reciprocity. *Prayer* is another dominant concern in Luke-Acts. Two primary emphases may be discerned. W. Ott has called attention to the evangelist's concern to foster prayer among his readers as they wait for the parousia so that they may escape temptation and be found faithful at the judgment. O'Brien (1973) and Trites (1978) focus on prayer in Luke-Acts as the instrument by which God directs the course of holy history both in the life of Jesus and in the development of the church. Since the latter is true, the former is desirable.

What Occasion Prompted the Lucan Response?

What was the occasion that prompted the Lucan response? When and where did it occur? J. C. O'Neill's second-century dating has been generally rejected. Determination of a Lucan locale—Rome, Ephesus, Achaia, Antioch of Syria, Caesarea—is mere guesswork. The list of problems that may have provoked the two-volume work includes the delay of the parousia, gnosticism (Klein; Roloff; Talbert, 1966; Schürmann, 1968b), suffering-persecution (Schütz), rich and poor (Karris, 1978), apology for Paul to Romans or Jews (Jervell; Mattill, 1970), or the need to defend the continuity of salvation history (Löning; Maddox). The list could go on. Redaction criticism has not been successful in describing the Lucan community and its *Sitz im Leben* ("life setting").

Though incomplete, an outline of the Lucan theological perspective seems to be emerging among scholars. Nevertheless, redaction criticism has been unable to delineate either the Lucan purpose or the Lucan *Sitz im Leben*. The usual procedure has been to trace a theological theme through Luke-Acts and then, on the basis of one's results, to infer an occasion for it. Problems arise (1) when one has to arbitrate among the many competing themes in the two-volume work and assign positions of relative importance to them; (2) when one has to do an analogous thing among the proposed occasions; and (3) when one has to decide an elementary question such as whether or not the readers are Gentile or Jewish Christians. In sum, redaction criticism has enabled us to see the author as a creative theologian with a perspective of his own and to discern parts of that point of view. It has not enabled us to grasp Luke's purpose in the context of his *Sitz im Leben*. The issue before us today is this: How can one discern the unity of the author's thought and thereby infer what are the central problems of his time and place?

III. IS THE ASSESSMENT OF THE LUCAN THEOLOGY CORRECT?

In the "new look" to Luke-Acts that emerged in Germany after 1950, Lucan theology was often regarded as suspect (so Käsemann and Vielhauer but not Conzelmann and Haenchen). It represented early Catholicism. After 1945 the predicate "early Catholic" was used by the Bultmann school in order to differentiate writings, layers, and elements in the NT from its kerygmatic center, the actual gospel. The roots again go back into Bultmann's *Theologie des Neuen Testaments*. This two-volume work must be read against the background of the old Protestant view of church history. According to this view, there was an originally ideal NT church that was followed by a falling away into Catholicism. So in Bultmann's *Theologie* one meets a normative Christian stance in Paul and John, after which there is a falling away. In contrast to the old Protestant view, however, in Bultmann's work this falling away already begins in the NT itself. In polity, doctrine, and ethics, the developments after Paul and alongside John reflect this falling away. This means that the NT contains at least two strata—a kerygmatic center (the true gospel) and a layer that has deserted the kerygmatic understanding of existence. In the Bultmann school this second layer has been called "early Catholicism." Into this early Catholic layer various scholars have included 2 Peter, Jude, Ephesians, the Pastorals, parts of Matthew, and Luke-Acts.

W. G. Kümmel has attempted a summary of the debate in Germany. To the five basic criticisms of Lucan theology [(1) Luke knows nothing of the near expectation of the kingdom, (2) does not understand Jesus' death as a saving event, (3) holds to the notion of "succession," and (4) therefore thinks there are guarantees for the Christian tradition so that faith's assurance is handed over to human accomplishment, and (5) misunderstands the kerygma evidenced by the existence of Acts after the Gospel], Kümmel has summarized the responses made: (1) Luke does know the expectation of the near end, (2) does not entirely remove the redemptive significance of Jesus' death (e.g., Luke 22:19b–20; Acts 20:28) though his chief emphasis is on Jesus' death as corresponding to God's will, (3) does not reflect on apostolic succession, and (4) recounts the history of Jesus not as a mere historian but as do Matthew and Mark, with the aim of proclamation. Finally, (5) since the kerygma Paul received (1 Cor 15:3ff.) presupposes that the resurrection experience of witnesses must also be portrayed in designating the basis of Christian faith, the presence of Acts is no betrayal of a primitive Christian stance. Kümmel concludes that it is wrong to say that Luke's theology is illegitimate/early Catholic. Luke remains, in the main lines of his theology, in agreement with the central proclamation of the NT (i.e., Jesus, Paul, John). Without a doubt, Luke belongs to the most important, and for us normative, witnesses to the NT proclamation.

The basic problem is the ambiguity of the term "early Catholic" (Barrett, 1972:99–100). Sometimes it is used so loosely that it can mean that Luke-Acts reflects a canon concept, a concept of a summary or summaries of faith, and a concept of episcopacy committed to preserving the true faith. In this case, Luke-Acts is probably early Catholic. At other times, however, the term is used to denote such things as (1) a moralization of the faith and a conception of the gospel as a new law (legalism), (2) a trend toward sacramentalism, and (3) a conception of the ministry as the authoritative teaching office which legitimates the word. In this case, Luke-Acts is not early Catholic (Talbert, 1970; Morris).

What is needed are two sets of categories: one to describe the new forms of Christianity that emerged after the first generation and the other to designate the varieties of Christianity possessing essential discontinuity with early Christianity's understanding of Christian life and faith. Early Catholic is an appropriate term for the emerging form of Christianity that was characterized by canon, creed, and episcopacy. It is necessary, however, to follow the lead of the old Catholic church in its process of canonization and to distinguish between two types of early Catholicism, normative and non-normative. When this is done, Luke-Acts can be accurately designated as normative early Catholic. Its view of Christian life and faith does not represent a falling away from Christian truth. In this we may agree with Kümmel.

IV. IS THE METHOD WORKABLE?

How does one arrive at the theology of Luke? The methodology varies in the Third Gospel and in Acts. Insofar as the Gospel is concerned,

Conzelmann says: "We must start from a methodological comparison with his [Luke's] sources, in so far as these are directly available or can be reconstructed" (4; Eng. trans. 12). Assuming the Two-Source theory, Conzelmann believed that Luke's theology could be discerned especially from Luke's alteration of Mark. This methodology has been widely accepted. The scholar notes a particular change made by Luke; if he is aware that the effect of this change is consistent with the effect of changes the author has made elsewhere, then he infers that the change reflects a tendency of the evangelist. Since the question of sources for Acts is impossible to settle with any finality (Dupont, 1960), the method used here is like one's work on Mark or the Fourth Gospel. One may infer something about a tradition behind the Lucan narrative, but there is no possibility of checking for minute changes by the author from some connected written source before him.

Questions about method focus primarily on work done in the Third Gospel. These questions group themselves in two categories: questions related to sources and questions about procedure generally. In the first place, the whole question of the sources behind the Third Gospel has become uncertain. Tim Schram argues that one must distinguish two groups of material in Luke where Luke runs parallel to Mark. Group 1 contains material that comes from Mark, so that all differences from Mark are due to the third evangelist. Group 2 consists of material that is under the influence of variant traditions. In this second group the task is to distinguish between Mark, the pre-Lucan tradition that is non-Marcan, and the redaction of the evangelist. Here divergences from Mark cannot, without further evidence, be taken as due to the evangelist. In this case, literary criticism attempts to serve as a corrective to redaction-critical work on Luke. Schram's point — that not every difference from Mark that one finds in Luke, where they run parallel, is a reflection of the evangelist's editorial activity — is one that has been made for years by advocates of the Proto-Luke hypothesis generally and by contenders for an independent Lucan passion narrative in particular (Taylor; Schürmann, 1953, 1955, 1957; Schneider, 1969). Given these contentions, deriving Luke's theology from an observation of changes he makes in his Marcan source becomes extremely difficult. Furthermore, in the last fifteen years there has been a significant assault on the Two-Source theory. British scholars like John Drury will accept the priority of Mark but not the existence of Q. Luke uses Mark and Matthew as his sources, along with the OT and a great deal of creativity. On such a literary theory, M. D. Goulder builds a picture of Luke as a liturgical book constructed on a calendrical pattern. Others, like W. R. Farmer, question even the priority of Mark: Luke uses Matthew and some independent tradition. Although these alternatives have not proved convincing, enough difficulties with Marcan priority have emerged to render its position as an "assured result" of criticism suspect and to make it a questionable control on redaction-critical work (Tyson). Employing Mark as a control today is about as compelling as using Colossians and 2 Thessalonians to describe Paul's theology. It may very well be legitimate to do so, but so many have problems with the procedure that such an assumption narrows considerably the scholarly circles within which one can converse. In the past, one has been able to use themes picked up in the Third Gospel by noting divergences of Luke from Mark as a control on one's reading of Acts. Now this control is removed, at least in the form that presupposes the priority of Mark.

In the second place, the entire procedure of noting an author's differences from his main source and deriving his theological perspective from that has been questioned. Marshall (1970:19–20) and Schütz (19) have asked whether Lucan theology should be sought only in the places where the evangelist differs from tradition instead of also in the areas where he reproduces tradition with little or no change. They argue that the fact that Luke took over the tradition shows that he regarded it as important. Hence, the traditions he took over should not be regarded as awkward intrusions into his work but rather as its basis. If we confine our attention to what can be clearly identified as redactional, we stand in danger of producing an eccentric picture of Lucan theology. Minear (1976:83) also rejects the effort to recover Luke's theology almost wholly by the use of a synoptic harmony and by careful scrutiny of every variant between the Lucan text and an earlier source. "The interdependence of these two volumes is such that the purposes of volume one can be most clearly discerned by observing the contents and sequences of volume two." This is certainly not the usual redaction-critical method. The fact that the same type of protest can be picked up in studies of Matthew (Waetjen: 18) and Mark (Donahue: 64) indicates that this is not a problem unique to Lucan study.

Since the question of Luke's sources is almost as debatable in the Third Gospel as in Acts, and since the entire procedure of basing Lucan theology on variants from Mark is questionable in any case, the issue before us today is this: How can one study the distinctive perspective of Luke-Acts without assuming any source theories? In this regard, the problem is the same as that faced with Mark and John all along.

Two questions have emerged from recent research on Luke-Acts: (1) How can one discern the unity of the evangelist's thought, given the many different themes isolated by redaction criticism? (2) How can one delineate the distinctive perspective of the author without assuming any source theories? Rohde has observed: "The history of the study of the synoptic gospels is . . . the history of the changing methods used in the endeavour to obtain fresh knowledge" (1). Since redaction criticism associated with the "new look" in Lucan studies has been unable to resolve the first issue and has not attempted to deal with the second, the question arises whether or not we are at a point where a new methodology would contribute significantly to our understanding of Luke-Acts? François Bovon speaks for many when he says that the redaction-critical method seems to be exhausting itself and that we stand on the brink of a new stage of Lucan study (1976).

Recent years have witnessed a good deal of experimentation in methodology designed to cope with the inadequacies of redaction criticism: (1) In vol. 58 of *Recherches de Science Religieuse* (1970) there appeared a series of articles devoted to structuralist analysis of Acts 10–11. Not only did these essays not assist with the problem of the author's thought taken as a whole, they offered little that was useful or new on the passage under consideration. (2) Literary criticism, not in the sense of source theory but in the sense in which it is practiced by nonbiblical literary critics, has been offered also as a way of moving beyond the redaction-critical impasse. Norman Petersen's *Literary Criticism for New Testament Critics* (1978) focuses on the narrative world of a document with its characters and plot. One of his examples of the working out of his method is Luke-Acts. He argues that the rejection of God's agents by God's people in connection with God's sanctuaries is *the* plot device by which the movement of the narrative *as a whole* is motivated. Certainly this method offers us a way to work on the text without assuming any source theories. What Petersen has isolated, however, is only one theme—and that hardly the central one in Luke-Acts. The method, moreover, leaves unanswered the basic question: How can one discern the unity of the evangelist's thought?

Alongside the new approaches attempted in the study of Luke, the legacy of Cadbury and Dibelius continues to bear fruit in the study of Acts. The comparison of Lucan forms and techniques of composition with those of the Mediterranean milieu, pagan and Jewish, has yielded major results: (1) Eckhard Plümacher (1972) has shown how in Acts the author used his missionary discourses, as did Dionysius of Halicarnassus and Livy, to indicate the motive forces behind crucial historical events; how Luke's use of Septuagintal style was analogous to the Hellenistic practice of imitation of Attic authors; how in Acts the use of archaism parallels what one finds in Livy; and how Luke's use of dramatic episode parallels what we find in Livy and certain romances. (2) Vernon Robbins (1975, 1978) and Plümacher (1977) have independently demonstrated that the "we-sections" of Acts are due to a literary convention found widely in Mediterranean antiquity and have nothing to say about any source the author may have used. (3) J. W. Bowker's analysis of the speeches in Acts 2; 3; 7; 12; and 15 in terms of the proem and *yelammedenu* (request for instruction) homilies of ancient Judaism casts fresh light on texts that have been worked on endlessly. (4) Lohfink's (1975) understanding of the three accounts of Paul's conversion in Acts in terms of the "apparition dialogue" form of the LXX and other Hellenistic Jewish writings is fresh and instructive. (5) The reading of Acts 27–28 in light of pagan and Jewish beliefs about divine retribution being mediated through storm at sea and snakebite has been established by Miles and Trompf and seconded by Ladonceur. This general type of approach works independently of any source theories. It draws its insights from a knowledge of the Greco-Roman milieu's literary conventions. Valuable as such an approach is, it has thus far stopped short of any attempt to deal with Luke-Acts as a whole.

It is at this point, the concern to grasp Luke-Acts as a whole but in terms of the literary conventions of its time, that genre criticism enters the picture. In the last decade literary critics have seen that a particular text standing alone is a problem because it lacks meaning. The interpretative rule "What is said must be understood in its context" works well for a word in a sentence, for a sentence in a paragraph, for a paragraph in a section, and for a section in a document as a whole. But what is the context for the whole? This question has led criticism to the attempt to view the individual text (i.e., the document as a whole) in terms of a universal type or configuration that is constructed on the basis of an inductive grouping of texts with common features. It is the particular text's participation in the universal type that gives it a first level of meaning. The particular text's transformation of the universal type-structure-genre is then seen as a further way of saying something about the meaning of the document taken as a whole. If the critic looks for those structures that have a definite function in a specific social and cultural context, as genre critics seem to do, then the boundaries of time, geography, and culture are crucial. The universal type-structure-genre is constructed from texts that come from a specific locale during a specific era. The critic's task is seen as viewing the individual writing in terms of a universal type or configuration constructed on the basis of an inductive grouping of texts with common features.

There are four main answers given to the question about the genre of Luke-Acts: it is (1) history, either in the tradition of Thucydides (Bruce) or Hellenistic historiography (Dahl: 88); (2) historical monograph (Conzelmann, 1963:6; Hengel: 36); (3) biography, either parallel biographies as in Plutarch's *Parallel Lives* (Radl) or the life of a founder followed by a list or narrative of his successors, as in some of the lives of philosophers used in Diogenes Laertius and the life of the monastic founder, Pachomius (Talbert, 1974, 1977; Schneider, 1977a); or (4) romance (Pervo). Only Pervo and Talbert have argued their cases with any thoroughness. The jury is still out on the issue. If the verdict can be reached, the genre of Luke-Acts might provide the clue for the relative ordering of the various themes isolated by redaction criticism and for the primary occasion that prompted the document. This methodology, moreover, need presuppose no source theories for Luke-Acts.

It is still too early to see the final shape of a methodology that will supersede redaction criticism. It is not unlikely, however, that it will combine elements of modern literary criticism, genre criticism, and the type of comparative study now being done in Acts.

V. WHAT ABOUT QUESTIONS NOT
ADDRESSED BY REDACTION CRITICISM?

The thrust of the "new look" in Lucan studies was that, at the very least, Luke-Acts reflects the faith of its author and of his community. In contrast to the views of William Ramsay at an earlier time, today's scholar sees Luke-Acts not as the product of a historian's careful work but as the composition of a preacher or theologian. At the very least, Luke is viewed as theologically interpreted tradition. At the extreme, Acts is regarded as a religiously motivated historical romance, an early Christian novel. This raises the question of how far Luke, and especially Acts, preserves reliable historical tradition about Jesus and the early church. Today the burden of proof rests on anyone who would read Acts as other than theology (Mattill, 1978). Wilckens's study (1961) of the missionary speeches in Acts is representative. Research on the speeches has moved from taking them as sermons of Peter and Paul, through taking them as examples of the earliest kerygma, to taking them as Lucan compositions.

Certain historical problems are assumed to be settled in favor of Lucan error (e.g., the date of the census [Moehring; R. E. Brown: 547–56]; the inverted order of Theudas and Judas in Acts 5 [Hanson: 86]) or are regarded as insoluble (e.g., the relation of Paul's visits to Jerusalem in Galatians and Acts, where at least eight solutions vie with one another [Talbert, 1967:26 n. 3; de Lacy]). In general, the quest for the historical Jesus is matched in difficulty by the quest for the historical apostolic age.

This state of affairs has brought protests from at least three quarters: (1) Jervell has argued successfully that apostolic traditions were preserved by the church for the same reasons that the Jesus materials were. This, however, says nothing about the reliability of the traditions. (2) Marshall (1970: chap. 3) repeats Ramsay's argument that accurate background information argues for Lucan historicity. Cadbury (120) has made it clear, however, that accurate local color in no way proves general historical accuracy. (3) Ward Gasque's tendentious history of the criticism of Acts serves as a useful bolt from the blue to jar research from its complacency, as does Hengel's critique of much critical orthodoxy, but they cannot do more than call us to a renewed sifting of the Lucan sands grain by grain.

Lucan research since World War II has been dominated by the quest for Luke the theologian using redaction criticism in Luke and style criticism in Acts. This has resulted in both a new appreciation of Luke as a theologian alongside Paul and John and in an increased skepticism about the historical accuracy of Luke's work. In recent years doubts have arisen about the adequacy of the redaction-critical method and a protest has been heard against current historical skepticism. A new methodology seems likely to emerge that will not depend on any source theories and that will be able to come to terms with the unity of Lucan thought. It is doubtful that any major breakthrough will occur in establishing the historicity of Acts, given our present knowledge. Of all contributions made by research since World War II, it is the working tools that may benefit us most in the end: histories of research (Bieder; Bovon, 1978; Conzelmann, 1978; Gasque; Grässer, 1976, 1977; Mattill, 1959; Rasco; Plümacher, 1983; Richard), bibliographies (Mattill, 1965; Rasco; Mills), critical concordances (Baird; Morton and Michaelson), and major commentaries on Acts (Haenchen; Conzelmann, 1963; Marshall, 1980; Roloff, 1981; Schneider, 1980–82) and on Luke (Schürmann, 1969; Marshall, 1977; Schneider, 1977b; Ernst; Fitzmyer, 1981–85). At the same time, dissatisfaction with the way commentaries are written foreshadows a change of format in the future (Oliver, 1982; Talbert, 1982).

BIBLIOGRAPHY

Achtemeier, Paul J.
1975   "The Lucan Perspective on the Miracles of Jesus: A Preliminary Sketch." *JBL* 94: 547–62.

Aland, Kurt
1964–65 "Neue Neutestamentliche Papyri II." *NTS* 11: 1–21.

Baird, J. A.
1971   *A Critical Concordance to the Synoptic Gospels.* Wooster, OH: Biblical Research Associates.

Barrett, Charles Kingsley
1961   *Luke the Historian in Recent Study.* London: Epworth.
1972   *New Testament Essays.* London: SPCK.

Bartsch, Hans-Werner
1963   *Wachet aber zu jeder Zeit! Entwurf einer Auslegung des Lukasevangeliums.* Hamburg: Herbert Reich.

Bieder, Werner
1960   *Die Apostelgeschichte in der Historie: Ein Beitrag zur Auslegungsgeschichte des Missionsbuches der Kirche.* ThStud 61. Zurich: EVZ Verlag.

Bovon, François
1976   "Orientations actuelles des études lucaniennes." *RTP* 26: 161–90.
1978   *Luc le théologien: Vingt-cinq ans de recherches (1950–75).* Le monde de la Bible. Neuchâtel and Paris: Delachaux & Niestlé.

Bowker, J. W.
1967   "Speeches in Acts: A Study in Proem and Yellammedenu Form." *NTS* 14: 96–110.

Brown, Raymond E.
1977   *The Birth of the Messiah: A Commentary on the Infancy Narratives in Matthew and Luke.* Garden City, NY: Doubleday.

Brown, Schuyler
1969   *Apostasy and Perseverance in the Theology of Luke.* AnBib 36. Rome: Biblical Institute Press.

Bruce, F. F.
1976 "The New Testament and Classical Studies." NTS 22: 229–42.

Bultmann, Rudolf Karl
1948–53 Theologie des Neuen Testaments. Tübingen: Mohr. Eng. trans. by K. Grobel: Theology of the New Testament. 2 vols. New York: Scribner, 1951–55.

Busse, Ulrich
1977 Die Wunder der Propheten Jesus: Die Rezeption, Komposition und Interpretation der Wundertradition im Evangelium des Lukas. Stuttgart: Katholisches Bibelwerk.

Cadbury, Henry Joel
1955 The Book of Acts in History. London: Adam & Charles Black.

Campenhausen, Hans von
1969 "Tradition and Succession in the Second Century." Pp. 149–77 in Ecclesiastical Authority and Spiritual Power. Trans. J. A. Baker. London: Black.

Conzelmann, Hans
1954 Die Mitte der Zeit: Studien zur Theologie des Lukas. BHT 17. Tübingen: Mohr-Siebeck. Eng. trans. by G. Buswell: The Theology of St. Luke. New York: Harper, 1960. Reprinted, Philadelphia: Fortress, 1982.
1963 Die Apostelgeschichte. HNT 7. Tübingen: Mohr-Siebeck. Eng. trans. by J. Limberg, A. T. Kraabel, and D. Juel: Acts of the Apostles. Hermeneia. Ed. E. J. Epp with C. R. Matthews. Philadelphia: Fortress, 1987.
1978 "Literatur zu den Synoptischen Evangelien." TRu 43: 3–51.

Crehan, Joseph
1957 "Peter according to the D-text of Acts." TS 18: 596–603.

Dahl, N. A.
1976 Jesus in the Memory of the Early Church: Essays by Nils Alstrup Dahl. Minneapolis: Augsburg.

Danker, Frederick W.
1972 Jesus and the New Age according to St. Luke. St. Louis: Clayton.

Degenhardt, Hans Joachim
1965 Lukas, Evangelist der Armen. Stuttgart: Katholisches Biblewerk.

Dibelius, Martin
1931 "Zur Formgeschichte des Neuen Testament (ausserhalb der Evangelien)." TRu 3: 207–42.
1951 Aufsätze zur Apostelgeschichte. Ed. Heinrich Greeven. Göttingen: Vandenhoeck & Ruprecht. Eng. trans. by Mary Ling: Studies in the Acts of the Apostles. London: SCM, 1956.

Donahue, John R.
1976 "Temple, Trial, and Royal Christology (Mark 14:53–65.)" Pp. 61–79 in The Passion in Mark. Ed. Werner H. Kelber. Philadelphia: Fortress.

Drury, John
1976 Tradition and Design in Luke's Gospel. Atlanta: John Knox.

Dupont, Jacques
1960   *Les sources du Livre des Actes: Etat de la question.* Bruges: Desclée
          de Brouwer. Eng. trans. by K. Pond: *The Sources of Acts: The Present
          Position.* London: Darton, Longman & Todd, 1964.
1973   *Les Béatitudes,* vol. 3. Paris: Gabalda.

Elliott, J. K.
1973–74   "The United Bible Societies Greek New Testament: An Evaluation."
          NovT 15: 278–300.

Ellis, E. Earle
1965–66   "Present and Future in Luke." *NTS* 12: 27–41.
1966   *The Gospel of Luke.* London: Nelson.

Epp, Eldon Jay
1966   *The Theological Tendency of Codex Bezae Cantabrigiensis in Acts.*
          SNTSMS 3. Cambridge: University Press.

Ernst, Josef
1977   *Das Evangelium nach Lukas.* Regensburg: Pustet.

Farmer, W. R.
1964   *The Synoptic Problem: A Critical Analysis.* New York: Macmillan.

Fitzmyer, Joseph A.
1962   "Papyrus Bodmer XIV: Some Features of Our Oldest Text of Luke."
          CBQ 24: 170–79.
1979   Review of *Das Evangelium nach Lukas* by Josef Ernst. *TS* 40: 349–51.
1981–85   *The Gospel according to Luke.* 2 vols. AB 28, 28A. Garden City, NY:
          Doubleday.

Flender, Helmut
1965   *Heil und Geschichte in der Theologie des Lukas.* Munich: Kaiser. Eng.
          trans. by R. H. and I. Fuller: *St. Luke: Theologian of Redemptive
          History.* Philadelphia: Fortress, 1967.

Francis, Fred O.
1969   "Eschatology and History in Luke-Acts." *JAAR* 37: 49–63.

Franklin, Eric
1975   *Christ the Lord: A Study in the Purpose and Theology of Luke-Acts.*
          London: SPCK.

Gasque, W. Ward
1975   *A History of the Criticism of the Acts of the Apostles.* Tübingen: Mohr-
          Siebeck. Reprinted, Grand Rapids: Eerdmans, 1975.

Geiger, Ruthild
1973   *Die lukanischen Endzeitreden: Studien zur Eschatologie des Lukas-
          Evangeliums.* Bern: H. Lang.

Glöckner, Richard
1976   *Die Verkündigung des Heils beim Evangelisten Lukas.* Mainz: Matthias
          Grünewald.

Goulder, Michael D.
1978   *The Evangelist's Calendar: A Lectionary Explanation of the Develop-
          ment of Scripture.* London: SPCK.

Grässer, Erich
1976   "Acta Forschung seit 1960." *TRu* ns 41: 141–94, 259–90; 42: 1–68.

Haenchen, Ernst
1956   *Die Apostelgeschichte neu übersetzt und erklärt.* MeyerK 3. Göttin-
           gen: Vandenhoeck & Ruprecht. Eng. trans.: *The Acts of the Apostles:
           A Commentary.* Philadelphia: Westminster, 1971.
Hanson, Richard P. C.
1967   *Acts.* New York: Oxford University Press.
Hengel, Martin
1979   *Acts and the History of Earliest Christianity.* Philadelphia: Fortress.
Hiers, Richard H.
1974   "The Problem of the Delay of the Parousia in Luke-Acts." *NTS* 20:
           145-54.
Jervell, Jacob
1972   *Luke and the People of God: A New Look at Luke-Acts.* Minneapolis:
           Augsburg.
Jones, Donald L.
1970   "The Title *Christos* in Luke-Acts." *CBQ* 32: 69-76.
1974   "The Title *Kyrios* in Luke-Acts." Pp. 85-101 in *SBL 1974 Seminar
           Papers.* Ed. George W. MacRae. Missoula, MT: Scholars Press.
Karris, Robert
1978   "Poor and Rich: The Lucan Sitz im Leben." Pp. 112-25 in *Perspec-
           tives on Luke-Acts.* Ed. Charles H. Talbert. Danville, VA: Association
           of Baptist Professors of Religion.
1979   "Missionary Communities: A New Paradigm for the Study of Luke-
           Acts." *CBQ* 41: 80-97.
Käsemann, Ernst
1960   "Amt und Gemeinde im Neuen Testament." Pp. 109-34 in *Exege-
           tische Versuche und Besinnungen,* vol. 1. Göttingen: Vandenhoeck &
           Ruprecht.
1963   "Paulus und der Frühkatholizismus." *ZTK* 60: 75-89. Reprinted,
           pp. 239-52 in *Exegetische Versuche und Besinnungen,* vol. 2. Göttin-
           gen: Vandenboeck & Ruprecht, 1964. Eng. trans.: "Paul and Early
           Catholicism." Pp. 236-51 in *New Testament Questions of Today.*
           Philadelphia: Fortress, 1969.
Kasser, Rodolphe, ed.
1961   *Papyrus Bodmer XVII: Actes des Apôtres, Epîtres de Jacques, Pierre,
           Jean et Jude.* Cologny-Genève: Bibliotheca Bodmeriana.
Kilpatrick, George D.
1966   Review of the *United Bible Societies Greek New Testament. JBL* 85:
           479-81.
Klein, Günter
1961   *Die zwölf Apostel: Ursprung und Gehalt einer Idee.* FRLANT 77.
           Göttingen: Vandenhoeck & Ruprecht.
Klijn, A. F. J.
1949   *A Survey of the Researches into the Western Text of the Gospels and
           Acts.* Utrecht: Kemink.
1959   "A Survey of the Researches into the Western Text of the Gospels
           and Acts (1949-59)." *NovT* 3: 1-27, 161-73.
1969   *A Survey of the Researches into the Western Text of the Gospels and
           Acts: Part Two, 1949-69.* NovTSup 21. Leiden: Brill.

Kränkl, E.
1972   *Jesus der Knecht Gottes: Die heilsgeschichtliche Stellung Jesu in den Reden der Apostelgeschichte.* Regensburg: Pustet.

Kümmel, Werner Georg
1972   "Lukas in der Anklage der heutigen Theologie." ZNW 63: 149–65.

Lacey, D. R. de
1973   "Paul in Jerusalem." NTS 20: 82–86.

Ladonceur, D.
1980   "Hellenistic Preconceptions of Shipwreck and Pollution as a Context for Acts 27–28." HTR 73: 435–49.

Lampe, G. W. H.
1969   *St. Luke and the Church of Jerusalem.* London: Athlone.

Lohfink, Gerhard
1967   *Paulus vor Damaskus.* 3d ed. Stuttgart: Katholisches Bibelwerk.
1975   *Die Sammlung Israels: Eine Untersuchung zur lukanischen Ekklesiologie.* Munich: Kösel.

Löning, Karl
1973   *Die Saulustradition in der Apostelgeschichte.* Münster: Aschendorff.

Lövestam, Evald
1961   *Son and Saviour: A Study of Acts 13,32–37.* Trans. M. J. Petry. ConNT 18. Lund: Gleerup.

McKnight, Edgar V.
1978   *Meaning in Texts: The Historical Shaping of a Narrative Hermeneutics.* Philadelphia: Fortress.

MacRae, George W.
1973   "Whom Heaven Must Receive Until the Time: Reflections on the Christology of Acts." Int 27: 151–65.

Maddox, Robert
1982   *The Purpose of Luke-Acts.* Edinburgh: T. & T. Clark.

Marshall, I. Howard
1970   *Luke: Historian and Theologian.* London: Paternoster.
1977   *The Gospel of Luke. A Commentary on the Greek Text.* Exeter: Paternoster.
1980   *The Acts of the Apostles.* Grand Rapids: Eerdmans.

Martin, Victor, and Rodolphe Kasser, eds.
1961   *Papyrus Bodmer XIV: Evangile de Luc chap. 3–24.* Cologny-Genève: Bibliotheca Bodmeriana.

Mattill, Andrew J., Jr.
1959   "Luke as a Historian in Criticism since 1840." Ph.D. diss., Vanderbilt University.
1965   (with Mary B. Mattill). *A Classified Bibliography of Literature on the Acts of the Apostles.* NTTS 7. Grand Rapids: Eerdmans.
1970   "The Purpose of Acts: Schneckenburger Reconsidered." Pp. 108–22 in *Apostolic History and the Gospel: Biblical and Historical Essays presented to F. F. Bruce.* Ed. W. Gasque and R. P. Martin. Grand Rapids: Eerdmans.
1972   "*Naherwartung, Fernerwartung,* and the Purpose of Luke-Acts." CBQ 34: 276–93.

1978 "The Value of Acts as a Source for the Study of Paul." Pp. 76–98 in *Perspectives on Luke-Acts*. Ed. Charles H. Talbert. Danville, VA: Association of Baptist Professors of Religion.

Menoud, Philippe
1951 "The Western Text and the Theology of Acts." *SNTS Bulletin* 2: 19–32.

Miles, Gary B., and Garry Trompf
1976 "Luke and Antiphon: The Theology of Acts 27–28 in the Light of Pagan Beliefs about Divine Retribution, Pollution, and Shipwreck." *HTR* 69: 259–67.

Mills, Watson E.
1986 *A Bibliography of the Periodical Literature on the Acts of the Apostles 1962–1984*. NovTSup 58. Leiden: Brill.

Minear, Paul S.
1966 "Luke's Use of the Birth Stories." Pp. 111–30 in *Studies in Luke-Acts*. Ed. L. E. Keck and J. L. Martyn. Nashville: Abingdon.
1976 *To Heal and To Reveal: The Prophetic Vocation according to Luke*. New York: Seabury.

Moehring, Horst R.
1972 "The Census in Luke as an Apologetic Device." Pp. 144–60 in *Studies in the New Testament and Early Christian Literature: Essays in Honor of Allen P. Wikgren*. Ed. D. E. Aune. NovTSup 33. Leiden: Brill.

Morris, Leon
1973 "Luke and Early Catholicism." *WTJ* 35: 121–36.

Morton, A. Q., and S. Michaelson
1976 *A Critical Concordance to the Acts of the Apostles*. Wooster, OH: Biblical Research Associates.

Moule, Charles F. D.
1966 "The Christology of Acts." Pp. 159–85 in *Studies in Luke-Acts*. Ed. L. E. Keck and J. L. Martyn. Nashville: Abingdon.

O'Brien, P. T.
1973 "Prayer in Luke-Acts." *TynBul* 24: 111–27.

Oliver, Harold H.
1963–64 "The Lucan Birth Stories and the Purpose of Luke-Acts." *NTS* 10: 202–26.
1982 Review of Fitzmyer, 1981, *Christian Century* 99: 65–67.

O'Neill, J. C.
1970 *The Theology of Acts*. 2d ed. London: SPCK.

O'Toole, Robert F.
1978 *Acts 26: The Christological Climax of Paul's Defense (Ac 22:1–26:32)*. AnBib 78. Rome: Biblical Institute Press.

Ott, Wilhelm
1965 *Gebet und Heil: Die Bedeutung der Gebetsparänese in der lukanischen Theologie*. Munich: Kösel.

Pervo, Richard
1979 "The Literary Genre of the Acts of the Apostles." Ph.D. diss., Harvard Divinity School. See now his *Profit with Delight: The Literary Genre of the Acts of the Apostles*. Philadelphia: Fortress, 1987.

Petersen, Norman R.
   1978   *Literary Criticism for New Testament Critics*. Philadelphia: Fortress.

Plümacher, Eckhard
   1972   *Lukas als hellenistischer Schriftsteller*. Göttingen: Vandenhoeck & Ruprecht.
   1977   "Wirklichkeitserfahrung und Geschichtsschreibung bei Lukas: Erwägungen zu den Wir-Stücken der Apostelgeschichte." *ZNW* 68: 2–22.

Prigent, Pierre
   1962   "Un nouveau texte des Actes: Le papyrus Bodmer XVII." *RHPR* 42: 169–74.

Radl, Walter
   1975   *Paulus und Jesus im lukanische Doppelwerk*. Bern: Lang.

Rasco, Emilio
   1976   *La teologia de Lucas: Origen, desarrollo, orientaciones*. Rome: Università Gregoriana Editrice.

Rese, Martin
   1969   *Alttestamentliche Motive in der Christologie des Lukas*. Gütersloh: Mohn.

Rice, George E.
   1974   "The Alterations of Luke's Tradition by the Textual Variants in Codex Bezae." Ph.D. diss., Case Western Reserve University.

Richard, Earl
   1938   "Luke—Writer, Theologian, Historian: Research and Orientation of the 1970's." *BTB* 13: 3–15.

Robbins, Vernon K.
   1975   "The We-Passages in Acts and Ancient Sea Voyages." *BR* 20: 1–14.
   1978   "By Land and By Sea." Pp. 215–42 in *Perspectives on Luke-Acts*. Ed. Charles H. Talbert. Danville, VA: Association of Baptist Professors of Religion.

Rohde, Joachim
   1966   *Die redaktionsgeshichtliche Methode*. Hamburg: Furche-Verlag. Eng. trans. by D. M. Barton: *Rediscovering the Teaching of the Evangelists*. NTL. Philadelphia: Westminster, 1968.

Roloff, Jürgen
   1965   *Apostolat—Verkündigung—Kirche: Ursprung, Inhalt und Funktion des kirchlichen Apostelamtes nach Paulus, Lukas und den Pastoralbriefen*. Gütersloh: Mohn.

Ross, J. M.
   1976   "The United Bible Societies' Greek New Testament." *JBL* 95: 112–21.

Schneider, Gerhard
   1969   *Verleugnung, Verspottung und Verhör Jesu nach Lukas 22:54–71*. Munich: Kösel.
   1973   *Die Passion Jesu nach den drei alteren Evangelien*. Munich: Kösel.
   1977a   "Der Zweck des lukanischen Doppelwerke." *BZ* n.s. 21: 45–66.
   1977b   *Das Evangelium nach Lukas*. 2 vols. Gütersloh: Mohn.
   1980–82 *Die Apostelgeschichte*. HTKNT 5. 2 vols. Freiburg: Herder.

Schram, Tim
1971   *Der Markus Stoff bei Lukas.* SNTSMS 14. Cambridge: University Press.

Schürmann, Heinz
1953,   *Einer quellenkritischen Untersuchung des Lucanischen Abendmahls-*
1955,   *berichtes, Lk 22:7–38.* 3 vols. Münster: Aschendorff.
1957
1968a   "Das Testament des Paulus für die Kirche (Apg. 20:18–35)." Pp. 310–40 in *Traditionsgeschichtliche Untersuchungen zu den synoptischen Evangelien.* Düsseldorf: Patmos.
1968b   "Die Warnung des Lukas vor der Falschlehre in der 'Predigt am Berge' Lk 6:20–49." Pp. 290–309 in *Traditionsgeschichtliche Untersuchungen zu den synoptischen Evangelien.* Düsseldorf: Patmos.
1969   *Das Lukasevangelium, Erster Teil.* HTKNT 3/1. Freiburg: Herder.

Schütz, Frieder
1969   *Der leidende Christus: Die angefochtene Gemeinde und das Christuskerygma der lukanischen Schriften.* Stuttgart: Kohlhammer.

Smalley, Stephen S.
1973   "The Christology of Acts Again." Pp. 79–93 in *Christ and Spirit in the New Testament: In Honour of C. F. D. Moule.* Ed. B. Lindars and S. S. Smalley. Cambridge: University Press.

Snodgrass, Klyne
1972   "Western Non-Interpolations." *JBL* 91: 369–79.

Stagg, Frank
1978   "Textual Criticism for Luke-Acts." *PIRS* 5: 152–65.

Talbert, Charles H.
1966   *Luke and the Gnostics.* Nashville: Abingdon.
1967   "Again: Paul's Visits to Jerusalem." *NovT* 9: 26–40.
1967–68   "An Anti-Gnostic Tendency in Lucan Christology." *NTS* 14: 259–71.
1970   "The Redaction Critical Quest for Luke the Theologian." Pp. 171–222 in *Jesus and Man's Hope,* vol. 1. Ed. D. G. Miller and D. Y. Hadidian. Pittsburgh: Pittsburgh Theological Seminary.
1974   *Literary Patterns, Theological Themes, and the Genre of Luke-Acts.* SBLMS 20. Missoula, MT: Scholars Press.
1975   "The Concept of Immortals in Mediterranean Antiquity." *JBL* 94: 419–36.
1977   *What Is a Gospel? The Genre of the Canonical Gospels.* Philadelphia: Fortress.
1982   *Reading Luke: A Literary and Theological Commentary on the Third Gospel.* New York: Crossroad.
1984   "Promise and Fulfillment in Lukan Theology." Pp. 91–103 in *Luke-Acts: New Perspectives from the Society of Biblical Literature Seminar.* Ed. C. H. Talbert. New York: Crossroad.

Tatum, W. Barnes
1966–67   "The Epoch of Israel: Luke 1–2 and the Theological Plan of Luke-Acts." *NTS* 13: 184–95.

Taylor, Vincent
1972   *The Passion Narrative of St. Luke.* Ed. O. E. Evans. Cambridge: University Press.

Throckmorton, Burton H.
1973   "Σώζειν σωτηρία in Luke-Acts." *SE* 6: 515–26.

Trites, Allison A.
1978   "The Prayer Motif in Luke-Acts." *Perspectives on Luke-Acts.* Ed. Charles H. Talbert. Danville, VA: Association of Baptist Professors of Religion.

Tyson, Joseph B.
1978   "Source Criticism of the Gospel of Luke." Pp. 24–39 in *Perspectives on Luke-Acts.* Ed. Charles H. Talbert. Danville, VA: Association of Baptist Professors of Religion.

Unnik, W. C. van
1966   "Luke-Acts, a Storm Center in Contemporary Scholarship." Pp. 15–32 in *Studies in Luke-Acts.* Ed. L. E. Keck and J. L. Martyn. Nashville: Abingdon.

Vielhauer, Philipp
1950–51   "Zum 'Paulinismus' der Apostelgeschichte." *EvT* 10: 1–15. Eng. trans.: pp. 33–50 in *Studies in Luke-Acts.* Ed. L. E. Keck and J. L. Martyn. Nashville: Abingdon, 1966.

Waetjen, Herman C.
1976   *The Origin and Destiny of Humanness: An Interpretation of the Gospel according to Matthew.* Corte Madera, CA: Omega.

Wainwright, Arthur W.
1977   "Luke and the Restoration of the Kingdom to Israel." *ExpTim* 89: 76–79.

Wanke, Joachim
1973   *Beobachtungen zum Eucharistieverständnis des Lukas auf Grund der lukanischen Mahlberichte.* Leipzig: St. Benno.

Wilckens, Ulrich
1961   *Die Missionsreden der Apostelgeschichte: Form- und traditionsgeschichtliche Untersuchungen.* WMANT 5. Neukirchen-Vluyn: Neukirchener Verlag.

Williams, R. R.
1965   "Church History in Acts: Is it Reliable?" Pp. 145–60 in *Historicity and Chronology in the New Testament.* London: SPCK.

Wilson, Stephen G.
1970   "Lucan Eschatology." *NTS* 15: 330–47.
1973   *The Gentiles and the Gentile Mission in Luke-Acts.* SNTSMS 23. Cambridge: University Press.

Yoder, James D.
1961   *A Concordance to the Distinctive Greek Text of Codex Bezae.* NTTS 2. Leiden: Brill.

Zehnle, Richard
1969   "The Salvific Character of Jesus' Death in Lucan Soteriology." *TS* 30: 420–44.

Zingg, Paul
1974   *Das Wachsen der Kirche: Beiträge zur Frage der lukanischen Redaktion und Theologie.* OBO 3. Göttingen: Vandenhoeck & Ruprecht.

12

PAULINE STUDIES

Victor Paul Furnish

The research agenda for Pauline studies that emerged from the nineteenth century and continued in force with relatively few modifications until World War II has undergone only modest changes and expansions since the war's conclusion. The developments in Pauline studies since F. C. Baur, and most especially since A. Schweitzer's survey (1912), were assessed by R. Bultmann in a series of articles published between the two world wars (1929, 1934, 1936). By and large, the topics that Bultmann identified as current and important in those two decades between the wars, have continued to dominate the discussion since 1945. These include such matters as Paul's religious background, the nature and meaning of his conversion, his early ministry, his last years, the relation of his gospel to the preaching of Jesus and, not least, Paul's understanding of faith and how that was related to his anthropology on the one hand and to his eschatology on the other. It would be wrong to say that no progress has been made on such topics in the years since Bultmann's articles, but it would be equally wrong to say that there is a general consensus about any one of them. The literature published in the field over the last 40 years demonstrates the contrary. What P. Schubert wrote a generation ago is just about as true today: "As regards Paul and his letters there is no notable agreement on any major issue" (1947:221).

Various surveys of recent contributions to Pauline studies have appeared during the period under review here. Of these, that by B. Rigaux (1968) is by far the most comprehensive, even though it does not deal as such with studies of Pauline theological themes or with attempts to organize and interpret Pauline theology as a whole. H. Conzelmann (1968) and G. Schneider, however, have focused particularly on discussions of Pauline theology. In two of the most recent surveys, J. Murphy-O'Connor (1975, 1977) deals with various sorts of studies, including commentaries, published between 1969 and 1976. What follows attempts to be at once more comprehensive and more selective than any of these others. It is more comprehensive in that it has in view the broad topics of Paul's letters, his life and ministry, and his thought, as these have been investigated from 1945 to the present. It is also more selective, however, because it must perforce be restricted to those areas under each of the main headings where, in the reviewer's opinion, the most significant developments have taken place.

321

I. THE PAULINE LETTERS

Formal, Structural and Literary Characteristics

Deissmann's famous distinction (1–59) between "epistles" (carefully composed literary productions meant for general publication) and "letters" (genuine correspondence addressed to specific persons and situations) exerted a significant influence on Pauline studies for many years. Because the apostle's letters, at least the ones judged to be authentic, were taken as real letters, they were studied mainly with reference to what they seemed to disclose about the addressees, on the one hand, and the author (Paul), on the other. Whatever the excesses of this approach (for instance, the tendency to read the letters for insight concerning Paul's "religious experience" and psychic condition), it correctly emphasized the situational character of the letters and of Paul's thought expressed in them. However, at the same time it drew attention away from questions about the form, the structure, and the literary style of those letters (Funk, 1966:252). As long as scholars presumed a clear distinction between "letters" and "epistles" — and that Paul wrote letters, not epistles — formal, structural, and stylistic questions were bound to seem inappropriate, or at least unimportant.

This picture was beginning to change, however, by the time M. Dibelius published his article on the application of form-critical methods to NT literature outside the Gospels (1931). There had already been some critical attempts to identify aspects of Paul's literary style (e.g., Weiss) and to illumine Paul's preaching by reference to the Cynic-Stoic diatribe (Bultmann, 1910). In the meantime, however, form criticism had focused attention on the individual units of oral tradition lying behind the written Gospels, and Dibelius argued that similar traditions — paraenetic, hymnic, and cultic — are recoverable from the letters. L. G. Champion carried out such a study in his dissertation, written under Dibelius, which showed how two particular liturgical forms found voice in the apostle's writing.

Such form-critical work was not itself concerned about the final *literary* form, structure, or style. But form-critical analysis did require one to reckon with literary features, insofar as they provided clues to the underlying oral traditions. Thus, almost despite its own objectives, the form-critical study of Paul's letters began to direct attention to the formal, structural, and stylistic characteristics of them. This was shown especially well by Schubert (1939), who demonstrated Paul's reliance on a particular ancient epistolary convention, the thanksgiving period. Schubert's work elicited even from Dibelius (1941) the acknowledgment that Paul's letters must henceforth be treated as at least "half-literary" (28). If this is so, then the compositional features of Paul's letters deserve study, no less than their historical settings. Indeed, as Schubert tentatively suggested with respect to the different types of thanksgiving periods in the letters, stylistic analysis may itself aid one's understanding of the writer's intentions and concerns (1939:183–84).

Schubert's study was published in the same year that Hitler told his generals war was inevitable and that events proved him right. Because of the intervention of that war, formal, functional, structural, and rhetorical studies of the Pauline letters have come into their own only since 1945. D. G. Bradley (1947, 1953) sought to follow out Dibelius's suggestions concerning Paul's use of paraenetic traditions; H. Thyen's treatment of the Jewish-Hellenistic homily was designed, like Bultmann's on the diatribe, to show Paul's indebtedness to a standardized form of oral address; G. Karlsson called attention to Paul's use of an epistolary formula identifying one's letter as written to substitute for a visit; and J. Jeremias explored the composition of several specific Pauline passages (1953) and the apostle's use of *chiasmus* (1958; cf. the earlier work of N. W. Lund and the subsequent study of K. Grobel).

Schubert's monograph on the Pauline thanksgivings has turned out to be the progenitor of a whole series of studies of other formal patterns and periods in the apostle's letters, most of these by Americans. Petitionary, disclosure, and greeting formulas (Mullins, 1962, 1964, 1968, respectively), the transitions from the thanksgivings to the letter bodies (J. T. Sanders), the autobiographical subscriptions (Bahr), homiletic benediction forms (Jewett, 1969), judgment forms (Roetzel), and, most recently, *Tobsprüche* ("'better . . . than' sayings") (Snyder) and oaths (Sampley) have all been identified and analyzed. C. J. Bjerkelund's monograph on the *parakalō*-periods ("comfort" or "encouragement sentences") was consciously modeled on Schubert's (1939). R. W. Funk's study of the "travelogue" material in Romans 15 (1967) helped to illumine that particular passage and to elaborate the point made more briefly by Karlsson, even though the same kind of period is not to be found in Paul's other letters. More recent studies of the thanksgiving periods (e.g., O'Brien) have suggested ways in which Schubert's work should perhaps be corrected, but they do not require any major alteration of the general conclusion toward which the many recent studies of forms and periods in Paul's letters seem to lead: the apostle was well acquainted with the epistolary conventions of his day, and he composed (or dictated) his letters with some degree of self-conscious concern that their form should be appropriate to their function. Studies of Paul's use of "parabolic language" (Riesenfeld) and various kinds of images and metaphors (e.g., Gale; Pfitzner; Malherbe, 1968) lend further support to this conclusion.

During the course of the work on specialized forms and periods within the Pauline letters, it has become increasingly clear that attention needs to be given as well to the overall structure and function of the letter as it existed in Paul's day (see Funk, 1966:254). M. L. Stirewalt's work in this area is still largely unpublished, but his analysis of the Greek "letter-essay" (1977) shows how much light the study of ancient handbooks of epistolary types and style, and of actual examples of ancient letters, can shed on Paul's practice (so also Bahr; Bandstra; Stirewalt, 1969; Doty; White, 1972a, 1972b; Kim). This kind of investigation has been greatly aided by some excellent monographs on Greek and Roman epistolography in general (e.g., Koskenniemi; Thraede). Jewish letters have so far been somewhat less intensively studied for the insight they may provide into Christian epistolography, but they, too, are bound to be helpful (Andresen; Fitzmyer, 1974). Meanwhile, there has been a growing interest in exploring the possibility that standard *rhetorical* patterns, as known from ancient handbooks on rhetoric as well as from ancient Greek and Latin examples, can shed light on Paul's manner of argument. H. D. Betz has sought to demonstrate this by his study of 2 Corinthians 10–13 (1972) and in his analysis of Galatians (1975, 1979), and W. Wuellner has argued for this approach in the interpretation of Romans. More recently, G. A. Kennedy has offered suggestions about the rhetorical characteristics not only of 2 Corinthians, Galatians, and Romans, but also of 1 Thessalonians (chaps. 4 and 7). A related concern is evident in J. Zmijewski's recent study of 2 Cor 11:1–12:10, which seeks to integrate rigorous stylistic analysis within the broader approach of historical criticism.

The recent blossoming of interest in identifying the literary characteristics of Paul's letters (their use of conventional literary formulas and periods, their proper epistolary functions, their patterns of argument, and their habits of style) has not meant the abandonment of interest in locating evidence there of preliterary forms and patterns. Form-critical analysis of the letters, as Dibelius (1931) had urged it, has continued along various fronts. There is by now general agreement that echoes of various sorts of hymnic, creedal, and other liturgical materials may be heard (e.g., Cullmann, 1949; Schille; Deichgräber; Martin, 1967; J. T. Sanders, 1971; Wengst). To be sure, serious questions remain about the extent of those, their origins, and how Paul has adapted and applied them within the several epistolary contexts. Nor is there any real agreement about the proper methodology for detecting them in the first place. On the other hand, the detection of paraenetic traditions behind the letters is somewhat less problematic, and the discovery of the Dead Sea Scrolls, as well as more careful investigation of Hellenistic ethical material in general, has made possible some real advances in our understanding of the ethical lists and codes that occur in the letters of the Pauline corpus (Wibbing; Kamlah; Schroeder; Crouch; Schrage).

Glosses and Interpolations

Hypotheses about textual glosses and the presence of even longer interpolated units have long been a part of textual and literary criticism. During the years under review, several older hypotheses have attracted new supporters, and some further passages have been added to the list of suspect texts. Of the several instances of glossing Bultmann found in Romans (1947), only his identification of a phrase in 6:17 has received much attention, and that has been persuasive to but a few (e.g., not to Käsemann, 1974:171).

There has been renewed discussion of 2 Cor 6:14–7:1 largely because of apparent affinities with ideas current among the Jewish sectarians at Qumran. W. K. M. Grossouw, J. A. Fitzmyer (1961), and J. Gnilka have judged it to be non-Pauline, and Betz (1973) has even argued that it derives from the polemic of the apostle's Galatian opponents. The long-suspected verse in 1 Thessalonians which indicts the Jews for killing "both the Lord Jesus and the prophets" (2:15) has been newly studied by B. Pearson and D. Schmidt, both of whom conclude that the whole of 2:13–16 should be attributed to an interpolator. G. Fitzer's detailed study of 1 Cor 14:34–35 has convinced a number of scholars of a gloss there, but proposals about the presence of interpolated material in Rom 3:24–26 (Talbert), Rom 13:1–7 (Kallas), 1 Cor 11:2–16 (Walker; Cope), 1 Corinthians 13 (Titus) and 1 Thess 5:1–11 (Friedrich) have so far received less support.

It is significant, in fact, that there has been no general scholarly agreement on the probability, or even on the plausibility, of any of these hypotheses about glosses and interpolations. For a while it appeared that some consensus might be possible about the non-Pauline character of 2 Cor 6:14–7:1, but the most recent studies have presented important reasons not only to reconsider its authenticity but also to reconsider its appropriateness to its present context in 2 Corinthians (Barrett, 1973:193–204; Dahl, 1977b:62–69; Fee; Thrall; Lambrecht). It is evident that so far no firm and convincing techniques or criteria have been developed to aid in the identification of glosses and interpolations. This is only confirmed by the wholesale resort to hypotheses about these which is characteristic of J. C. O'Neill's monograph on Galatians and his commentary on Romans. Highly subjective judgments about content and tone are intermixed with often-questionable generalizations about the apostle's style and vocabulary. What emerges is a Paul created in the interpreter's own image.

Integrity and Authenticity

Of the seven letters that are indisputably Paul's own, only Philemon seems able to be above suspicion of being a composite of two or more originally separate letters. There is general agreement that Rom 16:25–27 is a late addition to the text, and 16:24 continues to be suspect (Käsemann, 1974:401–7). The view, long held by many, that the remainder of chap. 16 is authentically Pauline but not integral to Romans, still finds support (e.g., Käsemann, 1974:390), but it has been increasingly challenged (Barrett, 1957; Donfried, 1970; Cranfield; Gamble, 1977, who also regards v 24 as authentic and integral).

Apart from the wide-ranging hypothesis of Schmithals about the Corinthian correspondence (1971; 1972:239–74), which is too problematic in too many respects to have gained much favor with other scholars, there have been few recent attempts to argue for the composite nature of 1 Corinthians.

2 Corinthians is, of course, another matter; even some of the more conservative commentators find themselves obliged to acknowledge that chaps. 1–9 and 10–13 represent two separate letters (e.g., Bruce, 1971; Barrett, 1973), while others separate out 2:14–7:4 (excluding 6:14–7:1) as yet a third (Bornkamm, 1961; Georgi, 1965; Collange). There have been serious recent proposals as well about the composite nature of our canonical Philippians (e.g., Beare) and 1 Thessalonians (e.g., Eckart).

Debates over the authenticity of various of the letters purporting to come from Paul have continued since 1945, but while certain arguments pro and con have been supplemented, modified, or abandoned, no genuinely new arguments have been advanced on either side. There are perhaps fewer who seek to defend the authenticity of the Pastoral epistles (among those Jeremias, 1975; Guthrie) and of Ephesians (especially van Roon; Barth, 1974), but one cannot speak of even an embryonic consensus about Colossians. Thus, recent commentators like R. P. Martin (1974) and G. B. Caird continue to defend its authenticity, even though E. Lohse's careful weighing of the evidence had earlier brought him to the opposite result (so also the stylistic analysis of W. Bujard). This situation also obtains for 2 Thessalonians: B. Rigaux (1956) and E. Best are among those who maintain its authenticity despite the challenge of scholars like C. Masson, W. Trilling, and J. A. Bailey.

There have been various attempts to employ a statistical method in the analysis of the linguistic features of the Pauline letters (e.g., Grayston and Herdan; Morton and McLeman). Questions remain, however, about how applicable this kind of method is to them (e.g., Johnson), and the results which may be obtained should be correlated with other kinds of literary-critical data (see, e.g., McArthur). One may perhaps expect more satisfactory results from the sort of objective stylistic analysis already carried out on Colossians by Bujard, as that can be extended and refined through application of the sophisticated methods of transformational-generative linguistics (see Schmidt).

Collection, Redaction, and Circulation

Questions about how the Pauline letters came to be collected into a corpus and then circulated as a group have usually been dealt with, and not inappropriately, as part of the larger topic of the development of the NT canon (see chapter 8 in this volume, by Harry Gamble). These questions also need to be faced, however, in the process of the literary-critical analysis of the individual letters. Where letters are judged to be deutero-Pauline, or composite, or where they are held to contain glosses and interpolations, there one must confront at least two fundamental problems: (1) Not only when and where, but how and why were Paul's letters first assembled and circulated? (2) Under what conditions, with what presuppositions, for what purpose(s), and to what extent did they undergo redactional modification? N. A. Dahl (1962) has called attention to these questions and others in an essay that deserves to be better known, and he has touched on them again in a recent study of the prologues to the Pauline letters (1978). Indeed, as hypotheses about glosses, interpolations, composite letters, and deutero-Pauline authorship have multiplied, it has become increasingly apparent that new investigations of the formation of the Pauline corpus need to be undertaken.

To many, at least in Britain and America, E. J. Goodspeed's hypothesis about Ephesians (1933) has seemed compelling. Ephesians, it has been held, was written by the collector of Paul's letters to serve as a covering, introductory letter to the corpus as it had been assembled by about 90 C.E. for general circulation (e.g., Mitton; Knox, 1959, who has sought to identify the collector as Onesimus, the runaway slave). There are, however, serious difficulties with this theory (see Zuntz: 228–29 n. 1; 276–77). For one thing, Ephesians seems never to have stood first in the collection (or even last), as the covering-letter hypothesis must presume it did at one time. Moreover, the Goodspeed hypothesis simply does not do justice to the actual contents of Ephesians. It is much more than a potpourri of Pauline thoughts and sentences. It has its own theme and its own theological standpoint and intention, which — however variously these may be defined (e.g., Chadwick; Fischer; Lindemann, 1975, 1976; Dahl, 1977a) — cannot be reduced to, and are not really compatible with, a concern to summarize and introduce the other Pauline letters. It is, therefore, no longer so easy to believe that Ephesians is the key that will unlock the many still-unanswered questions about the collection, redaction, and circulation of the Pauline letters.

There has been no one major study of these questions over the last forty years, despite the fact that no theory about glosses and interpolations, no partition theory, and no proposal to classify a letter as "deutero-Pauline" can be held to be reasonable unless such matters have been taken into account. Thus, for example, a very common defense of the integrity of a letter is to claim that no plausible explanation can be found for why originally separate letters or parts of letters have been joined together in the ways partition theories require. The argument has force where in fact the problem of redaction has not been faced. G. Bornkamm is one of the few to have faced this, specifically in the cases of 2 Corinthians (1961) and Philippians (1962). Schmithals (1972:239–74), more comprehensively, has argued that the Pauline corpus was formulated by a single individual for the purpose of counteracting gnosticism. Gamble (1975), however, has studied with special care the textual tradition of the Pauline letters, concluding that it goes back to multiple sources. In that case, he notes, it is the more remarkable how uniform that tradition is in all known witnesses. This would seem to require the conclusion that the kind of redactional work partition theories involve must have occurred before a given letter entered into the textual tradition.

Gamble (1977) agrees that such did occur in the case of Romans, but he thinks it significant that in this one exceptional instance traces of that work do occur in the textual tradition (1975:418).

II. PAUL'S LIFE AND MINISTRY

Chronology, Sequence of the Letters

All of the old questions about Paul's life and ministry have continued to be discussed since 1945. One still finds articles and monographs on Paul's conversion (e.g., Wilckens), his Roman citizenship (e.g., Kehnscherper), his collection for Jerusalem (e.g., Georgi, 1965; Nickle), and even on the state of his health (e.g., Binder). But of special importance in recent years are the contributions which have been made to the question of the Pauline chronology and — not to be separated from that — the question of the sequence of the letters.

J. Knox (1950) insisted that chronological data from Acts must be used only with the greatest caution and that they must in no case be allowed to assume precedence over data derived from Paul's own letters. He argued, specifically, that "Luke" was concerned with emphasizing the role of the Jerusalem church in the history of Christianity, that the Christian movement was politically innocuous, and that these Lucan interests have influenced the chronological framework provided for Paul's ministry in Acts. The historical reliability of Acts is, of course, a question in its own right, and several recent studies of Pauline chronology continue to be guided, to one degree or another, by the Lucan framework (e.g., Ogg; Gunther, 1972; Suhl; Dockx). On the other hand, J. C. Hurd (1965:3–42), C. Buck and G. Taylor, and G. Lüdemann (1984) have sought, like Knox, to develop a chronological framework for Paul's life from his letters alone. This has led Lüdemann, for example, to date Paul's first visit to Jerusalem in 33, his founding of the Corinthian church in 41, his letter to the Romans in 51–52, and his arrival in Jerusalem for the last time in 52, at least five years earlier than most other reconstructions. R. Jewett (1979) acknowledges the importance of staying free from the Lucan framework, but he is more willing to rely on data from Acts, at least insofar as these can be critically sifted and reasonably coordinated with data from Paul's letters and other kinds of external evidence. His method, which he calls "deductive-experimental," is to correlate the dates and time spans that may be reasonably ascertained from Paul's letters and Acts with those that are ascertainable "externally" from other ancient sources, both literary and archaeological.

This matter of the Pauline chronology has importance chiefly because of its direct bearing on the dating and the sequence of the letters (see Hurd, 1967, 1968), and the placement of the letters will in turn affect one's view of their several occasions. Moreover, it is vital that there be some consensus about chronology and sequence if discussions about the possible "development" of Paul's thought over the course of his ministry are to be more fruitful than they have been so far (Furnish, 1970). Hurd, Buck and Taylor, and Lüdemann (1984) have all been interested in demonstrating that there was some kind of development, and thus the old questions about the chronology of Paul's life and the sequence of his letters have taken on a new importance in the last several decades.

The Pauline Congregations

Although the standard "biographical" questions about Paul are still debated, these have in general been subordinated to questions about the Pauline congregations and his interaction with them as their apostle. One may judge this to be an altogether proper and indeed overdue refocusing of questions about Paul's life and ministry. It is Paul's interaction with his congregations, after all, for which his letters supply primary data—not for the reconstruction of his pre-Christian life, or for his theology in some systematic sense, or even, in the first instance, for his missionary preaching. The letters are addressed to the congregations which he had founded and for which he had assumed responsibility, or—in the case of Romans—to a congregation that he considered important for the present and future conduct of his ministry.

One of the long-standing issues that may be mentioned under this heading is the matter of the relation of Paul and his congregations to Jewish Christianity, and specifically to the church in Jerusalem. J. Munck's view that Jewish Christianity is not to be identified as "Judaistic" and the view that the Jerusalem apostles, like Paul, were devoted to the Gentile mission depended on a number of dubious exegetical judgments, especially in the case of Galatians (Bultmann, 1959). Munck was doubtless correct, however, in his judgment that Pauline studies were still too much under the spell of Baur's Hegelian portrait of earliest Christianity as a struggle between the "Pauline" and "Petrine" wings of the church. Yet Munck himself wanted to rewrite the history of earliest Christianity on the basis of his peculiar understanding of Paul as a "figure in the history of salvation" (*heilsgeschichtliche Gestalt*) who acted quite self-consciously as such. His evidence for this has not seemed persuasive to many, however, and his arguments are in large part dependent on O. Cullmann's (1951) problematic conclusions about the linear, temporal nature of salvation history (*Heilsgeschichte*) in the NT.

A more satisfactory approach to the question of Paul's role in the early church has been the attempt to identify with greater precision those by whom he was opposed. This is by no means a new topic for research (see Ellis, 1975), but it is one that has been taken up with renewed interest. The discovery of the Jewish and gnostic Christian libraries at Qumran and Nag Hammadi, respectively, has added to the resources available for studying this question (Murphy-O'Connor, 1968; Pagels). Moreover, since Walter

Bauer there has been a new appreciation of the theological diversity that obtained even among the churches of the first century and of the need to be alert to different local forms of Christianity (see Koester, 1965). Not all of the recent work on the question of Paul's opponents has taken adequate account of this diversity, however, and the tendency remains to identify one group as responsible for Paul's troubles in every church (e.g., Schmithals, 1972; Gunther, 1973; Lüdemann, 1983, who revives the hypothesis of F. C. Baur). The most promising studies have refrained from wholesale conclusions and have focused instead on the opposition to Paul reflected in particular letters, especially in 1 and 2 Corinthians (e.g., Georgi, 1964; Barrett, 1971; Machalet), Galatians (e.g., Tyson; Jewett, 1971a; Howard: 1–19) and Philippians (e.g., Koester, 1962; Klijn). The results of these various studies are exceedingly diverse, but there is broad agreement that as we are able to draw a more accurate picture of the opposition to Paul in his several churches, the better able we will be to understand his own conception of the gospel and of his apostolic mission.

Pauline studies in particular stand to benefit from rapidly growing interest in examining, with fresh questions, sharper tools, and new resources, the social history of earliest Christianity. Old questions about the environment of the early church are not just being revived but substantially redefined and refocused in an effort to probe more accurately the internal structure of early Christian groups and their position within and relationship to society at large. The Pauline letters are one crucial source of data for this kind of investigation, and its results should greatly enrich our understanding of his congregations and hence of his ministry. As Gager (1979:175, 179) has pointed out, one must distinguish between studies that seek mainly to *describe* the social world and characteristics of earliest Christianity, and those that propose to *analyze* these, making use of sociological methods. The pioneering studies of E. A. Judge belong to the former category, and his programmatic essay on Paul has been an important catalyst for other work, for instance, Hock's monograph on Paul as an artisan. Judge's own work has tended to use NT sources, especially Acts, too uncritically, making some of his conclusions less convincing than they might otherwise be. Hock, on the other hand, has been much more circumspect in this regard, so that his conclusions — which could probably be safely extended and developed — are considerably firmer.

The work of G. Theissen is also descriptive, but (like Gager, 1975) he wants in addition to employ sociological paradigms in analyzing the social data (1974; 1982:175ff.). His application of sociological methods to the study of social strata and relationships in the Corinthian church (1982:27ff., 69ff., 145ff.) shows how much can be learned in this way, even if, as Gager (1979:175) has observed with respect to another of Theissen's studies, one must be alert to the "theoretical infrastructure" of his work. W. A. Meeks has provided the first comprehensive "social description" of Pauline Christianity, and his work is certain to prompt further studies of the same type. There is no recent development in Pauline studies more promising than that represented by these scholars. Nevertheless, A. J. Malherbe (1983) has appropriately cautioned that sociological analysis must not be allowed to divert attention from those kinds of issues with which historical, literary, and theological analysis are properly concerned.

III. PAULINE THOUGHT

Paul's interpretation of the Christian message and of its implications for believers has always been—indeed, since the apostle's own lifetime—and will continue to be both an important and a difficult topic for discussion. The difficulty is not only to understand Paul's thought, but, more basic even than that, to know how to recover pertinent data from the sources and to know what recoverable data are in fact pertinent. Other phases of Pauline studies have shown that the interpreter must reckon with several hard realities: (1) Our sources are limited in their extent, especially since most scholars agree that Acts must be excluded entirely as a source for the content of Paul's preaching. (2) Not all of the letters attributed to Paul are certainly his. (3) The letters that can with confidence be regarded as authentic contain a mixture of traditional, Pauline and, perhaps in some cases post-Pauline, theologoumena. (4) The exact sequence of the letters remains problematic, as do many of the specifics of the situations in and for which they were written. (5) The letters themselves do not yield any specifically theological data. Paul's concern in them was not to summarize his "theology" (on the question of whether this might have been true of Romans to some extent, see especially the essays by Bornkamm, R. Karris, and Donfried in Donfried, 1977), but to deal with concrete situations in the life of the church, and most particularly in the life of his own congregations.

In view of these realities, it is not surprising that relatively few attempts have been made to organize Paul's thought in such a way that it may be presented as his "theology." To most it has seemed far more appropriate to deal with individual topics and themes of Pauline thought. Of the comprehensive treatments of Paul's thought, viewed as a whole, Bultmann's (1951) has unquestionably been the most important. Indeed, a great deal of the subsequent discussion of Pauline theology has gone on in more or less conscious dialogue with Bultmann's position. This brief survey cannot begin to do justice to the many and diverse studies of Pauline thought that have appeared since then. It may be useful, however, to make some brief comments about two absolutely fundamental issues. Each of these has received a good deal of attention in the period under review, and the two are closely related.

The Presuppositions of Paul's Thought

Historical analysis cannot rest content with any kind of view that finds the germ of Paul's theology in some private experience. The religious form of this view asserts that Paul's theology is rooted in his conversion, and thus in a sudden, direct revelation of Jesus as the Christ (e.g., Jeremias, 1971:20–27). The psychological, specifically Freudian, form of it claims that Paul's theology is rooted in his own psychic turmoil (Tarachow) and that his conversion is best described as "a profound emotional revolution" (Rubenstein: 113). The sources, however, are inadequate for pursuing this kind of analysis, and even if it were viable on this and other counts, the historical questions about Paul's general religious and cultural background, as well as his relationship to the earliest church, would still have to be faced.

One of the historical questions is sharply posed when W. C. van Unnik discusses whether Tarsus or Jerusalem was the place of Paul's upbringing. Shall one look to Hellenism or to Judaism as the decisive background of his thought? Van Unnik has concluded that Paul's most impressionable years were spent in Jerusalem, that Aramaic was the language he spoke at home (although he was bilingual), and that his main contacts with Hellenism came only after his conversion to Christianity. However, even if the exegetical foundations for these conclusions were more secure than they are, one would still have to take into account the increasingly well-documented fact that "Jewish Palestine was no hermetically sealed island in the sea of Hellenistic Oriental syncretism" (Hengel, 1:312).

Despite van Unnik, there is a general scholarly consensus that Paul must be thought of as a Jew of the Diaspora. Lively debate has continued, however, over what this means, and the old question of whether Paul was "more Jewish" or "more Greek" continues to be asked in various forms and answered in various ways. Bultmann did not treat Paul's non-Christian heritage as a special topic, but having distinguished between "earliest," that is, Jewish, and "Hellenistic" Christianity, he firmly identified the latter as "the historical presupposition for Paul's theology" (1951:63). In keeping with this, Bultmann's exposition of Paul's thought gives particular attention to the religious ideas and institutions of Hellenistic Judaism. W. D. Davies, on the other hand, has sought to demonstrate "that Paul belonged to the mainstream of first-century Judaism" (2) and that he regarded Christian faith as "the full flowering of Judaism,"—indeed, its "completion," with Christ as "a New Torah" (323).

Like Davies, H. J. Schoeps interprets Paul primarily in relation to the rabbis, although he believes that the apostle was influenced by Hellenistic Judaism when he failed to grasp the fundamental importance of the *covenant;* thus, Paul's polemic against the law was tragically misdirected. E. P. Sanders also stresses the importance of Paul's background in Palestinian Judaism, but he does not agree that Paul misunderstood the role of the law in Judaism, or experienced it as a frustration in his own life. Rather, he concludes, Paul gained "a new perspective" on the law when he became convinced that "Christ saves the Gentiles as well as the Jews" and that his own responsibility was to preach to the Gentiles (1977:496; cf. 1983: 149–54). According to Sanders, then, Paul's view of the law is the consequence of his commitment to a Gentile mission, not (as for Bultmann, 1951; Bornkamm, 1971; and many others) the cause of it.

L. Goppelt (362–90) is more aware than many of the need to take account of various kinds of presuppositions lying behind Pauline theology. Thus, he treats Paul's own religious experience (Galatians 1) in close connection with the apostle's acknowledged reliance on the Easter kerygma of the pre-Pauline church (1 Corinthians 15). The apostle's indebtedness to OT and Jewish apocalyptic thought and to various conceptions of Hellenistic syncretism is also affirmed, although Goppelt has recognized that such influences were only in part direct ones. They were also mediated to Paul through Hellenistic Judaism and the Hellenistic church. Already in his discussion of the presuppositions of Pauline theology, Goppelt emphasizes two points which recur in his subsequent presentation. The first of these is Paul's interpretation of scripture. Goppelt's view that Paul interpreted scripture as the "promise," and thus as the "Old Testament," is questionable, but there is no question about the important role Scripture played in his thinking about the gospel and in the argumentation of his letters (Bonsirven; Ellis, 1957; Hanson). Goppelt's other emphasis is on the importance of the Jesus traditions, both in the original Easter kerygma and subsequently in Paul's theology. He acknowledges that the apostle seldom refers to the kind of traditions we know from the Synoptic Gospels, but he argues that this is because Paul transforms them from a *geschichtlich* (historical) into a *heilsgeschichtlich* (salvation-historical) mode. In addition to raising the perennial question of whether—or, better, *in what way*—Jesus may be said to be one of the presuppositions of Paul's thought (e.g., Jüngel; Blank; Bruce; Fraser), Goppelt's formulation requires one to consider a second, absolutely fundamental question.

The Theological Center of Paul's Thought

One encounters this question in its most concrete form by simply observing the different ways recent interpreters have gone about organizing Paul's thought for purposes of analysis and presentation. With few exceptions (Whiteley is one), interpreters have recognized that it will not do to impose the standard doctrinal headings of systematic theology. There is general agreement that one must respect the apostle's own theological emphases, and so arrange those that his most fundamental interests and concerns are exhibited. There is genuine disagreement, however, about what those fundamental interests and concerns were and how the theological center of Paul's thought should be defined.

In Bultmann's presentation, the Reformation emphasis on Paul's preaching of the righteousness of God and justification by faith is given an existentialist twist. Paul's theology "is not a speculative system" that deals with God "as He is in Himself." It is centered, rather, on "God as He is significant for man" and on "man's responsibility and man's salvation." Since "every assertion about God is simultaneously an assertion about man and vice versa," and since the same thing exactly must be said concerning Paul's assertions about Christ, "Paul's theology is, at the same time, anthropology" and "Paul's christology is simultaneously soteriology" (1951:190–91). For this reason, Bultmann's presentation of Paul's thought is arranged under just two broad headings, "Man Prior to the Revelation of Faith" and "Man Under Faith." This arrangement represents a stunning departure from the traditional topical approach, and even Bultmann's closest followers have felt some need to modify it in order to give more attention to the nature and meaning of that "revelation of faith" by which salvation occurs (Conzelmann, 1969:164–65; Bornkamm, 1971:109–239). H. Schlier's organization is also noteworthy, even though he carefully describes his treatment of Pauline thought as more "systematic" than "historical" in intent (9). There is no section as such on "anthropology." Rather, the first chapter deals with God (properly "the first and last" topic of *theology*, 25), and subsequent chapters take up "the world," the coming of righteousness in Jesus Christ, the Spirit and the gospel, and—last of all—faith. (On this issue, see further chapter 19 in this volume by Reginald Fuller.)

Some interpreters have taken issue only with Bultmann's anthropologically oriented exposition of justification by faith, but others have questioned whether justification by faith is, in any case, the theological center of Paul's thought. For the latter group of interpreters, the most usual alternative is to identify that center as Paul's conception of salvation history (*Heilsgeschichte*). Munck, Davies, and Stendahl are representatives of this point of view, and it has also determined the way Kümmel, Ridderbos, and Ladd have organized their discussions of Pauline theology. Although Goppelt has specifically affiliated himself with the salvation-history approach to NT theology in general (50–51), he is unwilling to stretch Paul's thought across that conceptual framework. Because he believes Paul's conception of salvation history derived from his typological interpretation of the OT, Goppelt has opted for a presentation that more or less follows the design of the argument in Romans (389–90).

Käsemann's discussions of Pauline theology are best represented by several essays (1971) that criticize, on the one hand, what he believes is Bultmann's overemphasis on the anthropological side of Paul's thought (e.g., 1–31) and, on the other hand, the salvation-historical approach as represented by Stendahl and others (60–78). With regard to the latter, although Käsemann acknowledges that "salvation history forms the horizon of Pauline theology" (66), he insists that Paul's doctrine of justification is the heuristic key to it, just as justification is to Paul's thought overall (75). Although some of his criticisms of Stendahl may be misdirected (Stendahl: 129–33), it is clear that Käsemann, too, is concerned with doing justice to the salvation-historical aspects of Paul's thought, and he acknowledges that salvation history and the idea of justification belong together (76). The question remains, of course, whether Käsemann is correct in giving the priority to justification, or whether Stendahl is correct in giving it to salvation history.

Käsemann's differences with Bultmann center on the meaning of two Pauline expressions, δικαιοσύνη θεοῦ ("the righteousness of God") and σῶμα ("body," "human reality"). Bultmann has emphasized the forensic-eschatological meaning of "righteousness" and its use by Paul to describe the present reality of God's free gift of grace (1951:270–87). Faith, then, is the appropriation of the possibility for life opened up by God's justifying action (1951:314–30). Käsemann (1969), meanwhile, has argued that δικαιοσύνη θεοῦ is a technical term that derives especially from Jewish apocalyptic and that continues to be associated also in Paul's thought with God's establishment of and faithfulness to his covenant—a point Stuhlmacher has sought to verify and elaborate. Thus, Käsemann insists that the gift bestowed in justification "is never at any time separable from its Giver," and that "it partakes of the character of power [*Macht*], in so far as God himself enters the arena and remains in the arena with it" (1969:174). Against Bultmann, Käsemann argues that God's righteousness is not, in Pauline thought, a primarily anthropological concept, but rather an essentially apocalyptic one (1969:180–81). Pauline anthropology itself is described as a "crystallized cosmology" (1971:29), because Käsemann is convinced that Paul views human existence in terms of its "need to participate in creatureliness" and its "capacity for communication in the widest sense," viz., in its relationship to the world with which it is confronted (1971:21). The many recent studies that deal with Paul's idea of righteousness (e.g., Stuhlmacher; Müller; Kertelge; Barth, 1971; Conzelmann, 1968, 1971) and with his anthropology (e.g., Gundry; Jewett, 1971b; K.-A. Bauer; Sand; Heine) show how important these questions have become and also how complex the issues are that need resolution.

It is important to observe that the vast majority of works devoted to Pauline thought have sought to find its center in some particular *theological doctrine*. One must ask whether the diversity of proposals concerning that doctrinal center is not due at least as much to the character of Paul's thought and preaching as to the theological perspectives of Paul's interpreters. G. Eichholz has properly emphasized the dialogical character of Paul's thinking, how it takes shape in the course of his work as an apostle and in relation to the particular needs, conditions and concerns to which he had to be responsive. For this reason, Eichholz hesitates to present more than an "outline" (*Umriss*) of Paul's theology, and he chooses to orient this principle to Paul's own sense of apostolic vocation (14–40). Even so, because Eichholz has chosen the *themes* of Romans as the basis for his presentation (e.g., Christology, righteousness and faith, law, the church, and Israel), he is still trying to catch the butterfly of Pauline theology in a doctrinal net.

G. Howard's exposition of Galatians is not even intended as an "outline" of Paul's theology, but it deserves to be mentioned here because it is undertaken with the conviction that "Paul's genius is best seen when his theology is allowed to arise from the historical setting of his struggles with opponents and his methods in preaching the gospel" (ix). Whether or not one is able to agree with all of Howard's exegetical conclusions, his book stands as an interesting attempt to find a new way of "centering" Pauline thought—less in one or another theological doctrine or in a set of theological topics than in Paul's apostolic proclamation, interpretation, application, and defense of the gospel in particular missionary and pastoral contexts. Indeed, one major contribution of R. Jewett's study of Paul's anthropological terms (1971b) was to drive home this very point, at least with respect to one aspect of Pauline vocabulary.

More recently, J. C. Beker has quite rightly observed that the Pauline letters are artificially universalized and abstracted "away from their immediacy" whenever they are reduced "into a set of propositions, or doctrinal centers" (35). They must be understood, rather, as the instruments by which the apostle "was able to bring the gospel to speech in each new situation," not imposing the gospel's doctrinal core as if it were "a fixed, frozen message," but interpreting it "in the freedom of the Spirit" (33–34). This does not mean that the quest for the theological center of Paul's thought must be given up, only that it must be pursued in new ways and with revised objectives. Even if Beker's own location of that center in the apostle's apocalyptic world view is not fully convincing (see especially 11–19, 135ff.), he is surely on the right track in urging interpreters to focus their attention on the relationship between "contingency and coherence" in the Pauline letters (23–36).

IV. CONCLUDING REMARKS

Limitations of space permit only a few brief comments, in conclusion, about the prospects and opportunities for future work in the three areas of Pauline studies that have been surveyed here.

The Pauline Letters

We have learned a great deal about the various preliterary and literary formulas, patterns and rhetoric that have influenced Paul's writing. While this research continues, we must begin to learn how better to integrate its results with the fact that Paul's letters are, withal, those of an *apostle* whose understanding of his gospel and whose own sense of apostolic vocation have determined not only why but also how he has written those letters (see Berger). Moreover, it is imperative that we give more attention than we have so far to the collection, redaction, and circulation of the Pauline corpus. Questions about glosses, interpolations, integrity, and authenticity must be looked at in this larger framework if any real advances are to be made. This work must go on in tandem with efforts already initiated (e.g., Schenke; Lindemann, 1979) to track the influence of Paul on his earliest interpreters, beginning with the Book of Acts and the authors of the deutero-Pauline letters.

Paul's Life and Ministry

It has become clear that the nature of our sources requires us to approach these matters by way of Paul's interaction with his congregations, including of course his opponents. With respect to this latter, it is to be hoped that scholars may quickly pass through the phase of trying to identify every opposing or rival voice with some specific doctrinal position (e.g., "gnostic," "Judaistic"), thereby using known (and often later) doctrinal models to impose precision on evidence which, given Paul's letters alone, remains imprecise and enigmatic (see Hickling: 286–87). Indeed, one must resist the temptation to think that every sharp word or implied criticism in the letters requires an identifiable opponent on the other side. Scholarship in this area must not relax its efforts to follow out the smallest clues and test a wide range of hypotheses. But it must be more willing than it has sometimes been to regard every historical reconstruction as only provisional and to recognize that, in scholarship as in art, "less" is often "more" — that the less rigidly one holds to hypothetical identifications and reconstructions, the more alert one may become to new data and to new ways of interpreting and organizing the old. Investigation of the social world of earliest Christianity and of the social history and social structures of the movement itself is perhaps the single most promising development to be mentioned under this heading. It is important, however, that researchers in this area not press their Christian texts for data they cannot yield, and that they proceed with great caution in their application of data derived from other sources to the experiences and life of the Christian church. There is also a need for further discussion of the appropriateness of using specifically sociological methods and models for interpreting the data and for clarifying what the most pertinent of those may be. It is certain that students of Paul will be paying more attention than they have to the social, political, and economic features of Paul's world, to the social structures of the Christian congregations themselves, and to their place in the total spectrum of religious associations and movements in the first century.

Pauline Thought

With respect to the presuppositions of Paul's thought, I should like to stress the importance of pursuing the question about Paul's relation to Judaism, specifically the question about what kind of Jew he was. This is crucial if one hopes to be able to understand the significance of Paul's conversion to Christianity and of his own sense of apostolic vocation. It is not sufficient to compare the "whole pattern" of Paul's thought with the "whole pattern" of Palestinian Judaism. E. P. Sanders, who has tried to do this, leaves us with no convincing explanation of why Paul was *converted from* Judaism. When Paul says he had been "as to the law a Pharisee" (Phil 3:5; cf. Gal 1:13–14), that needs to be taken seriously. This is especially so if Rivkin is correct about what it would have meant to be a Pharisee in Paul's day, about the extent to which Pharisaism was itself indebted to Greco-Roman notions and institutions (242–43), and that the burning issue for the Pharisee was not moral purity but the authority of the twofold law and its correct interpretation (252–95). It will be important to ask what the implications are for Pauline studies of this, or any, revised picture of Pharisaism.

Finally, I should only like to emphasize that if the advances made in Pauline studies over the past forty years are to prove worthwhile, they must result eventually in some new models according to which "Pauline theology" can be analyzed and presented. The old models (which were developed largely as topics of "systematic theology," however much those were rearranged) did not recognize, or did not take sufficient account of, the profoundly situational character of Paul's letters. Nor did they attempt, with any seriousness or consistency, to interpret his message in relation to the multiple social, religious, ecclesiastical, and personal forces with which he was constantly and concretely engaged during the whole course of his ministry. The real challenge for interpreters of Paul's thought lies just here: to find ways of respecting the situational and dialogical character of his theology without abandoning the attempt to understand its most fundamental convictions and its most pervasive concerns.

BIBLIOGRAPHY

Andresen, Carl
1965   "Zum Formular frühchristlicher Gemeindebriefe." *ZNW* 56: 233–59.

Bahr, Gordon J.
1966   "Paul and Letter Writing in the First Century." *CBQ* 28: 465–77.

Bailey, John A.
1979   "Who Wrote II Thessalonians?" *NTS* 25: 131–45.

Bandstra, Andrew J.
1968   "Paul, the Letter Writer." *CJT* 3: 176–88.

Barrett, Charles Kingsley
1957   *A Commentary on the Epistle to the Romans.* HNTC. New York: Harper & Row.
1971   "Paul's Opponents in II Corinthians." *NTS* 17: 233–54.
1973   *A Commentary on the Second Epistle to the Corinthians.* HNTC. New York: Harper & Row.

Barth, Markus
1971   *Justification: Pauline Texts Interpreted in the Light of the Old and New Testaments.* Trans. A. M. Woodruff III. Grand Rapids: Eerdmans. [German, 1970.]
1974   *Ephesians.* AB 34, 34A. Garden City, NY: Doubleday.

Bauer, K.-A.
1971   *Leiblichkeit—das Ende aller Werke Gottes: Die Bedeutung der Leiblichkeit des Menschen bei Paulus.* SNT 4. Gütersloh: Mohn.

Bauer, Walter
1971   *Orthodoxy and Heresy in Earliest Christianity.* Trans. Philadelphia Seminar on Christian Origins. Ed. R. A. Kraft and G. Krodel. Philadelphia: Fortress. [1st German ed. 1934.]

Baur, Ferdinand Christian
1875–76   *Paul: His Life and Work.* 2 vols. Rev. A. Menzies. London: Williams & Norgate. [German 1845, 1866–67.]

Beare, Frank W.
1959   *A Commentary on the Epistle to the Philippians.* HNTC. New York: Harper & Row. [3d ed., London: Adam & Charles Black, 1973.]

Beker, J. Christiaan
1980   *Paul the Apostle: The Triumph of God in Life and Thought.* Philadelphia: Fortress.

Berger, Klaus
1974   "Apostelbrief und Apostolische Rede." *ZNW* 65: 190–231.

Best, Ernest
1972   *The First and Second Epistles to the Thessalonians.* HNTC. New York: Harper & Row.

Betz, Hans Dieter
1972   *Der Apostel Paulus und die sokratische Tradition.* BHT 45. Tübingen: Mohr-Siebeck.
1973   "2 Cor 6:14–7:1: An Anti-Pauline Fragment?" *JBL* 92: 88–108.
1975   "The Literary Composition and Function of Paul's Letter to the Galatians." *NTS* 21: 353–79.
1979   *Galatians.* Hermeneia. Philadelphia: Fortress.

Binder, H.
1976   "Die angebliche Krankheit des Paulus." *TZ* 32: 1–13.

Bjerkelund, Carl J.
1967   *Parakalō: Form, Funktion und Sinn der parakalō-Sätze in den paulinischen Briefen.* Bibliotheca Theologica Norvegica 1. Oslo/Bergen/Tromsö: Universitetsforlaget.

Blank, Josef
1968   *Paulus und Jesus: Eine theologische Grundlegung.* SANT 18. Munich: Kösel.

Bonsirven, Joseph
1938   *Exégèse Rabbinique et Exégèse Paulinienne.* Bibliotheque de Théologie historique. Paris: Beauchesne.

Bornkamm, Günther
1961   *Die Vorgeschichte des sogenannten Zweiten Korintherbriefes.* Sitzungsberichte der Heidelberger Akademie der Wissenschaften, Philosophisch-historische Klasse. Heidelberg: Winter. [Reprinted, with an addendum, in his *Geschichte und Glaube*, Zweiter Teil. Gesammelte Aufsätze, IV, 162–94. Munich: Kaiser, 1971.]
1962   "Der Philipperbrief als paulinische Briefsammlung." Pp. 192–202 in *Neotestamentica et Patristica: Eine Freundesgabe, Herrn Prof. Dr. Oscar Cullmann zu seinem 60. Geburtstag.* NovTSup 6. Leiden: Brill.
1971   *Paul.* New York: Harper & Row. [German 1969.]

Bradley, D. G.
1947   "The Origins of the Hortatory Materials in the Letters of Paul." Unpublished Yale dissertation.
1953   "The Topos as a Form in the Pauline Paraenesis." *JBL* 72: 238–46.

Bruce, Frederick Fyvie
1971   *1 and 2 Corinthians.* New Century Bible. London: Oliphants.
1974   *Paul and Jesus.* Grand Rapids: Baker.

Buck, Charles, and Greer Taylor
1969   *Saint Paul: A Study of the Development of His Thought.* New York: Scribner.

Bujard, W.
1973   *Stilanalytische Untersuchungen zum Kolosserbrief als Beitrag zur Methodik von Sprachvergleichen.* SUNT 11. Göttingen: Vandenhoeck & Ruprecht.

Bultmann, Rudolf
1910   *Der Stil der paulinischen Predigt und die kynisch-stoische Diatribe.* FRLANT 13. Göttingen: Vandenhoeck & Ruprecht.
1929   "Zur Geschichte der Paulus-Forschung." *TRu* 1: 26–59.
1934   "Neueste Paulusforschung." *TRu* 6: 229–46.
1936   "Neueste Paulusforschung." *TRu* 8: 1–22.
1947   "Glossen im Römerbrief." *TLZ* 72: 197–202.
1951   *Theology of the New Testament,* 1. Trans. K. Grobel. New York: Scribner. [German 1948]
1959   "Ein neues Paulus-Verständnis?" *TLZ* 84: 481–86.

Caird, George B.
1976   *Paul's Letters from Prison.* New Clarendon Bible. London: Oxford.

Chadwick, Henry
1960   "Die Absicht des Epheserbriefes." *ZNW* 51: 145–53.

Champion, Leonard G.
1934   *Benedictions and Doxologies in the Epistles of Paul.* Oxford: Kemp Hall.

Collange, J.-F.
1972   *Énigmes de la deuxième épître de Paul aux Corinthiens. Étude exégétique de 2 Cor. 2:14–7:4.* SNTSMS 18. Cambridge: University Press.

Conzelmann, Hans
1968   "Current Problems in Pauline Research." 22: 171–86. [German 1966]
1969   *An Outline of the Theology of the New Testament.* Trans. J. Bowden.
       London: SCM. [German 1967, 1968]
1971   "Paul's Doctrine of Justification: Theology or Anthropology?"
       Pp. 108-23 in *Theology of the Liberating Word.* Ed. F. Herzog.
       Nashville: Abingdon. [German 1968]

Cope, Lamar
1978   "I Cor 11:2–16: One Step Further." *JBL* 97: 435–36.

Cranfield, C. E. B.
1975   *A Critical and Exegetical Commentary on the Epistle to the Romans,*
       1. ICC. Edinburgh: T. & T. Clark.

Crouch, J. E.
1973   *The Origin and Intention of the Colossian Haustafel.* FRLANT 109.
       Göttingen: Vandenhoeck & Ruprecht.

Cullmann, Oscar
1949   *The Earliest Christian Confessions.* London: Lutterworth. [German
       1943]
1951   *Christ and Time.* Trans. F. V. Filson. London: SCM. [German 1946]

Dahl, Nils Alstrup
1962   "The Particularity of the Pauline Epistles as a Problem in the Ancient
       Church." Pp. 261–71 in *Neotestamentica et Patristica: Eine Freundes-
       gabe, Herrn Prof. Dr. Oscar Cullmann zu seinem 60. Geburtstag.*
       NovTSup 6. Leiden: Brill.
1977a "Interpreting Ephesians: Then and Now." *Theology Digest* 25:
       305–15.
1977b *Studies in Paul: Theology for the Early Christian Mission.* Minneapolis:
       Augsburg.
1978   "The Origin of the Earliest Prologues to the Pauline Letters."
       Pp. 233–77 in *The Poetics of Faith: Essays offered to A. N. Wilder.* Ed.
       W. A. Beardslee. *Semeia* 12. Missoula, MT: Scholars Press.

Daube, David
1956   *The New Testament and Rabbinic Judaism.* London: Athlone.

Davies, William D.
1948   *Paul and Rabbinic Judaism: Some Rabbinic Elements in Pauline
       Theology.* London: SPCK. [4th ed., Philadelphia: Fortress, 1980.]

Deichgräber, R.
1967   *Gotteshymnus und Christushymnus in der frühen Christenheit: Unter-
       suchungen zu Form, Sprache, und Stil der frühchristlichen Hymnen.*
       SUNT 5. Göttingen: Vandenhoeck & Ruprecht.

Deissmann, G. Adolf
1903   *Bible Studies.* 2d ed. trans. A. Grieve. Edinburgh: T. & T. Clark.
       [German 1895]

Dibelius, Martin
1931   "Zur Formgeschichte des neuen Testaments (ausserhalb der
       Evangelien)." *TRu* n.s. 3: 207–42.
1941   Review of Schubert, 1939, *TLZ* 66: 26–28.

Dockx, S.
1977   *Chronologies néotestamentaires et vie de l'Église primitive: Recherches
       exégétiques.* Gembloux: Duculot. [Reprinted Leuven: Peeters, 1984.]

Donfried, Karl P.
1970 "A Short Note on Romans 16." *JBL* 89: 441–49.
1977, ed. *The Romans Debate*. Minneapolis: Augsburg.
Doty, William G.
1969 "The Classification of Epistolary Literature." *CBQ* 31: 183–99.
Eckart, K.-G.
1961 "Der zweite echte Brief des Apostel Paulus an die Thessalonicher." *ZTK* 58: 30–44.
Eichholz, Georg
1972 *Die Theologie des Paulus im Umriss*. Neukirchen-Vluyn: Neukirchener Verlag. [2d ed. 1977.]
Ellis, E. Earle
1957 *Paul's Use of the Old Testament*. Edinburgh: Oliver & Boyd.
1975 "Paul and His Opponents." Pp. 264–98 in *Christianity, Judaism and Other Greco-Roman Cults: Studies for Morton Smith at Sixty*, 1. Ed. J. Neusner. SJLA 12. Leiden: Brill.
Fee, Gordon D.
1977 "II Corinthians vi.14–vii.1 and Food Offered to Idols." *NTS* 23: 140–61.
Fischer, Karl-Martin
1973 *Tendenz und Absicht des Epheserbriefes*. FRLANT 111. Göttingen: Vandenhoeck & Ruprecht.
Fitzer, Gerhard
1963 *Das Weib schweige in der Gemeinde: Über den unpaulinischen Charakter der mulier-taceat-Verse in 1. Korinther 14*. Theologische Existenz heute, n.s. 110. Munich: Kaiser.
Fitzmyer, Joseph A., S.J.
1961 "Qumran and the Interpolated Paragraph in 2 Cor. 6:14–7:1." *CBQ* 23: 271–80.
1974 "Some Notes on Aramaic Epistolography." *JBL* 93: 201–25.
Fraser, John W.
1974 *Jesus & Paul: Paul as Interpreter of Jesus from Harnack to Kümmel*. Appleford, Abingdon, Berkshire: Marcham Manor.
Friedrich, Gerhard
1973 "1. Thessalonicher 5, 1–11, der apologetische Einschub eines Späteren." *ZTK* 70: 288–315.
Funk, Robert W.
1966 *Language, Hermeneutic, and Word of God: The Problem of Language in the New Testament and Contemporary Theology*. New York: Harper & Row.
1967 "The Apostolic Parousia: Form and Significance." Pp. 246–68 in *Christian History and Interpretation: Studies Presented to John Knox*. Ed. W. R. Farmer, C. F. D. Moule, and R. R. Niebuhr. Cambridge: University Press.
Furnish, Victor Paul
1970 "Development in Paul's Thought." *JAAR* 38: 289–303.
1984 *II Corinthians*. AB 32A. Garden City, NY: Doubleday.
Gager, John G.
1975 *Kingdom and Community: The Social World of Early Christianity*. Englewood Cliffs, NJ: Prentice-Hall.

1979   Review essay of books by R. M. Grant, A. J. Malherbe, and G. Theissen. *RSR* 5: 174–80.

Gale, Herbert M.
1964   *The Use of Analogy in the Letters of Paul.* Philadelphia: Westminster.

Gamble, Harry
1975   "The Redaction of the Pauline Letters and the Formation of the Pauline Corpus." *JBL* 94: 403–18.
1977   *The Textual History of the Letter to the Romans.* SD 42. Grand Rapids: Eerdmans.

Georgi, Dieter
1964   *Die Gegner des Paulus im 2. Korintherbrief: Studien zur religiösen Propaganda in der Spätantike.* WMANT 11. Neukirchen-Vluyn: Neukirchener Verlag. Eng. trans. *The Opponents of Paul in Second Corinthians.* Philadelphia: Fortress, 1986
1965   *Die Geschichte der Kollekte des Paulus für Jerusalem.* TF 38. Hamburg-Bergstedt: H. Reich.

Gnilka, J.
1968   "2 Cor 6:14–7:1 in the Light of the Qumran Texts and the Testaments of the Twelve Patriarchs." Pp. 48–68 in *Paul and Qumran.* Ed. J. Murphy-O'Connor. London: Chapman.

Goodspeed, Edgar Johnson
1933   *The Meaning of Ephesians.* Chicago: University of Chicago Press.

Goppelt, Leonhard
1982   *Theology of the New Testament,* vol. 2. Trans. J. E. Alsup. Ed. J. Roloff. Grand Rapids: Eerdmans. [German 1976]

Grayston, Kenneth, and G. Herdan
1959   "The Authorship of the Pastorals in the Light of Statistical Linguistics." *NTS* 6: 1–15.

Grobel, Kendrick
1964   "A Chiastic Retribution-Formula in Romans 2." Pp. 255–61 in *Zeit und Geschichte: Dankesgabe an Rudolf Bultmann zum 80. Geburtstag.* Ed. E. Dinkler. Tübingen: Mohr-Siebeck.

Grossouw, W. K. M.
1951   "Over de echtheid van 2 Cor 6:14–7:1." *Studia Catholica* 26: 203–6.

Gundry, Robert H.
1976   *Sōma in Biblical Theology, with Emphasis on Pauline Anthropology.* SNTSMS 29. Cambridge: University Press.

Gunther, John J.
1972   *Paul: Messenger and Exile: A Study in the Chronology of His Life and Letters.* Valley Forge, PA: Judson.
1973   *St. Paul's Opponents and Their Background. A Study of Apocalyptic and Jewish Sectarian Teachings.* NovTSup 35. Leiden: Brill.

Guthrie, Donald
1957   *The Pastoral Epistles.* Tyndale NT Commentaries. Grand Rapids: Eerdmans.

Hanson, Anthony T.
1974   *Studies in Paul's Technique and Theology.* Grand Rapids: Eerdmans.

Heine, Susanne
1976   *Leibhafter Glaube: Ein Beitrag zum Verständnis der theologischen Konzeption des Paulus.* Vienna: Herder.

Hengel, Martin
1974   *Judaism and Hellenism: Studies in Their Encounter in Palestine during the Early Hellenistic Period.* Trans. J. Bowden. 2 vols. Philadelphia: Fortress. [2d German ed. 1973]

Hickling, C. J. A.
1975   "Is the Second Epistle to the Corinthians a Source for Early Church History?" *ZNW* 66: 284–87.

Hock, Ronald F.
1980   *The Social Context of Paul's Ministry: Tentmaking and Apostleship.* Philadelphia: Fortress.

Howard, George
1979   *Paul: Crisis in Galatia: A Study in Early Christian Theology.* SNTSMS 35. Cambridge: University Press.

Hurd, John C., Jr.
1965   *The Origin of I Corinthians.* New York: Seabury.
1967   "Pauline Chronology and Pauline Theology." Pp. 225–48 in *Christian History and Interpretation: Studies Presented to John Knox.* Ed. W. R. Farmer, C. F. D. Moule, and R. R. Niebuhr. Cambridge: University Press.
1968   "The Sequence of Paul's Letters." *CJT* 14: 189–200.

Jeremias, Joachim
1953   "Zur Gedankenführung in den paulinischen Briefen." Pp. 146–54 in *Studia Paulina in Honorem Johannes de Zwaan Septuagenarii.* Haarlem: Bohn.
1958   "Chiasmus in den Paulusbriefen." *ZNW* 49: 145–56.
1971   *Der Schlüssel zur Theologie des Apostels Paulus.* Calwer Hefte 115. Stuttgart: Calwer. [An earlier, briefer English version in *ExpTim* 76 (1964) 27–30.]
1975   *Die Briefe an Timotheus und Titus.* Rev. ed. NTD 9. Göttingen: Vandenhoeck & Ruprecht.

Jewett, Robert
1969   "The Form and Function of the Homiletic Benediction." *ATR* 51: 18–34.
1971a   "The Agitators and the Galatian Congregations." *NTS* 17: 198–212.
1971b   *Paul's Anthropological Terms: A Study of Their Use in Conflict Settings.* AGJU 10. Leiden: Brill.
1979   *A Chronology of Paul's Life.* Philadelphia: Fortress.

Johnson, P. F.
1973   "The Use of Statistics in the Analysis of the Characteristics of Pauline Writing." *NTS* 20: 92–100.

Judge, Edwin A.
1972   "St. Paul and Classical Society." *JAC* 15: 19–36.

Jüngel, E.
1962   *Paulus und Jesus: Eine Untersuchung zur Präzisierung der Frage nach dem Ursprung der Christologie.* Tübingen: Mohr-Siebeck.

Kallas, James
1965   "Romans xiii.1–7: An Interpolation." *NTS* 11: 365–74.

Kamlah, Ehrhard
1964   *Die Form der katalogischen Paränese im Neuen Testament.* WUNT 7. Tübingen: Mohr-Siebeck.

Karlsson, Gustav
1956   "Formelhaftes in Paulusbriefen?" *Eranos* 54: 138–41.

Käsemann, Ernst
1969   "The 'Righteousness of God' in Paul." Pp. 168–82 in his *New Testament Questions of Today.* Trans. W. J. Montague. Philadelphia: Fortress. [German 1961]
1971   *Perspectives on Paul.* Trans. M. Kohl. Philadelphia: Fortress. [German 1969]
1974   *An die Römer.* HNT 8a. Tübingen: Mohr-Siebeck.

Kehnscherper, G.
1964   "Der Apostel Paulus als römischer Bürger." *SE* 2: 411–40.

Kennedy, George A.
1984   *New Testament Interpretation through Rhetorical Criticism.* Chapel Hill and London: University of North Carolina Press.

Kertelge, Karl
1967   *"Rechtfertigung" bei Paulus: Studien zur Struktur und zum Bedeutungsgehalt des paulinischen Rechtfertigungsbegriffs.* NTAbh n.s. 3. Münster: Aschendorff.

Kim, Chan-Hie
1972   *Form and Structure of the Familiar Greek Letter of Recommendation.* SBLDS 4. Missoula, MT: Scholars Press.

Klijn, A. F. J.
1965   "Paul's Opponents in Philippians iii." *NovT* 7: 278–84.

Knox, John
1950   *Chapters in a Life of Paul.* Nashville: Abingdon. Rev. ed. Ed. R. A. Hare. Macon, GA: Mercer University Press, 1987.
1959   *Philemon Among the Letters of Paul.* Rev. ed. Nashville: Abingdon.

Koester, Helmut
1962   "The Purpose of the Polemic of a Pauline Fragment (Phil. iii)." *NTS* 8: 317–32.
1965   "GNOMAI DIAPHOROI: The Origin and Nature of Diversification in the History of Early Christianity." *HTR* 58: 279–318. Repr. in J. M. Robinson and H. Koester, *Trajectories through Early Christianity,* 114–57. Philadelphia: Fortress, 1971.

Koskenniemi, Heikki
1956   *Studien zur Idee und Phraseologie des griechischen Briefes bis 400 n. Chr.* Helsinki: Suomalaien Tiedeakatemie.

Kümmel, Werner Georg
1973   *The Theology of the New Testament according to Its Major Witnesses.* Trans. J. E. Steely. Nashville: Abingdon. [German 1969]

Ladd, G. E.
1974   *A Theology of the New Testament.* Grand Rapids: Eerdmans.

Lambrecht, J. L., S.J.
1978   "The Fragment 2 Cor vi 14–vii 1: A Plea for its Authenticity."
        Pp. 143–61 in *Miscellanea Neotestamentica*, vol. 2. Ed. T. Baarda,
        A. F. J. Klijn, and W. C. van Unnik. NovTSup 47. Leiden: Brill.

Lindemann, Andreas
1975   *Die Aufhebung der Zeit.* SNT 12. Gütersloh: Mohn.
1976   "Bemerkungen zu den Adressaten und zum Anlass des Epheser-
        briefes." *ZNW* 67: 235–51.
1980   *Paulus im ältesten Christentum: Das Bild des Apostels und die
        Rezeption der paulinischen Theologie in der frühchristlichen Literatur
        bis Marcion.* BHT 58. Tübingen: Mohr-Siebeck.

Lohse, Eduard
1971   *Colossians and Philemon.* Hermeneia. Philadelphia: Fortress.
        [German 1968]

Lüdemann, Gerd
1983   *Paulus, der Heidenapostel. II: Antipaulinismus im frühen Christentum.*
        FRLANT 130. Göttingen: Vandenhoeck & Ruprecht.
1984   *Paul, Apostle to the Gentiles: Studies in Chronology.* Trans. F. S. Jones.
        Philadelphia, Fortress. [German 1979]

Lund, Nils W.
1942   *Chiasmus in the New Testament.* Chapel Hill: University of North
        Carolina Press.

McArthur, H. K.
1969   "*Kai* Frequency in Greek Letters." *NTS* 15: 339–49.

Machalet, Christian
1973   "Paulus und seine Gegner: Eine Untersuchung zu den Korinther-
        briefen." Pp. 183–203 in *Theokratia: Jahrbuch des Inst. Judaicum
        Delitzschianum II. 1970–72. Festgabe für K. H. Rengstorf.* Ed. W.
        Dietrich et al. Leiden: Brill.

Malherbe, Abraham J.
1968   "The Beasts at Ephesus." *JBL* 87: 71–80.
1983   *Social Aspects of Early Christianity.* 2d ed. Philadelphia: Fortress.

Martin, Ralph P.
1967   *Carmen Christi: Philippians ii.5–11 in Recent Interpretation and in the
        Setting of Christian Worship.* SNTSMS 4. Cambridge: University
        Press.
1974   *Colossians and Philemon.* NCB. London: Oliphants.

Masson, C.
1957   *Les Deux Épîtres de S. Paul aux Thessaloniciens.* CNT. Paris:
        Delachaux & Niestlé.

Meeks, Wayne A.
1983   *The First Urban Christians: The Social World of the Apostle Paul.* New
        Haven and London: Yale University Press.

Mitton, C. Leslie
1955   *The Formation of the Pauline Corpus of Letters.* London: Epworth.

Morton, A. Q., and J. McLeman
1964   *Christianity and the Computer.* London: Hodder & Stoughton.
1966   *Paul: The Man and the Myth.* London: Hodder & Stoughton.

Müller, Christian
1964   *Gottes Gerechtigkeit und Gottes Volk: Eine Untersuchung zu Römer 9–11*. FRLANT 86. Göttingen: Vandenhoeck & Ruprecht.

Mullins, Terence Y.
1962   "Petition as a Literary Form." *NovT* 5: 46–54.
1964   "Disclosure: A Literary Form in the New Testament." *NovT* 7: 44–60.
1968   "Greeting as a New Testament Form." *JBL* 87: 418–26.

Munck, Johannes
1959   *Paul and the Salvation of Mankind*. Trans. F. Clarke. Richmond: John Knox. [German 1954]

Murphy-O'Connor, Jerome, O. P.
1968, ed.   *Paul and Qumran: Studies in New Testament Exegesis*. London: Chapman.
1975,   "Corpus paulinien." *RB* 82: 130–58; 84: 305–18.
1977

Nickle, Keith
1966   *The Collection: A Study in Paul's Strategy*. SBT 48. Naperville, IL: Allenson.

O'Brien, Peter T.
1977   *Introductory Thanksgivings in the Letters of Paul*. NovTSup 49. Leiden: Brill.

Ogg, George
1968   *The Chronology of the Life of Paul*. London: Epworth.

O'Neill, John C.
1972   *The Recovery of Paul's Letter to the Galatians*. London: SPCK.
1975   *Paul's Letter to the Romans*. Baltimore, MD: Penguin.

Pagels, Elaine
1975   *The Gnostic Paul: Gnostic Exegesis of the Pauline Letters*. Philadelphia: Fortress.

Pearson, Birger A.
1971   "1 Thessalonians 2:13–16: A Deutero-Pauline Interpolation." *HTR* 64: 79–94.

Pfitzner, Victor C.
1967   *Paul and the Agon Motif: Traditional Athletic Imagery in the Pauline Literature*. NovTSup 16. Leiden: Brill.

Riesenfeld, Harald
1960   "La langage parabolique dans les épîtres de Saint Paul." Pp. 47–59 in *Littérature et théologie pauliniennes* by A. Descamps et al. Recherches Bibliques 5. Louvain: Desclée.

Rigaux, Beda
1956   *Saint Paul: Les Épîtres aux Thessaloniciens*. EBib. Paris: Gabalda.
1968   *The Letters of St. Paul: Modern Studies*. Ed. and trans. S. Yonick. Chicago: Franciscan Herald Press. [French 1962]

Rivkin, Ellis
1978   *A Hidden Revolution: The Pharisees' Search for the Kingdom Within*. Nashville: Abingdon.

Roetzel, Calvin
1969   "The Judgment Form in Paul's Letters." *JBL* 88: 305–12.

Rubenstein, Richard L.
1972 *My Brother Paul*. New York: Harper & Row.

Sampley, J. Paul
1977 " 'Before God I do not lie' (Gal. I.20): Paul's Self-Defense in the Light of Roman Legal Praxis." *NTS* 23: 477–82.

Sand, A.
1967 *Der Begriff "Fleisch" in den paulinischen Hauptbriefen*. BU 2. Regensburg: Pustet.

Sanders, Ed Parish
1977 *Paul and Palestinian Judaism: A Comparison of Patterns of Religion*. Philadelphia: Fortress.
1983 *Paul, the Law, and the Jewish People*. Philadelphia: Fortress.

Sanders, Jack T.
1962 "The Transition from Opening Epistolary Thanksgivings to Body in the Letters of the Pauline Corpus." *JBL* 81: 348–62.
1971 *The New Testament Christological Hymns: Their Historical Background*. SNTSMS 15. Cambridge: University Press.

Sandmel, Samuel
1979 *The Genius of Paul*. Philadelphia: Fortress. [1st ed. 1958]

Schenke, H.-M.
1975 "Das Weiterwirken des Paulus und die Pflege seines Erbes durch die Paulus-Schule." *NTS* 21: 505–18.

Schille, G.
1965 *Frühchristliche Hymnen*. Berlin: Evangelische Verlagsanstalt.

Schlier, Heinrich
1978 *Grundzüge einer paulinischen Theologie*. Freiburg: Herder.

Schmidt, Daryl
1983 "1 Thess 2:13–16: Linguistic Evidence for an Interpolation." *JBL* 102: 269–79.

Schmithals, Walter
1971 *Gnosticism in Corinth*. Trans. J. E. Steely. Nashville: Abingdon. [German 1956]
1972 *Paul and the Gnostics*. Trans. J. E. Steely. Nashville: Abingdon. [German 1965]

Schneider, Gerhard
1974 "Paulus und sein Werk in der neuesten theologischen Forschung." *TPQ* 122: 375–82.

Schoeps, Hans Joachim
1961 *Paul: The Theology of the Apostle in the Light of Jewish Religious History*. Trans. H. Knight. Philadelphia: Westminster. [German 1959]

Schrage, Wolfgang
1974 "Zur Ethik der neutestamentlichen Haustafeln." *NTS* 21: 1–22.

Schroeder, David
1959 "Die Haustafeln des Neuen Testaments: Ihre Herkunft und ihr theologischer Sinn." Dissertation, Hamburg.

Schubert, Paul
1939 *Form and Function of the Pauline Thanksgivings*. BZNW 20. Berlin: Töpelmann.

1947 "Urgent Tasks for New Testament Research." Pp. 209–28 in *The Study of the Bible Today and Tomorrow*. Ed. H. R. Willoughby. Chicago: University of Chicago Press.

Schweitzer, Albert
1912 *Paul and His Interpreters: A Critical History*. Trans. W. Montgomery. London: Adam & Charles Black. [German 1912]

Snyder, Graydon F.
1976 "The 'Tobspruch' in the New Testament." *NTS* 23: 117–20.

Stendahl, Krister
1976 *Paul among Jews and Gentiles and Other Essays*. Philadelphia: Fortress.

Stirewalt, Martin Luther, Jr.
1969 "Paul's Evaluation of Letter-Writing." Pp. 186–90 in *Search the Scriptures*. Ed. J. M. Myers et al. Gettysburg Theological Studies 3. Leiden: Brill.
1977 "The Form and Function of the Greek Letter-Essay." Pp. 175–206 in *The Romans Debate*. Ed. K. P. Donfried. Minneapolis: Augsburg.

Stuhlmacher, Peter
1965 *Gerechtigkeit Gottes bei Paulus*. FRLANT 87. Göttingen: Vandenhoeck & Ruprecht.

Suhl, Alfred
1975 *Paulus und seine Briefe: Ein Beitrag zur paulinischen Chronologie*. Gütersloh: Mohn.

Talbert, Charles H.
1966 "A Non-Pauline Fragment at Romans 3:24–26?" *JBL* 85: 287–96.

Tarachow, Sidney
1955 "St. Paul and Early Christianity: A Psychoanalytic and Historical Study." Pp. 233–79 in *Psychoanalysis and the Social Sciences*, vol. 4. Ed. W. Muenstenberger. New York: International Universities.

Theissen, Gerd
1974 "Theoretische Probleme religions-soziologischer Forschung und die Analyse des Urchristentums." *Neue Zeitschrift für systematische Theologie und Religionsphilosophie* 16: 35–56.
1982 *The Social Setting of Pauline Christianity: Essays on Corinth*. Ed. and trans. with an introduction by J. H. Schütz. Philadelphia: Fortress. [Essays published in German in 1974 and 1975.]

Thraede, Klaus
1970 *Grundzüge griechischrömischer Brieftopik*. Zetemata 48. Munich: Beck.

Thrall, Margaret
1977 "The Problem of II Cor. vi.14–vii.1 in Some Recent Discussion." *NTS* 24: 132–48.

Thyen, Hartwig
1955 *Der Stil der jüdisch-hellenistischen Homilie*. FRLANT 47. Göttingen: Vandenhoeck & Ruprecht.

Titus, E. L.
1959 "Did Paul Write I Corinthians 13?" *JBR* 27: 299–302.

Trilling, W.
1972   *Untersuchungen zum zweiten Thessalonicherbrief.* ETS 27. Leipzig:
          St. Benno.

Tyson, Joseph B.
1968   "Paul's Opponents in Galatia." *NovT* 10: 241–54.

van Roon, A.
1974   *The Authenticity of Ephesians.* NovTSup 39. Leiden: Brill.

van Unnik, Willem C.
1962   *Tarsus or Jerusalem: The City of Paul's Youth.* London: Epworth.

Walker, William O.
1975   "1 Corinthians 11:2–16 and Paul's Views Regarding Women." *JBL* 94:
          94–110.

Weiss, Johannes
1897   "Beiträge zur paulinischen Rhetorik." *Theologische Studien, B. Weiss
          dargestellt.* Göttingen: Vandenhoeck & Ruprecht.

Wengst, Klaus
1972   "Der Apostel und die Tradition: Zur theologischen Bedeutung
          urchristlicher Formeln bei Paulus." *ZTK* 69: 145–62.

White, John L.
1972a   *The Form and Function of the Body of the Greek Letter: A Study of the
          Letter-Body in the Non-Literary Papyri and in Paul the Apostle.*
          SBLDS 2. Missoula, MT: Scholars Press.

1972b   *The Form and Structure of the Official Petition: A Study in Greek
          Epistolography.* SBLDS 5. Missoula, MT: Scholars Press.

Whiteley, Dennis E. H.
1964   *The Theology of St. Paul.* Philadelphia: Fortress.

Wibbing, Siegfried
1959   *Die Tugend- und Lasterkataloge im Neuen Testament und ihre Tradi-
          tionsgeschichte unter besonderer Berücksichtigung der Qumran-Texte.*
          BZNW 5. Berlin: Töpelmann.

Wilckens, Ulrich
1959   "Die Bekehrung des Paulus als religionsgeschichtliche Problem."
          ZTK 56: 273–93.

Wuellner, Wilhelm
1976   "Paul's Rhetoric of Argumentation in Romans: An Alternative to the
          Donfried-Karris Debate over Romans." *CBQ* 38: 330–51. Repr. in
          Donfried, 1977, ed. 152–74.

Zmijewski, Josef
1978   *Der Stil der paulinischen "Narrenrede": Analyse der Sprachgestaltung
          in 2 Kor 11, 1–12, 10 als Beitrag zur Methodik von Stiluntersuchungen
          neutestamentlicher Texte.* BBB 52. Cologne and Bonn: Peter
          Hanstein.

Zuntz, G.
1953   *The Text of the Epistles: A Disquisition upon the Corpus Paulinum.*
          Schweich Lectures, 1946. London: Oxford University Press for the
          British Academy.

13

THE EPISTLE TO THE HEBREWS

Philip Edgcumbe Hughes

In the modern postwar period, the discovery of the Dead Sea Scrolls contributed significantly to our understanding of Judaism in first-century Palestine and provided a fresh stimulus to the study of the writing known as the Epistle to the Hebrews. It is, indeed, the judgment of many scholars that the beliefs of the Qumran community offer a palpable clue, long sought in vain, to the situation that evoked the composition of this document.

I. HEBREWS AND QUMRAN

The thesis of the Jewish scholar Y. Yadin (1958) that Hebrews was written specifically for the purpose of counteracting certain distinctive teachings of the Dead Sea sect aroused immediate interest. The epistle's demonstration of the unique superiority of Jesus, the incarnate Son of God, to angels, Moses, and Aaron Yadin saw as a rejoinder to the beliefs of the Qumran brotherhood, who, cloistered in the wilderness, regarded themselves as dedicated observers of the Mosaic covenant as they awaited the setting up in Jerusalem of the eschatological kingdom under the hierarchical rule of the archangel Michael and two messianic personages — one priestly, who would restore to the temple the authentic Aaronic/Zadokite priesthood, and the other kingly, of the line of David (in that order of priority). Yadin concluded that the recipients of the epistle were converts to Christianity from the Dead Sea sect who had retained some of their previous beliefs and who, therefore, were in need of the instruction given in Hebrews. Some years later the publication of the text of the fragmented Melchizedek document found in Cave 11 was welcomed by Yadin (1965) as providing the answer to the hitherto unsolved question How and why did the writer come to use Melchizedek as his main theme?

M. de Jonge and A. S. van der Woude drew attention to the probability that in the Qumran perspective the archangel Michael and Melchizedek were one and the same (see also van der Woude, 1965). Special studies of Melchizedek and his significance have come from R. Rábanos; F. L. Horton (1976b), who disputes a connection here between Hebrews and Qumran, preferring to regard the Hebrews portrayal as in the main an original and independent interpretation of the OT material; B. Demarest, who surveys the interpretation of the Hebrews teaching from Erasmus to

11QMelchizedek; and P. J. Kobelski. Essays have been published by G. G. Lloyd; J. A. Fitzmyer (1963, 1967), who views Hebrews 7 as a midrash of Gen 14:18–20, similar in technique to that of 4QFlorilegium; M. Delcor; C. Spicq (1977b); and J. W. Thompson (1977), who argues for an affinity of the Hebrews picture with Philo rather than with 11QMelchizedek.

The case made out by Yadin for a connection between Hebrews and the teaching of Qumran seems to me a strong one, though my inclination is to work with a wider stage (Hughes, 1977). The teaching opposed in Hebrews may be regarded as characteristic of Essenism more generally, to which the Qumran documents bear important witness. The recipients need not be converts from Qumran in particular, but rather, again more generally, Hebrew Christians who, facing hostility in a Jewish setting, were tempted to ease their position by reverting in a compromising fashion to Judaism of the idealistic Qumran type.

C. Spicq (1952) approved the theory, previously advocated by J. V. Brown in 1923 and D. Bornhaüser in 1932 and in our period by M. E. Clarkson and P. Ketter, that Hebrews was addressed to a group of former Jerusalem priests belonging to the great number of priests who were "obedient to the faith" at the time preceding the martyrdom of Stephen (Acts 6:7) and who had left Jerusalem during the persecution that followed (Acts 8:1). F. V. Filson described the theory not unsympathetically as "interesting" but "incapable of proof." O. Cullmann suggested that the development mentioned in Acts 6:7 involved some priests from Qumran, and F.-M. Braun, who held that of all the NT writings Hebrews gave "the fullest answer to the basic tendencies" of Qumran, was of a similar opinion, but also envisaged another dispersal of priests during the disturbances leading up to A.D. 70, when the Qumran community was breaking up. Spicq, too, was impressed by the evidence accumulating from Qumran and found in Hebrews "a firm, almost aggressive, rejoinder to Qumranian speculations" (1959:381), and now classified the recipients as "Esseno-Christians, Jewish priests," among whom a number of "ex-Qumranians" could be found (390; see also 1977a:29ff.). J. Daniélou had favored a similar conclusion.

In the judgment of H. Kosmala, those addressed were not Christians but Jews of Essene persuasion, members of or sympathizers with the Qumran community, who were feeling their way toward Christianity. D. Flusser argued that the associations between Qumran and the NT go back to pre-Pauline Christianity and that Hebrews affords evidence to this effect. J. Bowman contended that the Dead Sea sect must have practiced the burning of the red heifer in accordance with the regulations for the preparation of the water for purification (Numbers 19); this being so, light is thrown on the otherwise puzzling mention of "the ashes of a heifer" in Hebrews 9:13 (see Hughes: 362ff.), though Bowman's article makes no attempt to connect Qumran and Hebrews. J. W. Bowman designated those to whom Hebrews was sent as belonging to the Hellenistic wing of early Palestianian Christianity who were influenced by the teachings of Qumran.

J. Coppens, however, was critical of the hypothesis of a close link between the content of Hebrews and the doctrines of Qumran and attributed any parallels to a common background, while affirming a much stronger connection between Hebrews and Hellenistic or Philonic Judaism. F. F. Bruce shared this skepticism and was of the opinion that "the most that can be said" is that the letter's recipients were "probably Jewish believers in Jesus" coming from "the nonconformist Judaism of which the Essenes and the Qumran community are outstanding representatives, but not the only representatives" (1963; 1964:xxix). But F. C. Fensham reaffirmed the likelihood of the Hebrews-Qumran connection and proposed the possibility of the letter's author having been associated in Egypt with a group responsive to the doctrines of Qumran and subsequently having written to Christians similarly influenced. R. Williamson (1976) looked elsewhere and, drawing attention to parallels between Hebrews and the concepts of the Merkabah mystics, suggested the probability that first-century Merkabah mysticism provided the best background for interpreting the thought and language of Hebrews.

II. DESTINATION

The destination of Hebrews has long been a matter of speculation: solutions proposed have spanned the Mediterranean world from east to west. It is impossible here to set forth and discuss all the different hypotheses propounded by recent authors; in general, however, it may be said that those who postulate a connection between Hebrews and Qumran understandably tend to locate the letter's recipients in Palestine or some neighboring territory, whereas those who think otherwise continue to range over a wide area.

The salutation at the conclusion of Hebrews (13:24), "Those from Italy send you greetings," has induced many to favor an Italian, or, more precisely, a Roman destination (though the phrase "those from Italy" is not free from ambiguity). Defenders of this supposition include R. C. H. Lenski, W. Manson, W. Neil, W. Barclay, and F. F. Bruce. W. Manson, for example, envisaged a separate congregation of Jewish Christians within the Roman church who were unprepared to acknowledge the unique supremacy of Jesus and to treat the customs of their fathers as obsolete and were, therefore, hesitant to commit themselves to the task of world evangelization (23–24 and passim). Spicq observes, however, that it is unthinkable that the Roman church, honored by the reception of this letter, should have been ignorant of its author and should for so long have refused to include it among the canonical writings (1952:233–34).

Thinking that the teaching opposed in Hebrews was similar to that denounced by Paul in Colossians—indeed, that Hebrews provided "a complete refutation of the Colossian heresy" and even perhaps stimulated Paul to write his letter—T. W. Manson decided that Hebrews was sent to the Lycus Valley, where Colossae was situated. But, as Bruce remarks, there is nothing in Hebrews to suggest that its recipients were addicted to angel-worship, and the admonition about foods in 13:9 could "equally well be related to the kind of situation with which Paul deals in Rom. xiv,2ff." (1963:218–19).

Others, among them Clarkson and W. F. Howard, have favored Ephesus as the *terminus ad quem*. The latter supposed that a number of Hebrew Christians in that city, who looked down on their Gentile fellow believers as inferior, were shaken in their faith when they received news of Paul's imprisonment and execution in Rome. Hebrews was written, Howard suggests, to encourage them and to inform them that Timothy, who, *ex hypothesi*, had also been imprisoned after complying with Paul's request to join him in Rome (2 Tim 4:9, 13, 21), had now been released and would soon be coming to them accompanied by the author of the letter (Heb 13:23).

F. Lo Bue, on the other hand, working from the assumption that Apollos was the writer of Hebrews, proposed Ephesus as the *terminus a quo*. "Those from Italy" he identified primarily with the "Roman refugees" Aquila and Priscilla, whom Apollos met and from whom he received instruction in Ephesus before traveling across to Corinth (Acts 18:24–19:1). Lo Bue's conclusion was that "the letter was addressed to a small but very lively Jewish-Christian section of the Corinthian church" (54). Other advocates of a Corinthian destination are H. Montefiore and J. H. Davies (1967). Adopting premises similar to those of Lo Bue, Montefiore suggested that Apollos wrote Hebrews to compensate for his inability to visit the Corinthian believers at the time of Paul's first letter to them (see 1 Cor 16:12), which the apostle sent soon afterward when he saw that the admonitions of Apollos's epistle had been disregarded. Montefiore believes that 1 Corinthians contains allusions to Hebrews, but, even granting his hypothesis, it must be regarded as strange that Paul makes no explicit reference to the missive of Apollos, the unsatisfactory response to which had, supposedly, been the occasion for his writing.

Spicq (1952:247ff.) came to the conclusion that Hebrews was "written by Apollos to a vast community of Jewish priests, converted by St. Stephen, exiled after his death and probably finding refuge in some large city on the Palestinian or Syrian coast, either Caesarea or, preferably, Antioch." The study of the Qumran documents led him to assert that "the Roman destination of Hebrews is becoming more and more improbable" (1959:390); and G. W. Buchanan has formed the judgment that "the author and recipients seem more closely related to monastic Zionists than has previously been thought" and that "there is more reason than before for locating both in Palestine before A.D. 70" (1975:329).

III. AUTHOR

It is not surprising that those who are persuaded that there is a strong Philonic influence in Hebrews have tended to advocate the candidacy of Apollos as its author. The chief reason for this choice is that Apollos, like Philo, was a native of Alexandria (Acts 18:24). It should be noted, however, that the authorship of Apollos has no place in the tradition of the early church; indeed, it was first advanced (according to the evidence at present available) in the sixteenth century by Martin Luther. No arguments were offered by Luther, but Spicq has presented the case for Apollos at some length (1952:210ff.) and seems to write with the assumption that the case is now to all intents and purposes closed. Montefiore apparently shares this conviction. Other supporters of the candidacy of Apollos are Lenski, T. W. Manson, Ketter, W. F. Howard, and Lo Bue.

Though over the centuries many different names have been proposed, most of these have dropped out of contention either because we know enough about them and their writings to rule them out or because we know little or nothing about their abilities. If the author is to be sought among those who appear in the pages of the NT, it is evident that two names stand out above the rest—those of Barnabas and Apollos. Both were Jewish Christians, outstanding leaders in the church, eloquent expounders of the scriptures, and companions of the apostle Paul. The Alexandrian origin of Apollos, if that is regarded as an advantage, is balanced by the information that Barnabas was a Levite (Acts 4:36). The tradition that Barnabas is the author of Hebrews, moreover, is ancient, earlier than Tertullian. In recent years it has been kept alive by scholars such as J. S. Javet, F. J. Badcock, H. Mulder (1965a, 1965b), and J. A. T. Robinson (217ff.).

But the realm is that of surmise and conjecture, not proven fact, and A. Vanhoye (1969c:39–40) has rightly sounded a caution regarding the association of Hebrews with Apollos: "Neither historical nor literary criticism provides sufficient facts. Indeed, there does not exist the least bit of ancient evidence in favor of the attribution to Apollos. No precise indication can be drawn from the epistle itself. And we possess no writing of Apollos which would permit a comparison. How, under these circumstances, is it possible to arrive at a firm conclusion?" Barnabas can claim a place in the patristic evidence, but otherwise Vanhoye's observations apply also to his name.

The hypothesis of a close connection linking Hebrews through Apollos to the conceptual world of Philo of Alexandria, of which Spicq (1951; 1952:39ff.; 1959) has been a vigorous champion, has been critically examined in a large volume by R. Williamson (1970b). S. G. Sowers was to some extent critical of Spicq's position, but still agreed with him that the author of Hebrews came from "the same school of Alexandrian Judaism as Philo" (66). The conclusion to which Williamson's detailed studies brought him, namely, that "the Writer of Hebrews had never been a Philonist, had never read Philo's works, had never come under the influence of Philo directly or indirectly" (579), has been seriously received as a challenge to the over-enthusiastic dogmatism of some modern speculation.

Doctrinal considerations have led to wide agreement that the writer of Hebrews was almost certainly within the orbit of Paul's influence, without in any way detracting from the personal individuality and originality with which his writing is stamped (see Javet; Spicq, 1952:144ff.; Kuss, 1953; Badcock; Grässer, 1965a, 1973; Schierse; Anderson, 1966, 1976). There are also interesting theological affinities between Hebrews and the Johannine writings (see F.-M. Braun; Spicq, 1952:109ff.). Spicq affirms "an intellectual and theological dependence on St. Paul" and "a spiritual affinity with St. John" (167) and sees Hebrews as a link between the theological systems of Paul and John (134). Bruce suggests that "one way forward in the attempt to understand the Letter may be to explore further than has yet been done its relationship to the teaching of the Fourth Gospel" (1969a:264). W. Manson discussed the question of the similarities between Hebrews and the theological perspective of Stephen as recorded in Acts 7 (25ff.) and decided that the teaching of Stephen was very likely "the matrix in which the main theological ideas elaborated in Hebrews were formed" (160). This continues to be a promising area of investigation, not least because of the congruity of eschatological outlook which involves the concept of the church as a pilgrim people (see Spicq, 1952:243ff., 1972; Fontecha; Obermüller; van der Waal; Johnsson, 1978b).

Names other than Apollos and Barnabas are still occasionally put forward as likely authors of Hebrews: Silvanus (Hewitt); Timothy (Legg); Epaphras (Anderson); and Priscilla (Hoppin, reviving Harnack's conjecture). The only novelty (and novelty confers no accolade) is the theory offered by J. Massyngbaerde Ford that Mary the mother of Jesus, perhaps with the help of John and Luke, composed the epistle.

IV. STRUCTURE

Interest in the literary structure of Hebrews has been stimulated by the intensive investigations of Vanhoye. There were, of course, earlier and less elaborate essays in structural analysis, such as those of F. Thien and L. Vaganay in the pre- and inter-war periods; in fact, Vanhoye sees himself as completing the inquiries of Vaganay, though not in an uncritical manner (1963:24ff.). Vanhoye found the contribution of A. Descamps, who stressed the significance of "thematic words," too brief and slight (31) and the governing distinction between exposition and parenesis propounded by R. Gyllen-berg less than satisfactory (20–21). Later (1974:366) Vanhoye dismissed the scheme of W. Nauck as "having too many gaps." Mention should also be made of the work of J. Bligh, who divided Hebrews into thirty-five sections in each of which, he maintained, the verses were chiastically arranged.

The system elaborated by Vanhoye consists of (1) the announcement of the subject, (2) *mots-crochets* or link-words, (3) *genre*, either exposition or parenesis, (4) characteristic terms, and (5) "inclusion" or verbal correspondence between the beginning and the end of a passage or development (1963:37). His analysis displays, he contends, a "clearly apparent *concentric symmetry*" (50). Vanhoye's scheme called forth a number of criticisms. Some found it incredible that the biblical author should have devised so intricately detailed a literary plan. J. Swetnam remarked that "the central weakness of Vanhoye's whole approach" is "its lack of concern for psychological plausibility" (1974:346); and he warned that "if form is too much divorced from content it can lead to a distortion of content, not a clarification" (1972:386–87). Gyllenberg's pupil J. Thurén (1973) offered similar and other critical observations. Vanhoye (1974) replied to his critics in an extensive article, denying the validity of their complaints and insisting that his formal construction enhanced the significance of the content.

Shortage of space precludes the consideration of other important themes, such as the author's method of interpreting the OT (Buchanan [1972:xix] describes Hebrews as "a homiletical midrash") and his teaching on Christology, priesthood, sacraments, eschatology, and the church. The bibliography indicates some of the literature available on these and other themes, but worthy articles, many of them devoted to the interpretation and discussion of particular verses or short passages in the epistle, have had to remain unmentioned.

BIBLIOGRAPHY

Anderson, C. P.
  1966   "The Epistle to the Hebrews and the Pauline Letter Collection." *HTR* 59: 429–38.
  1976   "Hebrews among the Letters of Paul." *SR* 5: 258–66.

Andriessen, P.
  1972   "L'Eucharistie dans L'Epître aux Hébreux." *NRT* 94: 269–77.
  1974   "Angoisse de la mort dans l'Epître aux Hébreux." *NRT* 96: 1054–66.
  1977   *En lisant l'épître aux Hébreux.* Vaals, Netherlands: St. Benedictusberg.

Andriessen, P., and A. Lenglet
  1971   *De Brief aan de Hebreeën.* Roermond: Roman.

Auffret, P.
  1980   "Essai sur la structure littéraire et l'interprétation d'Hébreux 3:1–6." *NTS* 26: 380–96.

Badcock, F. J.
  1957   *The Pauline Epistles and the Epistle to the Hebrews in Their Historical Setting.* London: SPCK.

Ballerini, T.
1978   "Il peccato nell'epistola agli Ebrei." *Scuola Cattolica* (Milan) 106: 358–71.

Barclay, William
1955   *The Letter to the Hebrews: Translated with an Introduction and Interpretation.* Daily Study Bible. Edinburgh: St. Andrew. [Rev. ed. 1976.]

Barrett, C. K.
1956   "The Eschatology of the Epistle to the Hebrews." Pp. 363–93 in *The Background of the New Testament and Its Eschatology.* Ed. W. D. Davies and D. Daube. Cambridge: University Press.

Barth, Markus
1962   "The Old Testament in Hebrews." Pp. 53–78 in *Current Issues in New Testament Interpretaion: Essays in Honor of Otto A. Piper.* Ed. W. Klassen and G. F. Snyder. New York: Harper.

Batdorf, Irvin W.
1972   "Hebrews and Qumran: Old Methods and New Directions." Pp. 16–35 in *Festschrift to Honor F. Wilbur Gingrich.* Ed. E. H. Barth and R. E. Cocroft. Leiden: Brill.

Black, Matthew
1961   *The Scrolls and Christian Origins: Studies in the Jewish Background of the New Testament.* New York: Scribner.

Bligh, J.
1966   *Chiastic Analysis of the Epistle to the Hebrews.* Heythrop College, Oxford: Athenaeum.

Bonnard, P.
1963   "Actualité de L'Epître aux Hébreux." *Foi et Vie* 62: 283–88.

Bowman, J.
1958   "Did the Qumran Sect Burn the Red Heifer?" *RevQ* 1: 73–84.

Bowman, J. W.
1962   *Hebrews, James, I and II Peter.* Richmond: John Knox.

Braun, F.-M.
1955   "L'arrière-fond judaïque du quatrième évangile et la communauté de l'alliance." *RB* 62: 5–44.

Braun, Herbert
1966   *Qumran und das Neue Testament.* Tübingen: Mohr-Siebeck.
1970   "Das himmlische Vaterland bei Philo und im Hebräerbrief." Pp. 319–27 in *Verborum Veritas: Festschrift für G. Stählin zu 70. Geburtstag.* Ed. O. Böcher and K. Haacker. Wuppertal: Brockhaus.
1971   "Die Gewinnung der Gewissheit in dem Hebräerbrief." *TLZ* 96: 322–29.
1984   *An die Hebräer.* HNT 14. Tübingen: Mohr-Siebeck.

Bristol, L. O.
1949   "Primitive Christian Preaching and the Epistle to the Hebrews." *JBL* 68: 89–98.

Brooks, W. E.
1970   "The Perpetuity of Christ's Sacrifice in the Epistle to the Hebrews." *JBL* 89: 205–14.

Bruce, F. F.
  1963   "'To the Hebrews' or 'To the Essenes'?" *NTS* 9: 217–32.
  1964   *The Epistle to the Hebrews.* New London Commentary. Grand
            Rapids: Eerdmans.
  1969a   "Recent Contributions to the Understanding of Hebrews." *ExpTim*
            80: 260–64.
  1969b   "The Kerygma of Hebrews." *Int* 23: 3–19.

Brys, B.
  1973   "Jesus, the High Priest of the New Law." *Jeevadhara* (Alleppey, India)
            3: 162–71.

Buchanan, George Wesley
  1972   *To the Hebrews.* AB 36. Garden City, NY: Doubleday.
  1975   "The Present State of Scholarship on Hebrews." Pp. 299–330 in
            *Christianity, Judaism and Other Greco-Roman Cults: Studies for
            Morton Smith at Sixty,* vol. 1. Ed. J. Neusner. 4 vols. SJLA 12. Leiden:
            Brill.

Caird, G. B.
  1959   "The Exegetical Method of the Epistle to the Hebrews." *CJT* 5:
            44–51.

Campbell, J. C.
  1956   "The Doctrine of the Incarnation in the Epistle to the Hebrews." *Int*
            10: 24–38.

Carlston, Charles E.
  1959   "Eschatology and Repentance in the Epistle to the Hebrews." *JBL* 78:
            296–302.

Carmignac, J.
  1970   "Le document de Qumrân sur Melkisédek." *RevQ* 27: 343–78.

Clarkson, M. E.
  1947   "The Antecedents of the High Priest Theme in Hebrews." *ATR* 29:
            89–95.

Clavier, H.
  1959   "Ο ΛΟΓΟΣ ΤΟΥ ΘΕΟΥ dans l'Epître aux Hébreux." Pp. 81–93 in
            New Testament Essays: Studies in Memory of Thomas Walter Manson.
            Ed. A. J. B. Higgins. Manchester: Manchester University Press.

Cody, A.
  1960   *Heavenly Sanctuary and Liturgy in the Epistle to the Hebrews.* St.
            Meinrad, IN: Grail.

Combrink, H. J. B.
  1971   "Some Thoughts on the Old Testament Citations in the Epistle to the
            Hebrews." *Neot* 5: 22–36.

Coppens, J.
  1962   "Les affinités qumrâniennes de l'Epître aux Hébreux." *NRT* 84:
            128–41, 257–82.

Cullmann, O.
  1955   "The Significance of the Qumran Texts for Research into the Begin-
            nings of Christianity." *JBL* 74: 213–26.

D'Angelo, Mary Rose
  1979   *Moses in the Letter to the Hebrews.* SBLDS 42. Missoula, MT:
            Scholars Press.

Daniélou, J.
1957   *Les manuscrits de la mer Morte et les origines du christianisme.* Paris: Orante.

Dautzenberg, G.
1973   "Der Glaube im Hebräerbrief." *BZ* 17: 161–77.

Davies, J. H.
1967   *A Letter to the Hebrews.* Cambridge Bible Commentary. London and New York: Cambridge.
1968   "The Heavenly Work of Christ in Hebrews." *SE* 4: 384–89.

Delcor, M.
1971   "Melchisedech from Genesis to the Qumran Texts and the Epistle to the Hebrews." *JSJ* 2: 115–35.

Demarest, B.
1976   *A History of the Interpretation of Hebrews 7:1–10 from the Reformation to the Present.* BGBE 19. Tübingen: Mohr-Siebeck.

Descamps, A.
1954   "La structure de l'Epître aux Hébreux." *Revue diocésaine de Tournai* 9: 251–58, 333–38.

Di Pinto, L.
1976   *Volontà di Dio e legge antica nell'Epistola agli Ebrei.* Naples: Aloisianum.

Dussaut, L.
1981   *Synopse structurelle de l'Epître aux Hébreux.* Paris: Cerf.

Eccles, Robert S.
1968   "The Purpose of the Hellenistic Patterns in the Epistle to the Hebrews." Pp. 207–26 in *Religions in Antiquity: Essays in Memory of Erwin Ramsdell Goodenough.* Ed. J. Neusner. Leiden: Brill.

Ellingworth, P.
1986   "Jesus and the Universe in Hebrews." *EvQ* 58: 337–50.

Feld, H.
1985   *Der Hebräerbrief.* Erträge der Forschung 228. Darmstadt: Wissenschaftliche Buchgesellschaft.

Fensham, F. C.
1971   "Hebrews and Qumran." *Neot* 5: 9–21.

Fernández, E. Lopez
1977   "Sacerdocio, Ministerio y Eucaristia en la Carta a los Hebreos." *Studium Ovetense* (Oviedo) 5: 99–136.

Feuillet, A.
1964   "Les points de vue nouveaux dans l'eschatologie de l'Epître aux Hébreux." *SE* 2: 369–87.
1984   "Une triple préparation du sacerdoce du Christ dans l'Ancien Testament. . . . Introduction à la doctrine sacerdotale de l'Epître aux Hébreux." *Divinitas* 28: 103–36.

Filson, F. V.
1954   "The Epistle to the Hebrews." *JBR* 22: 20–26.
1967   *'Yesterday': A Study of Hebrews in the Light of Chapter 13.* SBT n.s. 4. Naperville, IL: Allenson.

Fitzer, G.
   1969   "Auch der Hebräerbrief legitimiert nicht eine Opfertodchristologie:
                Zur Frage der Intention des Hebräerbriefes und seine Bedeutung für
                die Theologie." *KD* 15: 294–319.

Fitzmyer, Joseph A.
   1963   "Now This Melchizedek ..." *CBQ* 25: 305–21. [Reprinted pp. 221–43
                in his *Essays on the Semitic Background of the New Testament*.
                London: Chapman, 1971.]
   1967   "Further Light on Melchizedek from Qumran Cave 11." *JBL* 86:
                25–41. [Reprinted in *Essays on the Semitic Background of the New
                Testament*, 245–67. London: Chapman, 1971.]

Floor, L.
   1961   "The General Priesthood of Believers in the Epistle to the Hebrews."
                Neot 5: 72–82.

Flusser, D.
   1958   "The Dead Sea Sect and Pre-Pauline Christianity." Pp. 215–66 in
                Aspects of the Dead Sea Scrolls. Ed. C. Rabin and Y. Yadin. Scripta
                Hierosolymitana 4. Jerusalem: Magnes Press.

Fontecha, J. F.
   1961   "La Vida cristiana como Peregrinacion segun la Epistola a los
                Hebreos." *Studium Legionense* 2: 251–306.

Ford, J. Massyngbaerde
   1975   "The Mother of Jesus and the Authorship of the Epistle to the
                Hebrews." *University of Dayton Review* 11: 49–56. [Also published in
                Bible Today 82: 683–94.]

Fudge, E.
   1973   *Our Man in Heaven: An Exposition of the Epistle to Hebrews*. Athens,
                AL: C.E.I.

García del Moral, A.
   1973   *Carta a los Hebreos y Cartas católicas*. Madrid: P.P.C.

Gärtner, Bertil
   1965   *The Temple and the Community in Qumran and the New Testament*.
                SNTSMS 1. Cambridge: University Press.

Giles, P.
   1975   "The Son of Man in the Epistle to the Hebrews." *ExpTim* 86: 328–32.

Gnilka, J.
   1959   "Die Erwartung des messianischen Hohenpriester in dem Schriften
                von Qumran und im Neuen Testament." *RevQ* 2: 106–7.

Grant, F. C.
   1956   *The Epistle to the Hebrews*. New York: Harper.

Grässer, Erich
   1964   "Der Hebräerbrief 1938–1963." *TRu* 30: 138–236.
   1965a   *Der Glaube im Hebräerbrief*. Marburg: Elwert.
   1965b   "Der historische Jesus im Hebräerbrief." *ZNW* 56: 63–91.
   1973   "Zur Christologie des Hebräerbriefes." Pp. 195–206 in *Neues Testa-
                ment und christliche Existenz: Festschrift für Herbert Braun zum 70.
                Geburtstag*. Ed. H. D. Betz and L. Schottroff. Tübingen: Mohr-
                Siebeck.

1976   "Rechtfertigung im Hebräerbrief." Pp. 79–93 in *Rechtfertigung: Festschrift für Ernst Käsemann zum 70. Geburtstag.* Ed. J. Friedrich, W. Pöhlmann, and P. Stuhlmacher. Tübingen: Mohr-Siebeck; Göttingen: Vandenhoeck & Ruprecht.

Greer, R. A.
1973   *The Captain of our Salvation: A Study in the Patristic Exegesis of Hebrews.* BGBE 15. Tübingen: Mohr-Siebeck.

Grosheide, F. W.
1955   *De Brief aan de Hebreeën en de Brief van Jakobus.* Kampen: Kok.

Guthrie, D.
1983   *The Letter to the Hebrews.* Tyndale NT Commentary. Grand Rapids: Eerdmans.

Gyllenberg, R.
1957   "Die Komposition des Hebraerbriefs." *SEÅ* 22–23: 137–47.

Hagen, K.
1981   *Hebrews Commenting from Erasmus to Bèze, 1516–1598.* BGBE 23. Tübingen: Mohr-Siebeck.

Hagner, D. A.
1983   *Hebrews.* A Good News Commentary. San Francisco: Harper & Row.

Hanson, A. T.
1949   "The Gospel in the Old Testament according to the Hebrews." *Theology* 52: 248–52.
1964   "Christ in the Old Testament according to Hebrews." *SE* 2: 393–407.

Héring, J.
1964   *L'Epître aux Hébreux.* Neuchâtel and Paris: Delachaux & Niestlé. Eng. trans.: *The Epistle to the Hebrews.* London: SPCK, 1970.

Hession, R.
1977   *From Shadow to Substance: The Rediscovery of the Inner Message of the Epistle to the Hebrews, centered around the Words, "Let us go on."* Grand Rapids: Zondervan.

Hewitt, T.
1966   *The Epistle to the Hebrews.* Tyndale Bible Commentary: NT 15. Grand Rapids: Eerdmans.

Hillmann, W.
1965   *Der Brief an die Hebräer.* Düsseldorf: Patmos.

Hoekema, A. A.
1974   "The Perfection of Christ in Hebrews." *Calvin Theological Journal* 9: 31–37.

Hofius, O.
1970   *Katapausis: Die Vorstellung vom endzeitlichen Ruheort im Hebräerbrief.* WUNT 11. Tübingen: Mohr-Siebeck.
1973   "Die Unabänderlichkeit des göttlichen Heilsratschlusses." *ZNW* 64: 135–45.

Hoppin, R.
1969   *Priscilla, Author of the Epistle to the Hebrews and Other Essays.* New York: Exposition.

Horning, E. B.
1978   "Chiasmus, Creedal Structure, and Christology in Hebrews." *BR* 23: 37–48.

Horton, Fred L., Jr.
1976a   "The Background of the Epistle to the Hebrews." *ExpTim* 87: 232–37.
1976b   *The Melchizedek Tradition: A Crucial Examination of the Sources to the Fifth Century A.D. and in the Epistle to the Hebrews.* SNTSMS 30. Cambridge: University Press.

Howard, G.
1968   "Hebrews and the Old Testament Quotations." *NovT* 10: 208–16.

Howard, W. F.
1951   "The Epistle to the Hebrews." *Int* 5: 80–91.

Hugedé, N.
1983   *Le Sacerdoce du Fils: Commentaire de l'Epître aux Hébreux.* Paris: Fischbacher.

Hughes, Graham
1979   *Hebrews and Hermeneutics: The Epistle to the Hebrews as a New Testament Example of Biblical Interpretation.* SNTSMS 36. Cambridge: University Press.

Hughes, P. E.
1977   *A Commentary on the Epistle to the Hebrews.* Grand Rapids: Eerdmans.

Humphrey, J. F.
1945   "The Christology of the Epistle to the Hebrews." *London Quarterly and Holborn Review* 170: 427–32.

Hunt, B. P. W. S.
1964   "The 'Epistle to the Hebrews': An Anti-Judaic Treatise?" *SE* 2: 408–10.

Hurst, D. L.
1985   "Apollos, Hebrews, and Corinth: Bishop Montefiore's Theory Examined." *SJT* 38: 505–13.

Hutaff, M. D.
1978   "The Epistle to the Hebrews: An Early Christian Sermon." *Bible Today* 85: 1816–24.

Javet, J. S.
1945   *Dieu nous parla.* Neuchâtel: Delachaux & Niestlé.

Jeremias, J.
1958   "The Qumran Texts and the New Testament." *ExpTim* 70: 68–69.

Jewett, Robert
1981   *Letter to Pilgrims: A Commentary on the Epistle to the Hebrews.* New York: Pilgrim.

Johnsson, W. G.
1978a   "The Cultus of Hebrews in Twentieth-Century Scholarship." *ExpTim* 89: 104–8.
1978b   "The Pilgrimage Motif in the Book of Hebrews." *JBL* 97: 239–51.

Jones, C. P. M.
1955   "The Epistle to the Hebrews and the Lucan Writings." Pp. 113–42
        in *Studies in the Gospels: Essays in Memory of R. H. Lightfoot*. Ed.
        D. E. Nineham. Oxford: Blackwell.

Jones, P. R.
1979   "The Figure of Moses as a Heuristic Device for the Understanding of
        the Pastoral Intent of Hebrews." *RevExp* 76: 95–107.

Jonge, M. de, and A. S. van der Woude
1966   "11Q Melchizedek and the New Testament." *NTS* 12: 301–26.

Käsemann, E.
1984   *The Wandering People of God: An Investigation of the Letter to the
        Hebrews*. Minneapolis: Augsburg.

Katz, P.
1958   "The Quotations from Deuteronomy in Hebrews." *ZNW* 49: 213–23.

Kennedy, G. T.
1951   *St. Paul's Conception of the Priesthood of Melchizedek*. Washington:
        Catholic University of America.

Kent, H. A.
1972   *The Epistle to the Hebrews*. Grand Rapids: Baker.

Ketter, P.
1950   *Hebräerbrief*. Freiburg: Herder.

Kistemaker, Simon
1961   *The Psalm Quotations in the Epistle to the Hebrews*. Amsterdam: van
        Soest.
1984   *Exposition of the Epistle to the Hebrews*. Grand Rapids: Baker.

Klappert, B.
1969   *Die Eschatologie des Hebräerbriefs*. Theologische Existenz heute 156.
        Munich: Kaiser.

Kloker, G.
1947   "Das Hohepriestertum Christi nach dem Hebräerbrief." In *Zeugnis
        des Geistes: Gabe zum Benediktusjubilaum*. Beuron.

Kobelski, Paul J.
1981   *Melchizedek and Melchirešaʿ*. CBQMS 10. Washington, DC: Catholic
        Biblical Association,

Kosmala, Hans
1959   *Hebräer-Essener-Christen: Studien zur Vorgeschichte der frühchrist-
        lichen Verkündigung*. SPB 1. Leiden: Brill.

Köster, W.
1956   "Platonische Ideenwelt und Gnosis im Hebräerbrief." *Scholastik* 31:
        545–65.

Kuss, O.
1953   *Der Brief an die Hebräer*. RNT 8:1. Regensburg: Pustet. [A revised
        and enlarged edition was published in 1966.]
1963   "Der Verfasser des Hebräerbriefes als Seelsorger." Pp. 329–58 in his
        *Auslegung und Verkündigung: Aufsätze zur Exegese des Neuen
        Testaments*, vol. 1. Regensburg: Pustet.

Laubach, F.
1967   *Der Brief an die Hebräer*. Wuppertaler Studienbrief. Wuppertal:
        Brockhaus. [3d ed. 1974.]

Legg, J. D.
  1968   "Our Brother Timothy: A Suggested Solution to the Problem of the
            Authorship of the Epistle to the Hebrews." *EvQ* 40: 220–23.

Lenglet, A.
  1971   See Andriessen, P., and A. Lenglet.

Lenski, R. C. H.
  1946   *The Interpretation of the Epistle to the Hebrews.* Columbus, OH:
            Wartburg.

Lescow, T.
  1967   "Jesus in Gethsemane bei Lukas und im Hebräerbrief." *ZNW* 58:
            215–39.

Lightfoot, N. R.
  1976   *Jesus Christ Today: A Commentary on the Book of Hebrews.* Grand
            Rapids: Baker.

Loader, W. R. G.
  1981   *Sohn und Hoherpriester: Eine traditionsgeschichtliche Untersuchung
            zur Christologie des Hebräerbriefes.* WMANT 53. Neukirchen-Vluyn:
            Neukirchener Verlag.

Loane, M. L.
  1961   *Key-Texts in the Epistle to the Hebrews.* London: Marshall, Morgan,
            and Scott.

Lo Bue, F.
  1956   "The Historical Background of the Epistle to the Hebrews." *JBL* 75:
            52–57.

Luck, U.
  1963   "Himmlisches und irdisches Geschehen im Hebräerbrief." *NovT* 6:
            192–215.

Lussier, E.
  1975   *Christ's Priesthood according to the Epistle to the Hebrews.* College-
            ville, MN: Liturgical Press.

Luz, U.
  1967   "Der alte und der neue Bund bei Paulus und im Hebräerbrief." *EvT*
            27: 318–36.

MacDonald, W.
  1972   *The Epistle to the Hebrews: From Ritual to Reality.* New York:
            Loizeaux.

McConnell, J. F.
  1966   *Epístola a los Hebreos.* Conoce la Biblia, NT 12. Santander: Sal
            Terrae.

McCullough, J. C.
  1980a   "The Old Testament Quotations in Hebrews." *NTS* 26: 363–79.
  1980b   "Some Recent Developments in Research on the Epistle to the
            Hebrews: I." *Irish Biblical Studies* 2: 141–65.
  1981   "Some Recent Developments in Research on the Epistle to the
            Hebrews: II." *Irish Biblical Studies* 3: 28–45.

Mackay, C.
  1967   "The Argument of Hebrews." *CQR* 168: 325–38.

MacRae, George W.
1978 "Heavenly Temple and Eschatology in the Letter to the Hebrews." *Semeia* 12: 179–99.
1983 *Hebrews*. Bible Commentaries 10. Collegeville, MN: Liturgical Press.

Manson, T. W.
1949 "The Problem of the Epistle to the Hebrews." *BJRL* 32: 1–17.

Manson, W.
1951 *The Epistle to the Hebrews: An Historical and Theological Reconsideration*. London: Hodder & Stoughton.

Mercier, R.
1973 "La Perfección de Cristo y de los Cristianos en la carta a los Hebreos." *RevistB* 35: 229–36.

Michel, O.
1949 *Der Brief an die Hebräer*. MeyerK 13. Göttingen: Vandenhoeck & Ruprecht. [A revision of the 1936 edition.]

Moe, O.
1949 "Der Gedanke des allgemeinen Priestertums im Hebräerbrief." *TZ* 5: 161–68.
1951 "Das Abendmahl im Hebräerbrief: Zur Auslegung von Hebr. 13:9–16." *ST* 4: 102–8.
1953 "Das irdische und das himmlische Heiligtum (Hebr.9:4sq.)." *TZ* 9: 23–29.

Montefiore, Hugh
1964 *A Commentary on the Epistle to the Hebrews*. New York: Harper.

Mora, G.
1974 *La Carta a los Hebreos como escrito pastoral*. Colectánea San Paciano 20. Barcelona: Herder.
1976 "Ley y sacrificio en la carta a los Hebreos." *Revista Catalana de Teología* 1: 1–50.

Mulder, H.
1965a "De Schrijver van de Brief aan de Hebreeën." *Homiletica en Biblica* 24: 110–14.
1965b "Barnabas en de Gemeente te Jeruzalem." *Homiletica en Biblica* 24: 198–200.

Müller, P. G.
1973 ΧΡΙΣΤΟΣ ΑΡΧΗΓΟΣ. Frankfurt: Peter Lang.

Nash, R. H.
1977 "The Notion of Mediator in Alexandrian Judaism and the Epistle to the Hebrews." *WTJ* 40: 89–115.

Nauck, W.
1960 "Zum Aufbau des Hebräerbriefes." Pp. 199–206 in *Judentum-Urchristentum-Kirche: Festschrift für Joachim Jeremias*. Ed. W. Eltester. BZNW 26. Berlin: Töpelmann.

Neil, W.
1955 *The Epistle to the Hebrews*. London: SCM.

Nicolau, M.
1962 *Carta a los Hebreos*. Pp. 1–191 in vol. 3 of *La Sagrada Escritura: Nuevo Testamento*. B.A.C. Madrid: Editorial Católica.

Nomoto, S.
1968   "Herkunft und Struktur der Hohenpriestervorstellung im Hebräer-
            brief." *NovT* 10: 10–25.

Obermüller, R.
1971   "Una mística del camino: El tema de la peregrinación en la carta a
            los Hebreos." *RevistB* 33: 55–66.

Perez, G.
1956   "Autenticidad y canonicidad de la Carta a los Hebreos." *CB* 13:
            216–26.

Peterson, D.
1984   *Hebrews and Perfection*. SNTSMS 47. Cambridge: University Press.

Ploeg, J. van der
1947   "L'exégèse de l'ancien Testament dans l'Epître aux Hébreux." *RB* 54:
            187–228.

Pretorius, E. A. C.
1971   "Diathēkē in the Epistle to the Hebrews." *Neot* 5: 37–50.

Rábanos, R.
1961   *Sacerdote a semejanza de Melquisedec*. Salamanca: Seminario Misio-
            nero S. Vincente de Paul.

Robinson, J. A. T.
1976   *Redating the New Testament*. Philadelphia: Westminster. Pp. 200–
            220.

Robinson, W.
1961   "The Eschatology of the Epistle to the Hebrews: A Study in the
            Christian Doctrine of Hope." *Encounter* 22: 37–51.

Roloff, J.
1975   "Der mitleidende Hohepriester: Zur Frage nach der Bedeutung des
            irdischen Jesus für die Christologie des Hebräerbriefes." Pp. 143–66
            in *Jesus Christus in Historie und Theologie: Neutestamentliche Fest-
            schrift für Hans Conzelmann zum 60. Geburtstag*. Ed. G. Strecker.
            Tübingen: Mohr-Siebeck.

Sabourin, L.
1968a   "Sacrificium ut liturgia in Epistola ad Hebraeos." *VD* 46: 235–58.
1968b   "Auctor Epistolae ad Hebraeos ut interpres Scripturae." *VD* 46:
            275–85.

Samain, P.
1946   "L'Eucharistie dans l'Epître aux Hébreux." *Revue diocésaine de
            Tournai* 3: 408–10.

Schierse, F. J.
1968   *The Epistle to the Hebrews*. New York: Herder & Herder.

Schille, G.
1955   "Erwägungen zur Hohenpriesterlehre des Hebräerbriefes." *ZNW* 46:
            81–109.
1957   "Die Basis des Hebräerbriefes." *ZNW* 48: 270–80.
1960   "Katecheze und Taufliturgie: Erwägungen zu Hebr.11." *ZNW* 51:
            112–31.

Schröger, F.
1968   *Der Verfasser des Hebräerbriefes als Schriftausleger.* Biblische Unter-
          suchungen 4. Regensburg: Pustet.
1970   "Das hermeneutische Instrumentarium des Hebräerbriefverfassers."
          TGl 60: 344–59.

Silva, M.
1976   "Perfection and Eschatology in Hebrews." *WTJ* 39: 60–71.

Smith, J.
1969   *A Priest for Ever: A Study of Typology and Eschatology in Hebrews.*
          London and Sydney: Sheed & Ward.

Smith, R. H.
1984   *Hebrews.* Augsburg Commentary on the NT. Minneapolis: Augsburg.

Smits, C.
1963   *Oud-Testamentische Citaten in het Nieuwe Testament.* Part 4; *De Brief
          aan de Hebreeën.* 's-Hertogenbosch: Malmberg. Pp. 551–744.

Snell, A.
1959   *A New and Living Way: An Explanation of the Epistle to the Hebrews.*
          London: Faith.

Sowers, Sidney G.
1965   *The Hermeneutics of Philo and Hebrews.* Basel Studies of Theology.
          Richmond: John Knox.

Spicq, C.
1947   "L'authenticité du chapître 13 de l'Epître aux Hébreux." *ConNT* 11:
          226–36.
1951   "Alexandrinismes dans l'Epître aux Hébreux." *RB* 58: 481–502.
1952–53   *L'épître aux Hébreux.* 2 vols. Paris: Gabalda.
1959   "L'épître aux Hébreux: Apollos, Jean-Baptiste, les Hellénistes et
          Qumran." *RevQ* 1: 365–90.
1972   *Vie Chrétienne et pérégrination selon le Nouveau Testament.* Paris:
          Cerf.
1977a   *L'épître aux Hébreux.* SB. Paris: Gabalda. [A summary and an up-
          dating of the two-volume work.]
1977b   "Melchisédech et l'Epître aux Hébreux: La sacerdoce de la Nouvelle
          Alliance." *Esprit et Vie* 87: 206–8.

Stewart, R. A.
1966   "Creation and Matter in the Epistle to the Hebrews." *NTS* 12:
          284–93.

Stibbs, A. M.
1970   *So Great Salvation: The Meaning and Message of the Letter to the
          Hebrews.* Exeter: Paternoster.

Stott, W.
1962   "The Conception of 'Offering' in the Epistle to the Hebrews." *NTS* 9:
          62–67.

Strobel, A.
1975   *Der Brief an die Hebräer.* NTD 9. Göttingen: Vandenhoeck &
          Ruprecht.

Swetnam, J.
1972   "Form and Content in Hebrews 1–9." *Bib* 53: 368–85.
1974   "Form and Content in Hebrews 7–13." *Bib* 55: 333–48.

1981   *Jesus and Isaac: A Study of the Epistle to the Hebrews in the Light of Aqedah.* AnBib 94. Rome: Biblical Institute Press.

Synge, F. C.
1959   *Hebrews and the Scriptures.* London: SPCK.

Tasker, R. V. G.
1952   *The Gospel in the Epistle to the Hebrews.* London: Tyndale.

Teodorico da Castel San Pietro, P.
1945   *La Chiesa nella lettera agli Ebrei.* Turin: Marietti.
1952   *L'Epistola agli Ebrei.* Turin: Marietti.
1958   "Il sacerdozio celeste di Cristo nella lettera agli Ebrei." *Greg* 39: 319–34.

Terra, J. E. Martins
1978   "A Libertação Escatológica na Epistola aos Hebreus: O Povo de Deus a Caminho do Santuario." *RCB* 2: 325–43.

Thomas, K. J.
1965   "The Old Testament Citations in Hebrews." *NTS* 11: 303–25.

Thompson, J.
1971   *The Letter to the Hebrews.* Living Word Commentary. Austin: Sweet.

Thompson, James W.
1977   "The Conceptual Background and Purpose of the Midrash in Hebrews 7." *NovT* 19: 209–23.

1982   *The Beginnings of Christian Philosophy: The Epistle to the Hebrews.* CBQMS 13. Washington, DC: Catholic Biblical Association.

Thurén, J.
1964   "The Structure of Hebrews." *HeyJ* 5: 170–77.
1973   *Das Lobopfer der Hebräer: Studien zum Aufbau und Anliegen von Hebräerbrief 13.* Acta Academiae Åboensis, Ser. A: Humaniora 47,1. Åbo, Finland: Åbo Akademi.

Thurston, R. W.
1986   "Philo and the Epistle to the Hebrews." *EvQ* 58: 133–43.

Vanhoye, A.
1963   *La structure littéraire de l'Epître aux Hébreux.* Paris and Bruges: Descleé de Brouwer.

1968   *Exegesis Epistulae ad Hebraeos, cap.I-II.* Rome: Biblical Institute Press.

1969a   *Le Christ est notre Prêtre.* Toulouse: Éditions Prière et Vie. Eng. trans.: see 1977.

1969b   "De sacerdotio Christi in Hebraeis." *VD* 47: 22–30.

1969c   *Situation du Christ: Hébreux 1-2.* LD 58. Paris: Cerf.

1974   "Discussions sur la structure de l'Epître aux Hébreux." *Bib* 55: 349–80.

1976   "Le Dieu et la Nouvelle Alliance dans l'Epître aux Hébreux." In *La notion biblique de Dieu.* Ed. J. Coppens. Gembloux: Duculot.

1977   *Our Priest is Christ: The Doctrine of the Epistle to the Hebrews.* Trans. M. I. Richards. Rome: Biblical Institute Press.

1978   "Cristo Sumo Sacerdote." *RCB* 2: 313–23.

1979   "Literarische Struktur und theologische Botschaft des Hebräerbriefs." *Studien zum Neuen Testament und seiner Umwelt* 4: 119–47.

1981   "Sacerdoce du Christ et culte chrétien selon l'épître aux Hébreux." *Christus* 28: 216–30.

Venard, L.
1945   "L'utilisation des Psaumes dans l'Epître aux Hébreux." Pp. 253–64 in
        Mélanges E. Podechard: Etudes de sciences religieuses. Lyon: Facultes
        Catholiques.

Viard, A.
1981   "Le salut par la foi dans l'épître aux Hébreux." *Angelicum* 58: 115–36.

Villapadierna, C. de
1964   "Valor soteriológico de la Resurrección de Cristo según la carta a los
        Hebreos." In *Estudios Franciscanos* 65: 321–38.

Vine, W. E.
1952   *The Epistle to the Hebrews.* London: Oliphants.

Vos, G.
1956   *The Teaching of the Epistle to the Hebrews.* Grand Rapids: Eerdmans.

Waal, C. van der
1971   "The People of God in the Epistle to the Hebrews." *Neot* 5: 83–92.

Wikgren, A.
1960   "Patterns of Perfection in the Epistle to the Hebrews." *NTS* 6:
        159–67.

Williamson, R.
1970a   "Hebrews and Doctrine." *ExpTim* 81: 371–76.
1970b   *Philo and the Epistle to the Hebrews.* ALGHJ 4. Leiden: Brill.
1975   "The Eucharist and the Epistle to the Hebrews." *NTS* 21: 300–12.
1976   "The Background of the Epistle to the Hebrews." *ExpTim* 87:
        232–37.

Woschitz, K. M.
1981   "Das Priestertum Jesus Christi nach dem Hebräerbrief." *BLit* 54:
        139–50.

Woude, A. S. van der
1965   "Melchisedek als himmlische Erlösergestalt in den neugefundenen
        eschatologischen Midraschim aus Qumran Höhle XI." *OTS* 14:
        354–73.
1966   See Jonge, M. de, and A. S. van der Woude.

Yadin, Y.
1958   "The Dead Sea Scrolls and the Epistle to the Hebrews." Pp. 36–55
        in *Aspects of the Dead Sea Scrolls.* Ed. C. Rabin and Y. Yadin. Scripta
        Hierosolymitana 4. Jerusalem: Magnes Press.
1965   "A Note on Melchizedek and Qumran." *IEJ* 15: 152–54.

Young, N. H.
1981   "The Gospel according to Hebrews 9." *NTS* 27: 198–210.

Zedda, S.
1967   *Lettera agli Ebrei.* Rome: Paoline.

Zimmermann, H.
1964   *Die Hohepriester-Christologie des Hebräerbriefes.* Paderborn:
        Schöningh.
1977   *Das Bekenntnis der Hoffnung: Tradition und Redaktion im Hebräer-
        brief.* BBB 47. Cologne and Bonn: Hanstein.

14
JAMES, 1-2 PETER, JUDE

Birger A. Pearson

The four "catholic" epistles discussed in this article are sufficiently different, one from the others, to warrant separate and individual treatment. To be sure, from certain vantage points they might also be grouped together. They constitute, for example, the main NT witness to what German Protestant scholars refer to as "Early Catholicism" (see, e.g., Marxsen; and, from a Roman Catholic viewpoint, historically more defensible, Schelkle, 1963). They are also conveniently treated together in discussions of the history of the NT text (see, e.g., Kubo, 1963; Carder; Aland, 1970; Duplacy; Gallagher; Richards, 1974, 1975, 1976); but textual criticism is a subject to which a separate chapter is devoted (see chapter 4, by Eldon Jay Epp).

In what follows I shall try to cover, as completely but as briefly as possible, the scholarly work done on each of these four epistles since the end of World War II. Inasmuch as the "cutting edge" of scholarship is usually represented in monographs and articles, whereas commentaries (with some notable exceptions) tend more to present results of previous work, each section will treat first the monographs and articles and then, more briefly, the major commentaries. Although I have deliberately omitted treatment of works of a purely "popular" or "devotional" (or overly "apologetic") nature, I am probably open to criticism for casting as broad a net as I have. My aim here is, however, to present as broad a picture as possible.

I. JAMES

Monographs and Dissertations

Scholarly monographs on James in the period under consideration have predominantly been devoted to the chief theological problem of James, i.e., its doctrine of justification, faith, and works (vis-à-vis Paul). The dominant tendency has been to minimize the differences between James and Paul and to exonerate the epistle from Luther's charge that it is a "stroherne Epistel" ("strawy epistle") of no theological import. Thus, M. Lackmann, in his interpretation of Jas 2:14–26, argues that there is no real conflict between James and Paul and that the church should try to overcome the influence of Luther's "Missverständnis" ("misunderstanding"). G. Eichholz (1953) argues that, whereas Jas 2:14–26 is obviously directed against Paul, it is more exactly directed against a kind of "Paulinism" that is not authentically Pauline. James's message — "be doers of the word" — directed to a church in danger of secularization, is needed just as much as Paul's message of justification. The same author carries these arguments further in another monograph (1961): Without "harmonizing" Paul and James, who were speaking to different fronts with different concerns, it should be recognized that both of their messages are equally "canonical" and equally relevant for Christian existence today. Similar arguments are offered by Rendtorff. P. Stuhlmacher, on the other hand (191–94), states that Luther's clear No! to James's theology must be sustained. In his argumentation in 2:14–26 the epistle's author "falls back into Judaism" (194).

Another look at the same problem in James, by P. Bergauer, focuses on Augustine's use of James, with special attention to his interpretation of Jas 2:14–26. Augustine's solution to the problem of the relationship between faith and works was to differentiate between works *before* and *after* justification. James posits, in agreement with Paul, the necessity of "works which follow faith" (*opera quae fidem sequuntur*). Luther unfortunately overlooked or misunderstood Augustine's solution, which is still important today for the interpretation of Jas 2:14–26.

A more recent monograph focuses on the term "law of liberty" in Jas 1:25 and 2:12 (Fabris), interpreting the phrase, against an OT-Jewish background, to mean the "internal law" of love.

R. Hoppe, taking his cue from Dibelius's monumental commentary on James (1921; cf. Dibelius-Greeven), analyzes James as an example of early Christian paraenesis, with key emphases on "faith" and "wisdom." He sees three key motifs that James has in common with the synoptic tradition: perfection through fulfillment of the law (Jas 2:10; Matt 5:19), perfection through suffering (Jas 1:2–4; Matt 5:3, 11–12, 43–48), and wisdom "from above" (Jas 3:13–18; Matt 1:25–27; Luke 10:21–22). Dibelius's interpretation of James's emphasis on poverty as a Christian ideal is rejected by F. Kelly, who insists that James attempts to bring poor and rich together in the community, especially with the use of Job as a model of beneficence for the rich and of patience for the poor.

The composition of James is given special treatment by M. Rustler, who tries to show that James is organized into three main sections around the basic theme of the social problems and tensions between rich and poor (theological grounding, 1:2–27; practical ethics, 2:1–3:12; and eschatology, 3:13–5:20). An altogether different arrangement is seen in James by D. Beck, who attempts to show that the arrangement of themes in James, far from being random, actually follows the same order as is found in 1QS + 1QSa. In what appears to be something of a *tour de force*, Beck argues that the author of James had at his disposal a version of these two Qumran documents and derived the outline of his epistle from that source.

A number of important monographs bear partially on James. For example, L. Elliot-Binns (1956a:45–52) posits a Galilean background for James, and uses the epistle, together with the Synoptic Gospels, as evidence in his reconstruction of early Galilean Christianity. H.-J. Schoeps (343–49) argues that James is directed against a front of gnostic opponents, but in this view he is virtually alone among scholars of the postwar period (cf. Schammberger). The language of James is treated by K. Beyer (17 et passim), who finds a significant number of Semitisms and cases of "Semitic syntax" in James. J. Sevenster (esp. 3–21) shows that the use of Greek was sufficiently widespread in Palestine at the turn of the era, so that the "good Greek" of James poses no argument against a Palestinian origin for the epistle, or even its attribution to James, the Lord's brother. H. Thyen (14–16) accepts A. Meyer's theory of a Jewish *Grundschrift* ("underlying document") for James, pseudonymously attributed to the patriarch Jacob; Thyen can therefore use the epistle as one of his sources for reconstructing the homiletic style of synagogue preaching in the Jewish Diaspora. Finally, J. A. T. Robinson, as part of his daring project to "redate" the NT, proposes that James, the Lord's brother, wrote James in late 47 or early 48 (118–39).

Articles

A large number of scholarly articles on James have been devoted to the theological problem of faith and works, law and gospel, and the relationship of James to Paul. The preponderant tendency in recent scholarship is to play down the differences between James and Paul by showing that, though they argue on different fronts and with different terminology, they have more in common than Luther would have granted (e.g., with various emphases, Souček; Braumann; Ward, 1963; Noack, 1964a; Walker; Cranfield, 1965a, 1965b; Nicol, 1975; Lorenzen). One scholar (Hamann) comes up with the novel, if unconvincing, theory that Paul's formulations show a knowledge of James. By far the best treatment of the subject is still the short but important article by J. Jeremias (1955). On the other hand, D. O. Via is able to see contradictions not only between James and Paul but also between different passages within the Epistle of James itself (2:14–26 versus 1:18–24). For E. Trocmé, not only Jas 2:14–26 but indeed the whole central section of James (2:1–3:13) is directed by a postapostolic author against churches attached to the Pauline tradition.

Other theological studies of James focus on law and, in one case, Christology. For O. Seitz, "law" in James is the entire Mosaic law, understood as the divine *moral* (not cultic) standard. For J. Sánchez Bosch, "law" in James is equivalent to "gospel." For K.-G. Eckart, James has no original theology; its combination of the Decalogue with the love-command is entirely attributable to early Christian tradition. F. Mussner (1970) sees both "direct" Christology (2:1) and, especially, "indirect" Christology in James. M.

Shepherd discusses the theological similarities between James and Matthew and their mutual relationships.

A fruitful approach to James is to see it against the background of Jewish wisdom tradition. Indeed U. Luck sees the appropriation and use of wisdom traditions as the key to understanding not only James but also Paul and the relationship between them (1967, 1971). For R. Obermüller, James's overall hermeneutic is to be characterized as "sapiential." For J. Kirk, "Wisdom" and "Spirit" are virtually interchangeable in James. R. Halson argues on the basis of James's roots in OT-Jewish wisdom literature that the epistle as a whole should be understood as a collection of catechetical materials emanating from a catechetical school somehow connected with James of Jerusalem.

A liturgical setting is posited for James by a number of scholars, e.g., A. Hamman, who argues that James is directed to a liturgical assembly; and A. Strobel (1963a:8), who posits a cultic *Sitz im Leben* ("life-setting") for James (see also Strobel, 1961:254–64; and Boismard, 1957); R. M. Cooper compares the doctrine of prayer in James and Matthew. A. Cabaniss sees James as a "homily" addressed to a particular community of Jewish Christians ca. A.D. 100.

A majority of scholars would favor a postapostolic date for James, and pseudonymous authorship. E. Lohse, for example (1957), posits a date in the second or even third century. But other scholars hold out for a very early date for James, on the basis of its undeveloped theology (Kittel, 1942, 1950; Powell) and other factors (see Townsend; Feuillet, 1956). A. Geyser argues that James was written by James, the Lord's brother, to refugees in the Antioch area sometime after the martyrdom of Stephen but before the Council of Jerusalem in 48. S. Agourides posits an Aramaic *Grundschrift* ("underlying document") by James, the Lord's brother, written around A.D. 40–50, and subsequently rendered into Greek. A Palestinian environment for James is argued by D. Hadidian on the basis of its meteorological and geographical references. E. Stauffer (1952b) sees James as an encyclical letter, which, even if it cannot be ascribed directly to James the Lord's brother, coheres with other James traditions in representing him as "Princeps der Christenheit" ("leader of Christianity") (205, reacting against von Campenhausen). W. L. Knox suggests that James may be a collection of Genizah fragments from the church of Pella or of Jerusalem, with chaps. 4–5 attributable to James himself.

The language and style of James are studied by A. Wifstrand, who points in general to the influence of Jewish synagogue Greek and in particular to a number of "spontaneous semitisms" in James (176). In more recent years linguistic studies have taken a new turn, with the application of the methods of structural linguistics. Two studies by C.-B. Amphoux (1973, 1978) illustrate this development. At the same time older notions of literary "structure" still persist. For example, E. Fry sees a unity of thought — testing of faith, patience in trials — in James and divides the epistle into three main sections

(1:2–18; 1:19–4:12; 4:13–5:18). P. Forbes would divide the letter into two balanced sections (chaps. 1–2; 3–5).

Dibelius's designation of James as "paraenesis" ("exhortation") is universally accepted, but literary analysis can be carried further than he did. For example, H. Songer isolates and analyzes the characteristics of James's paraenesis. F. Francis applies form-critical analysis to James, using Hellenistic correspondence for comparative purposes. More recently, "rhetorical analysis" has been applied to James, with concomitant attention to social interactions reflected in it (Wuellner).

Miscellaneous exegetical and textual studies are too numerous to discuss in any detail. The most important ones, cited according to chapter and verse in James, are as follows: 1:1 (Baltzer and Koester, on ὠβλίας = δοῦλος θεοῦ; 1:2, 12 (Nauck, 1955); 1:2–18 (Thomas); 1:13 (Davids, on ἀπείραστος); 1:17 (Greeven; Amphoux, 1970); 1:18 (Elliott-Binns, 1957; Edsman, 1953); 1:21 (Elliott-Binns, 1955); 1:25 + 2:13 (Stauffer, 1952a, on νόμος ἐλευθερίας); 1:26–27 (Alonso Schökel); 1:27 (D. J. Roberts; Johanson); 2:1 (Brinktrine); 2:2–4 (Ward, 1969); 2:11 (Kilpatrick, proposing reading ἀποστάτης with P⁷⁴); 2:14–16 (Ward, 1968); 2:21–23 (Jacobs); 3:15 (Elliott-Binns, 1956b, on ὕλη); 4:1–4 (Townsend, proposing a Zealot-nationalistic background); 4:5 (Jeremias, 1959, on ἐπιποθεῖ; Michl, 1963, attributing the quotation to a Hellenistic Jewish hymn; Laws, on πνεῦμα); 4:13–5:6 (Noack, 1964b); 5:1–11 (Feuillet, 1956, on παρουσία); 5:11 (Gordon, on τὸ τέλος κυρίου); 5:12 (Minear, arguing that James and Justin *Apol.* 1.16.5 preserve an earlier form of the dominical saying than Matt 5:33–37; 23:16–22); 5:13–18 (Wilkinson); 5:14–16 (Condon; Reicke, 1973; Hoyos, and Luff discuss an Aramaic inscription found in Jerusalem which sheds light on this passage).

Much of the exegetical work on James in recent years has dealt with its use of the OT, frequently also with reference to Jewish targums and/or midrashim (e.g., Jeremias, 1959; Blenker, 1967; Ward, 1968, 1969; Gordon, 1975; Jacobs). M. Gertner goes further and refers to the whole epistle of James as a "midrash" based on Psalm 12. The use of the OT in James recently has been the subject of a working group of the SNTS (Studiorum Novi Testamenti Societas); A. Hanson's report provides a tantalizing suggestion of the extent to which James is influenced by interpretive traditions of contemporary Judaism.

The Qumran scrolls have provided a rich fund of comparative material which has been used to good advantage in the study of James. J. O'Callaghan, however, has gone so far as to suggest that some of the Greek papyrus fragments found in Qumran cave 7 can be identified as remnants of Greek NT texts, including James; he identifies 7Q8 as Jas 1:23–24 (1972a, 1972b). Although O'Callaghan's identifications have been greeted with some minimal acceptance (e.g., Martini, 1972), NT text critics have decisively rejected them (esp. Benoit, 1972; Baillet, 1972; Aland, 1973; C. H. Roberts; and Urbán; these scholars suggest more plausible identifications from LXX texts, but Roberts ultimately rejects the enterprise as a waste of time).

H. Quecke has edited a Bohairic papyrus fragment (*P. Heid. Kopt.* 452) containing Jas 2:15–19 and 3:2–6 and discusses some important unique readings.

Commentaries

Of the making of biblical commentaries there is no end, and there is not sufficient space to treat in any detail here even the most important ones. At the beginning of the period under discussion the commentary of M. Dibelius stood out as the most important one on James in any language (Dibelius, 1921). Although commentaries have multiplied in the meantime, the name of Dibelius is still predominant even now (Dibelius-Greeven; cf. Ward's review of the 1964 German ed., 1966). The most important of the other commentaries appearing since 1945 are Windisch and Preisker; Easton; Mussner, 1964 (see Lohse's review, 1966); perhaps Reicke, 1964 (because of its controversial socio-political interpretation [see Funk's review, 1965]); and Schrage, 1973. Other commentaries worth mentioning are those of Leconte; Michl, 1953; Garcia ab Orbiso; Warth; Schneider; Williams; Mitton, 1966; Sidebottom; Cantinat; Grünzweig; and Adamson.

A broad scholarly consensus on James is developing among recent commentators, in relation to such items as its literary genre ("paraenesis," without much discernible order of composition), its general intention (not to preach the kerygma but to call readers to live the Christian life), its language (good Koine Greek; but Mussner sees more "semitisms" in James than do Dibelius-Greeven), its relation to Paul (James, in polemicizing against a distorted "Paulinism," does not thereby contradict Paul), and its close dependence on the Gospel tradition, especially its close relation to, but literary independence of, Matthew. Though some postwar commentators are still attracted to Meyer's theory of a Jewish *Grundschrift* ("underlying document") (Windisch and Preisker; Easton), more recent commentators reject it. Most commentators favor a postapostolic date and pseudonymity; the strongest case for a pre-70 date and ascription to James, the Lord's brother, is made by Mussner (see also Garcia ab Orbiso, 6–23; a few others, e.g., Adamson, simply assume it without argument). There is no consensus on James's place of origin, except to say that no convincing case can be made for any particular locale. All agree on its "Jewish Christian" character.

II. 1 PETER

Monographs and Dissertations

1 Peter has been the subject of a rather large number of full-scale studies. One of the most-discussed monographs on 1 Peter in the last several years is that of F. L. Cross, who argues that it is not an epistle at all but a

baptismal liturgy tied to early Christian celebrations of Easter. The numerous references to suffering in the epistle reflect a wordplay on the festival (πάσχα-πάσχειν, otherwise first documented in Christian sources in Melito) — and not necessarily references to persecution. The epistle consists of various prayers, exhortations, and charges by the bishop, with actual baptism posited as occurring between 1:21 and 1:22. (Similar suggestions had already been made by R. Perdelwitz in 1911, but this was not referred to by Cross; Cross does refer to the Windisch and Preisker commentary; see below). M.-E. Boismard (1961) also sees baptismal liturgy reflected in 1 Peter and isolates four early baptismal hymns used by its author (1:3–5; 3:18–22; 2:22–25; 5:5–9); he sees traces of these same hymns in the Pauline epistles. Subsequent studies have tended to play down the liturgical explanation of 1 Peter and to see it instead as a real letter (e.g., Dalton, 1965; Watson; Ryan; Frederick).

The passages in 1 Peter traditionally associated with the *descensus ad inferos* ("descent into Hell") of Christ, 3:19 and 4:6, have been the focus of a number of studies. B. Reicke (1946) interprets the "spirits" of 3:19 as fallen angels, with reference to the background in *1 Enoch*. 1 Pet 4:6, on the other hand, refers to the dead sinners of the time of the flood. These basic distinctions are accepted by W. Bieder (1949:96–128), who points out also that 1 Peter does not really *locate* the post-crucifixion activity of Christ, that is, it is neither a *descensus* ("descent") nor an *ascensus* ("ascent"). W. Dalton (see the review by Holtz, 1967) convincingly answers this problem by affirming that an ascent is meant: Christ proclaimed his post-resurrection victory to the hostile angelic powers of the lower planetary spheres on the occasion of his ascension. 1 Pet 4:6 refers to the preaching of the gospel to Christians who have subsequently died. Dalton's conclusions are accepted by J. Price, but rejected by D. Spoto and H.-J. Vogels, both of whom equate the dead of 4:6 with the "spirits" of 3:19. Thus the debate goes on.

1 Pet 2:4–10 is the subject of an important monograph by J. H. Elliott (1966; see the reviews by Moule, 1967, and Schnackenburg, 1968). Elliott sees this passage as referring to the believing community as the elect and holy people of God, a βασίλειον ἱεράτευμα. The church is a royal dwelling place of God (βασίλειον; cf. οἶκος, which does not, according to Elliott, mean "temple"), whose priestly activity as a ἱεράτευμα has nothing to do with the Protestant slogan "priesthood of all believers." The same passage, esp. vv 3–6, is treated by B. Gärtner (72–88), who points out the close relationships between this passage and certain Qumran texts, esp. 1QS 8:4–10. Contrary to Elliott, Gärtner sees "temple" symbolism in this passage. G. Klinzing (191–96) also sees here, in parallel development with Qumran traditions, an *Umdeutung* ("new interpretation") of temple symbolism. The ecclesiology of 1 Peter is dealt with more generally by K. Philipps and by H. Goldstein; the latter sees the ecclesiology of 1 Peter as a practical development of that of Paul.

Exegetical monographs on individual passages in 1 Peter include the important study of πύρωσις in 1 Pet 4:12 by E. T. Sander, and the study of 1 Pet 2:1–3 by T. J. Ryan. Thematic studies include that of W. Bieder (1950a) on Christian mission in relation to baptism, that of D. Watson on church–state relations in 1 Peter, that of S. Frederick on the theme of obedience, and that of H. Millauer on the texts dealing with "suffering" in 1 Peter and the Jewish and early Christian traditions reflected in them.

The Old Latin text of 1 Peter is the subject of a thorough investigation by W. Thiele (see Sibinga's review, 1969). He sees Cyprian as the starting point for the study of the Latin Bible, Tertullian having translated his citations from the Greek. Augustine used a younger Old Latin text than that used by Cyprian. The Vulgate, not a creation of Jerome, is based on one of several European Old Latin texts.

Other monographs in which 1 Peter is partially in focus include the studies on early Christian hymns by R. Deichgräber (esp. 77–78, 140–43, 169–73), K. Wengst (esp. 83–85, 161–64), and J. T. Sanders (esp. 17–19, 95–96). The study by H. Baltensweiler on marriage and the place of women in the NT includes a section on the *Haustafel* ("tablet of household rules") in 1 Peter 3:1–6, which he takes to be a "backward step" in comparison to Eph 5:21–33 (243–55). J. A. T. Robinson, as part of his project of "redating," proposes the end of April, A.D. 65, for the writing of the letter by the apostle Peter (150–69). Finally, 1 Peter is briefly discussed in a joint Lutheran-Roman Catholic investigation of the role of Peter in the NT (Brown et al., 149–54).

Articles

The articles devoted to 1 Peter during the period under review are very numerous, and only the briefest possible sketch can be presented here. Other recent surveys of research on 1 Peter include the articles by J. H. Elliott (1976) and F. J. Schierse.

Although a majority of scholars favor a postapostolic origin for 1 Peter on the basis of content and historical allusions (e.g., J. Knox; Hunzinger; McCaughey; Brox, 1975, 1977, 1978a, 1978b), a significant number of studies have been devoted to arguments for the traditional dating and ascription. Selwyn (1950) and Carrington are satisfied simply to show that the case against authenticity has not been proved (see also Love). N. Hillyer (1970) offers a novel argument for the traditional view on the basis of 1 Peter's allusions to the Jewish festival of Tabernacles. C. Spicq (1966a) and R. Gundry (1967) argue for authenticity on the basis of the "eye-witness" character of the Gospel parallels in 1 Peter (see Best's critique of Gundry [1970] and Gundry's reply [1974]). F. Neugebauer has recently tried to show that the epistle's contents and historical allusions fit the traditional date and ascription better than a date and situation in the 90s or later. C. L. Mitton's case for the literary dependence of 1 Peter on Ephesians (1950) does not appear to have carried the day.

The literary structure of 1 Peter is studied by H. Combrink, who divides the letter into four major sections organized chiastically (1:3–2:10; 2:11–3:12; 3:13–4:19; 5:1–11). F. Schröger sees two letters in 1 Peter by different authors (1:1–4:11; 4:12–5:11). M.-A. Chevallier (1971) studies the structure of 1:1–2:10, and A. B. du Toit applies "discourse analysis" to 1 Peter, with special attention to 1:3–13.

A number of articles are devoted to the relationship of 1 Peter to early Christian liturgy; F. L. Cross's monograph plays a large role in these studies. M.-É. Boismard (1961) supports the interpretation of Cross and others that 1 Peter reproduces a baptismal liturgy; he devotes one article to the formula of the renunciation of Satan, which he sees reflected in 1 Pet 1:13–2:10 (1956a), and a two-part article to the liturgical elements 1 Peter has in common with the Pauline letters and with James (1956b, 1957). F. Gryglewicz (1958) accepts Boismard's views and attempts to expand the influence of baptismal liturgy on NT epistles to 1 John. S. I. Buse sees two baptismal homilies in 1 Peter, one delivered before and one after the rite itself. A. R. C. Leaney (1964) accepts Cross's theory that 1 Peter is a paschal liturgy and discusses a number of Jewish Passover traditions that he sees reflected in the epistle. According to O. Brooks, 1 Peter is a baptismal sermon, with its climax at 3:21. A. R. Jonsen sees echoes of primitive Christian eucharistic celebration in 1 Pet 2:1–11 and characterizes the moral teaching of 1 Peter as a whole as "sacramental morality."

On the other hand, many scholars remain unconvinced by Cross's arguments. T. Thornton strongly criticizes Cross's position, and rightly takes special issue with his theory of a πάσχα-πάσχειν wordplay in 1 Peter. C. F. D. Moule (1956) is also unconvinced by Cross's arguments and sees 1 Peter as a real letter sent out in two forms, one for those who are suffering under local persecutions and one for those who are not. W. C. van Unnik (1956) similarly rejects Cross's theories and similarly characterizes the persecutions referred to in 1 Peter as local harassments, rather than official state persecutions. D. Hill posits Christian suffering as the chief concern of 1 Peter; the references to baptism are theological, not liturgical.

General theological studies of 1 Peter include Lohse, 1954 (on its paraenesis); Filson (on its themes of suffering and hope); Miller (on its salvation doctrine); Selwyn, 1956 (on its eschatology); Davies (on its primitive-looking Christology); Delling (on its view of Christian existence); Goldstein, 1974 (on its doctrine of community); Chevallier (on its doctrine of salvation history in relation to actual conditions in the Roman empire); Wolff (on its view of Christians as "strangers" in the world); and Schröger (on the two concepts of church structure reflected in it). Special studies of ethics in 1 Peter include Brandt (on its use of ἀναστροφή); van Unnik, 1954 (on its doctrine of "good works"); Sleeper (strongly criticizing Reicke's commentary

[1964] for its interpretation of ethics in 1 Peter); Goppelt, 1972 (on the epistle's doctrine of the relationship between church and society); and Schrage (on the *Haustafeln* in 1 Peter [and Colossians and Ephesians]). D. Daube's important study of the use of imperative participles in the NT should also be mentioned here; he suggests that 1 Peter's use of imperative participles reflects the influence of the language of Hebrew rules for behavior, such as those in Mishna and Tosepta.

A number of exegetical studies cluster around the *descensus* passages in 1 Peter (cf. discussion of monographs above). R. Bultmann reconstructs what he takes to be a creedal formula behind 1:20 + 3:18–19, 22. J. Jeremias (1949) rejects Bultmann's reconstruction of the fragment and interprets 3:19–20 to refer to Christ's preaching of salvation, in contrast to Enoch's preaching of judgment. The πνεύματα of 3:19 are equated with the νεκροί of 4:6 by Schweizer; Cranfield, 1958; Johnson; and von Balthasar; these scholars also see the purpose of Christ's preaching as salvatory. W. J. Dalton, on the other hand (1964, 1968; see also his monograph, 1965) interprets 3:19–20 as Christ's proclamation of victory over the evil spirits and 4:6 as referring to Christians who have died.

1 Pet 2:4–10 has called forth a number of exegetical studies relating to the ecclesiology of 1 Peter. J. Blinzler studies the term ἱεράτευμα in 2:5, 9 and its OT background; he questions the applicability of this passage to the Protestant doctrine of the "priesthood of all believers." Blinzler's study has strongly influenced the work of J. H. Elliott on 1 Pet 2:4–10 (1968; see also his monograph, 1966). E. Best, on the other hand (1960), seems to accept that a "general priesthood" is taught in 1 Peter; in another article on the same passage (1969) he studies the background of the passage and its function in the total context of the epistle. W. Pesch supports Blinzler's interpretation. A. Feuillet (1974) takes issue with some of the arguments in Elliott's monograph; he sees both a personal and a communal aspect in 1 Pet 2:5–6 and argues that 1 Pet 2:4–10 should be interpreted against the background of Isaiah 53, Psalm 22, and Wisdom 2–5.

Miscellaneous exegetical and/or textual studies are far too numerous to discuss here. The most important ones, cited according to chapter and verse in 1 Peter, are as follows: 1:1 (Hemer; Schenke:517, reporting a suggestion by K.-M. Fischer); 1:1–12 (Furnish); 1:3–12 (Coutts); 1:1–20 (Arichea); 1:6 + 4:13–14 (Nauck, 1955; de Villiers); 1:9 (Dautzenberg); 1:18 (van Unnik, 1969, on πατροπαράδοτος); 1:20 (Le Déaut); 1:22–25 (Blendinger); 1:23 (LaVerdière; Bishop, 1953); 1:24–2:17 (Danker, 1967); 1:25 (Scharlemann); 2:1–10 (Snodgrass); 2:3–6 (Flusser:233–36); 2:6 (Hillyer, 1971); 2:9 (Deist); 2:11 (de Jonge); 2:11 (Adinolfi); 2:12 (Meecham, on ἐποπτεύοντες); 2:13 (Teichert, on ἀνθρωπίνη κτίσις; Kamlah on ὑποτάσσεσθαι); 2:13–17 (Bammel; Goldstein, 1973); 2:14, 20 (van Unnik, 1955, on ἀγαθοποιῶν); 2:18–25 (Thompson); 2:24 (Patsch); 2:24 (Wilcox); 3:6 (Rengstorf); 3:7 (Fridrichsen:127–31; Reicke, 1954, unsuccessfully opposing Fridrichsen's interpretation); 3:17 (Michaels); 3:18–21 (Synge, on baptism); 3:19 (Good-speed, supporting the conjectural reading, ΕΝΩΧ); 3:20 (Bishop, 1951, on ὀλίγοι); 3:20–21 (de Ru, 1966, on baptism); 3:21 (Arvedson; and Aalen, on ἐπερώτημα; Nixon, on baptism); 4:1–2 (Strobel, 1963b); 4:7–11 (Kline); 4:12 (Strugnell, on a Qumran parallel); 4:14 (García del Moral); 4:15 (Bauer, 1978, on κακόποιος and ἀλλοτριοεπίσκοπος; 4:18 (Barr, 1975, on μόλις); 5:1–5 (Nauck, 1957; Elliott, 1970); and 5:13 (Hunzinger, on "Babylon").

Important text-critical studies include Massaux, on the P[72] text of 1 Peter in relation to established text-families; Quinn, on the P[72] text of 2:3; 5:14; and 5:9; and Davey, on the Syriac versions of 1–2 Peter.

Commentaries

A large number of commentaries on 1 Peter have appeared in the period under discussion. Clearly the two most important ones published in the years just after the war are those of Selwyn (1946) and Beare (1947). Two extensive commentaries have recently appeared that will now be regarded as the best commentaries currently available on 1 Peter: Goppelt (1978) and Brox (1979). The most important commentaries in the intervening period are Windisch and Preisker; Schelkle, 1961; Spicq, 1966b; J. N. D. Kelly, 1969; and Schrage and Balz. Others worth mentioning are Cranfield, 1952; Leconte; Michl, 1953; Hunter; Schneider; Reicke, 1964; Leaney, 1967; Bauer, 1971; Best, 1971; and Holmer and de Boor.

The commentaries of Selwyn and Beare represent different trends in subsequent scholarship on 1 Peter. Selwyn is especially noteworthy as the first attempt to apply "form criticism" to the epistle, and his ground-breaking "Essay II: On the Inter-Relation of 1 Peter and other N.T. Epistles" (365–466) is still standard today. Selwyn defines 1 Peter as an encyclical letter, attributable to Peter with the secretarial assistance of Silvanus, and datable to A.D. 63 or 64. Beare, on the other hand, sees in 1 Peter a baptismal homily (1:3–4:11), capped by a later epistolary section reflecting the persecutions in northern Asia Minor documented in the Pliny-Trajan correspondence. 1 Peter is, therefore, a pseudepigraph, datable to the early second century.

That 1 Peter is more of a baptismal homily or liturgy than a letter is argued on form-critical grounds by Preisker (Windisch and Preisker). Leaney, utilizing insights gained from F. L. Cross's monograph (discussed above) sees 1 Peter as a paschal liturgy (1967). But more recent scholarship has tended to reject this view of 1 Peter, and there is now a growing consensus that it should be regarded as a letter after all, with liturgical, catechetical, and other varieties of early Christian tradition utilized in its formation (so Goppelt, Brox, Schrage, Kelly, Spicq, Schelkle, et al.). There is also a growing disinclination to attribute the letter to the apostle Peter, with a concomitant view of postapostolic origin (so the scholars just named, except Spicq). Although most recent commentators see a considerable degree of "Paulinism" reflected in 1 Peter, the most recent interpretations point out with greater clarity the distinctive traits in the theology of 1 Peter (so esp. Goppelt, Brox, Schrage), but these traits are not tied to any particular "Petrine" tradition; they represent a common early Christian tradition. Goppelt sees evidence of *Roman* church tradition in 1 Peter. Most recent commentators see as the destination and intended readership of 1 Peter predominantly Gentile churches of the five Roman provinces named in 1:1. The name "Babylon" (5:13) is taken to mean Rome, but this could just as well be a feature of the letter's baggage of pseudonymity (so Brox) as an indication of Roman origin (Goppelt, Schrage, et al.).

III. 2 PETER

Monographs and Dissertations

Very few monographs have been devoted to 2 Peter during the last several decades. E. M. B. Green (1961) examines the traditional arguments against the authenticity of 2 Peter; finding them wanting, he affirms the traditional ascription to the apostle. In a much more balanced study, T. Fornberg (see Pearson's review, 1978) sees 2 Peter as a product of the postapostolic church living in a Hellenistic environment somewhere in Asia Minor. With some cogency Fornberg takes issue with the usual view of the opponents of 2 Peter as "Gnostics," arguing that their denial of the parousia is more likely based on a Hellenistic determinist view of the universe. J. Neyrey subjects the form of the polemics in 2 Peter, in comparison with Jude, to close scrutiny and traces the patterns of argument back to a traditional Hellenistic polemic against Epicurean denials of divine providence. He finds such polemics reflected also in Jewish sources, both Greek (i.e., Philo) and rabbinic (e.g., targums and midrashim). The opponents in 2 Peter are accused of rejecting the parousia prophecy as a human fabrication and denying God's retributive judgment. Neyrey's view is preferable to the argument of A. Strobel (1961:87–97; see also 1963:3–4) that 2 Peter is reflecting a Jewish traditional exegesis of Hab 2:3. The language of 2 Pet 1:4, especially θεία φύσις and φθορά, is the subject of a dissertation by J. Thurén. He finds the most relevant parallels in Plato and Philo, but despite the Hellenistic terminology used in 2 Peter the basic theme of a "new nature," centered on the grace and promises of God, is rooted in Jewish apocalyptic. It is possible, argues Thurén, that the author of 2 Peter has taken over the terminology of his opponents.

2 Peter (together with 1 Peter, *Apocalypse of Peter*, and *Gospel of Peter*) is analyzed in connection with an investigation of early Peter traditions in a dissertation by D. Schmidt. He finds that the substantial differences among the four Petrine pseudepigraphs exclude the possibility of a use of common traditions, such as might be expected in a "school of Peter"; hence, no such

"school" ever existed. Schmidt places 2 Peter in Egypt, ca. A.D. 125-150. 2 Peter is briefly discussed in a joint Lutheran-Roman Catholic investigation of the role of Peter in the NT (Brown et al.:154–56). 2 Peter seems to address the same readership as 1 Peter (cf. 3:1) and presents the apostle as the chief guardian of orthodoxy. 2 Peter shows that the "Petrine trajectory" is outdistancing the Pauline in the second century. In a similar vein, 2 Peter is described and analyzed by O. Knoch as a postapostolic "testament" of Peter, contributing to the growing authority of Peter in the church (Knoch deals similarly with 2 Timothy as a "testament" of Paul).

Articles

Although an overwhelming majority of scholars favor the view that 2 Peter is a late pseudepigraph, attempts have occasionally been made in scholarly articles to overturn that view (see also Robinson:169–99, discussed below). For example, U. Holzmeister examines statistically the vocabulary of 2 Peter in comparison with 1 Peter, and, as a control sample, 2 Corinthians in comparison with 1 Corinthians; finding that there is a greater proportion of shared vocabulary between 1 and 2 Peter, he concludes that they were composed by the same author, namely, Peter. G. de Ru (1969) favors an early date for 2 Peter (late 60s), but ascribes the epistle to a disciple of Peter. F. Marín (1975) examines the main scholarly opinions and, in a reexamination of 2 Peter 3, comes to the conclusion that 2 Peter can indeed be dated to the time of the apostolic church. One of the most influential articles written on 2 Peter in the past several decades (Käsemann) presents a still-convincing case for viewing 2 Peter as a late pseudepigraph. According to Käsemann, 2 Peter is an "early catholic" document directed against gnostic opponents; as an "apology for primitive Christian eschatology," however, it is not completely successful, precisely because of its distance in time from the eschatological impulses of the early church.

The prevalent view regarding the opponents of 2 Peter is that they are "Gnostics" of some sort. This position is argued forcefully by C. Talbert; according to him these Gnostics justify their theology and ethical libertinism by appealing to the fact of the "delay of the parousia" and the concomitant experience of the stability of the universe.

The arguments of 2 Pet 3:1–13 are analyzed by D. von Allmen, who maintains that the author uses miscellaneous Jewish apocalyptic traditions to combat an extreme "hellenization" of the gospel. According to J. Klinger, 2 Peter borrows much of its ethical argument from Stoicism and attempts to synthesize the teachings of Peter and Paul in combatting libertinism. The most recent analysis of the eschatology of 2 Peter, that of E. Lövestam, argues for a unified structure in the argument in 2 Peter 3, with its emphasis on the generation of Noah and the flood; this argument goes back to a tradition that, perhaps via the apostle Peter, ultimately stems from Jesus (cf. Matthew 24).

The literary structure of 2 Peter is examined by M. McNamara, who views 2 Peter as a composite document made up of originally separate pieces. G. Boobyer (1959), assuming the usual view that 2 Peter is dependent on Jude, argues also for its dependence on 1 Peter, citing a number of specific examples in 2 Peter where passages in 1 Peter can be assumed to have been in the mind of the author. F. Danker (1978) has recently shown the extent to which the language of 2 Peter, specifically 1:1–11, reflects formulas found in Hellenistic civic and imperial decrees of the sort that extol the virtues of benefactors.

Miscellaneous textual and/or exegetical studies include the following, cited by chapter and verse in 2 Peter: 1:14 (Mariani, in connection with an analysis of the *Quo Vadis* legend); 1:12–15 (Vögtle, in relation to the canonization of apostolic tradition); 1:17 (Bretscher, relating it to Exod 4:22–23); 1:19 (Sibinga, 1966, relating it to Cant 2:17); 1:19–21 (Lønning, on the "prophetic word"); 1:20 (Louw; and Molland, both on ἰδίας ἐπιλύσεως); 2:1 (Meinertz, on αἵρεσις); 2:4 (Pearson, 1969, on ταρταρώσας); 2:13 (Skehan, supporting the readings ἀδικούμενοι and ἀπάταις); 2:14–15 (Rinaldi, on Balaam as "prophet" and *Tg. Neof.* Num 25:7); 2:18 (Hemmerdinger-Iliadou, proposing a reading found in Ephraim Syrus); 2:19 (Daniélou, relating it to early *testimonia* based on Num 24:17); 3:4 (Brinkman, on κτίσις); 3:7, 10, 12–13 (Gryglewicz; and Testa, relating the verses to Jewish apocalyptic traditions; cf. Barnard, who traces the Jewish conceptions to Iran); 3:10 (Danker, relating a proposed reading to *Pss. Sol.* 17:10; and Lenhard, proposing a new translation); 3:15 (Conti, relating σοφία to the Pauline χάρις).

As in the case of so many aspects of NT study, the analysis of 2 Peter and its background has been enormously enriched by the Qumran discoveries. But J. O'Callaghan has gone too far when he proposes to identify some of the Greek fragments of cave 7 as NT texts, especially in the case of 7Q10, which he identifies as 2 Pet 1:15 (O'Callaghan, 1972c). This proposal has been thoroughly demolished by P. Benoit (1973), M. Baillet (1973), and A. Urbán.

Commentaries

Comparatively few scholarly commentaries have been devoted to 2 Peter. The most important one to appear in the decade following the war is Windisch and Preisker; the best one currently available is Grundmann. The most important ones published in the intervening period are Schelkle, 1961; Spicq, 1966b; J. N. D. Kelly; and Schrage and Balz. Others worth mentioning are Leconte; Michl, 1953; Barnett, 1957a; Schneider; Reicke, 1964; Leaney, 1967; Sidebottom; Green, 1968; and Holmer and de Boor.

There is near unanimity among commentators on the character of 2 Peter as a late pseudepigraphical "testament" of Peter, championing an apostolically grounded orthodoxy; only theologically "fundamentalist" scholars regard it as a genuine epistle of the apostle Peter (e.g., Green). There is also near unanimity on the question of 2 Peter's dependence on Jude (Reicke, however, argues that Jude and 2 Peter are based on a common source). Most scholars also regard its polemics as directed against an early form of gnosticism. The intended readership is usually defined in terms of the addressees of 1 Pet 1:1; most scholars assume that 1 Peter is referred to at 3:1. No unanimity has been achieved on its place of origin, though Rome is frequently mentioned as a possibiity (e.g., Schelkle, Grundmann, Barnett, Reicke), as well as Egypt (J. N. D. Kelly, Schelkle). Considerable latitude is found regarding the date of 2 Peter, from the A.D. 90s (e.g., Spicq, Schelkle) to 150 (Grundmann, Barnett). Some commentators feel compelled to discuss its theological "questionability" (esp. Schrage), but this is a problem only for those who regard NT "early catholicism" in general as theologically problematical.

IV. JUDE

Monographs and Articles

Very few full-scale studies have been devoted to this "most neglected book in the New Testament" (see Rowston, 1975). Probably the longest study ever written on Jude is the Swedish dissertation by C. Albin (German abstract, 705–45). Albin deals with the traditions about Jude, most extensively with the text of Jude, and finally attempts a short interpretation of the epistle. The most important section of the book is the textual *apparatus criticus*, with commentary (590–631), but its importance is limited only to the accumulation of evidence, not its text-critical judgments. The other dissertation worth mentioning is that of D. Rowston (1971), dealing with the historical setting of Jude. Jude is seen as a postapostolic writing, attributed to a brother of the Lord, written ca. A.D. 90 to combat proto-gnostic antinomian heretics whose views are a distortion of the Pauline doctrine of grace. Rowston's findings are condensed in an article (1975).

A novel theory on the authorship and date of Jude and 2 Peter, and the relationship between them, has recently been put forward by Robinson (169–99). According to him, both Jude and 2 Peter were written by Jude to Jewish-Christians in Asia Minor between 60 and 62, or before Peter's departure for Rome. Jude wrote a general letter in the name of his colleague, Peter, and a more hurried short note on his own authority (referred to in 2 Pet 3:1!). More recently E. Ellis has attempted to show that Jude is an early (A.D. 55–65) "midrash" on the theme of judgment, attributable to the Jerusalem "brother" Jude mentioned in Acts 15:22. The false teachers condemned in Jude are opponents of the Apostolic Decree. The usual view of Jude's opponents —i.e., that they are "Gnostics" of some sort—is also called into question by I. Eybers and F. Wisse. W. Magass applies structural linguistics in an analysis of the polemics in Jude 12–13 and finds its polyvalence to be the most significant factor of the semiotics of this passage's polemics.

Miscellaneous textual and/or exegetical studies of Jude include the following, cited by verse: 5 (Black, reading ἅπαξ with the ὅτι clause; Wikgren, rejecting Black's solution); 6 (Dubarle, proposing that the "angels" are the spies sent into Canaan in Numbers 13); 8 (Szewc, proposing that the δόξαι are fallen angels); 9 (Berger, on the Jewish traditional motif of the struggle of good and evil angels over the soul or body of a righteous person); 11 (Boobyer, 1958, on the verbs in that verse, indicating the fate of the ungodly ones); 13 (Oleson, on the allusion in that verse to the myth of Aphrodite's birth in Hesiod's *Theogony* 190–92); 14 (Osburn, 1977, on the Aramaic text of *1 Enoch* used by Jude); 22–23 (Bieder, 1950b, accepting the three-part variant, and proposing ἐᾶτε for the second ἐλεᾶτε).

Other text-critical studies, in addition to Bieder's, focus on the notoriously difficult passage in Jude 22–23. C. Osburn (1972) argues that the P⁷² reading, the oldest manuscript evidence, also has the best claim to be the original. This view is favored by J. Birdsall, who also looks at the P⁷² text of other parts of Jude, in comparison with Clement of Alexandria and other church fathers. S. Kubo (1981) argues that the three-division form of 22–23, as read by Codex Sinaiticus, is original. M. King concludes that the P⁷² manuscript of Jude and 2 Peter, while not the most important NT papyrus, is a good witness to the full use of Jude and 2 Peter in third-century Egypt and to the predominance in that area of the "Alexandrian" text-type. Finally, M. Mees, studying Clement of Alexandria's quotations from Jude, shows how biblical texts in the early patristic period were changed and "corrected."

Commentaries

Few noteworthy commentaries on Jude exist. The most important ones published in the period under discussion are Windisch and Preisker; Schelkle, 1961; J. N. D. Kelly; Schrage and Balz; and Grundmann. Others worth mentioning are Leconte; Michl, 1953; Barnett, 1957b; Schneider; Reicke, 1964; Leaney, 1967; Sidebottom; Green, 1968; Cantinat; and Holmer and de Boor.

There is near unanimity among commentators on the character of Jude as an antiheretical tract, of Jewish-Christian provenience, pseudonymously attributed to Jude, brother of the Lord. A few scholars are compelled by their own theological conservatism to attribute the document to Jude himself and thus also to assign to it an early date (e.g., Leconte, Green, Cantinat; Schneider also leans in that direction). Most scholars date Jude to ca. A.D. 90, or toward the end of the first century (e.g., Windisch and Preisker, Schelkle, Kelly, Schrage, Grundmann); some, (e.g. Barnett, Sidebottom) date it as late as A.D. 125. A Palestinian provenience is considered likely by most commentators (Grundmann offers the best arguments for Galilee or its environs), though Rome has also been suggested (Barnett). The vast majority of commentators are willing to relate the opponents of Jude to emergent Christian gnosticism.

V. GENERAL CONCLUSIONS

From the foregoing sketch of over three decades of scholarship on James, 1–2 Peter, and Jude, some concluding observations are in order. The most obvious point to be made is that there is a bewildering variety of approaches and points of view in NT scholarship. Moreover, in the case of these particular epistles—in contrast to the Johannine materials, the Synoptic Gospels, and Paul—the towering figure of Rudolf Bultmann has not exerted any notable influence. His contemporary, Martin Dibelius, stands out as a giant in scholarship on James, but by and large no single "school" is dominant in the interpretation of these epistles.

It is of interest, too, to note two very important trends developing in the period under discussion, applicable to the entire NT: (1) the increasing contribution of *American* scholarship, and (2) the dramatic increase in ecumenism in NT scholarship, symbolized in Germany especially by the new commentary series, EKKNT. (3) To this might be added the increasingly "secular" character of biblical interpretation, especially in the U.S.A., where more and more scholarly work is being done in college and university settings, instead of exclusively in theological settings.

The last thirty-five years has also been a period of important new manuscript discoveries, some of revolutionary significance. The Qumran discoveries have provided a wealth of materials shedding much light on the background and religious world of all of our epistles, especially James, 1 Peter, and Jude. The Nag Hammadi Codices have not contributed much thus far to the elucidation of these epistles, but they may yet prove to be of some importance in this regard. The publication of Papyrus Bodmer 7 (P[72]) and other papyri is very important for the establishment of the Greek text of our epistles. And the publication of *Targum Neofiti* has been the catalyst for the reexamination of the Jewish targumim and midrashim in elucidating their background, and in arriving at solid exegetical advances in their interpretation.

Finally, there has been considerable development in the last thirty-five years in methods and approaches. Form criticism and tradition criticism, as applied to our epistles, have come into their own. In more recent years new tools in interpretation have developed, such as structural-linguistic analysis, literary and rhetorical criticism, and the application of the sociology of knowledge and other sociological methods to these epistles, especially in the case of James and 1 Peter. It is, therefore, to be expected that in the future the tried and true—and irreplaceable—methods of philological and historical-critical study of NT texts will be combined with newer methods to create a truly "interdisciplinary" science of biblical interpretation. In any case, it is safe to say that scholarship on James, 1–2 Peter, and Jude—as with the rest of the Bible—will not "stand still" in the years to come.

[*Postscript:* Although scholarship has not "stood still" since the end of 1979, when this chapter was completed, I think it is fair to say that the general conclusions reached here are still valid. Even so, I regret that I have not been able to bring the discussion up to date.]

BIBLIOGRAPHY

Aalen, S.
1972   "Oversittelsen av ordet ἐπερώτημα i dåpsstedet 1 Pet 3,21." *TTKi* 43: 161–75.

Adamson, J. B.
1976   *The Epistle of James.* NICNT. Grand Rapids: Eerdmans.

Adinolfi, M.
1967   "Stato civile dei cristiani 'forestieri e pellegrini' (1 Pt. 2,11)." *Antonianum* 42: 420–34.

Agourides, Savas C.
1963   "The Origin of the Epistle of St. James. Suggestions for a Fresh Approach." *Greek Orthodox Theological Review* 9: 67–78.

Aland, Kurt
1970   "Bemerkungen zu den gegenwärtigen Möglichkeiten text-kritischer Arbeit aus Anlass einer Untersuchung zum Cäsarea-Text der Katholischen Briefe." *NTS* 17: 1–9.
1973   "Neue neutestamentliche Papyri? Ein Nachwort zu den angeblichen Entdeckungen von Professor O'Callaghan." *BK* 28: 19–20.

Albin, C. A.
1962   *Judasbrevet: Traditionen, Texten, Tolkningen.* Lund: Håkan Ohlsson.

Allmen, D. von
1966   "L'apocalyptique juive et le retard de la parousie en II Pierre 3:1–13." *RTP* 99: 255–74.

Alonso Schökel, Luis
1975   "Culto y justicia en Sant 1,26–27." *Bib* 56: 537–44.

Amphoux, Christian-Bernard
1970   "A propos de Jacques I,17." *RHPR* 50: 127–36.
1973   "Études structurales: Langue de l'Épître de Jacques." *RHPR* 53: 7–45.
1978   "Vers un description linguistique de l'épître de Jacques." *NTS* 25: 58–92.

Arichea, D. C., Jr.
1977   "God or Christ? A Study of Implicit Information." *BT* 28: 412–18.

Arvedson, Tomas
1950   "Syneideseos agathes eperotema: En studie till 1 Petr. 3,21." *SEÅ* 15: 55–61.

Baillet, M.
1972, 1973   "Les manuscrits de la Grotte 7 de Qumrân et le Nouveau Testament." *Bib* 53: 508–16; 54: 340–50.

Baltensweiler, H.
1967   *Die Ehe im Neuen Testament: Exegetische Untersuchungen über Ehe, Ehelosigkeit und Ehescheidung.* ATANT 52. Zurich and Stuttgart: Zwingli.

Balthasar, H. U. von
1970   "Abstieg zur Hölle." *TQ* 150: 193–201.

Baltzer, Klaus, and Helmut Koester
1955   "Die Bezeichnung des Jakobus als 'ΩΒΛΙΑΣ." *ZNW* 46: 141–42.

Bammel, Ernest
1965   "The Commands in 1 Peter 2:17." *NTS* 11: 279–81.

Barnard, L. W.
1957   "The Judgment in 2 Peter iii." *ExpTim* 68: 302.

Barnett, A. E.
1957a   "The Second Epistle of Peter." *IB* 12. New York: Abingdon.
1957b   "The Epistle of Jude." *IB* 12. New York: Abingdon.

Barr, James
1975   "בארץ-ΜΟΛΙΣ: Prov. XI.31, I Pet. IV.18." *JSS* 20: 149–64.

Bauer, Johannes B.
1971   *Der erste Petrusbriefe.* Die Welt der Bibel, Kleinkommentar 14. Düsseldorf: Patmos.
1978   "Aut maleficus aut alieni speculator (1 Petr 4,14)." *BZ* 22: 109–15.

Beare, Francis Wright
1947   *The First Epistle of Peter.* Oxford: Blackwell.

Beck, David Lawrence
1973   "The Composition of the Epistle of James." Diss., Princeton Theological Seminary.

Benoit, Pierre
1972   "Note sur les fragments grecs de la grotte 7 de Qumrân." *RB* 79: 321–24.
1973   "Nouvelle note sur les fragments grecs de la grotte 7 de Qumrân." *RB* 80: 5–12.

Bergauer, Paulus
1962   *Der Jakobusbrief bei Augustinus und die damit verbundenen Probleme der Rechtfertigungslehre.* Vienna: Herder.

Berger, K.
1973   "Der Streit des guten und des bösen Engels um die Seele: Beobachtungen zu 4QAmr^b und Judas 9." *JSJ* 4: 1–18.

Best, Ernest
1960   "Spiritual Sacrifice: General Priesthood in the New Testament." *Int* 14: 273–99.
1969   "1 Peter II 4–10—A Reconsideration." *NovT* 11: 270–93.
1970   "1 Peter and the Gospel Tradition." *NTS* 16: 95–113.
1971   *1 Peter.* NCB. London: Oliphants.

Beyer, Klaus
1968   *Semitische Syntax im Neuen Testament.* SUNT 1. Göttingen: Vandenhoeck & Ruprecht.

Bieder, Werner
1949   *Die Vorstellung von der Höllenfahrt Jesu Christi.* ATANT 19. Zurich: Zwingli.

1950a   *Grund und Kraft der Mission nach dem 1 Petrusbrief.* Theologische
         Studien 29. Zurich: Evangelischer Verlag.
1950b   "Judas 22f: Οὓς δὲ ἐᾶτε ἐν φόβῳ." *TZ* 6: 75–77.

Birdsall, J. Neville
1963   "The Text of Jude in P⁷²." *JTS* 14: 394–99.

Bishop, Eric F. F.
1951   "Oligoi in 1 Peter 3:20." *CBQ* 13: 44–45.
1953   "A living and unchanging God: 1 Petr 1,23." *The Muslim World* 43:
         15–17.

Black, Matthew
1964   "Critical and Exegetical Notes on Three New Testament Texts,
         Hebrews xi.11, Jude 5, James i.27." Pp. 39–45 in *Apophoreta: Fest-
         schrift für Ernst Haenchen zu seinem siebzigsten Geburtstag.* Ed. W.
         Eltester and F. H. Kettler. BZNW 30. Berlin: Töpelmann.

Blendinger, C.
1967   "Kirche als Fremdlingschaft (1 Petrus 1,22–25)." *Communio
         Viatorum* 10: 123–34.

Blenker, Alfred
1967   "Jakobs brevs sammenhaeng." *DTT* 30: 193–202.

Blinzler, Josef
1949   "ΙΕΡΑΤΕΥΜΑ: Zur Exegese von 1 Petr 2,5 u. 9." Pp. 49–65 in
         *Episcopus: Studien über das Bischofsamt seiner Eminenz Michael
         Kardinal von Faulhaber.* Ed. Theologischer Fakultät der Universität
         München. Regensburg: Gregorius.

Boismard, M.-É.
1956a   "Je renonce à Satan, à ses pompes et à ses oeuvres." *Lumen Vitae* 26:
         105–10.
1956b,   "Une liturgie baptismale dans la *Prima Petri.*" *RB* 63: 182–208;
1957   64:161–83.
1961   *Quatre hymnes baptismales dans la première Épître de Pierre.* LD 30.
         Paris: Cerf.

Boobyer, G. H.
1958   "The Verbs in Jude 11." *NTS* 5: 45–47.
1959   "The Indebtedness of 2 Peter to 1 Peter." Pp. 34–53 in *New Testa-
         ment Essays: Studies in Memory of Thomas Walter Manson.* Ed.
         A. J. B. Higgins. Manchester: University Press.

Brandt, Wilhelm
1953   "Wandel als Zeugnis nach dem 1 Petrusbrief." Pp. 10–25 in *Verbum
         Dei manet in aeternum: Eine Festschrift für Prof. D. Otto Schmitz.* Ed.
         W. Foerster. Witten: Luther-Verlag.

Braumann, Georg
1963   "Der theologische Hintergrund des Jakobusbriefes." *TZ* 18: 401–10.

Bretscher, P. G.
1968   "Exodus 4:22–23 and the Voice from Heaven." *JBL* 87: 301–11.

Brinkman, B. R.
1957   " 'Creation' and 'Creature': Some Texts and Tendencies (excluding
         Romans)." *Bijdragen* 18: 129–39.

Brinktrine, J.
1954   "Zu Jak 2,1 [Genetivhäufung]." *Bib* 35: 40–42.

Brooks, O. S.
1974   "I Peter 3:21—The Clue to the Literary Structure of the Epistle."
            NovT 16: 290–305.

Brown, Raymond E., et al., eds.
1973   *Peter in the New Testament*. Minneapolis: Augsburg.

Brox, Norbert
1975   "Zur pseudepigraphischen Nahmung des ersten Petrusbriefes." *BZ*
            19: 78–96.
1977   "Situation und Sprache der Minderheit im ersten Petrusbrief." *Kairos*
            19: 1–13.
1978a   "Tendenz und Pseudepigraphie im ersten Petrusbrief." *Kairos* 20:
            110–20.
1978b   "Der erste Petrusbrief in der literarischen Tradition des Urchristen-
            tums." *Kairos* 20: 182–92.
1979   *Der erste Petrusbrief*. EKKNT 21. Cologne: Benziger; Neukirchen-
            Vluyn: Neukirchener Verlag.

Bultmann, Rudolf
1947   "Bekenntnis- und Liedfragmente im ersten Petrusbrief." *ConNT* 11:
            1–14.

Buse, S. I.
1959   "Baptism in Other New Testament Writings." Pp. 170–86 in *Chris-
            tian Baptism*. Ed. A. Gilmore. London: Lutterworth.

Cabaniss, A.
1975   "A note on Jacob's homily." *EvQ* 47: 219–22.

Campenhausen, Hans von
1950   "Die Nachfolge des Jakobus: Zur Frage eines urchristlichen
            'Kalifats.'" *ZKG* 63: 133–44.

Cantinat, Jean
1973   *Les Épîtres de Saint Jacques et de Saint Jude*. SB. Paris: Gabalda.

Carder, Muriel M.
1969   "A Caesarean Text in the Catholic Epistles?" *NTS* 16: 252–70.

Carrington, Philip
1951   "Saint Peter's Epistle." Pp. 57–63 in *The Joy of Study: Papers on New
            Testament and Related Subjects Presented to Honor Frederick Clifton
            Grant*. Ed. S. E. Johnson. New York: Macmillan.

Chevallier, M.-A.
1971   "I Pierre 1/1 à 2/10: Structure littéraire et conséquences exégé-
            tiques." *RHPR* 51: 129–42.
1974   "Condition et vocation des Chrétiens en diaspora: remarques exégé-
            tiques sur la Ire Épître de Pierre." *RevScRel* 48: 387–400.

Combrink, H. J. B.
1975   "The Structure of 1 Peter." *Neot* 9: 34–63.

Condon, K.
1959   "The Sacrament of Healing (Jas. 5:14–15)." *Scripture* 11: 33–42.

Conti, M.
1969   "La Sophia di 2 Petr. 3,15." *RivB* 17: 121–38.

Cooper, R. M.
1968   "Prayer: A Study in Matthew and James." *Encounter* 29: 268–77.

Coutts, J.
1957   "Ephesians 1:3–14 and I Peter 1:3–12." *NTS* 3: 115–27.

Cranfield, C. E. B.
1952   *The First Epistle of St. Peter.* London: SCM.
1958   "The Interpretation of 1 Peter 3:19 and 4:6." *ExpTim* 69: 369–72.
1965a,   "The Message of James." *SJT* 18: 182–93; 338–45.
1965b

Cross, F. L.
1954   *1 Peter: A Paschal Liturgy.* London: Mowbray.

Dalton, W. J.
1964   "Proclamatio Christi spiritibus facta: inquisitio in textum ex Prima
            Epistola S. Petri 3,18–4,6." *VD* 42: 225–40.
1965   *Christ's Proclamation to the Spirits: A Study of 1 Peter 3:18–4:6.*
            AnBib 23. Rome: Pontifical Biblical Institute.
1968   "Interpretation and Tradition: An Example from 1 Peter." *Greg* 49:
            11–37.

Daniélou, Jean
1957   "L'Étoile de Jacob et la mission chrétienne à Damas." *VC* 11: 121–38.

Danker, Frederick W.
1962   "II Peter 3:10 and Psalm of Solomon 17:10." *ZNW* 53: 82–86.
1967   "1 Peter 1:24–2:17 – A Consolatory Pericope." *ZNW* 58: 93–102.
1978   "2 Peter 1: A Solemn Decree." *CBQ* 40: 64–82.

Daube, David
1946   "Participle and Imperative in 1 Peter." Pp. 467–88 in Selwyn, 1946.

Dautzenberg, G.
1964   "Sōtēria psychōn (1 Petr. 1,9)." *BZ* 8: 262–76.

Davey, G. R.
1972   "Old Testament Quotations in the Syriac Version of I and II Peter."
            Parole de l'Orient 3: 353–64.

Davids, P. H.
1978   "The Meaning of ἀπείραστος in James 1,13." *NTS* 24: 386–92.

Davies, Paul E.
1972   "Primitive Christology in 1 Peter." Pp. 115–22 in *Festschrift to Honor
            F. Wilbur Gingrich.* Ed. E. H. Barth and R. E. Cocroft. Leiden: Brill.

Deichgräber, R.
1967   *Gotteshymnus und Christushymnus in der frühen Christenheit: Unter-
            suchungen zu Form, Sprache und Stil der frühchristlichen Hymnen.*
            SUNT 5. Göttingen: Vandenhoeck & Ruprecht.

Deist, F. E.
1970   "'Van die duisternis tot sy merkwaardige lig' (1 Petr. 2:9) in die lig
            van Elephantine." *Nederduitse Gereformeerde Teologiese Tydskrif* 11:
            44–48.

Delling, Gerhard
1973   "Der Bezug der christlichen Existenz auf das Heilshandeln Gottes
            nach dem ersten Petrusbrief." Pp. 95–113 in *Neues Testament und
            christliche Existenz: Festschrift für Herbert Braun zum 70. Geburts-
            tag.* Ed. H. D. Betz and L. Schottroff. Tübingen: Mohr-Siebeck.

Dibelius, Martin
    1921   *Der Brief des Jakobus.* MeyerK 9. Göttingen: Vandenhoeck &
             Ruprecht.

Dibelius, Martin, and Heinrich Greeven
    1976   *James: A Commentary on the Epistle of James.* Trans. Michael A.
             Williams. Hermeneia. Philadelphia: Fortress.

Dubarle, A.-M.
    1950   "Le péché des Anges dans L'Épître de Jude." Pp. 145–48 in *Memorial
             J. Chaine.* Bibliothèque de la Faculté Catholique de Théologie de
             Lyon 5. Lyon: Facultés Catholiques.

Duplacy, Jean
    1970   "'Le Texte Occidentale' des Épîtres Catholiques." *NTS* 16: 397–99.

Easton, Burton Scott
    1957   "The Epistle of James." *IB* 12. New York: Abingdon.

Eckart, Karl-Gottfried
    1961   "Zur Terminologie des Jakobusbriefes." *TLZ* 89: 521–26.

Edsman, Carl-Martin
    1953   "Schöpfung und Wiedergeburt: Nochmals Jac. 1,18." Pp. 43–55 in
             Spiritus et Veritas: Festschrift K. Kundsin. Eutin: Ozolin.

Eichholz, Georg
    1953   *Jakobus und Paulus: Ein Beitrag zum Problem des Kanons.* Theolo-
             gische Existenz heute, n.s. 39. Munich: Kaiser.
    1961   *Glaube und Werke bei Paulus und Jakobus.* Theologische Existenz
             heute, n.s. 88. Munich: Kaiser.

Elliott, John H.
    1966   *The Elect and the Holy: An Exegetical Examination of 1 Peter 2:4–10
             and the Phrase* βασίλειον ἱεράτευμα. NovTSup 12. Leiden: Brill.
    1968   "Death of a Slogan: From Royal Priests to Celebrating Community."
             Una Sancta 25: 18–31.
    1970   "Ministry and Church Order in the NT: A Traditio-Historical Analysis
             (1 Pt. 5,1–5 and Plls.)." *CBQ* 32: 367–91.
    1976   "The Rehabilitation of an Exegetical Step-Child: 1 Peter in Recent
             Research." *JBL* 95: 243–54.

Elliott-Binns, L. E.
    1955   "James I.21 and Ezekiel XVI.36: An Odd Coincidence." *ExpTim* 66:
             273.
    1956a   *Galilean Christianity.* SBT 16. Naperville, IL: Allenson.
    1956b   "The Meaning of ὕλη in Jas. III.5." *NTS* 2:48–50.
    1957   "James 1:18: Creation or Redemption?" *NTS* 3: 148–61.

Ellis, E. Earle
    1978   "Prophecy and Hermeneutic in Jude." Pp. 221–36 in *Prophecy and
             Hermeneutic in Early Christianity: New Testament Essays.* WUNT 18.
             Tübingen: Mohr-Siebeck. Reprinted, Grand Rapids: Eerdmans,
             1978.

Eybers, I. H.
    1975   "Aspects of the Background of the Letter of Jude." *Neot* 9: 113–23.

Fabris, R.
    1977   *Legge della libertà in Giacomo.* RivBSup 8. Brescia: Paideia.

Feuillet, André
1956 "Le sens du mot Parousie dans l'Evangile Matthieu — Comparison entre Matth. XXIV et Jac V, 1–11." Pp. 261–80 in *The Background of the New Testament and Its Eschatology: Studies in Honour of C. H. Dodd.* Ed. W. D. Davies and D. Daube. Cambridge: University Press.
1974 "Les 'sacrifices spirituels' du sacerdoce royal des baptisés (1 P 2,5) et leur préparation dans l'Ancien Testament." *NRT* 96: 704–28.

Filson, Floyd Vivian
1955 "Partakers with Christ: Suffering in First Peter." *Int* 9: 400–12.

Flusser, David
1958 "The Dead Sea Sect and Pre-Pauline Christianity." Pp. 215–66 in *Aspects of the Dead Sea Scrolls.* Ed. C. Rabin and Y. Yadin. Scripta Hierosolymitana 4. Jerusalem: Magnes Press.

Forbes, P. B. R.
1972 "The Structure of the Epistle of James." *EvQ* 44: 147–53.

Fornberg, Tord
1977 *An Early Church in a Pluralistic Society: A Study of 2 Peter.* ConBNT 9. Trans. Jean Gray. Lund: Gleerup.

Francis, Fred O.
1970 "The Form and Function of the Opening and Closing Paragraphs of James and 1 John." *ZNW* 61: 110–26.

Frederick, S. C.
1975 "The Theme of Obedience in the First Epistle of Peter." Diss., Duke University.

Fridrichsen, Anton
1947 "Scholia in Novum Testamentum." *SEÅ* 12: 124–31.

Fry, E.
1978 "The Testing of Faith: A Study of the Structure of the Book of James." *BT* 29: 427–35.

Funk, Robert W.
1965 "The Main Biblical Tradition?" *Int* 19: 468–72.

Furnish, Victor Paul
1975 "Elect Sojourners in Christ: An Approach to the Theology of I Peter." *PSTJ* 28: 1–11.

Gallagher, J.Tim
1970 "A Study of von Soden's H-Text in the Catholic Epistles." *AUSS* 8: 97–119.

Garcia ab Orbiso, T.
1954 *Epistola Sancti Jacobi. Introductio et Commentarius.* Lateranum 20. Rome: Facultas Theologica Pontificii Athenaei Lateranensis.

García del Moral, A.
1961 "Crítica textual de 1 Ptr. 4,14." *EstBib* 20: 45–77.

Gärtner, Bertil
1965 *The Temple and the Community in Qumran and the New Testament.* SNTSMS 1. Cambridge: University Press.

Gertner, M.
1962 "Midrashim in the New Testament." *JSS* 2: 267–92.

Geyser, A. S.
1975   "The Letter of James and the Social Condition of His Addressees."
            Neot 9: 25-33.

Goldstein, H.
1973   "Die politischen Paränesen in 1 Petr 2 und Röm 13." *BibLeb* 14:
            88-104.
1974   "Die Kirche als Schar derer, die ihrem leidenden Herrn mit dem Ziel
            der Gottesgemeinschaft nachfolgen: Zum Gemeindeverständnis von
            1 Petr. 2,21-25 und 3,18-22." *BibLeb* 15: 38-54.
1975   *Paulinische Gemeinde im Ersten Petrusbrief.* SBS 80. Stuttgart: Katho-
            lisches Bibelwerk.

Goodspeed, Edgar Johnson
1954   "Some Greek Notes." *JBL* 73: 84-92.

Goppelt, Leonhard
1972   "Prinzipien neutestamentlicher Sozialethik nach dem 1. Petrusbrief."
            Pp. 285-96 in *Neues Testament und Geschichte: Historischen
            Geschehen und Bedeutung im Neuen Testament: Oscar Cullmann zum
            70. Geburtstag.* Ed. H. Baltensweiler and B. Reicke. Zurich: Theolo-
            gischer Verlag.
1978   *Der erste Petrusbrief.* Ed. F. Hahn. MeyerK 13/1. Göttingen: Vanden-
            hoeck & Ruprecht.

Gordon, R. P.
1975   "ΚΑΙ ΤΟ ΤΕΛΟΣ ΚΥΡΙΟΥ ΕΙΔΕΤΕ (Jas V.11)." *JTS* 26: 91-95.

Green, E. M. B.
1961   *2 Peter Reconsidered.* Tyndale NT Lecture, 1960. London: Tyndale
            Press.
1968   *The Second Epistle General of Peter and the General Epistle of Jude.*
            Grand Rapids: Eerdmans.

Greeven, Heinrich
1958   "Jedes Gabe ist gut." *TZ* 14: 1-13.

Grundmann, Walter
1974   *Der Brief des Judas und der zweite Brief des Petrus.* THKNT 15.
            Berlin: Evangelische Verlagsanstalt.

Grünzweig, F.
1973   *Der Brief des Jakobus.* Wuppertaler Studienbibel. Wuppertal:
            Brockhaus.

Gryglewicz, Feliks
1958   "Pierwotna liturgia chrztu sw. jakozrodlo pierwszego listu sw.
            Piotra." *Ruch Biblijny i Liturgiczny* 11: 206-10.
1959   "Opis Konca swiata u sw. Piotra i w Qumran." *Ruch Biblijny i
            Liturgiczny* 12: 278-82.

Gundry, Robert H.
1967   " 'Verba Christi' in 1 Peter: Their Implications concerning the
            Authorship of 1 Peter and the Authenticity of the Gospel Tradition."
            NTS 13: 336-50.
1974   "Further *Verba* on *Verba Christi* in First Peter." *Bib* 55: 211-32.

Hadidian, Dikran Y.
1952   "Palestinian Pictures in the Epistle of James." *ExpTim* 63: 227-28.

Halson, R. R.
1968   "The Epistle of James: 'Christian Wisdom?'" *SE* 4:308–14.
Hamann, H. P.
1975   "Faith and Works: Paul and James." *Lutheran Theological Journal* 9:
           33–41.
Hamman, A.
1958   "Prière et culte dans la lettre de Saint-Jacques." *ETL* 34: 35–47.
Hanson, A.
1979   "Report on Working Group on 'The Use of the Old Testament in the
           Epistle of James' held during the Seminar on 'The Use of the Old
           Testament in the New' at Tübingen in 1977 and Châtenay-Malabry
           in 1978." *NTS* 25: 526–27.
Hemer, C. J.
1978   "The Address of 1 Peter." *ExpTim* 89: 239–43.
Hemmerdinger-Iliadou, D.
1957   "II Pierre ii,18, d'après l'Ephrem grec." *RB* 64: 399–401.
Hill, David
1976   "On Suffering and Baptism in I Peter." *NovT* 18: 181–89.
Hillyer, N.
1970   "First Peter and the Feast of Tabernacles." *TynBul* 21: 39–70.
1971   "'Rock-Stone' Imagery in I Peter." *TynBul* 22: 58–81.
Holmer, U., and W. de Boor
1976   *Die Briefe des Petrus und der Brief des Judas.* Wuppertaler Studien-
           bibel. Wuppertal: Brockhaus.
Holtz, T.
1967   Review of Dalton, 1965. *TLZ* 92: 359–60.
Holzmeister, U.
1949   "Vocabularium secundae epistolae S. Petri erroresque quidam de eo
           divulgati." *Bib* 30: 339–55.
Hoppe, R.
1977   *Der theologische Hintergrund des Jakobusbriefes.* Forschung zur Bibel
           28. Würzburg: Echter-Verlag.
Hoyos, P.
1963   "La Extrema Unción en el primer siglo: Santiago 5, 14–15 a la luz de
           un nuevo descubrimiento." *RevistB* 25: 34–42.
Hunter, A. M.
1957   "The First Epistle of Peter." *IB* 12. New York: Abingdon.
Hunzinger, C.-H.
1965   "Babylon als Deckname für Rom und die Datierung des 1 Petrus-
           briefe." Pp. 67–77 in *Gottes Wort und Gottes Land: H. W. Hertzberg
           zum 70. Geburtstag.* Ed. H. G. Reventlow. Göttingen: Vanden-
           hoeck & Ruprecht.
Jacobs, I.
1976   "The Midrashic Background for James ii.21–3." *NTS* 22: 457–64.
Jeremias, Joachim
1949   "Zwischen Karfreitag und Ostern: Descensus und Ascensus in der
           Karfreitagstheologie des Neuen Testamentes." *ZNW* 42: 194–201.
1955   "Paul and James." *ExpTim* 66: 368–71.
1959   "Jac 4:5: ἐπιποθεῖ." *ZNW* 50: 137–38.

Johanson, Bruce C.
1973   "The Definition of 'Pure Religion' in James 1:27 Reconsidered."
        ExpTim 84: 118-19.

Johnson, Sherman E.
1960   "The Preaching to the Dead." *JBL* 79: 48-51.

Jonge, Marinus de
1956   "Vreemdelingen en bijwoners: Enige opmerkingen naar aanheiding
        van 1 Pt. 2:11 en verwante Teksten." *NedTTs* 11: 18-36.

Jonsen, A. R.
1964   "The Moral Teaching of the First Epistle of St. Peter." *Sciences
        Ecclésiastiques* 16: 93-105.

Kamlah, E.
1970   "'Υποτάσσεσθαι in den neutestamentlichen 'Haustafeln.' " Pp. 237-43
        in *Verborum Veritas: Festschrift für G. Stählin zu 70. Geburtstag.* Ed.
        O. Böcher and K. Haacker. Wuppertal: Brockhaus.

Käsemann, Ernst
1952   "Eine Apologie der urchristlichen Eschatologie (2 Pe)." *ZTK* 49:
        272-96.

Kelly, F. X.
1973   "Poor and Rich in the Epistle of James." Diss., Temple University.

Kelly, J. N. D.
1969   *A Commentary on the Epistles of Peter and of Jude.* New York: Harper
        & Row.

Kilpatrick, G. D.
1967   "Übertreter des Gesetzes, Jak. 2,11." *TZ* 23: 433.

King, M. A.
1964   "Notes on the Bodmer Manuscript." *BSac* 121: 54-57.

Kirk, J. A.
1969   "The Meaning of Wisdom in James: Examination of a Hypothesis."
        NTS 16: 24-38.

Kittel, Gerhard
1942   "Der geschichtliche Ort des Jakobusbriefes." *ZNW* 41: 71-105.
1950   "Der Jakobusbrief und die Apostolischen Väter." *ZNW* 43: 54-112.

Kline, L.
1963   "Ethics for the End Time: An Exegesis of 1 Peter 4:7-11." *Restoration
        Quarterly* 3: 113-23.

Klinger, J.
1973   "The Second Epistle of Peter: An Essay in Understanding." *St.
        Vladimir's Theological Quarterly* 17: 152-69.

Klinzing, Georg
1971   *Die Umdeutung des Kultus in der Qumrangemeinde und im Neuen
        Testament.* SUNT 7. Göttingen: Vandenhoeck & Ruprecht.

Knoch, O.
1973   *Die "Testamente" des Petrus und Paulus: Die Sicherung der apostoli-
        schen Überlieferung in der spätneutestamentlichen Zeit.* SBS 62. Stutt-
        gart: Katholisches Bibelwerk.

Knox, John
1953   "Pliny and 1 Peter: A Note on 1 Peter 4, 14ff and 3,15." *JBL* 72:
        187-89.

Knox, W. L.
1945   "The Epistle of St. James." *JTS* 46: 10–17.

Kubo, Sakae
1963   "The Catholic Epistles in the Greek Lectionary: A Preliminary
            Investigation." *AUSS* 1: 65–70.
1981   "Jude 22–3: Two-division Form or Three?" Pp. 239–53 in *New Testa-
            ment Textual Criticism: Its Significance for Exegesis: Essays in Honour
            of Bruce M. Metzger.* Ed. E. J. Epp and G. D. Fee. Oxford: Clarendon.

Lackmann, Max
1949   *"Sola fide": Eine exegetische Studie über Jakobus 2 zur reformatori-
            schen Rechtfertigungslehre.* BFCT 50. Gütersloh: C. Bertelsmann.

LaVerdière, E. A.
1974   "A Grammatical Ambiguity in 1 Pet. 1:23." *CBQ* 36: 89–94.

Laws, Sophie S.
1974   "Does Scripture Speak in Vain? A Reconsideration of James IV:5."
            NTS 20: 210–15.

Leaney, A. R. C.
1964   "1 Peter and the Passover: An Interpretation." *NTS* 10: 238–51.
1967   *The Letters of Peter and Jude.* Cambridge: University Press.

Leconte, R.
1953   *Les épîtres catholiques des saint Jacques, saint Jude et saint Pierre.* SBJ.
            Paris: Cerf.

Le Déaut, R.
1961   "Le Targum de Gen. 22, 8 et 1 Pt. 1,20." *RSR* 49: 103–6.

Lenhard, H.
1961   "Ein Beitrag zur Übersetzung von II Ptr. 3:10d." *ZNW* 52: 128–29.

Lohse, Eduard
1954   "Paränese und Kerygma in 1 Petrusbrief." *ZNW* 45: 68–89.
1957   "Glaube und Werke: Zur Theologie des Jakobusbriefes." *ZNW* 48:
            1–22.
1966   Review of Mussner, 1964. *TLZ* 91: 112–14.

Lønning, I.
1971   "Tradisjon og skrift: Eksegese av 2 Petr. 1, 19–21." *NorTT* 72:
            129–54.

Lorenzen, T.
1978   "Faith without Works does not count before God! James 2:14–26."
            ExpTim 89: 231–35.

Louw, J.
1965   "Wat Wordt in II Petrus 1:20 gesteld?" *NedTTs* 19: 202–12.

Love, J. P.
1954   "The First Epistle of Peter." *Int* 8: 63–87.

Lövestam, Evald
1984   "Eschatologie und Tradition im 2. Petrusbrief." Pp. 287–300 in *The
            New Testament Age: Essays in Honor of Bo Reicke.* Ed. W. C.
            Weinrich. 2 vols. Macon, GA: Mercer University Press.

Luck, Ulrich
1967   "Weisheit und Leiden: Zum Problem Paulus und Jakobus." *TLZ* 92:
            253–58.
1971   "Der Jakobusbrief und die Theologie des Paulus." *TGl* 61: 161–79.

Luff, S. G. A.
1967   "The Sacrament of the Sick—A First Century Text." *Clergy Review*
            52: 56–60.

McCaughey, J. D.
1969   "Three 'Persecution Documents' of the New Testament." *AusBR* 17:
            27–40.

McNamara, M.
1960   "The Unity of Second Peter: A Reconsideration." *Scripture* 12: 13–19.

Magass, W.
1972   "Semiotik einer Ketzerpolemik am Beispiel von Judas 12f." *Linguis-
            tica Biblica* 19: 36–47.

Mariani, B.
1969   "La predizione del martirio di S. Pietro nel 'Quo Vadis?' e nella 2 Pe
            1,14." *Euntes Docete* 22: 565–86.

Marín, F.
1975   "Apostolicidad de los escritos neotestamentarios." *Estudios Ecclesias-
            ticos* 50: 211–39.

Martini, Carlo M.
1972   "Note sui papiri della grotta 7 di Qumrān." *Bib* 53: 101–4.

Marxsen, Willi
1958   Der *"Frühkatholizismus" im Neuen Testament*. Biblische Studien 21.
            Neukirchen: Neukirchener Verlag.

Massaux, É.
1963   "Le texte de la 1ª Petri du papyrus Bodmer VIII (P⁷²)." *ETL* 39:
            616–71.

Meecham, H. G.
1953   "A Note on 1 Pe 2,12 [ἐποπτεύοντες]." *ExpTim* 65: 93.

Mees, Michael
1968   "Papyrus Bodmer VII (P⁷²) und die Zitate aus dem Judasbrief bei
            Clemens von Alexandrien." *Ciudad de Dios* 181: 551–59.

Meinertz, Max
1957   "Schisma und Hairesis im Neuen Testament." *BZ* 1: 114–18.

Meyer, Arnold
1930   *Das Rätsel des Jacobusbriefes*. BZNW 10. Giessen: Töpelmann.

Michaels, J. Ramsey
1967   "Eschatology in 1 Peter III:17." *NTS* 13: 394–401.

Michl, Johann
1953   *Die katholischen Briefe*. RNT 8,2. Regensburg: Pustet.
1963   "Der Spruch Jakobusbrief 4,5." Pp. 167–74 in *Neutestamentliche Auf-
            sätze: Festschrift für Josef Schmid zum 70. Geburtstag*. Ed. J. Blinzler,
            O. Kuss, and F. Mussner. Regensburg: Pustet.

Millauer, H.
1976   *Leiden als Gnade: Eine traditionsgeschichtliche Untersuchung zur
            Leidenstheologie des ersten Petrusbriefes*. Europäische Hochschul-
            schriften, Reihe XXIII: Theologie 56. Bern: Herbert Lang.

Miller, Donald G.
1955   "Deliverance and Destiny: Salvation in 1 Peter." *Int* 9: 413–25.

Minear, Paul S.
1971   "Yes or No: The Demand for Honesty in the Early Church." *NovT* 13: 1–13.

Mitton, C. L.
1950   "The Relationship Between I Peter and Ephesians." *JTS* n.s. 1: 67–73.
1966   *The Epistle of James.* London: Marshall, Morgan & Scott.

Molland, E.
1955   "La Thèse 'La Prophetie n'est jamais venue de la volonté de l'homme' (2 Pe I,21) et les Pseudoclémentines." *ST* 9: 67–85.

Moule, C. F. D.
1956   "The Nature and Purpose of 1 Peter." *NTS* 3: 1–11.
1967   Review of Elliott, 1966. *JTS* 18: 471–74.

Mussner, Franz
1964   *Der Jakobusbrief.* HTKNT 13/1. Freiburg: Herder.
1970   " 'Direkte' und 'indirekte' Christologie im Jakobusbrief." *Catholica* 24: 111–17.

Nauck, Wolfgang
1955   "Freude im Leiden: Zum Problem einer urchristlichen Verfolgungs-tradition." *ZNW* 46: 68–80.
1957   "Probleme des frühchristlichen Amtsverständnisses (1 Petr. 5,2f)." *ZNW* 48: 200–20.

Neugebauer, F.
1979   "Zur Deutung und Bedeutung des 1. Petrusbriefes." *NTS* 26: 61–86.

Neyrey, Jerome H.
1977   "The Form and Background of the Polemic in 2 Peter." Diss., Yale University.

Nicol, W.
1975   "Faith and Works in the Letter of James." *Neot* 9: 7–24.

Nixon, R. E.
1968   "The Meaning of Baptism in 1 Peter 3,21." *SE* 4: 437–41.

Noack, Bent
1964a   "Jakobusbrevet som kanonisk skrift." *DTT* 27: 163–73.
1964b   "Jakobus wider die Reichen." *ST* 18: 10–25.

Obermüller, Rudolf
1972   "Hermeneutische Themen im Jakobusbrief." *Bib* 53: 234–44.

O'Callaghan, José
1972a   "¿Papiros neotestamentarios en la cueva 7 de Qumran?" *Bib* 53: 91–100.
1972b   "Notes sobre 7Q tomadas en el 'Rockefeller Museum' de Jerusalén." *Bib* 53: 517–33.
1972c   "Tres probables papiros neotestamentarios en la cueva 7 de Qumrān." *SPap* 11: 83–89.

Oleson, J. P.
1979   "An Echo of Hesiod's *Theogony* vv. 190–2 in Jude 13."*NTS* 25: 492–503.

Osburn, Carroll D.
1972   "The Text of Jude 22–23." *ZNW* 63: 139–44.
1977   "The Christological Use of 1 Enoch i.9 in Jude 14,15." *NTS* 23: 334–41.

Patsch, H.
1969   "Zum alttestamentlichen Hintergrund von Römer 4:25 und 1 Petrus
            2:24." *ZNW* 60: 273–79.

Pearson, Birger A.
1969   "A Reminiscence of Classical Myth at II Peter 2.4." *GRBS* 10: 71–80.
1978   Review of Fornberg. *JBL* 97: 602–4.

Perdelwitz, R.
1911   *Die Mysterienreligionen und das Problem des 1. Petrusbriefes.* Reli-
            gionsgeschichtliche Versuche und Vorarbeiten 11,3. Giessen:
            Töpelmann.

Pesch, Wilhelm
1970   "Zu Texten des Neuen Testaments über das Priestertum der
            Getauften." Pp. 303–15 in *Verborum Veritas: Festschrift für G.
            Stählin zum 70. Geburtstag.* Ed. O. Böcher and K. Haacker. Wupper-
            tal: Brockhaus.

Philipps, K.
1971   *Kirche und Gesellschaft nach dem 1 Petrusbrief.* Gütersloh: Mohn.

Powell, Cyril H.
1951   " 'Faith' in James and Its Bearing on the Problem of the Date of the
            Epistle." *ExpTim* 62: 311–14.

Price, J. J. H.
1977   "Submission in Humility in 1 Peter: An Exegetical Study." Diss.,
            Vanderbilt University.

Quecke, Hans
1974   "Ein altes bohairisches Fragment des Jakobusbriefes (P. Heid. Kopt.
            452)." *Or* 43: 382–92.

Quinn, Jerome D.
1965   "Notes on the Text of the P[72] 1 Pt. 2,3; 5,14; and 5,9." *CBQ* 27:
            241–49.

Reicke, Bo
1946   *The Disobedient Spirits and Christian Baptism: A Study of 1 Peter
            III.19 and Its Context.* ASNU 13. Copenhagen: Munksgaard.
1954   "Die Gnosis der Männer nach 1 Petr 3." Pp. 296–304 in *Neutesta-
            mentliche Studien für Rudolf Bultmann.* Ed. Walter Eltester. BZNW
            21. Berlin: Töpelmann.
1964   *The Epistles of James, Peter, and Jude.* AB 37. Garden City, NY:
            Doubleday.
1973   "L'onction des malades d'après Saint Jacques." *Maison-Dieu* 113:
            50–56.

Rendtorff, R.
1953   *Hörer und Täter: Eine Einführung in den Jakobusbrief.* Die urchrist-
            liche Botschaft 19. Hamburg: Furche.

Rengstorf, Karl Heinrich
1953   "Die neutestamentlichen Mahnungen an die Frau, sich dem Manne
            unterzuordnen." Pp. 131–45 in *Verbum Dei manet in aeternum: Eine
            Festschrift für Prof. D. Otto Schmitz.* Ed. W. Foerster. Witten:
            Luther-Verlag.

Richards, W. Larry
1974   "Textual Criticism on the Greek Text of the Catholic Epistles: A
            Bibliography." *AUSS* 12: 103–11.

1975   "The Present Status of Text Critical Studies in the Catholic Epistles."
         AUSS 13: 261–72.
1976   "The New Testament Greek Manuscripts of the Catholic Epistles."
         AUSS 14: 301–11.

Rinaldi, G.
1975   "Il Targum palestinese del Pentateuco." *BO* 17: 75–77.

Roberts, Colin H.
1972   "On Some Presumed Papyrus Fragments of the New Testament from
         Qumran." *JTS* 23: 446–47.

Roberts, David J., III
1972   "The Definition of 'Pure Religion' in James 1:27." *ExpTim* 83: 215–16.

Robinson, J. A. T.
1976   *Redating the New Testament*. London: SCM.

Rowston, D. J.
1971   "The Setting of the Letter of Jude." Diss., Southern Baptist Theologi-
         cal Seminary.
1975   "The Most Neglected Book in the New Testament." *NTS* 21: 554–63.

Ru, G. de
1966   "De Heilige Doop—gebed of gave? (1 Petrus 3:20b, 21)." *NedTTs* 20:
         255–68.
1969   "De authenticiteit van II Petrus." *NedTTs* 24: 1–12.

Rustler, M.
1952   "Thema und Disposition des Jakobusbriefes: Eine formkritische
         Studie." Diss., Vienna.

Ryan, T. J.
1973   "The Word of God in First Peter: A Critical Study of 1 Peter 2:1–3."
         Diss., School of Theology, Catholic University of America.

Sánchez Bosch, J.
1976   "Llei i Paraula de Déu en la carta de Jaume." *Revista Catalana de
         Teologia* 1: 51–78.

Sander, Emily T.
1966   "ΠΥΡΩΣΙΣ and the First Epistle of Peter 4:12." Diss., Harvard
         University.

Sanders, Jack T.
1971   *The New Testament Christological Hymns: Their Historical Back-
         ground*. SNTSMS 15: Cambridge: University Press.

Schammberger, Hermann
1936   *Die Einheitlichkeit des Jacobusbriefes im antignostischen Kampf*.
         Gotha: Klotz.

Scharlemann, Martin
1959   "Why the *Kuriou* in 1 Peter 1:25?" *CTM* 30: 352–56.

Schelkle, Karl Hermann
1961   *Die Petrusbriefe. Der Judasbrief*. HTKNT 13,2. Freiburg: Herder.
1963   "Spätapostolische Schriften als frühkatholisches Zeugnis." Pp.
         225–32 in *Neutestamentliche Aufsätze: Festschrift für Josef Schmid
         zum 70. Geburtstag*. Ed. J. Blinzler, O. Kuss, and F. Mussner.
         Regensburg: Pustet.

Schenke, Hans-Martin
1975   "Das Weiterwirken des Paulus und die Pflege seines Erbes durch die
          Paulus-Schule." *NTS* 21: 505–18.

Schierse, F. J.
1976   "Ein Hirtenbrief und viele Bücher. Neue Literatur zum Ersten
          Petrusbrief." *BK* 31: 86–88.

Schmidt, D. H.
1972   "The Peter Writings: Their Redactors and Their Relationships."
          Diss., Northwestern University.

Schnackenburg, Rudolf
1968   Review of Elliott, 1966. In *BZ* 12: 152–53.

Schneider, Johannes
1961   *Die Briefe des Jakobus, Petrus, Judas und Johannes.* NTD 10. Göttin-
          gen: Vandenhoeck & Ruprecht.

Schoeps, Hans-Joachim
1949   *Theologie und Geschichte des Judenchristentums.* Tübingen:
          Mohr-Siebeck.

Schrage, Wolfgang
1974   "Zur Ethik der neutestamentlichen Haustafeln." *NTS* 21: 1–22.

Schrage, Wolfgang, and Horst Balz
1973   *Die katholischen Briefe.* NTD 10. Göttingen: Vandenhoeck &
          Ruprecht.

Schröger, F.
1976   "Die Verfassung der Gemeinde des ersten Petrusbriefes." Pp. 239–52
          in *Kirche im Werden: Studien zum Thema Amt und Gemeinde im
          Neuen Testament.* Ed. J. Hainz. Munich, Paderborn, and Vienna: F.
          Schöningh.

Schweizer, Eduard
1952   "1 Petrus 4,6." *TZ* 8: 152–54.

Seitz, Otto J. F.
1964   "James and the Law." *SE* 2: 472–86.

Selwyn, E. G.
1946   *The First Epistle of St. Peter.* London: Macmillan.
1950   "The Persecutions in 1 Peter." *SNTS Bulletin* 1: 39–50.
1956   "Eschatology in 1 Peter." Pp. 394–401 in *The Background of the New
          Testament and Its Eschatology: Studies in Honour of C. H. Dodd.* Ed.
          W. D. Davies and D. Daube. Cambridge: University Press.

Sevenster, J. N.
1968   *Do You Know Greek? How Much Greek Could the First Jewish Chris-
          tians Have Known?* NovTSup 19. Leiden: Brill.

Shepherd, Massey H., Jr.
1956   "The Epistle of James and the Gospel of Matthew." *JBL* 75: 40–51.

Sibinga, J. Smit
1966   "Une Citation du Cantique dans la Secunda Petri." *RB* 73: 107–18.
1969   Review of Thiele. *VC* 23: 148–54.

Sidebottom, E. M.
1967   *James, Jude and 2 Peter.* NCB. New York and London: Nelson.

Skehan, Patrick W.
1960   "A Note on 2 Peter 2,13." *Bib* 41: 69–71.

Sleeper, C. Freeman
1968   "Political Responsibility according to 1 Peter." *NovT* 10: 270–86.

Snodgrass, Klyne R.
1977   "I Peter ii.1–10: Its Formation and Literary Affinities." *NTS* 24: 97–106.

Songer, H. S.
1969   "The Literary Character of the Book of James." *RevExp* 66: 379–89.

Souček, Josef B.
1958   "Zu den Problemen des Jk." *EvT* 18: 460–68.

Spicq, Ceslas
1966a   "La I^a Petri et le Témoignage évangélique de Saint Pierre." *ST* 20: 37–61.
1966b   *Les Épîtres de Saint Pierre.* SB. Paris: Gabalda.

Spoto, D. M.
1971   "Christ's Preaching to the Dead: An Exegesis of 1 Peter 3,19 and 4,6." Diss., Fordham University.

Stauffer, Ethelbert
1952a   "Das 'Gesetz der Freiheit' in der Ordensregel von Jericho." *TLZ* 77: 527–32.
1952b   "Zum Kalifat des Jacobus." *ZRGG* 4: 192–214.

Strobel, August
1961   *Untersuchungen zum eschatologischen Verzögerungsproblem auf Grund der spätjüdisch-urchristlichen Geschichte von Habakuk 2,2ff.* NovTSup 2. Leiden: Brill.
1963a   "Die Kirchenbriefe in der neuern Auslegung." *Lutherische Monatshefte* 3: Literaturheft 1–9.
1963b   "Macht Leiden von Sünde frei? Zur Problematik von 1, Petr. 4,1f." *TZ* 19: 412–25.

Strugnell, John
1967   "Notes on 1 QS 1,17–18; 8,3–4 and 1 QM 17,8–9." *CBQ* 29: 580–82.

Stuhlmacher, Peter
1965   *Gerechtigkeit Gottes bei Paulus.* FRLANT 87. Göttingen: Vandenhoeck & Ruprecht.

Synge, F.-C.
1971   "1 Peter 3:18–21." *ExpTim* 82: 311.

Szewc, E.
1976   " 'Chwaly' w listach Judy i 2 Piotra." *Collectanea Theologica* 46: 51–60.

Talbert, C. H.
1966   "II Peter and the Delay of the Parousia." *VC* 20: 137–45.

Teichert, H.
1949   "I Petr. 2,13—eine crux interpretum?" *TLZ* 74: 303–4.

Testa, P. E.
1962   "La distruzione del mondo per il fuoco nella 2 Ep. di Pietro 3,7.10.13." *RevistB* 10: 252–81.

Thiele, Walter
    1965   *Die lateinischen Texte des 1. Petrusbriefes.* Vetus Latina: Aus der
                Geschichte der lateinischen Bibel 5. Freiburg: Herder.

Thomas, Johannes
    1968   "Anfechtung und Vorfreude: Ein biblisches Thema nach Jakobus
                1,2–18, im Zusammenhang mit Psalm 126, Röm. 5,3–5 und 1 Petr.
                1,5–7, formkritisch untersucht und parakletisch ausgelegt." *KD* 14:
                183–206.

Thompson, J. W.
    1966   " 'Be Submissive to Your Masters': A Study of 1 Peter 2:18–25."
                Restoration Quarterly 9: 66–78.

Thornton, T. C. G.
    1961   "1 Peter, A Paschal Liturgy?" *JTS* 12: 14–26.

Thurén, J.
    1975   "Vergottung und Verderben im Zweiten Petrusbrief." Diss., Åbo.

Thyen, H.
    1956   *Der Stil der jüdisch-hellenistischen Homilie.* FRLANT 47. Göttingen:
                Vandenhoeck & Ruprecht.

Toit, A. B. du
    1974   "The Significance of Discourse Analysis for New Testament Interpre-
                tation and Translation: Introductory Remarks with Special Reference
                to 1 Peter 1:3–13." *Neot* 8: 54–79.

Townsend, M. J.
    1976   "James 4:1–14: A Warning against Zealotry?" *ExpTim* 87: 211–13.

Trocmé, E.
    1964   "Les Églises pauliniennes vues du dehors: Jacques 2,1 à 3,13." *SE* 2:
                660–69.

Unnik, Willem Cornelis van
    1954   "The Teaching of Good Works in 1 Peter." *NTS* 1: 92–110.
    1955   "A Classical Parallel [Diodorus Siculus XV,1,1] to 1 Pe. 2,14.20." *NTS*
                2: 198–202.
    1956   "Christianity according to 1 Peter." *ExpTim* 68: 79–83.
    1969   "The Critique of Paganism in 1 Peter 1:18." Pp. 129–42 in *Neotesta-
                mentica et semitica: Studies in Honour of Matthew Black.* Ed. E. E.
                Ellis and M. Wilcox. Edinburgh: T. & T. Clark.

Urbán, A. C.
    1973   "Observaciones sobre ciertos papiros de la cueva 7 de Qumran."
                RevQ 8: 233–51.

Via, D. O., Jr.
    1969   "The Right Strawy Epistle Reconsidered: A Study in Biblical Ethics
                and Hermeneutic." *JR* 49: 253–67.

Villiers, J. L. de
    1975   "Joy in Suffering in 1 Peter." *Neot* 9: 64–86.

Vogels, Heinrich Josef
    1976   *Christi Abstieg ins Totenreich und das Läuterungsgericht an den
                Toten.* Freiburger Theologische Studien 102. Freiburg: Herder.

Vögtle, A.
1972   "Die Schriftwerdung der apostolischen Paradosis nach 2 Petr.
        1,12–15." Pp. 297–305 in *Neues Testament und Geschichte: Histo-
        rischen Geschehen und Bedeutung im Neuen Testament: Oscar
        Cullmann zum 70. Geburtstag.* Ed. H. Baltensweiler and B. Reicke.
        Zurich: Theologischer Verlag.

Walker, R.
1964   "Allein aus Werken: Zur Auslegung von Jakobus 2, 14–26." *ZTK* 61:
        155–92.

Ward, Roy Bowen
1963   "James and Paul: Critical Review." *Restoration Quarterly* 7: 159–64.
1966   Review of Dibelius-Greeven. In *JBL* 85: 255–56.
1968   "The Works of Abraham: James 2:14–26." *HTR* 61: 283–90.
1969   "Partiality in the Assembly: James 2:2–4." *HTR* 62: 87–97.

Warth, W.
1959   *Der Jakobusbrief.* Stuttgarter Bibelhefte. Stuttgart: Quell.

Watson, D. L.
1970   "The Implications of Christology and Eschatology for a Christian
        Attitude toward the State in 1 Peter." Diss., Hartford Seminary
        Foundation.

Wengst, Klaus
1972   *Christologische Formeln und Lieder des Urchristentums.* SNT 7.
        Gütersloh: Mohn.

Wifstrand, Albert
1948   "Stylistic Problems in the Epistles of James and Peter." *ST 1: 170–82.*

Wikgren, Allen
1967   "Some Problems in Jude 5." Pp. 147–52 in *Studies in the History and
        Text of the New Testament in Honor of Kenneth Willis Clark, Ph.D.* Ed.
        B. L. Daniels and M. J. Suggs. SD 29. Salt Lake City: University of
        Utah Press.

Wilcox, Max
1977   " 'Upon the Tree'—Deut. 21:22–23 in the New Testament." *JBL* 96:
        85–99.

Wilkinson, John
1971   "Healing in the Epistle of James." *SJT* 24: 326–45.

Williams, R. R.
1965   *The Letters of John and James.* The Cambridge Bible Commentary.
        Cambridge: University Press.

Windisch, Hans, and Herbert Preisker
1951   *Die Katholischen Briefe.* HNT 15. Tübingen: Mohr-Siebeck.

Wisse, Frederik
1972   "The Epistle of Jude in the History of Heresiology." Pp. 133–43 in
        Essays on the Nag Hammadi Texts in Honour of Alexander Böhlig.
        NHS 3. Ed. M. Krause. Leiden: Brill.

Wolff, C.
1975   "Christ und Welt im 1. Petrusbrief." *TLZ* 100: 333–42.

Wuellner, Wilhelm H.
1978   "Der Jakobusbrief im Licht der Rhetorik und Textpragmatik,"
        Linguistica Biblica 43: 5–66.

15

REVELATION

Elisabeth Schüssler Fiorenza

Ernst Lohmeyer summed up the scholarly efforts during the research period 1920 to 1934 with the observation that very few early Christian writings have been so greatly courted by scholars but have so thoroughly eluded their methods of interpretation. The elusive meaning of Revelation might be one of the reasons why serious critical scholarship has largely neglected the book in the research period 1945 to 1980.* This is obvious if one compares research on Revelation, for example, with the number of publications, commentaries, monographs, and conferences on the Fourth Gospel, the Synoptics, or the Pauline literature. Except for some outstanding dissertations, serious research on Revelation is rather scant and mostly limited to articles. Although a plethora of very popular or semischolarly commentaries have appeared, no scientific commentary has been written that would embody the same research breadth as, for example, the works of W. Bousset, R. H. Charles, I. T. Beckwith, or E. B. Allo. H. Kraft's new commentary replacing that of Lohmeyer in the Handbuch zum Neuen Testament best approximates the format of a scientific commentary, whereas the most recent commentaries of J. M. Ford, R. H. Mounce, and J. P. M. Sweet, although more or less conversant with recent historical scholarship, aim at a more general audience.

Such a negative assessment of scholarly research on Revelation, however, does not imply that the book was neglected or overlooked. Several bibliographical essays indicate that much effort has been exerted to understand Revelation. Rather than duplicate these essays, I shall briefly discuss them and then focus on perspectives and issues in interpretation in order to sketch the paradigm shift that is taking place in the scholarly interpretation of Revelation.

I. RESEARCH ON REVELATION

A. Feuillet's research report (1965) first appeared in 1963 and covers the time between 1920 and 1960 in seven chapters: the general tendencies and methods of interpretation (chap. 1); composition and literary structure

---

* See *postscript* below.

(chap. 2); interpretation of Revelation 2–3 and 4–22 (chap. 3); the doctrine of the book (chap. 4); date and place of composition (chap. 5); and the author (chap. 6). Chapter 7 discusses various problems: the woman of Revelation 12, the problem of the millennium, and several other studies of special issues. Each of these chapters reviews first the opinions of the commentators, then discusses special studies, and finally concludes with an evaluation.

Although Feuillet's research report introduces an abundance of studies and problems, its selection and discussion of the literature are marred by its traditional, conservative tendencies. For instance, Feuillet argues that Revelation is written by the apostle John, who used a secretary. The objection that Rev 21:14 refers to the Twelve as the foundations of the New Jerusalem is rejected with the following argument: "But this is, after all, merely a reference to the will of Christ who has assigned a position of preeminence to the members of the apostolic college . . ."(107–8). In a similar fashion it is argued that the ecclesiological interpretation of Revelation 12 does not exclude the traditional mariological understanding (116–17).

H. Kraft's bibliographical essay (1973) is more like an extended book review than a comprehensive *Forschungsbericht* ("research report"). Kraft evaluates Feuillet's work positively, discusses the christological studies of T. Holtz and J. Comblin, critically analyzes U. B. Müller's *Messias und Menschensohn* (1972), and briefly refers to the studies of P. Prigent (1959), K. P. Jörns, and E. Schüssler Fiorenza (1972a). After a somewhat more lengthy review of M. Rissi's books (1966, 1972), he discusses the studies of U. Vanni (1971), A. Lancelotti, and G. Mussies. In his review of the more popular commentaries, he praises that of E. Lohse (1960) because of its combination of scientific accuracy with general intelligibility. The review concludes by treating H. H. Rowley's discussion of apocalyptic literature. Kraft's essay is very selective; it does not aim at a comprehensive discussion of scholarship on Revelation that would adequately reflect the *Stand der Forschung* ("state of research").

Otto Böcher's somewhat later bibliographical essay appears in a series entitled Erträge der Forschung (results of research); therefore, one expects a comprehensive review of scholarly methods and interpretations. The small book is divided into two main sections, one reviewing the history of research on Revelation from the eighteenth century until 1974 and the other discussing main problems of interpretation. The first section reviews the interpretations of the eighteenth and nineteenth centuries and discusses the history-of-religions approach of the twentieth century, as well as critical Anglo-Saxon exegesis (Ramsay; Charles), several Roman Catholic interpretations (Allo; Schmid; Olivier; Sickenberger; Ketter), Protestant research after Lohmeyer, and the combination of different interpretative methods in Roman Catholic scholarship.

The second section singles out exegetical problems of Revelation: the author and his historical-religious background, date and contemporary historical background, Christ the Lamb, the apocalyptic riders, the 144,000, the two witnesses, the woman of Revelation 12, the satanic trinity, the number 666, the harlot Babylon, the thousand-year reign, and the heavenly Jerusalem. The book concludes with a bibliography containing five hundred entries of publications that have appeared since 1700. For each of the enumerated exegetical-interpretational problems Böcher consults the commentaries of Bousset, Charles, Lohmeyer, Hadorn, Sickenberger, Wikenhauser, and Kraft, and he concludes with his own evaluative summary.

It is apparent that the small size of the book does not allow for any comprehensive presentation of the *status quaestionis* ("state of the question"). Not only does Böcher fail to take into account any of the foreign commentaries that have appeared after 1945, but he also neglects to review major articles and essays on Revelation. Only one page of the book is concerned with special studies and monographs, even though Böcher himself observes that the last three decades of research on Revelation are determined by studies of individual problems (23). He singles out the following areas of major scholarly interest: the history-of-religions and tradition-historical analysis, questions of form and redaction history, contemporary historical and political interpretations, and textual criticism and the history of interpretation. He concludes that studies focusing on the theology of Revelation are relatively rare and that research centers on ecclesiological problems. He points out briefly that further research is necessary on the relationship of Revelation to the Fourth Gospel and the Johannine Epistles, on the interrelationship between Revelation and Jewish apocalypticism and the Hebrew Scriptures, as well as on the prophetic realism and the specific Christian features of the book. Finally, according to him, the political conditions reflected in the language of Revelation and the social and pastoral aspects deserve further exploration.

Ugo Vanni (1980) has authored the most recent bibliographical essay on Revelation. His work presents a comprehensive listing of international scholarship on the book since 1963, although his strength lies in his familiarity with French, Italian, and Spanish literature. After a short introductory review of the development of scholarship (21) and of bibliography, he discusses the hermeneutics of Revelation, literary aspects, and the historical-religious milieu of the book (23–30). Next (31–43), he mentions studies on the relationship to the OT and on the biblical theology of Revelation, and lists commentaries and studies of various passages. In a final summary (43–46) he points to five different areas for future research: the literary analysis of Revelation, the hermeneutics of the book, its relationship to the OT and NT, its interrelation with Jewish and Christian apocalypticism, and, finally, the need for a new type of commentary that would integrate and profile present scholarly research on Revelation. Since this bibliographical essay includes articles and essays, it reflects more adequately the present state of scholarship on Revelation. The limitations of space as well as the nature of a bibliographical essay allow, however, only for an enumeration of problems, not for an overall integration.

The two most recent English review essays, by J. J. Pilch and J. J. Megivern, address a more general public. Whereas Pilch provides a short introduction rather than a comprehensive review of the literature, Megivern illustrates that the literature on Revelation ranges from "apocalyptic pornography" to dialectical philosophy (Ellul). Although serious scholarly works are rare, popular and fundamentalist writings abound. No wonder that Revelation is still considered to be the most difficult book in the NT (Caird; Ladd). Scholars seem to have arrived at the consensus that the book does not provide us with any details of church or world history or give us a calendar of future events; yet popular interest still focuses on such information. Nevertheless, R. H. Mounce concludes his discussion of the classical approaches to interpretation (the preterist, the historicist, the dispensationalist, and the timeless-symbolic) by insisting that "the predictions of John, while expressed in terms reflecting his own culture, will find their final and complete fulfillment in the last days of history" (44–45). Although most exegetes have replaced the classical approaches to the interpretation of Revelation with the historical-critical approach, they still maintain a combination of the preterist or futurist interpretation or that Revelation reveals the course of salvation history or timeless historical principles (Schüssler Fiorenza, 1968).

II. HISTORICAL-CRITICAL ANALYSES

It is universally acknowledged that Revelation has to be understood in its historical, cultural, and religious contexts. Therefore, historical-critical methods developed in other areas of NT research have also been employed for interpreting Revelation, though they have not achieved generally accepted results. The only exception is the text-critical work of J. Schmid, whose classification of the manuscripts and evaluation of the textual traditions seem to be generally accepted.

Grammar and Style

The grammar and style of Revelation are notoriously difficult because they are full of solecisms and Semitisms, repetitions, and logical breaks. Nevertheless, scholars have not accepted the thesis that Revelation is a rather deficient translation from Hebrew or Aramaic (Torrey) or that John's language is a ghetto language due to his inability to write Greek, since the text is neither interspersed with Aramaic expressions nor inconsistent in its linguistic offenses. A. Lancellotti's study of the author's syntax has substantiated Charles's dictum that although John "writes in Greek, he thinks in Hebrew" (1. cxliii). However, the bilingualism of the author (Mussies) needs to be studied more before a sociolinguistic evaluation can be attempted.

It is interesting, however, that not Aramaisms but Hebraisms (Lancellotti) are typical of the linguistic expression of Revelation. This Hebraic character of Revelation's language is due primarily to numerous allusions to the Hebrew text, which John never quotes explicitly but uses, in apocalyptic fashion, to express his own visions. H. Kraft has therefore proposed that the author deliberately created a hieratic language that was not spoken anywhere but which recreates the sentence melody of the Psalms for its liturgical setting (1974: 16). That the author was capable of writing poetic-hymnic language is substantiated by the research on the hymns in Revelation, which the author composed using traditional liturgical language in order to comment on the apocalyptic actions of the book (Jörns). Even though the attempts to render the text of Revelation in strophic form are not conclusive, they support the assumption that Revelation's style and language are intentionally created.

Source and Revision Hypotheses

Whereas traditional exegesis attributes the doublets, inconsistencies, and repetitions of the text either to the faulty memory of the author or to the incompetence of a student (Gaechter; Feuillet), historical-critical scholarship, particularly of the nineteenth century, proposes source-critical solutions or postulates various stages of revision, so that in this understanding Revelation manifests the same editorial processes as other Jewish or Christian apocalypses.

Because of the uniform language of Revelation, scholars tend, however, to stress the unity of Revelation and to reject source-critical manipulations. Yet U. B. Müller and J. M. Ford have recently challenged this scholarly consensus. Müller attempts to separate out sources with the help of christological criteria. He classifies those texts which refer to the messianic judgment of the nations as originally Jewish source texts, while those texts are Christian in which Christ relates to the community (1972). A more far-reaching source hypothesis was put forward by J. M. Ford, who argues that two Jewish apocalypses which she attributes to John the Baptist and his school were redacted by a Christian disciple of John. Yet these recent source-critical reconstructions have not received much support.

Source hypotheses tend to be replaced by revision hypotheses, since these can accommodate the view that Revelation has a style peculiar to itself and that a final redactor is responsible for the whole work. While M.-É. Boismard assumes that the final redactor combined two different works which were written by himself at different times, H. Stierlin proposes three such apocalypses that were fused together by a different redactor at the beginning of the second century. F. Rousseau, on the other hand, assumes five successive redactions of two Jewish and three Christian strata. Finally, H. Kraft suggests that the same author has revised and expanded an existing *Vorlage* ("copy") consisting of the seven-seal cycle. However, according to Kraft the final redactor of Revelation was such a skilled artist that he was able to combine and to integrate into his *Grundschrift* ("basic document") disparate traditions and *topoi* ("rhetorical commonplaces") in such a way that a unitary composition and optimal configuration of artistic form and theological content were achieved. However, if this is the case, then any reconstruction of the prehistory of Revelation must remain in the sphere of conjecture.

Form-Critical, Tradition-Historical, and History-of-Religions Analyses

Form-critical and tradition-historical, as well as history-of-religions analyses, have especially concentrated on the liturgical-hymnic materials and motifs and have explored their *Sitz im Leben* ("life setting") in Jewish and early Christian liturgy (Delling; Jörns; von der Osten Sacken; Schüssler Fiorenza, 1976b; Vanni, 1976b). Special attention was given to the judgment doxology (Betz) or vindication formula (Staples; Yarbro Collins, 1977b) in Rev 16:4–7, the worthy acclamation (van Unnik, 1970), the macarisms (Bieder), the heavenly journey (Yarbro Collins, 1979), and to prophetic-parenetic forms, especially in the so-called seven letters (U. B. Müller, 1975: 47–109; Hahn; van Unnik, 1963; and Käsemann). However, most of these form-critical studies are limited and selective. A comprehensive analysis and systematic evaluation of traditional forms and their redaction in Revelation needs still to be written.

The analysis of small formal units and their traditions must be supplemented by a pattern analysis, because the author has modeled whole visions and sections after OT, Jewish apocalyptic, mythological, and early Christian patterns (Harder). This procedure can best be traced with respect to OT texts, since they are still extant as written *Vorlagen* ("copies"/"patterns"). Such OT patterns are found throughout the book and are derived especially from Exodus, Ezekiel, Isaiah, and Daniel (Jenkins; H. P. Müller, 1960; Vanhoye; Cambier). Other patterns are taken over either from Jewish apocalyptic (judgment/salvation, cosmic week, messianic reign), from Hellenistic mythological patterns (divine child, sacred marriage, divine polis), or early Christian traditional patterns (e.g., the synoptic apocalypse or the apostolic letter form). Contemporary scholarship tends to elucidate especially the Jewish apocalyptic and OT matrix of Revelation's forms and patterns, but does not sufficiently acknowledge that the cultural-religious milieu of Revelation and its communities is Hellenistic-Oriental syncretism

(Betz). The scholarly attempts to determine the history-of-religions background and influences on Revelation 12 (Prigent, 1959; Gollinger; Yarbro Collins, 1976; Vögtle, 1972) elucidate how complex and inextricable the fusion and interaction of cultural-religious traditions and influences can be. Therefore, instead of trying to isolate different traditions and backgrounds, scholars might consider that the author consciously or not drew on and fused together traditions, motives, and patterns that were at home in very different cultures and mythologies (Halver).

Scholars have also attempted to chart the literary type or model John had in mind when writing his book. It was suggested that his overall pattern was a Jewish or Christian liturgy (Shepherd; Läuchli; Prigent, 1964), a festal calendar (Farrer), or a drama (Bowman; Stauffer). Most often it is assumed that John intended to write a prophetic book or an apocalypse, since Revelation gave the whole literary type or *Gattung* of apocalyptic literature its name. Yet we do not know whether the author already could have known a literary type "apocalypse." Scholars have not yet succeeded in delineating between the literary types of prophecy and apocalypse or in identifying essential component elements and stylistic characteristics of an apocalypse. The method in recent attempts to delineate the literary type of apocalypse (Yarbro Collins, 1979) is definitional—composite rather than literary-formal.

The Cultural-Political Milieu

It is generally agreed that the contemporary cultural-political milieu of Revelation is that of western Asia Minor and that its setting is early Christianity at the end of the first century, since Revelation is addressed to seven Christian communities in Asia Minor. However, some exegetes suggest that either the communities mentioned in Revelation or the author himself was alien to the church in Asia Minor because Revelation reflects a prophetic community order quite different from that known through the letters of Ignatius. It is suggested that the seven communities were Jewish apocalyptic conventicles within a predominantly Pauline missionary area (Satake) or that the prophet John, who had emigrated from Palestine-Syria, had nothing in common with these communities (U. B. Müller, 1976). However, both studies consider the letters of Ignatius but not Revelation to be descriptive of the ecclesial situation in Asia Minor. The issue can only be resolved, however, if a comprehensive study of the interaction between early Christian prophecy and developing local church leadership is written.

Although John understands himself as an early Christian prophet, who is probably the head of a prophetic circle (Hill; Schüssler Fiorenza, 1977b), scholars nevertheless still hold to the authorship of John, the apostle, or of the presbyter John mentioned by Papias, or they propose that Revelation belongs to the same school or circle as the Fourth Gospel and the Johannine Epistles. However, the Johannine school hypothesis is based on

the a priori assumption that the so-called Johannine writings must somehow
be related to each other because the ecclesiastical tradition ascribes them
to the same author. John's self-understanding and perception of authority,
however, are not apostolic but prophetic. He derives his authority not from
his fellowship with Jesus of Nazareth but, as Paul does, from the revelation
of the resurrected Lord. It seems necessary, therefore, that Revelation be
discussed not just in the context of the Johannine school but also as situated
within Pauline and post-Pauline, as well as prophetic-apocalyptic Christian,
school traditions (Schüssler Fiorenza, 1977b; Rousseau). Such a discussion
of Revelation within the context of early Christian development will shed
new light on debated theological issues, as for instance on the Christian
character of the book (Ford); its understanding of God (Vögtle), Christ
(Holtz; Comblin), or the Spirit (Schweizer; Bruce); the debate on whether
Revelation is prophetic or apocalyptic (Kallas); the book's understanding of
witness (Trites); or its relationship to synoptic (Vos) or gnostic traditions
(Schüssler Fiorenza, 1973; Prigent, 1977).

Date

H. Kraft dates the final redaction of the book by comparing the situation
of the communities in Revelation with that of Ignatius's letters. Since John
and Ignatius argue against two very similar groups of opponents, Kraft concludes that the so-called letters of Revelation and those of Ignatius reflect
the same theological-ecclesial situation. Whereas Revelation 13 and 17 were
written toward the end of Nerva's reign, the epistles and the final redaction
must be dated between 110 and 114. Further studies are needed to test
Kraft's claim that the comparison of the opponents in Ephesians, Colossians,
the Pastoral Epistles, and the letter of Polycarp would confirm this conclusion. However, the attempt to situate Revelation within the context of early
Christian development seems to be most promising.

In dating Revelation, the so-called letters have always played a major
role. Although we have several popular studies of them (e.g., Barclay;
Newman), new extensive scholarly investigation has been published recently
(cf. Hemer). Sherman Johnson's review article on early Christianity in Asia
Minor, however, suggests many promising avenues for further research.
Publication of A. T. Kraabel's work on Judaism in western Asia Minor is also
long overdue. The archaeological discoveries of the last decades would
provide the materials for a sociohistorical profile of cities like Ephesus,
Smyrna, or Pergamum. Similarly, Roman presence and especially the imperial cult need to be studied in more depth (see Stauffer's popular account).
Further mystery cults, private associations, and philosophical schools need
to be discussed with reference to Revelation. In short, a comprehensive
work like that of W. M. Ramsay needs to be written.

One of the main points of contention in evaluating Revelation's relationship to the Roman Empire still seems to be the question whether a persecution of Christians took place under Domitian. Although the majority of scholars still accept Irenaeus's dating of Revelation at the end of Domitian's reign, others have challenged this majority opinion (Bell). They propose that the book was written in the sixties when Jerusalem and the Temple were not yet destroyed. J. A. T. Robinson, for instance, argues that internal evidence speaks for a date between 64 and 70. Revelation 11, 17, and 18 link Revelation historically with events in Jerusalem and Rome during these years. Psychologically Revelation reflects the Neronic program, since no such bloody persecution is documented for Domitian's reign. He supports this contention also with a Neronic interpretation of the number 666 and with the *Nero redivivus* ("Nero restored to life") legend. However, it is difficult to decide whether a severe persecution is a reality or an impending danger, or whether it is just a part of the experience of the author, who attempts to shatter the complacency of Christians who prosper under Domitian and who forget the persecution of Nero (Sweet: 27). Moreover, scholars debate also whether John was exiled to Patmos or whether he had withdrawn to the island for the sake of prophetic experience (Saffrey).

In Rev 17:9–16 John supposedly points to his own historical standpoint. Yet scholars have not yet succeeded in decoding this information. They do not agree whether or not to begin with Caesar, Augustus, Caligula (Strobel) or Nero (Reicke). Some omit the short-term emperors from their count, whereas others suggest that only those emperors who were deified by the Senate should be counted. Another suggestion is that Rev 17:9–16 was inserted by a later redactor who thereby deliberately predates Revelation (Cerfaux and Cambier; Feuillet). Since these scholarly discussions have not yet arrived at a generally accepted solution, it must be asked whether they have misunderstood the language and intention of the author.

Conclusion

The current progress in the historical-critical analysis of Revelation moves in a way parallel to that of other NT writings. Just as in other areas the stress on source and form criticism has been replaced by a stress on redaction criticism, so in scholarship on Revelation the source and compilation theories of the last century have given way to the scholarly consensus that Revelation is the theological work of one author. Since linguistic analyses have established that the so-called seven letters form an integral part of the book, Revelation as a whole is no longer seen as a Jewish writing with superficial Christian additions. Instead, it must be evaluated as an authentic Christian prophetic-apocalyptic work addressed to the situation and problems of the Christian church in western Asia Minor (Schüssler Fiorenza, 1976a; Vanni, 1980).

Nevertheless the judgment of Ernst Lohmeyer applies also to the research period of the last three decades: "When one surveys even cursorily the scholarly literature of the last half-generation, the solutions that have been proposed and the directions that they take are so multifarious and heterogeneous that the inadequacies of the Book of Revelation appear to be almost insurmountable" (1934:271). All scholarly attempts to arrive at a definite interpretation of certain passages or of the whole book seem to have failed. This failure suggests that the historical-critical paradigm has to be complemented by a different approach that can do justice to the multivalent character of Revelation.

III. LITERARY-FUNCTIONAL INTERPRETATION

While redaction criticism elucidates the nature and extent of the author's activity in collecting, arranging, and editing traditional forms, sources, and patterns, literary analysis focuses on the compositional activity of the author and the aesthetic power of the work. Traditional patterns, sources, or stages of redaction may not be equated with the literary composition and expression of a work. The author's interests and intentions in writing the work are not something that lies behind the text, but they manifest themselves in the form-content configuration and social function of the book. Such literary analysis does not discard the results of historical-critical research but integrates them into the overall understanding of Revelation as a literary work. Revelation's language and overall composition are literary and not descriptive-factual. Small formal units, traditional patterns, and individual passages derive their meaning from the overall composition of the book.

Structural Analyses

Jacques Ellul claims that all scientific studies written in the last fifty years have erred completely because they applied a method to the interpretation of Revelation that is totally inappropriate to the book. According to him, Revelation must be understood as a whole and not analyzed verse by verse, because each part takes its import in its relation to the whole architecture of the work. Ellul's criticism is justified but overlooks the fact that structural analyses of Revelation have attempted to understand the overall composition of the book. While structuralist analyses of the deep structure of the book are rare (Calloud et al.; Schüssler Fiorenza, 1977a), scholarly analyses of the surface structure abound (see the overviews in Vanni, 1971; and Bowman). Scholars agree that in comparison with other Jewish and Christian apocalypses, Revelation's overall organization reveals a careful composition and definite plan in which the number seven plays a key role.

One can find almost as many different outlines of the composition as there are scholars studying the book. It is debated whether the so-called apocalyptic part (Revelation 4–22) is independent of the so-called letters, or whether the letters are an integral part of the architectonic structure of the book. Other issues of debate are whether the book is totally composed in seven cycles that recapitulate each other (Bornkamm; Yarbro Collins, 1976) or whether only the explicitly numbered visions are intended as seven cycles. It is also discussed whether Revelation consists of two rather even sections (1–11 and 12–22) or whether its architectonic pattern is the concentric ABCDC′B′A′ pattern. (Another issue is whether the narrative is cyclic, linear, or moves in a conic spiral).

Two methodological issues need to be clarified: first, it must be determined whether or not the structuration of the book is to be reconstrued on purely formalistic grounds (Vanni, 1971) or whether a morphological approach is more appropriate, one that elucidates the form-content configuration of Revelation (Schüssler Fiorenza, 1968, 1977a). Second, the following criteria formulated by architecture criticism need also to be applied to the structural analyses of Revelation: One has to show that the proposed architectonic or compositional structuration is not derived from the tradition, that it is also found in smaller units of Revelation, and, finally, that it is present in the art and literature of the time. The greatly differing proposals for the structuration of Revelation indicate that the formulation of such internal and external controls is necessary if structural analyses of the book are not to degenerate further into a purely subjectivistic enterprise.

The Evocative Power of the Book

Exegetes and theologians have still to discover what artists have long understood: The strength of Revelation's language and composition lies not in its theological argumentation or historical information but in its evocative power, inviting imaginative participation (Beardslee). The language and narrative flow of Revelation elicit emotions, reactions, and convictions that cannot and should not be fully conceptualized and phrased in propositional-logical language. Since the author does not employ discursive language and logical arguments but speaks in the language of symbol and myth, the often somewhat unsophisticated discussion of the imaginative, mythopoeic language of Revelation (see, e.g., Foerster) needs to be replaced by a literary approach and symbol analysis that would bring out the evocative power and "musicality" of Revelation's language, which was written to be read aloud and to be heard.

Such a literary approach would have to integrate literary-aesthetic analysis with historical-traditional research. It could not neglect traditional-historical and form-historical analyses since the author does not freely create his images and myths but reworks traditional materials into a new and unique literary composition. Nevertheless, the meaning of Revelation's mythopoeic language cannot be derived from its traditions but from its literary function in its present historical-literary context. To know the author's original reference points and cultural context helps us to approximate the multivalent meaning and emotive power of Revelation's imaginative language. Such an approximation, however, is possible only when individual passages of Revelation are interpreted within the context of the overall composition and theological perspective of the book.

Already in the eighteenth century scholars had recognized that apocalyptic language is poetic language and that therefore Revelation had to be interpreted as a work of poetry (see Schmidt: 87–97). However, because of the Jewish character of apocalyptic language, they had advocated a sharp distinction between literary form and theological content in order to maintain the genuine Christian character of Revelation. This dichotomy between Jewish apocalyptic language and Christian theological content, which reduces apocalyptic imagery to a mere container or cloak of timeless essences and propositional truth, has ever since marred the discussion of apocalyptic literature. Insofar as exegetes have understood Revelation as a descriptive or predictive account of factual events of the past and the future or of timeless theological statements and principles, they have tended to reduce the imaginative language of Revelation to a one-to-one meaning. They thus have historicized the sequence of images and visions, objectified symbolic-allegoric expressions, and reduced mythopoeic vision to abstract theological or philosophical principles.

Even those scholars who have championed a literary approach have tended to reduce the meaning of Revelation to archetypal (Farrer; Halver) or ontological (Minear; Schlier) concepts. However, such a de-historicization of Revelation neglects the theological interests of the author and the socio-theological function of the book. A purely formalistic literary understanding of Revelation overlooks the fact that John did not write art for art's sake, but that he had a definite purpose in mind when writing the book. It is necessary, therefore, to discuss briefly the communicative situation and literary social function of Revelation.

Theological Intention

If the theological intention and the social function of a work are not things that lie behind the texts but manifest themselves in the literary form-content configuration of a work, then it is significant that the apocalyptic visions of John are set within the framework of the apostolic letter-form and that they begin with a series of seven apocalyptic letters. The epistolary framework of Revelation is not an artificial and accidental setting for John's mythopoeic vision. John derived the authority of his work not from pseudonymity and fictional timetables but from the revelation of Jesus Christ. The form and the theological self-understanding of Revelation, therefore, come close to that of the Pauline letters (Schüssler Fiorenza; Kraft 1974).

In writing down the "words of prophecy," John wants to strengthen and encourage Christians in Asia Minor who were persecuted and still had to expect more suffering and harassment. He does so not simply by writing a hortatory treatise and letter but by creating a new "plausibility structure" and "symbolic universe."

The main concern of the author is not the interpretation of history but the issue of power. The focal point of the "already" and "not yet" of eschatological salvation is not history but the kingdom of God and the rule of Christ. Therefore, the main symbol of Revelation is the image of the throne and its main motif that of kingship (Schüssler Fiorenza, 1972, 1979; Lohse, 1971). The apocalyptic question "Who is Lord over the world?" is the central issue of Revelation. This question is expressed here in mythological and political images and language. Whereas Paul understood the question in terms of the alternative between the lordship of Christ and that of the cosmic powers, Revelation concretizes this alternative in political terms. Christians are the representatives of God's and Christ's eschatological power on earth and at the same time still subject to the political powers of their time. Those rejecting the beast and its cult are excluded from the economic and social life of their time and have to expect captivity and death (13:10–15). Revelation demands unfaltering resistance to the imperial cult because honoring the emperor would mean ratifying Rome's dominion over all people and denying the life-giving power of God and Christ.

The author appears to formulate this theology in opposition to an enthusiastic prophetic theology that seems to have advocated accommodation to the Roman civil religion (see the codewords "idolatry" and "immorality" in the so-called letters and in the central section of Revelation). His harsh rejection of the Nicolaitans and his denunciation of the beast and its cult have the same function. John can reject any accommodation to Roman civil religion and any participation in the imperial cult because he can "show" that the power of God and Christ will prevail over all anti-divine and anti-human forces. Without question, the symbolic universe of Revelation is genuinely Christian (see also Karner; Rissi, 1968; Nikolainen; Pesch). The central function of Revelation is the elaboration of God and the Lamb's power not only over the lives of individuals but over the whole world and its political powers.

Nevertheless, scholars have labeled the author's theological perspective and attempt at "social control" as sub-Christian because of his outcry for vengeance (Lawrence; Minear; Yarbro Collins; Barclay). Resentment and revenge are not compatible with Christian love and forgiveness. However, Revelation's demand for judgment must be understood as an outcry for justice for those who are exploited and killed today. John thus resounds the call of the prophets to repentance and justice. In doing so he continues the call and promise of the prophet, Jesus. Against the forces of economic, political, and religious oppression within the Roman Empire, the mythopoeic vision of Revelation shows that God and Christ's reign and salvation are different. The last chapters of Revelation (Rissi, 1972) picture a world free of evil and suffering in order to give hope to those who are suffering and oppressed now because they do not acknowledge the death-dealing political powers of their time.

In conclusion, this short essay has attempted to review the major approaches to the interpretation of Revelation that have been published before 1980. It seems that the theological-doctrinal and the historical-critical paradigms of interpretation need to be integrated into a new literary paradigm that could do justice to the symbolic-mythopoeic language as well as to the historical communicative situation of the book. Therefore, Revelation could emerge as one of the most interesting and challenging areas for NT scholarly research in the future.

[*Postscript:* Since the completion of this manuscript in 1980, the Book of Revelation has received lively scholarly attention. For further discussion and literature, see my volume, *The Book of Revelation: Justice and Judgment* (Philadelphia: Fortress, 1985). See also the collections of essays edited by David Hellholm, *Apocalypticism in the Mediterranean World and the Near East: Proceedings of the International Colloquium on Apocalypticism, Uppsala, August 12–17, 1979* (Tübingen: Mohr-Siebeck, 1983); J. Lambrecht, *L'Apocalypse johannique et l'Apocalyptique dans le Nouveau Testament* (BETL 53; Paris and Gembloux: Duculot; Leuven: Leuven University Press, 1980); and Adela Yarbro Collins, *Early Christian Apocalypticism: Genre and Social Setting* = *Semeia* 36 (1986); and the July issue of *Interpretation* 40 (1986) 227–301, which is devoted to the Book of Revelation.]

BIBLIOGRAPHY

Allo, E. B.
 1933 *Saint Jean, L'Apocalypse.* 4th ed. rev. EBib. Paris: Gabalda.

Barclay, William
 1957 *Letters to the Seven Churches: A Study of the Second and Third Chapters of the Book of Revelation.* New York: Abingdon.

Bauckham, Richard
 1977a "The Eschatological Earthquake in the Apocalypse of John." *NovT* 19: 224–33.
 1977b "Synoptic Parousia Parables and the Apocalypse." *NTS* 23: 162–76.

Beardslee, William A.
 1971 "New Testament Apocalyptic in Recent Interpretation." *Int* 25: 419–35.

Bell, Albert A.
 1978 "The Date of John's Apocalypse: The Evidence of Some Roman Historians Reconsidered." *NTS* 25: 93–102.

Betz, Hans Dieter
 1969 "On the Problem of the Religio-Historical Understanding of Apocalypticism." *JTC* 6: 134–56.

Bieder, Werner
1954   "Die sieben Seligpreisungen in der Offenbarung des Johannes." *TZ*
          10: 13–30.

Bietenhard, Hans
1955   *Das tausendjahrige Reich: Eine biblisch-theologische Studie.* 2d ed.
          Zurich: Zwingli.

Böcher, Otto
1975   *Die Johannesapokalypse.* Erträge der Forschung, 41. Darmstadt:
          Wissenschaftliche Buchgesellschaft.

Boismard, Marie-Émile
1949   " 'L'Apocalypse' ou 'les Apocalypses' de S. Jean." *RB* 56: 507–41.

Bousset, Wilhelm.
1906   *Die Offenbarung Johannis.* MeyerK 16. Göttingen: Vandenhoeck &
          Ruprecht.

Bowman, John Wick
1955   "The Revelation to John: Its Dramatic Structure and Message." *Int* 9:
          436–53.

Bruce, Frederick Fyvie
1973   "The Spirit in the Apocalypse." Pp. 333–44 in *Christ and Spirit in the
          New Testament: In Honour of C. F. D. Moule.* Ed. B. Lindars and S. S.
          Smalley. Cambridge: University Press.

Caird, George B.
1966   *A Commentary on the Revelation of St. John the Divine.* HNTC. New
          York: Harper & Row.

Calloud, Jean, Jean Delorme, and Jean-Pierre Duplantier
1977   "L'Apocalypse de Jean: Propositions pour une analyse structurale."
          Pp. 351–81 in *Apocalypses et Théologie de l'espérance.* Ed. L.
          Monloubou. LD 95. Paris: Cerf.

Cambier, Jules
1955   "Les images de l'Ancien Testament dans l'Apocalypse de Saint Jean."
          NRT 77: 113–22.

Cerfaux, Lucien, and Jules Cambier
1964   *L'Apocalypse de Saint Jean lue aux Chrétiens.* LD 17. Paris: Cerf.

Charles, Robert Henry
1920   *A Critical and Exegetical Commentary on the Revelation of St. John.*
          2 vols. ICC. Edinburgh: T. & T. Clark.

Comblin, Joseph
1965   *Le Christ dans l'Apocalypse.* Bibliothèque de Théologie 3:6. Paris:
          Desclée.

Delling, Gerhard
1959   "Zum gottesdienstlichen Stil der Johannes-Apokalypse." *NovT* 3:
          107–37. Reprinted in his *Studien zum Neuen Testament und zum
          hellenistischen Judentum,* 425–50. Ed. F. Hahn, T. Holtz, and N.
          Walter. Göttingen: Vandenhoeck & Ruprecht, 1970.

Ellul, Jacques
1977   *Apocalypse: The Book of Revelation.* A Crossroad Book. Trans. G. W.
          Schreiner. New York: Seabury.

Farrer, Austin
1949   A Rebirth of Images: The Making of St. John's Apocalypse. London:
            Dacre. Reprinted, Boston: Beacon, 1963, and Magnolia, MA: Peter
            Smith, 1970.

Feuillet, André
1965   The Apocalypse. Trans. T. E. Crane. Staten Island, NY: Alba House.
1974,   "Jelons pour une meilleure intelligence de l'Apocalypse." Esprit et
1975,   Vie 84:481-90; 85:65-72, 209-23, 432-43; 86:455-59, 471-79.
1976

Foerster, Werner
1970   "Bemerkungen zur Bildersprache der Offenbarung Johannis." Pp.
            225-36 in Verborum Veritas: Festschrift für G. Stählin zu 70.
            Geburtstag. Ed. O. Böcher and K. Haacker. Wuppertal: Brockhaus.

Ford, Josephine Massyngbaerde
1975   Revelation. AB 38. Garden City, NY: Doubleday.

Gaechter, P.
1949   "The Original Sequence of Apocalypse 20-22." TS 10: 485-521.

Giblin, Charles H.
1974   "Structural and Thematic Correlations in the Theology of Revelation
            16-22." Bib 55: 487-504.

Gollinger, Hildegard
1971   Das "grosse Zeichen" von Apokalypse 12. SBM 11. Stuttgart: Katho-
            lisches Bibelwerk; Würzburg: Echter-Verlag.

Hadorn, Wilhelm
1928   Die Offenbarung des Johannes. THKNT 18. Leipzig: Deichert.

Hahn, Ferdinand
1971   "Die Sendschreiben der Johannesapokalypse: Ein Beitrag zur Be-
            stimmung prophetischer Redeformen." Pp. 357-94 in Tradition und
            Glaube: Festgabe für Karl Georg Kuhn. Ed. G. Jeremias, H.-W. Kuhn,
            and H. Stegemann. Göttingen: Vandenhoeck & Ruprecht.

Halver, Rudolf
1964   Der Mythos im letzten Buch der Bibel: Eine Untersuchung der Bilder-
            sprache der Johannes-Apokalypse. TF 32. Hamburg and Bergstedt:
            Reich.

Harder, Günther
1963   "Eschatologische Schemata in der Johannes-Apokalypse." Theologia
            Viatorum 9: 70-87.

Hemer, C. J.
1969   "A Study of the Letters to the Seven Churches of Asia with Special
            Reference to Their Local Background." Ph.D. diss., University of
            Manchester.

Hill, David
1971-72   "Prophecy and Prophets in the Revelation of St John." NTS 18:
            401-18.

Holtz, Traugott
1971   Die Christologie der Apokalypse des Johannes. 2d ed. TU 85. Berlin:
            Akademie-Verlag.

Jenkins, F.
1976   *The Old Testament in the Book of Revelation.* Grand Rapids:
          Eerdmans.

Johnson, Sherman E.
1975   "Asia Minor and Early Christianity." Pp. 77–145 in *Christianity,
          Judaism and Other Greco-Roman Cults: Studies for Morton Smith at
          Sixty,* vol. 2. SJLA 12. Ed. J. Neusner. Leiden: Brill.

Jörns, Klaus Peter
1971   *Das hymnische Evangelium: Untersuchungen zu Aufbau, Funktion und
          Herkunft der hymnischen Stücke in der Johannesoffenbarung.* SNT 5.
          Gütersloh: Mohn.

Kallas, James
1967   "The Apocalypse—An Apocalyptic Book?" *JBL* 86: 69–80.

Karner, Karoly
1968   "Gegenwart und Endgeschichte in der Offenbarung des Johannes."
          TLZ 93: 641–52.

Ketter, Peter
1953   *Die Apokalypse.* 3d unchanged ed. Die Heilige Schrift für das Leben
          erklärt, Herders Bibelkommentar. Freiburg: Herder. Original 1942.

Klassen, William
1966   "Vengeance in the Apocalypse of John." *CBQ* 28: 300–11.

Kraft, Heinrich
1973   "Zur Offenbarung Johannes." *TRu* n.s. 38: 81–98.
1974   *Die Offenbarung des Johannes.* HNT 16a. Tübingen: Mohr-Siebeck.

Kümmel, Werner Georg
1957   "Der Text der Offenbarung des Johannes." *TLZ* 82: 249–54.

Ladd, George Eldon
1972   *A Commentary on the Revelation of John.* Grand Rapids: Eerdmans.

Lähnemann, Johannes
1978   "Die sieben Sendschreiben der Johannes-Apokalypse." Pp. 516–39 in
          *Studien zur Religion und Kultur Kleinasiens: Festschrift für Friedrich
          Karl Dörner zum 65. Geburtstag,* vol. 2. Ed. S. Sahin, E. Schwert-
          heim, and J. Wagner. EPRO 66. Leiden: Brill.

Lancellotti, Angelo
1964   *Sintassi ebraica nel greco dell'Apocalisse. I, Uso delle forme verbali.*
          Coll. Assisiensis 1. Assisi: Studio Teologico "Portiuncola."

Läuchli, Samuel
1960   "Eine Gottesdienststruktur in der Johannesoffenbarung." *TZ* 16:
          359–78.

Lawrence, D. H.
1976   *Apocalypse.* New York: Penguin Books and Heinemann. Original,
          1931.

Lohmeyer, Ernst
1926   *Die Offenbarung des Johannes.* HNT 16. Tübingen: Mohr-Siebeck.
          10th ed., 1971.
1934,   "Die Offenbarung des Johannes 1920–1934." *TRu* 6: 269–314; 7:
1935   28–62.

Lohse, Eduard
1960   *Die Offenbarung des Johannes.* NTD 11. Göttingen: Vandenhoeck & Ruprecht. 2d ed., 1953; 11th ed., 1976.
1971   "Apokalyptik und Christologie." *ZNW* 62: 48–67.

Megivern, James J.
1978   "Wrestling with Revelation." *BTB* 8: 147–54.

Minear, Paul
1968   *I Saw a New Earth: An Introduction to the Visions of the Apocalypse.* Washington, DC: Corpus.

Mounce, Robert H.
1977   *The Book of Revelation.* NICNT. Grand Rapids: Eerdmans.

Müller, Hans-Peter
1960   "Die Plagen der Apokalypse: Eine formgeschichtliche Untersuchung." *ZNW* 51: 268–78.
1963   "Die himmlische Ratsversammlung: Motivgeschichtliches zu Apc 5,1–5." *ZNW* 54: 254–67.

Müller, Ulrich B.
1972   *Messias und Menschensohn in den jüdischen Apokalypsen und in der Offenbarung des Johannes.* SNT 6. Gütersloh: Mohn.
1975   *Prophetie und Predigt im Neuen Testament: Formgeschichtliche Untersuchungen zur urchristlichen Prophetie.* SNT 10. Gütersloh: Mohn.
1976   *Zur frühchristlichen Theologiegeschichte: Judenchristentum und Paulinismus in Kleinasien an der Wende vom ersten zum zweiten Jahrhundert n. Chr.* Gütersloh: Mohn.

Mussies, Gerard
1971   *The Morphology of Koine Greek as Used in the Apocalypse of St. John: A Study in Bilingualism.* NovTSup 27. Leiden: Brill.

Newman, Barclay M., Jr.
1968   *Rediscovering the Book of Revelation.* Valley Forge, PA: Judson.

Nikolainen, Aimo T.
1968   "Über die theologische Eigenart der Offenbarung des Johannes." *TLZ* 93: 161–70.

Olivier, A.
1960   *Apocalypse et Evangiles.* Cahiers de littérature Sacrée 1. Saint-Maurice: [by the author].

Osten Sacken, P. von der
1967   " 'Christologie, Taufe, Homologie'—Ein Beitrag zu Apc Joh 1,5f." *ZNW* 58: 255–66.

Pesch, Rudolf
1970   "Offenbarung Jesu Christi: Eine Auslegung von Apk 1,1–3." *BibLeb* 11: 15–29.

Pilch, John J.
1978   *What Are They Saying about the Book of Revelation?* New York: Paulist.

Prigent, Pierre
1959   *Apocalypse 12: Histoire de l'exégèse.* BGBE 2. Tübingen: Mohr-Siebeck.
1964   *Apocalypse et liturgie.* Cahiers Théologique 52. Neuchâtel: Delachaux & Niestlé.

1974,   "Au temps de l'Apocalypse." *RHPR* 54: 455–83; 55: 215–35, 341–63.
1975
1977   "L'hérésie Asiate et l'église confessante de l'Apocalypse à Ignace." *VC* 31: 1–22.

Ramsay, William M.
1904   *The Letters to the Seven Churches of Asia.* London: Hodder & Stoughton. Reprinted, Grand Rapids: Baker, 1985.

Reicke, Bo
1972   "Die jüdische Apokalyptik und die johanneische Tiervision." *RSR* 60: 173–92.

Rissi, Mathias
1966   *Time and History: A Study on the Revelation.* Trans. G. Winsor. Richmond: John Knox. Original, 1952.
1968   "The Kerygma of the Revelation to John." *Int* 22: 3–17.
1972   *The Future of the World: An Exegetical Study of Revelation 19.11–22.15.* SBT 2/25. Naperville, IL: Allenson.

Robinson, John Arthur Thomas
1976   *Redating the New Testament.* Philadelphia: Westminster.

Rousseau, François
1971   *L'Apocalypse et le milieu prophétique du Nouveau Testament: Structure et préhistoire du texte.* Recherches 3. Paris and Tournai: Desclée; Montreal: Bellarmin.

Saffrey, H. D.
1975   "Relire l'Apocalypse à Patmos." *RB* 82: 384–417.

Sanders, J. N.
1962–63   "St. John on Patmos." *NTS* 9: 75–85.

Satake, Akira
1966   *Die Gemeindeordnung in der Johannes-Apokalypse.* WMANT 21. Neukirchen-Vluyn: Neukirchener Verlag.

Schlier, Heinrich
1956   "Zum Verständnis der Geschichte nach der Offenbarung des Johannis." Pp. 265–74 in *Die Zeit der Kirche: Exegetische Aufsätze und Vorträge.* Freiburg, Basel, and Vienna: Herder.

Schmid, Josef
1955–56   *Studien zur Geschichte des griechischen Apokalypse-Textes.* Münchener Theologische Studien, Historische Abteilung 1. 2 vols. in 3; Munich: Karl Zink.

Schmidt, J. M.
1969   *Die jüdische Apokalyptik: Die Geschichte ihrer Erforschung von den Anfängen bis zu den Textfunden von Qumran.* Neukirchen-Vluyn: Neukirchener Verlag.

Schmitt, Eugen
1960   "Die christologische Interpretation als das Grundlegende der Apokalypse." *TQ* 140: 257–90.

Schüssler Fiorenza, E.
1968   "The Eschatology and Composition of the Apocalypse." *CBQ* 30: 537–69.

1969   "Gericht und Heil: Zum theologischen Verständnis der Apokalypse."
        Pp. 330–48 in *Gestalt und Anspruch des Neuen Testaments*. Ed. J.
        Schreiner. Würzburg: Echter-Verlag.
1972a   *Priester für Gott: Studien zum Herrschafts- und Priestermotiv in der
        Apokalypse*. NTAbh 7. Münster: Aschendorff.
1972b   "Die tausendjährige Herrschaft der Auferstandenen (Apk 20,4–6)."
        BibLeb 13: 107–24.
1973   "Apocalyptic and Gnosis in the Book of Revelation and Paul." *JBL* 92:
        565–81.
1974a   "Religion und Politik in der Offenbarung des Johannes." Pp. 261–71
        in *Biblische Randbemerkungen: Schülerfestschrift für R. Schnacken-
        burg*. Würzburg: Echter-Verlag.
1974b   "Redemption as Liberation: Apoc 1:5f. and 5:9f." *CBQ* 36: 220–32.
1976a   *The Apocalypse*. Herald Biblical Booklets. Chicago: Franciscan
        Herald Press.
1976b   "Cultic Language in Qumran and in the New Testament." *CBQ* 38:
        159–77.
1977a   "Composition and Structure of the Book of Revelation." *CBQ* 39:
        344–66.
1977b   "The Quest for the Johannine School: The Apocalypse and the
        Fourth Gospel." *NTS* 23: 402–27.
1977c   "The Revelation to John." Pp. 99–120 in *Hebrews, James 1 and 2,
        Peter, Jude, Revelation*. Ed. G. Krodel. Proclamation Commentaries.
        Philadelphia: Fortress.

Schweizer, Eduard
1951–52 "Die sieben Geister in der Apokalypse." *EvT* 11: 502–12.

Shepherd, Massey H.
1960   *The Paschal Liturgy and the Apocalypse*. Richmond: John Knox.

Sickenberger, Joseph
1942   *Erklärung der Johannesapokalypse*. 2d ed. Bonn: Hanstein. 1st ed.,
        1940.

Staples, Peter
1972   "Rev. XVI 4–6 and Its Vindication Formula." *NovT* 14: 280–93.

Stauffer, Ethelbert
1964   *Christus und die Caesaren*. 2d ed. Hamburg: Wittig. Eng. trans.:
        Christ and the Caesars: Historical Sketches. Trans. K. and R. Gregor
        Smith. Philadelphia: Westminster, 1955.

Stierlin, Henri
1972   *La verité sur l'Apocalypse: Essai de reconstitution des textes originel*.
        Paris: Buchet-Castel.

Strobel, August
1964   "Abfassung und Geschichtstheologie der Apokalypse nach Kap.
        XVII. 9–12." *NTS* 10: 433–45.

Sweet, J. P. M.
1979   *Revelation*. Westminster Pelican Commentaries. Philadelphia:
        Westminster.

Thompson, Leonard
1969   "Cult and Eschatology in the Apocalypse of John." *JR* 49: 330–50.

Torrey, Charles C.
1959   *The Apocalypse of John.* New Haven, CT: Yale University Press.

Trites, A. A.
1973   "Μάρτυς and Martyrdom in the Apocalypse: A Semantic Study." *NovT* 15: 72–80.

Unnik, W. C. van
1963   "A Formula Describing Prophecy." *NTS* 9: 86–94.
1970   " 'Worthy is the Lamb': The Background of Apoc 5." Pp. 445–61 in *Mélanges bibliques en hommage au R. P. Béda Rigaux.* Ed. A. Descamps and A. de Halleux. Gembloux: Duculot.

Vanhoye, Albert
1962   "L'utilisation du livre d'Ezéchiel dans l'Apocalypse." *Bib* 43: 436–76.

Vanni, Ugo
1971   *La struttura letteraria dell'Apocalisse.* Aloisiana 8. Rome: Herder.
1976a   "Rassegna bibliographica sull'Apocalisse (1970–1975)." *RivB* 24: 277–301.
1976b   "Un esempio di dialogo liturgico in Ap 1,4–8." *Bib* 57: 453–67.
1980   "L'Apocalypse johannique: État de la question." Pp. 21–46 in *L'Apocalypse johannique et l'Apocalyptique dans le Nouveau Testament.* Ed. J. Lambrecht. BETL 53. Paris and Gembloux: Duculot; Louvain: Leuven University Press.

Vögtle, Anton
1971   "Mythos und Botschaft in Apokalypse 12." Pp. 395–415 in *Tradition und Glaube: Festgabe für Karl Georg Kuhn.* Ed. G. Jeremias, H.-W. Kuhn, and H. Stegemann. Göttingen: Vandenhoeck & Ruprecht.
1976   "Der Gott der Apokalypse: Wie redet die christliche Apokalypse von Gott?" Pp. 377–98 in *La notion biblique de Dieu.* Ed. J. Coppens. BETL 41. Leuven: Leuven University Press; Gembloux: Duculot.

Vos, Louis A.
1965   *The Synoptic Traditions in the Apocalypse.* Kampen: Kok.

Wikenhauser, A.
1959   *Die Offenbarung des Johannes.* 3d ed. RNT 9. Regensburg: Pustet.

Yarbro Collins, A.
1976   *The Combat Myth in the Book of Revelation.* HDR 9. Missoula, MT: Scholars Press.
1977a   "The Political Perspective of the Revelation to John." *JBL* 96: 241–56.
1977b   "The History-of-Religions Approach to Apocalypticism and the 'Angel of the Waters' (Rev 16:4–7)." *CBQ* 39: 367–81.
1979   "The Early Christian Apocalypses." Pp. 61–121 in *Apocalypse: The Morphology of a Genre.* Ed. J. J. Collins. Semeia 14. Missoula, MT: Scholars Press.

16

NEW TESTAMENT APOCRYPHA

R. McL. Wilson

At the end of World War II the standard work in English in this field was *The Apocryphal New Testament,* edited by M. R. James. There had been an older work by William Hone (1820), of which James has some severe things to say in his preface, and there was also a course of lectures by A. F. Findlay, *Byways in Early Christian Literature;* but apart from these and dictionary articles there was but little to guide the reader. The texts had to be sought in the even older editions of C. Tischendorf or R. A. Lipsius and M. Bonnet, or in the collections published by E. Klostermann, and the relevant literature was scattered over a wide range of periodicals in several different languages and not always easy of access. It is not surprising that interest in this field of study was comparatively slight: the material, after all, is secondary to the NT and does not add much to the information there contained, nor does it belong to the mainstream of the development of Christian theology. The field must, therefore, have seemed of no more than peripheral interest to NT scholars, to historians of doctrine, and to patristic scholars alike. In point of fact, the significance of this material lies in quite different directions, not in its contribution to the history of doctrine or the development of theology but in the glimpses it affords into trends and tendencies in popular Christianity of the early centuries, and also in the fact that it provides an insight into what can happen when imagination ranges uncontrolled, a standard of comparison by which to measure the relative sobriety and restraint of the books recognized as canonical, especially the Gospels.

Even today the work of James remains of value, as providing in a single volume a convenient and comprehensive collection of the most important texts in a serviceable English translation. Its deficiencies are, in the nature of the case, inevitable: with the passing of the years it has become dated, and in particular it takes no account of discoveries and developments in the interval, while the compression of so much material into one volume has left but little room for introductory material or discussion of the literature. Any such discussion, of course, would now after the lapse of half a century be likewise out of date. The German counterpart, edited by Edgar Hennecke, was already provided with a companion handbook, and the third edition, carried to completion after Hennecke's death by his collaborator Wilhelm

Schneemelcher, has grown to two substantial volumes. These contain, in addition to the texts, extensive introductions discussing the relevant problems and reviewing the literature devoted to them. These volumes, therefore, form the foundation and starting point for any further work in the field.

Five other works merit a mention at this point, to complete this general survey: *Los evangelios apocrifos*, by the Spanish scholar A. de Santos Otero, contains the Greek and Latin texts of the apocryphal gospels, as well as introductions, notes, and translations in Spanish. An Italian edition in three volumes was published by Mario Erbetta in 1966–1981. In 1975 Philipp Vielhauer devoted some chapters of his *Geschichte der urchristlichen Literatur* to discussion of the NT apocrypha, and in some cases he was able to take account of development beyond the stage documented in Hennecke-Schneemelcher. In the same year Martin McNamara, in *The Apocrypha in the Irish Church,* sought to make at least a start to the task of remedying the neglect of Irish apocrypha by students of this branch of literature, a neglect which, he says, "has been unfortunate as we have in Irish probably the richest crop of apocrypha in any of the European vernaculars, possibly in any vernacular language." In any case, some of the early Latin texts of the apocrypha come from Ireland. Very recently a subseries to Corpus Christianorum has been established: Series Apocryphorum, of which the *Acts of John* comprise the first two volumes (see Junod and Kaestli). The article "Apokryphen II" in *Theologische Realenzyklopädie* (3. 316–62) includes an extensive bibliography.

The postwar period has also seen some addition to our stock of original source material, particularly through the Coptic Gnostic library discovered near Nag Hammadi, which will concern us later. The Bodmer collection includes in Greek a copy of the *Protevangelium of James* and one of the apocryphal correspondence between Paul and the Corinthians (*3 Corinthians*), and in Coptic a fragment of the *Acts of Paul.* A Coptic papyrus in Utrecht contains part of the *Acts of Andrew,* and a parchment fragment in the Bodleian Library should also possibly be ascribed to the same work. Some fragments in Crum's British Museum catalogue have now been identified as belonging to one of the Nag Hammadi texts (Oeyen).

In view of the extent of the field, the accession of new material, and the ramifications of the secondary literature, it would be impossible in a single article to deal exhaustively and in detail with every aspect; nor is it necessary to repeat what may already be found in the pages of Hennecke-Schneemelcher. Attention will, therefore, be mainly concentrated on subsequent developments and on the areas in which there has been discussion and debate. At a few points, however, reference must be made to the discussion in these volumes and the questions therein raised, and it is with one of these that we begin.

I. DEFINITION AND DELIMITATION

The Greek word ἀπόκρυφος means "hidden," "secret," or "concealed." Its use for this literature has sometimes been explained on the assumption that these works, often attributed to figures from a distant past, were supposed to have been hidden away and only brought to light at a later date. This is in fact the case with the *Apocalypse of Paul* (Hennecke-Schneemelcher, 2. 759) and could be supported from the Nag Hammadi *Gospel of the Egyptians* (Codex III, 68.10ff.), but does not hold for all the NT apocrypha, in many of which no such claim is made. Nor can the term be adequately explained as a translation of the Hebrew *gānûz*, used of books that were excluded from use in public worship (Hennecke-Schneemelcher, 1. 25). More recent discoveries have set the question in a wholly different light, and, as Schneemelcher shows, it is to Gnosticism rather than to Judaism that we must look for the explanation of this usage. Clement of Alexandria (*Strom.* 1.15.69.6) speaks of Gnostics appealing to βίβλοι ἀπόκρυφοι ("hidden/secret books"), while one gnostic document bears the title *Apocryphon of John* and another twice uses the term with reference to secret and esoteric writings (*1 Apoc. Jas.* 10, 30–31).

In a gnostic context, therefore, the term is one of appreciation, referring to works that were valued as too sacred to be divulged to all and sundry. When it was taken over by Christian writers who rejected the gnostic doctrines, they gave it a pejorative connotation. Thus Irenaeus (*Adv. haer.* 1.13.1 [Harvey]) sets it alongside νόθος ("spurious"), whereas Tertullian (*De pud.* 10.12) uses *apocrypha* and *falsa* ("frauds") as synonyms. The word is, therefore, used in several different, although to some extent related, senses, and it is possible to trace development in its use: (a) the original sense of "hidden" or "secret," particularly with reference to gnostic texts; (b) the pejorative sense of "false," "spurious," "heretical," which lies at the root of the modern use of the adjective for something not really worthy of credence; and (c) as a description of certain books that were not accepted into the canon, although they might be accorded a limited recognition as suitable for private reading (see the Muratorian Canon on *Hermas*). Here the evidence shows that the usage and the selection of the books concerned were for a long time still fluctuating. As Schneemelcher notes (Hennecke-Schneemelcher, 1. 26), the use of the word for books preserved only in the Septuagint (i.e., the OT apocrypha) "prevailed only in Protestantism." The later canon catalogues differentiate these texts from those that were rejected, and only the latter are called ἀπόκρυφα. But when the *Decretum Gelasianum* (Hennecke-Schneemelcher, 1. 22–23) stigmatizes as apocryphal the *History* of Eusebius or the writings of Clement of Alexandria, Tertullian, and Lactantius, among others, this is much too wide an extension. Similarly, when such works as *Hermas, 1 Clement,* or the *Didache* were designated ἀπόκρυφα, they were not included in the canon, although some of them enjoyed a temporary or local canonicity. But they were permitted for reading. One point that should be specially noted here is the distinction that must be drawn between the OT and the NT apocrypha: the former are contained in the Septuagint, which was the Bible of the early church once it moved out from Palestine into the wider world. The OT apocrypha are still recognized by some branches of the church as forming part of Holy Scripture; the NT apocrypha, however, have never been accorded canonical status in the church at large, except that some of them (*Acts of Paul, Apocalypse of Peter*) for a time and in some areas enjoyed a measure of temporary or local canonicity.

The formulation of an adequate definition of the NT apocrypha is not a simple matter, since any such definition must be sufficiently comprehensive to include all the relevant material, yet at the same time sufficiently restrictive to exclude what does not belong in this category. As already noted, the usage of the *Decretum Gelasianum* is much too wide. Some of the writings there listed are frankly heretical, while others are theological treatises which may be perfectly orthodox but derive from a period long after the NT; in neither case can we think of these works as intended to rank alongside the NT. Early modern collections included the apostolic fathers, and for this there is at least the justification that some of these works (*Didache, Barnabas, 1 Clement, Hermas*) were for a time on the verge of acceptance into the NT canon. It is, however, open to question whether this does not still extend the range too widely. These works have their place in the history of early Christian literature, but they do not share one salient characteristic of the writings generally classed as NT apocrypha: they were not written to supplement or replace the canonical scripture. Accordingly, the more recent tendency (Schneemelcher, Vielhauer, 1975) has been to treat them separately.

Schneemelcher proposes a definition in terms of form criticism: "The New Testament Apocrypha are writings which have not been received into the canon, but which by title and other statements lay claim to be in the same class with the writings of the canon, and which from the point of view of Form Criticism further develop and mould the kinds of style created and received in the New Testament" (Hennecke-Schneemelcher, 1. 27). Later (p. 28) he speaks of "gospels which are distinguished by the fact not merely that they did not come into the NT but also that they were intended to take the place of the four gospels of the canon (this holds good for the earlier texts) or to stand as an enlargement of them," and further of pseudepigraphical epistles and of "elaborately fabricated Acts of Apostles, the writers of which have worked up in novelistic fashion the stories and legends about the apostles and so aimed at supplementing the deficient information which the NT communicates about the destinies of these men."

This definition, as Schneemelcher himself remarks, may be open to objection, and indeed, if strictly applied, it would exclude from consideration some of the material included in his volumes. It is, however, serviceable and delimits fairly clearly the kind of text with which we have to deal. In the nature of the case, documents do not always fall neatly into tidy categories, and there must be a certain flexibility with regard to material that stands at the fringe. The definition does, however, raise the question of the extent to which the Nag Hammadi library should be included with the apocrypha. As Krause notes (1974:8), it would not be difficult to put together a gnostic NT from the texts it contains: there are gospels of Philip, of Thomas, of the Egyptians, and the *Gospel of Truth*, Acts (of Peter and the Twelve), Letters (Peter to Philip) and Revelations (of James, of Paul, and of Peter). In addition to documents attributed to the disciples, there are others in which they appear in conversation with Jesus, while still others purport to be revelations given by the risen Jesus before his ascension. There are, however, other factors that need to be considered.

    1. One tractate (Codex VI.5) was discovered by H.-M. Schenke (1974:236–41) to be a defective translation of part of Plato's *Republic* (588b–589b); a second (XII.1) is the collection of ethical aphorisms already known as the *Sentences of Sextus*, while others were already known from the Corpus Hermeticum (VI.7 and 8) or are of a Hermetic type (VI.6). Some texts, again, have been classified as non-Christian gnostic, including (according to Krause) *Apocalypse of Adam* (V.5) and *Eugnostos* (III.3 and V.1). These should certainly not be included among NT apocrypha, although in the case of *Eugnostos* the problem is complicated by the fact that in the opinion of several scholars this document has been christianized in the *Sophia Jesu Christi* (BG 8502,3 and III.4). Are we to include *Sophia of Jesus Christ* among the NT apocrypha but not *Eugnostos*? What about documents which in their present form belong to the Christian gnostic period but are attributed to figures from the OT (Adam, Seth, Shem)? It is here that the problems of definition and delimitation become acute: Why include one document because it is definitely *Christian* gnostic and exclude another of the same character and genre?

    2. The titles assigned to the Nag Hammadi documents often give no clear indication of the contents. Thus, Vielhauer already notes (1965:599):

> Here there are writings with the titles Apocalypse of . . . or Revelation(s) of . . . , but the contents of these appear to be extensively cosmological and soteriological, and not of an eschatological-apocalyptic nature. On the other hand, apocalyptic material appears in writings with other labels (Gospel; Letter) or without any such title. . . . The designations of form (Gospel, Apocalypse) which these writings often carry in their titles should not be understood in the traditional sense as literary characterizations.

Similarly, none of the Nag Hammadi "gospels" is a gospel in the traditional sense: they contain no account of the life and ministry of Jesus, or of his death and resurrection. Only the *Gospel of Thomas* contains "sayings" of

Jesus, and here material familiar from the canonical Gospels is combined with other material, often of a very different character. The *Gospel of Truth* is rather a meditation on the theme of the gospel as "good news," the *Gospel of Philip* a rambling didactic and hortatory discourse, and the *Gospel of the Egyptians* a gnostic text presenting a system akin to that of *Apocryphon of John* but with elements derived from magic. Such works may merit inclusion among the NT apocrypha on other grounds, but not necessarily because of their titles.

3. It may be open to question how far the appearance of Jesus and/or his disciples in these works is sufficient to justify their inclusion. Most of the apocryphal Acts were fairly obviously designed to fill in the gaps and provide "information" about the apostles to supplement the deficiencies of the canonical Acts, but it is not so certain that this was the purpose of some other works. Often the form is only a device for the propagation of esoteric doctrine (usually more or less heretical) alleged to have been handed down from the apostles. As already noted, the problem becomes more acute when the person named in the title is not a NT figure but is from the OT.

Perhaps the best we can do is accept Schneemelcher's definition as describing a central core, yet recognize the existence of one or more "fringe groups" of related texts that must be taken into account if we are to see things in proper perspective: on the one hand, some of the documents that are included among the apostolic fathers; on the other, some forms of gnostic literature. The NT apocrypha, after all, did not exist in a vacuum: they are part of the corpus of early Christian literature as a whole. The purpose of definition and delimitation is to isolate specific categories within that literature which may be appropriately grouped and studied together, and such definition can never be entirely rigid and inflexible. With regard to the Nag Hammadi library in particular, two possibilities appear to be open: to classify the whole library, with such exceptions as those already noted, in a separate category as "gnostic apocrypha," distinct from the NT apocrypha proper; or to include in the NT apocrypha those texts that present a resemblance in type and form, and classify the rest apart as "tendency literature."

As already noted above, the titles of some of these works provide no real indication of their content. A further point in this connection is that in some cases we have two or more different texts bearing the same title: in Codex V from Nag Hammadi there are two quite different apocalypses of James. The *Gospel of Thomas* is completely different from the *Infancy Gospel* already known, and the *Apocalypse of Paul* from the apocalypse already included among the NT apocrypha. It is therefore dangerous to assume that identity of title means the same book. The *Gospel of Philip* bears no relation to the book cited by Epiphanius, nor is the *Gospel of the Egyptians* the document known to Clement of Alexandria. The *Gospel of Truth* may conceivably be the *Veritatis Evangelium* mentioned by Irenaeus (*Adv. haer.*

3.12.1 [Harvey]), but this has been disputed by some scholars; the manuscript has no title, and the title *Veritatis Evangelium* has been inferred from the opening words. In the same way, it is dangerous to assume that a document we now have is the one ascribed by the fathers to Valentinus or Heracleon, and even more dangerous to proceed on the strength of this identification to attribute other works to the same author.

II. THE NAG HAMMADI LIBRARY

It is not necessary to repeat the story of the discovery of the Nag Hammadi library or the long, slow process of editing or translating (see Robinson, 1978a; Rudolph, 1978; for bibliography, see Scholer). It may suffice to say that the library was discovered in 1945 but that for a variety of reasons only about half of it had been published by 1966, when the participants at the Messina Colloquium voiced their concern. Thanks to the energy and persistence of James M. Robinson, a new committee to supervise the work was convened in 1970 and the first volume of a facsimile edition appeared in 1972. At the same time a monograph series was launched with a bibliography covering the years 1948 to 1969 (Scholer), which has been regularly updated. An English translation of the whole library (although omitting parallel versions) appeared in 1978 (Robinson, 1978a), and a start has been made with a publication of volumes containing the full texts as well as translations (Böhlig and Wisse; Parrott). A parallel French series is being produced through the collaboration of scholars in Quebec and Strasbourg (see Ménard, 1978b), of which several fascicles have already appeared, while in Germany editions of a number of texts have been published, in collaboration with Pahor Labib and Victor Girgis of the Coptic Museum in Cairo, by Alexander Böhlig and Martin Krause. The Berliner Arbeitskreis für koptisch-gnostische Schriften has published translations of several texts in *TLZ* and plans a German translation of the complete collection to accompany Carl Schmidt's *Koptisch-gnostische Schriften* (Schenke, 1978).

As already indicated, not all of these texts belong to the NT apocrypha as defined above, and some therefore need not concern us further. Reference should be made, however, to certain ancillary areas of research that have been cultivated in this connection. Thus, the conservation and analysis of the codices led J. M. Robinson to carry out a series of studies in codicology, which he hopes may lead to the building of a science of papyrus codicology and help to avoid "another repetition of the less-than-ideal procedure of becoming at the end of the work scientifically equipped to begin it" (1978b:70).

Another area that affords abundant scope for investigation is that of the redaction of gnostic texts. Here a start has already been made, and it is to be expected that this question will increasingly engage the attention of scholars now that the Nag Hammadi texts are more readily accessible. The

Gospel of Mary, for example, appears to be composite, with Christian elements superimposed on originally non-Christian material (see Wilson, 1957; 1968:102-3). We now have four copies of the *Apocryphon of John* representing two different recensions, and there is also a cluster of other texts presenting related systems or variant forms of the same system (e.g., the *Hypostasis of the Archons, On the Origin of the World, Gospel of the Egyptians,* etc.), which provide abundant material for comparison. Even the analysis and investigation of particular pericopes may yield significant results (Tardieu; Fallon). The *Apocryphon of John* itself seems to present largely non-Christian material set in a Christian gnostic framework, which prompts the hope that by eliminating the Christian elements we may be able to recover a pre-Christian, or at least non-Christian, gnostic system (see Tröger, 1973:24).

Reference has already been made to the relationship that undoubtedly exists between the *Sophia of Jesus Christ* and *Eugnostos the Blessed,* where the question of priority has perhaps not yet been finally settled. H.-M. Schenke (1962), like others before him, argued for the priority of the *Sophia of Jesus Christ,* whereas Krause (1964) took the opposite view and seems to have carried most later scholars with him (see MacRae: 147-48). It is, however, by no means certain that *Eugnostos* is entirely free from Christian influence (see Wilson, 1968:111-17, esp. 115-16). Again, there is the question of possible sources underlying the *Gospel of the Egyptians;* Doresse (1968:370ff.) identifies as such sources certain parts of the *Apocryphon of John* and the *Apocalypse of Adam,* and Böhlig and Wisse (34-38) note other relevant parallels and regard the work as a compilation.

Here again, however, a word of warning is in place: (1) With many of these texts the only form known to us is the Christian gnostic. Any non-Christian form has to be recovered by removing the Christian "additions," and we can never be absolutely certain that the resultant "original" non-Christian form ever actually existed. (2) The current trend is to regard the gnostic form as primary and the christianized version as secondary. This appears to be correct in some cases (*Apocryphon of John, Gospel of Mary*), but it should not be assumed that the traffic was all in one direction: "Just as there are cases of Christianization among Nag Hammadi tractates, it is also conceivable that there was a process of de-christianization going on in gnostic circles, particularly at a relatively late date when the gnostic sects were losing the battle against the orthodox Church and were moving away from Christianity" (Wisse: 135). The problem here is to know how the original Christian gnostic text could be proved original, and the de-christianized version secondary. In this respect the relationship of the *Sophia of Jesus Christ* and *Eugnostos* is of some importance. (3) A text may be non-Christian without being chronologically pre-Christian. The latter term has sometimes been used in the sense of "prior to contact with Christianity," which can only lead to confusion: a text written ca. A.D. 130 by a Gnostic who had never come under Christian influence would be non-Christian, but is certainly not pre-Christian. This usage should, therefore, be avoided.

Finally, reference may be made to a point of direct relevance to NT studies. When the Berlin Arbeitskreis in 1974 published their translation of the *Trimorphic Protennoia* (XIII.1), reference was made to certain parallels with the prologue of the Fourth Gospel, with the suggestion that the light falls more from the *Protennoia* upon the prologue than in the reverse direction (G. Schenke, 1974). Assuming this to mean dependence of the prologue on the *Protennoia*, some scholars expressed reservations (Wilson, 1977; Janssens, 1975; see also Helderman: 206–11). These scholars, however, did not then have access to another study (Colpe), which presents a rather different picture: not of dependence but rather of a common background or, in Robinson's words (1978c: 131), of "parallel movements between Jewish wisdom literature and Sethian Gnosticism which . . . are converging as they provide the background of the Johannine Prologue" (see also Robinson, 1981).

III. NON-GNOSTIC APOCRYPHA

It is not possible to deal in detail with all these non-gnostic apocryphal works, nor is it necessary, since in some cases there is nothing to add to the discussion already available in Hennecke-Schneemelcher. With regard to apocryphal gospels in particular, however, one general point may be made at the outset—that it is only in the oldest surviving fragments that we have any real prospect of recovering authentic material about the life and teaching of Jesus. It is not, of course, impossible that some nugget of genuine tradition may have been handed down by means unknown to us, to emerge only in some fairly late document, but in general the later texts yield only imaginative elaboration, a delight in the miraculous, and sometimes sheer fantasy. All the material must be subjected to the most rigorous scrutiny.

The Agrapha

On the Agrapha, see Jeremias, 1963:85–90 [which provides a bibliography]; 1964; Vielhauer 1975:615ff. The title (literally, "unwritten" sayings) is strictly inexact, since all this material has come down to us in writing; but it is well established, has the advantage of brevity, and needs only one qualification: it refers to sayings not recorded in the four canonical Gospels. Our earliest source is the NT itself (e.g., Acts 20:35; 1 Cor 7:10; 9:14; 11:24–25), a second the additions and variant readings found at certain points in the text of the Gospels (e.g., the *pericope adulterae* [the narrative of the adulteress, usually found at John 7:53–8:11], the Freer Logion, or the additions at Luke 6:5; 9:55; 23:34a). Jeremias (1964:20–29) gives an extensive list of early Christian writers whose works contain Agrapha, and notes (25) that "even the Koran itself contains apocryphal material about Jesus."

By a process of elimination he reduces to twenty-one the number of sayings and stories whose authenticity deserves serious consideration. Here we are faced with the problem of subjective judgment: some readers may wish to retain what he rejects, or reject something he retains. The only proper course is to examine the evidence as objectively as possible and state the reasons upon which a judgment is based.

The Gospel of Thomas

See, in general, Ménard, 1975b; Puech: 278–307; Vielhauer, 1975:618ff. Although part of the Nag Hammadi library, this may conveniently be taken here as a collection of sayings attributed to Jesus. In 1897 a papyrus fragment containing sayings of Jesus was found at Oxyrhynchus in Egypt (P.Oxy. 1). Two others were found a year later (P.Oxy. 654, 655), and discussion of their contents and the relevant problems continued down to 1920 (see White; Hennecke-Schneemelcher, 1. 97–104, 110–13; Fitzmyer). All the sayings in these fragments are included in the Gospel of Thomas, although we cannot assume that they represent the Greek Vorlage ("exemplar") of the present Coptic text: logion 5 of P.Oxy. 1 is, in the Coptic, split into two widely separated parts (logia 30, 77), while line 31 of P.Oxy. 654 is missing from the Coptic altogether.

The text of the Gospel of Thomas was first made available in a German translation by J. Leipoldt from P. Labib's photographic edition of pages from Codex II. A transcription of the Coptic, with translations into several languages, appeared in 1959. The interest aroused can be seen from Scholer's Bibliography (135–65), which lists over a dozen books and some 230 articles (with others in the supplements).

The earliest studies, especially those of Puech, established three points that have been widely accepted (see Vielhauer, 1975:620–21): (a) the connection with the Oxyrhynchus papyri (see above); (b) the identity of the Gospel of Thomas with a document of the same title which ancient authorities number among the Manichean scriptures (Puech: 283; see his list of parallels, 299–304); (c) a connection with the Acts of Thomas and with "the great stream of the Thomas-tradition which has its origin in East Syria" (Vielhauer, 1965:621). Some authors (Baker; Quispel) have endeavored to trace further parallels in Syriac literature (see Ménard, 1968b; 1975b:13ff.), and Quispel in particular has gone on to develop a far-reaching theory of the influence of Jewish Christianity via the Gospel of Thomas on the whole development of early Syriac Christianity (1967). On the other side, B. Ehlers has challenged the whole theory of an Edessene origin (see Ménard, 1975a:78; Dehandschutter: 127).

About half the sayings in the Gospel of Thomas have parallels in the Synoptics (for Johannine elements, see Brown), but they appear often in completely different order and in nearly every case with some modification, not always readily explained by gnostic redaction. The earlier studies generally favored the theory that the *Gospel of Thomas* goes back to a tradition independent of our Gospels (e.g., Quispel, 1957, and elsewhere), but later the general tendency was to assume dependence. This, however, presents problems: the author must have known all three Synoptics; the modifications are not always gnostic in character; and sometimes it is the *Gospel of Thomas* that appears to be more primitive. Schrage endeavored to prove dependence on the Coptic NT, but again there are difficulties (see Wilson, 1966). The solution may lie in some modification of the independence hypothesis: in general terms we may speak of (1) an element of genuine early tradition; (2) an element parallel to but perhaps independent of our Gospels, but apparently from a later stage in the development of the tradition; and (3) an element derived from the Synoptics (see Wilson, 1960: esp. 147–48), in addition of course to the non-Synoptic material. H. Koester postulates a number of primitive sayings collections, in part incorporated into Q, in part directly accessible to Luke and Mark (the special traditions of Matthew seem to have no parallels in the *Gospel of Thomas*). These primitive collections were made for specific theological purposes and are closely related to the forms and types of the apocryphal gospel literature (Koester, 1971b:166). The *Gospel of Thomas* then continues "the most original gattung of the Jesus tradition . . . which, in the canonical gospels, became acceptable to the orthodox church only by radical critical alteration" (Koester, 1971a:135). Such a theory would account for the facts more adequately than one of direct dependence and, moreover, leaves room for growth and development in the tradition (see also Robinson, 1971).

It has often been taken for granted that the *Gospel of Thomas* is a gnostic work, but this view has been challenged by a number of scholars (e.g., Grobel). Quispel, for example, has consistently maintained that it is not gnostic but encratite. Here an important distinction must be drawn: there is no question that it can be read as a gnostic book (see Ménard, 1975b; also Grant; Gärtner; Haenchen), but does this mean that it is of gnostic *origin*, written by a Gnostic and intended to be understood in gnostic fashion? Puech (305–6) and Quispel (1967:11–12) have argued a theory of two versions, an orthodox represented by the Oxyrhynchus papyri and a gnostic represented by the *Gospel of Thomas;* but the opening lines, with their emphasis on finding the interpretation of these secret words, appear already to have been present in *P.Oxy.* 654. In the light of the studies of Robinson and Koester (1971), it may be that the *Gospel of Thomas* as we now have it is the result of a process of growth and development, the precise stages of which we can no longer determine with any confidence.

Quispel (1959) drew attention to parallels between the *Gospel of Thomas* and various Gospel harmonies which may derive ultimately from Tatian's *Diatessaron* (see now Quispel, 1975). His later extension of the argument to include the Anglo-Saxon *Heliand* (e.g., 1962) has, however, provoked opposition (Krogmann). If the *Gospel of Thomas* is correctly dated about A.D. 140, it must have been one of Tatian's sources, or dependent on the same tradition, but some scholars appear to assume dependence of the *Gospel of Thomas* upon Tatian. The point is of some importance for textual criticism, particularly in relation to the Western text (see Quispel, 1960). It should, however, be noted that if the *Gospel of Thomas* is to be cited as a witness to the text of the Gospels, this presupposes its dependence; if it is independent, then it can only serve as an indication of influences which may have operated during the transmission of the text.

In regard to the original language, the majority opinion is that the *Gospel of Thomas* was composed in Greek, although this does not exclude the possibility of underlying Semitic sources (see Guillaumont, 1958, but see also Kuhn). The connections with Syriac literature have led some to postulate a Syriac original, but this is in the realm of speculation. Garitte's opinion (1960b) that the Oxyrhynchus logia were translated from Coptic remains very much a minority view (see Guillaumont, 1960).

Apocryphal Gospels

These may be dealt with briefly, since in most cases there is little or nothing to add to the discussions in Hennecke-Schneemelcher and Vielhauer. It may be worth noting, however, that *P.Oxy.* 1081 has been identified as part of the *Sophia Jesu Christi* (Puech: 245) and that the evidence of Papyrus Egerton 2, an "unknown gospel with Johannine elements" (Jeremias 1963:94–97), and the Rylands Papyrus P[52] shows that the Fourth Gospel was known and used in Egypt in the first half of the second century and therefore cannot have been written much later than A.D. 100.

The Jewish-Christian gospels present a problem of some complexity, since our patristic sources mention three different names (*Gospel of the Hebrews*, the *Nazareans*, the *Ebionites*), and it is by no means clear whether we have to do with one, two, or three documents. The evidence points to at least one in a Semitic language and one in Greek, and the question is then whether Epiphanius is correct in identifying his *Gospel of the Ebionites* with the *Gospel of the Hebrews*. Since his testimony is suspect, it is preferable, with Vielhauer, to think of three. Vielhauer's redistribution of the fragments may, however, be open to question (in 1963:134 he says himself that no complete certainty can be arrived at, particularly with regard to the quotations in Jerome). A further question is that of the character of these works: the *Gospel of the Hebrews* is sometimes described as gnostic, but Quispel (1957 and elsewhere) ascribed the "Synoptic" material in the *Gospel of Thomas* to the *Gospel of the Hebrews* and more gnostic doublets to the *Gospel of the Egyptians* (against this, see Hennecke-Schneemelcher, 1. 177 n. 1; Vielhauer, 1975:662). A different distribution of the fragments in Jerome might make the *Gospel of the Nazareans* rather less "orthodox" and that of the *Hebrews* rather less "gnostic." It must be remembered that we have only fragments, which do not admit of a true appreciation of the character of these writings. On the other hand, there is something to be said for the view of W. Bauer (51–53) that the *Gospel of the Hebrews* was the gospel of Jewish Christians in Egypt, the *Gospel of the Egyptians* that of native Egyptian Christians.

This last question is complicated by the fact that we now know of two different works with the title *Gospel of the Egyptians,* one already known to Clement of Alexandria (see Vielhauer, 1975:662–65), the other in the Nag Hammadi library. The latter is not a gospel; its title is secondary, and it really belongs to the gnostic Seth literature (Vielhauer: 665). This is a case in which the problems of definition and delimitation become acute, but it is probably better, with Puech and Vielhauer, to exclude this book from the list of NT apocrypha. The text, from Codices III and IV, has now been published by Böhlig and Wisse.

The *Protevangelium of James* calls for somewhat fuller treatment, since the Bodmer collection has now yielded the oldest extant manuscript, dated by Testuz (1958) to the third century (de Strycker: 14 n. 3 corrects to the first half of the fourth). No complete Latin manuscript has survived, but there is evidence that a Latin version was once current (Cullmann: 370; cf. also de Aldama). The manuscript tradition has been exhaustively examined by de Strycker, who concludes that it shows a remarkable homogeneity and continuity (374–75), although even the Bodmer papyrus testifies to a fairly advanced stage of secondary expansion (Cullmann: 370). The place of origin is in doubt: de Strycker (423) argues for Egypt (so too Vielhauer, 1975:668), but Smid (20–22) disagrees and suggests Syria, although he admits that the evidence is not conclusive. A special problem is the integrity of the book: Vielhauer (1975:669) notes some indications of literary disunity, as the Bodmer version omits some of the dialogue in chaps. 18–21. De Strycker (391) argues that the long text alone is authentic and that the Bodmer version is the result of "a hasty and unintelligent abridgement."

On the *Infancy Gospel of Thomas* it need only be noted that this work has no connection with the Nag Hammadi gospel already mentioned. Thomas appears to have been a favorite choice as authority for apocryphal works, since in addition to these we have also the *Acts of Thomas* and the Nag Hammadi *Book of Thomas the Contender.* A variant of the story of the dyer appears in *Gos. Phil.* 54 (see Gaffron: 137ff.). The complicated textual tradition of this work still awaits detailed investigation: the versions in ancient languages show how the material has been sometimes enlarged, sometimes abridged, and occasionally adapted (see Vielhauer, 1975:673).

An edition of the Latin text of the *Gospel of Nicodemus* has been published by C.-H. Kim, who strangely ignores Hennecke-Schneemelcher. In this connection reference may be made to the Irish apocrypha listed by McNamara (68ff.) and to the medieval tradition of the Vision of Hell explored by Owen. The NT apocrypha may have been condemned by church authorities, but they were widely popular, as the numerous versions show, and exercised considerable influence on art and literature.

Conversations of the Risen Jesus
with His Disciples

Most of the documents under this head are of gnostic origin, and indeed Puech regards this as the usual or classic type of gnostic gospel (e.g., 246: *Sophia of Jesus Christ*; 320: *Apocryphon of John*). There is, however, an orthodox example in the *Epistula Apostolorum* (see also the Freer Logion in Codex W of Mark), which may justify their inclusion here. The basic structure has been frequently examined (Vielhauer, 1975:682 n. 8 refers to Rudolph, 1968:85ff. and Koester, 1971b:193-204): Jesus appears to one or more disciples, usually on a mountain, and conveys to them revelations in the form of answers to their questions. These answers frequently develop into lengthy discourses (in *Apocryphon of John*, for example, the discourse runs for twenty pages of the Berlin text before a question from John affords opportunity for correction of a "false" interpretation of Genesis). Koester links these documents with the OT theophanies and claims that these revelations continue the Jewish genre of "apocalypses," but Vielhauer (1975:691) objects that (a) the "vision report," which is constitutive for apocalyptic, rarely occurs in the "conversations" and (b) the "conversation" form is not constitutive for apocalyptic. Against Koester's arguments, he adheres to the view of a distinct literary *Gattung* (690–92). Part of the problem may lie in the ambiguity of the Greek word ἀποκάλυψις, which of course means "revelation"; but not all revelations are of an apocalyptic nature. At any rate, we require a distinct term to distinguish these revelation discourses from the apocalypses, which are often of different character and content. The discourses have a variety of titles (*Pistis Sophia, Books of Jeu, Apocryphon of John, Sophia of Jesus Christ, First Apocalypse of James, Apocryphon of James, Thomas the Contender*), but are all clearly of the same literary type. The chief orthodox example is the *Epistula Apostolorum* (Duensing; Hornschuh; Vielhauer, 1975:683–87), unmistakably intended to combat gnostic teaching (Vielhauer, 1975:686). If the *Gattung* is of gnostic origin, as Duensing (190) and Vielhauer (1975:687) hold (with some justification: this is the only full-scale "orthodox" example, while there are several gnostic), we have here an attempt to combat the Gnostics with their own weapons.

The closest literary parallel is the Nag Hammadi *Apocryphon of James* (Malinine; H.-M. Schenke, 1971). W. C. van Unnik questioned the gnostic character of this work, but the trend of opinion has gone against him (Zandee; Rudolph, 1969). If Schenke's restoration of the name Cerin [thus] is correct, there can be no further question. Fresh English translations of the *Pistis Sophia* and the *Books of Jeu* have been published, with Carl Schmidt's

Coptic text, by V. MacDermot. (For these revelation gospels, see also Pagels, 1978, 1979; Perkins, 1980; Rudolph, 1968).

Apocryphal Acts

With the passing of time we can trace a change in the status of the apostles and in the church's attitude to them (cf. Schneemelcher, Bauer, Hornschuh in Hennecke-Schneemelcher, 2. 25–87). Where Paul saw them as messengers of the gospel, Luke regards them as witnesses to the *historia Jesu* and hence as guarantors of the truth of the church's preaching (Hennecke-Schneemelcher, 2. 30). In the second century Luke's position was to be further developed: divergence and deviation entered in only with the departure of the apostles from the scene (see Hegesippus apud Eusebius *Hist. eccl.* 4.22), and the true and authentic faith could, therefore, be discovered only by a return to the apostles. This change of attitude opened the way for apostolic pseudepigrapha, for it was only when what was "apostolic" had become normative that there was any point in circulating writings under the names of the apostles (see Hennecke-Schneemelcher, 2. 31). It also led to an interest in the apostles themselves and to the growth of a literature about them in which the legendary element becomes more and more marked. Not only the "orthodox," however, appealed to the apostles, since the Gnostics also claimed to possess esoteric traditions handed down from them by various intermediaries. An apostolic name was, therefore, no longer a sufficient criterion for orthodoxy (see Eusebius *Hist. eccl.* 3.3 on writings ascribed to Peter), and other criteria had to be used as well.

In the light of Schneemelcher's discussion (Hennecke-Schneemelcher, 2. 169–74), the question of the relation between the apocryphal and the canonical Acts may now be regarded as settled (Vielhauer, 1975:694; for *Acts of Paul,* see Schneemelcher, 1964a). Though written from a definite theological standpoint, the apocryphal Acts are "essentially different . . . in genre and literary form as much as in content and theology" and cannot be put on a level with the Lucan work. Schneemelcher sets them rather in the *Gattung* of popular literature. As to their origins, they have often been described as gnostic, although A. Hamman claims that the Gnostics were the heirs rather than the fathers of this literature. Schneemelcher and Vielhauer offer a more nuanced view: the discussion of this question has suffered from too rigid a contrast of "Gnosis" and "early Catholicism," whereas in fact the boundaries were fluid; theological unity is not always preserved even in one and the same document (Hennecke-Schneemelcher, 2. 177). The several introductions to individual books in Hennecke-Schneemelcher show the *Acts of Peter* and the *Acts of Paul* to be non-gnostic, even in part anti-gnostic; the fragmentary character of the *Acts of Andrew* makes it more difficult to assess, while the gnostic element in the *Acts of John* is confined mainly to one section and the narrative material may be non-gnostic; the one document with the clearest claim to be called specifically gnostic is the *Acts of Thomas,* although here there are dissenting voices (Klijn, 1962; Quispel, 1964:234; 1967:115; cf. Rudolph, 1969). The problem is complicated by the existence of two versions, a Syriac (the basis for the translation in Klijn) and a Greek in which even Findlay sees "unmistakeable gnostic expressions" (288–89; earlier [278–79] he says it is a misuse of words to describe the book as a gnostic writing). It can be read as a gnostic work, but was it in origin and from the outset a gnostic composition?

A similar problem arises with the famous *Hymn of the Pearl* (cf. most recently Rudolph, 1969). It can be understood in gnostic terms, but there are inconsistencies that suggest revision and adaptation. Ménard (1968a), for example, distinguishes three layers, the earliest Jewish-Christian and the latest Manichean. Here final conclusions have not yet been reached.

The one example in the Nag Hammadi library is the *Acts of Peter and the Twelve Apostles* (see below). Coptic fragments of the *Acts of Andrew and Paul* have been published by X. Jacques, the Greek text of *3 Corinthians* by Testuz (1959), a fragment possibly from the *Acts of Andrew* by J. W. B. Barns. Translations of the Bodmer fragment of the *Acts of Paul* and the Utrecht papyrus of the *Acts of Andrew* (see Quispel, 1956) are included in Hennecke-Schneemelcher, but neither text has yet been published in full.

Apocryphal Epistles

The alleged correspondence of Paul and Seneca is briefly discussed by Sevenster, while a manuscript dated 1679 presents the *Epistle to the Laodiceans* in Latin, Greek, and Hebrew (Ebied). The Greek of this manuscript is, however, Elias Hutter's retroversion of 1599, with some transcriptional errors, which points a warning against hasty and uncritical judgment without thorough examination of all the relevant data. The Nag Hammadi library includes a *Letter of Peter to Philip* and the so-called *Letter to Rheginus,* the latter better classified as a gnostic *Treatise on the Resurrection* (see Peel).

Apocalypses

As already noted, not every work that bears this title is strictly an apocalypse. In particular, the two Nag Hammadi documents called *Apocalypse of James* do not belong to the *Gattung* (Vielhauer 1975:527; for *1 Apocalypse of James* see the section on conversations of the risen Jesus above; for *2 Apocalypse of James,* see Funk). Both contain revelations, but there are differences both in the content of these revelations and in the manner in which they are transmitted which distinguish these documents from the apocalypses proper. The library also contains an *Apocalypse of Paul,* which is not connected with the one already known. Some problems relating to apocalypses under the names of Zephaniah and Elias are discussed by Diebner, while gnostic elements in the *Ascension of Isaiah* are discussed by Helmbold.

IV. GNOSTIC APOCRYPHA

Of the works in Krause's "gnostic NT," the *Gospel of Thomas* has already been discussed above, as have the "revelation gospels." The two *Apocalypses of James* do not belong in the *Gattung* "apocalypse," while the *Gospel of Truth*, as a homily (Vielhauer, 1975:746–49), and the *Gospel of the Egyptians*, as predominantly cosmogonical (see the section on apocryphal gospels above) may be left out of consideration. Puech groups together various "gnostic gospels and related documents," but Koester (1971b:194 n. 122) finds the classification according to author "wholly unsatisfactory." What is common to all the documents in Puech's collection is that they are gnostic, but they belong to various types and genres and would now be better classified accordingly.

The *Gospel of Philip* is not a gospel in any accepted sense, but a didactic and hortatory treatise (Ménard, 1967; Gaffron). H.-M. Schenke (1959) originally divided it into 127 "sayings" but subsequently revised his opinion (1965). It is of importance as adding to our original sources for Valentinianism and for the way in which NT themes are taken up and transmuted in a gnostic context. The numerous references to sacraments give it significance for an aspect of Gnosticism not otherwise well documented (see esp. Gaffron).

The *Acts of Peter and the Twelve* (Krause, 1971, 1972; H.-M. Schenke, 1973) is the only example of the genre in the Nag Hammadi library. Krause (1972) explains the title as referring to two Acts, one of Peter and one of the twelve including Peter, and assumes (1972:50) that three originally independent parts have been worked together. This may be so, but when the work is read as an allegory some of the inconsistencies disappear; this seems to be a case in which the allegory has governed the composition. According to Schenke (1973:15) it contains nothing in itself gnostic, but read as an allegory it shows numerous motifs familiar from gnostic sources, and it is not difficult to see how it could appeal to gnostic readers. Krause (1972:56–58) finds agreement with the "Acts of Peter" in the Berlin Codex 8502, which Schmidt identified as part of the *Acts of Peter*. According to Schenke (1973:15), however, the text is hardly to be considered part of the *Acts of Peter*. One point of interest is that the name Lithargoel occurs as the name of an angel in a seventh-century text, but whether this indicates knowledge of our text (Krause, 1973:58) or a common tradition is by no means clear. Schenke thinks the name originally that of an angel, and its application to Jesus secondary (see also 1974:230).

The *Letter of Peter to Philip* has only recently become readily accessible

(Ménard, 1977; Robinson, 1978a), although summaries of its content were provided by Krause (1972) and Tröger (1973). Ménard (1978a:104) regards it as composed of two fragments, the first the remains of a letter, the second a gnostic explanation of humanity's situation in this world. Luttikhuizen (96) sees a more elaborate structure: it opens with a letter, but the main body is a narrative containing a revelation, followed by a conversation between the apostles, a sermon by Peter, and new appearances of Jesus to the assembled disciples. In some respects it recalls the conversations (see above), but it is not a dialogue of the usual type. The questions are asked at the beginning and answered in a continuous discourse, with a further question at the end. A notable feature for a gnostic text is that the apostles discuss among themselves the necessity of suffering (see also Tröger, 1978:144–66).

The *Apocalypse of Peter* (Krause, 1972, 1973; Werner; Tröger, 1973; H.-M. Schenke, 1975) has no connection with the apocalypse already known. It is not an apocalypse of the usual type but relates a revelation given to Peter, remarkably, before the arrest of Jesus. Points of interest in this document are the docetic Christology (the laughing Jesus on the cross, 81.15ff.) and the polemic against orthodoxy and other gnostic groups (Koschorke). Another is the place given to Peter: the prince of the apostles here appears as a secret founder of Gnosis (Tröger, 1973:62).

Finally, the *Apocalypse of Paul* again has no connection with the apocalypse already known, although there are some points of resemblance (see Böhlig and Labib; Wilson, 1968:132–33; Tröger, 1973:43–44). It starts from Paul's rapture to the third heaven (2 Cor 12:2–4) and continues to the tenth, although only two of the stages are described in any detail. For Böhlig (18) it offers an abundance of interesting details, whereas Tröger (1973:43) finds in it little of interest.

V. THE SIGNIFICANCE OF
THE NEW TESTAMENT APOCRYPHA

It is sometimes said that our NT is an arbitrary selection made by the church from a larger mass of documents which might equally have been included. As M. R. James noted long ago, the best answer to this assertion is provided by the texts themselves. Even a slight acquaintance is enough to make it clear that they cannot (apart from the earliest) be considered as reliable historical sources for the life of Jesus or the apostles. This does not, however, mean that they are unimportant or that they serve merely as a foil to set off the superiority of the canonical books (see Findlay: 4–7). Their significance lies in other directions. For one thing, they show that early Christianity was not monolithic nor merely to be divided into rigid categories of "orthodox" and "heretical." Again, they provide the documentation for trends and tendencies in popular Christianity (e.g., the ascetic element) of which we might otherwise know little or nothing. They show to some extent how the church adapted its beliefs, not always successfully, to meet the challenge of new situations. In this respect they reflect popular Christianity, not the mainstream of theological controversy and debate. They provide a reminder that the church almost from the beginning has been faced with the perennial task of making its message known in terms of contemporary culture, a problem still with us today. And finally they afford insights into the growth and development of asceticism, or of hagiography, of ideas about heaven and hell, or the cult of the Virgin Mary. In the realm of art and literature their influence has sometimes been almost as great as that of the Bible itself.

In comparison with the NT, they provide a standard by which to measure the comparative sobriety and restraint of the canonical books, especially the Gospels. Since the rise of form criticism it has been commonplace to speak of the molding and shaping, even of the creation, of the Jesus tradition, but curiously little has been done to correlate this with the evidence of the NT apocrypha. There may be cases in the canonical Gospels, as with Matthew's story of the guard at the tomb, where legendary development has already begun, but this is still short of the stage reached in the *Gospel of Peter*. On the other hand, rejection of a motif when it occurs in an apocryphal text must raise questions over its retention simply because it happens to appear in a canonical book. Are there other grounds to justify such retention, or should the motif not properly be rejected in both cases?

As will be evident, this survey has but scraped the surface: there is much more that could be recorded. Even so, it is hoped that enough has been said to show that much has been done in this field in recent years. Much, however, remains to be done before this material can be said to have been fully evaluated. The judgment that relegated these texts to a secondary place was sound, but that does not make them totally worthless and unimportant.

[*Postscript:* Since this chapter was completed, Gesine Schenke's edition of the *Trimorphic Protennoia* (TU 132; Berlin: Akademie-Verlag, 1984) has been published. A new edition of M. R. James, *The Apocryphal New Testament*, is being prepared by J. Keith Elliott, and the first volume of a 5th edition of *Neutestamentliche Apokryphen*, ed. by W. Schneemelcher, has appeared. James H. Charlesworth has published an extensive bibliography on *The New Testament Apocrypha and Pseudepigrapha: A Guide to Publications, with Excursuses on Apocalypses* (American Theological Library Association Bibliography Series, 17; Metuchen, NJ/London: American Theological Library Association/Scarecrow, 1987).]

BIBLIOGRAPHY

This list includes chiefly works mentioned in the text. For a more comprehensive bibliography see *TRE* 3. 316–62.

Baker, Aelred
    1964   "Pseudo-Makarius and the Gospel of Thomas." *VC* 18: 215–25.
    1965a   "The Gospel of Thomas and the Diatessaron." *JTS* 16: 449–54.

1965b   "The 'Gospel of Thomas' and the Syriac 'Liber Graduum.'" *NTS* 12: 49–55.

Barns, John Wintour Baldwin
1960   "A Coptic Apocryphal Fragment in the Bodleian Library." *JTS* 11: 70–76.

Bauer, Walter
1971   *Orthodoxy and Heresy in Earliest Christianity.* Trans. Philadelphia Seminar on Christian Origins. Ed. Robert Kraft and Gerhard Krodel (from 2d German edition by G. Strecker). Philadelphia: Fortress.

Böhlig, Alexander, and Pahor Labib
1963   *Koptisch-gnostische Apokalypsen aus Codex V von Nag Hammadi im Koptischen Museum zu Alt-Kairo.* Sonderband der Wissenschaftliche Zeitschrift d. Martin-Luther-Universität, Halle-Wittenberg.

Böhlig, Alexander, and Frederik Wisse
1975   *Nag Hammadi Codices III.2 and IV.2: The Gospel of the Egyptians.* NHS 4. Leiden: Brill.

Brown, Raymond E.
1963   "The Gospel of Thomas and St John's Gospel." *NTS* 9: 155–77.

Colpe, Carsten
1974   "Heidnische, jüdische und christliche Überlieferung in den Schriften aus Nag Hammadi III." *JAC* 17: 109–25.

Cullmann, Oscar
1963   "Infancy Gospels." Pp. 363–417 in Hennecke-Schneemelcher, vol. 1.

de Aldama, J. A.
1962   "Fragmentos de una versión latina del Protevangelio Santiago y una nueva adaptación de sus primeros capitulos." *Bib* 43: 57–74.

Dehandschutter, Boudewijn
1976   "Le lieu d'origine de l'évangile selon Thomas." *OLP* 6/7: 125–31.

de Santos Otero, A.
1956   *Los evangelios apocrifos.* Madrid: Editorial Catolica.

de Strycker, Emile
1961   *La forme la plus ancienne du Protévangile de Jacques.* Brussels: Société des Bollandistes.

Diebner, Bernd Jorg
1978   "Literarkritische Probleme der Zephanja-Apokalypse." Pp. 152–67 in *Nag Hammadi and Gnosis.* Ed. R. McL. Wilson. NHS 14. Leiden: Brill.

Doresse, Jean
1966,   "'Le livre sacré du grand Esprit invisible' ou 'L'Evangile des Egyp-
1968   tiens.'" *JA* 254: 317–435 (text); 256: 289–386 (commentary).

Duensing, Hugo
1963   "Epistula Apostolorum." Pp. 189–227 in Hennecke-Schneemelcher, vol. 1.

Ebied, Rifaat Yassa
1966   "A Triglot Volume of the Epistle to the Laodiceans, Psalm 151 and other Biblical Materials." *Bib* 47: 243–54.

Ehlers, Barbara
1970   "Kann das Thomasevangelium aus Edessa stammen?" *NT* 12: 284–317.

Erbetta, Mario
1966,   *Gli apocrifi del Nuovo Testamento.* 2 vols. in 3. Turin: Marietta. [1/1,
1975,   1975; 1/2, 1981; 2, 1966.]
1981

Fallon, Francis T.
1978   *The Enthronement of Sabaoth: Jewish Elements in Gnostic Creation
          Myths.* NHS 10. Leiden: Brill.

Findlay, Adam Fyfe
1923   *Byways in Early Christian Literature.* Edinburgh: T. & T. Clark.

Fitzmyer, Joseph A.
1959   "The Oxyrhynchus *logoi* of Jesus and the Coptic Gospel according to
          Thomas." *TS* 20: 505–60. Reprinted in Fitzmyer, *Essays on the
          Semitic Background of the New Testament,* 355–433. London:
          Chapman, 1971.

Funk, Wolf-Peter
1972   "Die zweite Apokalypse des Jakobus." *TLZ* 97: 947–50.
1974   "Probleme der zweiten Jakobus-Apokalypse aus Nag-Hammadi-
          Codex V." Pp. 147–58 in *Studia Coptica.* Ed. P. Nagel. Berlin:
          Akademie-Verlag.
1976, ed. *Die zweite Apokalypse des Jakobus aus Nag-Hammadi-Codex V.* TU
          119. Berlin: Akademie-Verlag.

Gaffron, Hans-Georg
1969   "Studien zum koptischen Philippusevangelium." Diss., Bonn.

Garitte, Gérard
1957   "Le 'Protévangile de Jacques' en géorgien." *Muséon* 70: 233–65.
1960a   "Les 'Logoi' d'Oxyrhynque et l'apocryphe copte dit 'Evangile de
          Thomas.'" *Muséon* 73: 151–72.
1960b   "Les 'Logoi' d'Oxyrhynque sont traduits du copte." *Muséon* 73:
          335–49.

Gärtner, Bertil
1961   *The Theology of the Gospel of Thomas.* London: Collins; New York:
          Harper.

Grant, Robert McQueen
1960   *The Secret Sayings of Jesus* London: Collins.

Grobel, William Kendrick
1962   "How Gnostic is the Gospel of Thomas?" *NTS* 8: 367–73.

Guillaumont, Antoine
1958   "Sémitismes dans les logia de Jesus." *JA* 246: 113–23.
1960   "Les logia d'Oxyrhynque sont-ils traduits du copte?" *Muséon* 73:
          325–33.

Haenchen, Ernst
1961   *Die Botschaft des Thomasevangeliums.* Berlin: Töpelmann.
1962   "Literatur zum Thomasevangelium." *TRu* 27: 147–78, 306–38.

Hamman, A.
1962   "'Sitz im Leben' des actes apocryphes du Nouveau Testament."
          Pp. 62–69 in *Studia Patristica* 8. TU 93. Berlin: Akademie-Verlag.

Helderman, Jan
1978 " 'In ihren Zelten . . .': Bemerkungen zu Codex XIII Nag Hammadi
p.47:14–18 im Hinblick auf Joh. i 14." Pp. 181–211 in *Miscellanea
Neotestamentica*, vol. 1. Ed. T. Baarda, A. F. J. Klijn, and W. C. van
Unnik. 2 vols. NovTSup 47, 48. Leiden: Brill.

Helmbold, Andrew K.
1972 "Gnostic Elements in the 'Ascension of Isaiah.' " *NTS* 18: 222–27.

Hennecke, Edgar, and Wilhelm Schneemelcher, eds.
1963, *New Testament Apocrypha*. 2 vols. London: Lutterworth. 2d impres-
1965 sion 1973, 1974. London: SCM. Eng. trans ed. by R. McL. Wilson.

Hornschuh, Manfred
1965 *Studien zur Epistula Apostolorum*. PTS 5. Berlin: de Gruyter.

Jacques, Xavier
1969 "Les deux fragments conservés des 'Actes d'André et de Paul.' " *Or*
38: 187–213.
1970 "Les 'Actes d'André et de Paul.' " *RSR* 58: 289–96.

James, Montague Rhodes
1924 *The Apocryphal New Testament*. Oxford: Clarendon. [Often
reprinted, with Appendixes from 5th impression on.]

Janssens, Yvonne
1975 "Une source gnostique du Prologue?" Pp. 355–58 in *L'Évangile de
Jean: Sources, rédaction, théologie*. Ed. M. de Jonge. BETL 44.
Gembloux: Duculot; Leuven: Leuven University Press.
1978 *La Protennoia Trimorphe*. Quebec: Université Laval.

Jeremias, Joachim
1963 "Papyrus Fragments of Apocryphal Gospels." With W. Schneemelcher. Pp. 91–116 in Hennecke-Schneemelcher, vol. 1.
1964 *Unknown Sayings of Jesus*. London: SPCK.

Junod, Eric, and Jean-D. Kaestli, eds.
1983 *Acta Johannis*. 2 vols. Corpus Christianorum: Series Apocryphorum
1–2. Turnhout: Brepols.

Kim, C.-H.
1973 *The Gospel of Nicodemus: Gesta Salvatoris*. Toronto Medieval Latin
Texts 2. Toronto: Pontifical Institute of Medieval Studies.

Klijn, Albert Frederick Johannes
1960 "The so-called Hymn of the Pearl." *VC* 14: 154–64.
1961 "Das Thomasevangelium und das altsyrische Christentum." *VC* 15:
146–59.
1962 *The Acts of Thomas*. NovTSup 5. Leiden: Brill.

Koester, Helmut
1971a "Gnomai Diaphoroi." Pp. 114–57 in *Trajectories through Early
Christianity*. By James M. Robinson and H. Koester. Philadelphia:
Fortress.
1971b "One Jesus and Four Primitive Gospels." Pp. 158–204 in *Trajectories
through Early Christianity*. By James M. Robinson and H. Koester.
Philadelphia: Fortress.

Koschorke, Klaus
1978 *Die Polemik der Gnostiker gegen das kirchliche Christentum*. NHS 12.
Leiden: Brill.

Krause, Martin
  1964   "Das literarische Verhältnis des Eugnostosbriefes zur Sophia Jesu Christi." *Mullus* (JAC Ergänzungsband) 1: 215–23.
  1971   With Pahor Labib. *Gnostische und hermetische Schriften in Codex II und VI von Nag Hammadi.* Gluckstadt: Augustin.
  1972   "Die Petrusakten in Codex VI von Nag Hammadi." Pp. 36–58 in *Essays on the Nag Hammadi Texts in Honour of Alexander Böhlig.* Ed. M. Krause. NHS 3. Leiden: Brill.
  1973   "Die Petrusapokalypse." Text and German translation by M. Krause and Victor Girgis. In *Christentum am Roten Meer.* Ed. F. Altheim and R. Stiehl. Berlin: de Gruyter.
  1974   "Coptic Sources." Pp. 1–120 in *Gnosis II: Coptic and Mandean Sources.* Ed. Werner Foerster, Eng. trans. ed. R. McL. Wilson. Oxford: Clarendon.

Krogmann, Willy
  1961   "Heliand, Tatian und Thomasevangelium." *ZNW* 51: 255–68.
  1964   "Heliand und Thomasevangelium," *VC* 18: 65–73.

Kuhn, K. H.
  1960   "Some Observations on the Coptic Gospel according to Thomas." *Muséon* 73: 317–23.

Leipoldt, Johannes
  1958   "Eine neues Evangelium? Das koptische Thomasevangelium übersetzt und besprochen." *TLZ* 83: 481–96. Reprinted, pp. 7–30 in Leipoldt-Schenke, *Koptisch-gnostische Schriften aus den Papyrus-Codices von Nag Hammadi.* Theologische Forschungen 20. Hamburg-Bergstedt: Herbert Reich, 1960.
  1967   *Das Evangelium nach Thomas.* TU 101. Berlin: Akademie-Verlag.

Luttikhuizen, G. P.
  1978   "The Letter of Peter to Philip and the New Testament." Pp. 96–102 in *Nag Hammadi and Gnosis.* Ed. R. McL. Wilson. NHS 14. Leiden: Brill.

MacDermot, Violet
  1978a   *Pistis Sophia.* Text ed. by Carl Schmidt. Translation and notes by Violet MacDermot. NHS 9. Leiden: Brill.
  1978b   *The Books of Jeu and the Untitled Text in the Bruce Codex.* Text ed. by Carl Schmidt. Translation and notes by Violet MacDermot. NHS 13. Leiden: Brill.

McNamara, Martin
  1975   *The Apocrypha in the Irish Church.* Dublin: Institute for Advanced Studies.

MacRae, George W.
  1978   "Nag Hammadi and the New Testament." Pp. 144–57 in *Gnosis: Festschrift für Hans Jonas.* Ed. B. Aland. Göttingen: Vandenhoeck & Ruprecht.

Malinine, Michel, et al.
  1968   *Epistula Jacobi Apocrypha.* Zurich and Stuttgart: Rascher.

Ménard, Jacques E.
  1967   *L'Evangile selon Philippe.* Strasbourg: Faculté de théologie catholique.
  1968a   "La chant de la Perle." *RevScRel* 42: 289–325.

1968b   "Le milieu syriaque de l'Evangile selon Thomas et de l'Evangile selon Philippe" *RevScRel* 42: 261–66.

1975a   "Der syrische Synkretismus und das Thomasevangelium." Pp. 65–79 in *Synkretismus im syrisch-persischen Kulturgebiet: Bericht über ein Symposion in Rheinhausen bei Göttingen in der Zeit vom 4. bis 8. Oktober 1971.* Ed. Albert Dietrich. Göttingen: Vandenhoeck & Ruprecht.

1975b   *L'Evangile selon Thomas.* NHS 5. Leiden: Brill.

1977   *La lettre de Pierre à Philippe.* Quebec: Université Laval.

1978a   "La lettre de Pierre à Philippe: Sa structure." Pp. 103–7 in *Nag Hammadi and Gnosis.* Ed. R. McL. Wilson. NHS 14. Leiden: Brill.

1978b   "La bibliothèque copte de Nag Hammadi." Pp. 108–12 in *Nag Hammadi and Gnosis.* Ed. R. McL. Wilson. NHS 14. Leiden: Brill.

Oeyen, Christian
1975   "Fragmente einer subachmimischen Version der gnostischen 'Schrift ohne Titel.'" Pp. 125–44 in *Essays on the Nag Hammadi Texts in Honour of Pahor Labib.* Ed. M. Krause. NHS 6. Leiden: Brill.

Owen, Douglas David Roy
1970   *The Vision of Hell.* Edinburgh and London: Scottish Academic Press.

Pagels, Elaine H.
1978   "Visions, Appearances and Apostolic Authority: Gnostic and Orthodox Traditions." Pp. 415–30 in *Gnosis: Festschrift für Hans Jonas.* Ed. B. Aland. Göttingen: Vandenhoeck & Ruprecht.

1979   *The Gnostic Gospels.* New York: Random House.

Parrott, Douglas M.
1979   *Nag Hammadi Codices V, 2–5 and VI with Papyrus Berolinensis 8502, 1 and 4.* Ed. Douglas M. Parrott. NHS 11. Leiden: Brill.

Peel, Malcolm L.
1969   *The Epistle to Rheginos: A Valentinian Letter on the Resurrection.* London: SCM; Philadelphia: Westminster.

Perkins, Pheme
1971   "Studies in the Form and Development of the Gnostic Revelation Dialogue." Diss., Harvard.

1980   *The Gnostic Dialogue.* New York: Paulist.

Puech, Henri-Charles
1963   "Gnostic Gospels and Related Documents." Pp. 231–362 in Hennecke and Schneemelcher, vol. 1.

Quispel, Gilles
1956   "An unknown Fragment of the Acts of Andrew." *VC* 10: 129–48. Reprinted in *Gnostic Studies* 2. 271–87.

1957   "The Gospel of Thomas and the New Testament." *VC* 11: 189–207. Reprinted in *Gnostic Studies* 2. 3–16.

1959   "L'évangile selon Thomas et le Diatessaron." *VC* 13: 87–117. Reprinted in *Gnostic Studies* 2. 31–55.

1960   "L'évangile selon Thomas et le 'Texte occidental' du Nouveau Testament." *VC* 14: 204–15.

1962   "Der Heliand und das Thomasevangelium." *VC* 16: 121–51. Reprinted in *Gnostic Studies* 2. 70–97.

1964   "The Syrian Thomas and the Syrian Makarius." *VC* 18: 226–35. Reprinted in *Gnostic Studies* 2. 113–21.

1967   *Makarius, das Thomasevangelium und das Lied von der Perle.* NovTSup 15. Leiden: Brill.

1975   *Tatian and the Gospel of Thomas: Studies in the History of the Western Diatessaron.* Leiden: Brill.

1975   *Gnostic Studies I, II.* 2 vols. Publications de l'institut historique et archéologique néerlandais de Stamboul 34: 1–2. Istanbul: Nederlands Historisch-Archaeologisch Instituut te Istanbul. [Includes most of the articles listed above, with others, see Scholer Supplement VI, No. 3514.]

Robinson, James McConkey

1971   "LOGOI SOPHON." Pp. 71–113 in *Trajectories through Early Christianity.* By J. M. Robinson and Helmut Koester. Philadelphia: Fortress.

1978a   Introduction to the *Nag Hammadi Library in English.* New York: Harper & Row.

1978b   "The Future of Papyrus Codicology." In *The Future of Coptic Studies.* Ed. R. McL. Wilson. Leiden: Brill.

1978c   "Gnosticism and the New Testament." Pp. 125–43 in *Gnosis: Festschrift für Hans Jonas.* Ed. B. Aland. Göttingen: Vandenhoeck & Ruprecht.

1981   "Sethians and Johannine Thought." Pp. 643–70 in *The Rediscovery of Gnosticism,* vol. 1. Ed. B. Layton. 2 vols. Studies in the History of Religions (Supplements to *Numen*) 41. Leiden: Brill.

Rudolph, Kurt

1968   "Der gnostische 'Dialog' als literarisches Genus." Pp. 85–107 in *Probleme der koptischen Literatur.* Ed. P. Nagel. Wissenschaftliche Beiträge der Martin-Luther-Universität, 1968:1[K2]. Halle-Wittenberg.

1969,   "Gnosis und Gnostizismus: Ein Forschungsbericht." *TRu* 34: 121–75,
1971   181–231, 358–61; 36: 1–61, 89–124.

1978   *Die Gnosis.* Leipzig: Koehler & Amelang. Eng. trans. by R. McL. Wilson: *Gnosis: The Nature and History of Gnosticism.* New York: Harper; Edinburgh: T. & T. Clark, 1983.

Schenke, Gesine

1974   "Die dreigestaltige Protennoia." *TLZ* 99: 731–46.

Schenke, Hans-Martin

1959   "Das Evangelium nach Philippus." *TLZ* 84: 1–26. Reprinted, pp. 31–65 in Leipoldt-Schenke, *Koptisch-gnostische Schriften aus den Papyrus-Codices von Nag Hammadi.* Theologische Forschungen 20. Hamburg-Bergstedt: Herbert Reich, 1960.

1962   "Das System der Sophia Jesu Christi." *ZRGG* 14: 263–78.

1965   "Die Arbeit am Philippus-Evangelium." *TLZ* 90: 321–32.

1971   "Der Jakobusbrief aus dem Codex Jung." *OLZ* 66: 117–30.

1973   "Die Taten des Petrus und der zwolf Apostel." *TLZ* 98: 13–19.

1974   "Zur Faksimile-Ausgabe der Nag-Hammadi-Schriften: Nag Hammadi Codex VI" *OLZ* 69: 229–43.

1975   "Bemerkungen zur Apokalypse des Petrus." Pp. 227–85 in *Essays on the Nag Hammadi Texts in Honour of Pahor Labib.* Ed. M. Krause. NHS 6. Leiden: Brill.

1978   "Koptisch-gnostiche Schriften, Volumes 2 and 3." Pp. 113–16 in *Nag Hammadi and Gnosis.* Ed. R.McL. Wilson. NHS 14. Leiden: Brill.

Schneemelcher, Wilhelm
1964a   "Die Apostelgeschichte des Lukas und die Acta Pauli." Pp. 236–50 in *Apophoreta: Festschrift für Ernst Haenchen zu seinem siebzigsten Geburtstag*. Ed. W. Eltester and F. H. Kettler. BZNW 30. Berlin: Töpelmann.
1964b   "Die Acta Pauli — Neue Funde und neue Aufgaben." *TLZ* 89: 241–54.

Scholer, David M.
1971   *Nag Hammadi Bibliography 1948–1969*. NHS 1. Leiden: Brill. [Annual Supplements in *Novum Testamentum*, except vol. 18.]

Schrage, Wolfgang
1964   *Das Verhältnis des Thomas-Evangeliums zur synoptischen Tradition und zu den koptischen Evangelienübersetzungen*. BZNW 29. Berlin: Töpelmann.

Sevenster, Jan N.
1961   *Paul and Seneca*. NovTSup 4. Leiden: Brill.

Smid, Harm Reinder
1965   *Protevangelium Jacobi: A Commentary*. Assen: Van Gorcum.

Tardieu, Michel
1974   *Trois mythes gnostiques: Adam, Eros et les animaux d'Egypte dans un écrit de Nag Hammadi [II,5]*. Paris: Etudes Augustiniennes.

Testuz, Michel
1958   *Papyrus Bodmer V: Nativité de Marie*. Geneva: Bibliotheca Bodmeriana.
1959   *Papyrus Bodmer X–XII*. Geneva: Bibliotheca Bodmeriana.

Tröger, Karl Wolfgang
1973, ed. *Gnosis und Neues Testament*. Berlin: Evangelische Verlagsanstalt.
1978   "Die Passion Jesu Christi in der Gnosis nach den Schriften von Nag Hammadi." Diss., Berlin.

Unnik, Willem Cornelis van
1956   "The Origin of the Recently Discovered 'Apocryphon Jacobi.'" *VC* 10: 149–56.

Vielhauer, Philipp
1963   "Jewish Christian Gospels." Pp. 117–65 in Hennecke and Schneemelcher, vol. 1.
1965   "Apocalypses and Related Subjects." Pp. 581–642 in Hennecke and Schneemelcher, vol. 2.
1975   *Geschichte der urchristlichen Literatur: Einleitung in das Neue Testament, die Apokryphen und die Apostolischen Väter*. Berlin and New York: de Gruyter.

Werner, Andreas
1974   "Die Apokalypse des Petrus — Die dritte Schrift aus Nag-Hammadi-Codex VII." *TLZ* 99: 575–84.

White, Hugh Gerard Evelyn
1920   *The Sayings of Jesus from Oxyrhynchus*. Cambridge: University Press.

Wilson, Robert McLachlan
1957   "The New Testament in the Gnostic Gospel of Mary." *NTS* 3: 236–43.
1960   *Studies in the Gospel of Thomas*. London: Mowbray.
1962   *The Gospel of Philip*. London: Mowbray; New York and Evanston: Harper & Row.

1966   Review of Schrage, *Das Thomasevangelium:* VC 20: 118–23.
1968   *Gnosis and the New Testament.* Oxford: Blackwell; Philadelphia: Fortress.
1977   "The Trimorphic Protennoia." Pp. 50–54 in *Gnosis and Gnosticism.* Ed. M. Krause. NHS 8. Leiden: Brill.
1978   "Apokryphen II." *TRE* 3. 316–62. Berlin: de Gruyter.

Wisse, Frederick
1970   "The Redeemer Figure in the Paraphrase of Shem." *NovT* 12: 130–40.

Zandee, Jan
1963   "Gnostische Trekken in een apokryphe Brief van Jakobus." *NedTTs* 17: 401–22.

17

THE APOSTOLIC FATHERS

William R. Schoedel

I. THE COLLECTION

Although mere inclusion in biblical codices of some of the books now counted among the apostolic fathers does not prove that they were regarded as scriptural, other evidence points decisively in that direction (Andry; Ruwet; cf. Grant, 1964b:13–33). The value of an appeal to the earliest fathers was not lost on theologians of the patristic period, and especially after Chalcedon many forgeries in their names are found (Grant, 1960, 1962, 1967c). In modern times it was the Reformation that provided the stimulus to a critical evaluation of these materials (Grant, 1967b). William Wake (and not J. B. Cotelier as is repeatedly stated) was the first to collect the writings of Barnabas, Clement, Ignatius, Polycarp, Hermas, and the martyrdoms of Ignatius and Polycarp and label them "the apostolic fathers" (de Jonge). Subsequently the writing addressed to Diognetus and the fragments of Papias (and Quadratus) were added to the group, and still later the *Didache* (Bihlmeyer: vii). Consistent criteria have not been operative in the formation of the collection, and the result must be regarded as artificial (Jouassard, 1957). The writing addressed to Diognetus — a later apologetic work — seems particularly out of place and is usually left to one side (so also the Quadratus fragment).

II. GENERAL STUDIES

Rich philological materials for the study of the apostolic fathers as a group continue to be provided: texts (Bihlmeyer; Fischer; Whittaker; Joly, 1958; Camelot, 1951; Jaubert, 1971; Prigent and Kraft, 1971;[1] Rordorf and Tuilier); versions (Lefort); English translations (Glimm et al.; Kleist, 1946, 1961); commentaries (Grant and Graham, 1965; Grant, 1966; R. A. Kraft, 1965; Schoedel, 1967; Snyder, 1968a); Hellenistic parallels (H. D. Betz, 1961, 1975, 1978); lexicography (Bauer, 1957; Bartelink); an excellent concordance (H. Kraft, 1963); bibliography (Quasten, 1950, 1961; Altaner, 1960; Altaner and Stuiber).

---

[1] For relevant papyrological publications, see Kilpatrick; Lappa-Zizicas; R. A. Kraft, 1967; Treu.

The theology of the apostolic fathers also continues to be treated as a whole. At the beginning of our period T. F. Torrance, writing from a Barthian perspective, drew a sharp line between the NT and the apostolic fathers in their teaching about grace. The book strongly reinforced typically Protestant views of the relation between the NT and the early church. Other studies also picture the apostolic fathers — exceptions (notably Ignatius) are sometimes admitted — as dissolving the tension between the indicative and the imperative (see Benoit; Bultmann, 1955: 2. 95–236; van Eijk) or as being derivative (Kittel, 1950/51). Yet not only have Catholic writers found resources in the apostolic fathers for healing the breach between dogma and morals (e.g., Hörmann, 1956), but Protestant commentators have also been impressed by the priority of grace in these writings (Lawson; Bakhuizen). The latter point is reinforced by J. Liébaert's study of ethics in the apostolic fathers (and related writings) yet without attention to Torrance or his understanding of the category of grace. Where there is less concern for anthropology, the NT and the apostolic fathers are more readily seen as sharing a similar Christianity (Grant, 1964b) and reflecting the same world of ideas on various points (Starck; Gokey; Martin, 1971a). Some Roman Catholic writers, however, continue to look (often in vain) for anticipations of later ecclesiastical developments in these early sources (see Jouassard, 1951–52; Noll, 1970, 1975; Rordorf, 1972, 1973; Hamman, 1973; Richter). And it is hard to deny that there were important shifts in emphasis from first-century Christianity: for example, the virtual denial of independent theological significance to ancient Israel through the identification of OT saints as Christians in everything but name (Flesseman-van Leer; Klevinghaus), or (in Ignatius) the influence of Greco-Roman theism (Pannenberg, 1959:39) and the shift from eschatological to incarnational categories (Pannenberg, 1977:118–19).[2]

Roman Catholic and Protestant evaluations of church order in the apostolic fathers have converged considerably (Knoch, 1961). To be sure, E. Schweizer (1961:139–62) still echoes the traditional Protestant view of the gulf between the NT and the apostolic fathers, and J. Colson (1956), though avoiding sacerdotal and juridical concepts, still finds support in the early period for basic Roman claims. But most Protestants have abandoned the contrast between "office" and "spirit" as theologically decisive (see von Campenhausen, 1969), and Roman Catholic scholars have begun to define church order in terms of "services" (see Lemaire, 1972). One reason for this convergence has been the recognition of the complexity of the development and the impact of H. Lietzmann's view (1941) that church order grew out of an amalgamation of a Jewish presbyterial system and another based on bishops and deacons (see von Campenhausen, 1969; Lemaire, 1971; Kraft, 1975).[3]

[2] For a shift (of uncertain significance) in the vocabulary of salvation, see Sachot.

[3] The situation has been further complicated by (tenuous) efforts to find support in the apostolic fathers for the Essene origin of the office of bishop (Nauck).

The scholarship of the period has more and more emphasized the importance of Jewish elements (independent of the NT) in the apostolic fathers, though the significance of this for the problem of continuity with first-century Christianity may be differently evaluated (Goppelt; Daniélou, 1964; Liébaert). The persistence of traditional eschatological themes has received special notice (O'Hagan, 1968; Bruce; van Eijk). Other influences — Hellenism and Gnosis— will be noted particularly in our comments on *1 Clement*, Ignatius, and Hermas.

The central issue regarding the literary relation between the apostolic fathers and the NT has been the use of the Synoptic Gospels.[4] L. E. Wright tended to interpret differences between the form of quotations in the NT and in the apostolic fathers as conscious modifications, and E. Massaux (1950) argued strongly for the literary influence of Matthew in this period. But H. Koester (1957b) has convinced many of the continued influence of the oral tradition in the apostolic fathers (with the notable exception of Polycarp). His views, however, have not gone unchallenged (see Grant, 1964b). Other studies will be noted below. For a thorough reexamination of the whole question, see now the study of Köhler.

Walter Bauer's views on orthodoxy and heresy (1971) have profoundly influenced the study of the apostolic fathers. Yet, although Koester (1965) and M. Elze (1974) have pushed Bauer's thesis still further, others have (with some reason) denied that forms of Christianity later regarded as heretical predominated everywhere and that the idea of normative Christianity played so restricted a role (Turner; Padberg, 1962; Rohde; Brunner: 11–15; Davids; Norris).[5]

Finally, it should be noted that histories of doctrine still attempt to assess the apostolic fathers in terms of the classical issues of Christian theology (e.g., Adam, 1965; Loofs; Kelly, 1960). It is the special merit of J. Daniélou's discussion of the apostolic fathers (1964), however, to have found a setting for them less distorted by the questions of later generations (however doubtful we may be about his use of the expression "Jewish Christianity"), to have consistently related the apostolic fathers to other early sources, and to have drawn attention to the importance of religious symbols (see also his essays of 1963) for our understanding of the period.

III. 1 CLEMENT

Since R. Knopf's important commentary of 1920, there have continued to appear studies devoted to the Greco-Roman elements (especially Stoicism)

---

[4] F.-M. Braun (1959) deals fully with the possibilities of the use of the Johannine literature by the apostolic fathers. He often greatly overestimates them.

[5] A. Garciadego (117–21) may be right (against J. B. Lightfoot) in attributing a certain "discriminating function" to Ignatius's use of the term "catholic" for the church (*Smyrn.* 8:2).

in *1 Clement:* the emphasis on the ordered cosmos (*1 Clem.* 20), the image of the spiritual athlete, political ideals of peace and concord, the call for voluntary exile, and so forth (Sanders; Eggenberger; Stuiber, 1955:195–97; Ziegler; Jaeger, 1959, 1961; Thierry; Mikat; van Unnik, 1970a).[6] A series of studies emphasizing the biblical setting provided for such elements cannot, however, be ignored (van Unnik, 1950; Eltester; Stockmeier; Helfritz; Lana; Wong; cf. Wickert, 1958).

Though L. Sanders professed to find in *1 Clement's* Hellenism support for the essential Paulinism of the letter, it seems more likely that it contributes to a flattening out of some of the most characteristic ideas of Paul and early Christianity in general. This view has been worked out in convincing detail by the Roman Catholic scholar Otto Knoch (1964; cf. van Eijk: 41–61). But Knoch himself elsewhere adopts a less critical stance toward *1 Clement* (1961; 1967), and others have found in *1 Clement* a persistence of biblical attitudes (see Kwa on humility in *1 Clement;* and for an interesting qualification, see van Unnik, 1952-53), apocalyptic themes (van Unnik, 1951, 1962; Bumpus), Essene notions (Jaubert, 1964a, 1964b, 1971:39–58), striking postbiblical Hebraisms (Werner; cf. Ponthot), Jewish epistolary conventions (Peterson, 1959b), Jewish liturgy (Werner: 799–802, 809–13; Cuming: 94; but see Rankin: 28), and the Hellenistic-Jewish homiletical style (Thyen: 11–12, 118). In any event it would be naïve to think that Hellenistic elements in *1 Clement* ruled out the possibility of an authentic restatement of Christian themes (see Padberg, 1966; Wickert, 1968:151–55). Nor, apparently, is *1 Clement's* treatment of such themes always without subtlety (see Hall on repentance in *1 Clement*).

1 Clement's relation to Judaism is put on an entirely different footing by K. Beyschlag in a rich and challenging book (1966). Beyschlag relies on "motif-historical comparison" to uncover the meaning of central themes in *1 Clement* primarily from their appearance in later Christian literature. The conclusion is that the author of *1 Clement* and those who came after him depended on a Hellenistic-Jewish apologetic tradition that had stamped itself on Roman Christianity. Despite many fascinating parallels and insights the method often leads Beyschlag to read too much back into *1 Clement* and to neglect less complex possibilities (Leder; Brunner: 21–26; van Unnik, 1970b, 1972; cf. Beyschlag, 1972). Also problematic is Beyschlag's identification of the world-affirming attitude of this apologetic tradition with a (non-Pauline) "early catholicism" out of touch with the most vital elements of first-century Christianity (see Knoch, 1967).

1 Clement's relation to OT and NT literature has been carefully studied by D. A. Hagner (see G. I. Davies). One important result is the admission from an author suspicious of form criticism that oral tradition explains most

---

[6] C. Eggenberger's further view that *1 Clement* is a forgery that uses Greco-Roman political concepts to proclaim Christian loyalty to the state is fantastic (see von Campenhausen, 1952).

of *1 Clement*'s use of synoptic materials. (Hagner: 135–51). The efforts of M.-É. Boismard and Tarelli to find Johannine influence in *1 Clement* are rightly regarded as bare possibilities (Hagner: 264–68). The use of James by *1 Clement* has been seen as probable (Hagner: 248–56; Young, 1948). A recent tendency to find a common liturgical tradition behind the high-priestly ideal of Hebrews and *1 Clement* (see now Mees) is not without its difficulties (Cockerill). There is a good possibility that *1 Clement* used biblical *testimonia* (Grant and Graham, 1965:10–13), but that is challenged by Hagner (93–103). As for other sources, serious doubts have been cast on *1 Clement*'s indebtedness to fixed Roman liturgy (van Unnik, 1951; Grant and Graham, 1965:92–96), but the dependence of *1 Clem.* 59–61 on a eucharistic prayer has been argued on new grounds by K. Gamber.

Attention has moved from sources to the literary structure of *1 Clement* in an important study by G. Brunner. Brunner shows that the theological center of *1 Clement* is the constituting of church order, and he successfully relates all parts of the letter to this concern. In this he builds especially on E. Peterson's demonstration of *1 Clement* as addressed both to Corinth and (on the model of the Jewish Diaspora) the whole church (1959b). *1 Clement*'s views, then, have a certain "public-legal significance" (see also Mikat[7]); yet (against traditionalists like A. M. Javierre) Brunner shows that *1 Clement* is conscious of bringing into being something new with its treatment of the apostolic appointment of successors. He also denies that Rome had any primacy of jurisdiction in this period (see McCue, 1964). Brunner concedes that *1 Clement*'s new ideas on order had their "dangers," but he sees the step as necessary (for a restatement of this point, see Weiss).

Another result of Brunner's study is a denial that there is any reference to persecution in *1 Clem.* 1:1 (101–2). This coheres with R. L. P. Milburn's denial of persecution under Diocletian (for the opposing view, see Barnard, 1966e). A wide range of possible dates for *1 Clement* is thus opened up.[8] The situation in the Corinthian church cannot be made out in any detail (Stuiber, 1955:190–91; Mikat: 12–14; cf. Chadwick, 1961). Most have denied that false teaching was involved (see van Eijk: 23–27), but B. Weiss now argues the contrary (and so justifies *1 Clement*'s emphasis on order).

Exegesis of *1 Clement* is involved in all studies that use the letter to explore the historicity of Peter's stay in Rome and the cause of the Neronian persecution there (see Schmutz; Fridrichsen; Altaner, 1950; Giet, 1955; Dinkler; Aland). The historicity of the Petrine tradition has generally been upheld (but see the interesting point made to the contrary by Morton Smith).

---

[7] P. Mikat draws attention to the importance of the political model in *1 Clement*'s description of disruption (*stasis*) in the church. Even so it seems best to view this stance as comparable to that of the rhetorician who gives political advice to cities in times of strife (van Unnik, 1970a:33–53).

[8] But the evidence brought by A. E. Wilhelm-Hooijbergh for a date as early as A.D. 69 seems strained.

Passages from *1 Clement* have also contributed directly to the solution of NT problems (see Bartsch, 1965; Cockerill; Quinn).

IV. 2 CLEMENT

2 Clement has received less attention than it deserves. Its importance "lies simply in its reflection of rather ordinary (essentially Jewish-Christian) life and thought in the early second century" (Grant and Graham, 1965:110). A similar view of *2 Clement* is reinforced in an important chapter by van Eijk (62–82; cf. van Unnik, 1973), who also succeeds in showing how the incarnational (and related ecclesiological) thinking of *2 Clement* coheres with its moralism.

Of fundamental importance now is K. P. Donfried's full-scale study of *2 Clement* (1973, 1974). It includes a careful delineation of genre (1974:19–48) based on Aristotelian categories (and fleshed out with the help of Baltzer: 132–36). Donfried's central thesis is that *2 Clement* represents a deliberate attempt to correct gnosticizing tendencies in its environment (1973, 1974:98–181). (Observe that van Eijk plays down such tendencies.) Highly speculative is the effort to prove that *2 Clement* was written by the presbyters reinstated at Corinth after the intervention of the first Clement in her affairs (1974:1–48). Finally, it is worth noting that Donfried goes even farther than Koester in emphasizing the role of the oral tradition in *2 Clement*'s use of synoptic materials (1974:49–97).

W. C. van Unnik's essay on Christian deference to public opinion through fear of "blaspheming the name" (1960) traces the history of the theme in the early period (involving Ignatius and Polycarp as well as *2 Clement*) and opens up an interesting social perspective on the times.

V. IGNATIUS

Ignatius represents a battleground for most of the central issues of the development of early Christianity. T. Zahn and J. B. Lightfoot have maintained their authority as defenders of the authenticity of the seven letters of the middle recension (see Brown; Trentin, 1972b).[9] R. Weijenborg's challenge (1969b) to this consensus fails (Perler, 1971, with attention to the Arabic version published by Basile; Wenger; Opelt), and that of J. Rius-Camps is not likely to fare better.[10] More weighty (though not, I think, decisive) are the objections to the received view by R. Joly (1979). Several contradictory views of the milieu of the longer recension have recently been

---

[9] J. H. Crehan's new fragment of the letter to Polycarp cannot be authentic.

[10] R. Weijenborg regards the middle recension as an abbreviation of the longer recension (which is itself inauthentic). Rius-Camps thinks that the letters of the middle recension from Troas are built up largely of materials from the other letters (for criticism, see Joly, 1979:121–27). For the relation between the letters from Troas (presupposing their authenticity), see Jouassard (1950).

advanced (Hannah; Perler, 1958; Woollcombe; Weijenborg, 1969a). For the short recension, see Lilienfeld.

The problem of the place of Ignatius in the history of religions has been dominated by the gnostic thesis set forth by H. Schlier (with special emphasis on the mythological background of *Eph.* 19) and (more modestly) H.-W. Bartsch (1940; though Käsemann doubts that the idea of divine unity without the gnostic myth qualifies as gnostic). For new suggestions along these lines, see especially Orbe, 1954, 1961; and Paulsen, 1978:110–87. The theme of God's and the bishop's silence in Ignatius (somewhat broadened by Daube) has often been connected with gnostic (see Chadwick, 1950; Paulsen, 1978:110–16) or Pythagorean (Mortley) ideas. But it is also common to emphasize the extent to which Ignatius refashions his gnostic heritage (e.g., Bieder, 1956b; Barnard, 1963; Rogge; Schoedel, 1964). And a strong challenge has been thrown down to the gnostic interpretation of the silence theme (Pizzolato). The view that the Hellenistic mysteries provide background for Ignatius's treatment of the savior's suffering and the eucharist is still occasionally met (Bartsch, 1940:113–32; cf. Elze, 1963:60–65) but is not compelling (van Eijk: 104–12).[11] Jewish sources — both apocalyptic (Daniélou, 1964) and Hellenistic (Cabaniss; Perler, 1949; Grant, 1967a:46–54) — must not be overworked but do seem relevant.[12] Not so the Essene backgrounds imagined by V. Corwin (cf. Musurillo). Direct contact with common Hellenistic themes and images has been too often neglected (but see Pannenberg, 1959:39; Riesenfeld, 1961; Pfitzner: 198–99).

As to Ignatius's opponents, it is still an open question whether he fights on one or two fronts (against Judaizers and docetists? or Judaizing docetists?) or more (including also pneumatics) and what the precise nature of the opposition was (see Molland; Meinhold, 1958b; Barrett; Prigent, 1977; Donahue; Schoedel, 1978).[13]

Ignatius is sometimes presented as a Paulinist (Grant, 1966) at least in essentials (Bultmann, 1960; cf. MacQuarrie). H. Rathke analyzes the literary and theological connections in detail and apparently finds in Ignatius a kind of late Paulinism moving off into Gnosis. C. Maurer represents a minority in arguing for a literary relationship between Ignatius and the Gospel of John. But he has more support in his view that the two theologies are fundamentally distinct (see Koester, 1957a; contrast Snyder, 1963). Koester's appeal to oral tradition for Ignatius's knowledge of synoptic material has been

---

[11] F. Normann's analysis of the theme of Christ as teacher in Ignatius (83–91) shows that the bishop does not forget other dimensions of the traditional picture of Christ when he reflects on the passion of Christ.

[12] M. Dibelius's neglected article of 1915 (on the Hellenistic and Hellenistic Jewish sources of the theme of unity in *Magn.* 7) deserves to be brought into the discussion more often.

[13] W. R. Schoedel's discussion is based in part on the discovery of a parallel in Josephus to Ignatius's designation of the OT as "archives" (*Phld.* 8:2).

opposed by Grant (1967a:41–43) but finds strong support in J. S. Sibinga's
analysis of the Matthaean parallels. (For *agrapha* in Ignatius, see now
Jeremias.)

There can be little doubt that whatever one thinks about Ignatius's
place in the history of religions, there is an emphasis not only on the divine
"reserve" (Corwin: 116) but also on the divine indwelling (Meinhold, 1958a)
and the "presence of salvation" (Paulsen, 1978:129–57).[14] Against this background many Roman Catholic writers ascribe a "spirituality" to Ignatius not
always very different from that established by means of the history of
religions, but the orientation is to theology and the life of the church rather
than to the Hellenistic milieu (see Padberg, 1963, 1972; Bosio; Camelot,
1971). A similar range of observations, however, led T. Preiss in a much-
cited article to discern in Ignatius a crucial shift from Paulinism toward a
(quasi-gnostic) emphasis on redemption uprooted from its biblical context
in creation, history, and eschatology. The reaction has been vigorous
(Tinsley; Winslow; Grant, 1966:5–6; Swartley), and many are now prepared
to credit Ignatius with a more biblical (Pauline or Johannine)—and very
often a more Protestant—theology (Rüsch; Corwin; Snyder, 1963; Haarlem;
Tarvainen; Meinhold, 1970; Bower). Lurking behind many of these discussions are contrasts akin to that of A. Nygren between *agape* and *eros* (cf.
Trentin, 1972a).[15] Ignatius's high view of the martyr has been felt to run a
special risk of distorting NT Christianity by presenting a rival to Christ (see
Preiss; von Campenhausen, 1964:56–106; Rathke: 68–75); but here too the
sharp distinctions of modern theology seem out of place (see Bouyer:
190–210; Bower; Swartley).[16] For a rejection of all overemphases (including
those of Schlier and Bartsch) on the role of the martyr in Ignatius, see
Bommes. Nevertheless, it is the special merit of H. Paulsen's study of
Ignatius to have seen that Ignatius's self-understanding as martyr has a
decided bearing on his theology (though Paulsen is unable to resolve the
apparent contradiction between the martyr's longing for redemption and, at
the same time, the emphasis on the presence of salvation in the Christian
communities).[17]

A similar tension exists in the understanding of the ministry in Ignatius. The analogy between God and the bishop is still given a maximalist

[14] This includes the emphasis on the presence of salvation in the eucharist (Paulsen, 1978:
155–57), though it is still uncertain whether Ignatius's sacramentalism is realistic (see Koester,
1957a), symbolic (see Bieder, 1956a; Snyder, 1968b), or both (Gribbard). For the literature, see
Zanetti, 1966.

[15] The contrast appears in Preiss as an opposition between Pauline "participation" in Christ
and Ignatius's "imitation" of Christ.

[16] The problem is illustrated by von Campenhausen's sharp distinction between "Nachfolge"
in the NT and "Nachahmung" in Ignatius.

[17] The link in Ignatius between anti-docetism and martyrdom is taken by N. Brox (1961,
1963) as the key to the redefinition of the term *martys* (from "witness" to "martyr") in the early
period. For a more traditional approach to the problem, see Günther.

interpretation by some (see Rathke: 76–80; Dassmann); many others (with good reason) find an emphasis on the shared authority of the three orders of ministry (Thurian; Vilela) or see the unity of the church as the dominant theme (Sauser; Padberg, 1972) with no sacerdotal overtones (Jourjon; McCue, 1967). But the fully Protestant reading of the matter by D. C. Lusk is hardly possible. More relevant perhaps are references to the pattern of church life in orthodoxy (von Campenhausen, 1969:106; Romanides; cf. McArthur). In any event, the charismatic element in Ignatius's person deserves attention (see Hörmann, 1956; Meinhold, 1963; Padberg, 1972). And the evidence is strong that Ignatius was not working out of a firmly established tradition in his view of monepiscopacy (Burke; yet see now Vogt). As for Ignatius's attitude toward Rome, traditional Roman Catholic claims (based on the inscription of the letter to the Romans) have been much modified (Perler, 1944) and even abandoned (McCue, 1964:171–75; cf. Staats).

Other traditional theological questions are still addressed to Ignatius. Thus, an incipient trinitarianism — as opposed to modalism (see Loofs: 73–77) or subordinationism (see Kettler, 1962:1025) — may (with some reason) be attributed to him (Sullivan; Berthouoz). But all such categories may well be misleading.[18]

Some of the most important work on Ignatius concerns literary matters. Perler (1949) has rightly connected Ignatius's style with Asianic rhetoric. The quasi-creedal elements (Kelly, 1950) and/or hymnic fragments (Schille, 1965; Deichgräber) have again been carefully studied. Although attempts have been made to trace their prehistory in several stages of development (Elze; Paulsen, 1978:29–59), von Campenhausen has (perhaps rightly) emphasized the creative role of Ignatius's rhetoric in their formation (1972). The relation between the form of Ignatius's letters and Hellenistic letters has begun to be explored (Bjerkelund: 104–6; Sieben).

New directions in research are suggested by J. P. Martin's use of a simple but illuminating structuralism in the analysis of the spirit/flesh polarity (1971b), S. Laeuchli's observations on the psychological import of Ignatius's language (questioned by S. L. Davies), and B. J. Malina's subjection of Ignatius to sociological scrutiny.[19]

The commentaries by Schoedel (1985) and Paulsen (1985) may be singled out from the studies published since the completion of this survey

---

[18] The reference to Sunday observance in Ignatius (*Magn.* 9:1) is probably secure, despite Guy; Lewis; and Bacchiocchi (213–18).

[19] Harrison's view that the restoration of "peace" in Antioch refers not to the end of persecution but to the vindication of Ignatius himself sets the stage for such questioning. To this may be added especially W. M. Swartley's analysis of Ignatius's self-understanding and the studies that flesh out the social background of items in Ignatius's letters (e.g., Niebergall; Gülzow: 76–100). Paulsen also works toward a sociological perspective on the relation between Ignatius's self-understanding and his theology (1978:88). For one way of putting such materials together, see Schoedel, 1980.

as thorough explorations of the problems affecting the interpretation of the letters of Ignatius.

VI. POLYCARP'S LETTER TO THE PHILIPPIANS

The authenticity of Polycarp's *Letter to the Phillippians* stands or falls with the authenticity of the letters of Ignatius. Most recent work assumes its authenticity but generally follows Harrison's magisterial study in splitting it into two (1–12 and 13–14; cf. Kleist, 1961:69–74). It appears, however, that the two letters must be closer to each other in time than Harrison thought (Barnard, 1966h), and it is possible that the division is after all unnecessary (Schoedel, 1967:9, 29, 37–41). Joly, however, challenges Harrison as well as Schoedel and presents more persuasively than before the view that chap. 13 (with its crucial reference to the collection of Ignatius's letters) is an interpolation (1979:17–37). Yet Joly's arguments are not necessarily decisive (Schoedel, 1987). The Christianity of *Phil.* is closely related to that of the Pastorals, but it seems unlikely that Polycarp was (as von Campenhausen suggests [1951]) the author of them as well.

Three studies (Meinhold, 1952; Schoedel, 1967:3–43; Steinmetz) have carefully probed the argument of the letter in search of its inner coherence. The last two reach very similar conclusions (especially regarding the relation between false teaching and Valens's love of money). The first moves in a somewhat different direction partly because of its commitment to Harrison's late dating of chaps. 1–12 and the related desire to find evidence that Marcionite heresy is combated in *Phil.*

The common view that Polycarp offers a moralized version of eschatological thinking is well presented by A. Bovon-Thurneyson (cf. van Eijk: 127–37).

For the wider problems (involving the Quartodeciman controversy) raised by Polycarp's visit to Anicetus, see especially Nautin, 1961; Brox, 1972; von Campenhausen, 1974.

We may note that Hagner (141–43, 279) regards the synoptic materials in *Phil.* 2:3 as dependent on oral tradition. For the possible light shed on John 8:44 by *Phil.* 7:1, see Dahl, 1964.

VII. MARTYRDOM OF POLYCARP

The *Martyrdom of Polycarp*, an account of Polycarp's death in a letter of the Smyrnaeans to all the churches, marks the emergence of hagiography. Although the document is generally taken to be historically reliable, von Campenhausen (1957) has argued strongly for the presence of interpolations in it. He has gone too far, however, especially because of his failure to understand what Eusebius was doing when he quoted *Mart. Pol.* and because of a too one-sided interpretation of the theme of the imitation of Christ in *Mart. Pol.* (Schoedel, 1967:47–82; Barnes, 1968:510–12; Barnard,

1970). In this connection the special problem raised by *Mart. Pol.* 4 (unnecessarily thought to be anti-Montanist) admits of more than one solution (Simonetti; Schoedel, 1967:57–58). For an interesting attempt to account for *Mart. Pol.* as an imaginative reconstruction based on Ignatius and (especially) Lucian, see Schwartz, 1972.

The late dating (A.D. 177) for *Mart. Pol.* by Grégoire and Orgels is open to many objections, and it now seems that a date in A.D. 155 or 156 or within about a decade after that is again taken as acceptable (Griffe, 1951, 1953; Telfer; Marrou; Syme; Schoedel, 1967:78–79; Barnes, 1967, 1968).

The Jewish roots of Christian martyrologies have been given special attention (Fischel; Perler, 1949). But the cult of martyrs—which seems already presupposed in *Mart. Pol.* (Rordorf, 1972)—almost certainly reflects the Hellenistic cult of the dead (cf. Nilsson: 545–47; and note that Klauser [1974a] withdraws his earlier emphasis on Jewish backgrounds). On the other hand, *Mart. Pol.*'s image of the martyr as a "bound ram" (14:1) is the starting point for a fascinating study by G. Kretschmar, which links martyrdom (and Christology) with Passover tradition and the Jewish theme of the binding of Isaac as it comes to expression in Melito of Sardis.

The book by Dehandschutter may be singled out from the studies published since the completion of this survey as a thorough investigation of all problems affecting the text and interpretation of *Mart. Pol.*

VIII. THE DIDACHE

With the *Didache* we turn to writings still closer to Judaism in substance. There is general agreement that the Two Ways teaching shared by *Did.* 1:1–6:2 and *Barn.* 18–21 goes back independently to a Jewish manual that has a close relation to the so-called *Doctrina Apostolorum* (see Goodspeed; Altaner, 1952; Audet, 1952, 1958:121–63; Barnard, 1958b, 1966g; R. A. Kraft, 1965:4–12; Giet, 1970b:39–170; Wengst: 58–67). A minority view on the relations involved is presented by B. C. Butler (1961). A connection between the Two Ways and the *Manual of Discipline* 3:13–4:26 is also generally accepted (see Audet, 1952; Barnard, 1958b, 1966g). Much more problematic is the attempt to trace the theme still farther back to the covenant formulary (Baltzer: 123–36) or even to Iranian dualism (Kamlah: 210–14; Suggs).

The directions for baptism in the *Didache* probably presuppose Jewish lore (Klauser, 1974b; Pillinger).[20] And the "eucharistic" prayers of *Did.* are surely Jewish in substance (Vööbus, 1968:159–71; contrast Rankin: 28–29). The special connection found by some between *Did.* 9:4 (the bread spread upon the mountains) and John 6 (Goodenough; Moule, 1955; Cerfaux) does not stand up (Riesenfeld, 1956; Vööbus, 1969), and the view that there is a

---

[20] On the complex matter of the ointment prayer in materials relevant to *Did.*, see the differing views of E. Peterson (1959e:156–68) and A. Vööbus (1968:41–50).

gnostic dimension in the text (Magne) seems even more strained. There is still much disagreement whether the prayers in *Did.* 9–10 and the reference in *Did.* 14 have to do with the *agape* or the eucharist or with both of them either separately or as overlapping rites (Adam, 1957:8–11; Peterson, 1959e:156–81; Vööbus, 1968:63–135; J. Betz; Giet, 1970b:203–17; Pillinger), or with something more distinctive (Audet, 1958:372–433).

In 1958, Audet, reacting against earlier opinion, placed *Did.* far back into the first century and developed a theory of literary strata to match. But his views are beset by many problems (Nautin, 1959a, 1959b), and there is room for alternatives in solving structural problems (see Giet, 1970a, 1970b). The role of the transitional material in *Did.* 6:2–3 (Stuiber, 1961) and the function of the apocalyptic conclusion (Butler, 1960; Bammel; Baltzer: 123–36; Kamlah: 210–14; Giet, 1970b:244–56) deserve the special attention they have received.

It is perhaps best to see *Did.* in its present form as hardly earlier than mid-second century (R. A. Kraft, 1965:76).[21] But there can be little doubt that it contains older materials. Relevant to the date is the still vexed question whether *Did.* uses books of the NT (Johnson; Massaux, 1949; Stommel; Vokes; Butler, 1960, 1961)[22] or not (Glover; cf. Vööbus, 1968:35–39)—or only in its later stratum (Audet, 1958:163–66). Note especially the careful development of criteria by B. Layton in arguing that *Did.* 1:3b–2:1 harmonizes elements from our Gospels. In all such problems the complexity of the textual materials must constantly be kept in mind (see Peterson, 1959e; Giet, 1970b:15–26). Nor should the possibility of deliberate archaizing or late borrowing of Jewish prayers be ruled out too easily.

The common view that the *Didache* emerged from a Syrian milieu (Adam; Audet, 1958:187–210; Walker) is not quite certain (see Vokes; Vööbus, 1968:14, 44–45).

IX. BARNABAS

There is growing agreement that Pseudo-Barnabas (*Barn.*) in its present form was put together ca. A.D. 130, when Hadrian considered rebuilding the Temple (Barnard, 1958a, 1958b), or such an attempt was made by the Jews (Wengst: 105–13). Other possibilities are not, however, excluded (see Burger; Prigent, 1961:76–78; Prigent and Kraft, 1971:25–27). Whereas the majority seem to presuppose an Alexandrian milieu (see R. A. Kraft, 1965:45–56; Barnard, 1966d, 1966f), Syria is not out of the question (Prigent and Kraft, 1971:20–24), and even Asia Minor has been cautiously suggested (Wengst: 113–18). *Barn.* may have been reacting to Jewish propaganda

[21] M. A. Smith (1966) thinks (tenuously) that *Did.* is reflected already by Justin.
[22] B. C. Butler (1960) also finds *Did.* dependent on *Barn.* (against which see R. A. Kraft, 1965:14–16).

attending the possibility of the rebuilding of the Temple (Lowy) but nothing so definite can really be made out (Wengst: 100–105).

The view that *Barn.* is heavily interpolated or made up of two or more strata is in decline.[23] But H. Windisch's theory that *Barn.* employs biblical *testimonia* has been renewed vigorously, especially by Prigent (1961; Prigent and Kraft, 1971:10–12; cf. R. A. Kraft, 1960, 1961; Barnard, 1964, 1966i). Although the hypothesis seems to invite one-sidedness and imprecision (see Froidevaux; Stegemann; Audet, 1963), a modest form of it is defensible, and Wengst admits too few instances in which *Barn.* appears dependent on *testimonia* (39–41).

Nevertheless, Wengst (following a suggestion by W. Bousset) has accounted more successfully than others for the overall unity and (at the same time) discontinuities[24] in *Barn.* by treating it as the product of school tradition. Note, however, that R. A. Kraft had already seen *Barn.* as a "'school' product" without feeling impelled also to abandon an emphasis on the use of *testimonia* (1965:19–22).

Efforts to read *Barn.* in terms of a tannaitic catechism (Barnard, 1959), a later Christian catechism (Schille, 1958), a paschal homily dominated by baptismal imagery (Barnard, 1961, 1966c), or the covenant formulary (Baltzer: 123–27) are too tenuous to be at all convincing (see Wengst: 5–9).

Though *Barn.*'s exegetical method is close to that of Philo, there is no clear dependence on that writer (Wengst: 113), and *Barn.*'s thought seems otherwise to be close to more conventional Jewish and Christian ideas. The author of *Barn.* knows a number of things about halakah (Barnard, 1966d:45–51; Wengst: 67); his eschatology is basically futuristic and virtually apocalyptic (R. A. Kraft, 1965:27–29; Prigent and Kraft, 1971:35–41). He seems to propound millennial ideas (Daniélou, 1948), though that is not quite certain (Hermans). Salvation, though made a possibility by the work of Jesus, is realized on the basis of obedience to the law properly understood (R. A. Kraft, 1965:29–32; Wengst: 82–95). *Barn.*'s interest in *gnōsis* has nothing gnostic about it, though it is emphasized in a new way (R. A. Kraft, 1965:22–27; Wengst: 95–99). Indeed, it is the key to scripture, which the author of *Barn.* sets forth more uncompromisingly than any other as an absolute, timeless authority (Wengst: 73–82) — an emphasis related to his radical elimination of the role of Israel in the history of salvation. The anticultic stance of *Barn.* has been linked with the circle of Stephen (Prigent, 1961:142–46; Barnard, 1966f), and there is at least no reason to doubt that such developments are possible in a Jewish or Jewish-Christian milieu. *Barn.*

---

[23] E. Robillard, however, now sets forth three strata, the earliest of which goes back to the historical Barnabas. The analysis depends on subtle theological distinctions not yet made in antiquity.

[24] It should be noted here that all interpretations of *Barn.* must keep in mind the author's tendency to mix theses, arguments, and digressions in a way that suggests more disunity and confusion than in fact exists (see Dahl, 1950).

shows no clear links with any of our NT writings, with the possible exception of Matthew (R. A. Kraft, 1965:19–20).[25] (For the Two Ways in *Barn.* see our remarks on the *Didache.*)

X. THE SHEPHERD OF HERMAS

Recent work on the *Shepherd of Hermas* has had to come to terms with the studies of Giet (1963, 1966a, 1966b). His book represents a mine of information and insight on many issues but is known particularly for the thesis that *Herm.* has three authors: (1) a Jewish-Christian visionary (*Vis.* 1–4), (2) a writer under Johannine influence (*Sim.* 9), (3) a Jewish-Christian adoptionist (*Vis.* 5, *Man.* 1–12, *Sim.* 1–8, 10). Although Giet's central thesis has met with more skepticism than belief (see Grant, 1964a; Pernveden; Joly, 1967; Hilhorst: 19–31), strong tensions in the theology of *Herm.* must be admitted, and it is clear that the book must have undergone editing. It is also possible that *Herm.* was written in stages over a period of time, and it may be best to see *Sim.* 9 as a later addition to it (Snyder, 1968a:3–7, 23–24). There is now a tendency to date at least the original materials early in the second century (Snyder, 1968a:22–24; Bauckham: 28; Hilhorst: 31–35).[26]

There is also growing agreement that *Herm.* is much indebted to Judaism (Pernveden; Snyder, 1968a; cf. Ford) and (by some uncertain path) to the two-spirits teaching of Qumran in particular (Audet, 1953; Lluis-Font; Barnard, 1966a, 1966b; Hanson). A. J. F. Seitz's research on the term "double-minded" in James, *1–2 Clement,* and *Herm.* proved to cohere well with such views of *Herm.*'s background (1944; 1947; 1958; Wolverton; yet see Snyder, 1968a:82–83). Also Jewish in inspiration is the use in *Herm.* of language borrowed from angelology for Christology (see Daniélou, 1957; 1964:119–27; Moxnes), though it is still a question whether this is actually what is found there (Giet, 1963:227–28; Pernveden: 58–64).

The importance of Judaism for *Herm.* may, however, have been exaggerated (Joly, 1953a; Reiling: 25–26).[27] In any event, there are undeniable reflections of Hellenism as well: echoes of divination and revelation (Peterson, 1959a, 1959b; Reiling: 21–22, 58–121; Aune), Hermetic ecstasy and professions of unworthiness (Festugière: 51–59), Arcadian scenery (Schmid), the life-speaking willow (H. Rahner, 1963:303–5), Cebes' *Tabula* (Joly, 1953a; 1958:51–53), and more (Schwartz, 1965). Peterson, however, sees the Hellenistic language of revelation as a facade behind which an

---

[25] F.-M. Braun's claim that the author of *Barn.* knew the Gospel of John (1958) is most tenuous.

[26] A. Hilhorst also includes a negative assessment of the even more daring theory of multiple authorship presented by W. Coleborne (1969, 1970).

[27] Reiling even calls for a reexamination of the sources of the two-spirits teaching (134 n. 1). He refers to materials collected by Dibelius.

eschatological-ascetic outlook is to be found (1959d). Reiling points more naturally to the phenomenon of prophecy but is likewise convinced that it is "a Christian concept expressed in the language and the pictures of the author's milieu" (173).

Such studies have helped to end the isolation of *Herm.*'s theology in the study of the early church and to cause it to be taken more seriously. It is symptomatic that Pernveden focuses attention on the church (rather than repentance) in *Herm.*, though it is likely that he makes *Herm.* more systematic and unified than it actually is (see Barnard, 1968:34). Less convincing are the efforts to deepen the theological categories of *Herm.* and have him speak Pauline language in the description of the believer's relation to Christ and the church (Barberet; Bausone; Flórez; cf. Hamman, 1961). The study of prophecy by Reiling seems closer to *Herm.*'s world, and it will be necessary to come to terms with his emphasis on the collective character of the phenomenon (122–54) and his denial of the role of the prophet to Hermas himself (155–70). The much-disputed problem of repentance in *Herm.* is not yet settled. The theory that *Herm.* proclaims an exceptional last call to repent still has much to commend it (Joly, 1955; 1958:22–30). Yet the research that finds something closer to the later ecclesiastical norm in *Herm.* is by no means without good arguments (Poschmann; Galtier; and with important amendments, K. Rahner, 1955; Giet, 1961). In any event, we must distinguish repentance in *Herm.* from much of what is conveyed by the term penance (see Frei, who builds especially on Young, 1946). Snyder finds a crude but healthy "dialectic" in *Herm.*'s view of the theme (1968a:36).

Hermas's Roman provenance is above dispute, and K. Grobel seems to have shown the author's familiarity with a viti-culture confined to central Italy. *Herm.* gives more information that is still sometimes taken as biographical (Clark), but it is likely that the author's "children" are members of the church and that Dibelius (1923) was right in seeing the opening scene with Rhoda as an adaptation from pagan erotic literature (Joly, 1953b; 1958:17–21).

A related question is whether the visions are only literary devices designed to lend urgency to exhortation (Snyder, 1968a:9–10). It seems at least clear that Peterson (1959c) was wrong in seeing eschatology in *Herm.* as individualized (cf. O'Hagan, 1961). Thus, even if the visions are literary devices, there is a genuine apocalyptic quality to the writing (Bauckham).

As to *Herm.*'s language, Hilhorst has shown that the Latinisms identified (see Mohrmann, 1949; Tanner) are not impressive. He has also shown that the Semitisms, though more numerous, are derived from the LXX or the (Greek) vocabulary of the early Christians. The (Latin) word *statio*, used by *Herm.* for a fixed time of fast, is a special case of borrowing which ultimately goes back to a Jewish model and Jewish terminology (Mohrmann, 1953; Hilhorst: 168–79).

The book by Osiek may be singled out from the studies published since the completion of this survey as an interesting exercise in the sociological analysis of Hermas and his community.

XI. PAPIAS

The fragments of Papias still continue to be looked at for more than they can possibly give. Yet progress has been made even here.

Eusebius's attitude toward Papias (in *Hist. eccl.* 3.39, the most important fragment) has been clarified. O. Giordano emphasizes the historian's hostility to the millennial ideas of Papias. B. Gustafsson notes that Eusebius uncharacteristically gives only vague references and may have been working with selections. Grant (1974) makes sense of some textual difficulties in Eusebius with the assumption that Eusebius's attitude toward Papias changed from favorable to hostile.

Elucidation of the meaning of Papias's prologue and his comments on Mark and Matthew (found in Eusebius) owes something now to the view that Papias was trained in rhetoric and used its categories to analyze the tradition and the literary character of the Gospels (Taylor: 75–90; Grant, 1961:14–19; Schoedel, 1967:97–98, 101, 106–07; Kürzinger, 1960, 1963, 1977). At the same time, the Jewish-Christian substance of Papias's thought has also received strong emphasis (Daniélou, 1964:45–49, 380–83; Schoedel, 1967:94– 127). L. Gry (1944, 1946) has carefully worked out the intricate background to the millennialism of the first fragment which is taken from Irenaeus (but is surely wrong in thinking that chiliastic ideas were interpolated into the work of Papias). K. Beyschlag's identification of gnostic themes that Papias has reoriented in a Jewish-Christian direction (1961) is ingenious but tenuous.[28]

There is some suggestion in the fragments that Papias had a polemical purpose in writing. He has long been viewed as an opponent of gnosticism (see Wotke: 976). But Paul has also been suggested (Annand: 46, 49; Nielsen). And W. Bauer names Paul, Luke, and John as well as gnosticism (1971:184–89, 214–15). But J. Munck is perhaps right in regarding the evidence as too slight for such conclusions (1959).

Papias is concerned, however, about the reliability of the tradition on the words and deeds of Jesus, and certain preferences are shown. A. F. Walls has made the useful point that the preference for oral tradition does not involve a negative evaluation of the written sources. Most think that Mark with his lack of "order" is being contrasted by Papias with Matthew. But

---

[28] The grotesque figure of Judas in the third fragment has been interpreted against a broader religio-historical background by J. Herber. It may also owe something to the exegesis of Psalm passages woven into the background of the story of Judas in the NT (Schweizer, 1958:46). And there are the standard Jewish parallels (Schoedel, 1967:112).

others have suggested Luke (Grant, 1943:218–22; Munck, 1962:251)[29] or John (Grant, 1961:14–19). But knowledge of Luke or John by Papias seems difficult to sustain (see Annand).[30]

The following suggestions about Papias's views of Mark have been made: that Papias was really speaking about John Mark as author of the Fourth Gospel (Parker); that he had in mind Q (Moule and Stephenson); that he was speaking about a gospel of Mark distinct from the one in the NT (Deeks); that the mention of Mark's disorder comes down to a complaint about its incompleteness (Kleist, 1945; Schoedel, 1967:106); that Papias is speaking about a second edition of the Gospel, to which the author added "some things"—that is, a few things (Mullins, 1960, 1976); that the text should be emended so that Mark is praised for having written "not at all hastily" (Rigg); that Papias does not refer to Mark as Peter's "translator" but is commenting on the literary form of Mark (Kürzinger, 1960, 1977; but the rhetorical categories are made to work too hard in denying the reference to translation); that Mark is seen as playing the role of methurgamen (Gächter; Stauffer); that the view just mentioned cannot appeal so assuredly to the appearance of the formula "neither adding or taking anything away" (van Unnik, 1949, 1963; cf. Schäublin); and that as far as the historical value of the note is concerned, there is some agreement only on the possibility that it is John Mark to whom Papias refers and that the former in fact wrote our Gospel of Mark (see Niederwimmer).

The following points on Papias's view of Matthew have been advanced: that Papias does not have in mind Matthew but Q (Solages); or (what is surely closer to the truth) that the term *logia* cannot be taken to refer to collections of sayings like Q (Gryson); that Papias is not referring to a translation of Matthew from a Semitic original (Kürzinger, 1960, 1963; but again this seems strained); that Papias is offering suggestions to account for the differences between the gospels known to him (Munck, 1962); and (against most NT introductions) that Papias has a good chance of being historically right about Matthew (Petrie).

Papias's presumed attestation to John in the "anti-Marcionite prologues" has been given some credence (see Grant, 1947; Braun, 1959:345–55), but it rests on a very fragile basis (Gutwenger, 1946; Heard, 1955). At the same time, the use of other notices in Papias definitely to sever the link between the apostle John and the Gospel of John also depends on very tenuous arguments (see Braun, 1959:357–64, 378–88, 407–11). There may in fact be traces of Papias's use of the Gospel and of Revelation (Grant, 1947).

---

[29] R. Annand (50–51) suggests that Luke was reacting to Papias in claiming to write an orderly account.

[30] R. G. Heard argues that the fragments of Papias show no actual use of any of our Gospels (1954a).

Papias probably found the *pericope adulterae* in the *Gospel according to the Hebrews* (Becker: 92–116). His use of 1 John and 1 Peter goes uncontested.

The chain of tradition in which Papias claims to stand for his knowledge of the primitive period was perhaps purposely constructed in an ambiguous way. In any event, the best analysis of the meaning of the terms involved (elders, disciples) is provided by Munck (1959). Although there are no lexical or grammatical reasons for denying that Papias claims direct as well as indirect contact with the apostles of Jesus, it is likely that he states the case more precisely when he claims only an indirect knowledge of what the "elders" (who may or may not be the apostles) said (see Beyschlag, 1961:277). It is still held that in this connection Papias did not refer to two Johns (Bligh), but this seems unlikely (Munck, 1959; cf. Braun, 1959:357-64).

Finally, it appears that a relatively early date for Papias (late first or early second century) is now preferable (Gutwenger, 1947; Schoedel, 1967:91–92).

The book by Körtner may be singled out from the studies published since the completion of this survey as a thorough investigation of all problems affecting the text and interpretation of the fragments of Papias.

BIBLIOGRAPHY

Adam, Alfred
1957   "Erwägungen zur Herkunft der Didache." *ZKG* 68: 1–47
1965   *Lehrbuch der Dogmengeschichte*, Vol. 1, *Die Zeit der alten Kirche*. Gütersloh: Mohn.

Aland, Kurt
1960   "Der Tod des Petrus in Rom: Bemerkungen zu seiner Bestreitung durch Karl Heussi." Pp. 35–104 in *Kirchengeschichtliche Entwürfe*. Gütersloh: Mohn.

Altaner, Berthold
1950   "Neues zum Verständnis von 1 Klemens 5,1–6,2." *Historisches Jahrbuch der Görresgesellschaft* 62: 25–30.
1952   "Zum Problem der Lateinischen Doctrina Apostolorum." *VC* 6: 160–67.
1960   *Patrology*. New York: Herder & Herder.

Altaner, Berthold, and Alfred Stuiber
1978   *Patrologie*. 8th ed. Freiburg im Breisgau: Herder.

Andrén, Olaf C. T.
1960   *Rättfärdighet och frid: en studie i det första Clemensbrevet*. Uppsala: Almquist & Wiksell. [English summary provided.]

Andry, Carl F.
1951   "Barnabae Epist. Ver. DCCCL." *JBL* 70: 233–38.

Annand, R.
1956   "Papias and the Four Gospels." *SJT* 9: 46–62.

Audet, Jean-Paul
1952 "Affinités littéraires et doctrinales du 'Manuel de Discipline.'" *RB* 59: 219–38.
1953 "Affinités littéraires et doctrinales du Manuel de Discipline." *RB* 60: 41–82.
1958 *La Didachè.* EBib. Paris: Gabalda.
1963 "L'hypothèse des Testimonia: Remarques autour d'un livre récent." *RB* 70: 381–405.

Aune, David E.
1978 "Herm. Man. 11.2: Christian False Prophets Who Say What People Wish to Hear." *JBL* 97: 103–4.

Bacchiocchi, Samuele
1977 *From Sabbath to Sunday: A Historical Investigation of the Rise of Sunday Observance in Early Christianity.* Rome: Pontifical Gregorian University.

Bakhuizen van den Brink, J. N.
1975 "Reconciliation in the Early Fathers." *Studia Patristica 13:* 90–106.

Baltzer, Klaus
1971 *The Covenant Formulary.* Philadelphia: Fortress.

Bammel, Ernst
1961 "Schema und Vorlage von Didache 16." *Studia Patristica 4:* 253–62.

Barberet, F.
1958 "La formule ZHN ΤΩΙ ΘΕΩΙ dans le Pasteur d'Hermas. *RSR* 46: 379–407.

Barnard, L. W.
1958a "The Date of the Epistle of Barnabas: A Document of Early Egyptian Christianity." *JEA* 44: 101–7.
1958b "The Problem of the Epistle of Barnabas." *CQR* 159: 211–30.
1959 "The Epistle of Barnabas and the Tannaitic Catechism." *ATR* 41: 177–90.
1961 "A Note in Barnabas 6,8–17." *Studia Patristica 4:* 263–67.
1963 "The Background of St. Ignatius of Antioch." *VC* 17: 193–206.
1964 "The Testimonium Concerning the Stone in the New Testament and in the Epistle of Barnabas." *SE* 3: 306–13.
1966a "Hermas and Judaism." *Studia Patristica 8:* 3–9.
1966b "Hermas, the Church and Judaism." Pp. 151–63 in Barnard, 1966j.
1966c "Is the Epistle of Barnabas a Paschal Homily?" Pp. 73–85 in Barnard, 1966j. [= *VC* 15 (1961) 8–22.]
1966d "Judaism in Egypt, A.D. 70–135." Pp. 41–55 in Barnard, 1966j.
1966e "St. Clement of Rome and the Persecution of Domitian." Pp. 5–18 in Barnard, 1966j.
1966f "St. Stephen and Early Alexandrian Christianity." Pp. 57–72 in Barnard, 1966j. [= *NTS* 7 (1960) 31–45.]
1966g "The Dead Sea Scrolls, Barnabas, the Didache, and the Later History of the 'Two Ways.'" Pp. 87–107 in Barnard, 1966j. [= *SJT* 13 (1960) 45–59.]
1966h "The Problem of Saint Polycarp's Epistle to the Philippians." Pp. 31–39 in Barnard, 1966j. [= *CQR* 163 (1962) 421–30.]
1966i "The Use of Testimonies in the Early Church and in the Epistle of Barnabas." Pp. 109–35 in Barnard, 1966j.

476 New Testament

1966j   *Studies in the Apostolic Fathers and Their Background.* Oxford: Blackwell.
1968   "The Shepherd of Hermas in Recent Study." *HeyJ* 9: 29–36.
1970   "In Defence of Pseudo-Pionius' Account of Saint Polycarp's Martyrdom." Pp. 192–204 in *Kyriakon: Festschrift Johannes Quasten*, vol. 1. 2 vols. Ed. P. Granfield and J. A. Jungmann. Münster: Aschendorff.

Barnes, Timothy D.
1967   "A Note on Polycarp." *JTS* n.s. 18: 433–37.
1968   "Pre-Decian Acta Martyrum." *JTS* n.s. 19: 510–14.

Barrett, Charles Kingsley
1976   "Jews and Judaizers in the Epistles of Ignatius." Pp. 220–44 in *Jews, Greeks and Christians: Religious Cultures in Late Antiquity: Essays in Honor of William David Davies.* Ed. R. Hamerton-Kelly and R. Scroggs. SJLA 21. Leiden: Brill.

Bartelink, Gerhardus Johanus Marinus
1952   *Lexicologisch-semantische studie over de taal van de Apostolische Vaders.* Utrecht: Beijers.

Bartsch, Hans-Werner
1940   *Gnostisches Gut und Gemeindetradition bei Ignatius von Antiochien.* Gütersloh: Bertelsmann.
1965   "Röm. 9,5 und 1. Clem. 32,4: Eine notwendige Konjektur im Römerbrief." *TZ* 21: 401–9.

Basile, Basile
1968   "Un ancien témoin arabe des lettres d'Ignace d'Antioche." *Melto, Recherches Orientales* 4: 107–91.

Bauckham, R. J.
1974   "The Great Tribulation in the Shepherd of Hermas." *JTS* n.s. 25: 27–40.

Bauer, Walter
1920   *Die Apostolischen Väter:* Vol. 2, *Die Briefe des Ignatius von Antiocheia und der Polykarpbrief.* HNTSup. Tübingen: Mohr-Siebeck.
1957   *A Greek-English Lexicon of the New Testament and Other Early Christian Literature.* Ed. W. F. Arndt and F. W. Gingrich. Chicago: University of Chicago Press. [2d ed., revised and augmented by F. W. Gingrich and F. W. Danker, 1979.]
1971   *Orthodoxy and Heresy in Earliest Christianity.* Trans. Philadelphia Seminar on Christian Origins. Ed. R. A. Kraft and G. Krodel. Philadelphia: Fortress. [The German original appeared in 1934 and was reprinted in 1964 with some corrections and additions by Georg Strecker.]

Bausone, Carla
1972   "Aspetti dell' ecclesiologia de Pastore di Hermas." *Studia Patristica* 11: 101–6.

Becker, Ulrich
1963   *Jesus und die Ehebrecherin: Untersuchungen zur Text- und Überlieferungsgeschichte von Joh. 7,53–8,11.* BZNW 28. Berlin: Töpelmann.

Benoit, André
1953   *Le baptême chrétien au second siècle: la théologie des pères.* Études d'histoire et de philosophie religieuses 43. Paris: Presses universitaires de France.

Berthouoz, Roger
1971   "Le père, le fils et le saint-esprit d'après les lettres d'Ignace d'Anti-
        oche." *Freiburger Zeitschrift für Philosophie und Theologie* 18:
        397–418.

Betz, Hans Dieter
1961   *Lukian von Samosata und das Neue Testament.* TU 76. Berlin:
        Akademie-Verlag.
1975, ed. *Plutarch's Theological Writings and Early Christian Literature.*
        SCHNT 3. Leiden: Brill.
1978, ed. *Plutarch's Ethical Writings and Early Christian Literature.* SCHNT 4.
        Leiden: Brill.

Betz, Johannes
1969   "Die Eucharistie in der Didache." *Archiv für Liturgiewissenschaft* 11:
        10–39.

Beyschlag, Karlmann
1961   "Herkunft und Eigenart der Papiasfragmente." *Studia Patristica 4:*
        268–80.
1966   *Clemens Romanus und der Frühkatholizismus.* BHT 35. Tübingen:
        Mohr-Siebeck.
1972   "Zur EIPHNH BAΘEIA (I Clem, 2,2)." *VC* 26: 18–23.

Bieder, Werner
1956a   "Das Abendmahl im christlichen Lebenszusammenhang bei Ignatius
        von Antiochia." *EvT* 16: 75–97.
1956b   "Zur Deutung des kirchlichen Schweigens bei Ignatius von Antio-
        chia." *TZ* 12: 28–43.

Bihlmeyer, Karl
1956   *Die Apostolischen Väter, Neubearbeitung der Funkschen Ausgabe.*
        Zweite Auflage, mit einem Nachtrag von Wilhelm Schneemelcher.
        Tübingen: Mohr-Siebeck.

Bjerkelund, Carl J.
1967   *Parakalô: Form, Funktion und Sinn der parakalô-Sätze in der pauli-
        nischen Briefen.* Oslo: Universitetsforlaget.

Bligh, J. F.
1952   "The Prologue of Papias." *TS* 13: 234–40.

Boismard, M.-É.
1948   "Clément de Rome et l'évangile de Jean." *RB* 55: 376–87.

Bommes, Karin
1976   *Weizen Gottes: Untersuchungen zur Theologie des Martyriums bei
        Ignatius von Antiochien.* Theophaneia 27. Cologne and Bonn: Peter
        Hanstein.

Bosio, C.
1966   "La dottrina spirituale di Sant' Ignazio d'Antiochia." *Salesianum* 28:
        519–51.

Bouyer, Louis
1963   *The Spirituality of the New Testament and the Fathers.* Paris and New
        York: Desclée de Brouwer.

Bovon-Thurneyson, A.
1973   "Ethik und Eschatologie im Philipperbrief des Polycarps von Smyr-
        na." *TZ* 29: 241–56.

Bower, Richard A.
1974   "The Meaning of ΕΠΙΤΥΓΧΑΝΩ in the Epistles of St. Ignatius of Antioch." *VC* 28: 1–14.

Braun, F.-M.
1958   "La lettre de Barnabé et l'évangile de Saint Jean." *NTS* 4: 119–24.
1959   *Jean le Théologien et son évangile dans l'église ancienne.* EBib. Paris: Gabalda.

Brown, Milton Perry
1963   *The Authentic Writings of Ignatius.* Durham, NC: Duke University Press.

Brox, Norbert
1961   *Zeuge und Märtyrer: Untersuchungen zur frühchristlichen Zeugnis-Terminologie.* SANT 5. Munich: Kösel.
1963   " 'Zeuge seiner Leiden': Zum Verständnis der Interpolation Ign. Röm. II,2." *ZKT* 85: 218–20.
1972   "The Conflict Between Anicetus and Polycarp." *Concilium* 71: 37–45.

Bruce, F. F.
1973   "Eschatology in the Apostolic Fathers." Pp. 77–89 in *The Heritage of the Early Church.* Ed. David Neiman and Margaret Schatkin. Orientalia Christiana Analecta 195. Rome: Pontificium Institutum Studiorum Orientalium.

Brunner, Gerbert
1972   *Die theologische Mitte des ersten Klemensbriefs.* Frankfurter Theologische Studien 11. Frankfurt am Main: Knecht.

Bultmann, Rudolf
1955   *Theology of the New Testament.* 2 vols. Tr. Kendrick Grobel. New York: Scribner.
1960   "Ignatius and Paul." Pp. 267–77 in his *Existence and Faith.* Ed. Shubert Ogden. New York: World.

Bumpus, Harold Bertram
1972   *The Christological Awareness of Clement of Rome and Its Sources.* New York: Cambridge University Press.

Burger, J.-D.
1946   "L'énigme de Barnabé." *Museum Helveticum* 3: 180–93.

Burke, P.
1970   "The Monarchical Episcopate at the End of the First Century." *JES* 7: 499–518.

Butler, B. C.
1960   "The Literary Relations of Didache Ch. XVI." *JTS* n.s. 11: 265–83.
1961   "The 'Two Ways' in the Didache." *JTS* n.s. 12: 27–38.

Cabaniss, Alan
1956   "Wisdom 18:14f.: An Early Christmas Text." *VC* 10: 97–102.

Camelot, Pierre-Thomas
1951   *Ignace d'Antioche, Polycarpe de Smyrne, Lettres, Martyre de Polycarpe.* SC 10. Paris: Cerf. [2d ed. 1957.]
1971   "Ignace d'Antioche." *Dictionnaire de Spiritualité 7. 1250–66.*

Campenhausen, Hans F. von
1951   *Polykarp von Smyrna und die Pastoralbriefe.* Jahrgang 1951, 2. Abteilung in Sitzungsberichte der Heidelberger Akademie der Wissenschaften, Philosophisch-historische Klasse 36. Heidelberg: Carl Winter.

1952   Review of Eggenberger. *TLZ* 77: 38–39.
1957   *Bearbeitungen und Interpolationen des Polykarpmartyriums.* Jahrgang 1957, 3. Abteilung in Sitzungsberichte der Heidelberger Akademie der Wissenschaften, Philosophisch-historische Klasse. Heidelberg: Carl Winter.
1964   *Die Idee des Martyriums in der alte Kirche.* 2d ed. Göttingen: Vandenhoeck & Ruprecht.
1969   *Ecclesiastical Authority and Spiritual Power in the Church of the First Three Centuries.* Trans. J. A. Baker. Stanford, CA: Stanford University Press. [Based on the edition of 1953 rather than on the extensively revised edition of 1963.]
1972   "Das Bekenntnis im Urchristentum." *ZNW* 63: 210–53.
1974   "Ostertermin oder Osterfasten? Zum Verständnis des Irenäusbriefs an Viktor (Eus. Hist. Eccl. 5, 24, 12–17)." *VC* 28: 114–38.

Cerfaux, Lucien
1959   "La multiplication des pains dans la liturgie de la Didachè (Did., IX, 4)." *Bib* 40: 943–58.

Chadwick, Henry
1950   "The Silence of Bishops in Ignatius." *HTR* 43: 169–72.
1961   "Justification by Faith and Hospitality." *Studia Patristica* 4: 281–85.

Clark, Kenneth Willis
1961   "The Sins of Hermas." Pp. 102–9 in *Early Christian Origins: Studies in Honor of Harold R. Willoughby.* Ed. Allen P. Wikgren. Chicago: Quadrangle.

Cockerill, Gareth L.
1978   "Heb 1:1–14, 1 Clem 36:1–6 and the High Priest Title." *JBL* 97: 437–40.

Coleborne, W.
1969   "A Linguistic Approach to the Problem of Structure and Composition of the Shepherd of Hermas." *Colloquium* 3: 133–42.
1970   "The Shepherd of Hermas, A Case for Multiple Authorship and Some Implications." *Studia Patristica* 10: 65–70.

Colson, Jean
1956   *Les fonctions écclesiales aux deux premiers siècles.* Textes et études théologiques. Paris: Desclée de Brouwer.
1961   "Agapè chez Saint-Ignace d'Antioche." *Studia Partistica* 3: 341–53.

Corwin, Virginia
1960   *St. Ignatius and Christianity in Antioch.* New Haven, CT: Yale University Press.

Crehan, J. H.
1957   "A New Fragment of Ignatius' *Ad Polycarpum.*" *Studia Patristica* 1: 23–32.

Cuming, Geoffrey J.
1974   "The New Testament Foundation for Common Prayer." *Studia Liturgica* 10: 88–105.

Dahl, Nils Alstrup
1950   "La terre où coulent le lait et le miel selon Barnabé 6.8–19." Pp. 62–70 in *Aux sources de la tradition Chrétienne: Mélanges offerts à M. Maurice Goguel.* Neuchâtel and Paris: Delachaux & Niestlé.
1964   "Der Erstgeborene Satans und der Vater des Teufels (Polyk. 7:1 und Joh. 8:44)." Pp. 70–84 in *Apophoreta: Festschrift für Ernst Haenchen*

zu seinem siebzigsten Geburtstag. Ed. W. Eltester and F. H. Kettler. BZNW 30. Berlin: Töpelmann.

Daniélou, Jean
1948   "La typologie millenariste de la semaine dans le Christianisme primitif." *VC* 2: 1–16.
1957   "Trinité et angelologie dans la théologie judeo-chrétienne." *RSR* 45: 5–41.
1963   *Primitive Christian Symbols.* Baltimore, MD: Helicon.
1964   *The Theology of Jewish Christianity.* A History of Early Christian Doctrine before the Council of Nicaea 1. Philadelphia: Westminster. [A revision of the French work of 1958.]

Dassmann, Ernst
1974   "Zur Entstehung des Monepiskopats." *JAC* 17: 74–90.

Daube, David
1965   "Τρία μυστήρια κραυγῆς: Ignatius, Ephesians, XIX,1." *JTS* n.s. 16: 128–29.

Davids, Adelbert
1973   "Irrtum und Häresie: 1 Clem.–Ignatius von Antiochien–Justinus." *Kairos* 15: 165–87.

Davies, G. I.
1977   Review of Hagner. *JTS* n.s. 28: 170–75.

Davies, Stevan L.
1976   "The Predicament of Ignatius of Antioch." *VC* 30: 175–80.

Deeks, David D.
1977   "Papias Revisited." *ExpTim* 88: 296–301, 324–29.

Dehandschutter, Boudewijn
1979   *Martyrium Polycarpi: Een literair-kritische studie.* BETL 52. Louvain: Leuven University Press.

Deichgräber, Reinhard
1967   *Gotteshymnus und Christushymnus in der frühen Christenheit: Untersuchungen zu Form, Sprache und Stil der früchristlichen Hymnen.* SUNT 5. Göttingen: Vandenhoeck & Ruprecht.

Dibelius, Martin
1915   "Die Christianisierung einer hellenistischen Formel." *Neue Jahrbucher für das klassische Altertumswissenschaft* 35/6: 224–36.
1923   *Die Apostolischen Väter:* Vol. 4, *Der Hirt des Hermas.* HNTSup. Tübingen: Mohr-Siebeck.

Dinkler, Erich
1959   "Die Petrus-Rom-Frage: Ein Forschungsbericht." *TRu* 25: 289–335.

Donahue, P. J.
1978   "Jewish Christianity in the Letters of Ignatius of Antioch." *VC* 32: 81–93.

Donfried, Karl Paul
1973   "The Theology of Second Clement." *HTR* 66: 487–501.
1974   *The Setting of Second Clement in Early Christianity.* NovTSup 38. Leiden: Brill.

Eggenberger, Christian
1951   *Die Quellen der politischen Ethik des 1. Klemensbriefes.* Zurich: Zwingli.

Eijk, Ton H. C. van
1974   *La résurrection des morts chez les pères apostoliques.* Théologie historique 25. Paris: Beauchesne.

Eltester, Walter
1957   "Schöpfungsoffenbarung und natürliche Theologie im frühen Christentum." *NTS* 3: 93–114.

Elze, Martin
1963   *Überlieferungsgeschichtliche Untersuchungen zur Christologie der Ignatiusbriefe.* Tübingen: Univ. Bibl.
1974   "Häresie und Einheit der Kirche im 2. Jahrhundert." *ZTK* 71: 389–409.

Festugière, André-Jean
1950   *La révélation d'Hermès Trismégiste:* Vol. 1, *L'astrologie et les sciences occultes.* 3d ed. EBib. Paris: Gabalda.

Fischel, H. A.
1946–47   "Martyr and Prophet." *JQR* 37: 265–80, 363–86.

Fischer, Joseph A.
1956   *Die Apostolischen Väter.* Darmstadt: Wissenschaftliche Buchgesellschaft. [5th ed. 1966.]

Flesseman-van Leer, E.
1954–55   "Het Oude Testament bij de Apostolische Vaders en de Apologeten." *NedTTs* 9: 230–44.

Flórez, S. Folgado
1972   "El binomio Cristo-Iglesia en el 'Pastor' de Hermas." *Cuidad de Dios* 185: 639–70.

Ford, J. Massyngbaerde
1969   "A Possible Liturgical Background to the Shepherd of Hermas." *RevQ* 6: 531–51.

Frei, Hans W.
1974,   "Metanoia in 'Hirten' des Hermas." *Internationale Kirchliche*
1975   *Zeitschrift* 64: 118–39, 189–202; 65: 120–38, 176–204.

Fridrichsen, Anton
1946   "Propter Invidiam: Note sur 1 Clem V." *Eranos* 44: 161–71.

Froidevaux, Léon-Marie
1956   "Sur trois textes cités par Saint Irenée." *RSR* 44: 408–21.

Gächter, P.
1936   "Die Dolmetscher des Apostel." *ZKT* 60: 161–87.

Galtier, Paul
1951   *Aux origines du sacrement de pénitence.* Rome: Gregorian University.

Gamber, Klaus
1959   "Das Papyrusfragment zur Markusliturgie und das Eucharistiegebet im Clemensbrief." *Ostkirchliche Studien* 8: 31–45.

Garciadego, Alejandro
1953   *Katholiké Ekklesía: El significado de epiteto "catholica" aplicado a "Iglesia" desde San Ignacio de Antioquía hasta Orígenes.* Mexico City: Editorial Jus.

Giet, Stanislas
1955   "Le témoignage de Clément de Rome, I: Sur la venue à Rome de saint Pierre." *RevScRel* 29: 123–36.

1955   "Le témoignage de Clément de Rome, II: Sur la cause des persécutions romaines." *RevScRel* 29: 333–45.
1961   "L'Apocalypse d'Hermas et la Pénitence." *Studia Patristica 3:* 214–18.
1963   *Hermas et les Pasteurs.* Paris: Presses universitaires de France.
1966a   "De trois expressions: auprès de la tour, la place inférieure, et les premiers murs, dans le Pasteur d'Hermas." *Studia Patristica 8:* 24–29.
1966b   "Les trois auteurs du Pasteur d'Hermas." *Studia Patristica 8:* 10–23.
1970a   "L'énigme de la Didachè." *Studia Patristica 10:* 84–94.
1970b   *L'énigme de la Didachè.* Publications de la faculté des lettres de l'université de Strasbourg 149. Paris: Ophrys.

Giordano, O.
1970   "I commentari di Papias di Ierapoli." *L'antiquité classique* 39: 106–46.

Glimm, Francis X., Joseph M. F. Marique and Gerald G. Walsh
1947   *The Apostolic Fathers.* The Fathers of the Church 1. Washington: Catholic University of America.

Glover, Richard
1958   "The Didache's Quotations and the Synoptic Gospels." *NTS* 5: 12–29.

Gokey, Francis X.
1961   *The Terminology for the Devil and Evil Spirits in the Apostolic Fathers.* Catholic University of America Patristic Studies 93. Washington: Catholic University of America.

Goodenough, Erwin R.
1945   "John a Primitive Gospel." *JBL* 64: 145–82.

Goodspeed, Edgar Johnson
1945   "The Didache, Barnabas and the Doctrina." *ATR* 27: 228–47.

Goppelt, Leonhard
1954   *Christentum und Judentum im ersten und zweiten Jahrhundert.* Gütersloh: Bertelsmann.

Grant, Robert M.
1943   "Papias and the Gospels." *ATR* 25: 218–22.
1947   "A Note on Papias." *ATR* 29: 171–72.
1960   "The Appeal to the Early Fathers." *JTS* n.s. 11: 13–24.
1961   *The Earliest Lives of Jesus.* New York: Harper.
1962   "The Apostolic Fathers' First Thousand Years." *CH* 31: 421–29.
1964a   Review of Giet, 1963. *Gnomon* 36: 357–59.
1964b   *The Apostolic Fathers:* Vol. 1, *An Introduction.* New York: Thomas Nelson.
1966   *The Apostolic Fathers:* Vol. 4, *Ignatius of Antioch.* Camden, NJ: Thomas Nelson.
1967a   "Scripture and Tradition in Ignatius of Antioch." Pp. 37–54 in Grant, *After the New Testament.* Philadelphia: Fortress.
1967b   "The Study of the Early Fathers in Modern Times." Pp. 3–19 in Grant, *After the New Testament.* Philadelphia: Fortress. [= *ATR* 44 (1967) 280–94.]
1967c   "The Use of the Early Fathers: From Irenaeus to John of Damascus." Pp. 20–34 in Grant, *After the New Testament.* Philadelphia: Fortress.
1974   "Papias in Eusebius' Church History." Pp. 209–13 in *Mélanges d'histoire des religions offerts à Henri-Charles Puech.* Paris: Presses universitaires de France.

Grant, Robert M., and Holt H. Graham
  1965   *The Apostolic Fathers:* Vol. 2, *First and Second Clement.* New York: Thomas Nelson.

Grégoire, H., and P. Orgels
  1951   "La veritable date du martyre de S. Polycarpe et le 'Corpus Poly-carpianum.'" *Analecta Bollandiana* 69: 1–38.

Gribbard, S. M.
  1966   "The Eucharist in the Ignatian Epistles." *Studia Patristica* 8: 214–18.

Griffe, E.
  1951   "Á propos de la date du martyre de saint Polycarpe." *Bulletin de littérature ecclésiastique* 52: 170–77.
  1953   "Un nouvel article sur la date du martyre de saint Polycarpe." *Bulletin de littérature ecclésiastique* 54: 178–81.

Grobel, Kendrick
  1951   "Shepherd of Hermas, Parable II." Pp. 50–55 in *Vanderbilt Studies in the Humanities I.* Ed. R. C. Beatty, J. P. Hyatt, and M. K. Spears. Nashville: Vanderbilt University Press.

Gry, L.
  1944   "Le Papias des belles promesses messianiques." *Vivre et penser* 3: 112–24.
  1946   "Henoch X, 19 et les belles promesses de Papias." *RB* 53: 197–206.

Gryson, R.
  1965   "Á propos du témoignage de Papias sur Matthieu: Le sens du mot *logion* chez les Pères du IIe siècle." *ETL* 41: 530–47.

Gülzow, Hennecke
  1969   *Christentum und Sklaverei in den ersten drei Jahrhunderten.* Bonn: Rudolf Habelt.

Günther, E.
  1956   "Zeuge und Martyrer." *ZNW* 47: 145–61.

Gustafsson, B.
  1961   "Eusebius' Principles in Handling his Sources as Found in his Church History." *Studia Patristica* 4: 429–41.

Gutwenger, E.
  1946   "The Anti-Marcionite Prologues." *TS* 7: 393–409.
  1947   "Papias, Eine chronologische Studie." *ZKT* 69: 385–416.

Guy, Fritz
  1964   " 'The Lord's Day' In the Letter of Ignatius to the Magnesians." *AUSS* 2: 1–17.

Haarlem, A. van
  1964–65 "De kerk in de brieven van S. Ignatius van Antiochië." *NedTTs* 19: 112–34.

Hagner, Donald A.
  1973   *The Use of the Old and New Testaments in Clement of Rome.* NovTSup 34. Leiden: Brill.

Hall, S. G.
  1966   "Repentance in I Clement." *Studia Patristica* 8: 30–43.

Hamman, A.
  1961   "La signification de σφραγίς dans le Pasteur d'Hermas." *Studia Patristica* 4: 286–90.

1973   "Existe-t-il un langage trinitaire chez les Pères Apostoliques."
        Augustinianum 13: 455–58.

Hannah, Jack W.
1960   "The Setting of the Ignatian Long Recension." *JBL* 79: 221–38.

Hanson, A. T.
1970   "Hodayoth vi and viii and Hermas *Sim.* VIII." *Studia Patristica 10*:
        105–8.

Harrison, Percy Neale
1936   *Polycarp's Two Epistles to the Philippians.* Cambridge: University
        Press.

Heard, R. G.
1954a   "Papias' Quotations from the New Testament." *NTS* 1: 130–34.
1954b   "The ἀπομνημονεύματα in Papias, Justin, and Irenaeus." *NTS* 1:
        122–29.
1955   "The Old Gospel Prologues." *JTS* n.s. 6: 1–16.

Helfritz, Hartwig
1968   "ΟΙ ΟΥΡΑΝΟΙ ΤΗΙ ΔΙΟΙΚΗΣΕΙ ΑΥΤΟΥ ΣΑΛΕΥΟΜΕΝΟΙ ΕΝ
        ΕΙΡΗΝΗΙ ΥΠΟΤΑΣΣΟΝΤΑΙ ΑΥΤΩΙ." *VC* 22: 1–7.

Herber, J.
1945   "La mort de Judas." *RHR* 129/30: 47–56.

Hermans, A.
1959   "Le Pseudo-Barnabé est-il millénariste?" *ETL* 35: 849–76.

Hilhorst, A.
1976   *Sémitismes et latinismes dans le Pasteur d'Hermas.* Graecitas Chris-
        tianorum Primaeva 5. Nijmegen: Dekker & van de Vegt.

Hörmann, Karl
1952   *Leben in Christus: Zusammenhänge zwischen Dogma und Sitte bei den
        apostolischen Vätern.* Vienna: Herold.
1956   "Das Geistreden des hl. Ignatius von Antiochien." *Jahrbuch für
        mystische Theologie* 2: 39–53.

Jaeger, Werner
1959   "Echo eines unerkannten Tragikerfragments in Clemens' Brief an die
        Korinther." *Rheinisches Museum für Philologie* 102: 330–40.
1961   *Early Christianity and Greek Paideia.* Cambridge, MA: Belknap Press
        of Harvard University.

Jaubert, Annie
1964a   "Les sources de la conception militaire de l'église en 1 Clement 37."
        VC 18: 74–84.
1964b   "Thèmes Lévitiques dans la Prima Clementis." *VC* 18: 193–203.
1971   *Clément de Rome, Épître aux Corinthiens.* SC 167. Paris: Cerf.

Javierre, Antonio M.
1958   *La primera 'diadoché' de la patristica y los 'ellogimoi' de Clemente
        Romano.* Turin: Societa editrice internazionale.

Jeremias, Joachim
1964   *Unknown Sayings of Jesus.* 2d English edition. London: SPCK.

Johnson, Sherman Elbridge
1946   "A Subsidiary Motive for the Writing of the Didache." Pp. 107–22 in
        Munera Studiosa. Studies Presented to W. H. P. Hatch. Ed. M. H.
        Shepherd and S. E. Johnson. Cambridge: Episcopal Theological
        School.

Joly, Robert
   1953a   "Judaisme, Christianisme et Hellénisme dans le Pasteur d'Hermas."
               La nouvelle Clio 5: 394–406.
   1953b   "Philologie et Psychanalyse: C. G. Jung et le 'Pasteur' d'Hermas."
               L'antiquité classique 22: 422–28.
   1955   "La doctrine pénitentielle du Pasteur d'Hermas et l'exégèse récente."
               RHR 147: 32–49.
   1958   *Hermas Le Pasteur.* SC 53. Paris: Cerf. [2d ed. 1968.]
   1967   "Hermas et le Pasteur." *VC* 21: 201–18.
   1979   *Le Dossier d'Ignace d'Antioche.* Université libre de Bruxelles, Faculté
               de Philosophie et Lettres 69. Brussels: Éditions de l'Université de
               Bruxelles.

Jonge, H. J. de
   1978   "On the Origin of the Term 'Apostolic Fathers'." *JTS* n.s. 29: 503–5.

Jouassard, G.
   1950   "Les épîtres expédiées de Troas par saint Ignace d'Antioche." Pp.
               213–21 in *Memorial J. Chaîne.* Bibliothèque de la faculté catholique
               de théologie de Lyon 5. Lyon: Facultés catholiques.
   1951–52 "Aux origines du culte des martyres dans le christianisme: Saint
               Ignace d'Antioche, Rom. II,2." *RSR* 39: 361–67.
   1957   "Le groupement des Pères dits apostoliques." *MScRel* 14: 129–34.

Jourjon, Maurice
   1967   "La présidence de l'eucharisté chez Ignace d'Antioche." *Lumière et
               vie* 84: 26–32.

Kamlah, Ehrhard
   1964   *Die Form der katalogischen Paränese im Neuen Testament.* WUNT 7.
               Tübingen: Mohr-Siebeck.

Käsemann, Ernst
   1946   Review of Bartsch, 1940. Pp. 131–36 in *Verkündigung und For-
               schung, Theologischer Jahresbericht 1942/46,* Lieferung 1/2. Munich:
               Kaiser.

Kelly, J. N. D.
   1950   *Early Christian Creeds.* London: Longmans. [2d ed. 1960.]
   1960   *Early Christian Doctrines.* New York: Harper & Row. [2d ed. 1978.]

Kettler, F. H.
   1954   "Enderwartung und himmlischer Stufenbau im Kirchenbegriff des
               nachapostolischen Zeitalters." *TLZ* 79: 385–92.
   1962   "Trinitäte." *RGG.* 3d ed. 6. 1025–32.

Kilpatrick, George D.
   1947   "A New Papyrus of the Shepherd of Hermas." *JTS* n.s. 48: 204–5.

Kittel, Gerhard
   1950/51 "Der Jakobusbrief und die Apostolischen Väter." *ZNW* 43: 54–112.

Klauser, Theodor
   1974a   "Christlicher Martyrerkult, heidnischer Heroenkult und spätjüdische
               Heiligenverehrung." Pp. 221–29 in *Gesammelte Arbeiten zur Litur-
               giegeschichte, Kirchengeschichte und Christlichen Archäologie.* Ed. E.
               Dassmann. JACSup 3. Münster: Aschendorff.
   1974b   "Taufet in lebendigen Wasser! Zum religions- und kulturgeschicht-
               lichen Verständnis von Didache 7,1–3." Pp. 177–83 in *Gesammelte
               Arbeiten.* Ed. E. Dassmann. JACSup 3. Münster: Aschendorff.

Kleist, James A.
1945   "Rereading the Papias Fragment on St. Mark." *Saint Louis University Studies*: Series A, Humanities 1, 1: 1–17. [St. Louis: St. Louis University.]
1946   *The Epistles of St. Clement of Rome and St. Ignatius of Antioch*. ACW 1. Westminster, MD: Newman.
1961   *The Didache, The Epistle of Barnabas, The Epistles and the Martyrdom of St. Polycarp, The Fragment of Papias, The Epistle to Diognetus.* ACW 6. Westminster, MD: Newman.

Klevinghaus, Johannes
1948   *Die theologische Stellung der apostolischen Väter zur alttestamentlichen Offenbarung.* BFCT 44,1. Gütersloh: Bertelsmann.

Knoch, Otto
1961   "Die Ausführungen des 1. Clemensbriefes über die kirchliche Verfassung im Spiegel der neueren Deutungen seit R. Sohm und A. Harnack." *TQ* 141: 385–407.
1964   *Eigenart und Bedeutung der Eschatologie im theologischen Aufriss des ersten Clemensbriefes.* Theophaneia 17. Bonn: Peter Hanstein.
1967   "Clemens Romanus und der Frühkatholizismus: Zu einem neuen Buch." *JAC* 10: 202–10.

Knopf, Rudolf
1920   *Die Apostolischen Väter:* Vol. 1, *Die Lehre der zwölf Apostel, Die zwei Clemensbriefe.* HNTSup. Tübingen: Mohr-Siebeck.

Koester, Helmut
1957a   "Geschichte und Kultus im Johannesevangelium und bei Ignatius von Antiochien." *ZTK* 54: 56–79. [English version in *JTC* 1 (1965) 111–23.]
1957b   *Synoptische Überlieferung bei den Apostolischen Vätern.* TU 65. Berlin: Akademie-Verlag.
1965   "GNOMAI DIAPHOROI: The Origin and Nature of Diversification in the History of Early Christianity." *HTR* 58: 279–318.

Köhler, Wolf-Dieter
1987   *Die Rezeption des Matthäusevangeliums in der Zeit vor Irenäus.* WUNT 2. Reihe 24. Tübingen: Mohr-Siebeck.

Körtner, Ulrich H. J.
1983   *Papias von Hierapolis: Ein Beitrag zur Geschichte des frühen Christentums.* FRLANT 133. Göttingen: Vandenhoeck & Ruprecht.

Kraft, Heinrich
1963   *Clavis Patrum Apostolicorum.* Munich: Kösel.
1975   "Die Anfänge des geistlichen Amts." *TLZ* 100: 81–98.

Kraft, Robert A.
1960   "Barnabas' Isaiah Text and the 'Testimony Book' Hypothesis." *JBL* 79: 336–50.
1961   "Barnabas' Isaiah Text and Melito's Paschal Homily." *JBL* 80: 371–73.
1965   *The Apostolic Fathers:* Vol. 3, *Barnabas and the Didache.* New York: Thomas Nelson.
1967   "An Unnoticed Papyrus Fragment of Barnabas." *VC* 21: 150–63.

Kretschmar, Georg
1972   "Christliches Passa im 2. Jahrhundert und die Ausbildung der christlichen Theologie." *RSR* 60: 287–323.

Kürzinger, Josef
1960   "Das Papiaszeugnis und die Erstgestalt des Matthäusevangelium." *BZ*
          n.s. 4: 19–38.
1963   "Irenaeus und sein Zeugnis zur Sprache des Matthäusevangeliums."
          NTS 10: 107–15.
1977   "Die Aussage des Papias von Hierapolis zur literarischen Form des
          Markusevangelium." *BZ* 21: 245–64.

Kwa, Joe Liang
1951   *Het begrip Deemoed in I Clemens.* Utrecht: Kemink.

Laeuchli, Samuel
1972   "The Drama of Replay." Pp. 69–126 in *Searching in the Syntax of
          Things: Essays by Maurice Friedman, T. Patrick Burke, and Samuel
          Laeuchli.* Philadelphia: Fortress Press.

Lana, Italo
1975   "La cristianizzazione di alcuni termini retorici nella lettera ai Corinti
          di Clemente." Pp. 110–18 in *Forma Futuri: Studi in onore del cardi-
          nale Michele Pellegrino.* Torino: Bottega d'Erasmo.

Lappa-Zizicas, Eurydice
1965   "Cinq fragments du Pasteur d'Hermas das un manuscrit de la biblio-
          thèque nationale de Paris." *RSR* 53: 251–56.

Lawson, John
1961   *A Theological and Historical Introduction to the Apostolic Fathers.*
          New York: Macmillan.

Layton, Bentley
1968   "The Source, Date and Transmission of Didache 1.3b-2.1." *HTR* 61:
          343–83.

Leder, Hans-Günter
1967   Review of Beyschlag, 1966. *TLZ* 92: 831–35.

Lefort, L.-Th.
1952   *Les Pères Apostoliques en Copte.* 2 vols. CSCO 135–36 (Scriptores
          Coptici, 17–18). Louvain: Durbecq.

Lemaire, André
1971   *Les ministères aux origines de l'église: Naissance de la triple hiérarchie:
          évêques, presbytres, diacres.* LD 68. Paris: Cerf.
1972   "From Services to Ministries: 'Diakoniai' in the First Two Centuries."
          Concilium 80: 35–49.

Lewis, Richard B.
1968   "Ignatius and the 'Lord's Day.' " *AUSS* 6: 46–59.

Liébaert, J.
1970   *Les enseignements moraux des Pères Apostoliques.* Recherches et
          synthèses, section de morale, 4. Gembloux: Duculot.

Lietzmann, Hans
1941   "Zur altchristlichen Verfassungsgeschichte." *ZWT* 55: 97–153.
          Reprinted, pp. 141–85 in *Kleine Schriften I.* TU 67. Berlin:
          Akademie-Verlag, 1958.

Lightfoot, Joseph B.
1889   *The Apostolic Fathers: Part 2, S. Ignatius, S. Polycarp.* 3 vols. 2d ed.
          London: Macmillan.

Lilienfeld, Fairy von
1966   "Zur syrischen Kurzrezension der Ignatianen: von Paulus bis zur
          Spiritualität des Mönchtums der Wüste." *Studia Patristica* 7: 233–47.

Lluis-Font, Pedro
1963   "Sources de la doctrine d'Hermas sur les deux esprits." *Revue d'ascé-
          tique et de mystique* 39: 83–98.

Loofs, Friedrich
1968   *Leitfaden zum Studium der Dogmengeschichte, 1. und 2. Teil: Alte
          Kirche, Mittelalter, und Katholizismus bis zur Gegenwart.* 7th ed., ed.
          Kurt Aland. Tübingen: Max Niemeyer.

Lowy, S.
1960   "The Confutation of Judaism in the Epistle of Barnabas." *JJS* 11: 1–33.

Lusk, D. C.
1950   "What is the Historic Episcopate?" *SJT* 3: 255–77.

McArthur, A. A.
1961   "The Office of Bishop in the Ignatian Epistles and in the Didascalia
          Apostolorum Compared." *Studia Patristica* 4: 298–304.

McCue, James F.
1964   "The Roman Primacy in the Second Century and the Problem of the
          Development of Dogma." *TS* 25: 161–96.
1967   "Bishops, Presbyters and Priests in Ignatius of Antioch." *TS* 28:
          828–34.

MacQuarrie, John
1963   "True Life in Death." *JBR* 31: 200–207.

Magne, Jean
1974   "Klasma, Sperma, Poimnion: Le voeu pour le rassemblement de
          Didachè IX,4." Pp. 197–208 in *Mélanges d'histoire des religions offerts
          à Henri-Charles Puech.* Paris: Presses universitaires de France.

Malina, Bruce J.
1978   "The Social World Implied in the Letters of the Christian Bishop-
          Martyr Named Ignatius of Antioch." Pp. 71–119 in *Society of Biblical
          Literature 1978 Seminar Papers,* vol. 2. Ed. Paul J. Achtemeier.
          Missoula, MT: Scholars Press.

Marrou, H.-I.
1953   "La date du martyre de S. Polycarpe." *Analecta Bollandiana* 71: 5–20.

Martin, José Pablo
1971a   *El Espiritu Santo en los origenes del Christianismo: Estudio sobre I
          Clemente, Ignacio, II Clemente y Justino Martir.* Biblioteca di scienze
          religiose, 2. Zurich: Pas.
1971b   "La pneumatologia en Ignazio de Antioquia." *Salesianum* 33:
          379–454.

Massaux, Édouard
1949   "L'influence de l'Évangile de St. Matthieu sur la Didachè." *ETL* 25:
          5–41.
1950   *Influence de l'évangile de saint Matthieu sur la littérature chrétienne
          avant saint Irenée.* Universitas catholica Lovanensis, 2,42. Louvain:
          Louvain University. (Reprinted with supplement and bibliography by
          B. Dehandschutter. BETL 75. Louvain: Leuven University Press,
          1986.)

Maurer, Christian
1949   *Ignatius von Antiochien und das Johannesevangelium.* ATANT 18. Zurich: Zwingli.

Mees, Michael
1978   "Die Hohepriester-Theologie des Hebräerbriefes im Vergleich mit dem Ersten Clemensbrief." *BZ* 22: 115–24.

Meinhold, Peter
1952   "Polykarpos." PW 21,2: 1662–93.
1958a "Die Ethik des Ignatius von Antiochien." *Historisches Jahrbuch* 77: 50–62.
1958b "Schweigende Bischöfe, die Gegensätze in den kleinasiatischen Gemeinden nach den Ignatianen." Pp. 467–90 in *Festgabe Joseph Lortz:* Vol. 2, *Glaube und Geschichte.* Ed. E. Iserloh and P. Manns. Baden-Baden: Bruno Grimm.
1963   "Episkope—Pneumatiker—Martyrer: Zur Deutung der Selbstaussagen des Ignatius von Antiochien." *Saeculum* 14: 308–24.
1970   "Die geschichtstheologischen Konzeptionen des Ignatius von Antiochien." Pp. 182–91 in *Kyriakon: Festschrift Johannes Quasten,* vol. 1. Ed. P. Granfield and J. A. Jungmann. Münster: Aschendorff.

Mikat, Paul
1969   *Die Bedeutung der Begriffe Stasis und Aponoia für das Verständnis des 1. Clemensbriefes.* Arbeitsgemeinschaft für Forschung des Landes Nordhein-Westfalen, Geisteswissenschaften, 155. Cologne and Opladen: Westdeutscher Verlag.

Milburn, R. L. P.
1944   "The Persecution of Domitian." *CQR* 139: 154–64.

Mohrmann, Christine
1949   "Les Origines de la latinité chrétienne à Rome." *VC* 3: 67–106.
1953   "Statio." *VC* 7: 221–45.

Molland, Einar
1954   "The Heretics Combatted by Ignatius of Antioch." *JEH* 5: 1–6.

Mortley, Raoul
1973   "The Theme of Silence in Clement of Alexandria." *JTS* n.s. 24: 197–202.

Moule, Charles F. D.
1955   "A Note on Didache 9,4." *JTS* n.s. 6: 240–43.

Moule, C. F. D., and A. M. G. Stephenson
1955b "R. G. Heard on Q and Mark." *NTS* 2: 114–18.

Moxnes, Halvor
1974   "God and His Angel in the Shepherd of Hermas." *ST* 28: 49–56.

Mullins, T.
1960   "Papias on Mark's Gospel." *VC* 14: 216–24.
1976   "Papias and Clement and Mark's Two Gospels." *VC* 30: 189–92.

Munck, Johannes
1959   "Presbyters and Disciples of the Lord in Papias." *HTR* 52: 223–43.
1962   "Die Tradition über das Matthäusevangelium bei Papias." Pp. 249–60 in *Neotestamentica et Patristica: Eine Freundesgabe, Herrn Prof. Dr. Oscar Cullmann zu seinem 60. Geburtstag.* NovTSup 6. Leiden: Brill.

Musurillo, Herbert J.
1961   "Ignatius of Antioch: Gnostic or Essene?" *TS* 22: 103–10.

Nauck, Wolfgang
    1957   "Probleme des frühchristlichen Amtsverständnisses (I Petr. 5,2f.)."
            ZNW 48: 200–20.

Nautin, Pierre
    1959a   "La composition de la 'Didachè' et son titre." *RHR* 155: 191–214.
    1959b   "Notes critiques sur la Didachè." *VC* 13: 118–20.
    1961   *Lettres et écrivains chrétiens des IIe et IIIe siècles.* Patristica 2. Paris:
            Cerf.

Niebergall, Alred
    1967   "Zur Entstehungsgeschichte der christlichen Eheschliessung:
            Bemerkungen zu Ignatius an Polykarp." Pp. 107–24 in *Glaube, Geist,
            Geschichte: Festschrift für Ernst Benz.* Ed. G. Müller and W. Zeller.
            Leiden: Brill.

Niederwimmer, K.
    1967   "Johannes Markus und die Frage nach dem Verfasser des zweiten
            Evangeliums." *ZNW* 58: 172–88.

Nielsen, C. M.
    1974   "Papias: Polemicist Against Whom? *TS* 35: 529–35.

Nilsson, Martin P.
    1974   *Geschichte der griechischen Religion:* Vol. 2, *Die hellenistische und
            römische Zeit.* 3d ed. Munich: Beck.

Noll, R. R.
    1970   "Recherches sur les origines du sacerdoce ministériel chez les Pères
            Apostoliques." Diss., Strasbourg.
    1975   "The Search for a Christian Ministerial Priesthood in I Clement."
            Studia Patristica 13: 250–54.

Normann, Friedrich
    1967   *Christos Didaskalos.* Münsterische Beiträge zur Theologie 32.
            Münster: Aschendorff.

Norris, Frederick W.
    1976   "Ignatius, Polycarp, and I Clement: Walter Bauer Reconsidered." *VC*
            30: 23–44.

O'Hagan, Angelo P.
    1961   "The Great Tribulation to Come in the Pastor of Hermas." *Studia
            Patristica 4:* 305–11.
    1968   *Material Re-Creation in the Apostolic Fathers.* TU 100. Berlin:
            Akademie-Verlag.

Opelt, I.
    1974   Review of Weijenborg, 1969b. *Gnomon* 46: 251–55.

Orbe, Antonio
    1954   "Variactiones gnosticas sobre las alas del Alma." *Greg* 35: 18–55.
    1961   *La uncion del Verbo: Estudios Valentinianos III.* Analecta Gregoriana
            113. Rome: Gregorian University.

Osiek, Carolyn
    1983   *Rich and Poor in the Shepherd of Hermas: An Exegetical-Social Investi-
            gation.* CBQMS 15. Washington: Catholic Biblical Association of
            America.

Padberg, Rudolf
    1962   "Geordnete Liebe, Amt, Pneuma und kirchliche Einheit bei Ignatius
            von Antiochien." Pp. 201–17 in *Unio Christianorum: Lorenz Jaeger*

zum 70. Geburtstag. Ed. O. Schilling and H. Zimmermann. Paderborn: Bonifacius.

1963   "Vom gottesdienstlichen Leben in den Briefen des Ignatius von
        Antiochien." *TGl* 53: 337–47.
1966   "Gottesdienst und Kirchenordnung im (ersten) Klemensbrief."
        Archiv für Liturgiewissenschaft 9,2: 367–74.
1972   "Das Amtsverständnis der Ignatiusbriefe." *TGl* 62: 47–54.

Pannenberg, Wolfhart
1959   "Die Aufnahme des philosophischen Gottesbegriffs als dogmatisches
        Problem des frühchristlichen Theologie." *ZKG* 70: 1–45.
1977   *Jesus—God and Man.* 2d ed. Philadelphia: Westminster.

Parker, Pierson
1960   "John and John Mark." *JBL* 79: 97–110.

Paulsen, Henning
1978   *Studien zur Theologie des Ignatius von Antiochien.* Forschungen zur
        Kirchen- und Dogmengeschichte 29. Göttingen: Vandenhoeck &
        Ruprecht.
1985   *Die Briefe des Ignatius von Antiochia und der Brief des Polykarp von
        Smyrna.* 2d rev. ed. of the publication of Walter Bauer. HNT. Tübin-
        gen: Mohr-Siebeck.

Perler, Othmar
1944   "Ignatius von Antiochien und die römische Christengemeinde."
        Freiburger Zeitschrift für Philosophie und Theologie 22: 413–51.
1949   "Das vierte Makkabäerbuch, Ignatius von Antiochien und die ältes-
        ten Martyrerberichte." *Rivista di archeologia cristiana* 25: 47–72.
1958   "Pseudo-Ignatius und Eusebius von Emesa." *Historisches Jahrbuch*
        77: 73–82.
1971   "Die Briefe des Ignatius von Antiochien: Frage der Echtheit—Neue
        Arabische Übersetzung." *Freiburger Zeitschrift für Philosophie und
        Theologie* 18: 381–96.

Pernveden, Lage
1966   *The Concept of the Church in the Shepherd of Hermas.* Studia
        Theologica Lundensia 27. Lund: Gleerup.

Peterson, Erik
1959a   "Beiträge zur Interpretation der Visionen im Pastor Hermae." Pp.
        254–70 in Peterson, 1959f. Also found in *Miscellanea Jerphanion,
        Orientalia christiana periodica* 13 (1947) 624ff.
1959b   "Das Praescriptum des 1. Clemens-Briefes." Pp. 129–36 in Peterson,
        1959f. Also found in *Pro regno, pro sancruario: Festschrift G. van der
        Leeuw* (Nijkerk: Callenbach, 1950) 351–57.
1959c   "Die Begegnung mit dem Ungeheuer." Pp. 285–309 in Peterson,
        1959f. Also found in *VC* 8 (1954) 52–71.
1959d   "Kritische Analyse der fünften Vision des Hermas." Pp. 271–84 in
        Peterson, 1959f. Also found in *Historisches Jahrbuch der Görresge-
        sellschaft* 77 (1958) 362–69.
1959e   "Über einige Probleme der Didache-Überlieferung." Pp. 146–82 in
        Peterson, 1959f. Also found in *Rivista di archeologia cristiana* 27
        (1951) 37–68.
1959f   *Frühkirche, Judentum, und Gnosis.* Rome, Freiburg, and Vienna:
        Herder.

Petrie, C. S.
1967   "The Authorship of 'The Gospel according to Matthew': A Recon-
        sideration of External Evidence." *NTS* 14: 15–33.

Pfitzner, Victor C.
1967   *Paul and the Agon Motif: Traditional Athletic Imagery in the Pauline
        Literature.* NovTSup 16. Leiden: Brill.

Pillinger, Renate
1975   "Die Taufe nach der Didache." *Wiener Studien* 9: 152–60.

Pizzolato, Luigi Franco
1970   "Silenzio del vescove e parola degli eretici in Ignazio d'Antiochia."
        Aevum 44: 205–19.

Ponthot, Joseph
1959   "La signification religieuse du 'nom' chez Clément de Rome et dans
        la Didachè." *ETL* 35: 339–61.

Poschmann, Bernard
1940   *Paenitentia secunda.* Theophaneia 1. Bonn: Peter Hanstein.

Preiss, T.
1938   "La mystique de l'imitation de Christ et de l'unité chez Ignace d'Anti-
        oche." *RHPR* 18: 197–241.

Prigent, Pierre
1961   *Les Testimonia dans le christianisme primitif: L'épître de Barnabé I-
        XVI et ses sources.* EBib. Paris: Gabalda.
1977   "L'hérésie Asiate et l'église confessante, de l'Apocalypse à Ignace."
        VC 31: 1–22.

Prigent, Pierre, and Robert A. Kraft
1971   *Épître de Barnabé.* SC 172. Paris: Cerf.

Quasten, Johannes
1950   *Patrology:* Vol. 1, *The Beginnings of Patristic Literature.* Utrecht and
        Brussels: Spectrum.
1961   *Patrologia:* Vol. 1, *Hasta el concilio de Nicea.* Ed. Ignacio Oñatibia
        with P. U. Farré and E. M. Llopart. Madrid: BAC.

Quinn, Jerome D.
1978   " 'Seven Times He Wore Chains' (1 Clem 5.6)." *JBL* 97: 574–76.

Rahner, Hugo
1963   *Greek Myths and Christian Mystery.* New York and Evanston, IL:
        Harper & Row.

Rahner, Karl
1955   "Die Busslehre im Hirten des Hermas." *ZKT* 45: 385–431.

Rankin, O. S.
1948   "The Extent of the Influence of the Synagogue Service upon Chris-
        tian Worship." *JJS* 1: 27–32.

Rathke, Heinrich
1967   *Ignatius von Antiochien und die Paulusbriefe.* TU 99. Berlin:
        Akademie-Verlag.

Reiling, J.
1973   *Hermas and Christian Prophecy: A Study of The Eleventh Mandate.*
        NovTSup 37. Leiden: Brill.

Richter, Klemens
1974   "Ansätze für die Entwicklung einer Weiheliturgie in Apostolischer Zeit." *Archiv für Liturgiewissenschaft* 16: 32–52.

Riesenfeld, Harald
1956   "Das Brot von den Bergen." *Eranos* 14: 142–50.
1961   "Reflections on the Style and the Theology of St. Ignatius of Antioch." *Studia Patristica* 4: 312–22.

Rigg, Horace A.
1956   "Papias on Mark." *NovT* 1: 161–83.

Rius-Camps, Josep
1979   *The Four Authentic Letters of Ignatius, the Martyr.* Christianismos 2. Rome: Pontificium Institutum Orientalium Studiorum.

Robillard, Edmond
1971   "L'épître de Barnabé: Trois époques, trois théologies, trois rédacteurs." *RB* 78: 184–209.

Rogge, Joachim
1964   ""Ενωσις und verwandte Begriffe in den Ignatiusbriefen ." Pp. 45–51 in . . . *und fragten nach Jesus: Beiträge aus Theologie, Kirche und Geschichte: Festschrift Ernst Barnikol.* Berlin: Evangelische Verlagsanstalt.

Rohde, J.
1968   "Häresie und Schisma im ersten Clemensbrief und in den Ignatius-Briefen." *NovT* 10: 217–33.

Romanides, John S.
1961-62   "The Ecclesiology of St. Ignatius of Antioch." *Greek Orthodox Theological Review* 7: 53–77.

Rordorf, Willy
1972   "Aux origines du culte des martyrs." *Irenikon* 45: 315–31.
1973   "La rémission des pechés selon la Didachè." *Irenikon* 46: 283–97.

Rordorf, Willy, and André Tuilier
1978   *La Doctrine des douze Apôtres (Didachè).* SC 248. Paris: Cerf.

Rüsch, Theodor
1952   *Die Entstehung der Lehre vom Heiligen Geist bei Ignatius von Antiochien, Theophilus von Antiocheia und Irenäus von Lyon.* Studien zur Dogmengeschichte und Systematischen Theologie 2. Zurich: Zwingli.

Ruwet, Jean
1952   "Le canon alexandrin des Éscritures, saint Athanase." *Bib* 33: 1–29.

Sachot, M.
1977   "Pour une étude de la notion de salut chez les Pères Apostoliques, Presentation du vocabulaire." *RevScRel* 51: 54–70.

Sanders, Louis
1943   *L'Hellénisme de saint Clément de Rome et le Paulinisme.* Studia Hellenistica 2. Louvain: Bibliotheca Universitatis Lovanii.

Sauser, Ekkart
1970   "Tritt der Bischof an die Stelle Christi? Zur Frage nach der Stellung des Bischofs in der Theologie des hl. Ignatius von Antiocheia." Pp. 325–39 in *Festschrift Franz Loidl,* vol. 1. Ed. Victor Flieder. Vienna: Hollinek.

Schäublin, Christof
1974   "Μήτε προσθεῖναι μήτ' ἀφαιρεῖν." *Museum Helveticum* 31: 144–49.

Schille, Gottfried
1958   "Zur urchristlichen Tauflehre: Stilistische Beobachtungen am Barna-basbrief." *ZNW* 49: 31–52.
1965   *Frühchristliche Hymnen.* Berlin: Evangelische Verlagsanstalt.

Schlier, Heinrich
1929   *Religionsgeschichtliche Untersuchungen zu den Ignatiusbriefen.* BZNW 8. Giessen: Töpelmann.

Schmid, Wolfgang
1954   "Eine frühchristliche Arkadienvorstellung." Pp. 121–30 in *Convivium: Festschrift Konrat Ziegler.* Stuttgart: Druckenmüller.

Schmutz, Stephan
1946   "Petrus war dennoch in Rom." *Benediktinische Monatsschrift* 22: 128–41.

Schoedel, William R.
1964   "A Blameless Mind 'Not on Loan' but 'By Nature' (Ignatius, *Trall.* 1.1)." *JTS* n.s. 15: 308–16.
1967   *The Apostolic Fathers:* Vol. 5, *Polycarp, Martyrdom of Polycarp, Fragments of Papias.* Camden, NJ: Thomas Nelson.
1978   "Ignatius and the Archives." *HTR* 71: 97–106.
1980   "Theological Norms and Social Perspectives in Ignatius of Antioch." Pp. 30–56, 220–25 in *Jewish and Christian Self-Definition: The Shaping of Christianity in the Second and Third Centuries.* Ed. E. P. Sanders. London: SCM; Philadelphia: Fortress.
1985   *Ignatius of Antioch: A Commentary on the Letters of Ignatius of Antioch.* Hermeneia. Philadelphia: Fortress.
1987   "Polycarp's Witness to Ignatius of Antioch." *VC* 41: 1–10

Schwartz, Jacques
1965   "Survivances littéraires paiennes dans le 'Pasteur' d'Hermas." *RB* 72: 240–47.
1972   "Note sur le martyre de Polycarpe de Smyrne." *RHPR* 52: 331–36.

Schweizer, Eduard
1958   "Zu Apg. 1,16–22." *TZ* 14: 46.
1961   *Church Order in the New Testament.* SBT 32. Naperville, IL: Allenson.

Seitz, Otto J. F.
1944   "Relationship of the Shepherd to the Epistle of James." *JBL* 63: 131–40.
1947   "Antecedents and Significance of the Term δίψυχος." *JBL* 66: 211–19.
1958   "Afterthoughts on the Term 'Dipsychos.'" *NTS* 4: 327–34.

Sibinga, J. Smit
1966   "Ignatius and Matthew." *NovT* 8: 262–83.

Sieben, Hermann Josef
1978   "Die Ignatianen als Briefe: Einige Formkritische Bemerkungen." *VC* 32: 1–18.

Simonetti, M.
1956   "Alcune osservazioni sul Martirio di S. Policarpo." *Giornale Italiano di Filologia* 9: 328–44.

Smith, M. A.
1966   "Did Justin Know the Didache?" *Studia Patristica* 7: 287–90.
Smith, Morton
1960–61   "The Report about Peter in 1 Clement v. 4." *NTS* 7: 86–88.
Snyder, Grayden F.
1963   "The Historical Jesus in the Letters of Ignatius of Antioch." *BR* 8:
            3–12.
1968a   *The Apostolic Fathers:* Vol. 6, *The Shepherd of Hermas.* Camden, NJ:
            Thomas Nelson.
1968b   "The Text and Syntax of Ignatius πρὸς Ἐφεσίους 20:2c." *VC* 22: 8–13.
Solages, B. de
1970   "Le témoignage de Papias." *Bulletin de littérature ecclésiastique* 71:
            3–14.

Staats, Reinhart
1976   "Die martyrologische Begründung des Romprimats bei Ignatius von
            Antiochien." *ZTK* 73: 461–70.

Starck, J.
1953   "L'Église de Pâques sur la Croix." *NRT* 4: 337–64.

Stauffer, Ethelbert
1963   "Der Methurgamen des Petrus." Pp. 283–93 in *Neutestamentliche
            Aufsätze: Festschrift für Josef Schmid zum 70. Geburtstag.* Ed. J.
            Blinzler, O. Kuss, F. Mussner. Regensburg: Pustet.

Stegemann, Hartmut
1962   Review of Prigent, 1961. *ZKG* 73: 142–53.

Steinmetz, Peter
1972   "Polykarp von Smyrna und die Gerechtigkeit." *Hermes* 100: 63–75.

Stockmeier, P.
1966   "Der Begriff παιδεία bei Klemens von Rom." *Studia Patristica* 7:
            401–8.

Stommel, Eduard
1953   "Σημεῖον ἐκπετάσεως (Didache 16,6)." *RQ* 48: 21–42.

Stuiber, A.
1955   "Clemens Romanus I." *RAC* 3: 188–97.
1961   " 'Das ganze Joch des Herrn' (Didache 6,2–3)." *Studia Patristica* 4:
            323–29.

Suggs, M. Jack
1972   "The Christian Two Ways Tradition: Its Antiquity, Form, and
            Function." Pp. 60–74 in *Studies in New Testament and Early Chris-
            tian Literature: Essays in Honor of Allen P. Wikgren.* Ed. D. E. Aune.
            NovTSup 33. Leiden: Brill.

Sullivan, J.
1957   *Trinitarian Analogies in St. Clement of Rome and St. Ignatius of
            Antioch.* Woodstock, MD: Woodstock College.

Swartley, Willard M.
1973   "The Imitatio Christi in the Ignatian Letters." *VC* 27: 81–103.

Syme, Ronald
1959   "Proconsuls d'Afrique sous Antonin le Pieux." *Revue des études
            anciennes* 61: 310–11.

Tanner, R. G.
1972   "Latinisms in the Text of Hermas." *Colloquium* 4: 12–23.

Tarelli, C. C.
1947   "Clement of Rome and the Fourth Gospel. *JTS* 48: 208–9.

Tarvainen, Olavi
1967   *Glaube und Liebe bei Ignatius von Antiochien.* Schriften der Luther-Agricola-Gesellschaft 14. Joensuu: Pohjois-Karjalan Kirjapaino Oy.

Taylor, Robert O. P.
1946   *The Groundwork of the Gospel.* Oxford: Blackwell.

Telfer, Walter
1952   "The Date of the Martyrdom of Polycarp." *JTS* n.s. 3: 79–83.

Thierry, J. J.
1960   "Note sur τὰ ἐλάχιστα τῶν ζώων au chapitre XX de la Ie Clementis." *VC* 14: 235–44.

Thurian, M.
1967   "L'organization du ministère dans l'église primitive selon saint Ignace d'Antioche." *Verbum caro* 21: 26–38.

Thyen, Hartwig
1955   *Der Stil der jüdisch-hellenistischen Homilie.* FRLANT 2,47. Göttingen: Vandenhoeck & Ruprecht.

Tinsley, E. J.
1957   "The *imitatio Christi* in the Mysticism of St. Ignatius of Antioch." *Studia Patristica* 2: 553–60.

Torrance, Thomas F.
1948   *The Doctrine of Grace in the Apostolic Fathers.* Edinburgh and London: Oliver & Boyd.

Trentin, G.
1972a   "Eros e Agape: A proposito di una interpretazione teologica della lettere di Ignazio di Antiochia." *Studia Patavina, Rivista di Scienze Religiose* 19: 495–538.
1972b   "Rassegna di studi su Ignazio di Antiochia." *Studia Patavina, Rivista di Scienze Religiose* 19: 75–87.

Treu, Kurt
1970   "Ein Neuer Hermas-Papyrus." *VC* 24: 34–39.

Turner, H. E. W.
1954   *The Pattern of Christian Truth.* Bampton Lectures. London: Mowbray.

Unnik, W. C. van
1949   "De la règle Μήτε προσθεῖναι μήτε ἀφαιρεῖν dans l'histoire du canon." *VC* 3: 1–36.
1950   "Is 1 Clement 20 Purely Stoic?" *VC* 4: 181–89.
1951   "1 Clement 34 and the 'Sanctus.'" *VC* 5: 204–48.
1952–53 "Zur Bedeutung von ταπεινοῦν τὴν ψυχήν bei den Apostolischen Vätern." *ZNW* 44: 250–55.
1960   "Die Rücksicht auf die Reaktion der Nicht-Christen als Motiv in der altchristlichen Paränese." Pp. 221–34 in *Judentum, Urchristentum, Kirche: Festschrift für Joachim Jeremias.* Ed. W. Eltester. BZNW 26. Berlin: Töpelmann.
1962   "Le nombre des élus dans la première épître de Clément." *RHPR* 42: 237–46.

1963	"Zur Papias-Notiz über Markus (Eusebius, *H.E.* III, 39, 15)." *ZNW* 54: 276–77.
1970a	"Studies over de Zogenaamde Eerste Brief van Clemens, I: Het litteraire genre." *Mededelingen der koninklijke Nederlandse Akademie van Wetenschappen, Afd. Leterkunde,* 33,4: 149–204.
1970b	" 'Tiefer Friede' (1. Klemens 2.2)." *VC* 24: 261–79.
1972	"Noch Einmal 'Tiefer Friede.' " *VC* 26: 24–28.
1973	"The Interpretation of 2 Clement 15,5." *VC* 27: 29–34.

Vilela, Albano
| 1973 | "Le Presbytérium selon saint Ignace d'Antioche." *Bulletin de littérature ecclésiastique* 74: 161–86. |

Vogt, Hermann J.
| 1978 | "Ignatius von Antiochien über den Bischof und seine Gemeinde." *TQ* 158: 15–27. |

Vokes, F. E.
| 1964 | "The Didache and the Canon of the New Testament." *SE* 3: 427–36. |

Vööbus, Arthur
| 1968 | *Liturgical Traditions in the Didache.* Papers of the Estonian Theological Society in Exile 16. Stockholm: ETSE. |
| 1969 | "Regarding the Background of the Liturgical Traditions in the Didache." *VC* 23: 81–87. |

Walker, Joan Hazelden
| 1966 | "An Argument from the Chinese for the Antiochene Origin of the Didache." *Studia Patristica* 8: 44–50. |

Walls, A. F.
| 1967 | "Papias and the Oral Tradition." *VC* 21: 137–40. |

Weijenborg, Reinoud
| 1969a | "Is Evagrius Ponticus the Author of the Longer Recension of the Ignatian Letters?" *Antonianum* 44: 339–47. |
| 1969b | *Les lettres d'Ignace d'Antioche.* Leiden: Brill. |

Weiss, Bardo
| 1975 | "Amt und Eschatologie im 1. Clemensbrief." *TP* 50: 70–83. |

Wenger, A.
| 1971 | "A propos des lettres d'Ignace d'Antioche." *Revue des études Byzantines* 29: 213–16. |

Wengst, Klaus
| 1971 | *Tradition und Theologie des Barnabasbriefes.* Arbeiten zur Kirchengeschichte 42. Berlin and New York: de Gruyter. |

Werner, Eric
| 1965 | "Post Biblical Hebraisms in the Prima Clementis." Pp. 793–818 in *Harry Austryn Wolfson Jubilee Volume,* vol. 2. Jerusalem: American Academy for Jewish Research. |

Whittaker, Molly
| 1956 | *Die apostolischen Väter:* Vol. 1, *Der Hirt des Hermas.* GCS 48. Berlin: Akademie-Verlag. [2d ed. 1967.] |

Wickert, Ulrich
| 1958 | "Eine Fehlübersetzung zu I Clem 19,2." *ZNW* 49: 270–75. |
| 1968 | "Paulus, der erste Klemens und Stephan von Rom: Drei Epochen der frühen Kirche aus ökumenischer Sicht." *ZKG* 79: 145–58. |

Wilhelm-Hooijbergh, A. E.
    1975   "A Different View of Clemens Romanus." *HeyJ* 16: 266–88.
Windisch, Hans
    1920   *Die apostolischen Väter:* Vol. 3, *Der Barnabasbrief.* HNTSup.
                Tübingen: Mohr-Siebeck.
Winslow, Donald F.
    1965   "The Idea of Redemption in the Epistles of St. Ignatius of Antioch."
                Greek Orthodox Theological Review 11: 119–31.
Wolverton, Wallace I.
    1956   "The Double-Minded Man in the Light of Essene Psychology." *ATR*
                38: 166–75.
Wong, D. W. F.
    1977   "Natural and Divine Order in I Clement." *VC* 31: 81–87.
Woollcombe, K. J.
    1962   "The Doctrinal Connexions of the Pseudo-Ignatian Letters." *Studia
                Patristica* 6: 269–73.
Wotke, F.
    1949   "Papias." PW 18,3: 965–76.
Wright, Leon E.
    1952   *Alterations of the Words of Jesus as Quoted in the Literature of the
                Second Century.* Harvard Historical Monographs 25. Cambridge,
                MA: Harvard University Press.
Young, Franklin Woodrow
    1946   "The Shepherd of Hermas: A Study of his Concepts of Repentance
                and of the Church." Diss., Duke University.
    1948   "The Relation of 1 Clement to the Epistle of James." *JBL* 67: 339–45.
Zahn, Theodor
    1873   *Ignatius von Antiochien.* Gotha: Perthes.
Zanetti, P. Serra
    1966   "Bibliografia eucaristica Ignaziana recente." Pp. 341–89 in *Miscel-
                lanea Liturgica in onore di sua eminenze il cardinale Giacomo Lercaro,*
                vol. 1. Rome: Desclée.
    1975   "Una nota Ignaziana: ΑΝΤΙΨΥΧΟΝ." Pp. 963–79 in *Forma Futuri:
                Studi in onore del cardinale Michele Pellegrino.* Turin: Bottega
                d'Erasmo.
Ziegler, Adolf W.
    1958   *Neue Studien zum ersten Klemensbrief.* Munich: Manz.

Part Four

New Testament Interpretation

18
JESUS AND CHRISTOLOGY

John Reumann

In the years following World War II, perhaps no area of biblical studies was quite so lively as *Leben-Jesu-Forschung* ("life of Jesus research") and the debate about Christology and the historical Jesus. The year 1953, in fact, introduced a fresh stage in the centuries-old search for "Jesus as he really was," for on October 20 of that year Ernst Käsemann called for what became known as "the New Quest of the Historical Jesus" (on the phrase, see J. M. Robinson, 1959 [1983 ed.: 5–6]).

This new quest, of course, inherited decades of intense work on Gospel sources and oral traditions, as well as the wartime discussion over "demythologization." Running concurrently with the interest in biblical theology through the fifties, it eventually helped give birth to the "New Hermeneutic" (Achtemeier, 1969). It felt in turn the impact of redaction criticism and emerging trends in literary study of the texts, like structuralism. Thus, as so often, Gospels study with regard to Jesus was a lightning rod, attracting almost every exegetical technique and religious-philosophical approach.

The net result of the new quest has by no means been an agreement about the man from Nazareth, for there are as many—and more—types of lives than previously, even if G. Aulén's surveying of the scene in 1973 saw an emerging scholarly consensus. But Jesus has been probed historically in this period as seldom, if ever, before. Only the decades before and just after 1900 provide real comparison. Albert Schweitzer felt that 1901 had been the fateful year, when his book on an eschatological Jesus and W. Wrede's skeptical account on the Marcan Jesus appeared. The years after 1953 mark a similar turn in the road or at least accelerated and heavier traffic.

The new quest was not an effort to present more data, biographically, about Jesus' appearance or mannerisms (as E. Stauffer offered). At bottom it represented a new interest in allowing or finding in Jesus some glint of Christology—the clear post-Easter belief of the Christian community that Jesus had claimed to be or in some way was "anointed of God" (messiah, *Christos*), son of man, God's son, lord, or, at least, (the) prophet, a figure of authority, thus warranting the later titles of honor given him. "It began with Jesus of Nazareth," Heinz Zahrnt called his book about the quest in 1960, "it" referring to Christology.

501

Ever since W. Bousset, it had been common to deal with Jesus in one volume and Christology (*Kyrios Christos*) in another (for a survey, see Boers, 1970, 1972; cf. Schillebeeckx). R. Bultmann (1920) had elevated to popularity Wrede's view that Christology arose only after Easter. Opinion about what could be recovered concerning the historical Jesus perhaps hit a low of negativity—apart from the "Christ myth school"—in C. Guignebert's *Jésus* (1933). If Bultmann's 1921 analysis of the Synoptics came into English (sometimes not clearly translated at that) only in 1963, his views and those of other form critics had long been disseminated (though often in more bland forms); and W. E. Bundy's commentary on the Synoptics, for example, made available in America the radical (German) views of previous decades. It was in the face of all this that the new quest wanted to restore some connection between Jesus and Christology. At the same time scholarship pointed more and more to variety in NT Christology (e.g., Braun, 1957a: 115 [Eng. trans.]: "For Paul anthropology is the constant. . . . Christology, on the other hand, is the variable").

The history of post-Enlightenment study of Jesus falls into three periods, it was commonly said in the late 1950s and 1960s, a time that gave increasing attention to the history of past questing (as witness McArthur, 1966; the translation of Kähler belatedly in 1964; of Wrede finally in 1971; Pelikan; and the "Lives of Jesus" reprint and translation series, ed. Keck). The epochs:

I. The Old Quest (from 1778, according to Schweitzer, with its four either/or decisions: Purely historical or supernatural? Synoptics or John? Eschatological Jesus or not? Mark as a whole the historical basis for a "life" or Christology as post-Easter?);

II. The No-Quest Period (Bultmann and the form critics: all Gospel accounts are colored by the church; or, the "no biography is possible" view);

III. Now, the New Quest *and its fragmentation* (Reumann, 1974).

For these most recent three decades there is no lack of literature (e.g., see Kümmel's research reports, covering 1950 on, though nothing comparable bridges the years from 1917 till then; Suggs, 1975; surveys like those of H. Anderson, 1964; C. C. Anderson; Leroy; Eichholz, 1984; O'Collins, 1977, 1983). The difficulty lies in covering and classifying the immense scholarly and not-so-scholarly production and, indeed, where to draw the line on what is included. It is well to remind ourselves again that virtually every trend in NT interpretation from 1945 to 1985 shows up in what people have written on Jesus and Christology. That includes modern Jewish and Israeli concerns (e.g., Isaac; Lapide); ancient archaeological finds and texts (on Qumran, see Braun, 1966; from Nag Hammadi, the *Gospel of Thomas* has been especially pertinent in the search for genuine parables and logia); and studies on individual gospels and NT theology (see chaps. 9, 10, 11, and 19 in this volume).

Needless to say, extra-biblical materials from the pagan and even Jewish worlds concerning Jesus are scanty (Conzelmann, 1959:12–16; but cf. Bammel, 1967, 1968). Noncanonical materials are often late, legendary, or still being assessed, even though the wall dividing them from what is "canonical" has been broken down for many (Koester). Comparatively little about the historical Jesus can be gleaned from the NT epistles and other books apart from the four Gospels. Therefore, the Synoptics and John remain our chief sources. They, of course, are subject to the winds of current theory.

In the decades under consideration, the Gospel of John has only rarely been used as a prime source, but perhaps more and more it has been employed eclectically (see Mussner, 1965; recall the contention of W. F. Albright, after discovery of the Dead Sea Scrolls, that John does *not* distort Jesus' teachings and may be the earliest Gospel of all [Davies and Daube: 171]). Among the Synoptics, in spite of efforts to reinstate the priority of Matthew and to set aside Q (e.g., Farmer), most investigations into the historical Jesus and Christology have continued to work with some sort of Two-Source hypothesis. Luke's special source (Jeremias) and Proto-Luke (Taylor, 1972) have sometimes been brought into play. Developments during the oral period and increasingly the evangelists' redaction have received priority, often at the expense of the historical Jesus. But increasingly there has been recognition of at least three stages in the tradition: "Jesus," "source," and "redaction";[1] (see Bea for a key statement in Roman Catholic circles); or, more important, in Christology, of a movement from Jesus to "Jewish-Christian" to "Hellenistic-Jewish-Christian" to the Hellenistic church (Fuller, 1965).

Besides diversion of interest into causes of the day ("God is dead," but Jesus is God's only Son, cf. Hamilton; "Jesus was a feminist," or, in liberation theology, he was a political revolutionist) and the lure of new techniques, the chief barrier to progress in the quest and to doing "Jesus and Christology" in any sort of traditional or classical sense had been the roadblock put up at Easter by the form critics: behind the barrier of Easter, Christology shall not be found! Some, of course, simply disregarded *die formgeschichtliche Methode* ("the form-critical method") and continued to appeal to eyewitness sources or traditions. So T. W. Manson and William Manson, but the phenomenon was common in Anglo-Saxon scholarship, and in Germany

---

[1] These three stages have often been referred to as *Sitz im Leben Jesu, Sitz im Leben der Kirche,* and *Sitz im Leben des Redakteurs* or of the evangelist (see Marxsen, 1956:23). But this is to confuse what was originally in form criticism *a repeated sociological situation* in the community life of the early church, like preaching, teaching, or aspects of worship, with what is taken to be a *specific, historical occurrence* during the ministry of Jesus in Galilee or Jerusalem and with *conditions* faced by the evangelist and his community in light of which he shapes his gospel. The confusion of usages is probably irreversible.

among those appealing to T. Zahn, A. Schlatter, and other giants of the past
(see Stauffer or now Stuhlmacher, 1975, 1979). Others, especially the Scandinavian scholars H. Riesenfeld, B. Gerhardsson, and T. Boman, attacked
form criticism itself, claiming that scribelike fidelity, urged by Jesus in
transmitting his words, kept his message intact. Their claims were countered
by M. Smith (1963), among others (see Davies, 1962). Still others, eschewing
the Bultmannian extremes, used scholarship, particularly appeal to Jewish
backgrounds, to establish a larger core of reliable knowledge about Jesus
(Jeremias; O. Betz; Barrett; Moule; a number of Americans and others;
Israeli scholarship generally). Nonetheless, Harvey McArthur (1969a:190n.*,
205) probably speaks for many in this period who have shifted away from the
notion that historical certainty is possible (via scripture, church, or
experience) and are wary of risking all of faith to ride upon the latest the
professors say, and are hoping instead for some way in which faith may be
"immune" from the results and vagaries of historical research.

I. THE SITUATION AFTER WORLD WAR II

C. C. McCown was completing his account of a century of historical
study on Jesus just as war was declared in 1939. A liberal who yearned for
social justice in which his Jesus, as "supreme Teacher," had "believed
passionately," McCown had no sympathy for "consistent eschatology" and
lamented that it had, for many, destroyed "the 'social gospel of the Carpenter
of Nazareth.' " There was, he had to say, "no concensus [sic] of scientific
opinion" about Jesus in the previous two decades, a fact he attributed to
"differences as to the rigor of historical method" and to "uncertainties as to
the philosophy of history into which to incorporate the historical Jesus"—the
latter problem far from solution "because it is essentially a Christological
problem" (306, 211–12, 284). But he was right that the search for "the real
Jesus" would go on.

McCown's survey should prevent us from being misled by the notion
that after 1906 every "life of Jesus" built in a hefty dose of eschatology, or
that after 1920 or so, even in Germany, everyone avoided biography in
writing on Jesus or followed implications of *Formgeschichte* ("form criticism"). Better put, "the quest" went on, and Schweitzer and Bultmann et al.
had introduced factors that in the long haul could not thereafter be ignored.
But by and large it was "The Quest of the Historical Jesus—*Continued*," as
T. W. Manson put it in 1949. A variety of the positions extant then (cf.
Kepler) may be seen in three lands especially identified with *Leben-Jesu* ("life
of Jesus") scholarship.

In Germany Bultmann had already in 1926 expressed his position that
behind the sources which the early church gives us we can work back to an
oldest layer where, with relative success, Jesus' teaching and message can
be marked off. As Jesus' words meet us, there can be a highly personal

encounter, but whoever wished to put "Jesus" in quotation marks "as an abbreviation for the historical phenomenon with which we are concerned, is free to do so" (14). The book was gradually influential, but not dominant. M. Dibelius's *Jesus* (1939) was a more positive portrait, even if E. F. Scott, in a later review (*Int* 4 [1950] 213–15) felt the human personality had been lost. Friedrich Büchsel's *Jesus,* published posthumously after the war, was far more conservative, still using a basically Johannine outline.

In France, it was not only the Renan-Loisy-Guignebert line that won attention but more particularly M. Goguel's lucid account, which refined the Germanic methods in a Gallic way. Typical of the Catholic "lives" was F. Prat's, which, like Goguel's, was influential in the English-speaking world also.

British methodology had been shaken somewhat by R. H. Lightfoot's contention in 1935 that, in the wake of form history, we can hear "little more" of the historical Jesus "than a whisper of his voice" since in the Gospels we trace "but the outskirts of his ways" (225, alluding to Job 26:14). But usually form criticism came there as a gentle illapse, not a violent disruption, upon the quest (e.g., Taylor). William Manson presented a sort of neo-orthodox, salvation-history Jesus. T. W. Manson (1953 especially) argued influentially for a personal Christology on Jesus' part that combined the Servant concept of Isaiah 53 with the Son-of-man idea in Daniel 7. See also Cadoux; Duncan.

It is surprising that in America the "name scholars" at certain famous institutions did *not* write lives of Jesus. Henry Cadbury contributed mostly marginal notes on Jesus and the quest. F. C. Grant wrote no real "life" (his *IDB* article comes closest; R. M. Grant approximates one in his *Introduction*). John Knox in his lectures had already by 1945 secured his Jesus-portrait from too rough a handling by criticism through enshrining it in the church's memory of him. Both J. Knox and F. C. Grant emphasized Jesus' basic sanity over against notions that he regarded himself as an apocalyptic Son of man. The "social-historical" method of the University of Chicago was by now somewhat in abeyance. E. J. Goodspeed's *Jesus* was popular, and his unexpected endorsement, late in his life, of Matthew as the author of the Gospel of Matthew, reflected a new conservatism.

For the American scene it is rightly to be noted that, while NT chairs in the great interdenominational seminary faculties were occupied by scholars of theologically liberal backgrounds, the multitude of students who came to them more likely took their theology from Reinhold Niebuhr, W. Pauck, P. Tillich, or neo-orthodoxy (W. Baird: 85). In Germany a new generation of giants came to chairs in the 1950s in an expanding university system, and most of them were Bultmannians. It was to these faculties that American graduate students and professors on sabbatical increasingly went to study. German influences were therefore picked up especially quickly in

America, and after 1960 or so the trans-Atlantic traffic was a bit more frequently two-way.

II. THE NEW QUEST:
A PROPOSAL AND AN UMBRELLA

Revitalization and a centripetal force in the then-existing quest came from an unexpected source: among Bultmann's own pupils and friends. At the annual gathering of these "old Marburgers" in 1953, Ernst Käsemann, then professor at Göttingen, proposed that precisely this group should give itself to a new quest as both scientifically possible and theologically necessary. Well aware of the dangers in "historification" and of the need for criteria to determine what is authentically of Jesus, Käsemann argued that our most rigorous scholarship nonetheless allows us to see distinctive features in Jesus and his mission, such as his sovereign freedom and authority. What is thus historically ascertainable must be emphasized because the early church did so (it was not enough to tell the story of Jesus simply in terms of Phil 2:6–11; Gospels were written about him too). We can thereby counter any "kerygma-theological docetism" (Dahl: 161, 167), the notion that a mere appearance of a Christ-figure suffices. The risen one is the crucified *Jesus*, who spoke as in the first, second, and fourth antitheses of the Sermon on the Mount, removed any distinction between "sacred" and "secular," and ate with sinners.

The next decade saw an amazing response. The clarion call was heard far outside the Bultmann school and beyond Germany (Jervell; Bouttier; cf. Dantine), even in Japan (Endo). Conservatives generally welcomed an emphasis that they had felt correct all along (Peter). The discussions in Germany were rather promptly reported in English (J. M. Robinson, 1959, 1962a), and lively reaction ensued especially in America. Meetings of learned societies and whole issues of journals were given over to the topic (*Int* 16/2 [April 1962]; *JBR* 30/3 [July 1962]; *TToday* 19/3 [Oct. 1962]; cf. Dupont, 1975). (By way of comparison, an SBL group on NT Christology began only in 1982; see Hurtado.) Hefty anthologies accommodated essays from varying viewpoints (Ristow and Matthiae; Schubert [1962a; cf. 1962b] reflects a Catholic reaction which saw an outgrowth from demythologizing here; Braaten and Harrisville, in English). Systematicians (e.g., Althaus; cf. Gloege) took up themes that had been smoldering since a *Neutestamentler-Dogmatiker*, Martin Kähler, had set himself against the quest in 1892. (Kähler's seminal essay finally made it into English in 1964, and there has been a revival of interest in his works in Germany.) For all this activity, it must be emphasized, however, that the new quest was really an umbrella term, covering a variety of approaches. Many attached themselves to it or were reckoned a part of the effort, even though they had little affinity to the extremes that E. Käsemann's proposal sought to rectify.

How can the new quest be characterized? Jesus' teachings were stressed far more than his career. Chronology, biography, and psychological development were never prominent, if present at all. It was said that whereas Bultmann had been content with the mere *dass* of Jesus' existence (the fact *that* he lived, taught, and died), the new quest was interested in the *Was* (what he was like) or the "*was*ness of the *dass*ness." Whereas the old quest, particularly under liberalism, had sought to jump from the Gospel portraits of Jesus, around the christological kerygma of the early church, to "*Jesus wie er eigentlich gewesen ist*" ("Jesus as he really was"), and Bultmann had been content to work back from the Gospel material to the kerygma (leaving "Jesus" a shadowy figure behind it), the new quest took aim at moving from the Gospel material through the kerygma to Jesus, about whose life history more could be said than had been customary in German circles. It was hoped that there would emerge a consistency of portraiture between the historical Jesus and the Christ of the kerygma and the Gospels. All the "criticisms" in modern scholarship were assumed. Often there was a strong appeal to existentialism, or at least to understanding of one's existence, and to a "theology of the word" and "language-events" for hearers then and now. J. M. Robinson (1962b) saw the venture as opening up the possibility of a second way in which a call to authentic existence can arise: in addition to the kerygma, now through the sayings of the historical Jesus.

Pride of place among the new quest lives fell to Günther Bornkamm's *Jesus of Nazareth* (1956; cf. 1964 and 1975 for further views; also Hahn, 1962), in many ways the chief and representative "life" from the movement. Widely read, it stood a bit to the right of Bultmann, for example, in allowing that Jesus made a deliberate decision to go up to Jerusalem and to his death. Jesus' directness and authority emerge strongly. But all christological titles are dealt with in an appendix; none goes back to the historical Jesus. Conzelmann produced the article on "Jesus Christ" for the new third edition of the German encyclopedia, *Die Religion in Geschichte und Gegenwart*, but otherwise abandoned the quest. Käsemann (1964) denounced as "dead-end streets" a number of efforts at "lives" (including Jeremias's work) and eventually withdrew from the venture (see 1975). His picture of Jesus' asserting "freedom" as a theme (1968), written during the enforced idleness of illness but reflecting personal battles in the German church, is as close to a "life" as Käsemann ever came. His Jesus was a revolutionary liberal. G. Ebeling and E. Fuchs moved into hermeneutics, James M. Robinson (after naming and championing the new quest) into Nag Hammadi studies. C. Burchard's *Kleine Pauly* article had, by the nature of that encyclopedia, to stress only "the historical side" (but cf. 1352–53).

Bultmann's reaction in 1959 was mixed but mostly negative. On the one hand, he went farther than he had in 1926 in listing what he would accept as authentic (1959:22–23), but he pressed home the embarrassment "that we cannot know how Jesus understood his end, his death." (On this point, contrast Schürmann, 1973, and Léon-Dufour, 1975.) Bultmann reiterated his fear, on the other hand, that the historical Jesus would again become a substitute for the word of kerygma.

A belated result of the new quest came in 1969 in the slim book, *Jesus*, by the scholar many feel most radically carried through Bultmann's anthropological intentions, Herbert Braun: Jesus becomes a kind of paradigm for the practice of grace, of openness to the neighbor, and "God" is a "process by which the wicked and hopeless person receives a future and a hope" (1969:136). Compare and contrast Schulz: theologically, "without the Pauline gospel, preaching of the historical Jesus must be misunderstood as 'law'" (1975:25).

III. SOME CHRISTOLOGICAL ALTERNATIVES

In its concern to link Jesus with a subsequent Christology, the new quest offered several approaches, quite apart from the question of honorific titles. One, already alluded to, centered in the *concept of existence* found in the teachings of Jesus. J. M. Robinson (1959, 1962b) argued that the pattern in authentic verses like Luke 14:11 and 17:33 is very much the same as that in Phil 2:6–11; 1 Pet 1:11, and elsewhere in post-Easter kerygma: humiliation/exaltation, lose life/gain life, suffering/glory. The logia thus offer a second avenue of access to the good news by historical research, paralleling the apostolic kerygma. The call to authentic existence can also come through the sayings of the historical Jesus, rightly grasped.

A second approach sought for the *ipsissima vox Jesu* ("the very voice of Jesus"). If his actual words (*verba*) are unrecoverable, at least we can sometimes clearly hear his "voice" (*vox*) (Jeremias, 1953). Actually, *verba* like *Abba* and *amēn* are usually involved. The aim here is to find a basis in what Jesus said during the ministry which leads into later Christology: if God is uniquely his Father, then he is Son; his use of *amēn* to begin a statement reflects his authority. H. Schürmann (1960) even speaks of a pre-Easter *Sitz im inneren Leben* ("setting of the inner life") of the disciples as a base for what happens afterwards ("sociological and confessional or witnessing continuity"), and W. Thüsing (1972:182–83 = Eng. trans. 121–22) of an *ipsissima intentio Jesu* ("the very intention of Jesus"). F. Mussner (1967, 1972) has even spoken of *ipsissima facta* ("the very facts") in connection with the miracles.

The third line of argument is to seek continuity in terms of something *implicit* in the historical ministry becoming *explicit* after Easter. Even if Jesus made use of none of the traditional titles, the way he confronted people with God through his message and himself, his conduct in receiving (and forgiving) sinners, and his claims to authority in the antitheses ("But *I* say to you . . .") or in words like *Abba/amēn* hold a Christology *in nuce* ("in a nutshell"), which is made more precise after the resurrection (Conzelmann,

1959:49–50, 93–96).[2] Roloff went farther in seeing implicit christological materials in passages like Mark 1:23–28 and 3:1–6, preserved and developed in the kerygma period.

Ebeling (1958) and Marxsen (1960) developed a fourth sort of link. The historical Jesus called for *faith* in God. The apostolic kerygma concluded with an appeal for *faith* in Jesus the Christ whom God has raised up. There is the link: in the continuity of the call for belief and trust, both before and after Easter (Achtemeier, 1969:101–15, 133–48). At times such research on Jesus seemed to return to older, psychologizing views on how Jesus himself believed (Fuchs). Later, Marxsen (1976b) presented the continuity in terms of an enacted *Jesus kerygma,* an explicit *Christ kerygma,* and in the Gospels' *Jesus Christ kerygma.* Thus, *die Sache Jesu* ("the business of Jesus"; 1976a) goes on. Sobrino's *Christology* (1976) also emphasizes "the faith of Jesus" (Eng., 79–145), but is an expression of Latin American "liberation theology," emphasizing "following Jesus" as the praxis whereby one gets to know Jesus; the approach especially derives from Sobrino's understanding (396–424) of Loyola's *Spiritual Exercises.*

Although some (V. Harvey and Ogden, 1962; cf. Harvey, 1966) suggested that there had been little advance beyond Bultmann in the new quest, the fact is that it reopened for Bultmannians the matter of a *pre*-Easter "messiology" in connection with Jesus, and for conservatives it brought home the possibility of Christology as *only* postresurrection, something they now had to consider more seriously (see Kertelge).

IV. THE CHRISTOLOGICAL TITLES

Already long before 1945 the various honorifics assigned to Jesus by the entire NT, Gospels included, had experienced a long and complex history of discussion. The years of the new quest, plus the Qumran finds and further exploration of the "gnostic myth" (Colpe, 1961; Borsch) in the history of religions accelerated the debates and production of theories. We can note here, only quite briefly, what was happening with regard to the Gospels and Jesus.

Besides sections in the general NT theologies (see chap. 19 in this volume; also Neill, 1976; cf. Lindemann; Stuhlmacher), several major books in our period were devoted specifically to Christology. Apart from V. Taylor's briefer treatments (1953, 1955, 1958), the first major one was by O. Cullmann (1957). One of the best reflections of the biblical theology movement, it was systematically organized around Jesus' earthly work (as prophet, suffering servant, and, surprisingly for some, "high priest"), future work (e.g., Son of man), present work (as lord and savior), and preexistence (Son of

---

[2] R. E. Brown (1974) sees the dividing line in much current scholarship to be between implicit and explicit Christology, most Catholics of the 1960s preferring the latter (Jesus used explicit titles), some Catholics of the 1970s the former (he employed no titles).

God). With regard to "messiah" as a title, Jesus was either extremely restrained or actually rejected it, according to Cullmann.

Ferdinand Hahn's dissertation under Bornkamm (published in 1963) was hailed as the most important study of many years on major titles, including Son of man, *kyrios*, Son of David, and Son of God. Development from Jewish backgrounds through Jesus to early Christian uses is traced. As for *Christos*, Hahn points out that any Zealotic tendency in Jesus is lacking and the concept of "kingly messiah" had no other significance for his work; yet he was accused and executed for messianic revolt (161). Behind Mark 8:27–33 Hahn found a biographical story telling how Jesus rejected the title as a Satanic temptation (similarly Dinkler). Hahn's theses were subjected to penetrating criticism by P. Vielhauer (1965), who argues, for instance, that the linkage of "Christ" with the atonement motif was Hellenistic-Jewish, rather than Palestinian, Christian. Yet see Hengel, 1980 (Eng. 71–73): the soteriological interpretation of Jesus' death as atoning goes back to Jesus' "person and actions." A. E. Harvey (120–53) argues that Jesus applied the name "anointed" to himself on the basis of Isaiah 61.

Change in position under the impact of new quest discussions, as exemplified by Hahn's work, is best seen in Reginald H. Fuller's two treatments. In 1954 he had allowed much closer connection between the historical Jesus and Christology. His 1965 treatment, after a period of study in Germany, reflects in a model way the course of development from Palestinian and Hellenistic Judaism and the Gentile world via Jesus through the Palestinian church, Hellenistic-Jewish and Hellenistic-Gentile missions, into the materials with which Paul, John, and others built. There is present a mini-life of Jesus along "implicit Christology" lines and a reexamination of what he had said eleven years before. Where previously Fuller had followed a modified version of the British view that Jesus combined Deutero-Isaiah's Servant with the Son of man, now he doubted that Jesus accepted Messiah as a title, let alone "spiritualized" it (1965:103–11). Fuller well illustrates how a number of scholars shifted position from the 1950s. Needless to say, the whole notion of neat "stages of development" in Christology has been questioned (I. H. Marshall, 1973; 1976:32–42, 51–58). Hengel (1983) points toward greater continuity in lines of development from Jesus' activity and the "saving event" of his cross and resurrection to the Christology of A.D. 30 to 60. On the topic and selected titles, see also Coppens; Kramer; and Sabourin, 1963; on methods generally, see Hahn, 1970.

Each christological title deserves a full research report of its own, and some have received such surveys. See Dunn, with special reference to "preexistence," especially "Last Adam" and "Wisdom." The view that Jesus used the (suffering) *Servant* concept of Isaiah as it had developed messianically in Judaism (Jeremias, 1952) was pretty much eclipsed in later discussion under the impact of investigations by M. Hooker (1959) and M. Rese. But P. Benoit defends it; see also L. Ruppert. A near consensus on *Messiah*, that Jesus did not employ or welcome the title or that he reinterpreted it (Moule: 35), has been noted—a consensus save of those scholars who identify him as a political revolutionist (see, e.g., Brandon). For the related notion of *Davidic sonship*, there is a strong tendency to grant that Jesus really was a Davidid but laid no emphasis on it (Fuller, 1965:111–14; Brown, 1977:505–12); Matthean emphasis on "Son of David" is redactional (Burger).

That *kyrios* in the form of Aramaic *mar/mārā'/mārê'* or/ *maranā'* was used of the historical Jesus, at least as a title of honor showing authority, like that of a rabbi (even if that term did not yet have a technical sense), is now more widely granted than in Bousset's view. F. Hahn saw a link here to post-Easter usages. S. Schulz (1962) pointed out that *mārā'* was by no means used in the same way as the Hebrew *'ādônāy*—let alone later Christian *kyrios* with its divine connotations—and could apply to Jesus as enthroned Son of man with royal authority as judge. J. A. Fitzmyer (1975a; 1981:201–2) situated the title in Palestinian Semitic religious usage. G. Vermes (1973:103–27) argued for a broader field of meanings for "lord" in Aramaic and that the term reflects the role of the historical Jesus as charismatic Hasid (holy man) as well as teacher. Moule (35–44) carries further "a cumulatively impressive case" that later acclamation of Jesus as Lord articulated what was "implicit all along."

"*Son of God*" is more complicated. B. M. F. van Iersel sought to preserve use of "the Son" by Jesus but termed "Son of God" a later application. But P. W. Schmiedel's old argument for Mark 13:32 as a "pillar passage" no longer finds wide acceptance. The possible allegorical reference to "a beloved son" in the parable at Mark 12:6 has been both defended as genuine and rejected as a later touch. The Q "thunderbolt from the Johannine blue" (Matt 11:25–27 par. Luke 10:21–22) has been so variously assessed that it is hard to build on it. Hahn, Fuller, and others concur in making it post-Easter. See Hengel, 1975, on development within a Jewish-Hellenistic background. On the other hand, an unusual filial consciousness on Jesus' part, seen in his use of *Abba,* is widely presumed. It is precisely such examples as when he is addressed by a heavenly voice as Son of God that Vermes makes his starting point, based on rabbinic analogies, for the contention that "Jesus could have spoken of himself as *son of God*" as a Galilean miracle-working Hasid (1973:210). References to a long-unpublished Qumran fragment (4QFlor 1–2 i 10) employing "son of God" and "son of the Most High," yet without reference to "messiah," tantalized scholars throughout the 1970s (Fitzmyer, 1971:121 n. 10; cf. 1974:391–94); it allows a home in Palestinian Judaism for the term, as well as in the Hellenistic world (Fitzmyer, 1981:206–7).

Opinions over Jesus and "*Son of man*" are almost too complex to analyze (see Higgins; Haufe; I. H. Marshall, 1966, 1970; and Vermes, 1978, for research reports; Pesch and Schnackenburg for a variety of views; Bietenhard; on background usage, Kearns; on history-of-religions setting, Borsch). It was long a commonplace to divide Jesus' Son-of-man sayings into three

groups and claim authenticity usually for one or the other group: (1) passion
sayings; (2) parousia or apocalyptic sayings; (3) present activity or miscellaneous sayings. H. E. Tödt's 1956 dissertation put clearly the classical
Bultmannian contention: only some of the parousia sayings come from Jesus
himself, and they are statements like Mark 8:38, where he distinguishes this
future figure from himself. P. Vielhauer (1957) took the position that none
of the Son-of-man sayings is genuine, because, among other reasons, none
of them refers also to his chief theme of the kingdom (a view argued fourteen
years earlier by H. B. Sharman). J. Gnilka insisted, however, that it was
precisely as Son of man that Jesus announced the kingdom.

E. Schweizer (1960, 1963) called genuine certain sayings dealing not
with the parousia but with the present activity of Jesus, and he entertained
the possibility of authentic aspects in some of the passion sayings. M.
Hooker's later book (1967), claiming that although Jesus did not employ
Suffering Servant categories he did understand himself as suffering Son of
man, was deemed by many to fit Mark's Gospel but not the historical Jesus.
C. Colpe, for the *TWNT* article (1964:429, 433–41), was led to posit a Jewish
Son-of-man tradition not found in Daniel 7, *1 Enoch*, or 4 Ezra, in order to
explain what he termed authentic sayings about a coming Son of man. N.
Perrin (1974:57–93) came to increasingly skeptical views on such sayings
and explained them as early Christian interpretative work applying Dan 7:13
to ascension, passion, and parousia. That, of course, is to remove all of them
from Jesus' own use. S. Kim (1983) on the other hand, maximizes Jesus' use
of the term in conjunction with Son of God.

In the past thirty years scholarship has thus moved from a position
where "Son of man" was widely regarded as "a connecting thread" holding
together Jesus' present and future work (Barrett: 32) to a view that the
problem is vastly more complicated or even insoluble or that the utterances
are all foreign to the historical Jesus (Conzelmann, 1967:135–36). But a
further dimension has been urged by R. Leivestad: the "apocalyptic Son of
man" was a phantom, occurring as a title neither in Jewish literature nor in
NT use. Vermes agreed that there was no pre-Christian Jewish concept (cf.
Colpe): Jesus simply employed it of himself as an Aramaic circumlocution
for "I"; disciples later read in the apocalyptic of Dan 7:13 by means of
midrash (1973:160–91; see also Casey). But Jeremias (1970:261 n. 1 [Eng.
trans.]) and Fitzmyer (*CBQ* 30 [1968] 427; 1975b:92–94), among others,
have objected to this conclusion on linguistic grounds. B. Lindars (1983)
finds no Danielic myth or titular use; Jesus employed *bar (ʿe)nāšaʾ* in the
sense of "man" for himself, with "teasing irony," in some sayings; linkage with
Daniel in a christological sense came only with Q and the evangelists. But
Moule (11–12) continues to be impressed by the presence of the definite
article in Greek, "*the* [or *that*] Son of man," indicating in Jesus' Aramaic a
reference to the human figure in Daniel 7 representing the people of God
destined to suffer and be vindicated. Thus, T. W. Manson's interpretation of

a "corporate Son of man" (Jesus and his disciples) still has defenders. Cf. Kümmel, 1984: Jesus proclaimed the kingdom, God working eschatological salvation in him as "the man" expected at the last times. All this work has brought no wide agreement on Son of man—or even on its importance for Jesus, if Vielhauer or Vermes is right.

Each christological title should be considered further within the theology of each author employing it—Paul, John, and so forth. Here some overall impressions may be noted. First, in place of the widely held supposition a generation or two ago, that Paul created Christology and foisted it upon Jesus, scholarship has moved to a greater recognition that key steps had been taken in the *pre-Pauline period* (see Kramer; Fuller, 1965; Wengst; Hengel, 1983). *Paul's own Christology* (see Cerfaux) worked chiefly with inherited concepts (Fuller, 1974). The impact of his "Damascus road experience" is often stressed as a formative factor (Thrall) and, indeed, overdone (Kim, 1981). For Paul's accenting of the tradition, see Eichholz, 1972:101–214; or Goppelt, 2:65–87 (Eng. trans.).

Second, under the impact of redaction criticism, there has been a more careful assessment of how each evangelist handles Christology in that community's situation. The *Johannine writings* provide the best example. Here early traditions about Jesus were enriched by the influx of Samaritan converts, extended in debate with the synagogue, and elevated into the NT's highest Christology, where Jesus is confessed as God (Brown, 1979, reflecting studies also by J. L. Martyn and others).

Mark's Gospel, which once labored under the assumption that it embodied little theology, has come to be viewed as expressing its own christological program. But what program? Mark has been said to reflect a Hellenistic Christ myth (like Phil 2:6–11; Bultmann, 1921:347–50 [Eng. trans.]) or an enthronement of the divine son (1:11; 9:7; 15:39, plus the textually uncertain "Son of God" at 1:1; Schreiber; but note also 14:61–62); or a Christology of Jesus as divine wonderworker that is either corrected as heretical (Weeden) or placed under a theology of the cross (Marxsen, 1956; Koester). Others see Jesus as God's apocalyptic agent (note "Son of man") in the divine plan to summon an end-time community of the new covenant (Kee, 1970, 1977). Different from all "corrective" theories about Mark, that in Kingsbury, 1983, holds that the rather contentless title "Son of man," used in public, complements the complex of terms "Messiah," "Son of David," "King," and "Son of God" that set forth the secret of who Jesus really is. Son of God functions as the norming or "evaluative" term, for it shows what God "thinks" about Jesus (1:11; 9:7). Of course, Marcan Christology is done by narrative as well as by titles. V. K. Robbins argues that Mark's achievement was to present the Jesus who fulfills royal messianic categories of Jewish expectations in a way that appealed to the Greco-Roman cultural world—as a disciple-gathering teacher. Mark does this by use of current rhetorical formulas, to assert, demonstrate, and lead on to conclusions about Jesus.

Christology looms relatively less large in the other two Gospels. *Matthew* is sometimes taken to have subordinated it to ecclesiology. Not so in Kingsbury's analysis (1975; 1981:61–93): "Son of God" is the chief "confessional" title, never used publicly but indicating that Jesus is Davidic Messiah, exalted since Easter; "Son of man" is the public title, showing what Jesus was during his ministry. J. Meier would stress more "Son of man," which, with "Son of God," forms an ellipse between whose two focuses "the Son" also is an important term. That Jesus is "wisdom" also comes into prominence in Matthew (11:19, cf. v 2; 11:25–27, 28–30; 23:34–36, 37–39), though it probably goes beyond the evidence to call Jesus wisdom's "incarnation" (Suggs, 1970:58, 96; cf. F. Christ). A further Matthean contribution is to regard Jesus, rather than the Spirit, as the ongoing presence of God (28:20; 18:20; cf. 1:23 "God with us"), particularly perhaps through the authoritative discourses of the Matthean Jesus and his being with disciples (Terrien: 429–31; Ziesler; cf. 8:23–27; 14:22–33).

The twin volumes of *Luke-Acts* not only heighten "a time of the church" after Pentecost but also allow the earthly ministry to be viewed as a *vita Jesu* ("life of Jesus"). While Luke somewhat separates into two stages his story of how the Christ had to suffer and then to enter into glory (Luke 24:26) — earthly and heavenly stages — his use of christological titles often straddles both periods. Indeed, terms like *kyrios* are retroverted into Jesus' life (e.g., Luke 10:1). Luke employs traditional terms intertwined with soteriology (including use of "savior" in Acts 5:31; 13:23; and Luke 2:11, alone of all the Synoptics), but often with twists of his own in describing the Spirit-led human figure with the more-than-human aspects of virginal conception (but not preexistence), ascension (after the resurrection), and future return as Messiah (Acts 3:19–21). For Luke, Jesus is especially a suffering Christ, Servant and Son, at times Elijah *redivivus* ("restored to life"), and Leader (*archēgos*, Acts 3:15; 5:31). For detailed survey and bibliography, see Fitzmyer, 1981:192–219, 263–65. F. Danker's "divine benefactor," while demonstrable as a theme in the Greco-Roman world, has too slim a data base in Luke-Acts to expect readers to pick it up as the overarching category.

On Christology in individual NT authors, one has two minds: on the one hand, to applaud the subtle nuances detected by some critics and, on the other, to regard titles as almost interchanging and promiscuously used (Conzelmann, 1967:199 [Eng. trans.]) by the time of the evangelist-redactors or even Paul.

V. SPECIAL AREAS OF STUDY

Constructing a *Leben Jesu* ("life of Jesus") inevitably reflects an understanding of a number of specialized topics concerning Jesus. Observation of what is happening in these areas, individually and collectively, also provides a barometer of trends.

The Kingdom of God

The kingdom of God has been regarded by scholars, virtually without exception, as Jesus' central theme. J. Bright has emphasized it, indeed, as "the total message of the Bible," the heart of its "gospel of salvation" (7). But since A. Ritschl a host of interpretations have flourished (Lundström). While the liberal view of Harnack had been shown to be one-sided by J. Weiss and A. Schweitzer, Schweitzer's eschatological interpretation proved convincing to few (the emphasis appears, however, in Strobel [1967]; and Hiers), though it did introduce a futurist element which almost no one has since ignored. Kümmel (1945) was influential in establishing the view exegetically that Jesus regarded the kingdom as both present and future (so, already in 1950, Wilder). Against the realized eschatology of Dodd (1935), Jeremias has argued consistently for an "eschatology in process of realization" (1964:32 n. 27, on the term). A trio of books in 1959–64 by H. N. Ridderbos, R. Schnackenburg, and G. E. Ladd agreed basically that God's kingly rule found a fulfillment in Jesus' mission but looked to a future consummation as well. Further on the kingdom, see Klein; and on eschatology, Grässer, 1957, 1973; J. A. T. Robinson, 1957; Thüsing, 1970; and on most aspects, Schlosser. On proclamation of the kingdom and Jesus' death, see Schürmann, 1983.

The work of Perrin, on both sides of the Atlantic, has been especially significant. From a position (1963) akin to that of his teachers, T. W. Manson and Jeremias, he was "converted" (Epp: 117), under the impact of form and then redaction criticism (1967:15–53; 1974:1–9), to a more minimalist position on what came authentically from Jesus, with the notion of the kingdom "not temporal, but experiential" (1967:205). Later, reckoning with myth (P. Ricoeur) and structuralism, he came to regard the kingdom in Jesus' message as a " 'tensive symbol' . . . used to evoke the myth of God acting as king" (1976:196).

The Parables of Jesus

Research on the parables (for a bibliographical report, see Kissinger, 1979), a key to any reconstruction of the message of Jesus, followed a course of development even clearer than that seen in connection with "the kingdom." It had long since been established that parables should be set in the context of Jesus' ministry, specifically his eschatological message (Dodd, 1935). The several editions of Jeremias's *The Parables of Jesus* (German original 1947) pioneered criteria for claiming the recovery of Jesus' *ipsissima vox* ("very voice") and applied form and redaction criticism to strip off churchly additions. Comparisons with parables in the *Gospel of Thomas* were weighed. A theology of Jesus was developed as the basis of genuine parables and other materials (1970).

In the early 1960s, however, the New Hermeneutic (Fuchs; Linnemann, 1961; Jüngel; and others) and literary concerns (Jones) moved parable study to a further stage: not merely the recovery of Jesus' "original" story but the course of development, the concept of existence involved, and the parable as art form or "metaphor" occupied scholarly attention (Funk, 1966:133–62; Via). The work of John Dominic Crossan has been particularly hailed: "parable is the house of God" (1973:32–33), and, appreciated as poetic metaphor, Jesus' parables can challenge us, as they once addressed Jesus' first hearers, to see the advent of new possibilities and the reversal of the past, and move us toward action. Crossan's view depends heavily, however, on the correctness of Perrin's view (1967:16–20) that verses like Mark 9:1 are early-church creations, so that the futuristic side of the kingdom in Jesus' teachings is undermined and a temporal understanding is replaced by an existential one. The Society of Biblical Literature Parables Seminar (1973–1978) wrestled especially with structuralism as an approach to the parables (*Semeia* 1; 2; 9: 1–73).

These efforts in the "post-Jeremias age" (for bibliography, see *Semeia* 1: 236–74) have been variously assessed. The SBL Seminar has been seen as letting "the parable speak for itself" afresh, in "the present of the interpreter," though there are reservations about whether some of the analysis "has helped us very much" (Perrin, 1976:181, 174). Does Luke 10:30–35 mean that hearers should identify with "the man in the ditch" (*Semeia* 2: 79 [Funk]) or with the Samaritan (Tannehill, as cited in Perrin, 1976:178)? Is Jesus precursor of Kafka (Funk, 1975) or of Gerard Manley Hopkins (*Semeia* 12: 37 [Breech])? But this is to move beyond Jesus and Christology to the history of the evocation of literary impressions. Breech (1983) limits his picture of a Jesus who is silent about himself to parables and core sayings that invite one to be human. Meanwhile, more conventional books about the parables continue to be written concerning Jesus and his death as seen from the parables (C. W. F. Smith) and on the development of meanings in the Synoptic versions (Carlston, 1975).

The Teachings of Jesus

The teachings of Jesus overall have only occasionally in this period found an expositor willing to tackle the topic the way T. W. Manson (1931, 1937) or H. Branscomb or B. S. Easton had. E. Percy took a position similar to that of Jeremias: the kingdom is still to come but has already begun, and Jesus is its bearer. S. Maclean Gilmour (1957) touched on Jesus' teaching. Note also R. Schäfer, on Jesus' view of God. On Q material, R. A. Edwards has given us an assembling of data, and S. Schulz (1972) a more detailed interpretation, but the interest has more often shifted to the theology of the source or the evangelist-editor— especially since the advent of *Redaktionsgeschichte* (redaction criticism)— rather than the teaching of Jesus. Schnackenburg (1962:15–167) and Jeremias (1970) are the most comprehensive, though most "lives" accentuate the topic. Perrin (1963:158–206; cf. 1967:11) gave promise of treating the matter, but his research took other directions. In the NT theologies of the period, Conzelmann (like Bultmann) and Schelkle have only brief presentations; Kümmel (1969:46–58) covers "fulfillment of the divine will" and "reward and punishment" on a popular level, along with Jesus' proclamation about God and his personal claim; Goppelt is on a more scholarly level, more conservative, but wins Kümmel's acclaim as "the best and most reliable presentation of Jesus' proclamation and activity" (*TRu* 41: 315).

The Ethics of Jesus

Studies of Jesus' ethics have moved in a similar direction. Prior to 1950, books like those of L. H. Marshall and L. Dewar presumed that they were able to present Jesus' view of God, evil, and problems in society, etc. rather positively. Some twenty years later, certain NT scholars stress instead how little is recoverable from Jesus and indeed comparatively little in the whole NT relates to us (Houlden: 101–14); "Jesus does not provide a valid ethics for today" (J. T. Sanders [29], who regards Jesus' teachings as so eschatological that the efforts of Wilder to find how they endure beyond the eschatological disappointment will not work; Bornkamm reverts to precritical solutions; Fuchs to a doctrinal answer; James M. Robinson to the kerygma; Herbert Braun to what a humanist can learn from Jesus-sans-eschatology). H.-D. Wendland (4–33), however, provides a unified eschatological ethic of Jesus, but it can be accused of some of the same failings, from J. T. Sanders's viewpoint. W. Schrage's *Ethik*, with its likewise eschatological view of Jesus, replaced Wendland's volume in the GNT series in 1982. It is probably no accident that recent discussion has concentrated on the "love-command" (Fuller, 1978; cf. Piper). K. Niederwimmer's *Jesus* especially stresses the radicality of Jesus against not only the law but also "against the whole sacred tradition of his people" (55). R. Newton Flew reflects the earlier outlook of biblical theology. John Knox (1961) and Paul Minear busied themselves in showing how Jesus' imperatives still apply, though they bring in fuller theological considerations.

The Sermon on the Mount

The Sermon-on-the-Mount material has always occupied pride of place in Jesus' teachings (for research report and bibliography, see Kissinger, 1975). Older studies by Windisch and Branscomb were translated or appeared in new editions in the early 1950s. The Qumran discoveries led to a flurry of comparisons with Jesus' sayings, Herbert Braun's bibliographical survey (1966) and analysis of "heightening of the Torah" at Qumran (1957b) being noteworthy. W. D. Davies, while concerned especially with the Matthean *Sitz im Leben* ("life setting") for the Sermon, stressed also Jesus' autonomous authority, assuming his messiahship (1964:430). By and large, however, concern has been with development of the tradition and redaction (Wrege: cf. Kümmel, *TRu* 43: 111–16), not with "a sermon of Jesus." The Beatitudes (Dupont, 1954) and antitheses have been treated more pertinently than other sections, though debate continues over which antithetical statements may go back to Jesus (usually 1, 2, and 4; see *TRu* 43: 116–20). On Matthew 5–7, see Guelich; and Strecker (1984), noting the role Matthew's Christology plays in the Sermon (Guelich: 25, 27–33, *passim;* Strecker: 185–87). However, notice should also be taken of the views of H. D. Betz, emerging in a number of essays, that the Sermon is a pre-Matthean unit from Jewish-Christian circles, not always agreeing with Matthew's own theology, but providing fragments of the teaching of Jesus and his Jewish thought (x–xi, 18–19, 55–56, 67, 90–95, and 151–54, presenting a minimalist "Christology" of Jesus in 7:21–23 as advocate for his disciples at the last judgment).

The Lord's Prayer

Of course, the Lord's Prayer has always been an object of special attention (Scott; Lohmeyer). Jeremias's reconstruction of an Aramaic "original" (1962) has fared better than his "recovered" eucharistic words of Jesus, but even his work here has been challenged (Goulder; Carmignac). That *"Abba"* and *"amēn"* are words showing us Jesus' "very voice" is widely accepted (e.g., Perrin, 1967:38–42), but each is disputed (Conzelmann, 1967:101–6, 127–29; Hasler; Berger, 1970 — the Jewish background does offer analogues to Jesus' usage, and early Christian prophets likely spoke "Amen-sayings" in the name of the risen Lord). Thus, all these areas still find varying assessment (see Hamerton-Kelly on God as "Father"). Even on so basic a matter as Jesus and the Mosaic law, three recent monographs fail to reach common convincing conclusions: Berger (1972) is but a prolegomenon on Jesus; Banks sees Jesus' authority (not the law) as the issue; and Hübner treats mainly the rejudaizing process (Stauffer) in the Gospels. See also Westerholm on Torah as loving expression of God's saving will. One can claim, however, that a greater understanding of Jesus' radicality in opposing at least aspects of the OT – Jewish law stands out. E. P. Sanders (1982:428) concludes that Jesus, living amid "covenantal nomism," "at least symbolically disrupted the sacrificial system which is commanded in the Torah" and "placed loyalty to his mission above at least some of the commandments of Moses."

The Activity of Jesus' Ministry

As for the activity of Jesus in his ministry, increasing emphasis has been put on the way he received sinners and ate with them (Haas) and, perhaps exaggerated by "liberation theology," his concern for the poor and outcasts (Schottroff and Stegemann). Generally, political involvement on Jesus' part – let alone overt Zealotism – has been denied. The "student rebellion" of the late 1960s made a "revolutionist Jesus" popular (see Cullmann, 1970;

Hengel), though even Brandon, who claimed that the Gospels are a post–A.D. 70 "cover-up," never quite made him a Zealot leader in an armed *Putsch* ("insurrection") the way Carmichael did. There has been a quiet minority literature claiming Jesus as a nonviolent peace leader (A. Trocmé; Yoder). Such views became increasingly popular in the early 1980s, claiming Jesus for peace causes (e.g., Beutler; Strecker, 1984:22–23).

The Miracle Stories

In this period the miracle stories were sometimes explained by modern psychology (McCasland, 1951), sometimes defended (van der Loos; Kallas — in the light of the "demonic"). The chief trends were (a) to subject them to the tradition-critical approach (e.g., Fuller, 1963) and (b) the "aretalogy"/ *theios anēr* ("divine man") debate (Achtemeier, 1972). It was contended that the Hellenistic world was rife with notions of wise teachers elevated to divinity (e.g., Socrates, Pythagoras), often credited with working wonders (such as Apollonius of Tyana) and that Judaism developed similar tales about Moses, Elijah, and others. Jesus, according to some, was so presented by the Gospels (Hadas and Smith) or by opponents of Paul in 2 Corinthians (Georgi) or of Mark (Weeden). Subsequent studies have questioned much of the evidence and approach (Kee, 1973; Tiede; Holladay). That Jesus freed sick people of demons, in terms of his day, remains probable, even in the opinion of a radical Bultmannian like Braun (1969:28 [Eng. trans.]). On Jesus' miracles as *facta* ("real happenings"), see further the Mussner-Pesch discussion.

The Passion of Jesus

The Passion narratives were subjected to redaction-critical studies emphasizing the version of each evangelist or source (e.g., Taylor on Proto-Luke; see the research report in Sloyan) and to form-critical questioning of the widespread assumption that one or several unified passion narratives circulated from the beginning (Linnemann, 1970: brief units have been combined). A complicating factor has been the question raised by Jewish and other scholars about anti-Semitic tendencies in the Gospels (noteworthily by Jules Isaac, a survivor of Nazi persecution) and indeed the historicity of any "Jewish trial" (Winter, following Lietzmann [*Judaism* 20 (1971) 6–74]; Cohn: Jewish authorities were trying to *save* Jesus' life!). The view that Jesus was a political revolutionist also surfaced in this connection (Brandon, 1968). Nonetheless, more traditional views had their defenders (Blinzler: a Sanhedrin trial according to *Sadducean* rules; Sherwin-White; Bammel, 1970, 1984; Strobel, 1980; and Catchpole). Perhaps the best popular account of (German) scholarly views came from Lohse (1964), while Wilson provided a more detailed report on Jesus' execution. See now also O. Betz (1982).

The Resurrection

The resurrection usually has not been treated as a part of Jesus' "life" (so Bornkamm; contrast Holtz), though more conservative lives often still include it, if only to indicate how resurrection-faith colors Gospel reports. Fuller (1971) offers a standard tradition-critical analysis of how resurrection accounts arose (earlier, see Grass). Marxsen (et al., 1966; 1968) has been especially in the center of the German discussion. R. R. Niebuhr made the resurrection a focal point in discussing historical and theological method.

The Infancy Material

For an area excluded from many "lives" (though not on the part of Catholics and some others), the infancy material has received surprising emphasis. Raymond E. Brown, *The Birth of the Messiah,* provides a magisterial analysis and report on varying views.

A controversy that developed in the late 1970s, particularly in Britain, concerned the place of the incarnation in NT Christology: Is it "myth"? (Hick; Goulder, 1979; Green). Dunn's *Christology in the Making* provided a response that minimalizes incarnational aspects of most titles for Jesus; "only with the Fourth Gospel" is there "a clear doctrine of incarnation" (258).

Others continue to devote their energies to the biographical, almost psychological problem of how Jesus of Nazareth came, humanly speaking, to his vocation. Schillebeeckx (1975:256–71 [Eng. trans.]) speaks of "Jesus' original *Abba* experience." Hollenbach claims that Jesus once practiced baptism as a follower of John but broke from the Baptist upon his "conversion" when he experienced the power to exorcise demons. On our ability to engage in a quest for the historical Baptizer, see Wink, 1968 (on sources and redaction); and Reumann, 1972. It is, however, of conclusions on such matters as those listed above that "lives" of Jesus are made.

VI. TYPES OF LIVES—SOME KEY EXAMPLES

For the period since 1900, Bowman (1970) has listed seven chief types of lives. Actually there are many more categories (Hayes), even since 1946 (see Deschner, Schierse), though not in the exotic profusion Martin has claimed over the centuries. We list twenty, possibly overlapping, categories.

(1) Probably no one since F. C. Burkitt in 1932 has attempted a "life" along the lines of Albert Schweitzer and his *apocalyptic messiah* figure, a Jesus of the heroic will, though few have been able to avoid the eschatology question, which Schweitzer brought to the fore. M. S. Enslin felt his *Prophet from Nazareth* reflected Schweitzer (123–25, 146, 170–71), but the book has more commonly been perceived as reflecting the stance of liberalism, the view exemplified in (2) Jesus as *the Great Teacher,* a category Bowman evidently felt to be dead. McCasland (1964) may be placed here, along with

Fosdick, D. F. Robinson, and others. The approach is by no means exhausted, especially where Wrede has been the signpost for the future. Neo-humanism (e.g., Braun) is not unrelated. But then Braun may better fit under the category that Bowman made for Bultmann, (3) Jesus as *existentialist rabbi.* Actually Bultmann later tended to see Jesus more as a prophet (1959:27).

(4) *The church's resurrected Lord* is Bowman's description for Born-kamm's Jesus. It picks up the fact that all Gospel pericopes are viewed in a postresurrection light, but does not indicate as fully as Bowman's own description does (1970:119–35) the emphasis on a Jesus of history. Bow-man's own predilection (1943, 1962, and as seen in other writings) is for a Jesus who fulfills God's plan as he saw it in the OT: (5) the *prophetic Suffering Servant-messiah.* Here he places W. Manson, T. W. Manson, V. Taylor (1951, 1955) and appeals to the writings of Dodd, Cullmann, and Kümmel. To this list could be added William Barclay and others. In the very year Bowman published his analysis, Dodd brought out *The Founder of Christianity,* which he had been polishing ever since the material was presented as lectures in 1954. The final three chapters offer with considerable confidence a chrono-logical "life," plus resurrection sequel. The eschatology is of the "realized" type. Jesus directed his followers to the Suffering-Servant theme (construed corporately) and interpreted "Messiah" and "Son of man" in light thereof. G. Vermes (1973:191) saluted Dodd for being the first, though an octogenarian, to rethink the Son-of-man problem and follow him in taking *bar nāšā* as a circumlocution for "I."

Two of Bowman's categories prove in retrospect to be but "flashes in the pan," of little enduring worth: (6) John Allegro (1957; cf. 1956) alleged that Jesus was an *Essene-like Teacher of Righteousness.* "Parallelomania" around 1956–57 led to charges that Jesus was but a copy of the Qumran leader. More careful sifting of the data soon dissipated such extreme views. We may add that Allegro later (1970) became more interested in advancing the view that "Jesus" was a codename for (7) the *Sacred Mushroom,* a hallucinatory drug which early Christians used and worshiped. (That Jesus never existed as a person takes us back to the "Christ myth" school; see Ory.) (8) The *Nazorean scheming Messiah* is Bowman's description for the Jesus of Schon-field (1966): Jesus plotted his own "death" and "resurrection" in a Machiavel-lian scheme, thwarted only by the chance Roman spear thrust on the cross. It is, in a way, type (5)'s OT scenario, carried to bizarre extremes. Need it be mentioned that Qumran was appealed to in supporting a vegetarian Jesus (Ewing) as well as a revolutionist figure (J. Lehmann)?

(9) Jesus as *political revolutionist* has been an approach since Reimarus. Brandon (especially 1967) and Carmichael championed it in this period, the former more cautiously than the latter (see also Harenberg; Hengel, 1970, bibliography; Petzke; Pike; Bammel, 1984). Bartsch recognized that Jesus expected the kingdom to come "exclusively as God's deed" but also saw it as "a utopia now to be realized," with change in social structures (73, 116).

In fairness, it must be said that a case, perhaps even better, can be made for (10) *Jesus as a pacifist* (G. Edwards; A. Trocmé; Yoder). A "Jesus of the business men," such as Bruce Barton had offered in the 1920s, has been lacking in more recent years, but (11) a *Marxist-atheist* interpretation of Jesus has emerged (Machoveč; Bloch; cf. Ratschow, 1970; Kern: 63–84). See also the popular volume by the Catholic university chaplain, Adolf Holl. Buchanan implies that Jesus taught a "conquest theology" and appears to have chosen voluntarily to suffer (312–13).

(12) Under the banner of *sexuality* we have had the case put for a married or at least romantically involved Jesus (Ben-Chorin; Phipps; Kazantzakis: Was Mary Magdalene "Mrs. Jesus"?); a pro-feminist Jesus (Swidler; Wahlberg; cf. Hamerton-Kelly); and discussion of Jesus and homosexuality (Horner). The fragment of "a Secret Gospel of Mark" published by Morton Smith has been taken by some to imply a homosexual relationship involving Jesus, at least in Carpocratian interpretation (1973b:185, cf. 154 and 295–350), but Smith employs the text to claim that Jesus is portrayed as teaching a secret baptismal rite that brings union with himself, the spirit, and ascent into the heavens, plus liberation from the law (1973a:101–14); see type (13) below. Of course, Qumran materials were used to argue also for a monastic, celibate Jesus (Vermes, 1973:99–102, prophetic celibacy; cf. Buchanan). Emergence (again) of such themes may be reflections of the times, but some found the emphasis to have scholarly grounding and to be of theological relevance. (13) Morton Smith, as noted above, has written on *Jesus the Magician,* an aspect he claims official records have ignored.

Far more important are the next two categories. (14) *Jesus the Jew and Jesus as seen by Jewish scholarship* (see Isaac; Lapide, already mentioned; Sandmel; Lindeskog, survey; Thoma; Aron). Forty years ago, in the wake of Houston Stewart Chamberlain and the Nazis, Dibelius (42–43) and others had to take pains to show that Jesus was Jewish, not Aryan, and there existed "German-Christian" lives (see Leipoldt; Ackermann; Grundmann earlier wrote on such topics, but his 1957 *Geschichte* is more conventionally biblical). Jewish interest in Jesus has moved from apologetics to a more positive reclaiming of him (*Heimholung Jesu,* Ben-Chorin, 1967, 1970, 1974). See Hagner for a negative judgment on such "reclamation." Flusser, with his own source analysis of the Gospels and notion that Jesus was an Essene, stresses congruities with the Judaism of his day and has produced the best-known Israeli "life" (but the reader who is unaware that he teaches at Hebrew University "would assume" that it is "by a Christian fundamentalist," S. Zeitlin, *JQR* 60 [1970] 188). Vermes's reading of the Gospels is perhaps the most significant in this class, in that he sets Jesus within charismatic Judaism in Galilee and sees him as a Hasidic *zaddiq,* helper, healer, teacher, and leader, taking "his stand among the pariahs of his world," venerated as "prophet, lord, and *son of God,*" unsurpassed in "laying bare . . . the essence of religion" (223–25). Cf. Hengel, 1968. E. P. Sanders concludes that Jesus preached the kingdom in a Jewish setting and may have died for his self-claims—a role in the kingdom, conceivably as a cosmic Son of man (326, 333). Islamic links have also been explored (Bammel, 1968; Räisänen; Osman).

(15) The *tradition-history* approach has emerged in the 1970s as the most feasible: something can be said of the historical Jesus, more can be said of how he was depicted in source materials, and most can be stated of what each Gospel presents on him. E. Trocmé has used form-critical categories to suggest how different groups looked on Jesus during his ministry. Kee (1970) sketches how Q and each evangelist regarded Jesus (see also Schulz, 1967). E. Schweizer (1968) has described the Jesus who emerges in the various strands of NT witness, from "the man who fits no formula" (see Ernst: 145–58, his "nonconformism") through each unsuing segment of the "trajectory" or lines of development. Others, e.g., Barnikol, have reconstructed a Jesus on the basis of quite individualistic source analysis; see also M. Lehmann (vs. E. Hirsch).

(16) A new form of the *social-historical emphasis* of the Chicago School has come to life in the treatment by Theissen of the "Jesus movement" (see also Duling: 295–97), and (17) *psychological, psychoanalytical* approaches have reappeared in Niederwimmer and Wolff (see also Kern: 84–100).

We dare not neglect the fact that (18) *classical, conservative* lives continue to be written; witness Stauffer, Turner, Carrington, Harrison, Guthrie, William Neil, and Mitton. Perhaps analyses from an audience standpoint (J. A. Baird, 1969; cf. 1963; Derrett) may fit here, or under (5) or as an aspect of (15). W. Phillips comes closet to a life from the perspective of the Albright archaeological school; see also Burrows. M. Grant writes as a student of ancient history who believes recovery of information about Jesus is possible.

(19) *Roman Catholic* lives have long formed a classification of their own. Fernández, Daniel-Rops, Steinmann, perhaps Léon-Dufour (1963), Bruckberger, and Geiselmann are in ways typical for our period. In recent years, however, as Catholics joined the quest, their results fall into other of the categories recognized above (De Rosa, Trilling, Gnilka, Grollenberg; Mackey [282 n. 1; cf. Reumann, 1968]; Fabris; Sloyan, 1983; Pfammalter, survey on the recent German literature). "Anticlerical" lives sometimes still appear, such as Craveri's. And while (20) *systematic theologians* carry Jesus and Christology far beyond the quest, the books of Pannenberg, J. A. T. Robinson, and Schillebeeckx surely try to reflect recent biblical scholarship. For literature in this area prior to 1966 Slenczka is not to be overlooked. W. A. Thompson provides an example of further theologizing in light of the historical Jesus; an overview of classical post-NT and current Christologies can be found in Fuller and Perkins (109–34, 135–61).

Student textbook "lives" which reflect the new quest include Connick, Saunders, Reumann, and Stein; earlier and to lesser degrees, Tilden,

Rowlingson, S. E. Johnson. Hayes (1976) and Duling (1979) provide recent surveys of the fuller quest (the former adds "the Black Messiah," the latter Eliade, structuralism, and analytical psychology as trends, but admittedly these — as yet — have not always given birth to "lives"). The "secular Christ" was a popular category in the late 1960s (Vincent, Todrank). Excerpts from the quest have been provided in textbooks by H. Anderson (1967) and McArthur (1969b). As always, and perhaps increasingly, the media (*Godspell, Jesus Christ Superstar*) and media people have been active in treating Jesus, e.g., Augstein, the publisher of *Der Spiegel*, or Muggeridge; see also Bauman (originally lectures for TV). There are, of course, other lives as good or better in quality than some examples cited above for illustrative purposes, of which space precludes mention.

VII. CONCLUSIONS, ISSUES, METHODOLOGY, AND ONWARD!

Aulén found emerging consensus in the period around 1970 by selective examination of a few leading scholars (Dodd, 1971; Braun, 1969; Jeremias, 1970; with references also to W. D. Davies, 1964; Perrin; Gerhardsson; and others). If Aulén had looked at more "lives," however, or additional specialized literature on Jesus, the results would have been more disparate. One can claim "consensus" only by ignoring or setting aside certain views. Indeed, as one examines the many attempts at lives, the chief function of historical-critical scholarship seems to be to exclude this one or that, but, within certain parameters of what is possible or likely, no final historical answer can be given on Jesus.

Quite apart from debate over this method or that, like form criticism (cf. Güttgemanns), there are often attacks on the scholarly approach today (Wink) and the quest as a whole (Gager; Hahn, 1972, 1974; A. E. Harvey). The basic question of criteria for isolating authentic Jesus-material has run through much recent discussion. While there has been some agreement on the criteria of dissimilarity, multiple attestation, consistency or coherence with proven Jesus-material, and linguistic or environmental tests (Aramaisms and Jewish background), one can scarcely speak of uncontested agreement here on either methods or results (see Kümmel, *TRu* 31: 15–46; 44: 345–59; Balz; on criteria specifically, Perrin, 1967:39–47; Fuller, 1966:94–98; Carlston, 1962; Gager: 256–60; Lührmann; Meyer).

Nonetheless, it is clear that the quest will go on. "They cannot kill Jesus — all the *Leben-Jesu* researchers" (Speicher). Meaningful work continues (Grässer, 1975). Keck's future for the historical Jesus, in preaching and theology, rests not only on the thesis that "we can know important things solidly" about him, but specifically on "the Jewishness of Jesus," the role of apocalyptic in his background, and his emphasis on "trust." In this somewhat anti-Kähler/Bultmann/New Hermeneutic approach, the link to a trustworthy

Jesus is a universal, social term, "trust" (more *fides qua creditur* ["faith which believes"] than *fides quae* ["faith which is believed"], almost "how Jesus trusted God"). This is to develop further the Ebeling-Marxsen-Fuchs alternative noted above (pp. 508–9), not to mention Wilhelm Herrmann (otherwise somewhat enigmatically included in the "lives of Jesus" series edited by Keck). But which Jesus, and what sort of "Jewishness" as background?

The new quest (along with other factors) has encouraged a "Christology from below" (Kasper; cf. Nolan; Lane; Schillebeeckx), for it develops from, or after, the man Jesus, not "from God" or "from above." Thus we have moved pointedly in the last thirty years from a more widespread emphasis on what the Gospels themselves present (namely, a Jesus who held a Christology) to, in many cases — and the title assigned to this article is significant — "Jesus *and* Christology." One may compare, among book titles of the period, Jesus *and* the Servant, Jesus *and* the Son of man, Jesus *and* his coming, Ethics *and* the New Testament. As the Christology in the Gospels became separated from Jesus, to be investigated concept by concept in the history-of-religions background and in his words, a result not altogether expected has occurred: scholarship became aware that there was no clear OT/rabbinic Jewish/or whatever concept to be found, as witness research on "messiah," "servant," and more recently on "apocalyptic son of man." The new quest was an attempt to redress this by finding links other than the christological titles. But the very method tends to exclude the possibility of any creative ability on Jesus' part, any significant personality who might have combined, and modified or reinterpreted messiological and eschatological ideas. Schweitzer did his utmost to reestablish a heroic Jesus. Dodd (1952 and over his long career) argued that the Gospels offer us a creative mind in Jesus and we need not reject their offer. The new quest was a modest effort to say more about the historical Jesus, but Christology remained the uncertain issue. R. Pesch (1978) is one recent example reflecting a new positivism; see also Goppelt. It remains to be seen how much future studies will stress, on the one hand, greater continuity from Jesus in these matters and/or, on the other hand, the newness of witness after Easter in the Christian community.

BIBLIOGRAPHY

Note: date cited below is for initial publication in original language, but pages cited above are for an English translation, where possible.

Research Reports, Surveys:

Kümmel, Werner Georg

    TRu 31   "Jesusforschung seit 1950." 1965–66: 15–46, 289–315.

    TRu 40   "Ein Jahrzehnt Jesusforschung (1965–75). I. Forschungsberichte, Ausserevangelische Quellen, Methodenfrage." 1975–76: 289–336.

TRu 41   (Continued) "II. Nicht-wissenschaftliche und Wissenschaftliche Gesamtdarstellungen." 1976–77: 197–258. (Continued as) "Jesusforschung seit 1965: III. Die Lehre Jesu (einschliesslich der Arbeiten über Einzeltexte)." 1976–77: 295–363.

TRu 43   (Continued) 1978–79: 105–61.
       (Continued) "IV. Bergpredigt—Gleichnisse—Wunderberichte (mit Nachträgen)." 1978–79: 233–65.

TRu 45   (Continued) "V. Der persönaliche Anspruch Jesu." 1980: 40–84.
       (Continued) "VI. Der Prozess und der Kreuzestod Jesu." 1980: 293–337.

TRu 46   (Continued) "Jesusforschung seit 1965: Nachträge 1975–80." 1981: 317–63.

Tru 47   (Continued) "Jesusforschung seit 1965: Nachträge 1975–80." 1982: 136–65; 348–83.

1985   *Dreissig Jahre Jesusforschung (1950–1980)*. Ed. H. Merklein. BBB 60. Bonn: Hanstein. [The research reports in *TRu* are combined in book form, with a postscript by the author and an index of writers.]

Piper, Otto A.
1953   "Das Problem des Lebens Jesu seit Schweitzer." Pp. 73–93 in *Verbum Dei manet in aeternum: Eine Festschrift für Prof. D. Otto Schmitz. . . .* Ed. W. Foerster. Witten: Luther-Verlag.

Leroy, Herbert
1978   *Jesus: Überlieferung und Deutung.* Erträge der Forschung 95. Darmstadt: Wissenschaftliche Buchgesellschaft. [Bibliography, pp. 139–54.]

Grässer, Erich
1973   "Motive und Methoden der neueren Jesus-Literatur." *VF* 18: 3–44. [Includes bibliography of Forschungsberichte.]

Reumann, John
1974   " 'Lives of Jesus' during the Great Quest for the Historical Jesus." *Indian Journal of Theology* 23: 33–59.

Ratschow, Carl Heinz
1959   "Jesusbild der Gegenwart." 3d ed. *RGG* 3. 655–63.

See also below: C. C. Anderson; H. Anderson; Conzelmann, 1959; Duling; Fuller, 1962; Genthe; I. H. Marshall, 1966, 1970; and McCown.

Achtemeier, Paul J.
1969   *An Introduction to the New Hermeneutic.* Philadelphia: Westminster.
1972   "Gospel Miracle Tradition and the Divine Man." *Int* 26: 174–97.

Ackermann, Heinrich (pseudonym)
1952   *Jesus: Seine Botschaft und ihre Aufnahme im Abendland.* Göttingen: Musterschmidt. [Stresses "Indo-Germanic" traits in Jesus.]

Albright, William Foxwell
1954   "Recent Discoveries in Palestine and the Gospel of St. John." Pp. 153–71 in *The Background of the New Testament and Its Eschatology.* Ed. W. D. Davies and D. Daube. Cambridge: University Press.

Allegro, John
1956   *The Dead Sea Scrolls.* Baltimore: Penguin. Rev. 1958. Rev. ed.: *The Dead Sea Scrolls: A Reappraisal* (1965).

1957   *The Dead Sea Scrolls and the Origins of Christianity.* New York: Criterion.
1970   *The Sacred Mushroom and the Cross: A Study of the Nature and Origins of Christianity within the Fertility Cults of the Ancient Near East.* Garden City, NY: Doubleday. See also *The End of the Road* (London: MacGibbon & Kee), "a companion volume." [Against Allegro, besides numerous reviews, see John C. King, *A Christian View of the Mushroom Myth* (London: Hodder & Stoughton, 1971) and John H. Jacques, *The Mushroom and the Bride* (Derby & London: Citadel, 1971).]

Althaus, Paul
1958   *Das sogenannte Kerygma und der historische Jesus: Zur Kritik der heutigen Kerygma-Theologie.* BFCT 48. Gütersloh: Bertelsmann. Eng. trans. by David Cairns: *The So-Called Kerygma and the Historical Jesus.* Edinburgh: Oliver & Boyd, 1959. USA ed.: *Fact and Faith in the Kerygma of Today.* Philadelphia: Muhlenberg, 1960. Reprinted, Westport, CT: Greenwood, 1979.

Anderson, Charles C.
1969   *Critical Quests of Jesus.* Grand Rapids: Eerdmans.
1972   *The Historical Jesus: A Continuing Quest.* Grand Rapids: Eerdmans. [Past efforts and continuing problems, from a conservative viewpoint.]

Anderson, Hugh
1964   *Jesus and Christian Origins: A Commentary on Modern Viewpoints.* New York: Oxford University Press.
1967   *Jesus.* "Great Lives Observed." Spectrum Books. Englewood Cliffs, NJ: Prentice-Hall. [Excerpts from famous "lives," for students.]

Aron, Robert
1968   *Ainsi priait Jésus enfant.* Paris: Bernard Grasset. Eng. trans. by A. H. Forsyth and A.-M. de Commaille, with H. T. Allen, Jr.: *The Jewish Jesus.* Maryknoll, NY: Orbis, 1971. See also *Jesus of Nazareth: The Hidden Years.* Trans. Frances Frenaye. New York: Wm. Morrow; London: Hamish Hamilton, 1962.

Augstein, Rudolf
1972   *Jesus, Menschensohn.* Munich: Bertelsmann. Eng. trans. by Hugh Young: *Jesus, Son of Man.* Preface by Gore Vidal; afterword by David Noel Freedman. New York: Urizen, 1977. Against the book: *Augsteins Jesus: Eine Dokumentation.* Ed. R. Pesch and G. Stachel. Zurich: Benziger, 1973.

Aulén, Gustaf
1973   *Jesus i nutida historisk forskning.* Stockholm: Verbum. 2d ed. 1974. Eng. trans. by Ingalill H. Hjelm: *Jesus in Contemporary Historical Research.* Philadelphia: Fortress, 1976.

Baird, J. Arthur
1963   *The Justice of God in the Teaching of Jesus.* Philadelphia: Westminster: London: SCM.
1969   *Audience Criticism and the Historical Jesus.* Philadelphia: Westminster. [Seeks to ascertain genuine logia by computer tests on style and listeners.]

Baird, William
　1977　　　*The Quest of the Christ of Faith: Reflections on the Bultmannian Era.*
　　　　　　Waco, TX: Word Books.

Balz, Horst Robert
　1967　　　*Methodische Probleme der neutestamentlichen Christologie.* WMANT
　　　　　　25. Neukirchen-Vluyn: Neukirchener Verlag.

Bammel, Ernst
　1967　　　"Christian Origins in Jewish Tradition." *NTS* 13: 317–35.
　1968　　　"Excerpts from a New Gospel?" *NovT* 10: 1–9.
　1970, ed.　*The Trial of Jesus: Cambridge Studies in Honour of C. F. D. Moule.* SBT
　　　　　　2/13. London: SCM.
　1984, ed.　(with C. F. D. Moule). *Jesus and the Politics of His Day.* New York:
　　　　　　Cambridge University Press. [Twenty-six essays, esp. on the Zealot
　　　　　　question.]

Banks, Robert
　1975　　　*Jesus and the Law in the Synoptic Tradition.* SNTSMS 28. London:
　　　　　　Cambridge University Press.

Barclay, William
　1960　　　*The Mind of Jesus.* London: SCM. [First published in *The British*
　　　　　　Weekly.]
　1961　　　*Crucified and Crowned.* London: SCM. USA ed.: 1960 and 1961 vols.
　　　　　　published as *The Mind of Jesus.* New York: Harper, 1961.
　1962　　　*Jesus As They Saw Him: New Testament Interpretations of Jesus.*
　　　　　　London: SCM. [Completes trilogy.]
　1966　　　*The Life of Jesus for Everyone.* New York: Harper & Row.

Bärnikol, Ernst
　1958　　　*Das Leben Jesu der Heilsgeschichte.* Halle: Niemeyer. [A reconstruc-
　　　　　　tion of Mark; Jesus dies A.D. 36; subsequent exaltation included.]

Barrett, Charles Kingsley
　1967　　　*Jesus and the Gospel Tradition.* London: SPCK; Philadelphia:
　　　　　　Fortress, 1968. [How Jesus spoke of his death and of the future.]

Barton, Bruce
　1924　　　*The Man Nobody Knows: A Discovery of the Real Jesus.* New York:
　　　　　　Grosset & Dunlap.

Bartsch, Hans-Werner
　1970　　　*Jesus, Prophet und Messias aus Galiläa.* Antworten 20. Frankfurt:
　　　　　　Stimme.

Bauman, Edward W.
　1960　　　*The Life and Teaching of Jesus.* Philadelphia: Westminster. [Based on
　　　　　　1958–59 TV series, for general reader.]

Bea, Augustin (Cardinal)
　1965　　　*The Study of the Synoptic Gospels: New Approaches and Outlooks.*
　　　　　　New York: Harper & Row. Trans. J. A. Fitzmyer, from *La Storicita*
　　　　　　dei Vangeli (Brescia: Morcelliana, 1964); originally articles in 1962
　　　　　　for the Second Vatican Council, published in *Civiltà cattolica* 115
　　　　　　(1964) 417–36, 526–45, with the Pontifical Biblical Commission's
　　　　　　"Instruction on the Historical Truth of the Gospels" of May 14, 1964,
　　　　　　Bib 45 (1964) 466–71.

Ben-Chorin, Schalom
1967   *Bruder Jesus: Der Nazarener in jüdischer Sicht.* Munich: Paul List. 2d
          ed. 1969. 3d ed. 1970. Paperback 1972. Stuttgart: Evangelische
          Buchgemeinde, 1976.
1970   *Jesus im Judentum.* Schriftreihe für christlich-jüdische Begegnung 4.
          Wuppertal: Brockhaus.
1974   "The Image of Jesus in Modern Judaism." *JES* 11: 401–30.

Benoit, Pierre
1975   "Jésus et le Serviteur de Dieu." In Dupont, 1975:111–40.

Berger, Klaus
1970   *Die Amen-Worte Jesu: Eine Untersuchung zum Problem der Legitima-
          tion in apokalyptischer Rede.* BZNW 39. Berlin: de Gruyter.
1972   *Die Gesetzesauslegung Jesu: Ihr historischer Hintergrund im Judentum
          und im Alten Testament: Teil I. Markus und Parallelen.* WMANT 40.
          Neukirchen-Vluyn: Neukirchener Verlag.

Betz, Hans Dieter
1985   *Essays on the Sermon on the Mount.* Philadelphia: Fortress. [Seven
          papers, five in Eng. trans. by L. L. Welborn.]

Betz, Otto
1965   *Was wissen wir von Jesus?* Stuttgart: Kreuz. Eng. trans. by Margaret
          Kohl: *What Do We Know About Jesus?* Philadelphia: Westminster;
          London: SCM, 1968. [A "bedrock of facts," especially in light of the
          Dead Sea scrolls.]
1982   "Probleme der Prozesses Jesu." *ANRW* 2.25.1: 565–647.

Beutler, J.
1982   "Friedenssehnsucht—Friedensengagement nach dem Neuen Testa-
          ment." *Stimmen der Zeit* 107: 291–306.

Bietenhard, Hans
1982   " 'Der Menschensohn'—*ho huios tou anthrōpou.* Sprachliche und
          religionsgeschichtliche Untersuchungen zu einem Begriff der synop-
          tischen Evangelien, I: Sprachlicher und religionsgeschichtlicher
          Teil." Pp. 265–350 in *ANRW* 2.25.1. [Continued in 2.26.]

Blinzler, Josef
1951   *Der Prozess Jesu: Das jüdische und das römische Gerichtsverfahren
          gegen Jesus Christus auf Grund der ältesten Zeugnisse dargestellt und
          beurteilt.* Regensburg: Pustet. 2d ed. 1955. Eng. trans. by Isabel and
          Florence McHugh: *The Trial of Jesus: The Jewish and Roman Pro-
          ceedings against Jesus Christ Described and Assessed from the Oldest
          Accounts.* Cork, Ireland: Mercier Press; Westminster, MD: Newman,
          1959. 4th Ger. ed. 1969.

Bloch, Ernst
1968   *Atheismus in Christentum.* Frankfurt: Suhrkamp. Eng. trans. by J. T.
          Swann: *Atheism in Christianity: The Religion of the Exodus and the
          Kingdom.* New York: Herder & Herder, 1972.

Boers, Hendrikus
1970   "Jesus and the Christian Faith: New Testament Christology since
          Bousset's *Kyrios Christos*." *JBL* 89: 450–56.
1972   "Where Christology Is Real: A Survey of Recent Research on New
          Testament Christology." *Int* 26: 300–327.

Boman, Thorlief
1967   *Die Jesus-Überlieferung im Lichte der neueren Volkskunde.* Göttingen: Vandenhoeck & Ruprecht.

Bornkamm, Günther
1956   *Jesus von Nazareth.* Urban Bücher. Stuttgart: Kohlhammer. 13th ed. 1983. Eng. trans. by Irene and Fraser McLuskey with James M. Robinson: *Jesus of Nazareth.* New York: Harper, 1960.
1962   See Hahn, 1962.
1964   "The Problem of the Historical Jesus and the Kerygmatic Christ." *SE* 3: 33–44.
1975   "Jesus Christ." *The New Encyclopaedia Britannica,* 15th ed. *Macropaedia,* Vol. 10: 145–55. Chicago: Encyclopaedia Britannica. [Replaces previous article by Jaroslav J. Pelikan, Vol. 13 (1964) 13–16.]

Borsch, Frederick Haupt
1967   *The Son of Man in Myth and History.* London: SCM; Philadelphia: Westminster.
1970   *The Christian and Gnostic Son of Man.* SBT 2/14. London: SCM.

Bousset, Wilhelm
1904   *Jesus.* Religionsgeschichtliche Volksbücher 1/2. Halle: Gebauer-Schwetschke. Eng. trans. by Janet Penrose Trevelyan: *Jesus.* London: Williams & Norgate; New York: Putnam, 1906.
1913   *Kyrios Christos: Geschichte des Christusglaubens von den Anfängen des Christentums bis Irenäus.* FRLANT n.s. 4. Göttingen: Vandenhoeck & Ruprecht. 2d ed. 1922. Eng. trans. by John E. Steely, from 5th ed. (1964) with introduction by Rudolf Bultmann: *Kyrios Christos: A History of the Belief in Christ from the Beginnings of Christianity to Irenaeus.* Nashville and New York: Abingdon, 1970.

Bouttier, Michel
1969   *Du Christ de l'histoire au Jésus des évangiles.* Avenir de la théologie. Paris: Cerf. [Popular analysis of Bultmann's position, Jeremias, and the quest.]

Bowman, John Wick
1943   *The Intention of Jesus.* Philadelphia: Westminster.
1962   "The Life and Teaching of Jesus." *PCB*: 733–47.
1963   *Jesus' Teaching in Its Environment.* Richmond: John Knox. [For the general reader.]
1970   *Which Jesus?* Philadelphia: Westminster.

Braaten, Carl E., and Roy A. Harrisville, eds.; trans.
1962   *Kerygma and History: A Symposium on the Theology of Rudolf Bultmann.* Nashville and New York: Abingdon.
1964   *The Historical Jesus and the Kerygmatic Christ: Essays on the New Quest of the Historical Jesus.* Nashville and New York: Abingdon.

Brandon, S. G. F.
1951   *The Fall of Jerusalem and the Christian Church: A Study of the Effects of the Jewish Overthrow of A.D. 70 on Christianity.* London: SPCK. 2d ed. 1957. Reprinted 1968.
1967   *Jesus and the Zealots: A Study of the Political Factor in Primitive Christianity.* Manchester: Manchester University Press; New York: Scribner, 1968.

1968   *The Trial of Jesus of Nazareth.* Historic Trials Series. London: Batsford; New York: Stein & Day. Paperback, London: Paladin, 1970.

Branscomb, Harvie
1931   *The Teachings of Jesus.* Nashville: Cokesbury. 2d ed. 1957.
1960   *The Message of Jesus: A Survey of the Teaching of Jesus Contained in the Synoptic Gospels.* Rev. by E. W. Saunders. Nashville: Abingdon.

Braun, Herbert
1957a   "Der Sinn der neutestamentlichen Christologie." *ZTK* 54: 341–77. Eng. trans. by Paul J. Achtemeier: "The Meaning of New Testament Christology." Pp. 89–127 in *God and Christ: Existence and Province.* *JTC* 5. Tübingen: Mohr-Siebeck; New York: Harper & Row, 1968.
1957b   *Spätjüdisch-häretischer und frühchristlicher Radikalismus: Jesus von Nazareth und die essenische Qumransekte.* 2 vols. BHT 24. Tübingen: Mohr-Siebeck. 2d ed. 1969.
1966   *Qumran und das Neue Testament.* 2 vols. Tübingen: Mohr-Siebeck. [See 1.1–138; 2.1–144.]
1969   *Jesus: Der Mann aus Nazareth und seine Zeit.* Themen der Theologie 1. Stuttgart & Berlin: Kreuz. 3d ed. 1972. Eng. trans. by Everett R. Kalin: *Jesus of Nazareth: The Man and His Time.* Philadelphia: Fortress, 1979.

Breech, James
1983   *The Silence of Jesus: The Authentic Voice of the Historical Man.* Philadelphia: Fortress.

Bright, John
1953   *The Kingdom of God: The Biblical Concept and Its Meaning.* Nashville: Abingdon-Cokesbury. British ed.: *The Kingdom of God in Bible and Church.* London: Lutterworth, 1955.

Brown, Raymond E., S.S.
1974   " 'Who Do Men Say That I Am?' — Modern Scholarship on Gospel Christology." *Horizons* 1: 35–50. Reprinted, pp. 20–37 in *Biblical Reflections on Crises Facing the Church.* New York: Paulist, 1975.
1977   *The Birth of the Messiah: A Commentary on the Infancy Narratives in Matthew and Luke.* Garden City, NY: Doubleday.
1979   *The Community of the Beloved Disciple.* New York: Paulist. Cf. his *The Epistles of John* (AB 30; Garden City, NY: Doubleday, 1982) 73–79.

Bruckberger, Raymond-Leopold
1965   *L'Histoire de Jésus-Christ.* Paris: Grasset. Eng. trans. by Denver Lindley: *The History of Jesus Christ.* New York: Viking, 1965. German trans. 1967. [By a French Dominican.]

Buchanan, George Wesley
1984   *Jesus the King and His Kingdom.* Macon, GA: Mercer University Press.

Büchsel, Friedrich
1947   *Jesus, Verkündigung und Geschichte.* Gütersloh: Bertelsmann.

Bultmann, Rudolf
1920   "Die Frage nach dem messianischen Bewusstsein Jesu und das Petrus-Bekenntnis." *ZNW* 19: 165–74. Reprinted pp. 1–9 in his *Exegetica: Aufsätze zur Erforschung des Neuen Testaments.* Ed. Erich Dinkler. Tübingen: Mohr-Siebeck, 1967.

1921   *Die Geschichte der synoptischen Tradition.* FRLANT n.s. 12. Göttin-
            gen: Vandenhoeck & Ruprecht. Eng. trans. by John Marsh, from the
            4th German ed. with Supplement, 1958: *The History of the Synoptic
            Tradition.* Oxford: Blackwell; New York: Harper & Row, 1963. Rev.
            ed. 1968.
1926   *Jesus.* Berlin: Deutsche Bibliothek. Eng. trans. by Louise Pettibone
            Smith and Erminie Huntress: *Jesus and the Word.* New York.
            Scribner, 1934. Paperback 1960.
1959   *Das Verhältnis der urchristlichen Christusbotschaft zum historischen
            Jesus.* SHAW, phil.-hist. Klasse, 1960: 3, 5–27. Reprinted, pp. 445–69
            in his *Exegetica* (see 1920, above). Eng. trans.: "The Primitive Chris-
            tian Kerygma and the Historical Jesus," in Braaten and Harrisville,
            1964:15–42.

Bundy, Walter Ernest
1955   *Jesus and the First Three Gospels: An Introduction to the Synoptic
            Tradition.* Cambridge, MA: Harvard University Press.

Burchard, Christoph. See also under Fuller, 1978.
1967   "Jesus." *Der Kleine Pauly: Lexicon der Antike,* 2: 1344–54. Stuttgart:
            Druckenmüller.

Burger, Christoph
1970   *Jesus als Davidssohn: Eine traditionsgeschichtliche Untersuchung.*
            FRLANT 98. Göttingen: Vandenhoeck & Ruprecht.

Burkitt, Francis Crawford
1932   *Jesus Christ: An Historical Introduction.* London: Blackie.

Burrows, Millar
1977   *Jesus in the First Three Gospels.* Nashville: Abingdon.

Cadbury, Henry Joel
1937   *The Peril of Modernizing Jesus.* New York: Macmillan. Reprinted
            London: SPCK, 1962.
1947   *Jesus: What Manner of Man?* New York: Macmillan. Reprinted
            London: SPCK, 1962.
1964   *The Eclipse of the Historical Jesus.* Wallingford, PA: Pendle Hill,
            Pamphlet No. 133.

Cadoux, Cecil John
1948   *The Life of Jesus.* West Drayton, Middlesex: Penguin Books. [Popular
            but based on more solid, earlier work, including *The Historic Mission
            of Jesus: A Constructive Reexamination of the Eschatological Teaching
            in the Synoptic Gospels* (London: Lutterworth; New York: Harper,
            1941).]

Carlston, Charles E.
1962   "A Positive Criterion of Authenticity?" *BR* 7: 33–44.
1975   *The Parables of the Triple Tradition.* Philadelphia: Fortress.

Carmichael, Joel
1963   *The Death of Jesus.* New York: Macmillan. Reprinted Penguin, 1966.
            German trans.: *Leben und Tod des Jesus von Nazareth* (Munich:
            Szczesny, 1965; Fischer Taschenbücher, 1968) [Discussed in *Der
            Spiegel,* Jan. 31, 1966, and following weeks. See Harenberg.]

Carmignac, Jean
1969   *Recherches sur le "Notre Père."* Paris: Letouzey & Ané. [Strong on
            Qumran parallels. Assumes a Hebrew Matthew, translated into
            Greek, with little emphasis on redaction.]

Carrington, Philip
1957   *The Story of the Christ.* London: SPCK. *Our Lord and Saviour: His
            Life and Teachings.* Greenwich, CT: Seabury, 1958. [For laity, by the
            Anglican Archbishop of Quebec, who also wrote on Mark and calen-
            dar theories.]

Casey, Maurice
1979   *Son of Man: The Interpretation and Influence of Daniel 7.* London:
            SPCK.

Catchpole, David R.
1971   *The Trial of Jesus: A Study in the Gospels and in Jewish Historiography
            from 1770 to the Present Day.* SPB 18. Leiden: Brill.

Cerfaux, Lucien
1954   *Le Christ dans la théologie de Saint Paul.* 2d ed. Paris: Cerf. Eng.
            trans. by G. Webb and A. Walker: *Christ in the Theology of St. Paul.*
            New York: Herder & Herder, 1959.

Christ, Felix
1970   *Jesus Sophia: Die Sophia-Christologie bei den Synoptikern.* ATANT 57.
            Zurich: Zwingli.

Cohn, Haim Hermann
1971   *The Trial and Death of Jesus.* New York: Harper & Row. Based in part
            on his *Mishpato u'Moto shel Yeshu ha-Notsri* (Tel-Aviv: Dvir, 1968).

Colpe, Carsten
1961   *Die religionsgeschichtliche Schule: Darstellung und Kritik ihres Bildes
            vom gnostischen Erlösermythus.* FRLANT 78, n.s. 60. Göttingen:
            Vandenhoeck & Ruprecht.
1969   "*Ho huios tou anthrōpou.*" *TWNT* 8: 403–81; *TDNT* 8: 400–477.

Connick, C. Milo
1963   *Jesus: The Man, the Mission, the Message.* Englewood Cliffs, NJ:
            Prentice-Hall.

Conzelmann, Hans
1959   "Jesus Christus." 3d ed. *RGG* 3: cols. 619–53. Eng. trans. by J.
            Raymond Lord: *Jesus.* Ed. with introduction and bibliography to
            1972 by J. Reumann. Philadelphia: Fortress, 1973.
1967   *Grundriss der Theologie des Neuen Testaments.* Munich: Kaiser. 3d
            ed. 1976. Eng. trans. by J. Bowden: *An Outline of the Theology of the
            New Testament.* New York: Harper & Row, 1969.

Coppens, Joseph
1968   *Le messianisme royal: Ses origines, son développement, son accom-
            plissement.* LD 54. Paris: Cerf. [With the following volumes, a history
            of messianic expectations and their unfolding.]
1974   *Le messianisme et sa relève prophétique: Les anticipations vétéro-
            testamentaires, leur accomplissement en Jésus.* BETL 38. Gembloux:
            Duculot.

1979   *La relève apocalyptique du messianisme royal: I. La royauté, le règne,*
         le royaume de Dieu, cadre de la relève apocalyptique. BETL 50.
         Louvain: Leuven University. [The three volumes of part three of
         Coppen's trilogy take up change but without break in the continuity
         of royal messianism as reread through apocalypticism (Jesus as Son
         of man).]

1981   *III. Le Fils de l'homme néotestamentaire.* BETL 55. Leuven: Leuven
         University.

1983   *II. Le Fils d'homme vétéro- et intertestamentaire.* BETL 61. Leuven:
         Leuven University.

Craveri, Marcello
1967   *The Life of Jesus.* Trans. C. L. Markham. New York: Grove Press;
         London: Secker & Warburg. Eng. trans. from the Italian, *La vita di*
         Gesù (1966). German trans. 1970.

Crossan, John Dominic
1973   *In Parables: The Challenge of the Historical Jesus.* New York: Harper
         & Row.

1975   *The Dark Interval: Toward a Theology of Story.* Niles, IL: Argus.

1979   *Finding Is the First Act: Trove Folktales and Jesus' Treasure Parable.*
         Semeia Supplements 9. Philadelphia: Fortress; Missoula, MT:
         Scholars Press.

1980   *Cliffs of Fall: Paradox and Polyvalence in the Parables of Jesus.* New
         York: Seabury.

Cullmann, Oscar
1957   *Die Christologie des Neuen Testaments.* Tübingen: Mohr-Siebeck. 2d
         ed. 1958. 5th ed. 1975. Eng. trans. by S. C. Guthrie and C. A. M. Hall:
         The Christology of the New Testament. Philadelphia: Westminster,
         1959. 2d ed. rev. 1963.

1970   *Jesus und die Revolutionären seiner Zeit: Gottesdienst, Gesellschaft,*
         Politick. Tübingen: Mohr-Siebeck. Eng. trans. by G. Putnam: *Jesus*
         and the Revolutionaries. New York: Harper & Row, 1970.

Dahl, Nils
1953   "Problemet den historiske Jesus." Pp. 156–202 in *Rett laere og*
         kjetterske meninger. Oslo: Land og Kirke. Expanded German version:
         "Der historische Jesus als geschichtswissenschaftliches und theolo-
         gisches Problem." *KD* 1 (1955) 104–32. Eng. trans.: "The Problem of
         the Historical Jesus." In Braaten and Harrisville, 1962:138–71.
         Reprinted pp. 48–89, 173–74 in Dahl, *The Crucified Messiah and*
         Other Essays. Minneapolis: Augsburg, 1974.

Daniel-Rops, Henri (Henri Petiot)
1954   *Jesus and His Times.* New York: Dutton; London: Burns & Oates,
         1955.

1964   *Brève histoire du Christ-Jésus.* Paris: Artheme Fayard. Eng. trans. by
         J. R. Foster: *The Life of Our Lord.* Twentieth-Century Encyclopedia
         of Catholicism 68. New York: Hawthorn Books. [In the same series,
         Daniel-Rops, along with F. Amiot, A. Brunot, and J. Daniélou, also
         did *The Sources for the Life of Christ.*]

Danker, Frederick
1976   *Luke.* Proclamation Commentaries. Philadelphia: Fortress. Pp. 6–43.

1982   *Benefactor: Epigraphic Study of a Greco-Roman and New Testament*
         Semantic Field. St. Louis: Clayton.

Dantine, Wilhelm
1974 *Jesus von Nazareth in der gegenwärtigen Diskussion.* Gütersloh: Mohn.

Davies, William David
1962 "Reflections on a Scandinavian Approach to 'The Gospel Tradition.' " Pp. 14–34 in *Neotestamentica et Patristica: Eine Freundesgabe Herrn Professor Dr. Oscar Cullmann zu seinem 60. Geburtstag.* NovTSup 6. Leiden: Brill. Reprinted in Davies, 1964:464–80.
1964 *The Setting of the Sermon on the Mount.* New York: Cambridge University Press.
1966 *The Sermon on the Mount.* New York: Cambridge University Press. [Simplified version of 1964.]

Davies, William David, and David Daube, eds.
1954 *The Background of the New Testament and Its Eschatology: Essays in Honour of Charles Harold Dodd.* New York: Cambridge University Press. Reprinted 1964.

De Rosa, Peter
1975 *Jesus Who Became Christ.* Denville, NJ: Dimension. [An intensely human Jesus, minus dogma, by a Roman Catholic.]

Derrett, J. Duncan M.
1973 *Jesus' Audience: The Social and Psychological Environment in which He Worked.* Crossroad Book. New York: Seabury.

Deschner, Karlheinz, ed.
1966 *Jesusbilder in theologischer Sicht.* Munich: List.

Dewar, Lindsay
1949 *An Outline of New Testament Ethics.* Philadelphia: Westminster.

Dibelius, Martin
1939 *Jesus.* Berlin: de Gruyter. 2d ed. 1949. 4th ed., with appendix, by W. G. Kümmel, Sammlung Göschen 1130 (1966). Eng. trans. by Charles B. Hedrick and F. C. Grant: *Jesus.* Philadelphia: Westminster, 1949.

Dinkler, Erich
1964 "Petrusbekenntnis und Satanswort: Das Problem der Messianität Jesu." Pp. 127–53 in *Zeit und Geschichte: Dankesgabe an Rudolf Bultmann zum 80. Geburtstag.* Ed. E. Dinkler. Tübingen: Mohr-Siebeck. Eng. trans. by C. E. Carlston: "Peter's Confession and the 'Satan' Saying: The Problem of Jesus' Messiahship." Pp. 169–202 in *The Future of Our Religious Past: Essays in Honour of Rudolf Bultmann.* Ed. J. M. Robinson. New York: Harper & Row, 1971.

Dodd, Charles Harold
1935 *The Parables of the Kingdom.* Shaffer Lectures, 1935. London: Nisbet. New York: Scribner. Rev. ed. 1961.
1952 *According to the Scriptures: The Substructure of New Testament Theology.* London: Nisbet. New York: Scribner, 1953.
1971 *The Founder of Christianity.* New York: Macmillan; London: Collins, ©1970; Fontana Books, 1973. Cf. Dodd's "The Life and Teachings of Jesus Christ." Pp. 367–89 in *A Companion to the Bible.* Ed. T. W. Manson. Edinburgh: T. & T. Clark, 1939.

Duling, Dennis C.
1979   *Jesus Christ through History.* New York: Harcourt Brace Jovanovich. [Textbook, surveying key interpreters from the NT to the present.]

Duncan, George S.
1974   *Jesus, Son of Man: Studies Contributory to a Modern Portrait.* London: Nisbet. [Maintains that a portrait is possible of the Man who accepted the divine mission to bring humanity home to God.]

Dunn, James D. G.
1980   *Christology in the Making: A New Testament Inquiry into the Origins of the Doctrine of the Incarnation.* Philadelphia: Westminster. [Cf. Dunn's remarks in *ExpTim* 95 (1984) 295–99.]

Dupont, Jacques
1954   *Les Béatitudes: Le problème littéraire, le message doctrinal.* Bruges: Abbaye de Saint-André. 2d ed. *Les Béatitudes: I. Le problème littéraire: Les deux versions du Sermon sur la montagne et des Béatitudes.* Bruges: Abbaye de Saint-André; Louvain: E. Nauwelaerts, 1958. *II. La bonne nouvelle.* Paris: Gabalda, 1969. *III. Les Evangélistes.* 1973.

Dupont, J., et al., eds.
1975   *Jésus aux origines de la christologie.* BETL 40. Louvain: Leuven University.

Easton, Burton Scott
1938   *What Jesus Taught: The Sayings Translated and Arranged with Expository Commentary.* Nashville: Abingdon.

Ebeling, Gerhard
1958   "Jesus und Glaube." *ZTK* 55: 64–110. Reprinted pp. 203–54 in his *Wort und Glaube,* vol. 1. Tübingen: Mohr-Siebeck, 1962. Eng. trans. by J. W. Leitch: "Jesus and Faith." Pp. 201–46 in *Word and Faith.* Philadelphia: Fortress, 1963.

Edwards, George R.
1972   *Jesus and the Politics of Violence.* New York: Harper & Row. [*Contra* Brandon.]

Edwards, Richard Alan
1976   *A Theology of Q: Eschatology, Prophecy, and Wisdom.* Philadelphia: Fortress.

Eichholz, Georg
1972   *Die Theologie des Paulus im Umriss.* Neukirchen-Vluyn: Neukirchener Verlag.
1984   *Das Rätsel des historischen Jesus und die Gegenwart Jesu Christi.* Ed. G. Sauter. TBü 72. Munich: Kaiser.

Endo, Shusaku
1978   *A Life of Jesus.* Trans. Richard A. Schuchert from the Japanese (1973). New York: Paulist.

Enslin, Morton Scott
1961   *The Prophet from Nazareth.* New York: McGraw-Hill. Reprinted New York: Schocken, 1968.

Epp, Eldon Jay
1971   "Norman Perrin on the Kingdom of God." Pp. 113–22 in *Christology and a Modern Pilgrimage: A Discussion with Norman Perrin.* Ed. H. D. Betz. Claremont, CA: SBL. Rev. ed. Missoula, MT: Scholars Press, 1974.

Ernst, Josef
1972   *Anfänge der Christologie.* SBS 57. Stuttgart: KBW. [Seeks bridges to post-Easter Christology in Jesus' nonconformism and through discipleship and the following of Jesus.]

Ewing, Upton Clary
1961   *The Essene Christ: A Rediscovery of the Historical Jesus and the Doctrines of Primitive Christianity.* New York: Philosophical Library.

Fabris, R.
1983   *Gesù di Nazareth: Storia e interpretazioni.* 2d ed. Assisi: Cittadella.

Farmer, William R.
1982   *Jesus and the Gospel: Tradition, Scripture, and Canon.* Philadelphia: Fortress.

Fernández, Andrés
1954   *Vida de Nuestro Señor Jesucristo.* . . . Madrid: Biblioteca de autores Cristianos. Eng. trans. by Paul Barrett, from the 2d ed.: *The Life of Christ.* Westminster, MD: Newman, 1959.

Fitzmyer, Joseph A.
1971   *Essays on the Semitic Background of the New Testament.* London: Chapman. New ed. SBLSBS 5. Missoula, MT: Scholars Press, 1974.
1974   "The Contribution of Qumran Aramaic to the Study of the New Testament." *NTS* 20: 382–407.
1975a   "Der semitische Hintergrund des neutestamentlichen Kyriostitels." Pp. 267–98 in Strecker, 1975.
1975b   "Methodology in the Study of the Aramaic Substratum of Jesus' Sayings in the New Testament." Pp. 73–102 in Dupont et al. Reprinted with slight revision in 1979:1–27.
1979   *A Wandering Aramean: Collected Aramaic Essays.* SBLMS 25. Missoula, MT: Scholars Press.
1981–85 *The Gospel according to Luke.* 2 vols. AB 28, 28A. Garden City, NY: Doubleday.
1982   *A Christological Catechism: New Testament Answers.* New York: Paulist.

Flew, R. Newton
1963   *Jesus and His Way: A Study of Ethics in the New Testament.* London: Epworth.

Flusser, David
1968   *Jesus in Selbstzeugnissen und Bilddokumenten.* Rowohlts Monographien 140. Reinbek: Rowohlt. Eng. trans. by R. Walls: *Jesus.* New York. Herder & Herder, 1969.

Fosdick, Harry Emerson
1949   *The Man from Nazareth as His Contemporaries Saw Him.* New York: Harper.

Fuchs, Ernst
1960   *Zur Frage nach dem historischen Jesus, Gesammelte Aufsätze II.* Tübingen: Mohr-Siebeck. 2d ed. 1965. Eng. trans. by Andrew Scobie: *Studies of the Historical Jesus.* SBT 42. London: SCM, 1964. [Especially 11–31, 48–64, and 167–90.]
1971   *Jesus: Wort und Tat.* Vorlesungen zum Neuen Testament 1. Tübingen: Mohr-Siebeck.

Fuller, Reginald H.
1954   *The Mission and Achievement of Jesus.* SBT 12. London: SCM.
1962   *The New Testament in Current Study.* New York: Scribner. [Pp. 25–53 on the quest.]
1963   *Interpreting the Miracles.* Philadelphia: Westminster.
1965   *The Foundations of New Testament Christology.* New York: Scribner; London: Lutterworth.
1966   *A Critical Introduction to the New Testament.* London: Duckworth.
1971   *The Formation of the Resurrection Narratives.* New York: Macmillan; London: SPCK, 1972. Reprinted with new Preface, Philadelphia: Fortress, 1980.
1974   "Aspects of Pauline Christology." *RevExp* 71: 5–18.
1978   "The Double Commandment of Love: A Test Case for the Criteria of Authenticity." Pp. 41–56 in *Essays on the Love Commandment.* By Luise Schottroff, C. Burchard, and M. J. Suggs. Philadelphia: Fortress.

Fuller, Reginald H., and Pheme Perkins
1982   *Who Is This Christ? Gospel Christology and Contemporary Faith.* Philadelphia: Fortress. [Includes creedal and modern developments. Annotated bibliography.]

Funk, Robert W.
1966   *Language, Hermeneutic, and Word of God: The Problem of Language in the New Testament and Contemporary Theology.* New York: Harper & Row.
1975   *Jesus as Precursor.* Semeia Supplements 2. Missoula, MT: Scholars Press; Philadelphia: Fortress.

Gager, John G.
1974   "The Gospels and Jesus: Some Doubts about Method." *JR* 54: 244–72. [Concerns limitation of sources to canon, scrutiny of form criticism, and criteria for authenticity.]

Geiselmann, J. R.
1951   *Jesus der Christus: Erster Teil: Die Frage nach dem historischen Jesus.* Munich: Kösel. 2d rev. ed. 1965.

Genthe, H. J.
1977   *Kleine Geschichte der neutestamentliche Wissenschaft.* Göttingen: Vandenhoeck & Ruprecht.

Georgi, Dieter
1964   *Die Gegner des Paulus im 2. Korintherbrief: Studien zur religiösen Propaganda.* WMANT 11. Neukirchen-Vluyn: Neukirchener Verlag. Eng. trans.: *The Opponents of Paul in 2 Corinthians: A Study of Religious Propaganda in Late Antiquity.* Philadelphia: Fortress, 1985.

Gerhardsson, Birger
1961   *Memory and Manuscript: Oral Tradition and Written Transmission in Rabbinic Judaism and Early Christianity.* ASNU 22. Eng. trans. by E. J. Sharpe. Lund: Gleerup. 2d ed. 1964.
1964   *Tradition and Transmission in Early Christianity.* ConNT 20. Lund: Gleerup.
1977   *Evangeliernas Förhistoria.* Lund: Verbum — Håkan Ohlssoms Förlag. Eng. trans.: *The Origins of the Gospel Traditions.* Philadelphia: Fortress, 1979. [Especially 15–18, 47–58, 67–78.] German trans. 1977.

Gilmour, S. Maclean
1957 *The Gospel Jesus Preached.* Philadelphia: Westminster.
1963 "Jesus Christ." Pp. 477–96 in *Dictionary of the Bible.* Ed. James Hastings. Rev. ed. by F. C. Grant and H. H. Rowley. New York: Scribner.

Gloege, Gerhard
1970 *Alle Tage Tag: Unsere Zeit im Neuen Testament.* Stuttgart: Kreuz. Eng. trans. by Stanley Rudman: *The Day of His Coming: The Man in the Gospels.* London: SCM. Philadelphia: Fortress, 1963. [Reflects new quest, as seen by a systematic theologian.]

Gnilka, Joachim
1970 *Jesus Christus nach frühen Zeugnissen des Glaubens.* Munich: Kösel. Pp. 159–74, "Die 'Christologie' Jesu von Nazareth."

Goguel, Maurice
1932 *La Vie de Jésus.* Paris: Payot. Eng. trans. by Olive Wyon: *The Life of Jesus.* New York: Macmillan, 1933. Reprinted with introduction by C. Leslie Mitton: *Jesus and the Origins of Christianity.* 2 vols. Harper Torchbooks. New York: Harper, 1960. [For Goguel's later views, see his "The Witness of a Historian," *HibJ* 60 (1962) 284–89.]

Goodspeed, Edgar J.
1950 *A Life of Jesus.* New York: Harper. [Popular account.]
1959 *Matthew, Apostle and Evangelist.* Philadelphia: Winston.

Goppelt, Leonhard
1975–76 *Theologie des Neuen Testaments.* Ed. Jürgen Roloff. 2 vols. Göttingen: Vandenhoeck & Ruprecht. 3d ed. 1980. Eng. trans. by John E. Alsup: *Theology of the New Testament.* 2 vols. Grand Rapids: Eerdmans, 1981–82.

Gouldner, M. D.
1963 "The Composition of the Lord's Prayer." *JTS* n.s. 14:32–45. [Mark recorded certain teachings of Jesus on prayer; Matthew wrote these into a formal prayer, which Luke abbreviated.]
1979, ed. *Incarnation and Myth: The Debate Continued.* London: SCM; Grand Rapids: Eerdmans. [Continues Hick, 1977, with a broader range of views.]

Grant, Frederick C.
1962 "Jesus Christ." *IDB* 2: 869–97.

Grant, Michael
1977 *Jesus.* London: Weidenfeld and Nicolson. USA ed.: *Jesus: An Historian's Review of the Gospels.* New York: Scribner.

Grant, Robert McQueen
1963 *A Historical Introduction to the New Testament.* New York: Harper & Row. Pp. 284–377, "The Problem of the Life of Jesus."

Grass, Hans
1956 *Ostergeschehen und Osterberichte.* Göttingen: Vandenhoeck & Ruprecht. 4th ed. 1970.

Grässer, Erich. See also above under "Research Reports, Surveys."
1957 *Das Problem der Parusieverzögerung in den synoptischen Evangelien und in der Apostelgeschichte.* BZNW 48. Berlin: Töpelmann. 3d ed., 1977.

1973   *Die Naherwartung Jesu*. SBS 61. Stuttgart: Katholisches Bibelwerk.
1975   "Der Mensch Jesus als Thema der Theologie." Pp. 129–50 in *Jesus und Paulus: Festschrift für Werner Georg Kümmel zum 70. Geburtstag.* Ed. E. E. Ellis and E. Grässer. Göttingen: Vandenhoeck & Ruprecht.

Green, E. W., ed.
1977   *The Truth of God Incarnate.* Grand Rapids: Eerdmans. (*Contra* Hicks, 1977.]

Grollenberg, Lucas Hendricus
1974   *Jezus, weg naar hoopvol samen leven.* Baarn, Holland: Bosch & Keuning. Eng. trans. by John Bowden: *Jesus.* Philadelphia: Westminster, 1978.

Grundmann, Walter
1957   *Die Geschichte Jesu Christi.* Berlin: Evangelische Verlagsanstalt. 2d ed. 1959. [By Protestant faculty member in DDR.]
1972   *Die Entscheidung Jesu: Zur geschichtlichen Bedeutung der Gestalt Jesu von Nazareth.* Berlin: Evangelische Verlagsanstalt. [Jesus as a model for people today.]
1975   *Jesus von Nazareth: Bürge zwischen Gott und Menschen.* Göttingen: Musterschmidt. [Popular, with use of modern art.]

Guelich, Robert A.
1982   *The Sermon on the Mount: A Fountain for Understanding.* Waco, TX: Word Books. [While concentrating on Matthean sense, this commentary also touches on the "Jesus level" behind the sources.]

Guignebert, Charles
1933   *Jésus.* Paris: La Renaissance du Livre. Eng. trans. by S. H. Hooke: *Jesus.* London: Kegan Paul, Trench, Trubner. New York: Knopf, 1935.

Guthrie, Donald
1972   *Jesus the Messiah: An Illustrated Life of Christ.* Grand Rapids: Zondervan. [The Gospels read directly as history.]

Güttgemanns, Erhardt
1970   *Offene Fragen zur Formgeschichte des Evangeliums: Eine methodologische Skizze der Grundlagenproblematik der Form- und Redaktionsgeschichte.* BEvT 54. Munich: Kaiser. 2d ed. 1971. Eng. trans. by W. G. Doty: *Candid Questions Concerning Gospel Form Criticism.* PTMS 26. Pittsburgh: Pickwick, 1979.

Haas, Jakob
1953   *Die Stellung Jesu zu Sünde und Sünder nach den vier Evangelien.* Studia Friburgensia n.s. 7. Freiburg (Schweiz): Universitätsverlag.

Hadas, Moses, and Morton Smith
1965   *Heroes and Gods: Spiritual Biographies in Antiquity.* Religious Perspectives 13. London: Routledge & Kegan Paul, New York: Harper & Row.

Hagner, Donald A.
1984   *The Jewish Reclamation of Jesus: An Analysis and Critique of Modern Jewish Study of Jesus.* Foreword by Gösta Lindeskog. Academie Books. Grand Rapids: Zondervan. [From an evangelical Christian perspective.]

Hahn, Ferdinand
1962 *Die Frage nach dem historischen Jesus.* Evangelisches Forum 2. Ed.
P. Rieger, with Wenzel Lohff and G. Bornkamm. Göttingen:
Vandenhoeck & Ruprecht. Eng. trans. by Grover Farley: *What Can
We Know about Jesus? Essays on the New Quest.* Philadelphia: Fortress, 1969.
1963 *Christologische Hoheitstitel: Ihre Geschichte im frühen Christentum.*
FRLANT 83. Göttingen: Vandenhoeck & Ruprecht. 4th ed. 1974.
Eng. trans. by Harold Knight and George Ogg: *The Titles of Jesus in
Christology: Their History in Early Christianity.* New York: World,
1969.
1970 "Methodenprobleme einer Christologie des Neuen Testaments." *VF*
15: 3–41.
1972 "Probleme historischer Kritik." *ZNW* 63: 1–17.
1974 "Methodologische Überlegungen zur Rückfrage nach Jesus." Pp.
11–77 in *Rückfrage nach Jesus: Zur Methodik und Bedeutung der
Frage nach dem historischen Jesus.* Ed. K. Kertelge. QD 63. Freiburg:
Herder.

Hamerton-Kelly, Robert G.
1979 *God the Father: Theology and Patriarchy in the Teachings of Jesus.*
Overtures to Biblical Theology. Philadelphia: Fortress.

Hamilton, Neill Q.
1968 *Jesus for a No-God World.* Philadelphia: Westminster.

Harenberg, Werner
1966 *Jesus und die Kirchen: Bibelkritik und Bekenntnis.* Stuttgart: Kreuz.
Eng. trans. by James H. Burtness: *Der Spiegel on the New Testament:
A Guide to the Struggle between Radical and Conservative in European
University and Parish.* New York: Macmillan; London: Collier-
Macmillan, 1970.

Harrison, Everett F.
1968 *A Short Life of Christ.* Grand Rapids: Eerdmans.

Harrisville, Roy A. See above under Braaten.

Harvey, A. E.
1982 *Jesus and the Constraints of History.* Philadelphia: Westminster.

Harvey, Van A.
1962 (with Schubert M. Ogden). "Wie neu ist die 'Neue Frage nach dem
historischen Jesus'?" *ZKT* 59: 46–87. Eng. trans. in Braaten and
Harrisville, 1964:197–242.
1966 *The Historian and the Believer: The Morality of Historical Knowledge
and Christian Belief.* New York: Macmillan.

Hasler, Victor
1969 *Amen: Redaktionsgeschichtliche Untersuchung zur Einführungsformel
der Herrenworte "Wahrlich ich sage euch."* Zurich: Gotthelf.

Haufe, Günter
1966 "Das Menschensohn-Problem in der gegenwärtigen wissenschaftli-
chen Diskussion." *EvT* 26: 131–41.

Hayes, John H.
1976 *Son of God to Superstar: Twentieth-Century Interpretations of Jesus.*
Nashville: Abingdon.

Hengel, Martin
    1968   *Nachfolge und Charisma: Eine exegetische-religionsgeschichtliche
                Studie zu Mt. 8,21f. und Jesu Ruf in die Nachfolge.* BZNW 34. Berlin:
                Töpelmann. Eng. trans. by J. Greig: *The Charismatic Leader and His
                Followers.* Edinburgh: T. & T. Clark; New York: Crossroad, 1981.
                [On the historical Jesus and discipleship.]
    1970   *War Jesus Revolutionär?* Calwer Hefte 110. Stuttgart: Calwer. Eng.
                trans. by W. Klassen: *Was Jesus a Revolutionist?* FBBS 28. Phila-
                delphia: Fortress, 1971.
    1975   *Der Sohn Gottes: Die Entstehung der Christologie und die jüdisch-
                hellenistische Religionsgeschichte.* Tübingen: Mohr-Siebeck. 2d ed.
                1977. Eng. trans. by J. Bowden: *The Son of God: The Origin of
                Christology and the History of Jewish-Hellenistic Religion.* London:
                SCM; Philadelphia: Fortress, 1976. [A two-stage Christology devel-
                oped within a few years after Easter and a Christology of "sending"
                and preexistence by A.D. 50.]
    1980   "Der stellvertretende Sühnetod Jesu. Ein Beitrag zur Entstehung des
                urchristlichen Kerygmas." *Internationale katholische Zeitschrift* 9:
                1–25, 135–47. Expanded, Eng. trans. by J. Bowden: *The Atonement:
                The Origins of the Doctrine in the New Testament.* London: SCM;
                Philadelphia: Fortress, 1981. [Part of "the prolegomena to a compre-
                hensive *Christology of the New Testament*" (xi).]
    1983   *Between Jesus and Paul: Studies in the Earliest History of Christianity.*
                London: SCM; Philadelphia: Fortress. Eng. trans. by J. Bowden of six
                articles, including "Christologie und neutestamentliche Chronolo-
                gie," in *Neues Testament und Geschichte* (Cullmann Festschrift, Tü-
                bingen, 1972) 43–67; "Hymnus und Christologie," in *Wort in der Zeit*
                (Rengstorf Festschrift, Leiden, 1980) 1–23; and "Erwägungen zum
                Sprachgebrauch von *Christos* bei Paulus und in der 'vorpaulinischen'
                Überlieferung," in *Paul and Paulinism* (Barrett Festschrift, London,
                1982) 135–59.

Herbst, Karl
    1979   *Was wollte Jesus selbst? Vorkirchliche Jesusworte in den Evangelien.*
                Düsseldorf: Patmos. Vol. 2, 1981.

Hick, John, ed.
    1977   *The Myth of God Incarnate.* London: SCM; Philadelphia: Westmin-
                ster. [Jesus was "a man approved by God" (Acts 2:21); "incarnation"
                is a later concept.]

Hiers, Richard H.
    1970   *The Kingdom of God in the Synoptic Tradition.* Gainesville: University
                of Florida Press. [Staunchly eschatological (in J. Weiss's sense).]
    1973   *The Historical Jesus and the Kingdom of God: Present and Future in
                the Message and Ministry of Jesus.* Gainesville: University of Florida
                Press.

Higgins, A. J. B.
    1959   "Son of Man-*Forschung* since 'The Teaching of Jesus.'" Pp. 119–35
                in *New Testament Essays: Studies in Memory of Thomas Walter
                Manson.* Ed. A. J. B. Higgins. Manchester: Manchester University
                Press.
    1964   *Jesus and the Son of Man.* Philadelphia: Fortress.

1980   *The Son of Man in the Teaching of Jesus.* SNTSMS 39. New York: Cambridge University Press.

Hirsch, Emanuel
1941   *Frühgeschichte des Evangeliums.* 2 vols. Tübingen: Mohr-Siebeck. 2d ed. 1951.

Holl, Adolf
1971   *Jesus in schlechter Gesellschaft.* Stuttgart: Deutsche Verlags-Anstalt. Eng. trans. by Simon King: *Jesus in Bad Company.* London: Collins, 1972. New York: Holt, Rinehart & Winston, 1973.

Holladay, Carl R.
1977   *THEIOS ANER in Hellenistic Judaism: A Critique of the Use of This Category in New Testament Christology.* SBLDS 40. Missoula, MT: Scholars Press.

Hollenbach, Paul W.
1982   "The Conversion of Jesus: From Jesus the Baptizer to Jesus the Healer." Pp. 196–219 in *ANRW* 2.25.1. [Cf. pp. 850–75 in *ANRW* 2.19.1.]

Holtz, Traugott
1977   *Jesus aus Nazareth.* Berlin: Union. 2d ed. 1979. Reprinted as *Jesus aus Nazaret: Was wissen wir von ihm?* Zurich, Einsiedeln and Cologne: Benziger, 1981.

Hooker, Morna
1959   *Jesus and the Servant: The Influence of the Servant Concept of Deutero-Isaiah in the New Testament.* London: SPCK.
1967   *The Son of Man in Mark: A Study of the Background of the Term 'Son of Man' and Its Use in St. Mark's Gospel.* London: SPCK; Montreal: McGill University Press.

Horner, Tom
1978   *Jonathan Loved David: Homosexuality in Biblical Times.* Philadelphia: Westminster. [Pp. 110–26, on Jesus' possible attitudes toward sexuality.]

Houlden, J. L.
1973   *Ethics and the New Testament.* Harmondsworth, Middlesex: Penguin. New York: Oxford University Press, 1977.

Howard, V.
1975   *Das Ego Jesu in den synoptischen Evangelien: Untersuchungen zum Sprachgebrauch Jesu.* MTS 14. Marburg: Elwert.

Hübner, Hans
1973   *Das Gesetz in der synoptischen Tradition: Studien zur These einer progressiven Qumranisierung und Judaisierung innerhalb der synoptischen Tradition.* Witten: Luther.

Hultgren, Arland J.
1979   *Jesus and His Adversaries: The Form and Function of the Conflict Stories in the Synoptic Tradition.* Minneapolis: Augsburg.

Hurtado, Larry W.
1981   "The Study of New Testament Christology: Notes for the Agenda." Pp. 185–98 in *Society of Biblical Literature 1981 Seminar Papers.* Ed. K. H. Richards. Chico, CA: Scholars Press.

Isaac, Jules

1946   *Jésus et Israël.* Paris: A. Michel. New ed. Paris: Fasquette, 1959. Eng. trans. by S. Gran; ed. Claire Hachet Bishop: *Jesus and Israel.* New York: Holt, Rinehart & Winston, 1971. German trans. 1967.

Jeremias, Joachim

1935   *Die Abendmahlsworte Jesu.* Göttingen: Vandenhoeck & Ruprecht. 2d ed. 1949; 3d ed. 1960. 4th ed. 1967. Eng. trans. by A. Ehrhardt: *The Eucharistic Words of Jesus.* Oxford: Blackwell, 1955. Rev. ed., trans. Norman Perrin: London: SCM; New York: Scribner, 1966. Reprinted Philadelphia: Fortress, 1978.

1947   *Die Gleichnisse Jesu.* ATANT 11. Zurich: Zwingli. 2d ed. rev. Göttingen: Vandenhoeck & Ruprecht, 1952. 3d ed. Berlin: Evangelische Verlagsanstalt. 9th ed. 1977. Eng. trans. by S. H. Hooke from the 3d German ed.: *The Parables of Jesus.* London: SCM, 1954. Rev. ed. from the 6th German ed. of 1962, London: SCM; New York: Scribner, 1963. Abbreviated version, ed. B. Schaller: *Die Gleichnisse Jesu.* Munich-Hamburg: Siebenstern Taschenbuch, 1965: Eng. trans., adapted by F. Clarke: *Rediscovering the Parables,* London: SCM; New York: Scribner, 1966.

1952   "*Pais Theou.*" TWNT 5: 676–713. Eng. trans. by H. Knight: *The Servant of God* (with W. Zimmerli). SBT 20. London: SCM, 1957. Rev. ed. 1965. TDNT 5: 677–717.

1953   "Kennzeichen der ipsissima vox Jesu." Pp. 86–93 in *Synoptische Studien: Alfred Wikenhauser zum siebzigsten Geburtstag am 22. Februar 1953 dargebracht.* Munich: Karl Zink, 1954. Reprinted pp. 145–51 in Jeremias's *Abba: Studien zur neutestamentlichen Theologie und Zeitgeschichte.* Göttingen: Vandenhoeck & Ruprecht, 1966. Eng. trans. by J. Bowden: "Characteristics of the ipsissima vox Jesu." Pp. 108–15 in *The Prayers of Jesus.* SBT 2/6. London: SCM, 1967. Philadelphia: Fortress, 1978.

1957   "Der gegenwärtige Stand der Debatte um das Problem des historischen Jesus." Pp. 12–65 in Ristow and Matthiae. Also: *Das Problem des historischen Jesus.* Calwer Hefte 32. Stuttgart: Calwer, 1960. Eng. trans.: "The Present Position in the Controversy Concerning the Problem of the Historical Jesus." *ExpTim* 69 (1957–58) 333–39. Rev. trans. by N. Perrin: *The Problem of the Historical Jesus.* FBBS 13. Philadelphia: Fortress, 1964. Rev. ed. 1969.

1962   *Das Vater-Unser im Lichte der neueren Forschung.* Calwer Hefte 50. Stuttgart: Calwer. Eng. trans. by J. Reumann: *The Lord's Prayer.* FBBS 8. Philadelphia: Fortress, 1964. Reprinted pp. 82–107 in *The Prayers of Jesus* (cited above, 1953).

1970   *Neutestamentliche Theologie: I. Teil: Die Verkündigung Jesu.* Gütersloh: Mohn. 3d ed. 1979. Eng. trans. by J. Bowden: *New Testament Theology: Part 1: The Proclamation of Jesus.* London: SCM; New York: Scribner, 1971.

Jervell, Jakob

1965   *The Continuing Search for the Historical Jesus.* Minneapolis: Augsburg. Eng. trans. by H. Kaasa from the Norwegian, *Den historiske Jesus* (1962).

Johnson, Sherman E.

1957   *Jesus in His Own Times.* New York: Scribner.

Jones, Geraint Vaughan
1964   *The Art and Truth of the Parables: A Study in Their Literary Form and Modern Interpretation*. London: SPCK.

Jüngel, Eberhard
1962   *Paulus und Jesus: Eine Untersuchung zur Präzisierung der Frage nach dem Ursprung der Christologie*. HUT 2. Tübingen: Mohr-Siebeck. 2d ed. 1964. [Pp. 87–135 on parables. Review article by James M. Robinson, *Int* 18 (1964) 347–59.]

Kähler, Martin
1892   *Der sogenannte historische Jesus und der geschichtliche, biblische Christus*. Leipzig: Deichert. 2d rev. ed. 1896, 1926. New ed., TBü 2, Systematische Theologie; Munich: Kaiser, 1953; 4th ed. 1969. Ed. and Eng. trans. by C. E. Braaten: *The So-Called Historical Jesus and the Historic, Biblical Christ*. Philadelphia: Fortress, 1964.

Kallas, James
1961   *The Significance of the Synoptic Miracles*. SPCK Biblical Monographs 2. London: SPCK.

Käsemann, Ernst
1954   "Das Problem des historischen Jesus." *ZTK* 51: 125–53. Reprinted pp. 187–214 in his *Exegetische Versuche und Besinnungen*, vol. 1. Göttingen: Vandenhoeck & Ruprecht, 1960. Eng. trans. by W. J. Montague: "The Problem of the Historical Jesus." Pp. 15–47 in Käsemann's *Essays on New Testament Themes*. SBT 41. London: SCM, 1964. Reprinted Philadelphia: Fortress, 1982.
1964   "Sackgassen im Streit um den historischen Jesus." Pp. 31–68 in *Exegetische Versuche und Besinnungen*, vol. 2. Eng. trans. by W. J. Montague: "Blind Alleys in the 'Jesus of History' Controversy." Pp. 23–65 in Käsemann's *New Testament Questions of Today*. London: SCM; Philadelphia: Fortress, 1969.
1968   *Der Ruf der Freiheit*. Tübingen: Mohr-Siebeck. 5th ed. 1972. Eng. trans. by F. Clarke: *Jesus Means Freedom*. Philadelphia: Fortress, 1970.
1975   "Die neue Jesus-Frage." In Dupont et al.: 47–57.

Kasper, Walter
1974   *Jesus der Christus*. Mainz: Matthias-Grünewald. 7th ed. 1979. Eng. trans. by V. Green: *Jesus the Christ*. London: Burns & Oates; New York: Paulist, 1976.

Kazantzakis, Nikos
1960   *The Last Temptation of Christ*. Eng. trans. by P. A. Bien. New York: Simon & Schuster; New York: Bantam Books, 1971.

Kearns, Rollin
1978   *Vorfragen zur Christologie. I: Morphologische und Semasiologische Studie zur Vorgeschichte eines christologischen Hoheitstitels*. Tübingen: Mohr-Siebeck. *II: Überlieferungsgeschichtliche und Rezeptionsgeschichtliche Studie zur Vorgeschichte eines christologischen Hoheitstitels*. 1980. [Pre-New Testament use of Son-of-man terminology.]

Keck, Leander
    1970–77,   "Lives of Jesus Series." Philadelphia: Fortress. [New introductions to
    ed.   reprints of D. F. Strauss's *Leben Jesu*, Loisy, Herrmann, and Shailer
                Mathews, and new translations of Reimarus, J. Weiss, and D. F.
                Strauss on Schleiermacher, as historical landmarks in the quest.
                Review by J. A. Duke and D. L. Dungan, *RSR* 4 (1978) 259–73.]
    1971   *A Future for the Historical Jesus: The Place of Jesus in Teaching and
                Theology.* Nashville and New York: Abingdon. Reprinted Philadel-
                phia: Fortress, 1981.

Kee, Howard Clark
    1970   *Jesus in History: An Approach to the Study of the Gospels.* New York:
                Harcourt Brace Jovanovich. 2d ed. 1977.
    1973   "Aretalogy and Gospel." *JBL* 92: 402–22.
    1977   *Community of the New Age: Studies in Mark's Gospel.* Philadelphia:
                Westminster.

Kepler, Thomas S., ed.
    1944   *Contemporary Thinking about Jesus: An Anthology.* New York and
                Nashville: Abingdon-Cokesbury.

Kern, Walter
    1978   "Jesus — marxistisch und tiefenpsychologisch." Pp. 63–100 in *Theolo-
                gische Berichte VII: Zugänge zu Jesus.* Zurich: Benzinger.

Kertelge, Karl, ed.
    1974   *Rückfrage nach Jesus: Zur Methodik und Bedeutung der Frage nach
                dem historischen Jesus.* By F. Hahn, K. Kertelge, F. Lentzen-Deis, F.
                Mussner, R. Pesch, R. Schnackenburg. QD 63. Freiburg: Herder.

Kim, Seyoon
    1981   *The Origin of Paul's Gospel.* WUNT 2/4. Tübingen: Mohr-Siebeck.
    1983   *"The Son of Man" as the Son of God.* WUNT 30. Tübingen:
                Mohr-Siebeck.

Kingsbury, Jack Dean
    1975   *Matthew: Structure, Christology, Kingdom.* Philadelphia: Fortress.
    1981   *Jesus Christ in Matthew, Mark, and Luke.* Proclamation Commen-
                taries. Philadelphia: Fortress.
    1983   *The Christology of Mark's Gospel.* Philadelphia: Fortress.

Kissinger, Warren
    1975   *The Sermon on the Mount: A History of Interpretation and Bibliogra-
                phy.* ATLA Bibliographical Series 3. Metuchen, NJ: Scarecrow;
                American Theological Library Association.
    1979   *The Parables of Jesus: A History of Interpretation and Bibliography.*
                ATLA Bibliographical Series 4. Metuchen, NJ: Scarecrow Press;
                American Theological Library Association.

Klein, Günter
    1970   " 'Reich Gottes' als biblischer Zentralbegriff." *EvT* 30: 642–70. Eng.
                trans.: "The Biblical Understanding of 'the Kingdom of God.'" *Int* 26
                (1972) 387–418.

Knox, John
    1941   *The Man Christ Jesus.* Chicago: Willett, Clark.
    1945   *Christ the Lord: The Meaning of Jesus in the Early Church.* Chicago:
                Willett, Clark.
    1947   *On the Meaning of Christ.* New York: Scribner.

1958a   *Jesus, Lord and Christ: A Trilogy.* New York: Harper. [Combines 1941, 1945, 1947.]
1958b   *The Death of Christ: The Cross in New Testament History and Faith.* New York/Nashville: Abingdon.
1961   *The Ethic of Jesus in the Teaching of the Church: Its Authority and Its Relevance.* New York and Nashville: Abingdon.
1967   *The Humanity and Divinity of Christ: A Study of Pattern in Christology.* New York: Cambridge University Press.

Koester, Helmut
1968   "One Jesus and Four Primitive Gospels." *HTR* 61: 203–47. Reprinted pp. 158–204 in J. M. Robinson and H. Koester, *Trajectories through Early Christianity.* Philadelphia: Fortress, 1971. German trans.: *Entwicklungslinien durch die Welt des frühen Christentums* (Tübingen: Mohr-Siebeck, 1971) 147–90.

Kramer, Werner
1963   *Christos, Kyrios, Gottessohn.* Zurich: Zwingli. Eng. trans. by B. Hardy: *Christ, Lord, Son of God.* SBT 50. London: SCM, 1966.

Kümmel, Werner Georg. See also under "Research Reports, Surveys" and Dibelius.
1945   *Verheissung und Erfüllung: Untersuchungen zur eschatologischen Verkündigung Jesu.* ATANT 6. Basel: Zwingli. Rev. ed. Zurich: Zwingli, 1953. 3d ed. 1956. Eng. trans. by D. M. Barton: *Promise and Fulfillment: The Eschatological Message of Jesus.* SBT 23. London: SCM, 1957. 2d ed. 1961.
1969   *Die Theologie des Neuen Testaments nach seinen Hauptzeugen, Jesus, Paulus, Johannes.* GNT, NTD Ergänzungsreihe 3. Göttingen: Vandenhoeck & Ruprecht. Eng. trans. by John E. Steely: *The Theology of the New Testament According to Its Major Witnesses: Jesus—Paul—John.* Nashville and New York: Abingdon, 1973.
1984   *Jesus der Menschensohn?* SWG Frankfurt 20,3. Wiesbaden: Steiner.

Küng, Hans. See Lapide, 1976b.

Ladd, George Eldon
1952   *Crucial Questions about the Kingdom of God.* Grand Rapids: Eerdmans. [A conservative approach but with increasing use of the historical-critical method.]
1959   *The Gospel of the Kingdom: Scriptural Studies in the Kingdom of God.* Grand Rapids: Eerdmans.
1964   *Jesus and the Kingdom: The Eschatology of Biblical Realism.* New York: Harper & Row; London: SPCK, 1966. Republished as *The Presence of the Future: The Eschatology of Biblical Realism.* Grand Rapids: Eerdmans, 1974.
1974   *A Theology of the New Testament.* Grand Rapids: Eerdmans. [Especially "Part I: The Synoptic Gospels," 13–212.]

Lane, Dermot A.
1975   *The Reality of Jesus: An Essay in Christology.* Dublin: Veritas Publications; New York: Paulist, 1977. [The quest and a "low-ascending" Christology. See also Osman.]

Lapide, Pinchas E. (Phinn Erwin)
1970   "Jesus in Israeli Literature." *Christian Century* 87: 1248–53 (Oct. 21, 1970).
1971   "Jesus in Israel." *Orientierung* (Zurich) 35: 212–16. [Book of same title. German trans. by U. Bohn. Gladbeck: Schriftenmissionsverlag.]

1974   *Der Rabbi von Nazareth: Wandlungen des jüdischen Jesusbildes.* Trier: Spee.

1976a   *Ist das nicht Josephs Sohn? Jesus im heutigen Judentum.* Stuttgart: Calwer. Eng. trans. by P. Heinegg: *Israelis, Jews and Jesus.* Garden City, NY: Doubleday, 1979.

1976b   (with Hans Küng). *Jesus im Widerstreit: Ein jüdisch-christlicher Dialog.* Stuttgart: Calwer; Munich: Kösel. Eng. trans. by E. Quinn: *Brother or Lord? A Jew and a Christian Talk Together about Jesus.* London: Collins, Fount Paperbacks; Garden City, NY: Doubleday, 1977. [1975 radio broadcast.] Also printed in abbreviated form as "Is Jesus a Bond or Barrier? A Jewish-Christian Dialogue." *JES* 14 (1977) 466–83: and in Küng's *Signposts for the Future* (Garden City, NY: Doubleday, 1978), pp. 64–87, "Jesus in Conflict: A Jewish-Christian Dialogue."

1979   (with U. Luz). *Der Jude Jesus: Thesen eines Juden: Antworten eines Christen.* Zurich, Eisiedeln and Cologne: Benziger.

Lehmann, Johannes

1970   *Jesus-Report: Protokoll einer Verfälschung.* Düsseldorf and Vienna: Econ. Knaur-Taschenbuch 301; Munich: Droemersche Verlagsanstalt, 1972. Eng. trans. by M. Heron: *Rabbi J.* New York: Stein & Day; London: Souvenir, 1971. [Reply, *Rabbi J.: Eine Auseinandersetzung mit Johannes Lehmanns Jesus Report,* by Rudolf Schnackenburg, Karlheinz Müller, Gerhard Dautzenberg (ed. K. Müller; Würzburg: Echter, 1970).]

1972   *Die Jesus G.M.B.H. Was Jesus wirklich wollte. Wie Paulus Christus schuf.* Düsseldorf and Vienna: Econ. Eng. trans. by M. Ebon: *The Jesus Establishment.* Garden City, NY: Doubleday, 1974.

Lehmann, Martin

1970   *Synoptische Quellenanalyse und die Frage nach dem historischen Jesus: Kriterien der Jesusforschung untersucht in Auseinandersetzung mit Emanuel Hirschs "Frühgeschichte des Evangeliums."* BZNW 38. Berlin: de Gruyter.

Leipoldt, Wilhelm Johannes

1935   *Gegenwartsfragen in der neutestamentlichen Wissenschaft.* Leipzig: Deichert. Pp. 17–64, "War Jesus Jude?"

Leivestad, Ragnar

1968   "Der apokalyptische Menschensohn ein theologisches Phantom." *ASTI* 6: 49–105.

1972   "Exit the Apocalyptic Son of Man." *NTS* 18: 243–67.

1982   "Jesus — Messias — Menschensohn: Die jüdischen Heilandserwartungen zur Zeit der ersten römischen Kaiser und die Frage nach dem messianischen Selbstbewusstsein Jesu." Pp. 220–64 in *ANRW* 2.25.1.

Léon-Dufour, Xavier

1963   *Les évangiles et l'histoire de Jésus.* Paris: Seuil. Abbreviated Eng. trans. by J. McHugh: *The Gospels and the Jesus of History.* New York and Tournai: Desclée; London: Collins, 1968. Garden City, NY: Doubleday, Image Books; London: Fontana, 1970.

1975   "Jésus devant sa mort, à la lumière des textes de l'Institution eucharistique et des discours d'adieu." In Dupont et al.: 141–68.

Leroy, Herbert. See under "Research Reports, Surveys."

Lightfoot, Robert Henry
1935   *History and Interpretation in the Gospels.* London: Hodder & Stoughton.

Lindars, Barnabas
1975   "Re-Enter the Apocalyptic Son of Man." *NTS* 22: 52–72.
1983   *Jesus Son of Man: A Fresh Examination of the Son of Man Sayings in the Gospels in the Light of Recent Research.* London: SPCK.

Lindemann, Andreas
1975   "Jesus in der Theologie des Neuen Testaments." In Strecker, 1975:27–58.

Lindeskog, Gösta
1938   *Die Jesusfrage im neuzeitlichen Judentum: Ein Beitrag zur Geschichte der Leben-Jesu Forschung.* Arbeiten und Mitteilungen aus dem neutestamentlichen Seminar zu Uppsala 8. Ed. A. Fridrichsen. Uppsala: Almqvist & Wiksells. Reprinted with postscript by the author (pp. 370–73) Darmstadt: Wissenschaftliche Buchgesellschaft, 1973.

Linnemann, Eta
1961   *Gleichnisse Jesu: Einführung und Auslegung.* Göttingen: Vandenhoeck & Ruprecht. 7th ed. 1979. Eng. trans. by J. Sturdy: *Parables of Jesus: Introduction and Exposition.* London: SPCK, 1966. USA ed.: *Jesus of the Parables: Introduction and Exposition.* New York: Harper & Row, 1967.
1970   *Studien zur Passionsgeschichte.* Göttingen: Vandenhoeck & Ruprecht.

Lohmeyer, Ernst
1946   *Das Vater-unser.* Göttingen: Vandenhoeck & Ruprecht. 2d ed. 1947. Eng. trans. by J. Bowden: *"Our Father": An Introduction to the Lord's Prayer.* New York: Harper & Row, 1965.

Lohse, Eduard
1964   *Die Geschichte des Leidens und Sterbens Jesu Christi.* Gütersloh: Mohn. New ed. 1979. Eng. trans. by M. O. Dietrich: *History of the Suffering and Death of Jesus Christ.* Philadelphia: Fortress, 1967.

Longenecker, Richard N.
1970   *The Christology of Early Jewish Christianity.* SBT 2/17. London: SCM.

Lührmann, Dieter
1975   "Die Frage nach Kriterien für ursprüngliche Jesusworte — eine Problemskizze." In Dupont et al.: 59–72.

Lundström, Gösta
1963   *The Kingdom of God in the Teaching of Jesus: A History of Interpretation from the Last Decades of the Nineteenth Century to the Present Day.* Eng. trans. by J. Bulman from the Swedish, *Guds Rike i Jesu Förkunnelse; tolkningens historia från 1800-talets sista decennier till våra dagar* (Lund: Svenska Kyrkans Diakonistyrelses Bokförlag, 1947), plus Postscript 1947–62 by the author. Edinburgh: Oliver & Boyd; Richmond: John Knox.

Luz, Ulrich. See Lapide, 1979.

McArthur, Harvey K.
1964   "Basic Issues, A Survey of Recent Gospel Research." *Int* 18: 39–45. Reprinted in 1969b: 131–44.

1966   *The Quest through the Centuries: The Search for the Historical Jesus.* Philadelphia: Fortress.

1969a   "From the Historical Jesus to Christology." *Int* 23: 190–206.

1969b, ed.   *In Search of the Historical Jesus.* New York: Scribner. [Textbook, excerpting important books and articles.]

McCasland, S. Vernon

1951   *By the Finger of God: Demon Possession and Exorcism in Early Christianity in the Light of Modern Views of Mental Illness.* New York: Macmillan. [See also McCasland's articles, "Miracle," *IDB* 3: 392–401; "Miracles," *Hastings' Dictionary of the Bible,* rev. ed (1963) 663–66.]

1964   *The Pioneer of Our Faith: A New Life of Jesus.* New York: McGraw-Hill.

McCown, Chester Charlton

1940   *The Search for the Real Jesus: A Century of Historical Study.* New York: Scribner.

Machoveč, Milan

1972   *Jesus für Atheisten.* Mit einem Geleitwort von Helmut Gollwitzer. Stuttgart: Kreuz. 2d ed. 1973. 5th ed. 1977. [Chapters 2–6 are translated from the original Czech by P. Kruntorad; chap. 1 is written in German by the author.] Eng. trans. *A Marxist Looks at Jesus.* Intro. by Peter Hebblethwaite. London: Darton, Longman & Todd; Philadelphia: Fortress, 1976.

1974, ed.   (with Iring Fetscher). *Marxisten und die Sache Jesu.* Gesellschaft und Theologie, Abteilung: Systematische Beiträge 14. Munich: Kaiser.

Mackey, James P.

1979   *Jesus the Man and the Myth: A Contemporary Christology.* New York: Paulist.

Manson, Thomas Walter

1931   *The Teaching of Jesus: Studies of its Form and Content.* New York: Cambridge University Press. 2d ed. 1935. Reprinted 1961.

1937   "The Sayings of Jesus," Part 2 (pp. 299–639) of *The Mission and Message of Jesus,* with H. D. A. Major and C. J. Wright. London: Nicholson & Watson; New York: Dutton. Separately published, with some additional notes, as *The Sayings of Jesus.* London: SCM, 1949.

1949   "The Quest of the Historical Jesus—Continued." Pp. 3–12 in Manson's *Studies in the Gospels and Epistles.* Ed. M. Black. Philadelphia: Westminster, 1962. [Address delivered in Cambridge in 1949 not previously published.]

1953   *The Servant-Messiah: A Study of the Public Ministry of Jesus.* New York: Cambridge University Press. Reprinted 1961.

1954   "The Life of Jesus: Some Tendencies in Present-Day Research." In Davies and Daube: 211–21.

Manson, William

1946   *Jesus the Messiah: The Synoptic Tradition of the Revelation of God in Christ: With Special Reference to Form-Criticism.* Philadelphia: Westminster. [Originally the Cunningham Lectures, 1940.] German trans. by F. Keienburg: *Bist Du, der da kommen soll? Das Zeugnis der drei ersten Evangelien von der Offenbarung Gottes in Christo unter Berücksichtigung der Formgeschichte.* Zollikon and Zurich: Evangelischer Verlag, 1952.

Marshall, I. Howard
  1966   "The Synoptic Son of Man Sayings in Recent Discussion." *NTS* 12:
            327–51.
  1970   "The Son of Man in Contemporary Debate." *EvQ* 42: 67–87.
  1973   "Palestinian and Hellenistic Christianity: Some Critical Comments."
            NTS 19: 271–87.
  1976   *The Origins of New Testament Christology.* London & Downer's
            Grove, IL: Inter-Varsity.

Marshall, L. H.
  1946   *The Challenge of New Testament Ethics.* London: Macmillan. Pp.
            1–215.

Martin, Malachi
  1973   *Jesus Now.* New York: Dutton. Reprinted New York: Popular Library,
            n.d.

Martyn, James Louis
  1968   *History and Theology in the Fourth Gospel.* New York: Harper & Row.
            2d rev. ed. Nashville: Abingdon, 1979.

Marxsen, Willi
  1956   *Der Evangelist Markus: Studien zur Redaktionsgeschichte des
            Evangeliums.* FRLANT 67. Göttingen: Vandenhoeck & Ruprecht. 2d
            ed. 1959. Eng. trans. by R. A. Harrisville: *Mark the Evangelist: Studies
            on the Redaction History of the Gospel.* Nashville and New York:
            Abingdon, 1969.
  1960   *Anfangsprobleme der Christologie.* Gütersloh: Mohn. Eng. trans. by
            P. J. Achtemeier; introduction by J. Reumann: *The Beginnings of
            Christology: A Study in Its Problems.* FBBS 22. Philadelphia: Fortress,
            1969. Reprinted with new introduction: *The Beginnings of Christol-
            ogy, Together with The Lord's Supper as a Christological Problem* (the
            latter, German 1963, Eng. trans. by L. Nieting, FBBS 25, 1970),
            1979.
  1966   (with Ulrich Wilckens, Gerhard Delling, Hans-Georg Geyer). *Die
            Bedeutung der Auferstehungsbotschaft für den Glauben an Jesus
            Christus.* Ed. F. Viering. Gütersloh: Mohn. Eng. trans. by D. M.
            Barton and R. A. Wilson: *The Significance of the Message of the Resur-
            rection for Faith in Jesus Christ.* Ed. C. F. D. Moule. SBT 2/8. London:
            SCM, 1968.
  1968   *Die Auferstehung Jesu von Nazareth.* Gütersloh: Mohn. 7th ed. 1969.
            Eng. trans. by M. Kohl: *The Resurrection of Jesus of Nazareth.*
            London: SCM, Philadelphia: Fortress, 1970.
  1976a   *Die Sache Jesu geht weiter.* Gütersloh: Mohn.
  1976b   "Christology in the NT." *IDBSup* 146–56.

Matthiae, K. See Ristow.

Mayer, A.
  1983   *Der zensierte Jesus: Soziologie des Neuen Testaments.* 2d ed. Olten,
            Switzerland and Freiburg: Walter. [A sociological analysis of Jesus'
            proletarian origins, "from below." Review article by H.-J. Venetz,
            "Der zensierte Jesus," *Orientierung* 47 (1983) 250–52.]

Meier, John
  1979   *The Vision of Matthew: Christ, Church, and Morality in the First
            Gospel.* Theological Inquiries: New York: Paulist. Pp. 1, 3, 42–51, and
            passim.

Meyer, Ben
1979   *The Aims of Jesus.* London: SCM.

Minear, Paul S.
1972   *Commands of Christ.* Nashville and New York: Abingdon.

Mitton, C. Leslie
1974   *Jesus. The Fact Behind the Faith.* Grand Rapids: Eerdmans.

Moule, C. F. D. See also Bammel, Ernst, 1984.
1977   *The Origin of Christology.* New York: Cambridge University Press. Reprinted 1978.

Muggeridge, Malcolm
1969   *Jesus Rediscovered.* London: Collins, Fontana Books. Garden City, NY: Doubleday.

Mussner, Franz
1965   *Die johanneische Sehweise und die Frage nach dem historischen Jesus.* QD 19. Freiburg: Herder. Eng. trans. by W. J. O'Hara: *The Historical Jesus in the Gospel of John.* New York: Herder & Herder, 1967.
1967   *Die Wunder Jesu: Eine Hinführung.* Munich. Kösel. Eng. trans. by A. Wimmer: *The Miracles of Jesus: An Introduction.* Notre Dame, IN: University of Notre Dame Press, 1968.
1972   "Ipsissima facta Jesu?" *TRev* 68: cols. 177–84. [Review of Pesch, 1970.]

Neil, William
1965   *The Life and Teaching of Jesus.* "Knowing Christianity" series. Philadelphia: Lippincott.

Neill, Stephen
1970   *What We Know about Jesus.* London: Lutterworth. Grand Rapids: Eerdmans, 1972. [Originally for the World Council of Churches, Commission on World Mission and Evangelism.]
1976   *Jesus through Many Eyes: Introduction to the Theology of the New Testament.* Philadelphia: Fortress.

Niebuhr, Richard R.
1957   *Resurrection and Historical Reason: A Study of Theological Method.* New York: Scribner.

Niederwimmer, Kurt
1968   *Jesus.* Göttingen: Vandenhoeck & Ruprecht. [Uses depth psychology as a hermeneutical tool.]

Nolan, Albert
1976   *Jesus before Christianity.* London: Darton, Longman & Todd, 1977 (originally published in South Africa). Maryknoll, NY: Orbis, 1978. [By a Dominican.]

O'Collins, Gerald
1977   *What Are They Saying about Jesus?* New York: Paulist. 2d ed. rev. 1983.
1983   *Interpreting Jesus.* Introducing Catholic Theology 2. London: Chapman; New York: Paulist.

Ogden, Schubert. See V. A. Harvey, 1962.

Ory, Georges
1968   *Le Christ et Jésus.* Paris: Pavillon. [Reflects the Christ-myth view. The Gospels are fictional, of no historical value.]

Osman, Fathi
1977   (with Zalman Schachter, Gerard S. Sloyan, Dermot A. Lane). "Jesus in Jewish-Christian-Muslim Dialogue." *JES* 14: 448–65.

Pannenberg, Wolfhart
1964   *Grundzüge der Christologie.* Gütersloh: Mohn. Eng. trans. by L. Wilkens and D. Priebe: *Jesus, God and Man.* Philadelphia: Westminster, 1968. 2d ed. 1977.

Pelikan, Jaroslav. See also Bornkamm, 1975.
1985   *Jesus through the Centuries: His Place in the History of Culture.* New Haven: Yale University Press. German trans. by C. Hermanns: *Jesus Christus: Erscheinungsbild und Wirkung in 2000 Jahren Kulturgeschichte.* Zurich: Benziger, 1986; Darmstadt: Wissenschaftliche Buchgesellschaft, 1987.

Percy, Ernst
1953   *Die Botschaft Jesu: Eine traditionskritische und exegetische Untersuchung.* Lunds universitets årsskrift, n.s. 1, Vol. 49, No. 5. Lund: Gleerup.

Perkins, Pheme. See Fuller, 1982.

Perrin, Norman
1963   *The Kingdom of God in the Teaching of Jesus.* London: SCM; Philadelphia: Westminster.
1967   *Rediscovering the Teaching of Jesus.* London: SCM; New York: Harper & Row. Annotated Bibl., pp. 249–66. German trans. by P. G. Pohl: *Was lehrte Jesus wirklich? Rekonstruktion und Deutung.* Göttingen: Vandenhoeck & Ruprecht, 1972.
1974   *A Modern Pilgrimage in New Testament Christology.* Philadelphia: Fortress.
1976   *Jesus and the Language of the Kingdom: Symbol and Metaphor in New Testament Interpretation.* Philadelphia: Fortress. Annotated Bibl., pp. 209–15.

Pesch, Rudolf. See also Augstein.
1970   *Jesu ureigene Taten? Ein Beitrag zur Wunderfrage.* QD 52. Freiburg: Herder. [See also Mussner, 1972.]
1978   *Das Abendmahl und Jesu Todverständnis.* QD 80. Freiburg: Herder.

Pesch, Rudolf, and Rudolf Schnackenburg, eds.
1975   *Jesus und der Menschensohn: Für Anton Vögtle.* Freiburg, Basel, and Vienna: Herder.

Peter, James F.
1965   *Finding the Historial Jesus: A Statement of the Principles Involved.* New York: Harper & Row. [Conservative, nonspecialist account of the new quest.]

Petzke, Gerd
1975   "Der historische Jesus in der sozial-ethischen Diskussion: Mk 12, 13–17 par." In Strecker, 1975:223–36.

Pfammalter, Josef
1978   "Katholische Jesusforschung im deutschen Sprachraum. 200 Jahre nach Reimarus." Pp. 101–48 in *Theologische Berichte VII: Zugänge zu Jesus.* Zurich: Benziger. [A thorough survey, showing the extent of recent Catholic activity in German, though no significant "life" has yet appeared.]

Phillips, Wendell
1975   *An Explorer's Life of Jesus*. New York: Two Continents and Morgan Press. ["The biography of the Founder of Christianity that is true to fact as to faith."]

Phipps, William E.
1970   *Was Jesus Married? The Distortion of Sexuality in the Christian Tradition*. New York: Harper & Row.
1973   *The Sexuality of Jesus: Theological and Literary Perspectives*. New York: Harper & Row.

Pike, Dianne (Kennedy) and R. Scott Kennedy
1972   *The Wilderness Revolt: A New View of the Life and Death of Jesus based on ideas and notes of the late Bishop James A. Pike*. Garden City, NY: Doubleday. [Jesus as revolutionist; from Pike's seminar at the Esalen Institute, San Francisco, 1969.]

Piper, John
1979   *Love Your Enemies: Jesus' Love Command in the Synoptic Gospels and the Early Christian Paraenesis*. SNTSMS 38. New York: Cambridge University Press.

Prat, Ferdinand
1933   *Jésus-Christ, sa vie, sa doctrine, son oeuvre*. Paris: Beauchesne. Eng. trans. from the 16th French ed. by J. J. Heenan: *Jesus Christ: His Life, His Teaching, and His Work*. 2 vols. Milwaukee: Bruce, 1950.

Rahner, Karl. See Thüsing, 1972.

Räisänen, Heikki
1971   *Das Koranische Jesusbild: Ein Beitrag zur Theologie des Korans*. Helsinki: Missiologian ja Ekumeniikan Seura/Finnische Gessellschaft für Missiologie und Ökumenik.

Ratschow, Carl Heinz. See also above, under "Research Reports, Surveys."
1970   *Atheismus in Christentum? Eine Auseinandersetzung mit Ernst Bloch*. Gütersloh: Mohn.

Rese, Martin
1963   "Überprüfung einiger Thesen von Joachim Jeremias zum Thema des Gottesknechtes im Judentum." *ZTK* 60: 21–41.

Reumann, John. See also above, under "Research Reports, Surveys."
1968   *Jesus in the Church's Gospels: Modern Scholarship and the Earliest Sources*. Philadelphia: Fortress. Paperback 1973. 4th ed. 1982. London: SPCK, 1970. See Kümmel, *TRu* 41 (1976) 240.
1972   "The Quest of the Historical Baptist." Pp. 181–200 in *Understanding the Sacred Text: Essays in Honor of Morton S. Enslin*. Ed. J. Reumann. Valley Forge, PA: Judson.

Ridderbos, Herman N.
1962   *The Coming of the Kingdom*. Eng. trans. from the Dutch, by H. de Jongste. Ed. R. A. Zorn. Philadelphia: Presbyterian & Reformed.

Riesenfeld, Harald
1957   *The Gospel Tradition and Its Beginnings: A Study in the Limits of "Formgeschichte."* London: Mowbray. Reprinted pp. 1–29 in his collected essays, *The Gospel Tradition*. Philadelphia: Fortress, 1970.

Ristow, H., and K. Matthiae, eds.
1961   *Der historische Jesus und der kerygmatische Christus*. Berlin: Evangelische Verlagsanstalt. [Forty-eight essays.]

Robbins, Vernon K.
1984   *Jesus the Teacher: A Socio-Rhetorical Interpretation of Mark.* Philadelphia: Fortress.

Robinson, Donald F.
1964   *Jesus, Son of Joseph: A Reexamination of the New Testament Record.* Boston: Beacon. [Influenced by M. S. Enslin, a pastor writes for those "for whom traditional Christianity has lost its impact."]

Robinson, James McConkey. See also Bornkamm, 1956; Jüngel; and Koester.
1959   *A New Quest of the Historical Jesus.* SBT 25. London: SCM. Expanded German trans. *Kerygma und historischer Jesus.* Zurich: Zwingli, 1960. 2d ed. 1967. English reprinted, Scholars Press Reprint Series; Missoula, MT: Scholars Press, 1979. Reprinted, *A New Quest of the Historical Jesus and Other Essays* (Philadelphia: Fortress, 1983), with 1962a and 1962b, below, plus his introduction to Schweitzer, 1968.
1962a   "The Recent Debate on the 'New Quest.'" *JBR* 30: 198–208.
1962b   "The Formal Structure of Jesus' Message." Pp. 91–110 in *Current Issues in New Testament Interpretation: Essays in Honor of Otto A. Piper.* Ed. W. Klassen and G. Snyder. New York: Harper.

Robinson, John A. T.
1957   *Jesus and His Coming: The Emergence of a Doctrine.* London: SCM; Nashville: Abingdon. Reprinted Philadelphia: Westminster, 1979.
1973   *The Human Face of God.* Philadelphia: Westminster.

Roloff, Jürgen
1970   *Das Kerygma und der irdische Jesus: Historische Motive in den Jesus-Erzählungen der Evangelien.* Göttingen: Vandenhoeck & Ruprecht. [Habilitationsschrift under L. Goppelt.]

Rowlingson, Donald T.
1961   *Jesus, the Religious Ultimate.* New York: Macmillan. [Not a "life," but "the historical Jesus" in "present tense vividness."]

Ruppert, Lothar
1972   *Jesus als der leidende Gerechte? Der Weg Jesu im Lichte eines alt- und zwischentestamentlichen Motivs.* SBS 59. Stuttgart: Katholisches Bibelwerk.

Sabourin, Léopold
1963   *Les noms et les titres de Jésus: Thèmes de theologie biblique.* Paris: Desclée. Eng. trans. by M. Carroll: *The Names and Titles of Jesus: Themes of Biblical Theology.* New York: Macmillan, 1967.
1977   *The Divine Miracles, Discussed and Defended.* Rome: Catholic Book Agency. [Salvation history and the "criterion of necessary explanation."]

Sanders, Ed Parish
1982   "Jesus, Paul and Judaism." Pp. 390–450 in *ANRW* 2.25.1. [Against the background analysis of "covenantal nomism" and Paul's "pattern of religion" viewed as "eschatological participation," Sanders discusses Jesus' position on Temple and Law, his proclamation, and his death.]
1983   "The Search for Bedrock in the Jesus Material." *Proceedings of the Irish Biblical Association* 7: 74–86.
1985   *Jesus and Judaism.* Philadelphia: Fortress. [Jesus looked for eschatological restoration of Israel, the kingdom to come by a miracle, himself as "king"; he likely died for his (christological) claim.]

Sanders, Jack T.
1975   *Ethics in the New Testament: Change and Development.* Philadelphia: Fortress.

Sandmel, Samuel
1965   *We Jews and Jesus.* New York: Oxford University Press. British ed.: *A Jew Looks at Jesus.* London: Gollancz, 1966.

Saunders, Ernest W. See also Branscomb, 1960.
1967   *Jesus in the Gospels.* Englewood Cliffs, NJ: Prentice-Hall. [College-level text. Jesus' career seen in the context of "the community that he brought to life."]

Schachter, Zalman. See Osman.

Schäfer, Rolf
1970   *Jesus und der Gottesglaube: Ein christologischer Entwurf.* Tübingen: Mohr-Siebeck. [By a systematician, for a wider audience. Jesus' teachings grew out of his faith in God.]

Schelkle, Karl Hermann
1968–76   *Theologie des Neuen Testaments.* Düsseldorf: Patmos. I. *Schöpfung. Welt — Zeit — Mensche* (1968). II. *Gott war in Christus* (1973). III. *Ethos* (1970). IV.1. *Vollendung von Schöpfung und Erlösung* (1974). IV.2. *Jüngergemeinde und Kirche* (1976). Eng. trans. by W. A. Jurgens: *Theology of the New Testament.* Collegeville, MN: Liturgical Press. I. *Creation. World — Time — Man* (1971). II. *Salvation History — Revelation* (1976). III. *Morality* (1973). IV. *The Rule of God: Church — Eschatology.* (1978).

Schierse, Franz Joseph, ed.
1972   *Jesus von Nazareth.* Mainz: Matthias-Grünewald.

Schillebeeckx, Edward C. F.
1975   *Jezus: Het verhaal van een levende.* Bloemendaal: Nelissen. Eng. trans. by H. Hoskins: *Jesus: An Experiment in Christology.* New York: Seabury, 1979.
1977   *Gerechtigheid en liefde: Gnade en bevrijding.* Bloemendaal: Nelissen. Eng. trans. by J. Bowden: *Christ: The Experience of Jesus as Lord.* New York: Crossroad (© Seabury), 1980.
1978   *Tussentijds verhaal over Jezus boeken.* Bloemendaal: Nelissen. Eng. trans. by J. Bowden: *Interim Report on the books Jesus & Christ.* New York: Crossroad, 1982. [See R. H. Fuller, *Thomist* 48 (1984) 368–82.]

Schlosser, Jacques
1980   *La règne de Dieu dans les dits de Jésus.* EBib. 2 vols. Paris: Gabalda.

Schmiedel, Paul W.
1901   "Gospels." Cols. 1761–1898 in *Encyclopaedia Biblica,* vol. 2. Ed. T. K. Cheyne and J. S. Black. London: A. & C. Black. Reprinted separately, 1908. [Nine "pillar passages" isolated for a "truly scientific" life of Christ.]

Schnackenburg, Rudolf
1959   *Gottes Herrschaft und Reich.* Freiburg: Herder. Eng. trans. by J. Murray: *God's Rule and Kingdom.* New York: Herder & Herder; London: Nelson, 1963. Reprinted London: Search, 1968. ["Probably the best discussion of the subject" (Perrin, 1976:210).]
1960   (with Anton Vögtle). "Jesus Christus." *LTK* 5:922–40. 2d ed. Freiburg: Herder.

1962   *Die sittliche Botschaft des Neuen Testaments.* Handbuch der
          Moraltheologie VI, 2. Munich: Huebner. Eng. trans. by J. Holland-
          Smith and W. J. O'Hara: *The Moral Teaching of the New Testament.*
          London: Burns & Oates; New York: Herder & Herder, 1965.

Schonfield, Hugh
1966   *The Passover Plot: New Light on the History of Jesus.* London: Hutch-
          inson; New York: Geis (Random House). Paperback, Bantam Books
          1967. Sequels: *Those Incredible Christians* (1968) and *The Jesus Party*
          (New York: Macmillan, 1974). [*Contra,* e.g., Clifford Wilson, *The
          Passover Plot Exposed* (San Diego: Master, 1977).]

Schottroff, Luise, and Wolfgang Stegemann. For Schottroff, see also Fuller, 1978.
1978   *Jesus von Nazareth — Hoffnung der Armen.* Stuttgart: Kohlhammer.

Schrage, Wolfgang
1982   *Ethik des Neuen Testaments.* GNT, NTD Ergänzungsreihe 4. Göttin-
          gen: Vandenhoeck & Ruprecht. Eng. trans. by D. E. Green: *The
          Ethics of the New Testament.* Philadelphia: Fortress, 1988.

Schreiber, Johannes
1961   "Die Christologie des Markusevangeliums: Beobachtungen zur
          Theologie und Komposition des zweiten Evangeliums." *ZTK* 58:
          154–83.
1967   *Theologie des Vertrauens: Eine redaktionsgeschichtliche Untersuchung
          des Markusevangeliums.* Hamburg: Furche.

Schubert, Kurt
1962a, ed. *Der historische Jesus und der Christus unseres Glaubens: Eine katho-
          lische Auseinandersetzung mit den Folgen der Entmythologisierungs-
          theorie.* Vienna and Freiburg: Herder.
1962b, ed. *Vom Messias zum Christus. Die Fülle der Zeit in religionsgeschicht-
          licher und theologischer Sicht.* Vienna and Freiburg: Herder.
          [Especially on eschatology and Jesus' self-understanding.]

Schulz, Siegfried
1962   "Maranatha und Kyrios Jesus." *ZNW* 53: 125–44.
1967   *Die Stunde der Botschaft: Einführung in die Theologie der vier
          Evangelisten.* Hamburg: Furche.
1972   *Q, Die Spruchquelle der Evangelisten.* Zurich: Theologischer Verlag.
          [See also *Griechisch-Deutsch Synopse der Q-Überlieferungen.* The
          synopsis is a separate volume from the same publisher.]
1975   "Der historische Jesus: Bilanz der Fragen und Lösungen." In
          Strecker, 1975:3–26.

Schürmann, Heinz
1960   "Die vorösterlichen Anfänge der Logientradition: Versuch eines
          formgeschichtlichen Zugangs zum Leben Jesu." Pp. 342–70 in
          Ristow and Matthiae. Reprinted pp. 39–63 in his collected essays,
          *Traditionsgeschichtliche Untersuchungen zu den synoptischen Evange-
          lien: Beiträge.* Düsseldorf: Patmos, 1968.
1973   "Wie hat Jesus seinen Tod bestanden und verstanden? Eine metho-
          denkritische Besinnung." Pp. 325–63 in *Orientierung an Jesus: Zur
          Theologie der Synoptiker: Für Josef Schmid.* Ed. P. Hoffmann. Frei-
          burg: Herder. Reprinted pp. 16–65 in his *Jesu ureigener Tod: Exe-
          getische Besinnungen und Ausblick.* Freiburg, Basel, and Vienna,
          1975.

1983   *Gottes Reich—Jesu Geschick: Jesu ureigener Tod im Licht seiner Basileia-Verkündigung.* Freiburg, Basel, and Vienna: Herder.

Schweitzer, Albert
1901   *Kritische Darstellung unterschiedlicher neuerer historischer Abendmahlsauffassungen.* Freiburg: Wagner. [Dissertation for licentiate degree; part 1 of his 2-vol. work.] *Das Abendmahl im Zusammenhang mit dem Leben Jesu und der Geschichte des Urchristentums.* Tübingen: Mohr-Siebeck, 1901. 2d ed., 1929.
        1. *Das Abendmahlsproblem auf Grund der wissenschaftlichen Forschung des 19. Jahrhunderts und der historischen Berichte.* Eng. trans. by A. J. Mattill, Jr., ed. with introduction by J. Reumann: *The Problem of the Lord's Supper according to the Scholarly Research of the Nineteenth Century and the Historical Accounts:* Vol. 1: *The Lord's Supper in Relationship to the Life of Jesus and the History of the Early Church.* Macon, GA: Mercer University Press, 1982.
        2. *Das Messianitäts- und Leidensgeheimnis: Eine Skizze des Lebens Jesu.* Eng. trans. by W. Lowrie: *The Mystery of the Kingdom of God: The Secret of Jesus' Messiahship and Passion.* London: A. & C. Black; New York: Dodd, Mead, 1914. Reprinted 1925; New York: Macmillan, 1950; New York: Schocken, 1964.
1967   *Reich Gottes und Christentum.* Ed. Ulrich Neuenschwander. Tübingen: Mohr-Siebeck. Eng. trans. by L. A. Garrard: *The Kingdom of God and Primitive Christianity.* London: A. & C. Black; New York: Seabury, 1968. [Written 1951, published posthumously. On Jesus, see pp. 68–129.]
1968   *The Quest of the Historical Jesus: A Critical Study of Its Progress from Reimarus to Wrede.* Eng. trans. by W. Montgomery from the German original, *Von Reimarus zu Wrede* (Tübingen: Mohr-Siebeck, 1906), first published in English 1910 (London: A. & C. Black) and often reprinted. The 1968 paperback ed. contains a new introduction by James M. Robinson (pp. xi-xxxiii), reprinted in J. M. Robinson, 1959 (1983 ed. 172–95), first published in the German paperback ed., *Geschichte der Leben-Jesu-Forschung* (Hamburg: Siebenstern Taschenbuch, 1966) 7–24.

Schweizer, Eduard
1955   *Erniedrigung und Erhöhung bei Jesus und seiner Nachfolgern.* ATANT 28. Zurich: Zwingli. Eng. trans. *Lordship and Discipleship.* SBT 28. London: SCM, 1960.
1960   "The Son of Man." *JBL* 79: 119–29.
1963   "The Son of Man Again." *NTS* 9: 256–61. [Both Son-of-man articles are reprinted pp. 56–92 in his *Neotestamentica: German and English Essays 1951-1963.* Zurich: Zwingli.]
1968   *Jesus Christus im vielfältigen Zeugnis des Neuen Testaments.* Munich: Siebenstern. Eng. trans. by D. E. Green: *Jesus.* London: SCM; Richmond: John Knox, 1971.

Scott, Ernest Findlay
1951   *The Lord's Prayer: Its Character, Purpose, and Interpretation.* New York: Scribner.

Semeia 1
1974   *A Structuralist Approach to the Parables.* Ed. Robert W. Funk. Missoula, MT: Scholars' Press. Bibl., pp. 236–74.

Semeia 2
1974   *The Good Samaritan.* Ed. J. D. Crossan.

Semeia 9
1977   *Polyvalent Narration.* Ed. J. D. Crossan.

Semeia 12–13
1978   *The Poetics of Faith: Essays Offered to Amos Niven Wilder.* Ed. William A. Beardslee. 2 vols.

Semeia 30
1985   *Christology and Exegesis: New Approaches.* Ed. Robert Jewett. [Treats the work of Fuller and Dunn as well as narrative and sociological approaches.]

Sharman, Henry Burton
1943   *Son of Man and Kingdom of God: A Critical Study.* New York: Harper.

Sherwin-White, A. N.
1963   *Roman Law in the New Testament.* Oxford: Clarendon. Reprinted Grand Rapids: Baker, 1979. [Especially pp. 24–47 on the trial of Jesus.]

1965   "The Trial of Christ." Pp. 97–116 in *Historicity and Chronology in the New Testament.* SPCK Theological Collections 6. London: SPCK.

Slenczka, Reinhard
1967   *Geschichtlichkeit und Personsein Jesu Christi: Studien zur Christologischen Problematik der historischen Jesusfrage.* Forschungen zur systematischen und ökumenischen Theologie 18. Göttingen: Vandenhoeck & Ruprecht.

Sloyan, Gerard S.
1973   *Jesus on Trial: The Development of the Passion Narratives and their Historical and Ecumenical Implications.* Edited, with introduction by J. Reumann. Philadelphia: Fortress.

1977   See Osman.

1983   *Jesus in Focus: A Life in Its Setting.* Mystic, CT: Twenty-Third Publications.

Smith, Charles W. F.
1948   *The Jesus of the Parables.* Philadelphia: Westminster. Rev. ed. Philadelphia: Pilgrim, 1975.

1969   *The Paradox of Jesus in the Gospels.* Philadelphia: Westminster.

Smith, Morton. See also Hadas.
1963   "A Comparison of Early Christian and Early Rabbinic Tradition." *JBL* 82: 169–76.

1973a   *The Secret Gospel: The Discovery and Interpretation of the Secret Gospel According to Mark.* New York: Harper & Row. [Popular account.]

1973b   *Clement of Alexandria and a Secret Gospel of Mark.* Cambridge, MA: Harvard University Press, 1973. Critical text and discussion.

1978   *Jesus the Magician.* New York: Harper & Row.

Sobrino, Jon
1976   *Christologia desde américa latina (esbozo a partir del seguimento del Jésus histórico).* Río Hondo, Mexico: Centro de Reflexíon Teológia. Eng. trans. by J. Drury: *Christology at the Crossroads: A Latin American Approach.* Maryknoll, NY: Orbis, 1978.

Speicher, Günter
1966   *Doch sie können Ihn nicht töten: Forscher und Theologen auf den Spuren Jesu.* Düsseldorf: Econ.

Stauffer, Ethelbert
1956   "Geschichte Jesu." In *Historia Mundi: Ein Handbuch der Weltgeschichte in zehn Bänden,* begründet von Fritz Kern. Ed. Fritz Valjavec. Bern: Francke, 1952–61. Vol. IV, *Römisches Weltreich und Christentum,* 129–89.
1957   *Jesus: Gestalt und Geschichte.* Delp Taschenbücher. Bern: Francke. British trans. by D. M. Barton: *Jesus and His Story.* London: SCM, 1960. American trans. by Richard and Clara Winston: *Jesus and His Story.* New York: Knopf, 1960. [Part of a German trilogy, with *Jerusalem und Rom im Zeitalter Jesu Christi* (1957) and *Die Botschaft Jesu: Damals und Heute* (1959).]
1967   *Jesus war ganz anders.* Hamburg: Friedrich Witte.
1982   "Jesus, Geschichte und Verkündigung." Pp. 3–130 in *ANRW* 2.25.1.

Stegemann, Wolfgang. See Schottroff.

Stein, Robert H.
1978   *The Method and Message of Jesus' Teachings.* Philadelphia: Westminster. [Introductory textbook.]

Steinmann, Jean
1959   *La vie de Jésus.* Paris: Club des Librairies de France.

Strecker, Georg
1975, ed.   *Jesus Christus in Historie und Theologie: Neutestamentliche Festschrift für Hans Conzelmann zum 60. Geburtstag.* Tübingen: Mohr-Siebeck.
1984   *Die Bergpredigt: Ein exegetischer Kommentar.* Göttingen: Vandenhoeck & Ruprecht. [A "criterium of growth" (11) allows one to trace development of Matthew's sermon from a historical core of three macarisms, antitheses 1–3, the command to love enemies, the Lord's Prayer, and other sayings (181–85).]

Strobel, August
1966   *Die moderne Jesusforschung.* Calwer Hefte 83. Stuttgart: Calwer. 2d ed. 1968. [Brief research report.]
1967   *Kerygma und Apokalyptik: Ein religionsgeschichtlicher und theologischer Beitrag zur Christologie.* Göttingen: Vandenhoeck & Ruprecht.
1980   *Die Stunde der Wahrheit: Untersuchung zum Strafverfahren gegen Jesus.* WUNT 21. Tübingen: Mohr-Siebeck.

Stuhlmacher, Peter
1975   "Jesus als Versöhner: Überlegungen zum Problem der Darstellung Jesu im Rahmen einer biblischen Theologie des Neuen Testaments." In Strecker, 1975:87–104. Reprinted pp. 9–26 in Stuhlmacher's *Versöhnung, Gesetz und Gerechtigkeit: Aufsätze zur biblischen Theologie.* Göttingen: Vandenhoeck & Ruprecht, 1981. Eng. trans. by E. R. Kalin: pp. 1–15 in *Reconciliation, Law, & Righteousness: Essays in Biblical Theology.* Philadelphia: Fortress, 1986. See also Stuhlmacher's *Vom Verstehen des Neuen Testaments: Eine Hermeneutik.* GNT, NTD Ergänzungsreihe 6. Göttingen: Vandenhoeck & Ruprecht, 1979. Pp. 229–31.
1979   (with Helmut Class). *Das Evangelium von der Versöhnung in Christus.* Stuttgart: Calwer. Pp. 13–54. Eng. trans. in *Horizons* 1 (1979) 161–90.

Suggs, M. Jack. See also Fuller, 1978.
1970   *Wisdom, Christology, and Law in Matthew's Gospel.* Cambridge, MA:
         Harvard University Press.
1975   "Bibliography" to G. Bornkamm's 1975 article on "Jesus Christ,"
         Encyclopaedia Britannica, 15th ed., 10: 155.

Swidler, Leonard J.
1971   "Jesus was a Feminist." *SEAJournTheol* 13: 102–10. *Catholic World*
         212 (Jan. 1971) 177–83. Reprinted in *Dimensions of Man.* Ed.
         Harold P. Simonson and John P. Magee. New York: Harper & Row,
         1973. Expanded in his *Biblical Affirmations of Women.* Philadelphia:
         Westminster, 1979. German trans.: "Jesu Begegnung mit Frauen:
         Jesus als Feminist." Pp. 130–46 in *Menschenrechte für die Frauen.* Ed.
         Elisabeth Moltmann-Wendel. Munich: Kaiser, 1974.

Taylor, Vincent
1951   "The Life and Ministry of Jesus." *IB* 7: 114–44.
1953   *The Names of Jesus.* New York: St. Martin's.
1955   *The Life and Ministry of Jesus.* New York and Nashville: Abingdon.
         Paperback 1968. Expanded version of 1951.
1958   *The Person of Christ in New Testament Teaching.* New York: St.
         Martin's.
1972   *The Passion Narrative of St Luke: A Critical and Historical Investiga-
         tion.* Ed. O. E. Evans. SNTSMS 19. New York: Cambridge University
         Press.

Terrien, Samuel
1978   *The Elusive Presence: Toward a New Biblical Theology.* Religious
         Perspectives 26. New York: Harper & Row.

Theissen, Gerd
1977   *Soziologie der Jesusbewegung: Ein Beitrag zur Entstehungsgeschichte
         des Urchristentums.* Theologische Existenz heute 194. Munich:
         Kaiser. Eng. trans. by J. Bowden: *Sociology of Early Palestinian Chris-
         tianity.* Philadelphia: Fortress, 1978. British ed.: *The First Followers
         of Jesus.* London: SCM, 1978.

Thoma, Clemens
1978   "Jüdische Zugänge zu Jesus Christus." Pp. 149–76 in *Theologische
         Berichte VII: Zugänge zu Jesus.* Zurich: Benziger.

Thompson, W. A.
1980   *Jesus, Lord and Savior: A Theopathic Christology and Soteriology.*
         New York: Paulist. [Development of human consciousness is the
         framework for the quest; God is "Jesuslike"; Christ must be trans-
         cultural.]

Thrall, Margaret E.
1970   "The Origin of Pauline Christology." Pp. 304–16 in *Apostolic History
         and the Gospel: Biblical and Historical Essays presented to F. F. Bruce.*
         Ed. W. Gasque and R. P. Martin. Exeter: Paternoster; Grand Rapids:
         Eerdmans.

Thüsing, Wilhelm
1970   *Erhöhungsvorstellung und Parusieerwartung in der ältesten nachöster-
         lichen Christologie.* SBS 42. Stuttgart: Katholisches Bibelwerk.

1972   (with Karl Rahner). *Christologie, systematisch und exegetisch: Arbeits-grundlagen für eine interdisziplinäre Vorlesung.* QD 55. Freiburg: Herder. Eng. trans. by D. Smith and V. Green: *A New Christology.* Crossroad Book. New York: Seabury, 1980.

Tiede, David L.
1972   *The Charismatic Figure as Miracle Worker.* SBLDS 1. Missoula, MT: SBL.

Tilden, Elwyn E., Jr.
1956   *Toward Understanding Jesus.* Englewood Cliffs, NJ: Prentice-Hall. [College text on Gospels and Jesus, for (freshmen) students seeking "life dedication."]

Todrank, Gustave H.
1969   *The Secular Search for a New Christ.* Philadelphia: Westminster.

Tödt, Heinz Eduard
1959   *Der Menschensohn in der synoptischen Überlieferung.* Gütersloh: Mohn. 2d ed. 1963. Eng. trans. by D. M. Barton: *The Son of Man in the Synoptic Tradition.* London: SCM; Philadelphia: Westminster, 1965.

Trilling, Wolfgang
1966   *Fragen zur Geschichtlichkeit Jesu.* Düsseldorf: Patmos. 3d ed. 1969. [Deals with various questions like Jesus and the law, the Last Supper, his trial, etc.]

Trocmé, André
1961   *Jésus et la révolution non violente.* Geneva: Labor et Fides. Eng. trans. by M. H. Shank and M. E. Miller: *Jesus and the Nonviolent Revolution.* Scottdale, PA: Herald, 1973.

Trocmé, Etienne
1972   *Jésus de Nazareth vu par les témoins de sa vie.* Neuchâtel: Delachaux & Niestlé. Eng. trans. R. A. Wilson: *Jesus and His Contemporaries.* London: SCM, 1973. USA ed.: *Jesus as Seen by his Contemporaries.* Philadelphia: Westminster, 1973.

Turner, Henry Ernest William
1953   *Jesus, Master and Lord: A Study in the Historical Truth of the Gospels.* London: Mowbray; New York: Morehouse-Gorham. [Conservative, conventional, for students.]
1963   *Historicity and the Gospels: A Sketch of the Historical Method and its Application to the Gospels.* London: Mowbray. [On criteria for authentic materials, pp. 58–108.]

van der Loos, Hendrik
1965   *The Miracles of Jesus.* NovTSup 9. Leiden: Brill.

van Iersel, Bas M. F.
1961   *'Der Sohn' in den synoptischen Jesusworten: Christusbezeichnung der Gemeinde oder Selbstbezeichnung Jesu?* NovTSup 3. Leiden: Brill.

Vermes, Geza
1973   *Jesus the Jew: A Historian's Reading of the Gospels.* London: Collins. Fontana paperback 1976. 2d ed. 1983. Reprinted Philadelphia: Fortress, 1981.
1978   "The Present State of the 'Son of Man' Debate." *JJS* 29: 123–34. Abridged version, "The 'Son of Man' Debate." *JSNT* 1 (1978) 19–32.

1983   *Jesus and the World of Judaism.* London: SCM; Philadelphia: Fortress. [Reprints ten papers, including Vermes's 1974 Montefiore lecture (summarizing the 1973 book) and the 1981 Riddell Memorial Lectures, published as *The Gospel of Jesus the Jew* (University of Newcastle upon Tyne), intended as "prolegomenon to the second part of the Jesus trilogy" (viii) announced in the 1976 paperback (10).]

Via, Dan Otto, Jr.
1967   *The Parables: Their Literary and Existential Dimension.* Philadelphia: Fortress.

Vielhauer, Philipp
1957   "Gottesreich und Menschensohn in der Verkündigung Jesu." Pp. 51–79 in *Festschrift für Günther Dehn.* Ed. W. Schneemelcher. Neukirchen: Verlag der Buchhandlung des Erziehungsvereins. Reprinted pp. 55–91 in Vielhauer's *Aufsätze zum Neuen Testament.* TBü 31. Munich: Kaiser, 1965. Cf. also pp. 92–140, "Jesus und der Menschensohn," originally *ZTK* 60 (1963) 133–77, vs. views of Schweizer, Tödt, and Hahn.
1965   "Ein Weg zur neutestamentlichen Christologie? Prüfung der Thesen Ferdinand Hahns." *EvT* 25: 24–72. Reprinted with minor revisions in his *Aufsätze:* 141–98.

Vincent, John J.
1968   *Secular Christ: A Contemporary Interpretation of Jesus.* Nashville and New York: Abingdon.

Vögtle, Anton. See Schnackenburg, 1960.

Wahlberg, Rachel Conrad
1975   *Jesus according to a Woman.* New York: Paulist.

Weeden, Theodore
1971   *Mark — Traditions in Conflict.* Philadelphia: Fortress.

Weiss, Johannes
1971   *Jesus' Proclamation of the Kingdom of God.* Eng. trans. from German 1st ed., 1892, with Introduction by R. H. Hiers and D. L. Holland. "Lives of Jesus" series. Philadelphia: Fortress. Reprinted Scholars Press Reprints and Translations Series, Chico, CA: Scholars Press, 1985.

Wendland, Heinz-Dietrich
1970   *Ethik des Neuen Testaments: Eine Einführung.* GNT, NDT Ergänzungsreihe 4. Göttingen: Vandenhoeck & Ruprecht.

Wengst, Klaus
1972   *Christologie Formeln und Lieder des Urchristentums.* SNT 7. Gütersloh: Mohn. [Diss. under Vielhauer on catechetical and hymnic formulas about Jesus' death and person.]

Westerholm, Stephen
1978   *Jesus and Scribal Authority.* ConBNT 10. Lund: Gleerup. [Jesus, no Pharisee, regarded Torah not as statutory legislation but as loving expression of God's saving will. Discusses criteria for authenticity also.]

Wilder, Amos Niven. For his bibliography, see *Semeia* 13: 263–87.
1950   *Eschatology and Ethics in the Teaching of Jesus.* New York: Harper. Rev. from 1939 ed. Reprinted Westport, CT: Greenwood Press, 1979.

Wilson, William Riley
    1970   *The Execution of Jesus: A Judicial, Literary, and Historical Investigation.* New York: Scribner.
Windisch, Hans
    1929   *Der Sinn der Bergpredigt.* Leipzig: Hinrichs. 2d ed. 1937. Eng. trans. by S. M. Gilmour: *The Meaning of the Sermon on the Mount: A Contribution to the Historical Understanding of the Gospels and to the Problem of Their True Exegesis.* Philadelphia: Westminster, 1951.
Wink, Walter
    1968   *John the Baptist in the Gospel Tradition.* SNTSMS 7. New York: Cambridge University Press.
    1973   *The Bible in Human Transformation: Toward a New Paradigm for Biblical Study.* Philadelphia: Fortress.
Winter, Paul
    1961   *On the Trial of Jesus.* Studia Judaica 1. Berlin: de Gruyter.
Wolff, Hanna
    1975   *Jesus der Mann: Die Gestalt Jesu in tiefpsychologischer Sicht.* Stuttgart: Radius. 3d ed. 1977.
Wrede, William
    1901   *Das Messiasgeheimnis in den Evangelien: Zugleich ein Beitrag zum Verständnis des Markusevangeliums.* Göttingen: Vandenhoeck & Ruprecht. 2d ed. 1913. 3d ed. 1963. Eng. trans. with introduction by J. D. G. Greig: *The Messianic Secret.* Cambridge and London: James Clarke, 1971; Greenwood, SC: Attic, 1972.
Wrege, Hans Theo
    1968   *Die Überlieferungsgeschichte der Bergpredigt.* WUNT 9. Tübingen: Mohr-Siebeck.
Yoder, John Howard
    1972   *The Politics of Jesus: vicit Agnus noster.* Grand Rapids: Eerdmans.
Zahrnt, Heinz
    1960   *Es begann mit Jesus von Nazareth: Die Frage nach dem historischen Jesus.* Stuttgart: Kreuz. Paperback ed. Gütersloh: Mohn. 3d ed. 1969. Eng. trans. by J. Bowden: *The Historical Jesus.* New York: Harper & Row; London: Collins, 1963.
Ziesler, J. A.
    1984   "Matthew and the Presence of Jesus (1), (2)," *Epworth Review* 11: 55–63, 90–97.

19

NEW TESTAMENT THEOLOGY

Reginald H. Fuller

I. FROM WREDE TO BULTMANN

In the first half of the twentieth century few fresh Theologies of the NT saw the light of day. Most scholars were frightened off the enterprise because of the dilemma posed by the Wrede–Schlatter debate over the nature of the discipline (Morgan, 1973). W. Wrede, a leading representative of the history-of-religions school, held that it was a historical and descriptive discipline, not normative for faith, and that it should therefore go beyond the confines of the dogmatically determined canon to embrace the whole of early Christian literature. Moreover, it had better be called "the history of primitive Christianity." For A. Schlatter, on the other hand, NT theology was a prolegomenon to dogmatic theology, which formulated the present proclamation of the believing community. Schlatter agreed that NT theology was a historical discipline, but on theological grounds: history was the arena of God's actions, which the historian could discern (cf. Pannenberg). Schlatter actually wrote both a NT Theology (1909–10) and a Dogmatics (1911) at the same time.

Until the end of World War I, Wrede's influence remained in the ascendant, and scholars, in Germany at least, generally confined themselves to historical monographs written from a history-of-religions perspective (e.g., Bousset, Weiss). The rise of dialectical theology diverted attention to dogmatics in the inter-war period (Piper), and at this time also there was no return to the writing of theologies, except for one or two students' textbooks (Feine).

II. RUDOLF BULTMANN

As a result of this same dialectical theology, Schlatter's concern received new appreciation between the wars, bearing fruit initially in the "Kittel *Wörterbuch*." It was not, however, until the late forties that Bultmann produced his epoch-making NT theology (Eng. trans. 1951–1955), solving the Wrede–Schlatter dilemma by treating part of the NT as history of religion and part as theologically meaningful for contemporary faith. Bultmann's chapter headings are instructive: (1) "The Message of Jesus"; (2) "The

Kerygma of the Earliest Church"; (3) "The Kerygma of the Hellenistic Church Aside from Paul." Similarly, Part IV is headed "The Development Toward the Ancient Church." But Parts II and III are headed respectively — and significantly — "The *Theology* of Paul" and "The *Theology* of the Gospel of John and the Johannine Epistles." Only Paul and the Johannine literature have a theology; the rest of the NT is dealt with purely as history. In Part IV, Bultmann, as Wrede had recommended, includes material from the apostolic fathers, thus going beyond the canon. To put it another way, only Paul and the Johannine literature are considered normative for contemporary faith — that is, as Schlatter conceived NT theology. Bultmann was able to make these distinctions because he viewed Paul and John as susceptible of a demythologizing-existentialist interpretation as he had proposed earlier (1941; Eng. trans. 1953). This has consequences for his treatment of the various parts. The message of Jesus is treated as "a presupposition for the theology of the New Testament rather than a part of that theology itself" (1951:3). The confining of the Jesus section to his message and the need for only thirty pages to cover it are understandable from the methodological skepticism about the historical Jesus that Bultmann had developed in his form-critical work (Bultmann, 1968). The kerygma of the earliest church is critically reconstructed from the data of Acts, the Pauline letters, and the Synoptic tradition. As in W. Bousset, the kerygma of the Hellenistic church is reconstructed from data in the Antiochene (?) source in Acts, from inferences from the Pauline letters, and from inferences from later sources within and beyond the canon. In view of Bultmann's treatment of this material, one may legitimately ask why these two chapters on the Palestinian and Hellenistic communities aside from Paul should not, like the message of Jesus, have been designated as "presuppositions of NT Theology" — or, more accurately, "of Pauline and Johannine Theology," and Part IV as chapter 1 in the history of dogma.

Paul's theology is constructed exclusively — and properly — from the Pauline homologoumena. It is organized in two parts: "Man Prior to the Revelation of Faith" and "Man under Faith." For Bultmann, "every assertion about God is simultaneously an assertion about man and vice versa," and "therefore Paul's theology can best be treated as his doctrine of man" (Bultmann, 1951:191). Critics claimed that Bultmann did not give us the vice versa or, alternatively, that he had confined Pauline theology to an anthropological straitjacket (Barth, 1962:114). A more discerning reviewer (Dahl: 113–14) pointed out that much of what would normally go into a treatment of Pauline theology actually appears in the chapter on the Hellenistic community aside from Paul (e.g., God, Christology, pneumatology). But there, of course, it is treated descriptively — not as normative for contemporary faith.

Bultmann's treatment of Johannine theology is naturally based on the work he had done for his commentary on the Gospel (Eng. trans. 1971). He deals with the Johannine dualism of decision, the concept of world and the gospel as "de-worldlification" (*Entweltlichung*) and faith as hearing of the Word and consequent translation into eschatological existence. Such a treatment is purchased in part by the elimination of "objective" elements such as sacraments and future eschatology as additions of the ecclesiastical redactor. His treatment of Johannine Christology is in terms of paradox and humiliation in the *sarx* ("flesh") — an interpretation that E. Käsemann was later to criticize as too Pauline (1968:12 etc.)

Part IV deals with those institutional, doctrinal, and ethical developments that were later to be characterized, and in the Bultmann school stigmatized, as "early" or "emergent catholicism" (*Frühkatholizismus*) (see especially Käsemann, 1964:63–107, 236–517).

III. AFTER BULTMANN, WHAT?

Bultmann's *Theology* is now dated so far as its historical reconstructions are concerned. A palace revolt among his pupils in 1953 led to the so-called new quest of the historical Jesus (Robinson, 1959, 1960), and few today would be content to confine the treatment of Jesus to his message. Thus G. Bornkamm in his Jesus book (contrast Bultmann, 1934) includes chapters on "Discipleship," "Jesus' Journey to Jerusalem," and "Suffering and Death," while L. E. Keck would command widespread assent when he speaks of "the whole configuration of word, deed, and career capped by death" (1971:177). H. Conzelmann (1969) is an exception (see below).

The sharp distinction between Palestinian and Hellenistic Christianity has become blurred (Davies: 1–16; Hengel). Some have postulated an intermediate stratum of Hellenistic Jewish Christianity (Hahn; Fuller, 1965). The Qumran and Nag Hammadi finds of the forties have added considerably to our knowledge of the environment of early Christianity and have thrown doubt on the theory of a pre-Christian gnostic redeemer myth as the clue to Hellenistic Christology (Colpe). It is much more common to find the origins of preexistence Christology in Jewish wisdom speculation (Schweizer, 1959, 1966). A great deal more work has been done and new perspectives gained on the history of the Johannine tradition (Martyn, 1979a, 1979b; Brown, 1966, 1970, 1979).

But the theological questions raised by Bultmann's *Theology* are still very much alive. They include the following: (1) the place and role of the historical Jesus in a NT theology; (2) the adequacy of the anthropological interpretation of Paul and of "deworldlification" as a hermeneutical key for John; (3) the problem of variety and unity in the NT; (4) whether the NT contains a stratum to be designated "early catholicism," and if this is admitted, how that stratum is to be assessed. There are doubtless other questions too, but these will have to suffice for this paper.

The Place of the Historical Jesus

Our concern here is not with the possibility or legitimacy of the quest of the historical Jesus, new or old, but with the relation of Jesus to NT theology. Conzelmann, a pupil of Bultmann who had participated in the early stages of the new quest and had contributed a highly appraised article, "Jesus Christus," to *RGG*[3] (Eng. trans. 1973), later withdrew from the quest and consequently has no section on Jesus' message at the beginning of his NT theology (1969). He treats Jesus under "Synoptic Kerygma" (97–139) — an appropriate procedure for a pioneer of redaction criticism. Bultmann, on the other hand, who wrote his *Theology* before the rise of redaction criticism, had had no section on the theology of the evangelists. In this Conzelmann provides a valuable supplement to Bultmann. Here we may contrast G. E. Ladd. Writing twenty years after the beginnings of redaction criticism as a self-conscious method, Ladd has a long section (Part 1, 200 pages) entitled "The Synoptic Gospels." This, however, is not, as the reader would expect, an exposition of the redactional theology of the evangelists, but a reconstruction of the message and mission of the earthly Jesus. Any treatment of the evangelists as theologians is completely lacking, a major weakness that reviewers have not been slow to point out.

W. G. Kümmel (1973), unlike Ladd, is deliberately and self-consciously selective, which explains why *he* has no section on the redactional theology of the evangelists. He covers only the "major witnesses" in the NT. These are Jesus (!), Paul, and John, with a transitional chapter on the faith of the earliest community between Jesus and Paul. This assignment of the role of a major witness to the earthly Jesus is problematical. Kümmel addresses himself briefly to the theological relevance of the historical Jesus (1973: 24–27) and concludes that since faith is centered on the kerygma, it is directly concerned with the question whether there is an agreement between the kerygma and historical reality of Jesus. The person and preaching of Jesus are the "presupposition" for the confession of the risen Lord and for the preaching of the community. Hence, if we enquire into the message of the NT, we are bound to enquire after the historical Jesus, who is the ground of its faith (1973:25). But this explanation still leaves unexplained why Jesus should be included among the "witnesses." Witness to what? Only the Johannine Christ, whom Kümmel excludes from this chapter, is a witness — to himself.

In one way it is a tragedy that age and health prevented J. Jeremias (1971) from completing his NT theology, of which we have only the first of two volumes (1971). This volume (311 pages + index; contrast Bultmann's 30 pages) covers only "The Proclamation of Jesus." Jeremias is clearly much more optimistic than Bultmann about the chances of recovering the historical Jesus. He relies mainly on the criteria of Palestinian language and milieu, of the knowledge of which J. M. Robinson has called him the "custodian." Unfortunately, these criteria yield inconclusive results. Yet Jeremias is not uncritical; indeed, in his work on the parables he had used form-critical method to strip away the applications of the post-Easter community and to get back to the historical Jesus. Also, he follows the form critics in not attempting a "life" of Jesus, but only his "message." But for Jeremias, Jesus' message includes much more than it does for Bultmann: Jesus' call (1971:49–56), his use of *Abba* (on which Jeremias had spent years of research) (36–37, 66–68), the gathering of the community (167–78), the mission of the disciples (231–40), an explicit self-understanding involving the use of "Son of man" as a self-designation (257–76), and an explicit self-interpretation of his death as a salvific event (277–99). He thus goes far beyond Bornkamm and Bultmann. But Jeremias offers no indication of the place of the historical Jesus in a NT theology, or of how volume 2 would have related to volume 1. We have to infer this relationship from his earlier writings, especially from his essay on the problem of the historical Jesus (1964; cf. Käsemann, 1973:239). Here we discover that "the good news of Jesus and the early church's witness of faith are inseparable from one another [sadly, his *Theology* does just that]. . . . Neither can the kerygma be treated in isolation" (1964:22–23). Compare also the title of the Jeremias *Festschrift, The Call of God and the Response of the Community* (Lohse, 1970). But for all its inadequacies as a NT theology, Jeremias's work is a magnificent summary of his life's work on the Palestinian milieu of the Synoptic tradition. As a NT theology, the title is a misnomer.

S. Neill (1976:164–95) interestingly treats Jesus in a final chapter entitled "What Lies Behind It All?"

Alternatives to Existentialist Interpretation

The two chief competitors to Bultmann's existentialist interpretation were realized eschatology and salvation history. C. H. Dodd (1935) first worked out realized eschatology in opposition to the thoroughgoing eschatology of Albert Schweitzer. Dodd later modified his position, coming close to the Haenchen-Jeremias formula, *sich realisierende Eschatologie* ("eschatology in process of realization") (Dodd, 1951). Consistent with this basis, Dodd interpreted Jesus' self-understanding as an explicit Christology in which the Danielic Son of man and Isaianic Suffering Servant were combined (Dodd, 1970), a view that he shared in various nuances with his British contemporaries, V. Taylor and the two Mansons. Realized eschatology also provided the interpretive framework for the third element in Dodd's NT theology, namely, the kerygma. By this he meant not the act of proclaiming the word as address (Bultmann), but a creedlike summary reconstructed from pre-Pauline elements in Paul (cf. Hunter, 1961) and from the early speeches in Acts (Dodd, 1936).

In this congenial reconstruction the continuity between the historical Jesus and the kerygma was assured, and the radical consequences of form criticism blunted. Since this theology fed in so perfectly to the British and particularly the Anglican emphasis on the incarnation and the church, it was very popular.

Dodd never wrote a NT theology himself. The nearest he came to it was in a study of its "sub-structure," namely, the use of OT *testimonia* in early Christian tradition (1952). But Hunter (1957) produced a very slim introduction to NT theology along Doddian lines, and A. Richardson shares many of Dodd's positions (1958). So too does Neill (1976), though he allows more weight to future eschatology (1976:174).

A second and somewhat kindred alternative to Bultmann's existentialist theology was the German school of salvation history. This was popularized by Oscar Cullmann. The Bible operates with a linear conception of history. This line begins with creation and terminates with the parousia (1951). The NT message is that the end has occurred in principle in the Christ-event (the "already") and awaits final consummation at the end (the "not yet"). Later (1967) Cullmann developed further insights, especially the constant revision of salvation history that takes place as a result of further acts of God. E. Stauffer and Ladd made salvation history the framework for their NT theologies.

Both realized eschatology and salvation history have come under fire. It is impossible to eliminate the future from Jesus' eschatological preaching, and both present and future elements must be held in tension (Kümmel, 1953). Dodd's kerygma was an artificial construct of disparate elements and obscured the variations in the kerygma. Salvation history is not NT theology but Lucan theology (Conzelmann, 1960). Such exegetical questions, especially the last point, are open to debate. More serious is the criticism of Robinson (1974–75). These NT theologies have ignored the hermeneutical problem. They do not offer NT faith as a life option for today. They reduced the discipline to historical description and made it an "antique shop."

Dissatisfaction with the existentialist interpretation of the NT in general and with the anthropological interpretation of Paul in particular was voiced even within the Bultmann school. Notably, Käsemann argued that "Apocalyptic was the mother [*Mutterboden;* better, "matrix"] of all Christian theology" (Käsemann, 1969:102). This thesis was supported mainly from the special Matthean material. But it is true also of Paul, whose theology has a salvation-historical, communal, and cosmic breadth which the anthropological concentration of Bultmann obscured (Käsemann, 1971:1–31). Moreover, in his study of the righteousness of God in Paul, Käsemann (1969:168–82) showed that this concept is more objective-theological than subjective-anthropological. But does all this mean that Käsemann has lapsed back into Wrede's view of NT theology as historical and descriptive? Can apocalyptic and objective theology be appropriated today? The long footnote at the conclusion of the essay "Primitive Christian Apocalyptic" (Käsemann, 1969: 109–10 n. 2) shows that he is not oblivious to the hermeneutical problem, but he is mainly concerned that we should first listen to the text. It was left to others to develop the hermeneutical aspects of this emphasis on apocalyptic, to the Pannenberg school, to Moltmann and the theology of hope, and to the political theology of Dorothee Sölle. Such theologies would not have been possible on a purely existential-theological basis. But Käsemann himself has not written a NT theology.

A second alternative to existentialist interpretation has been proposed by Walter Wink, who is concerned like the Bultmannians that NT exegesis and theology should not be purely antiquarian; he proposes instead to use the insights of psychology as practiced at the Guild for Psychological Studies (San Francisco). Wink's work has not found much favor in the United States among the NT guild, but it is mentioned positively by Stuhlmacher (1977:86 n. 32).

Variety and Unity in the New Testament: The Canon within the Canon

In the liberal period of NT scholarship, prior to the revival of Biblical Theology, there was much stress upon the variety of the NT. Typical of this period was the title of E. F. Scott's book, *The Varieties of New Testament Religion* (1944). Then, in the inter-war period, especially in Britain (Hunter, 1943), there was jubilant emphasis on the underlying unity of the NT. The clues to that unity seemed to lie in a consistently realized eschatology (already/not yet) running through the message of Jesus, the earliest church, and the NT theologians. Or it lay in Christology. Even the smallest items of tradition isolated by the form critics were "shot through with christology" (Hoskyns and Davey, 1931:206–7) and the same basic Christology was expressed in every strand of the NT. Or with Dodd and Hunter, as we have seen, it lay in the same underlying kerygma: "Under all variations of form, they [i.e., the great thinkers of the NT] continued to affirm that in the events out of which the Christian Church arose there was a conclusive act of God, who in them visited and redeemed His people" (Dodd, 1935:77). Bultmann's *Theology* shattered that confidence. He denied all continuity between Jesus and the kerygma: "the proclaimer became the proclaimed" (Bultmann, 1951:33). The earliest church, Hellenistic Christianity aside from Paul, and the development toward the ancient church were relegated to the antique shop. The only unity within the NT was between Paul and John, in the possibilities of existential self-understanding they offered. It was Käsemann who raised the question of pluralism in the NT more radically and acutely than any before him. In a paper delivered at an ecumenical symposium at Göttingen in 1951 (1964:95–107), he began by pointing out the variations and contradictions between the Gospels, then moved to the situation and polemical character of the Epistles and our exclusive reliance upon them for knowledge of the "other side." This brought him to three conclusions: (1) the variability within the NT kerygma; (2) the variety of the theologies constructed on the basis of this kerygma; (3) the irreconcilability of these theologies. Hence the NT provides a basis for the multiplicity of confessions rather than for the unity of the church. This led Käsemann to speak of a "Canon within the Canon," his canon being the Pauline-Lutheran message of justification by grace through faith alone and along with it a charismatic concept of ministry (1964:63–164). We shall deal further with the questions raised here in the ensuing section on early catholicism, but for the moment we note that Küng (135–51) in his controversy with Käsemann over early catholicism raised the question of pluralism, unity, and authority in respect to the canon. He protested against this confessionally determined, à la carte treatment of the canon, arguing that for the church and faith the *whole* canon remains authoritative despite and in fact *with* its pluralism: the Pauline message and the charismata along with the institutional features of early catholicism.

A completely different line is taken by the more radical Bultmann pupil H. Braun. He eliminates the kerygma of an act of God and reduces the NT message to a self-understanding expressing itself as "ich soll und ich darf" (I ought and I can—the sense of moral obligation and empowerment to fulfill it) (1965). The Christology of the NT is variable, the self-understanding constant (1968). This purchases the unity of the NT at the cost of forfeiting its evangelical message. It is the German-Lutheran equivalent of the death-of-God theology.

In America there has been a steady emphasis on the NT's varieties all through—a fact that disturbed me as relativistic when I came to this country in 1955 in the heyday of Dodd's kerygmatic theology. Actually, a quite balanced view was presented by F. C. Grant. The heading to chapter 3 section 1 of his NT theology reads: "Unity in Diversity," with a citation of 1 Cor 12:4–6. Sections 2–5 do emphasize diversity much more strongly than was usual in Britain at that time: variety in literary form, Christology, soteriology, church organization and practice. But then in chapter 4 there is a section entitled "The Unity of the New Testament" (45–49). *This* is "the most significant thing," not the variety in NT theology; "its main body of doctrine is *kath' holon* ["of a whole"] . . . found—or presupposed—everywhere, and held by all." Contrast Käsemann (1964:175), who cites the Vincentian canon, *quod ubique, quod semper, quod ab omnibus* ("that which [has been believed] everywhere, always, and by all") as a reflection of Jude 3, "the faith once delivered to the saints," and a product of early catholic synthesis. Has Grant solved the problem too easily?

A less facile solution to the problem of pluralism is offered in a recent work by a British theologian who gives full weight to the variety of NT theology, namely J. D. G. Dunn. His work shows how much the climate has changed even in Britain in recent years. Part 1 of his book is headed "Unity in Diversity?" and Part 2 "Diversity in Unity?" He is prepared with Käsemann to recognize the presence of kerygmata rather than a single kerygma in the NT (Jesus, Acts, Paul, and John). The NT writings provide evidence for Jewish Christianity, Hellenistic Christianity, apocalyptic Christianity, and early catholicism. Dunn takes no short cuts, as Grant did. Instead, he pleads not for a canon within the canon but for a "canon *through* the canon" (382), a *center* in the Jesus of history, access to whom is only available through the pluralistic writings of the NT.

If Dunn finds the answer to the problem of variety in the NT in lines that converge backward to the historical Jesus, Robinson and Koester, with their theory of trajectories, provide a possibility of converging lines that move forward. At first they leave us with the picture of a manifold variety of trajectories, and so enhance the impression of relativism. However, although Robinson and Koester are not concerned with the question of unity *versus* diversity, their work is patient of being used in the manner here suggested, and was in fact so used in the Lutheran-Catholic studies on Peter (Brown et al., 1973:166–68) and Mary (Brown et al., 1978:25) in the NT. A further example is suggested by Brown. The pluralistic and distinct Christologies, the "low" one of the virginal conception and the "high" one of the incarnation of the preexistent Logos, lie on trajectories that converge in the second century (Brown, 1977:141). Such a solution to the problem is likely to appeal only to those who believe that NT theology should be a churchly discipline, related to dogmatic theology (see below).

Early Catholicism

We have already spoken of early catholicism as a recognized stratum in the NT, a recognition that in recent discussion goes back to Bultmann's *Theology*, Part IV, and was developed by Käsemann. Early catholicism in the NT is recognizable only when criticism is seen to require a post-(or sub-) apostolic dating of certain NT books: the Pauline antilegomena, the redactional work of Matthew and Luke-Acts, and the General Epistles aside from the Johannines. A conservative scholar like Ladd, who uses the Pastorals as evidence for Pauline theology and, though hesitantly, accepts 2 Peter as authentic, has no place for early catholicism in the NT.

This stratum of the NT, where recognized, is seen as a response to the exigencies of the post-(or sub-) apostolic age: the need to preserve the apostolic tradition, to cope with "heresy" (really, to sift out from the pluralistic possibilities of the apostolic age what was regarded as permanently viable); to face up to persecution; and to adapt to the world in response to the delay in the parousia. These needs were met by developing such institutional features as canon, creed, a regular ministry, and liturgical and catechetical forms. Such elements are to be found embryonically in the later NT writings (hence, precisely, *early* or *emerging* catholicism).

But how is this (quite considerable) stratum of the NT to be evaluated? In what way, if any, is it normative? For the Bultmannians it is at worst "der grosse Abfall," ("the great fall") at best a temporary necessity in a situation long since past (Marxsen). Such views are possible for those who operate with a clearly defined canon within the canon. There are other assessments. H. Diem altogether denies the presence of early catholicism in the NT by means of conservative datings and a different exegesis of the relevant literature (229–34). Küng recognizes an early catholic stratum in the NT and its difference from apostolic Christianity, but argues that both strata should be normative and that early catholicism points to and sanctions the development of later catholicism (135–51). Yet another assessment is that early catholicism should not be regarded as a blueprint but that it points to the need of institutional features if the apostolic gospel is to be preserved, although the precise form of these institutional features must be adapted to the needs of any particular age (Fuller, 1966:196–97; 1983:39). Richardson devotes four and a half chapters to what we would call early catholicism: "One, holy, catholic Church" (286–90); "Ministries within the Church" (312–36); the theology and practice of baptism (337–63) and eucharist (364–87). But he regards the whole NT as a repository of normative theology and does not differentiate between the historical settings of the various strata. Early catholicism is jumbled up with apostolic Christianity, yet he instinctively gives a high assessment to precisely this stratum of the NT. His treatment is very definitely Anglican!

New Testament and Dogmatic Theology

Of all the German-speaking scholars of the nineteenth and early twentieth centuries, only Baur and Schlatter sought consciously—in different ways—to treat NT and dogmatic theology as related disciplines. For Baur, NT theology was the beginning of the "unfolding of Christian consciousness" (Bultmann, 1955:244), a state in "the movement through history of the divine or infinite spirit" (Morgan, 1973:13). Dogmatics was the continuation of this. But dogmatics was really for Baur the history of dogma, and it is significant that he produced not a dogmatics but a *History* of Christian dogma (1847). Thus, for Baur NT theology was neither replacement nor norm for dogmatic theology, but its source in the Hegelian sense. Schlatter, by contrast, distinguished the two disciplines yet related them. Indeed, we have seen that he has the unique distinction of producing both a NT theology (1909–10) and a dogmatic theology (1911). In an age when the dominant trend, exemplified by Wrede, was to reduce NT theology to a historical-descriptive discipline, Schlatter vindicated its character as *also* a theological discipline, as a disclosure of divine truth *through history*. Unfortunately the historical aspect of his work was vitiated by his conservatism, and as a result his contemporaries paid less attention to it than they might have.

Theologically, though, his work was much more constructive. He saw that NT Theology, though a disclosure of truth, nevertheless could not stand on its own feet as a replacement for dogmatics, but as its prolegomenon was also its source and norm.

Bultmann had a high regard for the theological side of Schlatter's exegesis and theology, though he was poles apart from him in matters of historical criticism and NT introduction. But he only took up part of Schlatter's theological inheritance, that aspect of it which finds within the NT truth for contemporary faith. And, as we have seen, Bultmann restricted this to the theology of Paul and John. As a discipline, NT theology in Bultmann's hands was as isolated from dogmatics as it was from the OT.

One would have expected that Conzelmann, the first (1969) to write a NT Theology in the Bultmann school since Bultmann, would have developed Bultmann's work on its theological side, perhaps with the help of Käsemann's critique of the existentialist interpretation, and have widened it to include the historical, communal-political, and cosmic dimensions of NT theology. Instead, Conzelmann drops most of the interpretive elements from his presentation of Paul and John and confines himself mainly to historical description (1969:xiv). This could have one of two results. Either the biblical concepts will be taken over uninterpreted for contemporary faith as in pietism, or, alternatively, the whole study will become completely antiquarian, as was the case with Wrede. Robinson (1974–75:181–82) sees the rebellious German students of 1968, the year after Conzelmann's *Outline,* as drawing the latter conclusion: "The inevitable result of Conzelmann's flight into the historical . . . was a decided turn by the students to the claims of life itself upon us, the claims to which, according to Bultmann (but not according to Conzelmann), New Testament Theology is supposed to direct us." But Robinson clearly expects NT Theology to do the whole job. He envisages it as a replacement for dogmatic theology and as itself systematic, as Bultmann did. Is it possible for NT theology to be historical-descriptive, yet at the same time a theological discipline, which, however, does not aim at replacing dogmatics and systematics but feeds into them as source and norm? Such would seem to be the program enunciated for our discipline by K. Stendahl. Where and how has such a program been attempted?

Here we may fittingly turn our attention to NT theology in Roman Catholicism. Our discipline originated in Protestantism, being motivated by the Reformation scriptural principle as revived in Pietism and by the rise of historical method in the Enlightenment. Roman Catholicism initially lacked these motivations. Since Trent, Scripture and church tradition had been accepted as sources and norms of equal weight for doctrine, and Vatican I had placed the sole responsibility for the exposition of this doctrine on the infallible magisterium. A few Catholic voices, such as J. A. Möller and the Catholic Tübingen school and Newman in his Roman days, opened up possibilities for a more historical approach to the Bible by means of a developmental or evolutionary understanding of tradition. These possibilities remained for long aborted owing to the repressive measures taken against Catholic Modernism. But Pius XII's encyclical *Divino afflante spiritu* of 1944 at last freed Scripture scholars to employ historical-critical methods, subject of course to the *caveat* that their results must conform to the teachings of the church. And to a lesser degree the same pope's encyclical *Humani generis* of 1950 freed Catholic theologians to adopt a more developmental and evolutionary approach to doctrine. Thus, the stage was set for the rise of NT theology as a discipline in Roman Catholic circles.

The effects were first felt in France and Germany. Much ground had first to be recovered in exegesis, but then came the NT theologies of Meinertz (1950) and of Bonsirven (1963, originally 1951), each author setting forth the theological ideas of the NT as they developed historically. A decade later came R. Schnackenburg's *Forschungsbericht* on NT theology (1963), first published in French, and then a limited study of certain aspects of NT theology (1974). A more ambitious effort was the four-volume and only recently finished NT Theology of Schelkle, who seeks to trace the development of each theological doctrine through the NT. Catholic theologians can afford to be less concerned than Protestants about the historical-descriptive approach to NT theology. For them NT theology is not and cannot be a replacement for dogmatic theology, since truth comes not directly from scripture, but through the living voice of the magisterium. Nor is scripture the norm as it was for the Reformation. Rather, it is the source and font from which developing dogma flows. It can, therefore, fructify understanding and lead to fresh interpretations of dogma, but it cannot correct it. The Roman Catholic NT scholar can thus live with the tension between historical-critical exegesis and the dogmas of the church. For example, Brown can take a thoroughly critical view of the birth narratives and yet affirm his acceptance of the Marian dogmas (1977:484 n. 9). How does he do this? In answer to an inquiry from me he explained his position in a letter dated 15 December 1977. He recognizes that the NT nowhere refers even implicitly to the Immaculate Conception or the Assumption of the Virgin. But Luke inaugurates a trajectory of Mary as the ideal disciple. Christian disciples are delivered from original sin through Christ in baptism and will rise from the dead in Christ. The church teaches that the first of these privileges was granted to Mary in advance of her conception, and the second at her death.

For a Protestant scholar who sees in the NT not a replacement for dogmatics but its norm as well as its source, the solution is not so easy. A possible way forward has been recently proposed by Stuhlmacher (1977). As a pupil of Käsemann at Tübingen and his successor in the chair earlier held by Schlatter, he seeks to integrate Käsemann's overcoming of the a-historical individualism of existentialist interpretation with the churchly-dogmatic concerns of Schlatter. NT theology should be done as a historical-theological discipline related backward to its roots in OT theology and forward to the creeds and confessions. Stuhlmacher's proposals remain programmatic. To date he has been long on diagnosis, but short on construction. In the translated essay (1977:76–77) he has a tantalizingly brief section entitled "The Connection with Dogmatics." He desiderates a dogmatics which will "correct and guide" exegesis (and therefore presumably NT theology) and "above all a dogmatics which moves on to its own affirmations and judgments." This means that for him NT theology is not a substitute for the work of the systematician or dogmatician, as it was for Bultmann and more recently for Robinson. Historical exegesis is to be distinguished from dogmatics, for it is the latter that "is charged with a contemporary account of the faith." The exegete must not monopolize the tasks of the dogmatician. Stuhlmacher has not as yet produced his own NT theology, his major work to date being a study of righteousness in Paul (1965). Meanwhile we do have the posthumously published and unfinished two-volume *Theology* of Goppelt (1981, 1982), which Stuhlmacher welcomes as being on the right lines. One sees here a real openness to the biblical theology of the OT, which was sadly lacking in Bultmann. But the openness to the confessions I find more problematical when, for example, Goppelt corrects Jeremias's interpretation of the eucharistic words in the direction of the Lutheran doctrine of the Supper (1981:267–68). What we need, rather, I think, in this churchly type of NT theology is a constant dialogue between dogmatics and systematics on the one side and NT theology on the other.

The Organization of New Testament Theologies

There are two basic ways of organizing a NT theology—the topical or thematic and the historical-chronological. In our period most Protestant NT theologies have followed the historical-chronological arrangement. All Roman Catholics thus far—but in our period only Stauffer, Grant, and Richardson among the Protestants—have followed the thematic and topical.

Each method has its advantages and its perils. The historical-chronological can easily lead to pure antiquarianism on the one hand or to the obscuring of the problem of present meaning on the other (see Robinson [1974–75] on Conzelmann). It is arguable that this method produces NT theologies rather than a NT theology, but this seems an inevitable consequence of the NT's pluralism and really an advantage. The way to avoid these problems, in my opinion, is to include a final chapter, stating what the NT theologian wishes to hand over to the dogmatician and systematician for meaningful interpretation, and how the author conceives the unity behind the diversity (see Kümmel, 1973:323–33).

The thematic or topical organization also exposes the NT theologian to two major perils. First, there is a compulsion to deal with *every* topic in the traditional dogmatic scheme, whether present in the NT or not (see Schelkle; Richardson wisely omits the doctrine of God [but see Schlosser], but inexplicably fails to deal with future eschatology). Second, it can lead to false harmonization of differences and the obscuring of development—for example, Richardson's failure to distinguish between the charismatic ministries of the Pauline churches and the institutional ministry of the Pastorals.

IV. A FUTURE FOR NEW TESTAMENT THEOLOGY?

Wrede tried to kill the discipline and to substitute the History of Early Christian Religion. Similarly, after Conzelmann, Robinson exulted over its impending demise as a historical discipline (1974–75:176). If it becomes that, as Conzelmann in effect made it, die it will.

But there are other possibilities. NT theology shows every sign of continuing in Roman Catholicism and in churchly oriented Protestantism. In both instances it will be not a replacement for dogmatics, but its prolegomenon. But it will be related to dogmatics differently in Protestantism from the way it will be in Roman Catholicism. For both confessions it will be the source, but for Protestants it will also be the norm. Their problem is, how can a pluralistic and temporally conditioned norm function? Their temptation will be to do violence to exegesis by conforming it to the confession, maybe unconsciously as we saw happening in Goppelt in connection with the eucharistic words. Dialogue with the Roman Catholic colleagues will help keep Protestants honest in their exegesis, for Catholics can more easily tolerate apparent rifts between exegesis and church dogma. Protestants in turn can challenge Catholics to clarify the relationship between developed dogma and the NT font—as Brown did in response to my challenge over the Marian dogmas. Protestants can help keep Roman Catholics honest over the way they hold dogma.

There is another possibility for NT theology. In a controversial address delivered at the SNTS meeting at Duke University in 1976, Robert Funk contended that the scene of NT scholarship in America was shifting from the great interdenominational seminaries to the departments of religion in the secular universities. Here NT studies, freed from the shackles of ecclesiastical control, could be pursued in a humanistic context. If NT theology, and not merely the historical study of early Christian thought or religion, is to flourish in such an environment, it must be study which makes some kind of faith claim. This would be the claim of Christianity as part of the religious past of humanity. This assumes that modern humanity, specifically American humanity (I don't think this would be so true in Europe; there the lines are drawn more sharply between a nonreligious secularism and churchly faith), is "religious" and that religion today can and must be nourished from the human religious past. If NT theology thrives in such a context it should remain in dialogue with its churchly opposite numbers, both Catholic and Protestant. For the great temptations of NT theology done in a humanistic context are the perils of modernization on the one hand and of historicism on the other. It is the same peril that besets the study of all antiquity. Catholics and churchly Protestants, with their delight in the strangeness of the biblical world, will challenge their humanistic colleagues not to gloss it over, or alternatively they will insist that ultimately the reason for studying the NT is for the sake of contemporary meaning. And, on the other hand, the humanists will constantly remind their churchly colleagues where the shoe pinches for men and women today.

BIBLIOGRAPHY

Barth, Karl
    1962   "Rudolf Bultmann—An Attempt to Understand Him." Pp. 83–132 in *Kerygma and Myth*. Vol. 2. Ed. Hans-Werner Bartsch. London: SPCK. German orig.: *Rudolf Bultmann: Ein Versuch ihn zu verstehen*. Theologische Studien 34. Zollikon and Zurich: Evangelischer Verlag. 2d ed. 1953.

Baur, Ferdinand Christian
    1863   *Vorlesungen über neutestamentliche Theologie*. Reprinted Darmstadt: Wissenschaftliche Buchgesellschaft, 1973.
    1874   *Lehrbuch der christlichen Dogmengeschichte*. Reprinted Darmstadt: Wissenschaftliche Buchgesellschaft, 1968.

Boers, Hendrikus
    1979   *What is New Testament Theology? The Rise of Criticism and the Problem of a Theology of the New Testament*. Guides to Biblical Scholarship. Philadelphia: Fortress.

Bonsirven, Joseph
    1963   *Theology of the New Testament*. Westminster, MD: Newman. French orig.: *Théologie du Nouveau Testament*. Paris: Aubier.

Bornkamm, Günther
    1960   *Jesus of Nazareth*. New York: Harper. German orig.: *Jesus von Nazareth*. Stuttgart: Kohlhammer, 1956.

Bousset, Wilhelm
    1971   *Kyrios Christos*. Nashville and New York: Abingdon. German orig.: *Kyrios Christos*. Göttingen: Vandenhoeck & Ruprecht. 2d ed. 1921.

Braun, Herbert
    1965   "The Problem of a Theology of the New Testament." *JTC* 1: 169–83. German orig.: "Die Problematik einer Theologie des Neuen Testaments." Pp. 325–41 in *Gesammelte Studien zum Neuen Testament und seiner Umwelt*. Tübingen: Mohr-Siebeck, 1962.
    1968   "The Meaning of New Testament Christology." *JTC* 5: 89–127.

Brown, Raymond Edward
    1966,   *The Gospel According to John*. 2 vols. AB 29, 29A. Garden City, NY:
    1970   Doubleday.
    1977   *The Birth of the Messiah: A Commentary on the Infancy Narratives in Matthew and Luke*. Garden City, NY: Doubleday.
    1979   *The Community of the Beloved Disciple*. New York: Paulist.

Bultmann, Rudolf Karl
1934   *Jesus and the Word.* New York: Scribner. German orig.: *Jesus.* Berlin: Deutsche Bibliothek, 1926.
1941   "Neues Testament und Mythologie." See 1953.
1951,   *Theology of the New Testament.* 2 vols. New York: Scribner. German
1955   orig.: *Theologie des Neuen Testaments.* Tübingen: Mohr, 1948, 1951.
1953   "New Testament and Mythology." Pp. 1–44 in *Kerygma and Myth.* Ed. Hans-Werner Bartsch. London: SPCK. German orig.: "Neues Testament und Mythologie." Pp. 15–48 in *Kerygma und Mythos.* TF 1. Hamburg: Reich & Heydrich, 1948. [The essay was written in 1941 but first published in 1948.]
1968   *History of the Synoptic Tradition.* Rev. ed. Oxford: Blackwell; New York: Harper & Row. German orig.: *Geschichte der synoptischen Tradition.* FRLANT 29. Göttingen: Vandenhoeck & Ruprecht, 1921.
1971   *The Gospel of John: A Commentary.* Philadelphia: Westminster. German orig.: *Das Evangelium des Johannes.* MeyerK. Göttingen: Vandenhoeck & Ruprecht, 1941.

Colpe, Carsten
1961   *Die religionsgeschichtliche Schule: Darstellung und Kritik ihres Bildes vom gnostischen Erlösermythus.* FRLANT 78. Göttingen: Vandenhoeck & Ruprecht.

Conzelmann, Hans
1960   *The Theology of Luke.* London: Faber & Faber. German orig.: *Die Mitte der Zeit: Studien zur Theologie des Lukas.* BHT 17. Tübingen: Mohr-Siebeck, 1954.
1969   *An Outline of the Theology of the New Testament.* London: SCM. German orig.: *Grundriss der Theologie des Neuen Testaments.* Munich: Kaiser, 1968.
1973   *Jesus: The Classic Article from RGG³ Expanded and Updated.* Philadelphia: Fortress.

Cullmann, Oscar
1951   *Christ and Time.* London: SCM. German orig.: *Christus und die Zeit.* Zollikon and Zurich: Evangelischer Verlag, 1946.
1967   *Salvation in History.* London: SCM. German orig.: *Heil als Geschichte.* Tübingen: Mohr-Siebeck, 1965.

Dahl, Nils Alstrup
1974   "Rudolf Bultmann's Theology of the New Testament." Pp. 90–128 in *The Crucified Messiah.* Minneapolis: Augsburg, 1974. German orig.: "Die Theologie des Neuen Testaments." *TRu* 22 (1954) 21–49.

Davies, W. D.
1948   *Paul and Rabbinic Judaism: Some Rabbinic Elements in Pauline Theology.* London: SPCK.

Diem, Hermann
1959   *Dogmatics.* London: Oliver & Boyd. German orig.: *Theologie als kirchliche Wissenschaft.* Bd 2. Munich: Kaiser, 1955.

Dodd, Charles Harold
1935   *The Parables of the Kingdom.* London: Nisbet.
1936   *The Apostolic Preaching and Its Developments.* London: Hodder & Stoughton.
1951   *The Coming of Christ.* Cambridge: University Press.

1952   *According to the Scriptures: The Substructure of New Testament Theology.* London: Nisbet.
1970   *The Founder of Christianity.* New York: Macmillan.

Dunn, James D. G.
1977   *Unity and Diversity in the New Testament.* Philadelphia: Westminster.

Feine, Paul
1953   *Theologie des Neuen Testaments.* 8th ed. Berlin: Evangelische Verlagsanstalt.

Fuller, Reginald Horace
1965   *The Foundations of New Testament Christology.* London: Lutterworth.
1966   *A Critical Introduction to the New Testament.* London: Duckworth.
1983   "Early Catholicism: An Anglican Reaction to a German Debate." Pp. 34–41 in *Die Mitte des Neuen Testaments: Einheit und Vielfalt neutestamentlicher Theologie: Festschrift für Eduard Schweizer.* Ed. U. Luz and H. Weder. Göttingen: Vandenhoeck & Ruprecht.

Goppelt, Leonhard
1968   *Christologie und Ethik: Aufsätze zum Neuen Testament.* Göttingen: Vandenhoeck & Ruprecht.
1981,   *Theology of the New Testament.* Ed. Jürgen Roloff. 2 vols. Grand
1982   Rapids: Eerdmans. German orig.: *Theologie des Neuen Testaments.* 2 vols. Göttingen: Vandenhoeck & Ruprecht, 1975, 1976.

Grant, Frederick Clifton
1950   *An Introduction to New Testament Thought.* New York and Nashville: Abingdon.

Hahn, Ferdinand
1969   *The Titles of Jesus in Christology.* London: Lutterworth. German orig.: *Christologische Hoheitstitel.* FRLANT 83. Göttingen: Vandenhoeck & Ruprecht, 1963.

Hasel, Gerhard
1978   *New Testament Theology: Basic Issues in the Current Debate.* Grand Rapids: Eerdmans.

Hengel, Martin
1974   *Judaism and Hellenism: Studies in Their Encounter in Palestine during the Early Hellenistic Period.* London: SCM. German orig.: *Judentum und Hellenismus: Studien zu ihrer Begegnung unter besonderer Berücksichtigung Palästinas bis zur Mitte des zweiten Jahrhunderts vor Christus.* WUNT 10. Tübingen: Mohr-Siebeck, 1969.

Hoskyns, Edwyn Clement, and Francis Noel Davey
1931   *The Riddle of the New Testament.* London: Faber.
1981   *Crucifixion-Resurrection: The Pattern of the Theology and Ethics of the New Testament.* Ed. Gordon S. Wakefield. London: SPCK.

Hunter, Archibald M.
1943   *The Unity of the New Testament.* London: SCM.
1957   *Introducing New Testament Theology.* London: SCM.
1961   *Paul and His Predecessors.* London: SCM.

Jeremias, Joachim
1964   *The Problem of the Historical Jesus.* Facet Books, Biblical Series 13; Philadelphia: Fortress. German orig.: "Der gegenwärtige Stand der Debatte um das Problem des historischen Jesus." Pp. 12–25 in *Der historische Jesus und der kerygmatische Christus.* Ed. H. Ristow and K. Matthiae. Berlin: Evangelischer Verlag, 1964.
1965   "Abba." Pp. 9–30 in *The Central Message of the New Testament.* New York: Scribner. English version based on "Abba." *Untersuchungen zur neutestamentlichen Theologie und Zeitgeschichte.* Göttingen: Vandenhoeck & Ruprecht, 1965.
1971   *New Testament Theology: The Proclamation of Jesus.* New York: Scribner. German orig.: *Die neutestamentliche Theologie. I. Teil: Die Verkündigung Jesu.* Gütersloh: Mohn, 1971.

Käsemann, Ernst
1964   *Essays on New Testament Themes.* SBT 41. London: SCM.
1968   *The Testament of Jesus.* London: SCM. German orig.: *Jesu letzter Wille nach Johannes 17.* Tübingen: Mohr-Siebeck, 1966.
1969   *New Testament Questions of Today.* London: SCM.
1971   *Perspectives on Paul.* Philadelphia: Fortress. German orig.: *Paulinische Perspektiven.* Tübingen: Mohr-Siebeck, 1969.
1973   "The Problem of a New Testament Theology." *NTS* 19: 235–45.

Keck, Leander E.
1964–65   "Problems of New Testament Theology," *NovT* 7: 217–41.
1971   *A Future for the Historical Jesus: The Place of Jesus in Teaching and Theology.* New York and Nashville: Abingdon.

Kittel, Gerhard, and Gerhard Friedrich, eds.
1964–76   *TDNT.*

Kümmel, Werner Georg
1957   *Promise and Fulfilment: The Eschatological Message of Jesus.* SBT 23. London: SCM. German orig.: *Verheissung und Erfüllung: Untersuchung zur eschatologischen Verkündigung Jesu.* ATANT 6. Zurich: Zwingli, 1945. 2d ed. 1953.
1972   *The New Testament: A History of the Investigation of Its Problems.* Nashville: Abingdon. German orig.: *Das Neue Testament: Geschichte der Erforschung seiner Probleme.* Freiburg: Alber, 1958.
1973   *The Theology of the New Testament according to Its Major Witnesses.* Nashville and New York: Abingdon. German orig.: *Die Theologie des Neuen Testaments nach seinen Hauptzeugen.* NTD Ergänzungsreihe 3. Göttingen: Vandenhoeck & Ruprecht, 1969.

Küng, Hans
1965   *Structures of the Church.* London: Burns & Oates. German orig.: *Strukturen der Kirche.* Freiburg: Herder, 1962.

Ladd, George Eldon
1971   "The Search for Perspective." *Int* 25: 41–62
1974   *A Theology of the New Testament.* Grand Rapids: Eerdmans.

Lohse, Eduard, ed.
1970   *Der Ruf Jesu und die Antwort der Gemeinde: Exegetische Untersuchungen Joachim Jeremias zum 70. Geburtstag.* Göttingen: Vandenhoeck & Ruprecht.

Martyn, J. Louis
   1979a   *History and Theology in the Fourth Gospel.* Rev. ed. Nashville and New York: Abingdon.
   1979b   *The Gospel of John in Christian History.* New York: Paulist.

Marxsen, Willi
   1958   *Der "Frükatholizismus" im Neuen Testament.* Biblische Studien 21. Neukirchen: Neukirchener Verlag.

Meinertz, Max
   1950   *Theologie des Neuen Testaments.* Bonn: Hanstein.

Moltmann, Jürgen
   1967   *Theology of Hope: On the Ground and Implications of a Christian Eschatology.* New York and Evanston: Harper & Row. German orig.: *Theologie der Hoffnung.* Munich: Kaiser, 1965.

Morgan, Robert C.
   1973   *The Nature of New Testament Theology: The Contribution of William Wrede and Adolf Schlatter.* SBT 2d ser. 25. London: SCM.
   1977   "A Straussian Question to 'New Testament Theology.'" *NTS* 23: 243–65.

Neill, Stephen
   1964   *The Interpretation of the New Testament.* London: Oxford University Press.
   1976   *Jesus through Many Eyes: Introduction to the Theology of the New Testament.* Philadelphia: Fortress.

Pannenberg, Wolfhart
   1968   *Revelation in History.* New York: Macmillan. German orig.: *Offenbarung als Geschichte.* Göttingen: Vandenhoeck & Ruprecht, 1961.

Piper, Otto A.
   1957   "Biblical Theology and Systematic Theology." *JBR* 25: 106–11.

Richardson, Alan
   1958   *An Introduction to the Theology of the New Testament.* London: SCM.

Robinson, James M.
   1959   *A New Quest of the Historical Jesus.* SBT 25. Naperville, IL: Allenson.
   1960   *Kerygma und historischer Jesus.* Zurich and Stuttgart: Zwingli. [Expanded edition of the 1959 work.]
   1974–75   "The Future of New Testament Theology." *Drew Gateway* 45: 175–87.

Robinson, James M., and Helmut Koester
   1971   *Trajectories through Early Christianity.* Philadelphia: Fortress.

Schelkle, Karl Hermann
   1971–78   *Theology of the New Testament.* 4 vols. Collegeville, MN: Liturgical Press. German orig.: *Theologie des Neuen Testaments.* Düsseldorf: Patmos, 1968–76.

Schlatter, Adolf
   1909–10   *Theologie des Neuen Testaments.* I, *Das Wort Jesu.* II, *Die Lehre der Apostel.* Stuttgart: Calwer.
   1973   "The Theology of the New Testament and Dogmatics." In Morgan, 1973:117–66. German orig.: *Die Theologie des Neuen Testaments.* BFCT 13. Gütersloh: Bertelsmann, 1909.

Schlier, Hans
  1957   "Über Sinn und Aufgabe einer Theologie des Neuen Testaments." *BZ*
          1: 6–23.
Schlosser, Jacques
  1987   *Le Dieu de Jésus: Etude exégètique.* LD 129. Paris: Cerf.
Schnackenburg, Rudolf
  1963   *New Testament Theology Today.* New York: Herder & Herder.
          French orig.: *Le Théologie du Nouveau Testament.* StudNeot, Subsidia
          1. Bruges: Desclée de Brouwer, 1961.
Schweizer, Eduard
  1959   "Zur Herkunft der Präexistenzvorstellung bei Paulus." *EvT* 19:
          65–70.
  1966   "Zum religionsgeschichtlichen Hintergrund der Sendungsformel."
          ZNW 56: 99–210.
Scott, Ernest Findlay
  1944   *The Varieties of New Testament Religion.* New York: Scribner.
Sölle, Dorothee
  1974   *Political Theology.* Philadelphia: Fortress. German orig.: *Politische
          Theologie: Auseinandersetzung mit Rudolf Bultmann.* Stuttgart:
          Kreuz, 1971.
Stauffer, Ethelbert
  1955   *New Testament Theology.* New York: Macmillan. German orig.: *Die
          Theologie des Neuen Testaments.* Stuttgart: Kohlhammer, 1941.
Stendahl, Krister
  1962   "Biblical Theology," *IDB* 1. 418–32.
Strecker, Georg, ed.
  1975   *Das Problem der Theologie des Neuen Testaments.* Wege der For-
          schung, 367. Darmstadt: Wissenschaftliche Buchgesellschaft.
Stuhlmacher, Peter
  1965   *Gerechtigkeit Gottes bei Paulus.* FRLANT 87. Göttingen: Vanden-
          hoeck & Ruprecht.
  1977   *Historical Criticism and Theological Interpretation of Scripture:
          Towards a Hermeneutics of Consent.* Philadelphia: Fortress. German
          orig.: "Historische Kritik und theologische Auslegung." Pp. 59–127
          in *Schriftauslegung auf dem Wege zur biblischen Theologie.* Göttin-
          gen: Vandenhoeck & Ruprecht, 1975.
Weiss, Johannes
  1959   *Earliest Christianity.* 2 vols. New York: Harper. German orig.: *Das
          Urchristentum.* 2 vols. Göttingen: Vandenhoeck & Ruprecht, 1917.
Wink, Walter
  1973   *The Bible in Human Transformation: Toward a New Paradigm for
          Biblical Study.* Philadelphia: Fortress.
Wrede, William
  1973   "The Task and Methods of New Testament Theology." In Morgan,
          1973:68–116. German orig.: *Über die Aufgabe und Methode der soge-
          nannten neutestamentlichen Theologie.* Göttingen: Vandenhoeck &
          Ruprecht, 1897.

GRECO-ROMAN WORLD

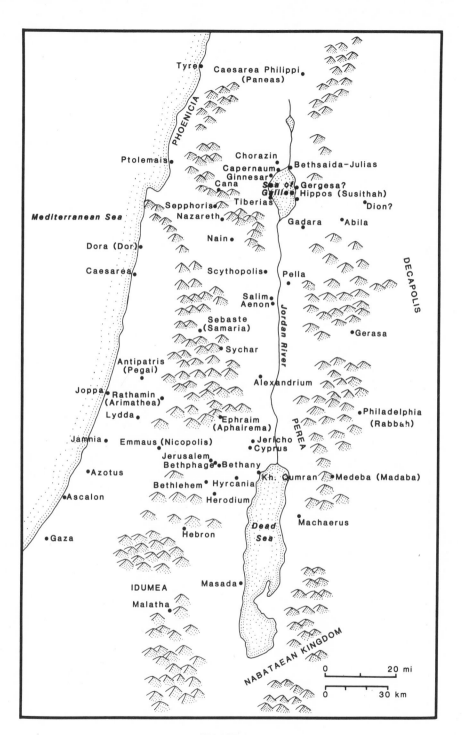

Tyre●
Caesarea Philippi
(Paneas)●

PHOENICIA

Ptolemais●

Chorazin
Capernaum●
Ginnesar●
Cana
Nazareth●
Sepphoris
Tiberias●
Sea of
Galilee
Bethsaida–Julias
Gergesa?
Hippos (Susithah)
Dion?

Mediterranean Sea

Dora (Dor)●

Caesarea●

Nain●

Gadara
●Abila

Scythopolis●
Pella

Salim●
Aenon

Sebaste
(Samaria)●

●Gerasa

Jordan River

Sychar●

Antipatris
(Pegai)●

Alexandrium

Joppa●
Rathamin
(Arimathea)●
Lydda●

PEREA

Philadelphia
(Rabbah)●

Jamnia●
Emmaus (Nicopolis)●

Ephraim
(Aphairema)●

Jericho●
Cyprus●

Jerusalem●
Bethphage●Bethany
Bethlehem●
Hyrcania●
Herodium●

●Azotus

Kh. Qumran
●Medeba (Madaba)

●Ascalon

Dead
Sea

DECAPOLIS

Hebron●

Machaerus●

●Gaza

IDUMEA
Malatha●

Masada●

NABATAEAN KINGDOM

0   20 mi

0   30 km

PALESTINE

INDEX OF MODERN AUTHORS